MODERN ACCOUNTING RESEARCH: HISTORY, SURVEY, AND GUIDE

Co-authored and edited by

Richard Mattessich

University of British Columbia

with a Foreword by Yuji Ijiri

and contributions by:
S. Baiman, M. J. Bryant,
J. E. Butterworth, C. J. Christenson,
P. M. Clarkson, M. Darrough,
T. R. Dyckman, G. A. Feltham,
M. Gibbins, N. H. Hakansson,
S. Haribhakti, P. J. Hughes, J. Joyce,
R. S. Kaplan, R. D. King, R. Libby,
S. Sunder, D. B. Thornton,
W. J. Vatter, R. L. Watts,
M. C. Wells, and J. L. Zimmerman;

The Canadian Certified
General Accountants' Research
Foundation

La Foundation de recherche de
l'Association des comptables
généraux licenciés du Canada

ISBN 0-920167-15-2

Additional copies of this monograph may be obtained by writing:
Director of Research
Canadian Certified General Accountants' Research Foundation
740-1176 West Georgia Street
Vancouver, British Columbia
V6E 4A2

Typography by:
R.E. Type-A-Graphic Inc., Vancouver, British Columbia
Printed by:
Pegasus Press Inc., Vancouver, British Columbia

To Maurice Moonitz, mentor and friend, and other eminent *members* and students of the "Berkeley School of Accounting"*

*Especially *Philip W. Bell*, Earl R. Blaine, *Wayne S. Boutell*, William J. Bruns, Jr., John E. Butterworth, Edwin H. Caplan, Donald G. A. Carter, *Alan R. Cerf, C. West Churchman*, Robert H. Crandall, *Carl T. Devine, Thomas R. Dyckman*, Gerald A. Feltham, Ronald Fraser, George Gorelik, *Henry R. Hatfield, Nils H. Hakansson*, Loyd C. Heath, Eldon S. Hendriksen, Carol Inberg, Vernon T. Kam, Greg Kunkel, Yu-Ku Li, James J. Linn, *Perry Mason*, Theodore J. Mock, W. A. Morehouse, Gerhard G. Mueller, Denis P. Neilson, David S. P. Ng, *James A. Ohlson*, C. Alan Prentice, Alexander A. Robichek, Janet R. M. Smith, *Robert T. Sprouse, George J. Staubus*, Russell A. Taussig, *John A. Tracy, Lawrence L. Vance, William J. Vatter, Robin Wagner, John T. Wheeler*, and Jerold L. Zimmerman.

vi

The Canadian Certified General Accountants' Research Foundation was incorporated and registered as a charitable foundation on May 30, 1979. The creation of the Foundation grew from the desire of members of the Canadian Certified General Accountants' Association to make a meaningful contribution to accounting research in Canada by supporting research which would advance the accounting community as a whole. It is our desire to encourage pure and applied research in the areas of auditing, accounting and finance.

This monograph is the seventh in a series to be published by the Certified General Accountants' Research Foundation as part of CGA Canada's continuing research effort. Each monograph expresses the viewpoint of its author(s), and has been neither approved nor disapproved by CGA Canada. These monographs are intended to stimulate thought discussion and debate on matters relating to accounting, auditing and finance. The Foundation welcomes comments from readers.

Gérald Sinotte, FCGA
President
Canadian Certified General Accountants'
Research Foundation
June 1984

Preface

THIS book is written for all those who are bewildered, or ought to be, by the large number of accounting research publications that have burst upon the scene during the last decade or so. It offers an overview and wants to serve as a guide for students, practitioners, and academics alike.

Contrary to other anthologies, this book contains many *research survey articles* and is more than a mere collection of essays. First, it is steeped in tradition and reflects an important phase of contemporary accounting history; it may therefore be of some permanent relevance. And second, it sums up forty years of my personal professional experience (I should say "the first forty years," because I do not intend it to be a swan song). Thus I beg the reader to make allowance for my personal bias and the occasional self-reference in the General Introduction as well as in the introductory commentaries attached to the various Parts of this anthology. But had I spared you my deep-rooted beliefs about the essence of accounting and the task of accounting research, the "soul" or unifying force of this book might have been lost. And since the agony and ecstasy of doing accounting research for three decades shine through the veneer of this book, I might just as well summarize them at this early stage:

On the *asset side* there is, first of all, the research atmosphere and most pleasant cooperation that I have found among my colleagues at the Faculty of Commerce and Business Administration of the University of British Columbia during the last sixteen years.

Second, related to this, is the deep satisfaction of having many of my former students teaching at the universities of a dozen countries; above all, knowing that several of them, notably John Butterworth, Bill Bruns, Jerry Feltham, Ted Mock, Eduardo Schwartz (in Finance), and others, have become prominent researchers in their own right.

Third, there is the fact that the analytical approach has thrived in our discipline during the last two decades and that my own work, particularly *Accounting and Analytical Methods*, has received wide international response in spite of (or perhaps because of) much controversy with Professor Ray Chambers on *multi-value* vs. *uni-value* (e.g., exit-value) accounting and other issues.

Fourth, the recent current value legislations in the United States (FASB, *Accounting Standard No.*

33) and in Canada (Section 4510, CICA *Handbook*) have finally put into practice something for which I have been struggling and pleading for a quarter of a century. I do not merely refer to legislating inflation accounting, but, above all, to the establishment of standards that are tolerant and flexible enough to permit *a choice among different accounting hypotheses for different information requirements* (for details, see Section 3 of the General Introduction and introductory commentary to Part II, especially footnote 3).

Fifth, I refer to the valuable contact with experts from actual practice through Arthur Andersen & Co., the American Institute of Certified Public Accountants, the Canadian Institute of Chartered Accountants, the Canadian Certified General Accountants' Research Foundation, the Financial Accounting Standards Board, the Institute of Chartered Accountants of British Columbia, and the latter's School of Chartered Accountancy.

As to the *agony and tribulations*, my greatest concern belongs to the regrettable constellation of circumstances that makes many young and a few older scholars believe that accounting can be treated as a pure or positive science. If this trend continues, there is a danger that accounting will fall into the trap of a clerisy and super-academism that, for example, proved to be disastrous to modern architecture.[1] Unless it is realized that *accounting is an applied discipline*, like architecture, engineering, and medicine, its theory will be able to fulfill neither its predominantly practical goals nor the genuine needs of its users.

A second difficulty lies in our failure, up to this point at least, to develop a set of interpretations capable of matching, rigorously and reliably, specific accounting hypotheses to specific information requirements. Although this matching process does go on in actual practice and is even accelerated by current legislation, it is based more on informal rationalization than on systematic analytical reasoning and empirically testable hypotheses.

The third point is closely related to the two preceding ones; it concerns the lack of rigor and generality (e.g., excluding macro-accounting systems) on the side of accounting bodies in formulating a conceptual framework, and the loss of nerves on the part of some academics in the search for a full-fledged general theory of accounting. The current efforts of the FASB and the CICA, and the *Statement of Accounting Theory and Theory Acceptance* (SATTA 1977), respectively, offer evidence in support of this complaint.

Finally, it seems surprising that our discipline — which is beset by many *methodological* problems — harbours so small a number of scholars interested in methodology as part of the philosophy of science. Admittedly, many methodological questions, which accounting shares with the other applied sciences, still loom in darkness and have as yet to be formulated. But it should be an incentive, rather than a deterrent, to concern oneself with this academic stepchild. And it was for this reason that I devoted a decade to the writing of *Instrumental Reasoning and Systems Methodology* (1978), which probes deeper into the foundations of applied science than any of my previous writings. But notwithstanding a surprisingly favourable response from behaviourists, economists, medical experts, philosophers, sociologists, and, above all, from systems experts, this book found hardly any echo within the accounting camp — a favourable discussion in *The Accounting Review* and an odd one in a German journal, the rare quote in some papers, and a few encouraging remarks from friends is all that came to my notice from this particular quarter. But the last point is the least of my worries; sooner or later, academic accountants too are bound to discover the need for a methodology of applied science.

Finally, let me thank all those who have made the publication of this book possible. First of all, thanks to the Canadian Certified General Accountants' Research Foundation, which has sponsored this project; also to my colleague and Division Chairman, Professor George Gorelik, as one of the Foundation's officials; and to its present and its former Director of Research, Messrs. Tom Abbott and R. C. Bell, respectively, as well as to Miss Barbara Hemphill and Mr. Len Webster, its editors. Further thanks go to the Social Sciences and Humanities Research Council, which supported research closely connected with this endeavour. Furthermore, I am most grateful to all the authors who contributed to this book through their personal efforts (above all, to Jerry Feltham, CGA-Professor of U.B.C., who wrote, particularly for the anthology, one of its finest essays), to our long-standing and eminent friend, Yuji Ijiri, leading accounting theorist and past President of the American Accounting

Association, for writing the Foreword to this book, and to the editors and publishers (listed separately) who gave copyright permissions for the reprinted articles. This prompts me to apologize to all those whose survey articles might well have been worth including but were barred by nothing more than the constraint of space — indeed, it was difficult to make the right selection.

Special thanks go to my research assistant, Mrs. Pamela Fraser, M.A., who contributed to the readability of the commentaries and without whose competence on the Word Processor, some of the manuscripts would not have come into being; furthermore, to Professor Masako Darrough, who joined me in writing the commentary to Part IV; also to Mr. Peter Clarkson, MBA, Ms. Valerie Kinnear, C.A., Mr. Rikard Smistad, C.A., and Mr. David Lee for assisting me in various jobs connected with this book; and finally, to my wife, Hermi, not only for reading and correcting commentaries and proofs, but also for her great patience and understanding.

Vancouver, B. C.
March, 1983

Richard Mattessich
"Arthur Andersen & Co.
Alumni Professor" of U.B.C.

FOOTNOTES

[1] For details, see the exciting and revealing book by Tom Wolfe, *From Bauhaus to Our House* (New York: Simon and Schuster, 1982).

Acknowledgements

ACKNOWLEDGEMENT is made to all publishers and editors of the books and journals in which the texts of most parts of this anthology were first published. We are grateful to them for their permissions to reprint.

Part II: Richard Mattessich, "An Evaluation of the Statement on Accounting Theory and Theory Acceptance: Summary," in *Collected Papers of the American Accounting Association's Annual Meeting, 1978* (Sarasota, Fla.: AAA, 1978), pp. 597-600; Richard Mattessich, "On the Evolution of Theory Construction in Accounting: A Personal Account," *Accounting and Business Research* 10 (Special Accounting History Issue 1980), pp. 158-173; Murray C. Wells, "A Revolution in Accounting Thought?" *The Accounting Review* 51 (July 1976), pp. 471-482; Nils H. Hakansson, "On the Interaction of Accounting, Economics, and Finance and the Economic Consequences of Accounting," Plenary Address given at the Annual Meeting of the American Accounting Association — Honolulu, Hawaii, August 21-25, 1979 (Berkeley, Calif.: Institute of Business and Economic Research for the Professional Accounting Program); Nils H. Hakansson, "Where We Are in Accounting: A Review of 'Statement on Accounting Theory and Theory Acceptance,'" *The Accounting Review* 53 (July 1978), pp. 717-725.

Part III: Ross. L. Watts and Jerold L. Zimmerman, "Towards a Positive Theory of the Determination of Accounting Standards," *The Accounting Review* 53 (January 1978), pp. 112-134; Ross L. Watts and Jerold L. Zimmerman, "The Demand for and Supply of Accounting Theories: The Market for Excuses," *The Accounting Review* 54 (April 1979), pp. 273-305; Charles Christenson, "The Methodology of Positive Accounting," *The Accounting Review* 58 (January 1983), pp. 1-22.

Part IV: John E. Butterworth, Michael Gibbins, and Raymond D. King, "The Structure of Accounting Theory: Some Basic Conceptual and Methodological Issues," in *Research to Support Standard Setting in Financial Accounting: A Canadian Perspective, Proceedings of the 1981 Research Symposium*, ed. Sanjoy Basu and J. Alex Milburn (Toronto: Clarkson, Gordon Foundation, 1982), pp. 1-65; Stanley Baiman, "Agency Research in Managerial

Accounting: A Survey," *Journal of Accounting Literature* 1 (Spring 1982), pp. 154-213.

Part V: Thomas R. Dyckman, Michael Gibbins, and Robert J. Swieringa, "Experimental and Survey Research in Financial Accounting: A Review and Evaluation," in *The Impact of Accounting Research on Practice and Disclosure*, ed. A. Rashad Abdel-khalik and Thomas F. Keller (Durham, N. C.: Duke University Press, 1978), pp. 48-105; Robert S. Kaplan, "The Information Content of Financial Accounting Numbers: A Survey of Empirical Evidence," in *The Impact of Accounting Research on Practice and Disclosure*, ed. A. Rashad Abdel-khalik and Thomas F. Keller (Durham, N. C.: Duke University Press, 1978), pp. 134-173; Michael Gibbins and Patricia Hughes, "Behavioral Research And Financial Accounting Standards," in *Usefulness to Investors and Creditors of Information Provided by Financial Reporting: A Review of Empirical Accounting Research*, ed. Paul A. Griffin (Stamford, Conn.: Financial Accounting Standards Board, 1982), pp. 99-134.

Part VI: Richard Mattessich, "Management Accounting, Past, Present, and Future," in *Management Accounting 1980: Proceedings of the University of Illinois Management Accounting Symposium*, ed. H. Peter Holzer (Urbana-Champaign: University of Illinois, 1980), pp. 209-240; Robert S. Kaplan, "Application of Quantitative Models in Managerial Accounting: A State of the Art Survey," in *Management Accounting — State of the Art*, Beyer Lecture Series 1976-77 (Madison, Wisconsin: University of Wisconsin Graduate School of Business, 1977), pp. 29-71; William J. Vatter, "State of the Art — Non-Business Accounting," *The Accounting Review* 54 (July 1979), pp. 574-584; Edward J. Joyce and Robert Libby, "Behavioral Studies of Audit Decision Making," *Journal of Accounting Literature* 1 (Spring 1982), pp. 103-123.

Foreword

by Yuji Ijiri

WHEN Professor Richard Mattessich invited me to write a Foreword to his new book, *Modern Accounting Research: History, Survey, and Guide*, I felt that our roles should have been reversed, since I am junior to him, both in age and in accomplishments. But my prior association with the Canadian Certified General Accountants Research Foundation, sponsoring this project, persuaded me to accept this honor.

Professor Mattessich's phenomenal breadth and depth of knowledge in science provides an extremely valuable source to draw upon when judging accounting issues. He is a rare accounting scholar indeed, who has published on Philosophy, Logic, and Methodology.

The present volume represents his attempt to develop a framework of accounting research in collaboration with a number of outstanding accounting scholars. In fact, this book is a "supermodel" of accounting research. It is a collection of articles, together with a carefully written General Introduction and Commentaries preceding the individual sections. Each article is a survey of some accounting research area or else deals with a particular aspect, thus presenting different models of accounting research.

Choosing rigorous criteria, Professor Mattessich selected these articles out of numerous publications that have appeared during the last decade or so. He has structured them in such a way that a "supermodel" emerges which expresses his personal conviction about what accounting and accounting research ought to be. The anthology reflects his strong belief that accounting is an *applied science* — a science and not an art, an applied science and not a pure science, a science because of its *methodology*, an applied one because of its *goal-orientation*. These are two fundamental aspects of accounting that Professor Mattessich has highlighted throughout his previous writings. Consequently, he emphasizes that accounting research must be based on a rigorous methodology and must be guided by a normative and teleological prospect — just as in any other applied science, such as engineering or medicine.

The work also reflects the fact that accounting as a discipline goes far beyond the practice in any given country. The contributors to this volume represent many countries, and Professor

Mattessich himself has a multiple representation through his vast international experience. This anthology is most indicative of the truly international nature of modern accounting.

As a long-time friend and colleague of Professor Mattessich and many of the contributors to this volume, I sincerely hope that the viewpoints on accounting and accounting research embedded in this book will receive wide and serious attention from the accounting community.

Part I

GENERAL
INTRODUCTION

THE SCIENTIFIC APPROACH TO ACCOUNTING

by Richard Mattessich

SOME GENERAL AND HISTORICAL REMARKS

TWO periods in the history of modern accounting theory[1] might be characterized as particularly exciting and full of fermenting, novel ideas. The first of these covers the twenties and early thirties of this century, while the second began in the late fifties and extends into the present. The earlier period is marked, in America, by such prestigious names as William A. Paton, John B. Canning, Arthur C. Littleton, Stephen Gilman, Henry R. Hatfield, Roy B. Kester, Kenneth F. MacNeal, George O. May, Thomas H. Sanders, Maurice E. Peloubet, D. R. Scott, Charles E. Sprague, and Henry W. Sweeney, as well as that of the eminent economist, Irving Fisher, and by a galaxy of no lesser names in Europe: Heinrich Nicklisch, Eugen Schmalenbach, Fritz Schmidt, Johann F. Schär, Wilhelm Rieger, Léon Gomberg, Walter Le Coutre, Walter Mahlberg, Heinrich Sommerfeld, and Ernst Walb in the German language area; Fabio Besta, S. Rossi, and Gino Zappa in Italy; Theo Limperg in Holland; and E. Gomberg, L. Quesnot, and others in the French language area.

If, during this first period, the impetus and major international influence came from Germany,[2] there can be no doubt that the second period has been dominated from the very beginning by the Anglo-American literature (for an overview of recent accounting research in Great Britain, see Bromwich and Hopwood [1981]). A somewhat subjective picture of how this second period began is offered in our first article of Part II, "On the Evolution of Theory Construction in Accounting: A Personal Account." The background offered there (and in the remaining papers of Part II) must be considered a prerequisite for comprehending the present state of theoretical accounting, but the main focus of this anthology is on the research activity of the seventies and dawning eighties.

There is presently an urgent need to bridge the constantly widening gap between accounting research and professional accountants (including accounting students), because accounting literature is becoming ever more technical and mathematical. Indeed, due to the highly sophisticated statistical, probabilistic, and empirical tools employed in present-day research, the situation has become so incongruous that a good deal of this literature is inaccessible, not only to accounting practitioners and undergraduates, but even to our graduate students at the master level. It seems that only a doctoral degree in business administration or economics would provide sufficient background to fully comprehend some of this literature. Obviously, this book offers no crash programme for obtaining such an understanding, and the reader might wonder how the gap between research and practice can ever be bridged. But we hope that this collection of *survey articles*, in combination with the *short commentaries* to the various Parts and the *current General Introduction*, will serve as a first step toward clarifying the endeavours of present-day academic literature for practitioners and students of accounting as well as for more traditionally oriented academics. However, without an honest desire and some serious effort on the part of practitioners to overcome their diffidence toward academic literature, the chasm between practice and research will continue to grow and, in time, must affect the social and intellectual climate as well as the long-run economic conditions of countries afflicted by this kind of alienation.

Yet the burden of a changing attitude lies equally on the shoulders of the academic community. Even if some of its research tools surpass the skill of practitioners, its literary presentations ought to be comprehensible to a wider spectrum of accountants — at least to those who seriously endeavour to digest academic literature. Furthermore, *academics must pay greater attention to the goals and needs of accounting practice*. For these reasons, we hope that the present anthology will be of interest not only to the profession and to students, but also to academic accountants. And it is for the same reasons that we feel compelled in our commentaries to question the present quest for an exclusively *positive* theory of accounting. It has recently become fashionable among accounting researchers to deride *normative theory* in the same way as the Victorians derided sex: namely, without being able to dispense with it.

Can an *applied* discipline like accounting refuse to deal with *goals*, *norms*, and *prescriptive* conclusions? Does not the broad spectrum of information goals manifested by different accounting user groups necessitate a *search for the means by which each of these ends can be achieved*? Does accounting not have the major dual task of demonstrating, on one side, *which accounting standards satisfy which national economic and social goals*, and, on the other side, *which specific accounting systems serve which information purposes*? If these questions are to be affirmed, then surely accounting theory must be conditionally prescriptive. This does not mean a rejection of positive models and subtheories. Partial theories and hypotheses may prove highly useful for accounting, even if purely descriptive; but a theory serving the ultimate purpose of our discipline cannot renounce prescriptions based on preconceived goals. Twenty-five years ago, when game theory came into its own, similar thoughts were expressed by Luce and Raiffa in the following passage, which we may accept verbatim provided one substitutes "accounting theory" for the expression "game theory:"

> We belabor this point because we feel that it is crucial that the social scientists recognize that game theory is not *descriptive*, but rather (conditionally) *normative*. It states neither how people do behave nor how they should behave in an absolute sense, but how they should behave if they wish to achieve certain ends. [Luce and Raiffa 1957, p. 63]

And even such a positivistically oriented scholar as Herbert Simon warns of the onesided research training in present-day professional schools and appeals for a science of design, i.e., for teleologically oriented research:

> Engineering schools have become schools of physics and mathematics; medical schools have become schools of biological science; business schools have become schools of finite mathematics. . . .
> The problem is widely recognized in engineering and medicine today and to a lesser extent in business. . . . The older kind of professional school did not know how to educate for professional design at an intellectual level appropriate to a university; the newer kind of school has nearly abdicated responsibility for training in the core professional skill. Thus we are faced with a problem of devising a professional school that can attain two objectives simultaneously: education in both artificial and natural science at a high intellectual level. This too is a problem of design — organizational design. [Simon 1981, pp. 130-131]

ACCOUNTING AS AN APPLIED SCIENCE

Many people, including practitioners, question the usefulness of a scientific approach to accounting. They may ask whether our discipline has not always been an "art" rather than a "science". Apart from the fact that the terms "art" and "science" (or their equivalents) are nowadays differently understood in most European languages than in traditional English, we must bear in mind that accounting is in a similar position as engineering and medicine. In the past, both of these have been considered arts but are presently accepted as applied sciences. In the end, it is the *methodology* that determines whether a discipline manifests itself as an art, a science, or a mere skill. And it is this criterion that is responsible for the transition which such arts as medicine and engineering have undergone to become applied sciences. A glance into the cultural history of the last hundred fifty years leaves little doubt that scientific methods have progressively penetrated these two areas as well as other disciplines, converting them from arts to applied sciences. During the twentieth century, these same scientific methods have gradually been adopted by our discipline, and the inclusion of academic accounting among the applied sciences seems to be well justified. *General* theories of applied sciences are relatively novel; they have, in spite of their generality, a specific focus and also find increasing support in the accelerating trend towards computerization. In medicine, it is the general theory of diagnosis and therapy as well as of the determination and prevention of vectors of disease; in architecture and engineering, there is the endeavour towards a general theory of design; and in accounting, the pivot can hardly be anything else but the flow and aggregation of wealth and their representation through input-output models.

But two things must be borne in mind: (i) scientific-academic training alone makes neither every physician nor every engineer nor every accountant a scientist; and (ii) the adoption of a scientific methodology will never convert accounting into a *pure* science. This latter fact, coupled with an insufficient distinction between applied and pure science by the young Turks of accounting research, is a potential source of misunderstanding our discipline and its raison d'être. Of course, there are parallels with pure sciences: just as bubble chamber photography and nuclear physics are recording and analyzing the interactions involved in the creation, distribution, and destruction of *particles*, accounting is recording and analyzing the interactions involved in the creation, distribution, and destruction of *"values"* (not merely as "value measures," but in the sense of "bearers of utility"). And, in the face of modern physics, no one can claim that values are more volatile or elusive than are nuclear and subnuclear particles. Yet there is one major difference: physics looks at the world from a positive and nonteleologic point of view, while accounting regards it from a *normative and teleologic* prospect. The reason for this lies in the fact that particles belong to the realm of matter and energy, while "values" are part of the realm of mind, information, and purpose.

If accounting is a science, or ever becomes one, it will by its very nature be an *applied* (or *instrumental*) science but not a pure one. The major difference between pure and applied science lies in the fact that a pure science is *disinterested*, that is, *purely cognitively* oriented, and does *not directly* serve practical ends. Whereas an applied science *directly* pursues such practical purposes as fighting diseases, or building machinery and edifices, or measuring aggregates and increments of wealth attributed to some micro- or macro-economic entity to facilitate decisions and choices.[3] Thus every applied science, besides pursuing a cognitive end and doing some *fundamental* research, becomes an *instrument* for attaining "efficiently" a fairly well defined area of goals beyond the satisfaction of mere scientific curiosity. In the pure sciences, *teleologic thinking* is still prohibited, while in the applied sciences it is a necessity. Familiarity with the dichotomy between pure and applied science and comprehension of the latter's essential nature are paramount for a genuine insight into the major problems confronting present-day accounting.[4]

Schreuder, for example, states that:

> accounting is neither a "pure" nor an "applied" science — nor a combination of the two.
> . . . However, accounting is no applied science either since its "applications" hardly ever
> are direct translations of insights from pure theory.[5]

The first part of this statement is not acceptable to us as it contradicts the deeply-rooted customary division of all sciences into pure and applied ones, and the second part is no more acceptable. It not only implies that most of accounting theory is practically irrelevant, but makes the characterization of an *applied* science dependent on the degree to which practitioners are willing and sophisticated enough to apply it. The recent legislation of current cost accounting in several industrialized countries — after a research period of no less than six decades — is only one among many instances demonstrating that accounting theory is decisively influential in actual practice, and increasingly so. To this extent, accounting is already an applied science and undoubtedly has considerable growth potential.

THE SPECIAL CASE OF INFLATION ACCOUNTING

Although this book touches upon the most important core areas of modern accounting research (excluding taxation, management information systems, and other peripheral areas), some omissions were unavoidable. The most crucial of these concerns are the broad field of inflation accounting and closely related areas.[6] The following reasons prompted us to omit such fashionable topics from this book:
• Inflation accounting and its recent literature constitutes such a vast and important field that it deserves a separate book, which hopefully will materialize in the not-too-distant future.
• Although dealing with many subtle and intricate problems, the most original research in this area was done in the twenties and thirties and, to some extent, in the sixties.[7]
• Practitioners might be more familiar with problems and research on inflation accounting than with the more recent research in information economics, behavioural accounting, agency theory, etc. Hence inflation accounting requires a different kind of presentation than that offered in this book; it might need more emphasis on historical and analytical aspects rather than on a collection of surveys or similar articles.[8]

However, there is one aspect of inflation accounting that is of some relevance to the previously mentioned need for a conditional-normative or purpose-oriented accounting theory, because the *means-end relationships* are especially transparent in the case of basic inflation accounting models. At first, it might even seem that there exists a one-to-one correspondence between model and information purpose. Does not the *historical cost* model satisfy the need for maintaining *nominal* financial capital, the *general purchasing power* model that for *real* financial capital, and the *simple (nominal) current cost* model that for *physical capital*? Are not the two issues of "income model structure" and "a particular capital maintenance notion" two sides of the same coin? We would hesitate to give an affirmative answer, because the situation is more intricate than it might at first appear (for further details, see Mattessich [1981a]). Since there exists a means-end relationship between a special inflation accounting model and the income measurement under a particular capital maintenance requirement, the problem is not trivial; yet it is simple enough to serve as a starting point for exploring *the fundamental and more general problem of relating a specific accounting system to a particular information requirement.*[9] To determine *ex post* which of two investments afforded a higher yield, can often (at least in times of shifting prices) not be answered without first answering another question: namely, whether the required income measurement ought to be based on real financial or on physical capital maintenance or on any other assumption. The absolute-normatists have long quarreled with each other about the question: which of these bases is the correct one? But, in principle, *only a conditional answer is appropriate*. In a certain context, real financial capital maintenance offers the proper income figure and physical capital maintenance a distorted one, while in another context it may well be vice versa. Although there exist some obvious examples to confirm this assertion, accountants have not sufficiently explored the various contexts to realize that, here too, a *conditional-normative* approach is indispensable. Yet the *preference and effective demand* for more differentiated accounting information *relevant to a variety of different conditions* is now overt enough to call for its general acceptance by practitioners and academics alike.

The formulation of this approach may be either in terms of *preference* and *demand* or, more fundamentally, in terms of basic and derived *needs*, the diversity of which grows with the complexity of the economy. The basic needs are for *energy* (in the form of different nutritional and other substances for sustenance, protection, propagation, etc.) and for *information*, without which the sources of energy, etc., could not be perceived. Unfortunately, present-day economics has shied away from recognizing these subjective needs (which are neither absolute nor perfectly inelastic) as the roots of its more objective and aggregate notions of preference and demand. But accounting must also draw upon the behavioural sciences, in which the concept of need figures prominently (e.g., Maslow [1970], Merton [1973], and Sorokin [1937, vol.I]).

Such explorations might lead to answers more scientific and more systematic than those previously offered when addressing such questions as the following: Which particular inflation accounting model is satisfactory or optimal for a specific firm? Which inflation accounting standards are most appropriate under particular welfare goals? Which electronic data processing system is most desirable in a special situation? And the answers to these questions might be complemented by extending the frame of reference in such a way that the information requirement itself becomes the means, and the more basic economic goal the end. This leads to an extension of the notion of *rational behaviour*, which then refers not only to the choice of a particular means for attaining a particular end, but also to the shifting from one end to another depending upon circumstances (see Harsanyi [1976, pp. 92 ff.]). In accounting, this results in such questions as: When shall a particular firm pursue the maintenance of real financial capital (for the purpose of identifying the profit figure), when of physical capital, or when of economic earning power? The answers to all these questions are *conditionally prescriptive* and cannot be supplied by a *positive* accounting theory, because, contrary to a popular fallacy, a normative theory is more than a positive theory supplemented by some goal statements and simple inferences. Although there is a need for positive models in *limited areas of accounting, the major and ultimate problems of accounting will not be solved without resorting to a conditional-normative theory*. Ultimately, this is rooted in the *fundamental dilemma of the economic sciences* (pure as well as applied). Too often they are assumed to be rigorous empirical sciences, without, however, having reached that stage. Most of them are *quasi-empirical sciences*, with a more or less heavy analytical framework resting on a host of unrealistic assumptions.

Therefore, this apologetic subsection is hopefully serving a second purpose: namely, to remind the reader that, in digesting the subsequent material, the crucial quest for *relating means to ends on various levels* must not be forgotten. Every hypothesis or model or theory of accounting ought to be seen as an instrument for attaining a particular goal as "efficiently" as possible; and awareness of the complexity of inferring the pertinent means from this end is of paramount importance.

VARIOUS ASPECTS OF MODERN ACCOUNTING RESEARCH

In this book we have tried to offer a representative, though by no means exhaustive, picture of modern accounting research. The major vehicle to reach this goal is "the survey article," and most of the papers included are reprints of this kind or of a related type. But there are *five hitherto unpublished papers* included in this book: our present paper on "The Scientific Approach to Accounting;" an article by M. J. Bryant and D. B. Thornton on "Public Choice of Corporate Accounting Standards," one by S. Sunder and S. Haribhakti on "Economic Interests and Accounting Standards" (both in *Part III*); the superb article by Gerald Feltham (in *Part IV*), "Financial Accounting Research: Contributions of Information Economics and Agency Theory;" and that by Peter Clarkson and myself (in *Part V*), "A Review of Market Research in Financial Accounting," pointing to some of the empirical accounting literature not indicated in the other papers of *Part V*.

Part II (Evolution or Revolution of Modern Accounting Theory?) sets the stage by hinting at the evolutionary background and the recent predicaments of accounting research. Our own article illuminates the events out of which present accounting research arose, partly as a consequence of and partly as a reaction to the original trend towards reform and axiomatization. The article by Wells then examines the possible occurrence of a paradigm shift in modern accounting; while one article by Hakansson discusses the interrelations between economics, finance, and accounting so crucial for modern research, his other article offers a frank and pertinent criticism of SATTA (the American Accounting Association's latest decennial report, the *Statement on Accounting Theory and Theory Acceptance*).

Part III (Positive versus Normative Accounting Theory and Standard Setting) deals with an issue most decisive for the future of our discipline. Is a general positive theory of accounting indispensable, necessary, desirable, or even possible? The two articles by Watts and Zimmerman seem to plead strongly for such a positive theory (or do they plead only for a "positive theory of lobbying behaviour"?), while Christenson's article offers strong arguments against it, claiming that Watts and Zimmerman's "positive theory" is based on a methodological misunderstanding. Bryant and Thornton's paper might be taken as more neutral, but offers a novel approach towards constructing an accounting theory different from that of Watts and Zimmerman. Finally, the paper by Sunder and Haribhakti offers lucid insight into the problems of setting accounting standards and some reasonable suggestions.

Part IV (Agency Theory and Information Economics) emphasizes the *analytical* aspects of modern accounting research. The three comprehensive papers by Feltham, by Butterworth, Gibbins, and King, and by Baiman — although all dealing with the integrated areas of agency theory and information economics — complement each other and should offer an excellent insight into this newly emerging and exciting subdiscipline.

Part V (Empirical Accounting Research) begins with two classic survey papers, one by Dyckman, Gibbins, and Swieringa, the other by Robert Kaplan. These papers reveal the wealth of *empirical* research in the sixties and seventies, especially in *financial* accounting on the basis of experimental or survey research. They are complemented and updated through an article by Gibbins and Hughes (formerly Brennan). The last paper by Clarkson and myself, with special emphasis on the research efforts based on stock market data, attempts to round out the picture of this novel and vigorous research area.

Part VI (Managerial and Institutional Accounting, and Auditing). Although *financial* accounting research stood in the forefront during the last decade or more, this research has important implications for *managerial* accounting and possibly for *institutional* ("non-business" accounting). Our own paper, beginning with a concise historical glance, may shed some light on these implications and on the possible impact of information economics and agency theory upon cost and management accounting, while the paper by Robert Kaplan is a classic survey paper for this area. The paper by Vatter summarizes the area of institutional accounting, which might well become more prominent in the future, while the paper by Joyce and Libby offers insight into the highly fashionable behavioural research efforts within the area of auditing.

ACCOUNTING AND METHODOLOGY

In the second *Section 2*, we referred to the particular methodology as the criterion for designating a discipline as a science, pure or applied. But what is this methodology, of what does it consist, and what is its relation to the ultimate theory? Although there is a trend toward methodological pluralism (see Caldwell [1982] for its promotion in economics), it seems that every empirical science requires the following six methodological components, but the weight which each step bears may vary greatly from discipline to discipline:

- Observation, experimentation, and their design.
- Qualitative and quantitative description.
- Generalization (usually through inductive inferences or other conjectures).
- Analysis (through mathematical and other deductive inferences).

- Interpretation and model-building (further specification and linking of theoretical terms to observational terms by means of rules of correspondence or indicator hypotheses).
- Testing and revising (usually through some confirming or corroborating evidence, attempts of refutation, and demonstration of coherence with neighbouring theories or hypotheses).

OBSERVATION, EXPERIMENTATION AND THEIR DESIGN

Direct or indirect observation of some naturally occurring or experimentally induced phenomena is the beginning of every empirical-scientific undertaking. Accounting too is based on observation, but can hardly be called an experimental science. Nevertheless, the behavioural-experimental approach has been introduced to budgeting by Argyris [1952], has been developed by Stedry [1960] and others, and has found application in further areas of accounting. Occasionally, it is discussed under a combined heading together with the survey approach — see the article by Dyckman, Gibbins, and Swieringa in *Part V.* Yet the results of experiments in accounting may be doubtful for the following reasons: (1) the selection of the subjects may not be representative enough, or the task-surrogation may be inadequate (e.g., in experiments about managerial decisions where students instead of managers are being observed); (2) the resulting generalizations may not hold universally but may be valid only for a narrowly restricted universe of discourse (e.g., certain budgetary incentives leading to higher performance of the managers may be effective only with persons of a certain educational background — a limitation the experimenter may not be aware of); (3) control groups, permitting a comparison between subjects experiencing the experimental impact and those not experiencing it, may not have been provided for or properly arranged (e.g., stockholders may be deemed to be influenced in their investment decisions by a certain accounting practice, while actually those not affected by this practice may react no differently).

At any rate, a good deal of empirical accounting research is nonexperimental and relies on observations of things and facts occurring in the ordinary course of accounting activity in the broadest sense. This may include professional observations carried out by both the practitioner (and his aids) as well as the scientist. More often than not, *the observations made by the practicing accountants* are vicarious and rely on written evidence contained in documents, reports, vouchers, and other scraps of paper that are actual but not ultimate objects of observation.

Academic accountants, in contrast, try to observe directly by means of surveys, questionnaires, etc., and by the reactions of persons, groups of persons, and systems (shareholders, creditors, managers, accountants, employees, consumers, unions, governmental agencies, computers, etc.) to certain events and alternative structures of accounting systems (e.g., to competing accounting *goals* and standards). Of course, these observations often assume the very impersonal form of prices, values, and quantities transacted, of mathematical functions with more or less reliable parameters expressing the "behavioural" nature of the hypotheses inferred. But, not all academic accountants are, or need be, empiricists, just as not all physicists are experimentalists. The need for good analytical accountants is no less than that for empiricists.

Before discussing the next methodological step of the scientific approach, the question may be raised whether *values*, so prominent in accounting, can be scientifically observed in spite of their ultimately subjective nature. Traditionally, purely introspective experiences were excluded from the pure sciences, since the required *objective confirmation* is not feasible. Values have their roots in needs of people and possibly also in those of other creatures. The urge to satisfy those needs creates *preferences* (and, if quantified, *utilities*) vis-à-vis various objects of gratification, and the manifestation of these preferences are *subjective values* (or values in use). These subjective values (interacting with the scarcity, i.e., the demand and supply situation for the commodities satisfying those needs) lead to a price which becomes the *"objective" value* (or value in exchange) negotiated between a seller and a buyer. Thus all genuine values (as distinct from mere "value labels") are ultimately based on subjective values. Indeed, the adjective "objective" rather refers here to an objectification attempt of two or more different subjective values within a market, rather than to something objective in the scientific sense. What is observable is the choice behaviour and the agreement on a price that, through more or less "accidental" circumstances, may lie anywhere between the subjective value of the seller and the subjective value of the buyer, provided the latter value is higher than the former (otherwise, it is obvious that no agreement can be attained). Thus, although a price actually paid can usually be confirmed objectively, grave doubts arise (1) whether this event of price formation, even when occurring in a perfect market, can be used as *exclusive* standards for the values of all commodities of the same kind *but not presently traded in this market*,[10] and (2) whether subjective values (e.g., discounted expected future net benefits of the asset) should not be equally accepted in accounting since they are indispensable for any investment or disinvestment decision. Indeed, in theory and practice, many financial experts extend their interest to subjective values no less than to subjective probabilities, i.e., introspection and its manifestation in preferences, beliefs, and actual choices. This *value-ladenness of accounting observation* is also found on higher levels where the objects of observation, as well as the methods and experiments, have to be selected on the basis of subjective choices.

QUALITATIVE AND QUANTITATIVE DESCRIPTION

Observations have to be recorded and systematically described. This can be done verbally, by various classification schemes, by graphical or algebraic devices and, above all, by measurement. The latter is regarded by some experts as nothing but numerical description (also called quantification) and is often considered the most precise way of describing something. But caution as to the limitations and deceptions of quantification is advised. In accounting practice, classification and valuation, both of which might be considered special kinds of measurement, are predominant; while in accounting theory, in addition to valuation and classification, verbal description still abounds, although mathematical or symbolic representations have steadily increased during the last two decades.

Various *scales of measurement* [see Mattessich, 1964/1977 and Mock, 1976] have been employed in accounting no less than in other areas for the purpose of quantitative description, yet the distinction of various measurement scales is not sufficient. To understand a measure, one must also be able to discriminate between various types of measurement. One scheme distinguishes between fundamental, derived, and fiat measurement (see Torgerson [1958]), the other between deterministic and probabilistic measurement. Figure 1 combines both categories in a two-dimensional presentation.

Typical *fundamental measures* are those of weight, length, and volume. All these properties are directly accessible, and the rules of measurement are based on scientific laws. In contrast to this are *derived measures* like those of density or specific weight, where weight and volume have to be measured before the density measure can be derived. In accounting and other economic sciences, *measurement by fiat* plays an important role because its rules of measurement are not scientific laws but less rigorous hypotheses. Take *acquisition cost valuation*, *current market valuation*, and *"present value" valuation*; in each case, a different valuation hypothesis is employed, but none can be considered a law statement. Nevertheless, each valuation hypothesis fulfills a specific purpose, and its use can be justified under particular circumstances.

The distinction between *deterministic* and *probabilistic* measures refers more to the technique than to the scientific basis, because measurement, by its very nature, is bound to be a probabilistic activity. That is to say, every measure, if carried to an extreme degree of accuracy, is fraught with error. To convey this unreliability, one would have to measure the same property not once, but often enough to establish a frequency distribution to indicate the meanvalue together with some measure of dispersion. In accounting, the closest to probabilistic measurement is the statement of some error estimates immediately after the figures representing the actual or supposed (mean) values. For example, the value $350,000 $\pm$ 10,000 would indicate that the actual value would range between $340,000 and $360,000, although the pertinent degree of confidence (e.g., 95 per cent) might not be explicitly indicated. Such error estimates "measured" on a ratio, scale, or even ordinal scale (e.g., A...for high,

B. . .for medium, and C. . .for low accuracy) have been presented in some national income account-ing systems and might be desirable in other areas of accounting. More recently, Oliver [1972] and several dissertations used behavioural experiments to study the effect of "confidence intervals" in financial statements for hypothetical lending decisions by bankers, etc. On the level of behavioural accounting research, highly sophisticated statistical measurement procedures have been introduced.

A two-dimensional Classification:	Fundamental Measurement	Derived Measurement	Measurement by fiat
Deterministic Measurement	(1) Based on scien-tific laws. (2) Properties are directly measurable. No error estimates are available.	(1) Based on scien-tific laws. (2) Properties are derived. No er-ror estimates are available.	(1) Based on less rigorous hypotheses. (2) Properties are directly or in-directly measurable. (3) No error estimates.
Probabilistic Measurement	(1) Based on scien-tific law. (2) Properties are directly measurable. Er-ror estimates are available.	(1) Based on scien-tific laws. (2) Properties are derived. Error estimates are available.	(1) Based on less rigorous hypotheses. (2) Properties are directly or in-directly measurable. (3) Error estimates available.

Figure 1: *Types of Measurement*

Although measurement may be defined as the assignment of numerals to objects or events accor-ding to (determinative and nondegenerate) rules (cf. Stevens [1946] and Ellis [1968, pp. 39-42]), fur-ther requirements are usually stipulated (cf. Mock [1976]). Since quantification always involves the comparison between some property of an object or event (called the Empirical Relational System [ERS]), on one side, and a numerical scale (the Numerical Relational System [NRS]), on the other side, measure-ment is regarded as a homomorphic (many-to-one) or even isomorphic (one-to-one) mapping of an ERS into an NRS. But the quality of this mapping is judged by some or all the criteria listed in the following: *valid representation* (how well or "fine" the relations of the NRS represent those of the ERS); *uniqueness* (the lack or the availability of alternative measures); *meaningfulness* (being infor-mative and relevant to the measurement purpose, standardization, consistency, uniformity, etc.); *reliability* (relative freedom from error or noise, low statistical variance); *simplicity* (avoidance of unnecessarily complicated scales or methods).

"Measure theory" is another area of increasing importance for accountants. It must not be confus-ed with the general theory of measurement but is a part of modern mathematics and deals with measure functions and measurable sets (see also Mock [1976, pp. 9-26]). Demski [1980, pp. 11-22 and 23-41] devotes several sections of his book to a special application of measure theory: namely, to the quan-tification of preferences in form of utilities and utility functions as well as to the problem of fineness vs. coarseness of the classificational system available to express the information (a problem equally valid in measurement).

GENERALIZATION AND INDUCTION

One of the most commonly encountered *fallacies* in texts of accounting theory and other methodological treatises of administrative studies is the view that induction must proceed from the particular to the general, whereas deduction must proceed from the general to the particular. This misconception becomes obvious if one considers the well-known fact that it is not only possible to induce the constitution of the universe of discourse from a representative sample, but also the constitution of the sample from that of the universe. Actually, both inductive and deductive inferences can be drawn from the particular (or the more particular) to the general or from the general to the (more) particular or from the general to the general or from the particular to the particular. Therefore, inductive inference (which requires not only logic but also psychology for its full comprehension) should be regarded as an inference, the outcome of which is less than certain.

But generalization, or, more precisely, the formulation of *universal propositions* expressing causal regularities of natural and social behaviour, is the most crucial step in scientific methodology. Some scholars consider it so important as to exclude the study of history from the *sciences* because history is dominated by so-called *singular and existential* propositions (which make statements merely about a particular thing or the *existence* of *particular* things or events, and rarely, if ever, are capable of pronouncing law-like generalizations). This leads to the precarious question of how general must a generalization be to be acceptable to science? The laws of physics, with some stretch of imagination, might be formulated as *unbounded* universal propositions, asserting validity for the entire universe. Although the social and administrative sciences also generate universal propositions, the boundaries of their universe of discourse are set so much tighter that one no longer dares to speak of law statements, and the question arises whether a science without a respectable number of law statements can be justified. Some scholars try to resolve the dilemma by accepting more narrowly bounded universal propositions under such expressions as "quasi laws," "lawlike propositions," etc. The ultimate boldness is found in the substitution of mere correlations (without any assurance of *causal* relations) for scientific laws. Although this proves to be most precarious, it is done without much ado in econometrics, even in physics, and is often accepted in accounting and other administrative sciences where instrumental goals, beyond mere cognition, are pursued. Indeed, for an applied science, mere correlations often constitute useful substitutes for rigorous hypotheses, proving the fragility of our knowledge.

Frequently encountered generalizations in traditional accounting involve the formulation of hypotheses as regards depreciation, the aging of accounts, allocation, classification, cost curves, valuations, etc., while in modern empirical accounting research, many hypotheses deal with the behaviour of users and producers of accounting data as well as with market behaviour. In most cases, some kind of inductive procedure is involved in such generalizations (this, however, means neither that generalization can be attained only by induction, nor that induction must always result in a universal proposition). Let us illustrate the inductive process as applied to the construction of an (imaginary) cost curve.

A cost curve expresses the total cost (or the cost of a particular item) as a function of some output variable (in dollars, units, weights, etc.). The knowledge of such functions can be of great benefit to managerial accounting and decision making (for determining breakeven points, price setting, measures of cost reductions, etc.) and also has proved most interesting from a theoretical point of view (e.g., whether linear approximations to cost functions prove, in general, realistic enough). In practice, the cost curve is constructed by determining the pertinent cost at least at two points, at a relatively low output level and at a relatively high output level, and by connecting these two or more points. This primitive procedure yields only crude results that, however — under the required cost-benefit consideration of small firms — might prove to be within the orbit of acceptability. Occasionally, and most likely in scientific studies, more sophisticated techniques like regression analysis, maximum likelihood estimates, etc., are employed for fitting a curve into a large number of individual data. These are derived from individual observations which, by means of one or the other statistical-inductive inference, are generalized to a linear or nonlinear cost function (or production function, from which the cost function can be easily derived). Thus the data represent the factual evidence, while the cost curve represents the generalized hypothesis. Another example of an inductive generalization is the inference of the "cash collection formula" for budgeting purposes. If it were observed that, during the past five years (prior to a budgeting period), approximately 95 percent of the beginning balance of Accounts Receivable plus 80 percent of all Sales on Account (of each accounting period) were collected, a pertinent budgeting formula for future projections might well be inferred. But it is quite obvious that, in spite of the fact that the resulting hypotheses are "universal" propositions, they are *narrowly bounded* and are a far cry from genuine law statements.

Although verification of universal propositions is rarely possible and *confirmation* often difficult (for further details, see p. 13 ff.), *a single case of refutation is capable of falsifying* an hypothesis. Thus one might aim not so much at verifying or confirming an hypothesis but at trying to falsify it. What previously was deemed an act of confirmation might now be considered an act of attempted refutation. And as long as an hypothesis is not falsified, it might be accepted for the time being. Apart from the fact that deeper methodological analysis reveals that all these connections are much more complex than can here be explained (for details, see Mattessich [1978/1980, pp. 141-191] and a series of recent books dealing with the methodology of economics: Latsis [1976], Machlup [1978], Stewart [1979], Blaug [1980], Boland [1982], Caldwell [1982], and Stegmüller, Balzer, and Spohn [1982]), falsification procedures too have many weaknesses and one major drawback. Often, the scientist is confronted with several competing hypotheses, all of which are unfalsified. Which hypothesis should then be accepted? Recourse to some kind of measure — establishing the degree of confidence or confirmation or corroboration or coherence — might be inevitable.

So far, all the inductive arguments mentioned have involved a move from the particular to the more general. But let us take the example of some statistics covering age and sex distributions of all the public accountants of a country. Thus we assume that the essential properties (like age, sex, etc.) of the universe of discourse are known. On the basis of this information, we may now conjecture the distribution of the properties of a particular population. This too is inductive inference, but it proceeds from the universe, or the more general, to the sample, or the less general. From the known universe, we may even infer the likelihood which a particular event has; then we are dealing with *an inductive argument inferring the particular from the general*, and not, as it is often asserted, the other way round.[11] By the way, the latter inference is not a deductive one, as some might think; it is inductive, because the resulting conclusion is not certain but merely probable.

Since no inductive argument can confirm the hypothesis with certainty on the basis of the evidence, it follows that no empirical law is fully reliable. The attempts to quantify the *degree of confirmation*, through a probability measure expressing the support which evidence gives to hypothesis h, encountered great conceptual problems and have not had much practical success. Scientists instead, rank their hypothesis according to various criteria on an ordinal scale as having very *strong, strong, weak, very weak, or nil* evidence. Where statistical procedures are applicable, probabilities of random *events* (instead of probabilities of *proportions*, as in the case of the degree of confirmation) are used to evaluate hypotheses. One attempts to refute the *rival* (or *null*) hypothesis under the assumption of a *preconceived* significance level (e.g. $p=0.05$). If such a refutation of the *rival* hypothesis is successful, the main hypothesis is assumed to be *confirmed* (inverting, in a way, Popper's methodology -- see Bunge [1983] pp. 133-135). All this offers a hint on how shaky a foundation science rests and gives an idea of the value-ladenness of such an enterprise.

But there exists an important parallel between the hopeless search for a rigorous foundation of inductive science and for the foundations of accounting. Since the time of David Hume's sceptical assertion of the "non-rationality" of inductive inference, philosophers have been trying to refute Hume. But all attempts to create a rational basis of induction failed (most notably Carnap's [1962] attempt to provide a practicable, *analytical* measure of the degree to which an evidence *confirms* an hypothesis), until Bertrand Russell [1948] (and ultimately even Carnap[12]) turned the question around. Instead of asking what justifies the assumption underlying inductive inference, they asked: *what do we have to assume to justify the present state of inductive-scientific inference*? Russell's answer is given in five postulates which form the purely *normative* credo of modern science. Similarly, in recognizing the futility of searching for a positivistic justification of accounting, twenty years ago we began to ask: *what do accountants assume when doing accounting*? This was the grossly misunderstood quintessence of the eighteen (and later nineteen[13]) basic assumptions of our book, *Accounting and Analytical Methods*. The fact is that these assumptions were inductively inferred from the extant micro- and macro-accounting systems; not only do they form a rigorous semantic-axiomatic definition of contemporary accounting, they also indicate *the assumptions that underlie the past and present practice of accountants*.[14]

ANALYSIS AND DEDUCTION

Once basic assumptions have been induced from general information needs, a series of consequences follows from those premises. It is the task of logical and mathematical analysis to infer deductively the major and minor conclusions, which are called *theorems* and *lemmas*, respectively. But deduction is much more extensive and penetrates into all corners of the scientific hulk. Whether one is inserting some data and solving the pertinent formula or arguing verbally some specific case, deductive inference (occasionally referred to as consistent or "rational thinking") is ubiquitous. Although the indispensability of deduction in accounting cannot be questioned, it is *a matter of dispute how formal and rigorous these deductive inferences and their proofs ought to be in accounting research*. Formality and rigor, both of which are matters of degree, are by no means mere criteria of scientific esthetics and prestige; they serve important functions of reliability, accuracy, pedagogy, and even creativity. An informal deduction may occasionally harbour hidden fallacies, the demonstration of which requires contradictions by formal proof. Sometimes, a conclusion is taken to be the result of *deductive* inference, while a formal contradiction reveals it to be, at best, an *inductive* inference.[15] Other times, a more or less formal deductive framework (like the axiomatic presentation of a theory) constitutes a most valuable pedagogic means for revealing the basic assumptions as well as the connections and interrelations of various notions and propositions of the entire theory. Often, new aspects or hitherto unsuspected consequences are disclosed by rigorous deductive proofs. The analytical or "theoretical" scientist plays a crucial role in any scientific discipline; he is concerned with foundational, logical, and methodological problems and tries to reveal the often unexpected but testable *consequences* following from the conceptual framework together with the generalized observations. His contributions can be of fundamental importance, which is illustrated in physics, for example, by the theories of such purely theoretically and philosophically oriented scientists as Maxwell, Einstein, Gell-Mann, and many others.

In the first half of this century, the *analytical part* of accounting theory consisted in the prescription of a considerable number of classificational schemes and accounting identities and in depreciation and valuation procedures, etc., while the *empirical part* concerned itself with the description and generalization of actually existing accounting systems. Such classificational and descriptive activities are typical of the juvenile state of an academic discipline. Since the fifties, however, the analytical as well as empirical activities of many academic accountants have become more sophisticated. By extending the boundaries of accounting and widening the area of interest to include a much greater number of environmental and behavioural variables, accounting theory has become a kind of *meta-accounting* that observes the observers, the recorders and manipulators of accounting data, as well as the data users, and examines the social-cybernetic function of accounting in a much broader context.

In accounting and economics, the most commonly used tools for deductive and inductive inferences are not borrowed from symbolic logic but from mathematics and statistics, respectively. The increasing popularity of mathematics lies, not least, in the fact that its algorithms offer a relatively convenient way to solve a host of deductive inferences, just as statistics offers a practical tool to perform inductive inferences relatively painlessly. But the use of such tools requires a thorough mathematical training on the part of the researcher and often impedes the ultimate user's control of the research process as well as his full understanding of the results. This, more than any other reason, causes the suspicion of practitioners and traditional academics against the modern scientific approach in accounting.

INTERPRETATION AND MODEL BUILDING

Although model building has become a favourite activity in the economic and administrative sciences, the notion of interpretation as a separate and important step in the scientific process is not sufficiently understood. In many cases, it is highly desirable to formulate a theory as generally as possible. In such a case, one speaks of an uninterpreted (or semi-interpreted) "calculus." This is to say that not all (or some) terms and relations of this theory have as yet been assigned any definite meaning in the semantic sense. Usually, such a "calculus" can serve a variety of purposes as soon as the general theory is given the appropriate specific interpretation. Every interpretation reduces the degree of abstraction of the theory by providing a more concrete model. Thus interpretation is a matter of degree; even a purely mathematical theory may lend itself to further analytical interpretation without becoming an empirical theory (e.g., the first step of interpreting a formula like $y=f(x)$ might be found in the following specification $y=a+bx$, while further interpretation might be achieved by specifying $y=10+3x$ without stating the meaning of x and y, which would require the assignment of data). For us, the interpretation extending from the theoretical level to the empirical one is of special interest. Indeed, the interpretation is often given by "rules of correspondence" that connect the purely *theoretical notions* of a theory (with which the theoretical scientist operates) to the *observational notions* (with which the empirical or experimental scientist operates).[16] We thus recognize that the distinction between syntactical, semantic, and pragmatic interpretation is advisable. Often, a specific interpretation is called a model, and the development of all the paraphenalia for such an interpretation is called model building (but this is only one among several meanings of the term "model"). Comparatively little attention has been paid to the problem of interpretation by accounting researchers, and we have previously pointed out that:

> Systematic attempts to create a series of clearly defined uninterpreted concepts of the major accounting notions (for value, income, etc.) and alternative interpretations (for specific or standardized needs) of each concept have not been made in our discipline. But in an informal, vague and incomplete manner such interpretations have been customary in traditional accounting for a long time. One could well argue that the acquisition cost basis, the market value basis and the present value basis are nothing but 'interpretations' of a general uninterpreted value concept. But the essence of the methodological achievement of distinguishing between uninterpreted and interpreted concepts and theories (calculi) lies in the specification of the conditions characterizing every uninterpreted concept. These rules are rarely if ever spelled out. Thus the practice of distinguishing various species of one and the same super-concept, as encountered in our discipline, is merely a first step in the direction of fulfilling this important methodological prerequisite. [Mattessich 1972, pp. 471-472.]

On this level too, a series of crucial decisions and value judgements have to be made. Above all, the specific purposes and intended applications of the individual interpretations and models must be chosen. Indeed, pragmatic *interpretation* becomes, for an applied science, a convenient way to convert a *descriptive* and cognitive theoretical framework into a conditionally *prescriptive* and purpose-oriented theory.

TESTING, ACCEPTANCE, AND REJECTION

The testing of an hypothesis or entire theory constitutes the *control process* that distinguishes a science from a body of mere dogmas. For the purely analytical theories (logic and mathematics) and the analytical parts of the empirical theories, there are rigorous *proofs*, each of which must demonstrate a theorem to be either true or false (a third possibility, like "probable," is not feasible here; and although proofs are also control features, they belong to "analysis" rather than to the empirical area of testing). However, the factual parts of an empirical theory are, precisely speaking, neither true nor false, but only "probable" to a higher or lower degree. They can be tested in various ways.

(1) Through *"verification,"* a term that is often loosely used but in its precise meaning refers either to the testing of a *singular* (or an *existential*) proposition or, in the case of a universal proposition, to the testing of *all* members of the pertinent universe of discourse. Due to the usual vastness of this universe, such comprehensive testing is hardly ever possible.

(2) Through *confirmation*, which in its precise meaning refers to a measurement technique developed by Carnap [1950/1962] and others that attempts to determine the *degree of confirmation* by means of which some evidence supports an hypothesis. But since this involves subjective assumptions and is possible only within a highly simplified and artificial language system, the term "confirmation" is usually used in a loose and vague sense. The related, yet essentially different, statistical measure of *confidence coefficient* is most commonly used but is also dependent on subjective assumptions and is a purely conventional means, fraught with many methodological weaknesses; furthermore, it is inapplicable in situations where mass phenomena do not occur or cannot be measured. Under such circumstances, the *subjective degree of belief* (somewhat more closely related to the degree of confirmation but definitely not identical with it) occasionally constitutes a last resort in spite of its strong personal bias.

(3) Through attempts *to refute* the hypothesis and thus the entire inductive argument. The three major shortcomings of this neo-rationalistic philosophy of falsificationism are the following. (a) If all or several of a set of competing hypotheses have successfully withstood falsification, one must decide which one to accept; to help in this choice, Popper [1935/1959] suggested the notion of *degree of corroboration*, which, however, turns out to be similar to the degree of confirmation — cf. Kyburg [1970, pp. 160-162] — and is just as difficult to determine. (b) A single instance of refutation may not always be acceptable as a final falsification because of possible observation and measurement errors, which merely *seem* to refute the argument. And (c) a theory is actually a mathematical structure and instrument, and such instruments, unlike propositions, can be neither true nor false but can merely be more or less useful or downright useless. According to this instrumental or structuralistic viewpoint [see Stegmüller 1979], a theory may be accepted or rejected for a specific purpose but cannot be falsified, as it can no longer be assigned a truth value.

(4) Through attempts to show the *coherence* of the pertinent hypothesis or theory with neighbouring theories or disciplines. This *holistic* approach may be compared to a jigsaw puzzle in which an hypothesis or a theory represents the "stone" or cluster of stones fitting an empty spot or area so far left open in the integral structure of science. Although no formal procedures are applied in such a test, most sciences find this the ultimate test (often supplemented by others) for keeping or eliminating an hypothesis or a theory in the long run. But it may take considerable time to find the surrounding "stones" to show that the one confronting us really fits, or does not fit, the puzzle. The widely accepted "Copenhagen Interpretation" — that science is nothing but a framework for correlating, organizing, and expanding human experience — has, by now, sufficiently undermined the positivistic view that science is capable of *depicting reality* by one-to-one correspondences; quantum theory (whose essential message to *all* sciences is the *interdependence between observer and the observed*) has helped considerably in replacing the *correspondence theory* of truth by the *coherence theory*, which is much more in tune with the knowledge and the needs of our time (for a recent version of the coherence theory, see the excellent book by Rescher [1979]).

All of this indicates that decisive value judgements must be made at the stage of testing. Even a student engaged in the routine task of simple hypothesis testing has to choose (consciously or subconsciously) an arbitrary level of confidence. Although this choice is usually dictated by convention, it constitutes a value judgement on which the acceptance or rejection of the hypothesis may well depend.

Before closing this Section, a word about the testing of *instrumental* or *means-end hypotheses*. It has been objected that our or any other *teleologic* (i.e., purpose-oriented) theory is not testable. This argument rests on a gross misunderstanding and confuses "difficulty" with "impossibility." As we have tried to show in this Section, a theory is tested by indicating its coherence with neighbouring areas and by "confirming" its individual hypotheses. In cognitive science, this means to supply "sufficient" evidence that either "under circumstance C, the occurrence A *always causes* occurrence B," or, more frequently, that "under circumstance C, the occurrence A is *most of the time, or at a certain relative frequency, followed by* occurrence B" (most laws in quantum physics and the social sciences are based on statistical correlations of the latter type — for further differences between cognitive and instrumental hypotheses, see Mattessich [1978/80, pp. 12-16, 128-140]). Although evidence supporting such hypotheses is often difficult to come by, it is even more difficult to obtain sufficient evidence supporting instrumental hypotheses of the following basic structure: "under circumstance C, the means A attains goal B most of the time, or at a certain relative frequency, more efficiently than any alternative means." But in everyday life, competing means are constantly compared and tested as to the efficiency of achieving certain ends; and it is a great challenge for the methodology of applied science to analyze, explain, and systematize these informal procedures, and hopefully to convert them into a scientific instrument.

THE SIGNIFICANCE OF METHODOLOGY

The previous Section hopefully conveyed to the reader that all of science, especially the social and applied sciences, are fraught with unsolved methodological problems. Indeed, the question arises whether the solution of some of these problems (e.g., the inference of specific accounting structures from particular information requirements) is not a prerequisite for any useful kind of empirical accounting research. In spite of highly sophisticated statistical techniques and rigorous hypothesis testing, a good deal of present-day empirical accounting research yields little more than self-evident results. Why was it then necessary to invest considerable resources and to apply such high-powered mathematical and statistical tools?

One answer lies in the need for confirmation. Although the significance of the scientific approach becomes more obvious in unexpected results, the confirmation of something commonplace is often prerequisite for further empirical investigations. Indeed, it would be most shortsighted to dismiss the efforts of modern accounting research merely because many of its immediate results do nothing but confirm what has long been taken for granted. The scientific approach to accounting is fairly young, and it would be unreasonable to question its significance. At this stage, accounting research must be taken as an exciting cultural development that is by no means without promise for the future. One of the positive indications, for example, is the emerging *cooperation* between *analytical* and *empirical* research. This dichotomy and its interplay, so crucial for most scientific disciplines, has begun to take hold of our discipline, and instances emerge in which analytical and empirical accounting research cross-fertilize each other and go hand in hand. All this has contributed to a rigor in accounting research unmatched by any previous generation of accounting scholars.

But where the sun is shining, shadows fall, and the question arises whether this rigor has not prevented many of our young academics from seeing that accounting is an *applied* science. Furthermore, rigorous training in pure science is not necessarily a balanced training for an applied scientist. This may be illustrated by the following example: many accountants identify the term "methodology" with "statistical methodology," in which the best of our young scholars have been well trained; but their education is often insufficient in the core of general methodology; above all, too few resources are devoted to the methodology of means-end relationships and deontic (i.e., "normative") inferences without which the raison d'être of an applied science cannot be fully understood.

Finally, modern accounting research tends towards the periphery, towards specialization and fragmentation. This explains why many of the younger generation have abandoned the search for a unifying general theory of accounting. But, as David [1972, p. 45] says: "The apparent thirst of the mind for unity and coherence is most persistent. The quest for unity is of great intensity and seems to lie at the very root . . . of intellectual activity of any kind." Thus, in spite of the strong centrifugal forces presently at work, and in spite of the American Accounting Association's SATTA [1977] (for further details, see the commentary to *Part VI*), the attempt to forge all the generally accepted premises of accounting into a unified but flexible theory can be expected to continue.[17]

We hope that this book may be helpful to practitioners and students of accounting, as well as to academics, as a survey of the "state of the art," as a stimulus to further research, and as a reference work to an exciting episode in the evolution of accounting. It is for the latter reason that we have compiled a comprehensive index of authors, a practice not customary in anthologies. Short biographies of the various contributors to this book are also provided. The reference function may be of particular significance because, unlike textbooks on accounting theory, an anthology of survey articles can afford to pay attention to further details, to research in the making, and to literature in the forefront of our discipline.

FOOTNOTES

[1] Apart from bookkeeping and its "theory" which goes back to the fifteenth century.

[2] Regrettably, this decisive German influence on accounting literature during the first three decades of our century has been ignored in the recent historical work by Gaffikin and Aitken [1982] presenting the "Significant Contributors to Accounting Thought in the 20th Century." For a survey of *recent* accounting research in Europe, see Hopwood and Schreuder [1984 forthcoming].

[3] The "measurement of income and wealth" shifts from positive economics to normative accounting as soon as this measurement becomes *an approximation based on surrogates and on a cost-benefit criterion and is used to satisfy various information requirements.*

[4] For further details on applied science and its instrumental reasoning, see our book and articles [Mattessich 1978/1980; 1979, 1980a].

[5] Hein Schreuder, "Accounting Research and Practice," a paper presented at the Conference on "New Challenges to Management Research" of the European Institute for Advanced Studies in Management, Brussels, 23-24 May 1984, p. 20.

[6] Another area deliberately omitted here is "the search for a conceptual framework" (not to be confused with the "lobbying" for accounting standards) as presently pursued by some public accounting bodies (e.g., in the U.S.A., the Financial Accounting Standards Board: *Scope and Implications of the Conceptual Framework Project* [FASB 1976], and *Statements of Financial Accounting Concepts* Nos. 1-4 [FASB 1978-80]; in Canada, the Canadian Institute of Chartered Accountants: *Corporate Reporting: Its Future Evolution* [Toronto 1980]). But the most important part of the *academic* research in this area was done in the sixties, and it is no coincidence that the pertinent publications and other writings have recently been compiled and reprinted by Zeff [1982], one of the leading accounting historians.

[7] For an anthology of the early development of inflation accounting, see Zeff [1976], and for an overview of the entire development, see Mattessich [1980b, 1982].

[8] See R. Mattessich, *Price Level Changes and Purpose Oriented Income Measurement — A Teleologic Interpretation of Accounting Theory* (in preparation).

[9] The recent legislation of the United States, Great Britain, Canada, Australia, New Zealand, etc., to enforce the publication of income statements (and other financial data for larger publicly held firms) not only on an *historical*, but simultaneously on a *current* cost basis, *is indication that our fight and long-standing plea* [cf. Mattessich 1964/1977, pp. 161-168, 213-226, 232-237] *for a teleologic approach has been accepted in modern accounting practice.* This is reinforced by the fact that both the U.S. legislation [*Statement of Financial Accounting Standards No. 33*, 1979] and the Canadian legislation [CICA *Handbook*, Section 4510, 1982] are flexible enough to permit a choice of measuring income on the basis of either physical or real financial capital maintenance. Here too the recommended principle of "different accounting hypotheses for different purposes" has been victorious.

[10] This *question* is related to the *unrealism* of general equilibrium theory and its *completeness assumption* and is frequently raised in various forms, e.g., by Aumann [1962] and Kötter [1982]: "What could completeness of the preference ordering mean? This postulate means that at any moment of decision a consumer is exposed to all those needs, for the satisfaction of which goods are produced. Or, in other words: at any given moment of decision, all feasible commodities are relevant for the consumer. But why should the need of a single person always cover the whole feasible supply?" [Kötter 1982, p. 106]

11 Skyrms [1966, p. 14] offers further examples illustrating the fact that inductive arguments need not necessarily proceed from the specific to the general.

12 For details see Mattessich [1978/1980, pp. 161-169 and 176-179].

13 See, for example, Mattessich [1977, pp. xx-xxi; 1979, pp. 335-351 (especially pp. 343-348)].

14 That this attempt is still not generally appreciated seems to be evidenced by some loaded questions which Gaffikin and Aitken [1982, p. 194] recently posed in connection with the criticism which their former teacher and colleague, Professor Chambers [1966, pp. 101-118] advanced against our theory. Of course, to accept the latter, one must be aware of the great impact which *semantic-axiomatic definitions* (quite different from *nominal* definitions with which Gaffikin and Aitken obviously confuse them) have had in mathematics, physics, and epistemology, and of the advantage which the drawing of precise boundaries has for an analytical presentation of accounting.

15 As for the differences between inductive and deductive arguments, we may point out that, in both cases, one deals with premises and conclusions (but, to avoid confusion, one often addresses the premises of the inductive arguments as "evidence" and their conclusions as "hypotheses"); in both cases, one *infers* the "conclusion" from the premises. Indeed, words like "consequently," "hence," "therefore," "thus," etc., are used *to indicate the presence of a deductive or inductive inference* in our everyday language. And it might be worth examining how many verbal inferences in accounting texts, assumed to be deductive by the reader, are actually inductive.

16 In accounting, such notions as income, capital, value, debt, etc., are considered to be *theoretical*, while a $100 bill, the paper on which an IOU is written, a bushel of wheat, a barrel of crude oil, or a machine are *observational* notions.

17 Several authors have recently approached this problem from different corners and have illuminated various aspects of the move towards a rigorous unified theory of accounting: Carlson and Lamb [1981] from an axiomatic viewpoint (by means of *predicate logic* instead of set-theory as done by Mattessich [1964/77, Appendix A]); Tanaka [1982] from a linguistic or semantic-axiomatic viewpoint; Lee [1982] and Ortner [1983] from the viewpoint of semantics and (electronic) data processing; and, more indirectly, by ljiri [1982] through a theory of triple-entry.

BIBLIOGRAPHY

American Accounting Association. *Statement on Accounting Theory and Theory Acceptance* (SATTA). Saratoga, Fla.: AAA, 1977.

Argyris, Chris. *The Impact of Budgets on People*. Ithaca, New York: The Controllorship Foundation, 1952.

Aumann, R.J. "Utility Theory Without the Completeness Axiom." *Econometrica* Vol. 30 (1962): 445-462.

Blaug, Mark. *The Methodology of Economics*. Cambridge, U.K.: Cambridge University Press, 1980.

Boland, Lawrence A. *The Foundations of Economic Method*. London, U.K.: George Allen & Unwin, 1982.

Bromwich, Michael, and Hopwood, Anthony G., eds. *Essays in British Accounting Research*. London: Pitman, 1981.

Bunge, Mario. *Treatise on Basic Philosophy, Vol 6—Epistemology & Methodology II*. Dordrecht - Holland/Boston, Mass.: D. Reidel Publ. Co., 1983.

Caldwell, Bruce J. *Beyond Positivism: Economic Methodology in the Twentieth Century*. London: George Allen & Unwin, 1982.

Canadian Institute of Chartered Accountants: *Exposure Draft, Current Value Accounting*. Toronto: CICA, 1980. *Corporate Reporting: Its Future Evolution — A Research Study* by Edward Stamp and his Study Group. Toronto: CICA, 1980. *Re-Exposure Draft, Reporting the Effects of Changing Prices*. Toronto: CICA, 1981. *Section 4510 (Reporting the Effects of Changing Prices)*. *CICA Handbook*. Toronto: CICA, 1982.

Carnap, Rudolph. *Logical Foundations of Probability*. Chicago: University of Chicago Press, 1950. 2d ed., 1962.

Carlson, Marvin L., and Lamb, James W. "Constructing a Theory of Accounting — An Axiomatic Approach." *The Accounting Review* 56 (July 1981):554-573.

Chambers, Raymond J. "Accounting and Analytical Methods: A Review Article." *Journal of Accounting Research* (Spring 1966):101-118.

David, William H. *Peirce's Epistemology*. The Hague, 1972.

Demski, Joel. *Information Analysis*. 2nd ed. Reading, Mass.: Addison-Wesley Co., 1980.

Ellis, Brian. *Basic Concepts of Measurement*. Cambridge, U.K.: Cambridge University Press, 1968.

Financial Accounting Standards Board: *Scope and Implications of the Conceptual Framework Project*. Stamford, Conn.: FASB, 1976. *Statements of Financial Accounting Concepts*, Nos. 1-4 and 33. Stamford, Conn.: FASB, 1978-80.

Gaffikin, Michael J., and Aitken, Michael J., eds. *The Development of Accounting Theory: Significant Contributors to Accounting Thought in the 20th Century*. New York and London: Garland Publishing, Inc., 1982.

18

Harsanyi, John C. *Essays on Ethics, Social Behavior, and Scientific Explanation*. Dordrecht-Holland: D. Reidel Co., 1976.

Hopwood, Anthony G., and Schreuder, Hein, eds. *European Contributions to Accounting Research: The Achievements of the Last Decade*. Amsterdam: Vrije Universiteit Boekhandel/Uitgeverij, forthcoming 1984.

Ijiri, Yuji. *Triple-Entry Bookkeeping and Income Momentum*. Sarasota, Fla.: American Accounting Association, 1982.

Kötter, Rudolf. "General Equilibrium Theory — An Empirical Theory?" In *Philosophy of Economics*, pp. 103-117. Edited by W. Stegmüller, W. Balzer, and W. Spohn. New York: Springer-Verlag, 1982.

Kyburg, Henry E., Jr. *Probability and Inductive Logic*. New York: MacMillan, 1970.

Latsis, S., ed. *Method and Appraisal in Economics*. Cambridge, U.K.: Cambridge University Press, 1976.

Lee, Ronald M. *CANDID Description of Commercial and Financial Concepts: A Formal Semantics Approach to Knowledge Representation*, WP-81-162. Laxenburg, Austria: International Institute for Applied Systems Analysis, 1982.

Luce, R.D., and Raiffa, H. *Games and Decisions: Introduction and Critical Survey*. New York: J. Wiley, 1957.

Machlup, Fritz. *Methodology of Economics and Other Social Sciences*. New York: Academic Press, 1978.

Maslow, Abraham H. *Motivation and Personality*. Rev. ed. New York: Harper and Row, 1970.

Maslow, Abraham H. *The Farther Reaches of Human Nature*. New York: Penguin Books, 1976.

Mattessich, Richard. *Accounting and Analytical Methods — Measurement and Projection of Income and Wealth in the Micro- and Macro-Economy*. Homewood, Illinois: R.D. Irwin, Inc., 1964. Reprint edition in the "Series of Accounting Classics." Houston: Scholars Book Co., 1977.

Mattessich, Richard. "Methodological Preconditions and Problems of a General Theory of Accounting." *The Accounting Review* 47 (July 1972):469-487.

Mattessich, Richard. *Instrumental Reasoning and Systems Methodology — An Epistemology of the Applied and Social Sciences*. Dordrecht, Holland and Boston, U.S.A.: D. Reidel & Co., 1978. Paperback ed., 1980.

Mattessich, Richard. "Instrumental Aspects of Accounting: Illustrated on Professor Sterling's Fictitious Taxi Company." In *Accounting for a Simplified Firm Owning Depreciable Assets: Seventeen Essays and a Synthesis Based on a Common Case*, pp. 335-351. Edited by R.R. Sterling and A.L. Thomas. Houston: Scholars Book Co., 1979.

Mattessich, Richard. "On the Essence of Basic and Applied Research in the Administrative and Other Instrumental Sciences." In Appendix G of *University Management Education and Research: A Developing Crisis*, pp. 61-81 L. Picard, R. Mattessich, et al. Ottawa: S.S.H.R.C., 1980a.

Mattessich, Richard. "The Canadian Current Cost Accounting Exposure Draft: A Flawed Approach." *CA Magazine* (November 1980b):48-52.

Mattessich, Richard. "Major Concepts and Problems of Inflation Accounting: Part I." *CGA Magazine* (May 1981a):10-15.

Mattessich, Richard. "Major Concepts and Problems of Inflation Accounting: Part II, General Purchasing Power, Capital Maintenance, and the Canadian CCA Exposure Draft." *CGA Magazine* (June/July 1981b):20-27.

Mattessich, Richard. "On the Evolution of Inflation Accounting — With a Comparison of Seven Major Models." *Economia Aziendale* Vol. 1, No. 3 (October 1982): 349-381.

Merton, Robert K. *The Sociology of Science — Theoretical and Empirical Investigations*. Chicago: University of Chicago Press, 1973.

Mock, Theodore J. *Measurement and Accounting Information Criteria*. Studies in Accounting Research No. 13. Sarasota, Florida: American Accounting Association, 1976.

Oliver, B.L. "A Study of Confidence Interval Financial Statements." *Journal of Accounting Research* (Spring 1972):154-166.

Ortner, Erich. *Aspekte einer Konstrucktionssprache für den Datenbankentwurf*. Darmstadt: S. Toeche-Mittler Verlag, 1983.

Popper, Karl R. *Logik der Forschung*. Töbingen: J.C.B. Mohr, 1935. English ed.: *The Logic of Scientific Discovery*. New York: Basic Books, 1959.

Rescher, Nicholas. *Cognitive Systemization: A System-Theoretic Approach to a Coherentist Theory of Knowledge*. Totowa, N. J.: Rowan and Littlefield, 1979.

Russell, Bertrand. *Human Knowledge, its Scope and Limits*. New York: Simon and Schuster, 1948.

Simon, Herbert A. *The Sciences of the Artificial*. 2nd ed. Cambridge, Mass. The MIT Press, 1981.

Skyrms, B. *Choice and Chance: An Introduction to Inductive Logic*. Belmont, California: Dickenson Publishing, 1966.

Sorokin, Pitirim A. *Social and Cultural Dynamics*. 4 Vols. New York: American Book Co., 1937.

Stedry, Andrew C. *Budget Control and Cost Behavior*. Englewood Cliffs, New Jersey: Prentice-Hall, Inc., 1960.

Stegmüller, Wolfgang. *The Structuralist View of Theories*. New York: Springer Verlag, 1979.

Stegmüller, Wolfgang; Balzer, W.; and Spohn, W., eds. *Philosophy of Economics*. New York: Springer-Verlag, 1982.

Stevens, S.S. "On the Theory of Scales of Measurement." *Science*, Vol. 103 (1946):677-80.

Stewart, I.M.T. *Reasoning and Method in Economics*. London, U.K.: McGraw-Hill, 1979.

Tanaka, Shigetsugu. *The Structure of Accounting Language*. Tokyo: Chuo University Press, 1982 (in English).

Torgerson, W.S. *Theory and Measurement of Scaling*. New York: Wiley & Sons, Inc., 1958.

Zeff, Stephen A., ed. *Asset Appreciation, Business Income and Price-Level Accounting: 1918-1935*. The History of Accounting Series. New York: Arno Press, 1976.

Zeff, Stephen A., ed. *The Accounting Postulates and Principles Controversy of the 1960's*. New York: Garland Publishing, Inc., 1982.

Part II

EVOLUTION OR REVOLUTION OF MODERN ACCOUNTING THEORY?

THE search for a systematic basis and a deductive framework constitutes one of the core activities of modern accounting research. As our first article of Part II shows, this search began, or at least was revived, in the late fifties with four articles (two by Chambers and two by Mattessich)[1] and continued during the sixties in several books by these and other authors (e.g., Moonitz, Ijiri). Indeed, accounting historians and theoreticians usually deal with Chambers and Mattessich under a common label, without articulating the great divergence between their views.[2] Here, the attempt to formulate the postulates or basic assumptions of accounting, and the different views and aspects emerging from this effort, are discussed. Our discipline, unlike a natural science, cannot extract its premises from an *experimentum crucis* and from the observation of *fundamental* empirical regularities. Thus the following alternatives offer themselves: (1) to borrow some (or a great number of) more or less basic statements from other social disciplines and to accept them in an *absolute-normative* way as a foundation — as Chambers did; or (2) to accept empirical regularities of a *low* and often coincidental order as premises for *partial* accounting theories of limited scope — as it is nowadays done in "positive accounting theory." But there is a third possibility; namely, to invert the question and to ask *what basic methodological assumptions underlie present-day accounting practice*, and to what extent can these assumptions be subjected to *different interpretations (i.e., specific models) matching different information purposes*. This approach — which *we* have adopted recognizes the important information function which traditional accounting fulfills and thus is also normative, but *conditional-normative* and not dogmatic.

The second important core activity is closely connected with the first and concerns the question: Which valuation (and related) hypotheses ought to be accepted in accounting practice? Here too, our views diverge from those of Chambers, the explanation again lying in the difference between *absolute* versus *conditional* prescription. Chambers admits as "correct" only current values based predominantly (or even exclusively) on exit values, while we have been pleading for the acceptance of *various* valuation bases[3] (e.g., historical cost basis *supplemented* by a flexible scheme of current *entry* and *exit* values similar to the recently accepted current value accounting legislations in the U.S.A. and Canada and, to some extent, in the U.K., Australia, and New Zealand), each serving any one among different information purposes, such as income determination under nominal *and* real financial capital maintenance *as well as* under physical capital maintenance. As previously hinted at, this kind of current value legislation, and the fact that public accounting bodies have resumed their search for a *systematic* conceptual framework, provide excellent evidence that accounting theory has not failed to serve actual practice.

Wells' article is an attempt to apply to accounting the distinction between *ordinary* and *revolutionary* science, as developed by the well-known philosopher and historiographer Thomas S. Kuhn. For Wells, the old paradigm (disciplinary matrix), consolidated during the thirties and forties, is the *historical cost doctrine* with all its paraphenalia of cost and revenue matching, realization at sales, going concern notion, and, of course, depreciation adjusted acquisition cost valuation. He notes the striking similarities between Kuhn's chronological schema of an existing paradigm, emerging anomalies and professional crises, the development of emerging alternatives, competing new schools of thought fighting with each other to displace the old paradigm by forming a new one which, in time, ought to be generally accepted — and the happenings in accounting during recent decades. All this becomes evidence supporting Wells' argument that the (normative) *a priori* research emerging during the "golden age" of the sixties were by no means vain attempts, but important historical manifestations of a scientific-cultural process in search of a new paradigm of accounting. Has this paradigm emerged by now? And, if so, what is it called and what does it imply? Wells does not say; seven years ago, when his article was written, he believed it was too soon to give an answer. Is this still true today?

We think that the single most decisive set of events in the direction of the acceptance of a new paradigm of accounting is the legislation introducing — *supplementary to the historical cost approach — a fairly flexible scheme of current value accounting* in the United States (1979)[4] and Canada (1982), and a similar but less flexible scheme in the United Kingdom (1980) as well as Australia and New Zealand.[5] If this turns out to be the major manifestation of a new paradigm, then the latter is characterized by the following features:

- Simultaneous acceptance of different valuation, realization, and classification hypotheses for different information uses.
- Continuing use of the historical cost method for legalistic and contractual purposes and as a basis for taxation.
- Utilization of the *nominal* current cost model for income measurement under physical capital maintenance (e.g., in firms the *specific* prices of which tend to advance beyond the inflationary rate) and related purposes. The remarks in parentheses of this and the next item constitute an extension *of the principle of conservatism to current value accounting*.
- Utilization of the *real* current cost or value model for income measurement under real financial capital maintenance (e.g., in firms the *specific* prices of which tend to advance below or in conformity with the inflationary rate) and related purposes.
- The possible extension of the above-mentioned flexibility by utilizing also the *present value method* (discounted net future cash flows) especially for internal investment calculations and management accounting decisions (while items 2 to 4 are provided for in Section 4510 of the Canadian CICA *Handbook*, no provisions are, or were expected to be, made for this last item).[6]

But the difficulty of applying Kuhn's thesis to accounting lies in the fact that, for him, as well as for Stegmüller,[7] who made decisive contributions and improvements upon Kuhn's thesis, a paradigm shift requires a new scientific core in form of a new fundamental law. Obviously, accounting lacks such a fundamental law, and the question arises whether, in this situation, the distinction between ordinary and revolutionary science is still meaningful. Yet our discipline is dominated by methodology, and we seem to be dealing with the shift of a *methodological* rather than a scientific accounting paradigm. For an applied discipline, such a shift may be no less revolutionary than a scientific paradigm displacement in a pure science, especially if it promises to lead to a fundamentally novel scientific outlook, posing and solving previously unquestioned or unanswerable questions and problems (e.g., "Which specific accounting system is satisfactory or even optimal for which purpose?'' and ''Which set of accounting standards is satisfactory to which social group?'').

The two topics, ''accounting on the crossroads'' and ''the need for the present value method,'' are continued in the next and first article by Nils H. Hakansson, in which the relationship of our discipline to economics and finance is illuminated. In discussing the relevance of the capital pricing model, the option pricing model, decision theory, as well as the theory of private and public information to accounting and crucial public policy issues, this paper prepares the reader for further and more detailed discussions of these and related topics in *Parts III, IV, and V*. Hakansson also emphasizes the ''imbalance,'' or net export, of knowledge from our sister areas to accounting. He even raises the question of whether accounting research might not be an underdeveloped country in which foreigners (from Finance) harvest profitably; but he envisages rich export potentials for accounting through its multidimensionality, its institutional richness, and further intellectual growth. The redistributive and productive effects of inflation, standard setting, and other public policy decisions receive special attention in this paper.

The last article, also by Nils H. Hakansson, is a response to and critique of the last of the American Accounting Association reports on ''the state of the art,'' which this association is committed to publish every decade or so. As much as one may be dissatisfied with this report, it is interesting to note that it, like the previously discussed article by M. C. Wells, refers to Thomas S. Kuhn's thesis and distinguishes between different competing accounting paradigms.[8] Although this *Statement on Accounting Theory and Theory Acceptance* [SATTA 1977] suffers from the two major curses of our discipline (an *insufficient grounding in methodological background* and the *perennial confusion of ''accounting'' with ''financial accounting''*), it is praiseworthy in many respects:

- It is a much more sophisticated and possibly more profound statement than its precursor, *A Statement of Basic Accounting Theory* [ASOBAT 1966], although it might not prove to be as influential.
- It asks some of the right questions and constitutes a major contribution to present accounting theory.
- It emphasizes information economics and behavioural accounting, two of the most prominent novel aspects of our discipline.
- It mirrors the broadening of the new accounting horizon and gives recognition to some accomplishments of past and present-day accounting theory.
- Its authors are a most distinguished group of scholars.

If the criticism of SATTA, brought forth by various reviews, is more detailed and more passionate than the praise, the reason is found partly in the very nature of a critical evaluation and partly in the state of crisis that has beset accounting theory for several decades. Ours is not only an applied discipline, but, as an academic endeavour, it is also a relatively young one. Thus, to offer an overview of its present state is a difficult task and can hardly avoid controversy.

Among the *minor criticism*, the following (items 1 to 6) were mentioned by our panel or in Professor Hakansson's above-mentioned paper:

1. The classifications, categorizing different theories, are confusing, inappropriate, and without articulate basis.
2. The logic and clarity of presentation leaves something to be desired.
3. It lacks creative and synthetic power, as is to be expected from any committee work.
4. The assertion that reported information is always a public commodity was questioned by at least one member of our panel.
5. Partial (in contrast to complete) ordering, which may well lead to Pareto optimality, is neglected in ranking alternative public accounting policies (for details, see Hakansson).
6. Some neglect of the welfare impact from public accountants' potential for monopolizing their market is evident (see Hakansson).

Of somewhat heavier caliber are the following items (7 to 11):

7. The distinction between positive and normative theories is not made in an appropriate way, and this leads to confusion. This seems to be the most unanimous criticism and might suggest that similar committees, in future, should consult experts competent in methodology.
8. After paying lip service to "classical thought" and previous contributions, subsequent discussions disregard them.
9. SATTA ignores the incentives and goals behind the profession's search for an accounting theory, and, contrary to its title, does not concern itself with theory acceptance by *practitioners*.
10. The choice of literature dealt with in SATTA is biased or, at least, is not broad enough to give a survey of the present state of accounting theory.
11. The ultimate message of SATTA is trite, disappointing, and perhaps even self-contradictory (possibly the second and third items taken together — see also Hakansson).

These are the points of critique advanced by Hakansson and other "reviewers on the panel" to which the panel's defender of SATTA (Lawrence Revsine) gave some replies.[9] We personally sympathize with several of these objections but must admit that some of them might rest on misunderstandings. However, since it is not the task of a panel chairman to offer a major presentation of his own, let us restrict ourselves to a single additional criticism:

12. We cannot agree with SATTA's pessimistic view that "a general theory does not exist at this time" (p. 1). Before one makes such a pronouncement, one ought to survey the many assumptions underlying every present-day accounting practice, together with the general consequences that follow from these assumptions. Indeed, if such general assumptions and consequences did not exist, accounting could hardly be taught at universities.

This does not deny the considerable amount of disagreement among practicing as well as academic accountants; but *the theory of any scientific discipline is made up of the common ground and not of the controversies among its members.* Furthermore, we believe that the controversial parts of various conflicting theories concern a limited number of hypotheses and that the misunderstanding arises out of the accountants' failure to specify the action goals and information purposes that a "specific theory" is supposed to serve. As we have shown elsewhere, one can get around most of the conflicting areas by formulating some of the basic assumptions as "empirically empty shells," holding a place for specific hypotheses. This deployment of *surrogate assumptions* is much more than a cheap trick; it is a device to harness the area of agreement within a general theory and, at the same time, to separate it from the area of disagreement. In this way, a detailed purpose-oriented interpretation becomes possible, which in turn opens the door to an *instrumental theory* (in contrast to a cognitive theory) of accounting. When we *look at accounting as it actually is*, we run much less risk of missing the common ground than when *guessing what accounting ought to be*. To our mind, we are not at all lacking a generally accepted theoretical basis of accounting (in spite of the fact that SATTA makes neither any effort to expose this common basis or its formulations in the literature, nor to attempt a formulation of its own, as might have been its original task). But what accounting is lacking is a systematic development of various *interpretations* (of this general, theoretical basis) for different information purposes. Although the difference between an un- or semi-interpreted theory and its interpretation is a very important one, accountants seem to continue to disregard it. But, in defense of the SATTA Committee, it must be pointed out that one could not have expected this committee to develop such interpretations, because the effort to do so would be great, and the time required to accomplish such a task would stretch over several years. Furthermore, this committee should not entirely be blamed for not having offered a formulation of the basic assumptions and consequences common to all present-day accounting systems or for not having accepted the idea of place-holder assumptions (including the distinction between a theory and its interpretations). The research pertinent to this dual task goes back to the sixties and thus belonged to the responsibility of ASOBAT [1966]. It was the latter that ignored those possibilities, setting the switches in a particular direction. And it can only be hoped that the next "state of the art report" of the AAA (to be expected in 1987) improves upon this situation by taking the following items into consideration:

- That accounting as an academic undertaking belongs to the applied sciences, the theories of which have a *normative* structure and (although partly based on positive theories) are very different from those of the pure sciences.
- That there exists sufficient literature preparing the ground for a conditional-normative theory of accounting that is general enough to embrace the common basis of all contemporary accounting systems but flexible enough to allow for specific purpose-oriented models or interpretations.
- That the present trend in practice and public policy is towards flexible standards that allow a choice of different accounting hypotheses for different information purposes, as evidenced by the supplementary current value legislations of the United States (FASB: *FAS No. 33*) and Canada (CICA *Handbook*: Section 4510).
- That a general theory of accounting cannot be limited to financial accounting but must comprise management accounting (including budgeting) and hopefully also macro-accounting models.

Of special interest is Butterworth and Falk's[10] recent distinction between various "valuation paradigms," asserting that the major task of financial accounting is the *determination of values* serving investment purposes, and various "stewardship paradigms," defending the position that accounting's major task lies in the appropriate *allocation* of depreciation or similar costs and in supplying other information for the purpose of attaining an optimal or satisfactory contract between principal (e.g., shareholders) and agent (e.g., management). However, there arises the question whether these two categories are really mutually exclusive and ought therefore to be addressed as paradigms in the Kuhnian sense of a revolutionary science. It seems to us that these paradigms and their versions rather form a "theory-net" as proposed in the epistemology of Sneed and Stegmüller or a series of "research programmes" in Lakatos' sense.[11] The latter would rather speak in favour of a *normal*, hence evolutionary, scientific activity; it would also take into consideration that accounting is to serve both (1) the contracting between owners and management through "incentive information," as well as (2) the investment function through "predictive information." R.M.

FOOTNOTES

[1] One article of each of these authors ("Detail for a Blueprint" by R. Chambers [1957] and "Towards a General and Axiomatic Foundation of Accountancy — With an Introduction to the Matrix Formulation of Accounting Systems" by R. Mattessich [1957]) was recently reprinted in S. Zeff's historical collection, *The Accounting Postulates and Principles Controversy of the 1960's* (New York: Garland Publishing, Inc., 1982) as having influenced the AICPA Accounting Research Study No. 1, *The Basic Postulates of Accounting*, by M. Moonitz [1961], which is also reprinted in Zeff's [1982] book.

[2] E.g., Michael Chatfield, *History of Accounting Thought*, rev. ed. (New York: R. E. Krieger Publishing Co., 1977), pp. 300-301; G. J. Previts and B. D. Merino, *A History of Accounting in America* (New York: Ronald Press, 1979), pp. 292-294; S. Hendriksen, *Accounting Theory*, 4th ed. (Homewood, Illinois: R. D. Irwin, Inc., 1982), pp. 53-55.

[3] Cf. R. Mattessich, *Accounting and Analytical Methods* (Homewood, Illinois: R. D. Irwin, Inc., 1964; reprinted, Houston: Scholars Book Co., 1977), pp. 42-43, 158-183, 215-237; *idem*, "The Canadian CCA Exposure Draft — A Flawed Approach," *CA Magazine* (Nov. 1980), pp. 48-57; *idem*, "Major Concepts and Problems of Inflation Accounting — Part I and Part II," *CGA Magazine* (May 1981), pp. 10-15 and (June/July 1981), pp. 20-27; *idem*, "Still Shooting with Bow and Arrow — To the CICA Re-Exposure Draft on 'Reporting the Effects of Changing Prices'," *Cost and Management* (Nov. 1982), pp. 16-19; *idem*, "On the Evolution of Inflation Accounting — With a Comparison of Seven Major Models" *Economia Aziendale* 1/3 (December 1982), pp. 349-381. In Canada, all these efforts seem to have been accompanied by success, as a very reasonable and flexible solution was ultimately adopted in Sect. 4510 (Nov. 1982) of the *Handbook* of the Canadian Institute of Chartered Accountants.

4 But *current value legislation* is only a single aspect of the "enormous increase in the financial reporting required of corporations," and one might well regard the consequences of *all* this new legislation a paradigm shift, as it is implicit in W. H. Beaver's book, *Financial Reporting: An Accounting Revolution* (Englewood Cliffs, N.J.: Prentice-Hall, Inc., 1981).

5 Cf. *Statement — Financial Accounting Standards No. 33 — Financial Reporting and Changing Prices* (Stamford, Conn.: Financial Accounting Standards Board, 1979); " Section 4510 — Reporting the Effects of Changing Prices" of the CICA *Handbook* (Toronto: Canadian Institute of Chartered Accountants, 1982); *Statement of Standard Accounting Practice No. 16: Current Cost Accounting* (London: Institute of Chartered Accountants of England and Wales, 1980); and *Guidance Notes on SSAP 16: CCA* (London: ICAEW — ASC, 1980).

6 In our repeated plea for the simultaneous use of *several valuation methods*, we have also emphasized the need for the *present value hypothesis* (see our controversy with Chambers in *Cost and Management* (March/April 1970, March/April 1971, and July/August 1971) as well as for a consideration of alternative accounting hypotheses beyond the mere valuation issue. Some alternative realization and classification hypotheses have indeed been taken into consideration in Section 4510 of the CICA *Handbook*).

7 See Wolfgang Stegmüller, *The Structure and Dynamics of Theories* (New York: Springer, 1975); *idem*, *The Structuralist View of Theories* (New York: Springer, 1979). Stegmüller's contributions to Kuhn's thesis are not taken into consideration in Wells' article, here reproduced, but most of them are discussed on pp. 260-272 of Mattessich's *Instrumental Reasoning and Systems Methodology*.

8 What follows is an adaptation and expansion of our paper, "An Evaluation of the Statement on Accounting Theory and Theory Acceptance: Summary," in *Collected Papers of the American Accounting Association's Annual Meeting, 1978* (Sarasota, Fla.: AAA, 1978), pp. 597-600. This summarizes not only Hakansson's critique, but also that by Barbara Merino, Murray Wells, and Jerold Zimmerman, whose pertinent contributions are also contained in the *Collected Papers, 1978*.

9 Another excellent critique of SATTA is by K. V. Peasnell, "Statement of Accounting Theory and Theory Acceptance: A Review Article," *Accounting and Business Research* 8 (Summer 1978), pp. 217-225.

10 See John E. Butterworth and Haim Falk. "The Methodological Implications of a Contractual Theory of Accounting," Working Paper, University of British Columbia, Oct. 1983.

11 Cf. T.S. Kuhn, *The Structure of Scientific Revolutions* (Chicago: Univ. of Chicago Press, 1962); W.S. Stegmüller, *The Structure and Dynamics of Theories* (New York: Springer-Verlag, 1976); *idem*, *The Structuralist View of Theories* (New York: Springer-Verlag, 1979); and I. Lakatos, "Falsification and the Methodology of Scientific Research Programmes," in *Criticism and the Growth of Knowledge*, edited by I. Lakatos and A. Musgrave (Cambridge, 1970), pp. 91-95; *idem*, "History of Science and its Rational Reconstruction," in *Boston Studies in the Philosophy of Science*, Vol. 8 (1972), pp. 91-136.

ON THE EVOLUTION OF THEORY CONSTRUCTION IN ACCOUNTING: A PERSONAL ACCOUNT*

by Richard Mattessich

*Reprinted from *Accounting and Business Research* 10 (Special Accounting History Issue 1980): 158-173

INTRODUCTION

ACCOUNTANTS seem to make insufficient distinction between 'theory construction' and 'theory or hypotheses annunciation'.[1] By the latter I mean the exposition of an idea deemed to be powerful enough to form *the nucleus* of an entire theory. This idea will usually consist of one or a few hypotheses capable of sustaining the theoretical structure still missing. 'Theory construction', in contrast, refers to *the search for this very structure*; it comprises the systematic development of (1) *all* the basic underlying *assumptions* through some kind of *inductive process* (including *intuition*) together with a presentation of supporting evidence (testing), (2) the *deductive derivation* of at least the most essential of the theorems following from these assumptions together with pertinent proofs, and in time, (3) the *interpretation* of this theory to enable as many practical applications (models) as feasible.[2] But this is precisely what is meant by an axiomatic or postulational approach of an empirical discipline. The deductive process thereby invoked is greatly facilitated by mathematically or otherwise formalised tools, but contrary to popular misconception, such tools do not constitute the essence of the postulational approach. The decisive matter is that the theoretical framework is comprehensive and systematic enough and follows a flawless way of reasoning. Once the distinction between the fragmentary notion of theory or hypotheses annunciation, and the all-embracing notion of theory construction is fully comprehended, it comes as a shock to notice how popular the former, unsystematic and narrow approach has traditionally been in accounting, and how seldom the latter, systematic and comprehensive approach is encountered in our field.

However, it cannot be denied that attempts to formulate accounting theory by means of a general and postulational framework gained considerable glamour during the fifties and sixties (e.g. Chambers, 1955, 1957, 1966/75; Mattessich, 1956, 1957, 1964/77; Moonitz, 1961; Ijiri, 1967/77, 1975) and that the application of information economics and related approaches to accounting — e.g.: Hakansson (1966, 1969a, b, 1977, 1978a), Butterworth (1967, 1972), Feltham (1967, 1968, 1976),

Mock (1969, 1971, 1976), Feltham and Demski (1970), Butterworth and Feltham (1972), Demski (1972a, b, 1974), Demski and Feltham (1976), Itami (1977), Mattessich (1975, 1978c, 1979a)—continues to carry the banner of genuine accounting theory construction since the late sixties. There is, furthermore, some hope that the recent *Statement on Accounting Theory and Theory Acceptance* (SATTA-AAA, 1977)—with its pessimistic assertion about the present lack of a *general theory of accounting*—might stimulate interest in theory construction, perhaps even rekindle the enthusiasm for an overtly postulational approach exploiting the flexibility created by the strict distinction between a theory and its interpretations (for details see Section III). After all, accounting, like any other art or science rides on the waves of academic fashion and thus is subject to a recurrent cyclical trend. And the fascination with accounting postulates, being more than half a century old, might prove to be of greater intellectual benefit than is presently envisaged by our academic community. Hence, there seems to be some justification for sketching the evolution of the postulational approach in accounting.

EARLY DEVELOPMENT

The endeavour to cast the foundations of accounting into postulates forming the logical bases for other statements, goes back to Paton's *Accounting Theory* (1922/73).[3] At the end of his book (in Chapter 20), we find what its author believed to be 'all the important postulates of accounting' (cf. Moonitz and Littleton, 1965, p. 65). Actually, however, we are presented with a detailed discussion of the following notions: The Business Entity, The 'Going Concern' (Assumption), The Balance Sheet Equation, Financial Condition and the Balance Sheet, Cost and Book Value, Cost Accrual and Income, and Sequence. Though only *some* of these notions might nowadays be considered fundamental enough to form a postulational basis, the mere fact that *Paton was the first to search for the analytical and empirical premises on which accounting rests*, deserves highest recognition. Of course, his presentation lacks rigour as well as systematics. Perhaps worse, he puts the cart before the horse by presenting the conclusions in the first nineteen chapters of his book and summarising the presmises at the very end instead of showing how to derive the conclusions from the premises. Furthermore, he mixes different strata of generalizations, thereby putting general and specific assumptions into one pot, and occasionally even confusing conclusions with premises. He also seems to have started from the following somewhat narrow question: Which assumptions underly the activity of business accountants? Whereas he could have attained a clearer and more comprehensive picture by asking the altogether different question: Which assumptions must be fulfilled to make an accounting system operational? But this is not so much to criticise the pioneer as all those accounting theoreticians who for five decades accepted this more narrow kind of question, thereby neglecting many accounting systems beyond the boundaries of business. Thus his epigones, not unlike Paton himself, formulated specific *interpretations* of accounting without attaining a truly general theory. Let me illustrate the situation: Paton accepts the *acquisition cost principle* (which is hardly general enough to be regarded as a postulate) as an equal to such a genuine postulate as the one asserting the *existence of the (economic) entity*. While the latter assumption cannot be abandoned without destroying the operability of an accounting system, the former could well be changed into the market value hypothesis or the present value hypothesis, etc., without rendering the accounting system inoperable, provided a place holder postulate for various valuation alternatives is supplied. Yet all those objections do not diminsh Paton's indelible merit. We must not forget that he wrote at a time when the business and economic conditions, as well as the academic climate, were utterly different from those prevailing today.

What seems to me surprising is the fact that the Continental (European) literature of accounting, quite prominent in the first third of this century, does not present us with any serious postulational attempt. The reason for this might be found in the preoccupation of Continental accounting scholars with three problem areas:

1. The principles of accounting (*Grundsätze des Rechnungswesens*) which were loosely connected, practical norms rather than tightly knit premises and theorems (e.g. Schär, 1890, 1911, 1914; Nicklisch, 1911, 1912; Töndury, 1933).
2. The valuation and price level problems. Schmidt (1921/29), for example, anticipated the work of Edwards and Bell (1961) by four decades.[4] Other Continental accounting theorists heavily concerned with valuation problems were Zappa (1910/27), Schmalenbach (1919),[5] Le Coutre (1922), Walb (1922, 1926), Limperg (1925/46), Onida (1935), and Rieger (1936).
3. The issue of *Kontenrahmen* (basic charts of accounts) and closely related classification problems (e.g. Schmalenbach, 1927). From the viewpoint of English accounting literature the intense concern with basic charts of accounts in Continental Europe may well seem excessive, the more so since in English speaking countries very little attention has been paid to this particular issue.

To be exhaustive, I should finally mention a slim German monograph by Hans Holzer (1936) bearing the promising title *Zur Axiomatik der Buchführungs- und Bilanztheorie*. Alas, this title is a misnomer; neither does this author seem to possess knowledge of the current meaning behind the term 'axiomatic', nor does one find in this monograph any attempt at presenting a structural revelation of accounting.

THE GOLDEN AGE OF A PRIORI RESEARCH IN ACCOUNTING

In spite of Paton's (1922/62) early endeavour to introduce the notion of 'postulate' to accounting, the idea did not catch on, and it took more than a third of a century before the first attempt was made to construct a postulational theory of accounting by rigorous means. *The preparatory phase* to what Carl Nelson (1973) called the 'golden age of *a priori* research of accounting' (thereby referring mainly to the sixties), began as early as the mid-fifties. This preparatory phase might be characterised by a series of articles by Chambers (1955, 1957) and myself (Mattessich, 1956, 1957) that were ambitious enough to aim at the construction of a postulational as well as a general theory of accounting.[6] Chambers' 'Blueprint for a Theory of Accounting' (1955) set the stage by first distinguishing clearly between 'systems of rules relating to the practice of accounting and a theory of accounting', pointing out that even the works of 'early analytical writers' like Gilman (1939), Sanders, Hatfield and Moore (1938), Paton and Littleton (1940), and of later analytical writers such as Morris and Bray are systems of rules rather than theories. Chambers then calls for a set of 'more fundamental propositions', and produces the following three 'premises':

*   Certain organized activities are carried out by entities which exist by the will or with the cooperation of contributing parties;
*   These entities are managed rationally, that is, with a view to meeting the demands of the contributing parties efficiently;
*   Statements in monetary terms of the transactions and relationships of the entity are one means of facilitating rational management;
*   The derivation of such statements is a service function. (Chambers, 1955, p. 19.)

He then goes on discussing these premises in some detail and emphasizes the advantages of such a system. In his 'Detail for a Blueprint' (1957) Chambers reiterates these premises as well as the need for 'the scientific study of accounting' (p. 208—209). He goes a step further by presenting what he deemed to be a proof of the following 'theorem': *'In the case of continuing ventures, periodical accounting is a necessary conditional of rational action.'* Furthermore, he takes issue with Littleton's (1956) criticism of his first Blueprint article and with Littleton's aversion to what I initially called 'accounting theory construction'.[7]

Similar to Chambers, with whom I wholeheartedly agreed on the need for the construction of a 'scientific' accounting theory, I too started from economics and in 'The Constellation of Accountancy and Economics' (Mattessich, 1956) presented a plea for a theory general enough to integrate business accounting with national income and other accounting systems. My subsequent paper, 'Towards a General and Axiomatic Foundation of Accountancy' (Mattessich, 1957) strengthened this plea by presenting a series of concise axioms and definitions from which I was able *to derive and prove rigorously* (in matrix algebraic terms) *eight accounting theorems.* For my taste, Chambers' 'premises' were neither fundamental enough nor were they formulated concisely enough to lend themselves to the derivation of theorems;[8] and the proof he supplied for the single 'theorem' presented (in Chambers, 1957, p. 209—210) would hardly be acceptable to a logician or mathematician. Indeed, it was more than a decade later that Montague (1970) showed for the first time (at the end of his *Universal Grammar*) how to prove rigorously theorems within the framework of *ordinary* language systems (i.e. beyond the artificial systems of logic and mathematics). Stegmüller, for example, regards Montague's simple examples as historical landmarks *'because these are the first cases of natural sentences* in the over 2,500 year old history of western logic and grammar . . . for which proof of (deductive) inference could be established or denied' (cf. Stegmüller, 1975, p. 64 translated). Thus Chambers did not progress much beyond Paton's (1922/62) postulational attempt of which Chambers seemed to have been, at this time, as unaware as I was. But one should not be too harsh on Chambers, for it is in the nature of fundamental accounting propositions to resist simplification and reduction to mathematical or logical formulation. In my own attempts, I not only had to simplify the axioms sufficiently, but had to choose carefully those theorems that lend themselves to mathematical formulation and thus to deductive proofs. Probably for this reason Hakansson, later referring to my work (in particular to Mattessich 1964/78), paid the following tribute:

> Various postulate systems with reference to accounting have of course been suggested in the literature . . . However, only in [24] (i.e. by Mattessich) do the postulates appear to be motivated by a desire to explore the *implications* of the postulates by deducing, in a rigorous fashion, logical consequences, thereby providing a further basis for their evaluation. To specify postulates in English is relatively easy; the process of extracting consequences from them and demonstrating their consistency and independence (up to some point) is far more challenging and requires, in most instances, a complete 'reformulation' of the postulates. However, to advance knowledge significantly in normative accounting, the method of postulation and deduction cannot be dispensed with (Hakansson, 1969a, pp. 38—39).

In passing, it might be mentioned that this article (Mattessich, 1957) has been most significant for my personal fate. Not only was it (during the fifties and sixties) often enough referred to in the pertinent literature as well as translated into foreign languages, above all, it secured me two important things: a tenure position in Berkeley and Maurice Moonitz' close friendship which ultimately proved to be the more permanent of the two. Yet the fact that this paper has not been made available in any of the English accounting anthologies,[9] and thus has now almost fallen into oblivion (with the exception of some mention in Chatfield's *History of Accounting Thought*, 1974/77), has been a matter of much regret to me—not because of a longing for more recognition, but because of a hope for a better comprehension by our contemporaries. Apart from the fact that papers of this kind (together with much effort on the part of a small group of us) helped to bring about a more rigorous mathematical background of the subsequent generations of accounting scholars, I think that this paper offered the following novelties: (1) it *generalized* Leontief's matrix-algebraic formulation, making it applicable to all micro-and macro-accounting systems, (2) for the first time in accounting evolution, it proved a series of accounting theorems *rigorously,* and by doing so, (3) finally showed that even in accounting instruction *we no longer need to rely on mere illustrations* (which by necessity are always specific), *but are in a position to demonstrate at least some of our conclusions by general and scientifically acceptable means.* It will be up to our historians to test whether my claims are mistaken or whether accountants simply forgot that this twenty-odd year old paper marks a turning point in accounting education and academic research.[10]

Yet in spite of the fairly comprehensive basis of twenty-seven axioms, definitions and other requirements (in Mattessich, 1957), much of the content of this paper was programmatic and required further analysis—had I realized that twenty years later I would still be working on it, I might never have begun in the first place. Immediately after my invitation to Berkeley (1958)—where a mutually stimulating atmosphere facilitated my own research and at the same time enabled me to share, with such eminent colleagues as Maurice Moonitz, the conviction that a postulational approach would facilitate the construction of a fairly tight and general accounting theory—I set out writing *Accounting and Analytical Methods* (Mattessich, 1964/77). Meanwhile Moonitz was appointed Director of Accounting Research of the American Institute of Certified Public Accountants (AICPA) and published his Accounting Research Study No. 1 under the title *The Basic Postulates of Accounting* (Moonitz, 1961). The immense merit of this publication is to be found in the impact this study had upon a large number of academic as well as practical accountants. Even if objections and hostilities were encountered towards the postulational approach, nevertheless, attention was drawn to the issue of and the need for theory construction in our field.

Of course, Moonitz, in writing his monograph, had to make the difficult choice between an altogether rigorous approach or a version that abandoned rigour in favour of a more widespread understanding. Under the impact of his position as Research Director of a body of public accountants, and due to his profound insight into the mentality of practitioners, the choice had to be for a less rigorous version. Whether this was the right way or not, even nowadays, is difficult to assess. Today, after much of the interest in the postulational approach has ebbed away, many accountants might think it would not have mattered, one way or the other. I personally regret that the rigorous version was not feasible under the circumstances and that the postulates were limited to business accounting. The consequences of these shortcomings were probably more obvious in the subsequent AICPA study on *A Tentative Set of Broad Accounting Principles for Business Enterprise* (Sprouse and Moonitz, 1962). It was hoped that these principles could either be derived logically as theorems from the postulates or that some of them would be presented as specific interpretations of a general theory. Unfortunately this was not the case and criticism made itself felt along such lines. Among the nine appended comments predominantly by practitioners in and about Sprouse and Moonitz (1962), the one by Spacek points out that 'there is very little attempt to demonstrate how these principles flow from or are based on the postulates set forth in the previous study'[11] (Spacek, 1962, p. 77). A similar thought was reiterated by Buckley, Kircher and Mathews (1968, pp. 280—281). Beyond this, from our point of view justified, criticism, Sprouse and Moonitz (1962) were heavily criticised for their courageous act of attempting to introduce current (exit and entry) valuation methods into financial accounting (see the various 'Comments' at the end of their research study).

Meanwhile Edwards and Bell's (1961) influential work was published. Though neither written by accountants nor employing an explicitly postulational approach, it played and still plays an important role in accounting theory construction and has special significance in connection with the 'Berkeley School of Accounting'[12] (an expression favoured by Most, 1977, and justified by a tradition of several generations of eminent accounting researchers reaching from Henry Rand Hatfield to Nils H. Hakansson). At first one may have the impression that the book by Edwards and Bell (1961) belongs to the category of mere 'theory annunciation'. Indeed, this book pivots upon the combination of *two major but specific hypotheses:* (1) the current (replacement or entry) value hypothesis (one version *with* and the other *without* general price level adjustments), and (2) the classificational hypothesis of strictly separating operating and holding gains. Yet this work offers a good deal of theory construction because it systematically develops a broad spectrum of *individual consequences, tying tightly to each other* many important notions such as accounting profit, business profit, realizable profit, realized profit, subjective profit, subjective goodwill, market value of the firm, subjective value of the firm, etc.[13] Elsewhere (Mattessich, 1971c, p. 193) I compared this work to the structure of a Gothic cathedral in which one element inevitably depends on and grows out of the other—a comparison holding for only a few books in the realm of accounting literature. Apart from this structural ingenuity and the broad influence it has exercised, it has essentially contributed to major a victory of theory in accounting practice.[14]

A few years later two of my books *Accounting and Analytical Methods* (Mattessich, 1964/77) and *Simulation of the Firm Through a Budget Computer-Program* (Mattessich, 1964) were published. Both publications belong together; while the first one improves and develops the foundations conceived in my 1957 article, the second book offers an interpretation and detailed illustration of this theory within the area of budgeting (simultaneously initiating computer simulation in this accounting area).[15] In AAM (the abbreviation used in the following for Mattessich, 1964/77) I utilized the same *predicative form of axiomatization* as sometimes used in mathematics (e.g. Birkoff and MacLane, 1953) and logic (e.g. Suppes, 1957). It permits the representation of the axiom system as a logical *structure,* i.e. as a series of predicative conditions of a specific definition. In our case, *the predicate*: 'is an accounting system' (or equivalently 'is the quantitative description and projection of income and wealth aggregates') is determined by a series of eighteen basic assumptions (monetary values, time intervals, structure, duality, aggregation, economic objects, inequity of monetary classes, economic agents, entities, economic transactions, valuation, realization, classification, data input, duration, extension, materiality and allocation). These assumptions were presented *verbally* in the text of AAM, *and set-theoretically* (together with theorems and their proofs) in its Appendix A. Furthermore, AAM is concerned with important historical connections (e.g. a macro-accounting interpretation of Quesnay's *tableau économique*) and relations to other micro- and macro-systems including planning systems. Yet above all, its postulational attempt is characterized by a *great flexibility* and an *instrumental* nature, both of which are possible by introducing *place-holder assumptions*. As this is still the least understood, though most important, aspect of AAM, I may be permitted to offer a few hints: *The basic assumptions were gained inductively by examining a large number of micro- and macro-accounting systems.* Thereby only those propositions were included which constitute *necessary* conditions for measuring income and wealth by double classification (i.e. necessary for operating an accounting system). Whereas the first nine of those basic assumptions need no further intepretations, *the remaining nine assumptions* (ten in the German version: Mattessich, 1970a) require interpretation, since they *are mere place-holders*. Depending on the information purpose pursued, every place-holder assumption (also called stop-gap or surrogate assumption in AAM) invokes one or several pragmatic or instrumental hypotheses matching this particular purpose. Such a procedure was designed to avoid a second criticism, directed by Spacek (1961, p. 77) against Moonitz and Sprouse (1961), that the various 'purposes and objectives of accounting' are not taken into consideration. In contrast to my 1957 article, where the teleologic orientation was only implicit though present nevertheless (e.g. it can be discerned from the graphical presentation on p. 331 as well as in 'requirements' Nos. 0.29 to 0.35 on pp. 346—347 of Mattessich, 1957),[16] the improved version in AAM repeatedly emphasizes *purposes* and *objectives* (see AAM, pp. 31, 41-42, (49-50), 234—237). It is for these reasons (the separation of the general theory from its interpretation, and the required purpose-orientation of the latter) that

> we cannot accept . . . the pessimistic view of the AAA Committee Report (1977) which asserts that 'a single universally accepted basic accounting theory does not exist at this time' (p. 1). Of course, this controversy might resemble the comparison between the optimist and the pessimist both of whom are looking at a partly filled mug of beer: the first says 'it is half full', the second 'it is half empty'. But we believe that accounting could not be taught as an academic discipline, if there were not a series of basic assumptions which the vast majority of accountants either consciously or subconsciously accept in their professional activity. This does not mean to deny that there exists a considerable amount of disagreement among accountants. But the controversial parts of various conflicting 'theories' usually concern a very limited number of hypotheses (e.g. valuation, realization or allocation hypotheses); and second, misunderstandings arise out of a failure to clearly specify the action goal or information purpose which a specific 'theory' is supposed to serve; and third, a disregard of the fact that one can get around most of the conflicting areas by formulating some of the basic assumptions as 'empirically empty shells holding place' for specific hypotheses . . . . The choice of such 'surrogate assumptions' is by no means a cheap trick but a device to harness the area of agreement within a general theory, and simultaneously to separate it from the area of disagreement. This also makes detailed teleologic interpretation possible and opens the door to a truly purpose oriented theory of accounting.[17]

The reception of AAM was very mixed; it ranged from great enthusiasm, through utter indifference and incomprehension, to wholesale rejection. The epitome of the latter was Chambers' (1966) lengthy review article. I foresaw a good deal of reaction to such an iconoclastic work as AAM which I described as 'being plagued with all the shortcomings of a pioneering attempt' (AAM, p. 434). But I was naive enough not to expect it from those who themselves were promoting the postulational approach. Nevertheless Chambers paid a compliment to AAM by the mere length (over 18 pages) of his devastating criticism. Apart from the many misunderstandings which this review contains, it must be said, in retrospect, that Chambers was by no means the only one who failed to comprehend or appreciate the following three important aspects of AAM: (1) *the strict separation of the general theoretical framework from the interpretation through specific purpose oriented hypotheses* (today I am inclined to regard this separation as the decisive achievement of AAM and as its most important potential contribution for future, *general* accounting theories); (2) *the attempt to develop the general framework before and independently of the specific hypotheses;* and (3) *the deliberate postponement of the systematic development of teleologic interpretations to a later time* (when hopefully the methodological and empirical prerequisites for such interpretations are available). My own response to Chambers' review appeared in the following year and may here be summarized by its last sentence: 'I have great sympathy for the reaction to such a seditious work as AAM. It is a book with many imperfections, but I ask the reader to judge it without prejudice and after careful study. Above all, I ask him not to be obsessed with trivialities, but to penetrate to the essence of its results and its message', Mattessich (1967), p. 123.

But Chambers' (1966) criticism can be much better understood in terms of his own ultimate and comprehensive postulational attempt: *Accounting, Evaluation and Economic Behavior* (Chambers, 1966/75). Whereas I tried to infer inductively the basic assumptions by studying various extant micro- and macro-accounting systems (thus respecting the preferences manifested by current users and producers of those information systems), Chambers started from a preconceived, and to my mind, dogmatic objective. For him the major task of accounting is the representation of *market prices*[18] in financial reports and statements ultimately serving managerial actions, whereas for me the objective of accounting was and still is the *valuation* of assets, liabilities, owner's equities, flow of services, etc. by that evaluation procedure which is appropriate for the pertinent purpose. *Yet, according to Chambers, valuation can never be measurement* ('What is past and present may be able to be measured, but what is future can only be evaluated.' Chambers, 1966/75, p. 42). *For me, however, valuation is the measurement of preferences; and nobody can deny that having a preference is a 'present state' of mind about the future, not a future state in itself.*[19] Furthermore, I regard the current market exit price merely as one value among several alternatives, and not, like Chambers, as something special, something sacrosanct, something free of value judgement. Let no one forget that every price actually paid is the result of nothing but two or more personal preferences, both or all of which are *purely subjective.* Unfortunately, the term 'market value' is used equally for two entirely different things: (1) for the (unit) price of a commodity *actually traded,* and (2) for the (unit) value of all the units of the same commodity *not traded. Yet only the former is objectively verifiable, not the latter* (I call this the *economic Heisenberg principle* which is best illustrated by the well-known example in which the actual market value of a firm fails to correspond to the product of outstanding shares times share price, when the latter was determined at a much smaller trading volume).

There are many more aspects of divergence between Professor Chambers and myself (e.g. his exclusion versus my inclusion of budgeting and macro-accounting systems in the 'general' accounting theory), but for this paper the following is the most decisive: Chambers (1966/75) presents a vast number of postulates *and* definitions without clearly indicating which are which. The processes of inductive inferences leading to the postulates, and of the deductive inferences, leading to the many theorems thereby presented, cannot be traced by the reader. My own attempts to prove several of his theorems on the basis of the reference numbers given as hints by Chambers, were a complete failure—but this may be due to my own limitations. Finally, Chambers' theory is not an uninterpreted or semi-interpreted calculus. Theory and interpretation are completely fused, hence the range of application is by necessity fairly limited.

The third comprehensive book containing a major postulational attempt in accounting is that of Ijiri (1967/78). He is by far the youngest of the three of us, and thus had the benefit of the best mathematical training, well reflected in his work. The hallmark of Ijiri's theory is its orientation towards traditional *acquistion cost valuation* and his reliance on *merely three valuation axioms* (control, quantities, and exchange) from which he deduces five extremely simple 'valuation rules' (extended to eight in his new version: Ijiri, 1975). Apart from the many valuable contributions made by Ijiri (1967/78 and 1975), I believe that his axiomatic basis is too small, and thus would regard his theory as a partial, not a fully-fledged, postulational system (in the rigorous sense of this word). Indeed, in his improved version he openly admits this by appropriately calling his postulational approach in Chapter 5 'The Axiomatic Structure of Historical Cost Valuation'. Nevertheless, from the point of view of theory construction, his work is *coherent and broad enough* to be considered as one of the most impressive contemporary accounting theories.

INTERNATIONAL REACTION IN THE LATE SIXTIES AND SEVENTIES

A comparison of Ijiri's or Chambers' theory with my own will demonstrate that I have been concerned with a problem neglected by those theoreticians, an issue which they did not regard as crucial or even as relevant. This is the problem of (1) *separating the general theory* (uninterpreted or semi-interpreted calculus) *from its interpretations,* and of (2) *creating the foundation of such a general theory* as an indispensable prerequisite for attaining a common denominator for feasible interpretations. In this way it becomes possible to construct under a single theory various interpretations on the basis of different information objectives. To devote one's concern to the interpretations (as most accountants did) before the foundations are solved, may be a useful stop-gap solution for practical purposes, but it is no solution leading to a *general* accounting theory. If the latter can ever be attained, it is by developing both the uninterpreted framework as well as the specific interpretations in the right order. I do not claim that this will necessarily lead to a *generally satisfactory* theory, but I believe that it is the only way towards a *generally applicable* theory. It is characteristic of my approach that, in contrast to others (e.g. to Alexander who used present values, Edwards and Bell who stressed replacement values, Chambers who championed exit market values, Ijiri who defended acquisition cost values), I introduced a *general* valuation assumption, thus *tolerating all specific valuation hypotheses,* but envisaging that one day sufficient empirical-deontic evidence would be available to select not only the proper valuation hypothesis for a particular information purpose but all the other specific hypotheses (for realization, classification, allocation, etc.) as well:

> Yet I did not make any attempt to present a *body of systematic interpretations* of my theoretical framework. The reason for this omission rested in my conviction that I lacked the methodological and empirical prerequisites to tackle such a complex task. To overcome this handicap I concerned myself during the last decade predominantly with general methodological questions. The outcome is a comprehensive recent book: *Instrumental Reasoning and Systems Methodology* (Mattessich, 1978a), with the publication of which I consider a decade of methodological apprenticeship terminated.[20]

Although I have gained many valuable methodological insights, a systematic *interpretation* of the general accounting theory [21] will require much empirical research, impossible to be mastered by a single person. By deliberately abstaining (e.g. Mattessich, 1964/77) from formulating those specific interpretations, I admitted my ignorance about the pertinent means-end relations. By so doing I was in full expectation of falling out of favour with many experts. Socrates did not endear himself to his colleagues (the 'sophists') by telling them that he at least knows that he does not know. And instead of the hemlock, I was administered a good deal of disregard from some quarters.

On the one side, all these postulational attempts by Chambers, Ijiri, Moonitz and myself, as well as the Edwards and Bell study, led during the sixties to a considerable number of further, related publications by other individual scholars: e.g., Bray (1966), Buckley, Kircher and Mathews (1968), Devine (1960), Gordon (1964), Hakansson (1966, 1969a, b), Parker (1969), Parker and Harcourt (1969), Prince (1963), Richards (1960), Storey (1963), and by various committees: e.g. American Accounting Association (ASOBAT 1966), Center for International Education and Research in Accounting (1964), as well as by the original authors: e.g., Bell (1966/69), Chambers (1963, 1965, 1967), Ijiri (1965), Mattessich (1962, 1966), Moonitz and Littleton (1965). On the other side, decisive works in the area of theory construction and its evaluation, such as Chambers (1966/75), AAA (ASOBAT 1966), Dopuch and Revsine (1973a, b), Nelson (1973), AAA (SATTA 1977) avoided my name and failed to list any of my contributions. This, however, is not a complaint against the academic accounting community in general. In the seventies, important books summarizing the evolution of accounting theory such as Chatfield (1974/77), Hendriksen (1965/70/77), Most (1977) did by no means close themselves to my ideas on basic assumptions and other contributions. Chatfield's (1974/77) accounting history, for example, devoted a common section to Chambers and myself, merely skipping the great abyss that separates our divergent views.

Especially favourable was the international response in Japan. Apart from Japanese translations (of Chambers, 1966/75, Ijiri, 1967/78 and Mattessich, 1964/77), and personal invitations as well as published profiles, etc., I there encountered the first and, thus far, only substantial evidence that my *set-theoretical* axiomatization (Appendix A of AAM) has been comprehended and constructively improved upon. Professor Saito (1972, 1973), who now is with Tokyo University, pointed at some weaknesses of this set-theoretical formulation to which I gratefully responded (Mattessich, 1973a) by further clarification and improvements.

In Italy, the leading expert, Professor Onida of the University of Rome published in Italian (1970) and English (1974) a monograph under the title *Modern Developments of the North American Accounting Doctrine and the Studies of Business Economics* (Onida, 1970/74) in which the theories of Chambers, Ijiri and myself are compared and discussed. As Onida is very much disposed towards my position, but quite critical of that of Chambers, a further exchange (in Italian) between Chambers (1973) and Onida (1973a, b) ensued. Professor Galassi's recent book on *Axiomatic Accounting Systems and Theoretical Deductive Systems* (1978, in Italian) pursues ideas similar to my own and fully acknowledges the influence of my own research in accounting as well as in the philosophy of science upon his book.

In Germany, where an improved German version of Part I and II of AAM (Mattessich, 1970a) was published,[22] it was Kosiol (1970, 1978, pp. 182—207) and Schweitzer (1970, 1972) who, under the influence of the Anglo-American trend in the sixties, began to develop their own postulates of accounting.

In Spain the interest in the axiomatization of accounting began relatively early when a Spanish translation of my 1957 article appeared (Mattessich, 1958). This interest (especially in some methodological and mathematical aspects) was revived when a series of articles by Garcia (1972), Requena-Rodriquez (1972), and Buenos-Campos (1972) in the inaugural issue of the *Revista Española de Financiacion y Contabilidad* took reference to Chambers' and Ijiri's work as well as to my own. Thereupon I was invited by the editors of this journal to submit an article on recent improvements of my theory which was published in Spanish (Mattessich, 1973).

In the United Kingdom it was Professor Gambling (1974) who based his argument for recognition of other cultural values, besides those based on purely economic criteria, on my nineteen basic assumptions which penetrate a considerable part of his book. Furthermore Laughlin (1979), from the University of Sheffield, refers to the need for approaching accounting theory from both ends, the general (uninterpreted) theory as well as the specific interpretations, and perceptively remarks that 'undoubtedly such a stand makes an immense amount of sense and yet it is surprising, even alarming, how little Mattessich's ideas have been developed over the years.' (p.22). I hope that my remarks in the second paragraph of the current section have explained why these ideas were difficult to pursue thus far, or more precisely, why only one end of them could approach solution.

In the United States, however, the inevitable reaction to *a priori* research and the postulational approach began in the sixties with Vatter (1963) but made itself felt mainly in the early seventies. Although one further substantial contribution to accounting theory construction by Sterling (1970)[23] was still to appear, and although various publications on the postulational approach by Chambers, Ijiri and myself received the AICPA literature award for notable contributions, the reaction of the dialectical process of academic fashion had to come, and manifested itself in the following two ways:

(1) *An overt criticism of accounting research of the sixties.* As early as 1968 Buckley, Kircher and Mathews—who analysed and juxtaposed various attempts at formulating accounting postulates and principles—pointed out that: 'Absence of methodology is probably the major cause of isolation of most new endeavours in our field. The objective of too many authors appears to be uniqueness or originality. Progress is retarded by this attitude.' Buckley *et al* (1968), p. 278. I wholeheartedly agree with this criticism and believe that, by now, we would have been much farther in the construction of a general theory of accounting, had we behaved less individualistically. But such individualism is characteristic of the 'childhood phase' of theory construction in general, and I personally am convinced that the 'manhood phase' still lies ahead of us. We ourselves, as well as future generations, may learn from our errors.

But the heavy guns of opposition moved forward with the monograph *Accounting Research 1960—1970: A Critical Evaluation* (ed. by Dopuch and Revsine, 1973a). There, specific criticism is found by Nelson (1973), Dopuch and Revsine (1973b), and in a separate study by Gonedes and Dopuch (1974), pp. 49—50. Probably many accountants shared Nelson's view expressed in the following words.

> The new writers have applied logic, other philosophic techniques, economics, and mathematics to the accounting problem at a level exceeding that of their predecessors . . . But at this point we must stop. We may have a more logical structure today, but we really have not moved very far, in substance from the earlier writings. Impressive as the scholarship is, we are not significantly advanced from where we were in 1950. (Nelson, 1973, p. 15).

However, it seems that Nelson and others overlooked that *accounting, as a whole, is a most schizophrenic discipline* in which academicians work towards more and better information to erect a structure able to fulfill an important social cybernetic function, while many practitioners and managers effectively oppose such endeavours and, with it, the practical application of new theoretical insights. Wells, illuminating another aspect, answers Nelson with the following words:

> Some of the authors proposing these systems which appeared during the golden age already have been identified—Edwards and Bell (1961) and Chambers (1966); others include Sprouse and Moonitz (1962), Mattessich (1964/77), and Mathews (1965). The works of these authors were debated throughout the 1960s, and that debate served to clarify and identify the alternatives. Without that identification, the next step of the revolutionary process could not proceed. It *has* proceeded, as shown by the published evaluations of the alternatives . . . The fact that the evaluation process has taken place, and is continuing, is evidence of the imprtance of the so-called *a priori* works; hence our disagreement with Nelson's comment that these works are of doubtful value. (Wells, 1976, p. 477.)

(2) *A reorientation of many young scholars, away from the a priori approach,* [24] *towards empirical research.* The inevitable reaction to the heavy emphasis upon *a priori* and analytical research in accounting during the fifties and early sixties manifested itself in an increasing need for, and interest in, behavioural accounting research in the late sixties and seventies. This was a very natural and wholesome phenomenon. Indeed, competent empirical research could enormously enrich theory construction and theory testing in accounting; above all, empirical research is indispensable for the teleologic *interpretations* of the general theory.

The beginnings of systematic empirical accounting research might be traced to Argyris (1952). This research gained momentum with Stedry (1960), was stimulated by Cyert and March's renowned book on *A Behavioral Theory of the Firm* (1963), and received special promotion through the 'Chicago School of Accounting' and its *Journal of Accounting Research* together with its supplementary volumes on *Empirical Research in Accounting* (1966-1973) and related topics, such as *Studies in Financial Accounting Objectives* (1974). Clarification of accounting objectives and information goals, the application of novel insights of investment and finance theory to accounting, as well as the development of human resource accounting, seem to be most important areas of behavioural accounting research. Since it is not possible to list here the many significant contributions in this area, we refer the reader to such anthologies as Bruns and De Coster (1969), Dopuch and Revsine (1973), Sterling (1972b), Abdel-khalik and Keller (1978), and to such summaries as Williams and Griffin (1969), Hakansson

(1973), Green (1973), Gonedes and Dopuch (1974), and most recently Dyckman, Gibbins and Swieringa (1978). Although most of these publications reveal the limitations of the present state of empirical accounting research, it is doubtful that most accountants are aware of the enormous methodological difficulties which the empirical approach encounters in such applied sciences as accounting and business administration in general. If even the natural sciences (which enjoy the benefit of *practically unbounded* universal law statements) are severely plagued by foundational problems,[25] how much graver is the situation in our discipline where law-like propositions are practically non-existent? This is because they are not truly universal statements but are *severely bounded,* and constitute *means-end relations* (e.g. instrumental hypotheses) which are much more difficult to handle, logically as well as empirically, than assertoric or descriptive law statements (cf. Mattessich, 1978a, pp. 13—16, 128—140, 191—192, 317—322).

Once accounting theorists come to realize these and many other difficulties of the empirical approach in our discipline, they will acknowledge that a minimum of *a priori* assumptions in accounting are indispensable. It might turn out, for example, that the accounting users' information needs cannot satisfactorily be established by empirical research alone, and that certain *a priori* assumptions about rationality criteria of those users will have to be accepted. In other words *a priori* reasoning might not remain restricted to the purely analytical procedures of accounting, but might continue to compete with empirical research and supply more or less legitimate substitutes. Indeed, this may be one reason why in the seventies several academic accountants are pioneering information economics for the purpose of *testing* accounting systems through analytical evaluation.

APPLICATION OF INFORMATION ECONOMICS

Most recently the aversion to the *a priori* approach seems to yield to a more reasonable attitude. This is not merely expressed in such survey articles on *a priori* research as Bedford's (1978), but finds manifestation in the increasing interest in the application of information economics within our own discipline. Such an application reveals that accounting theoreticians feel the need for recognising explicitly the following aspects: (1) *a priori* assumptions on choice and rationality criteria, (2) a rigorous *analytical* framework (based on modern economics and decision theory), (3) the employment of *stochastic* models, and thus the abandoning of the traditional deterministic outlook, (4) the explicit recognition of such *subjective* forces as *preferences* and *beliefs* of accountants, managers and other information users, (5) further *conceptual clarification,* (6) the *evaluation* of information costs as well as benefits, and (7) the distinction between the *unrealistic* 'ideal information' system and *realistic* 'modifications' and 'simplifications'.

As hinted at in the beginning of this paper, the new breed of 'information economics accountants' of the late sixties and seventies are the direct descendants of 'the more rigorous among the postulational accountants'. Indeed, some similarities are striking since both groups are using: (1) a set of basic premises—while the older approach presents 'basic assumptions' at the outset, the information economic approach introduces at various stages the Neumann-Morgenstern axioms of expected utility (together with the often implied axioms of the probability calculus and some decision criterion—e.g. the Bayes-Bernoulli criterion) together with additional assumptions (cf. Demski and Feltham, 1976, pp. 31—39 ff., or Mattessich, 1975, pp. 350—353); (2) a *formal* conceptual apparatus for deducing rigorously theorems or 'propositions' with proofs (cf. Demski and Feltham, 1976, pp. 26, 38, 45, 47—50, ff.); (3) a presentation of a semi-interpreted calculus, postponing the specific interpretations to a time when the pertinent empirical information is available. Just as the postulational approach presents place-holder assumptions without specifying the actual hypotheses, so the information economic approach offers, for example, merely empty shells for the preference and probability functions without specifying the actual shapes of these functions.

Thus the information economics approach and related attempts—as encountered by Butterworth (1967, 1972, etc.), Demski (1970, 1972, etc.), Feltham (1967, 1968, 1972, etc.), Hakansson (1969a, b,

1977, 1976), Itami (1977), Mattessich (1975, 1978c), Mock (1971, 1976), etc.—are just as much concerned with theory construction as the postulational approaches of the fifties and early sixties; and it might be no coincidence that Butterworth, Feltham and Mock studied for their doctoral degrees in Berkeley at a time when the postulational approach to accounting reached its climax [26] and when Marschak and Radner advanced the fairly novel ideas on information economics and team theory.[27]

Two well-known papers on 'Theory Construction and Verification' by Sterling (1970) and the American Accounting Association (1971) have called for a fusion of the accounting measurement model with a decision theoretic model, thereby demanding the following specification of the decision settings:

1. an optimization rule, decision criterion, and/or goals of the decision make (constraints, if any),
2. all feasible acts available to the decision maker,
3. all possible events or states that may occur over the decision horizon,
4. probability distributions relating to the set of possible events, and
5. a set of payoffs, conditional upon the state and act. (AAA, 1971, p. 62.)

Although neither Sterling (1970) nor the AAA (1971) explicitly invoked the information economics approach, the models of Demski and Feltham (1976) which result from it, seem to fulfill all of those requirements.

As Demski and Feltham (1976) have excellently demonstrated, such an approach can be most helpful in clarifying many important conceptual and methodological issues (and even more helpful if juxtaposed to or coordinated with behavioural research). This approach could become the key to a theory determining both the quasi-optimal structure of a goal-directed accounting system and its degree of efficiency. Furthermore, it might be able to answer questions of the following kind: When is it meaningful and when senseless to operate in accounting with *a priori* probabilities? When is it advisable to subdivide an action goal or an information purpose? Under which circumstances is it possible to define sharply an information need and to match it to a specific accounting structure? When and in which way can cost and benefit of an accounting system be measured meaningfully? What kinds of modifications and simplifications are commendable or acceptable in a specific situation? How can the logical link between an ideal system and its practicable simplification be conceived and represented?

Yet in spite of its desirability and its promising features, the information economics approach most likely is too abstract and too far away from the deeply rooted double-classification approach; furthermore, the need for well-determined utility and preference functions, etc., is too forbidding to sustain a generally acceptable theory of accounting. A truly general, well-constructed theory must be flexible enough to serve the small shopkeeper as well as the chief accountant of the large multinational corporation, the individual practitioner as well as the international public accounting firm, the cost minimizing managerial accountant as well as the profit maximizing chief executive, the individual shareholder as well as the financial analyst, the government accountant as well as the national income statistician. I believe that such flexibility can be attained only by a combination of a holistic overall framework with a large set of variegated goal-directed interpretations. Though I am not at all convinced that the set of basic assumptions suggested by myself (be it in Mattessich, 1957, 1964/77, 1970, or 1978/79a) will ultimately prove satisfactory, I firmly believe that *it must be a set of assumptions common to all accounting systems. Otherwise the fatal game of atomistic, nonteleologic and isolated interpretations*[28] *with its one-sided orientation, its intolerant belief in a unique solution, its confusing duplications, and its ineffectual rivalry between different valuation approaches,* will begin all over again.

FOOTNOTES

[1] This distinction resembles, but is *not* identical with, T. Kuhn's (1962) distinction between 'normal science' and 'revolutionary science'—see also Wells (1976) and Mattessich (1978a), pp. 11, 155-156, 263-272—because 'theory construction' may constitute either normal or revolutionary scientific activity. If it involves an ap-

proach or some hypotheses that are capable of bringing about *a fundamental theoretical change,* it is revolutionary, otherwise normal.

[2] Thus expressions like 'entity theory', 'fund theory', 'replacement value theory', 'events theory', etc., might be considered *misnomers,* as they do not refer to the construction of a whole theory, but to the annunciation of individual hypotheses or other specific theory aspects.

[3] The concern with *'accounting principles'* is one or two decades older: see Niklisch (1911) and Sprague (1907/72). But for us accounting principles are formulations of guiding norms for practical or even technical purposes; they do not possess the fundamental nature of postulates and often turn out to be mere interpretations.

[4] Although Edwards and Bell's excellent book (1961) clarifies many conceptual and technical issues of the market value method beyond Schmidt's (1921/29) contribution (e.g. the introduction of the notion of 'current operating profit'), Edwards and Bell seem to underrate the originality and the pioneering effort of Schmidt's contribution (in which not only are replacement values most prominent, but where such ideas as 'capital maintenance', 'fictitious gains', 'smoothing business cycles through current valuation in accounting', etc. are presented in a comprehensive and well-integrated system). Apart from a single footnote (Edwards and Bell, 1961, pp. 26-27), they neither relate Schmidt's very detailed elaborations to their own research, nor do they bother to list *most* of Schmidt's many pertinent publications in their bibliography. This remark is not so much intended to castigate those two well-known authors, as it is to characterize the parochial attitude of accounting literature in general (whether it is American, German, or of any other provenance). The trend towards a truly international accounting literature, though existing, seems to progress at an extremely slow pace.

[5] Schmalenbach's *Dynamic Accounting* (1959) still seems to be the only English translation of early German accounting theories.

[6] If Hendriksen (1977, p. 104) asserts that 'the current interest in this area was sparked by the recommendations in 1958 of the AICPA Special Committee on Research Program', it should be added that this committee in turn was sparked by the publications of Chambers and myself which appeared between 1955 and 1957. Experts like Moonitz (e.g. 1961) and Storey (e.g. 1963), who kept close ties with the AICPA, might be invoked as competent witnesses. An even earlier reaction is found by Devine (1960).

[7] One might point out that in spite of the suggestive title of Littleton's *Structure of Accounting Theory* (1953), Littleton makes no attempt to present an analytical, i.e. postulational, structure of accounting. In Littleton (1956) he openly admits his opposition to such attempts by listing alternative premises to those presented by Chambers, trying to demonstrate the arbitrariness of Chambers' premises, stressing the dangers of too high a generalization and making a plea for the historical cost basis.

[8] In a recent German paper of mine (Mattessich, 1978b) which was written abroad when several relevant publications were not available to me, I asserted that my 1957 article was written without knowledge of Chambers' (1955) article. I meanwhile discovered that this article came to my attention shortly before dispatching my own to the editor. I hope this sets the matter straight, and I should like to point out that in my 1978b article (written for a lecture I gave in Darmstadt in 1977), I explicitly drew attention to the fact that it was written 'under circumstances which prevented me from having access to my private library as well as to important relevant literature' (cf.Mattessich, 1978b, p. 172, translated).

[9] It was merely duplicated in a *mimeographed* English manuscript by Devine (1962) in Indonesia, but has been made available in a Japanese anthology (Koshimura, 1969).

[10] To show that it is not my name but a particular article I am here promoting, I freely admit that none of my accounting articles actually reprinted or published in anthologies, can match either the historical significance (as regards impact on Moonitz and others) or the originality of this 1957 paper.

[11] By 'previous study', Moonitz (1961) is meant.

[12] Edwards and Bell (1961) was not merely published at the University of California Press in Berkeley, Bell was also a member of Berkeley's Economics Faculty keeping good contact with our Accounting Division.

[13] As regards interpretation, Edwards and Bell (1961) cover a more limited spectrum, but at least offer two sub-interpretations of one major version, namely the interpretation of *nominal* and of *real* values.

[14] On March 23, 1976 the *Accounting Series Release* No. 190 of the US Security Exchange Commission (SEC) *ruled,* effective December 24, 1976, *that registrant corporations* (with inventories and gross property, plant and equipment of more than $100 million, representing more that 10% of total assets) have to submit at fiscal year ends to the SEC financial statements based on *replacement costs* as well as acquisition costs, and in September 1977 *Statement of Financial Accounting Standards* No. 33 prescribed for the larger corporations complementary adjustments to the Income Statement as to general inflation and current cost effects, as well as separate reports on gains or losses from holding monetary and non-monetary items.

[15] The idea of budget computer simulation was first advanced 3 years before (Mattessich, 1961).

[16] The term 'requirement' in Mattessich (1957) is fairly equivalent to the expression 'surrogate assumption' in AAM, pp. 340, 346-347.

[17] Mattessich (1978/79a), p. 8.

[18] Chambers' *current cash equivalent* (CCE) basically is a market exit price which for him is the major objective accounting measure.

[19] For details on this issue the reader is referred to another, even more lengthy controversy between Chambers (1971a, b) and myself (Mattessich, 1970b, 1971a, b).

[20] Mattessich (1978/79b), pp. 58-59.

[21] Similar to Thomas (1974), p. 4, such interpretation would *not* favour general-purpose financial statements and allocations.

[22] The most crucial aspect of this improvement (Mattessich, 1970) consists of the *explicit* recognition of various information purposes through an additional place-holder assumption (involving specific information hypotheses) and leading to a set of *nineteen,* instead of eighteen, basic assumptions (cf. Mattessich, 1978/79a).

[23] Emphasizing, like Chambers, current market exit values. For details see my review article, Mattessich (1971), and Sterling's (1972a) reply.

[24] Although my work is usually categorized as '*a priori* research', I personally am most reluctant to accept this label for two major reasons: (1) The basic assumptions of my general framework are derived *inductive-empirically* from the many extant micro- and macro-accounting systems. If I thereby accept *a priori* the double classificational structure, it is in consideration of the well manifested preferences and needs of present accounting system users. (2) My theory, unlike the *a priori* theories of Chambers, Ijiri, Moonitz, etc., is based on the idea that the specific hypotheses (i.e. the '*fine* structure' of an accounting system, in contrast to the '*gross* structure') is to be inferred from the pertinent *information purpose,* instead of being imposed upon the user in an *a priori* fashion. This has been grossly misunderstood, as remarks by Most (1977), p. 55 and others indicate. The reason for this misunderstanding probably lies in the fact that I did not attempt to supply *systematic interpretations* of accounting theory.

[25] Philosophers of science as well as scientists had to abandon the well cherished notion of *verification,* substituting first the much weaker notion of *confirmation*; but this too was abandoned in favour of the precarious notion of *falsification* which in turn proved to be inapplicable for existential statements for the same reason for which universal statements could be verified. (Try to *verify* such a statement as 'all ravens are black' or to *falsify* the statement 'There exists an apple the natural colour of which is golden'. In both cases *all* ravens or apples, past, present, and future, would have to be examined.)

[26] Indeed, in the Spring of 1965, Butterworth, Feltham, Mock and others attended *simultaneously* my Graduate Seminar in Accounting Theory at the University of California in Berkeley.

[27] Provisional manuscripts of various chapters of Marschak and Radner (1972) were circulating in Berkeley from the early sixties onwards.

[28] These atomistic interpretations correspond to Hendriksen's (1977), pp. 4-5, 'Interpretational Theories', which should be strictly distinguished from the *interpretations of an uninterpreted or semi-interpreted theory* which we are pleading for.

BIBLIOGRAPHY

Abdel-khalik, A. R. and T. F. Keller (eds.), *The Impact of Accounting Research on Practice and Disclosure* (Durham, N. C.: Duke University Press, 1978).

American Accounting Association, *A Statement of Basic Accounting Theory* (ASOBAT) (Evanston, Ill.: AAA, 1966).

idem., Committee Report on 'Accounting Theory Construction and Verification,' *Accounting Review,* Supplement to Vol. 46, 1971, pp. 50-79.

idem., Statement on Accounting Theory and Theory Acceptance (SATTA) (Sarasota: AAA, 1977).

American Institute of Certified Public Accountants, Accountants Objectives Study Group, *Objectives of Financial Statements* (New York: AICPA, 1973) (Trueblood Report).

Argyris, C., *The Impact of Budgets on People* (Ithaca: School of Business and Public Administration, Cornell University, 1952).

Backer, Morton (ed.), *Modern Accounting Theory* (Englewood Cliffs, NJ: Prentice-Hall, 1966).

Baxter, W. T. and S. Davidson (eds.), *Studies in Accounting Theory* (Homewood, Ill.: R. D. Irwin, 1962).

Bedford, Norton, *Income Determination Theory* (Reading, Mass.: Addison-Wesley Publishing Co., 1965).

Bedford, Norton, 'The Impact of *A Priori* Research', *The Impact of Accounting Research on Practice and Disclosure,* ed. by Abdel-khalik and T. F. Keller (Durham, NC: Duke University, 1978), pp. 2-31.

Bell, P. W., (1966/69), 'Price Changes and Income Measurement', *Modern Accounting Theory* (Englewood Cliffs, NJ: Prentice-Hall, 1966), pp. 91-97, reprinted in Parker and Harcourt (1969), pp. 185-192.

Birkoff, G. and S. MacLane, *A Survey of Modern Algebra,* rev. ed. (New York: Macmillan Co., 1953).

Bray, F. Sewell, 'Accounting Postulates and Principles', *Modern Accounting Theory,* ed. by M. Backer (Englewood Cliffs, NJ: Prentice-Hall, 1966), pp. 28-47.

Brummet, R. L., E. G. Flamholtz and W. C. Pyle, *Human Resource Accounting: Development and Implementation in Industry* (Ann Arbor: Foundation for Research in Human Behavior, 1969).

Bruns, W. J. and D. T. De Coster, *Accounting and its Behavioral Implications* (New York: McGraw-Hill Co., 1969).

Buckley, J. W., Paul Kircher and R. L. Mathews, 'Methodology in Accounting Theory', *Accounting Review*, April 1968, pp. 274-283.

Burns, T. J. (ed.), *Behavioral Experiments in Accounting* (Columbus, Ohio: Ohio State University, 1972).

Buenos-Campos, E., 'Analisis Conceptual de la Planificacion Contable', *Revista Española de Financiación y Contabilidad*, Jan.-April 1972, pp.73-94.

Butterworth, J. E., *Accounting Systems and Management Decision: An Analysis of the Role of Information in the Management Decision Process* (Berkeley: Doct. Diss., 1967).

idem., 'The Accounting System as an Information Function, *Journal of Accounting Research*, Spring 1972, pp. 1-27.

idem., 'The Evaluation of Information Alternatives for Uncertain Decision Problems', Working Paper 73-47 (European Institute for Advanced Studies in Management, Brussels, 1973).

Butterworth, J. E. and G. A. Feltham, 'Mathematical Decision Models in Managerial Accounting', Working Paper No. 204. Faculty of Commerce and Business Administration. University of British Columbia, Vancouver, 1972.

Center for International Education and Research in Accounting (Study Group at the University of Illinois), *A Statement of Basic Accounting Postulates and Principles* (Urbana: University of Illinois, 1964).

Chambers, R. J., 'Blueprint for a Theory of Accounting', *Accounting Research*, January 1955, pp. 17-25.

Idem., 'Detail for a Blueprint', *Accounting Review*, April 1957, pp. 206-215.

Idem., 'Why Bother with Postulates?', *Journal of Accounting Research*, Spring, 1963, pp. 3-15.

Idem., 'Edwards and Bell on Business Income', *Accounting Review*, October 1965, pp. 731-740.

Idem., (1966/75), *Accounting, Evaluation and Economic Behavior* (Englewood Cliffs, NJ: Prentice-Hall, 1966/Reprint ed., Houston: 'Accounting Classics Series', Scholars Book Co., 1975).

Idem., 'Accounting and Analytical Methods: A Review Article', *Journal of Accounting Research*, Spring 1966, pp. 101-118.

Idem., 'Continuously Contemporary Accounting—Additivity and Action', *Accounting Review*, October 1967, pp. 751-757.

Idem., 'Asset Measurement and Valuation', *Cost and Management*, March/April 1971a, pp. 30-35.

Idem., 'Measurement and Valuation Again', *Cost and Management*, July/August 1971b, pp. 12-17.

Idem., 'Misurazioni, stime e valutazioni nelle decisioni finanziarie', *Rivista dei Dottori Commercialisti*, Nov.-Dec. 1973, pp. 1002-1022.

Chatfield, Michael, *A History of Accounting Thought* (Hindsdale, Ill.: Dryden Pr., 1974. Revised ed. Krieger Co. 1977).

Cyert, R. and J. March, *A Behavioral Theory of the Firm* (Englewood Cliffs, NJ: Prentice-Hall, 1963).

Demski, J. S., 'Some Decomposition Results for Information Evaluation', *Journal of Accounting Research*, Autumn 1970, pp. 178-198.

Idem., *Information Analysis* (Reading, Mass.: Addison-Wesley Publishing Co., 1972a).

Idem., 'Information Improvement Bounds', *Journal of Accounting Research*, Spring, 1972b, pp. 58-76.

Idem., 'The General Impossibility of Normative Standards', *Accounting Review*, October 1973, pp. 718-723.

Idem., 'Choice among Financial Reporting Alternatives', *Accounting Review*, April 1974, pp. 221-232.

Demski, J. S. and G. A. Feltham, 'Forecast Evaluation', *Accounting Review*, April 1972, pp. 533-548.

Idem., *Cost Determination—A Conceptual Approach* (Ames, Iowa: Iowa State University Press, 1976).

Devine, Carl, 'Research Methodology and Accounting Theory Formation', *Accounting Review*, July 1960, pp. 387-399.

Idem., *Readings in Accounting Theory, Vol. I.* mimeograph (Djakarta: 1962).

Dopuch, N. and L. Revsine (eds.), *Accounting Research 1960-1970: A Critical Evaluation* (Urbana: Center for International Education and Research in Accounting, 1973a).

Idem., (1973b), 'Editors' Preface' in Dopuch and Revsine (1973a), pp. iv-v.

Dyckman, T. R., M. Gibbins and R. J. Swieringa, 'Experimental and Survey Research in Financial Accounting: A Review and Evaluation', *The Impact of Accounting Research on Practice and Disclosure*, ed. by A. R. Abdel-khalik and T. F. Keller (Durham, NC: Duke University Press, 1978), pp. 48-105.

Edwards, E. O. and P. W. Bell, *The Theory and Measurement of Business Income* (Berkeley: University of California Press, 1961).

Feltham, G. A., *A Theoretical Framework for Evaluating Changes in Accounting Information for Managerial Decisions* (Berkeley: Doct. Diss., 1967).

Idem., 'The Value of Information', *Accounting Review*, Vol. 42, No. 4, October 1968, pp. 684-696.

Idem., *Information Evaluation.* (Sarasota, Fla.: American Accounting Association, SAR No. 5, 1972).

Feltham, G. A. and J. S. Demski,' The Use of Models in Information Evaluation', *Accounting Review*, October 1970, pp. 623-640.

Gambling, T., *Societal Accounting* (London: George Allen & Unwin, 1974).

42

Galassi, G., *Sistemi Contabili Assiomatici e Sistemi Teorici Deduttivi* (Bologna: Pàtron Editore, 1978).

Garcia-Garcia, M., 'Modernas Tendencias Metodologicas en Contabilidad', *Revista Española de Financiación y Contabilidad,* Jan.-April 1972, pp. 23-44.

Gilman, Stephen, *Accounting Concepts of Profit* (New York: Ronald Press, 1939).

Gonedes, N. J. and N. Dopuch, 'Capital Market Equilibrium, Information Production and Selected Accounting Techniques: Theoretical Framework and Review of Empirical Work', *Studies in Financial Accounting Objectives.* Supplement to Vol. 12 of *Journal of Accounting Research,* 1974, pp. 48-129.

Gordon, M. J., 'Postulates, Principles and Research in Accounting', *Accounting Review,* April 1964, pp. 251-263.

Green, D. O., 'Behavioral Science and Accounting Research' in *Accounting Research 1960-1970: A Critical Evaluation,* ed. by N. Dopuch and L. Revsine (Urbana: Center for International Education and Research in Accounting, 1973), pp. 93-115.

Hakansson, N. H., 'Optimal Investment and Consumption Strategies for a Class of Utility Functions'. Doct. Diss. (Los Angeles: University of California at Los Angeles, Working Paper No. 101, WMSI, 1966).

Idem., 'Normative Accounting Theory and the Theory of Decision', *International Journal of Accounting Education and Research,* Spring 1969a, pp. 33-47.

Idem., 'An Induced Theory of Accounting under Risk', *Accounting Review,* 1969b, pp. 495-514.

Idem., 'Empirical Research in Accounting', in *Accounting Research 1960-1970: A Critical Evaluation,* ed. by N. Dopuch and L. Revsine (Urbana: Center for International Education and Research in Accounting, 1973), pp. 137-173.

Idem., 'Interim Disclosure and Forecasts: An Economic Analysis and a Framework for Choice', *Accounting Review,* April 1977, pp. 396-416.

Idem., 'Information Needs for Portfolio Choice: Some Normative Aspects', *Financial Information of Business Administration,* ed. by A. R. Abdel-khalik and T. F. Keller (Durham, NC: Duke University, 1978a).

Idem., 'Where we are in Accounting: A Review of 'Statement on Accounting Theory and Theory Acceptance',' *Accounting Review,* July 1978b, pp. 717-725.

Hendriksen, E. S., *Accounting Theory* (Homewood: R. D. Irwin, 1st ed. 1965, 2nd ed. 1970, 3rd ed. 1977).

Hermanson, R. H., *Accounting for Human Assets.* Occasional Paper No. 14, Michigan State University, 1964.

Holzer, Hans, *Zur Axiomatik der Buchführungs- und Bilanztheorie* (Stuttgart, 1936).

Ijiri, Yuji, 'Axioms and Structures of Conventional Accounting Measurement', *Accounting Review,* January 1965, pp. 36-53.

Idem., (1967/78) *The Foundations of Accounting Measurement* (Englewood Cliffs, NJ: Prentice-Hall, 1967/Reprint ed., Houston: 'Accounting Classics Series', Scholars Book Co., 1978).

Idem., Theory of Accounting Measurement (Sarasota, Fla.: American Accounting Association, Studies in Accounting Research No. 10, 1975).

Itami, H., *Adaptive Behavior: Management Control and Information Analysis* (Sarasota, Fla.: American Accounting Association, 1977).

Koshimura, S. (ed.), *Matrix Accounting* (in Japanese) (Tokyo: Daisan Shuppan, 1969).

Kosiol, Erich, 'Der pagatorische Charakter des Anschaffungswertes' in *Zeitschrift für handelswissenschaftliche Forschung,* Vol. 38, 1944a, pp. 47-54.

Idem., Bilanzreform und Einheitsbilanz (Stuttgart, 1944b).

Idem., 'Pagatorische Bilanz', *Lexikon des kaufmännischen Rechnungswesens,* Vol. 3, 1956.

Idem., 'Zur Axiomatik der Theorie der pagatorischen Erfolgsrechnung', *Zeitschrift für Betriebswirtschaft,* Vol. 22, 1970, pp. 135-162.

Idem., Pagatoric Theory of Financial Income Determination (Urbana, Ill.: Center for Education and Research in Accounting, 1978).

Kuhn, T. S., *The Structure of Scientific Revolutions* (Chicago: University of Chicago Press, 1962).

Laughlin, R. C., 'On the Construction of a Paradigm for Accounting Science', Working paper, Division of Economic Studies, University of Sheffield, 1979.

LeCoutre, Walter, *Grundzüge der Bilanzkunde* (Leipzig, 1922).

Littleton, A. C., *Structure of Accounting Theory* (Menasha: American Accounting Association, 1953).

Idem., 'Choice among Alternatives', *Accounting Review,* July 1956, pp. 363-370.

Limperg, Theodor, Jr., *Het Object der Betrijfshuishoudkunde* (Purmerend, Netherlands: J. Muusses 1925(?), 3rd printing 1946).

Marschak, J. and R. Radner, *Economic Theory of Teams* (New Haven: Yale University Press, 1972).

Mathews, R. L., 'Price-Level Accounting and Useless Information', *Journal of Accounting Research,* Spring 1965, pp. 133-155.

Mattessich, Richard, 'The Constellation of Accountancy and Economics', *Accounting Review,* October 1956, pp. 551-564.

Idem., 'Towards a General and Axiomatic Foundation of Accountancy—With an Introduction to the Matrix Formulation of Accounting Systems', *Accounting Research,* October 1957, pp. 328-355.

Idem., Spanish translation of Mattessich (1957) in *Technica Economica,* April 1958, pp. 106-127.

Idem., 'Budgeting Models and System Simulation', *Accounting Review,* July 1961, pp. 384-397.

Idem., 'Operations Research and Accounting—Competitors or Partners?' *Quarterly Review of Economics and Business*, August 1962, pp. 7-14.

Idem., (1964/77), *Accounting and Analytical Methods* (AAM) (Homewood, Ill.: R. D. Irwin, Inc., 1964/Reprint ed., Houston:'Accounting Classics Series', Scholars Book Co, 1977).

Idem., *Simulation of the Firm through a Budget Computer Program* (Homewood, Ill.: R. D. Irwin, 1964).

Idem., 'The Impact of Electronic Data Processing and Management Science Upon Accounting Theory', *Modern Accounting Theory*, ed. by M. Backer (Englewood Cliffs, NJ: Prentice-Hall, 1966), pp. 511-534.

Idem., 'Accounting and Analytical Methods: A Comment on Chambers' Review', *Journal of Accounting Research*, Spring 1967, pp. 119-123.

Idem., *Die wissenschaftlichen Grundlagen des Rechnungswesens* (Düsseldorf: Bertelsmann Universitätsverlag, 1970a).

Idem., 'On the Perennial Misunderstanding of Asset Measurement by Means of "Present Values"', *Cost and Management*, March/April 1970b, pp. 29-31.

Idem., 'On Further Misunderstandings About Asset "Measurement" and Valuation: A Rejoinder to Chambers' Article', *Cost and Management*, March/April 1971a, pp. 36-42.

Idem., 'Asset Measurement and Valuation—A Final Reply to Chambers', *Cost and Management*, July/August 1971b, pp. 18-23.

Idem., 'The Market Value According to Sterling', *Abacus*, December 1971c, pp. 176-193.

Idem., On The Axiomatic Formulation of Accounting: Comment on Prof. S. Saito's Considerations. Originally in Japanese in *Sangyo Keiri*, Tokyo, Vol. 33, No. 3, pp. 70-77, and No. 4, pp. 71-75, English translation in *Musashi University Journal*, Vol. 21, No. 1-2, 1973a, pp. 77-94.

Idem., 'Recientes Perfeccionamientos en la Presentacion Axiomatica de los Sistemas Contables', *Revista Española de Financiación y Contabilidad*, Jan.-April 1973b, pp. 444-465.

Idem., 'Information Economics and the Notion of "Management Information System"', *Information Systems and Organizational Structure*, ed. by E. Grochla and N. Szyperski (Berlin and New York: Walter de Gruyter, 1975), pp. 342-364.

Idem., *Instrumental Reasoning and Systems Methodology—An Epistemology of the Applied and Social Sciences* (Dordrecht: D. Reidel Co., 1978a).

Idem., 'Axiomatisierungsversuche des Rechnungswesens im Lichte neuer Erkenntnisforschung' in *Quantitative Ansätze in der Betriebswirtschaftslehre*, ed. by H. Müller-Merbach (Munich: Vahlen Verlag, 1978b), pp. 160-172.

Idem., 'Instrumentelle Bilanztheorie: Voraussetzungen und erste Ansätze', *Zeitschrift für betriebswirtschaftliche Forschung*, Oct./Nov. 1978c, pp. 792-800.

Idem., (1978/79a), 'Instrumental Aspects of Accounting: Illustrated on Professor Sterling's Fictitious Taxi Company', *Accounting for a Simplified Firm—Seventeen Essays Based on a Common Example*, ed. by R. R. Sterling and A. L. Thomas (Houston: Scholars Book Co., 1979), quotations are from the manuscript contained in the preliminary, mimeographed version of 1978.

Idem., (1978/79b), 'What Effect Does the Time Period Assumption have upon Disclosure? A Questionable Question and its Meaningful Alternative', *1978 Accounting Research Convocation*, ed. by J. J. Davies (The University of Alabama, 1979), pp. 55-67.

Mock, T. J., 'Comparative Values of Information Structures', *Journal of Accounting Research*, 1969. Supplement, pp. 124-159.

Idem., 'Concepts of Information Value and Accounting,' *Accounting Review*, October, 1971, pp. 765-778.

Idem., *Measurement and Accounting Information Criteria* (Sarasota, Fla.: American Accounting Association, ARS No. 13, 1976).

Montague, Richard, 'Universal Grammar', *Theoria*, Vol. 36, 1970, pp. 373-398.

Moonitz, Maurice, *The Basic Postulates of Accounting* (New York: American Institute of CPAs, Accounting Research Study No. l, 1961).

Moonitz, M. and A. C. Littleton (eds.), *Significant Accounting Essays* (Englewood Cliffs, NJ: Prentice-Hall, 1965).

Most, K. S., *Accounting Theory.* (Columbus, Ohio: Grid, 1977).

Nelson, C. L., '*A Priori* Research in Accounting', *Accounting Research 1960-1970: A Critical Evaluation*, ed. by N. Dopuch and L. Revsine (Urbana: Center for International Education and Research in Accounting, 1973).

Nicklisch, Heinrich, 'Die Konten des fremden Kapitals', *Zeitschrift für handelswissenschaftliche Forschung*, Vol. 4, 1911.

Idem., *Allgemeine kaufmännische Betriebswirtschaftslehre als Privatwirtschaftslehre des Handels* (Stuttgart, 1912).

Onida, P., *Il bilancio delle aziende commerciali—La determinazione di bilancio* (Milano, 1935).

Idem., (1970/74), *I moderni sviluppi della dottrina contabile nordamericana e gli studi economia aziendale* (Milano: Guiffré, 1970). English translation: 'Modern Developments of the North American Accounting Doctrine and the Studies of Business Economics' in *Academia Nazionale di Ragioneria—Papers on Business Administration*, Vol. 1 (Milano: Guiffré, 1974), pp. 149-222.

Idem., 'Alcuni punti di dissenso col pensiero di R. J. Chambers, espressi in una mia publicazione del 1970: I moderni sviluppi della dottrina contabile nord-americana e gli studi di economia aziendale', *Rivista dei Dottori Commercialisti*, Nov.-Dec., 1973a (Milano), pp. 996-1000.

Idem., 'Replica all' articolo di R. J. Chambers', *Rivista dei Dottori Commercialisti*, Nov.-Dec., 1973b, (Milano), pp. 1024-1033.

Parker, W. M., 'Business Combinations and Accounting Valuation', *Journal of Accounting Research*, Autumn 1966, pp. 149-154.

Parker, R. H. and G. C. Harcourt, 'Introduction' (pp. 1-30) to *Readings in the Concept and Measurement of Income* (ed. by same authors) (Cambridge: Cambridge University Press, 1969).

Paton, William A., 'Theory of the Double-Entry System', *Journal of Accountancy*, 1917, pp. 7-26.

Idem., (1922/62), *Accounting Theory—With Special Reference to the Corporate Enterprise* (New York: Ronald Press, 1922. Reprint ed., Lawrence, Kans.: Scholars Book Co., 1962).

Paton, W. A. and A. C. Littleton, *Introduction to Corporate Accounting Standards* (Iowa City: American Accounting Association, 1940).

Prince, T. R., *Extension of the Boundaries of Accounting Theory* (Cincinnati: South Western Publ. Co., 1963).

Requena-Rodriguez, J. U., 'Theoria de la Contabilidad: Analisis Dimensional', *Revista Española de Financiación y Contabilidad*, Jan.-April 1972, pp. 45-53.

Richards, A. B., 'Input-Output Accounting for Business', *Accounting Review*, July 1960, pp. 429-436.

Rieger, Wilhelm, *Schmalenbachs Dynamische Bilanz—Eine kritische Untersuchung* (Stuttgart, 1936).

Saito, S., 'Some Considerations on the Axiomatic Formulation of Accounting'. Originally in Japanese in *Kaikei*, Vol. 101, pp. 45-65, English translation in *The Mushashi University Journal*, Vol. 20, 1972, pp. 81-99.

Idem., 'Further Considerations on the Axiomatic Formulation of Accounting: A Reply to Prof. R. Mattessich' in *The Mushashi University Journal*, Vol. 21, No. 1-2, 1973, pp. 95-107.

Sanders, T. H., H. R. Hatfield and U. Moore, *A Statement of Accounting Principles* (New York: American Institute of Accountants, 1938).

Schär, Johann F., *Versuch einer wissenschaftlichen Behandlung der Buchhaltung* (Basel, 1890).

Idem., *Allgemeine Handelsbetriebslehre* (Berlin, 1911).

Idem., *Buchhaltung und Bilanz auf wirtschaftlicher, rechtlicher und mathematischer Grundlage* (Berlin, 1914).

Schmalenbach, Eugen, *Die Dynamische Bilanz im Rahmen der Wirtschaft* (Leipzig, 1919, 3rd revised edition, 1929).

Idem., *Der Kontenrahmen* (Leipzig, 1927).

Idem., *Dynamic Accounting* (London: Gee and Co., 1959). Translation of the 11th ed. of *Die Dynamische Bilanz*.

Schmidt, Fritz, *Die organische Bilanz in Rahmen der Wirtschaft* (Leipzig: 1921, 3rd revised edition, 1929).

Schweitzer, Marcell, 'Axiomatik des Rechnungswesens' *Handwörterbuch des Rechnungswesens*, ed. by E. Kosiol (Stuttgart: Poeschel Verlag, 1970), pp. 83-90.

Idem., *Struktur und Funktion der Bilanz* (Berlin: Duncker & Humblot, 1972).

Securities and Exchange Commission, Accounting Series Release, No. *190* (New York: SEC, March 23, 1976).

Spacek, Leonard, 'Comments' in Sprouse and Moonitz (1962), pp. 77-79.

Staubus, George, *A Theory of Accounting to Investors* (Homewood, Ill.: R. D. Irwin, 1961).

Sprague, C. E., (1907/72), *The Philosophy of Accounts* (New York: Ronald Press, 1907. Reprint ed. Lawrence, Kans.: Scholars Book Co., 1972).

Sprouse, R. J. and M. Moonitz, *A Tentative Set of Broad Accounting Principles for Business Enterprise* (New York: American Institute of CPAs, Accounting Research Study No. 3, 1962).

Stedry, A. C., *Budget Control and Cost Behavior* (Englewood Cliffs, NJ: Prentice-Hall, 1960).

Stegmüller, Wolfgang, *Hauptströmungen der Gegenwartsphilosophie*, Vol. II (Stuttgart: A. Kröner, 1975).

Sterling, R. R., *Theory of the Measurement of Enterprise Income* (Lawrence, Kans.: University Press of Kansas, 1970a).

Idem., 'On Theory Construction and Verification', *Accounting Review*, July 1970b, pp. 444-457.

Idem., 'The Market Value Method According to Sterling: A Reply', *Abacus*, June 1972a, pp. 91-101.

Sterling, R. R. (ed.), *Research Methodology in Accounting* (Lawrence, Kans.: Scholars Book Co., 1972b).

Storey, R. K., *The Search for Accounting Principles* (American Accounting Association, 1963).

Suppes, Patrick, *Introduction to Logic* (Princeton: D. Van Nostrand Co., 1957).

Thomas, A. L., *The Allocation Problem in Financial Accounting*, Studies in Accounting Research, No. 3 (Sarasota, Fla.: American Accounting Association, 1969).

Thomas, A. L., *The Allocation Problem: Part Two*, Studies in Accounting Research, No. 9 (Sarasota, Fla.: American Accounting Association, 1974).

Töndury, H., 'Die Grundlagen betrieblicher Verrechnung', *Festgabe für Julius Ziegler*, K. Meithner (ed.), 1933.

Vatter, W. J., 'Postulates and Principles', *Journal of Accounting Research*, Autumn 1963, pp. 179-197.

Walb, Ernst, *Die kaufmännische Buchhaltungslehre* (Leipzig, 1922).

Idem., *Die Erfolgsrechnung privater und öffentlicher Betriebe* (Berlin, 1926).

Wells, M. C., 'A Revolution in Accounting Thought?', *Accounting Review*, July 1976, pp. 471-482.

Wheeler, J. T., 'Accounting Theory and Research in Perspective', *Accounting Review*, January 1970, pp. 1-10.

Williams, T. H. and C. H. Griffin, 'On the Nature of Empirical Verification in Accounting', *Abacus*, Dec. 1969, pp. 157-78.

Zappa, G., *Le valutazioni di bilancio con particolare riguardo ai bilanci delle società per azioni* (Milano, 1910. Reprint ed. 1927).

A REVOLUTION IN ACCOUNTING THOUGHT?*

by M. C. Wells

ALTHOUGH the decade of the 1960s has been described by Carl Nelson as a "golden age in the history of a piori research in accounting" [Nelson, 1973, p.4], the works cited as examples of that kind of research also have been severely criticized.[1] Nelson states that, "impressive as the scholarship is, we are not significantly advanced from where we were in 1960" [Nelson, 1973, p.15]. He also is reported as having "contended that the existing a priori studies are of doubtful value" [Dopuch and Revsine, 1973, p. 32]. In similar vein, Gonedes and Dopuch are critical because, they allege, the same works are theoretically deficient, and it is possible "to declare the superiority of just about any set of accounting procedures, depending on the particular a priori model adopted" [Gonedes and Dopuch, 1974, pp. 49-50].

It will be argued here that those criticisms are based on a misunderstanding of the role of so-called *a priori research* in the overthrow of outdated ideas and practices. Far from being unproductive, the works referred to were a necessary step in the revolution currently underway in accounting thought. Far from being of doubtful value, those works have helped to place us in a significantly different position from that of 1960. Whether the works were theoretically deficient is, to some extent, irrelevant in this context, and the circularity implied by Gonedes and Dopuch's second criticism is a normal and healthy characteristic of theoretical works of that kind.

SCIENTIFIC REVOLUTIONS

The notion of a revolution in accounting is taken from Kuhn's *The Structure of Scientific Revolutions* [1970].[2] His thesis is that science does not progress through accumulation. Rather, a series of tradition-shattering revolutions occur in which one "time-honored scientific theory is rejected in favour of another incompatible with it" [Kuhn, 1970, p. 6]. The new theory, or set of ideas, is unique in that it is not derived from the previously accepted dogma. It is "seldom or never just an increment

*Reprinted from *The Accounting Review* 51 (July 1976): 471-482

to what is already known'' [Kuhn, 1970, p. 7], and in the process of moving from the old set of ideas to the new, the community of scientists follows a number of identifiable steps:

- Recognition of anomalies
- A period of insecurity
- Development of alternative sets of ideas
- Identification of schools of thought
- Domination of the new practices or ideas

The first step is a precursor to the whole process; it initiates the period of crisis which follows. During that period, scientists become increasingly dissatisfied with the existing theoretical framework, and a search for alternatives begins. Therefore, the second and third steps are mutually interactive. As dissatisfaction grows, the search for alternatives gains impetus; as alternatives are discerned and discussed, the dissatisfaction is heightened. Schools of thought emerge, and one set of ideas gradually gains ascendency over the alternatives

Because these steps involve such fundamental changes in the outlook and practices of the community of scholars, Kuhn applies the political metaphor of revolution to the process. He argues that the change takes place only after a serious malfunction has occurred in the sense that ''existing institutions [or practices] have ceased adequately to meet the problems posed by an environment that they have in part created'' Kuhn, 1970, p. 92]. Just as political revolutions ''aim to change political institutions in ways that those institutions themselves prohibit'' [Kuhn, 1970, p. 93], so do scientific revolutions change previously held concepts of the field of enquiry in a way which is incompatible with those concepts. Such a fundamental change cannot take place within the existing institutional or conceptual framework. The challenger is incompatible with the incumbent. ''The parties to a revolutionary conflict must resort to the techniques of mass persuasion'' [Kuhn, 1970, p. 93], and, ''like the choice between competing political institutions, that between competing paradigms proves to be a choice between incompatible modes of community life'' [Kuhn, 1970, p. 94].

The process, or revolution, is unlikely to be completed quickly. The assimilation of new ideas will not be complete until previously accepted theories have been reconstructed and previously held facts have been re-evaluated. This is ''an intrinsically revolutionary process that is seldom completed by a single man and never overnight'' [Kuhn, 1970, p. 7].

There is, of course, no necessary reason why the pattern of developments in science (and particularly the physical sciences from which Kuhn derives most of his examples) should be found also in accounting. Kuhn does consider the possibility of his thesis being applicable in other fields, despite some obvious differences [p. 208]. Nevertheless, just as scientific theories may both describe and prescribe physical phenomena, so may accounting theories describe and prescribe financial phenomena. Furthermore, if the pattern of events in accounting can be seen to be following the pattern of successful revolutions described by Kuhn, then we will be able to explain the reasons for and the importance of the ''golden age of a priori research'' referred to above. In doing that, we also will answer the criticisms made of the works which appeared during that golden age.

It should be emphasized that the analogy here is to accounting thought.[3] Given the political difficulties of initiating change in accounting practices, that may well be an evolutionary rather than a revolutionary process. But it will not, I suspect, take place until the revolution described here is complete.

However, to apply the analogy to accounting thought, one initial condition must be satisfied: a community of scholars must be identified. This was emphasized by Kuhn in his postscript. He pointed out that ''scientific communities can and should be isolated without prior recourse to paradigms'' [Kuhn, 1970, p. 176]. Accordingly, I will specify the community to which this paper relates as comprising the members of academic and research organizations such as the American Accounting Association, the Association of University Teachers of Accounting of the United Kingdom, the Accounting Association of Australia and New Zealand, the Research Division of the AICPA and the Australian Accountancy Research Foundation.

THE ACCOUNTING DISCIPLINARY MATRIX

The basic techniques used for keeping accounting records can be traced back more than 500 years, but the information conventionally stored within those records is largely a product of this century. Only within the last 75 years did the historical cost doctrine crystalize and come to dominate the literature and practices of accounting. More recently still, during the late 1930s and the 1940s, attempts were made to formalize the framework underlying the rules for recording and reporting financial matters. The works of Gilman (1939), Sanders, Hatfield and Moore (1938), Paton and Littleton (1940)[4] and others[5] attempted to rationalize existing practices and to set the framework within which alternative ideas and procedures might be evaluated.

The framework of ideas which emerged during this period has characteristics of a paradigm. However, note that Kuhn used the term *paradigm* in a number of different ways. As this was a cause of considerable confusion and a matter he delt with at length in the postscript appended to the 1970 edition of his essay, we will avoid the use of the term here. Instead, substitute terms introduced in the postscript will be used as far as possible. For the general set of ideas that binds together a community of scientists, Kuhn uses the term *disciplinary matrix* [p. 182]. There are several features which distinguish a disciplinary matrix (disciplinary because it refers to the common possession by the members of a particular discipline; matrix because it comprises ordered elements of various sorts, each requiring further specification) [Kuhn, 1970, p. 182]. There are: (1) symbolic generalizations—readily understood and undisputed symbolic representations common to the discipline [p. 182]; (2) shared commitments—beliefs which help determine what will be accepted as explanations or solutions [p. 184]; (3) values—the various qualities which members of the community expect in the work of their colleagues [pp. 184-186]; and (4) exemplars—the concrete problem—solutions which students entering the community encounter and which show by example how they are to go about seeking solutions [p. 187].

Following these descriptions, the disciplinary matrix of accountants which emerged during the 1940s may be described as follows: (1) The symbolic generalization included accepted notions and formulations such as the double entry equation, representations of income, current asset/fixed asset classifications and calculations of working capital, rate of return and debt/equity ratios. (2) The shared commitments included the so-called realization and matching principles, the notion of going concern and the cost basis of asset valuation. (3) The values included conservatism, consistency, materiality, etc.[6] (4) Finally, the exemplars were seen in the textbooks and expositions of the period. There was (and still is) a remarkable similarity in the contents of most texts—so much so that the content of academic courses and examinations had become almost completely predictable.

Once a student has absorbed the elements of a disciplinary matrix, he or she views all problem situations in the same way as other members of his or her specialist group. Writers and researchers have a common standard of practice, and problems tend to have common solutions, or shared examples [Kuhn, 1970, p. 187]. Thus, we have the commonality of training and outlook which helps to bind together a community of scholars.

However, the existence of a disciplinary matrix does not imply that a rigid, inviolable set of rules also exists. Rather, and because members of the community have been trained in problem-solutions (or as Kuhn expresses it "learning by finger exercises or by doing," p. 471), they do not need a full set of rules. Accounting was in this position prior to 1930. Writers took for granted, or simply explained, general principles.[7] Only after the criticisms of the 1920s and early 1930s were efforts made to formalize the framework of accounting ideas and were authoritative bodies set up for that purpose.[8] This development, too, is foreseen by Kuhn who suggests that only when accepted procedures come under attack, does consideration of the rules become important [p. 47].

However, the formalization of rules did not eliminate all of the contradictions and conflicts that had plagued accounting expositions in the past. Neither accounting writers nor practitioners apparently saw any conflict in certain departures from a strict application of the historical cost rule, such as the valuation of inventory at the lower of cost or market or the deduction of depreciation charges from the cost of fixed assets.[9] Even this is to be expected, according to Kuhn. Because the rules are learned through their application in specific contexts, any diversity either is not apparent or may be explained away by the different facts of each case. Therefore, what the rules serve to do is to "limit both the nature of acceptable solutions and the steps by which they are obtained" [Kuhn, 1970, p.38].

ANOMALIES AND PROFESSIONAL INSECURITY

> Discovery commences with the awareness of anomaly, i.e., with the recognition that nature has somehow violated the paradigm-induced expectations that govern normal science [or conventional practice] (Kuhn, 1970, pp. 52-53).

There have long been critics of conventional accounting practices and of solutions to problems proposed within the conventional framework [Brief, 1975; and Chatfield, 1974, pp. 273-276]. Outstanding examples in the period before the historical cost disciplinary matrix crystalized were Paton [1922], Sweeney [1936] and MacNeal [1939]. However, their criticisms appear to have had little impact on the subsequent ascendancy of the historical cost model. Recognition was not given in the literature of accounting to the great number of anomalies which defied resolution and which brought the accounting profession into public opprobrium until the 1960s and early 1970s. During this period, and since, the fundamental defects in the historical cost model repeatedly were identified and criticized by scholars, by businesspersons and in the courts.[10] The criticisms culminated in the almost simultaneous publication of Briloff's *Unaccountable Accounting* [1972] and Chambers' *Securities and Obscurities* [1973]. Leasco, Westec, Lockheed, Four Seasons, I.O.S., Rolls Royce, Reid Murray, Minsec and a host of other companies which were involved in cases which highlighted the "gap in GAAP" [Briloff, 1966, p. 484; 1972, pp. 31-33] became almost household names.

The reaction by theorists to the evidence thrust before them precisely follows that predicted by Kuhn; it corresponds to the period of *professional insecurity* [Kuhn, 1970, pp. 67-68] wherein the rules are subject to increasing scrutiny and occasional amendment. The disciplinary matrix is questioned, but not abandoned:

> . . . when confronted by anomaly [scientists] will devise numerous articulations and *ad hoc* modifications of their theory in order to eliminate any apparent conflict [Kuhn, 1970, p. 78].

During the 1960s and 1970s, the Accounting Principles Board in the United States and equivalent committees in other countries and innumerable authors proposed amendments to the rules to cope with the anomalies and criticisms.[11] Pronouncements, monographs and journal articles on problem areas such as purchase versus pooling, equity accounting, tax effect accounting and materiality followed. There were even attempts to increase the solidarity of the practicing profession. Carey wrote disparagingly of CPAs who gave evidence against their professional brethren [Briloff, 1972, p. 351], and the professional bodies issued statements requiring stricter conformance with official pronouncements [Zeff, 1972, pp. 76, 180-182, 294-295; 1973, pp. 22-23].

The ad hoc solutions which emerge during a period of crisis have a far-reaching consequence; they make it possible to contemplate rules which previously would have been unacceptable. That is, ". . . by proliferating versions of the [disciplinary matrix], crisis loosens the rules of normal puzzle-solving in ways that ultimately permit a new [disciplinary matrix] to emerge" [Kuhn, 1970, p. 80]. For example, the purchase versus pooling debate provoked discussion of asset values which were not original costs; equity accounting involved revaluing investments in associated companies; tax effect accounting extended the acceptance of nontransaction-based debits and credits. If accounting follows the revolutionary sequence of events, the acceptance of the techniques adopted in response to these problems will have hastened the ultimate acceptance of an alternative disciplinary matrix.

However, there is one class of anomaly which has proved to be intractable. The historical-cost based system fails to take account of changes in asset prices and changes in the purchasing power of the monetary unit. That failure has been a source of criticism, particularly during periods of inflation. It is anomalous in that, despite the going concern values in the financial statements, those statements no longer represent the state of affairs of the corporation. There have been numerous instances of the abuse of privilege by people in possession of current price data which have been denied to others [Chambers, 1973, Chapter 10]. Yet, accounting for the effects of inflation requires a substantial revision of the conventional thought in accounting. Partial solutions, such as equity accounting or, in the U.K. and Australia, occasional revaluations, are only partially successful.[12] The specific price and price-level problems are the sorts of anomalies which lead, finally, to the overthrow of the existing set of rules. Their "characteristic feature is their stubborn refusal to be assimilated to existing paradigms. This type alone gives rise to new theories" [Kuhn, 1970, p. 97].

There is one further feature of the periods of crisis described by Kuhn for which we may find a parallel in accounting:

> It is, I think, particularly in periods of acknowledged crisis that scientists have turned to philosophical analysis as a device for unlocking the riddles of their field. . . . To the extent that normal . . . work can be conducted by using the paradigm as a model, rules and assumptions need not be made explicit. . . . But that is not to say that the search for assumptions (even for non-existent ones) cannot be an effective way to weaken the grip of tradition upon the mind and to suggest the basis for a new one [Kuhn, 1970, p. 88].

Again, there has long been concern for the theoretical foundations of accounting practices [Chatfield, 1974, Chapter 16; Hendriksen, 1970, Chapter 2]. However, it is possible to discern two related developments like those referred to in the quotation above. The first is the search for assumptions. Of particular interest here are Littleton's *The Structure of Accounting Theory* [1953], Moonitz's *The Basic Postulates of Accounting* [1961], the American Accounting Association's *A Statement of Basic Accounting Theory* [1966], Ijiri's *The Foundations of Accounting Measurement* [1967] and various shorter contributions and comments.[13] These were, in varying degrees, attempts to define the underlying assumptions of accounting. Yet they did not lead to a widely recognized set of basic ideas. Rather, as Kuhn suggests, they served to highlight the defects of the disciplinary matrix and loosen the grip of tradition. Therefore, perhaps we should not be surprised to find that, despite the vast expenditure of time and money, the AICPA belatedly (in 1971) recognized a need for a statement of, and initiated a study of, the "objectives" of financial statements.[14] That the Trueblood Study fits the pattern of events is evident; the report includes discussion of both objectives and alternatives to generally accepted accounting principles. Those alternatives would have been rejected out of hand even 10 years previously.[15]

The other development which is particularly noticeable throughout this period is the concern with principles and theory construction generally. Commencing, perhaps, with Chambers' "Blueprint for a Theory of Accounting" [1955], notable contributions or comments by Mattessich [1957], Devine [1960], Chambers [1963], Vatter [1963] and Sterling [1970] followed. These philosophical discussions have served to increase the rigour of the discipline,[16] but hopefully, they also have helped to unlock the riddles of the field.

ALTERNATIVE PROPOSALS AND THEIR EVALUATION

One direct consequence of the philosophical discussions has been the emergence and refinement of alternatives to the disciplinary matrix of, e.g., asset values based on historical costs. There have been various attempts to derive logically consistent systems which overcome the defects of the historical cost system. Some of the authors proposing these systems which appeared during the golden age already have been identified—Edwards and Bell [1961] and Chambers [1966]; others include Sprouse and Moonitz [1962], Mattessich [1964] and Mathews [1965]. The works of these authors were debated throughout the 1960s, and that debate served to clarify and identify the alternatives. Without that identification, the next step of the revolutionary process could not proceed. It *has* proceeded, as shown by the published evaluations of the alternatives. The Trueblood Study report contained some discussion. More comprehensive evaluations have been undertaken by Chambers [1970], Macdonald [1974], McDonald [1972], Hanna [1974] and others, while the Price Waterhouse Study [Mueller, 1971] gives attention to the need for introducing consideration of the alternatives into regular teaching programmes.[17]

The fact that the evaluation process has taken place, and is continuing, is evidence of the importance of the so-called a priori works; hence, our disagreement with Nelson's comment that these works are of doubtful value. In the pattern of events described here, the works fulfill a critically important role; they are both a natural reaction to the recognition of anomalies and a vital step in the selection of a new disciplinary matrix. Furthermore, having those works to consider, and having the alternatives thus laid out, we are in a fundamentally different position from that of 1960. For while schools of thought embracing the various alternatives might now appear, that would not have been possible in 1960.

However, before discussing that possibility, there are some other characteristics of the evaluative stage which were described by Kuhn and which may be seen also in accounting. Kuhn drew attention to the similarities of the evaluative stage to the pre-paradigm period. It is the stage at which "frequent and deep debates over legitimate methods, problems and standards of solution" take place, although "these tend to define schools rather than to produce agreement" [Kuhn, 1970, p. 48].[18] In accounting, this stage has been marked by debates about the admissability of data relating to events external to the firm and data based on managers' intentions; on the presentation of cash flow statements, earnings per share calculations, etc.; the raising of problems, such as the translation of holdings of foreign currencies, the reporting for diversified companies, long-term contracts and land development projects; the legitimacy of cost allocations; and reconsideration of the standards which the solutions must meet such as objectivity, independence and freedom from bias.

It is also because of the importance of these debates, and the evaluative process generally, that we contended that the alleged theoretical defects in the works published in the 1960s were, in a sense, irrelevant. This is not to suggest that "anything goes." On the contrary, tightly reasoned and empirically valid theoretical prescriptions have a greater chance of being adopted than do loosely constructed sets of ideas. However, theoretical defects will, presumably, be discovered during the evaluation process, and their existence may even add to the extent and heat of the debate, thus aiding this part of the revolutionary process.

Yet another characteristic of this step in the process identified by Kuhn and found in accounting is the diversity of activity:

> In the absence of a paradigm or some candidate for a paradigm, all of the facts that could possibly pertain to the development of a given science are likely to seem equally relevant. As a result early fact-gathering is a far more random activity than the one that subsequent scientific activity makes familiar [Kuhn, 1970, p. 15].

This perhaps, is the reason why so many proposals have emerged in recent years. They include suggestions for publication of multicolumn financial statements and forecasts; the development of human resource accounting; and, on a different level, the far-ranging research into share price movements and their information theory and cost benefit analyses to the provision of financial information.

SCHOOLS OF THOUGHT

It may be possible to identify schools of thought in respect of some or all of the matters of interest just referred to. However, one example will suffice—asset measurement alternatives. Four schools may be identified[19]:

- Price-Level Adjusted (or Current Purchasing Power) Accounting
- Replacement Cost Accounting
- Deprival Value Accounting
- Continuously Contemporary (or Net Realizable Value) Accounting

Strong or widespread support for these schools is not yet discernible,[20] which is understandable. For, as Kuhn points out:

> The man who embraces a new paradigm at an early stage must often do so in defiance of the evidence provided by problem solving. He must, that is, have faith that the new paradigm will succeed with the many large problems that confront it, knowing only that the older paradigm has failed with a few. A decision of that kind can only be made on faith [Kuhn, 1970, p. 158].

Accounting researchers are not likely to rely on faith or make that decision lightly. But there are sufficient examples of dispute in the literature for us to identify some of the characteristics of "paradigm debates" [Kuhn, 1970, p. 110]. For example, "each group uses its own paradigm to argue in that paradigm's defense" [Kuhn, 1970, p. 94]. The Provisional Statement of Accounting Practice, No. 7, issued by the I.C.A. in England & Wales, refers to the need for a method which shows the "effect of changes in the purchasing power of money on accounts prepared on the basis of existing conventions" [para. 3] in arguing for Constant Purchasing Power Accounting; the Replacement Price School relies on the notion of "maintenance of productive capacity" which implies the need to replace assets in kind, in support of replacement cost accounting [Edwards and Bell, 1961, p. 99]; Wright [1971, pp. 60-61], refers to the possible loss which a firm might suffer if deprived of an asset when arguing for deprival value (or value to the owner) accounting; and Chambers [1966, p. 190] stresses the importance of adaptive behaviour when arguing for a measure of assets which is indicative of the firm's capacity to adapt.

These examples of apparent circularity are not intended as criticisms. Obviously, different systems of ideas can be evaluated only in the context to which those systems apply[21]; hence, the comment at the beginning of this paper that the charge of circularity by Gonedes and Dopuch is misplaced. The point is that arguments of this sort are a necessary and inevitable part of the process of trying to win support for the competing points of view [Kuhn, 1970, p. 94]. Like Nelson, Gonedes and Dopuch's error lies in their failure to identify the place of a priori research works in the transition to a new disciplinary matrix.

These debates have other characteristics. Adoption of a new disciplinary matrix will, normally, require a fundamental shift in the view which theorists have of the world. Thus, in accounting there have been changes: the view that the value of the monetary unit is stable has changed to acceptance of the view that it is variable; the view that the point of realization should be the point of recognition of gains is giving way to the view that other evidence of gains is admissible; and the view that only actual transactions give rise to objective data is giving way to a less restricted notion of objectivity.

Similarly, members of competing schools will have diferent views of the phenomena which are the subject of their discipline:

> Practicing in different worlds, the two groups of scientists see different things when they look from the same point in the same direction. Again that is not to say that they can see anything they please. Both are looking at the world, and what they look at has not changed. But in some areas they see different things, and they see them in different relations one to the other. That is why a law that cannot even be demonstrated to one group of scientists may occasionally seem intuitively obvious to another [Kuhn, 1970, p. 150].

Hence Gynther's view of firms is of ongoing nonadaptive organizations while Chambers sees organizations as being fluid and constantly adapting to environmental changes.[22] And, it seems, debate between them serves only to convince each of the validity of his own argument.

A NEW DISCIPLINARY MATRIX?

The analysis presented here suggests that financial accounting thought is undergoing a revolution. If that is so, then the criticisms of a priori research cited at the beginning of this paper are misplaced.

The criticisms fail to recognize the importance of research which leads to the delineation of alternative sets of ideas. Those alternatives are candidates for a new disciplinary matrix; they are the basis of competing schools of thought.

If the analogy presented above is correct, i.e., if Kuhn's notion of a revolution can be applied to accounting, then it appears that accounting is emerging from a state of crisis [Kuhn, 1970, Chapter VIII]. Alternative sets of ideas have been proposed and debated, and schools of thought are beginning to emerge. Admittedly, the analysis does not enable us to identify neat periods of time which correspond with Kuhn's steps in the revolution. Yet, the characteristics of an accepted disciplinary matrix, the period of insecurity and the development of alternative sets of ideas appear to be well recognizable in accounting.

What will be the outcome? In accounting it is too soon to say. Researchers cannot be observed rushing to adopt any of the alternative sets of ideas. Continued debate, primarily amongst academics but increasingly involving the research organizations of the professional bodies is, however, serving to identify schools of thought. The next stage, according to Kuhn, will be "an increasing shift in allegiances" [p. 158] in favour of one of the alternatives. However, this is a process which takes time. After all, it involves the assimilation of a new theory, and that in turn involves a "reconstruction of prior theory and the reevaluation of prior fact"; i.e., "an intrinsically revolutionary process." But note, "it is seldom completed by a single man and never overnight" [Kuhn, 1970, p. 7].

FOOTNOTES

1 The examples given were, "the writings of Chambers, Edwards and Bell, Sterling, and Ijiri" [Nelson, 1973, p. 3].

2 Kuhn's exposition has been subject to widespread criticism. See for example Shapere [1964] and Lakatos and Musgrave [1974]. However, references in this paper are to the enlarged edition of Kuhn's monograph. The postscript to that edition contains Kuhn's reply to his critics.

3 Other attempts to apply Kuhn's thesis to financial accounting may be seen in Chambers [1966, pp. 373-376] and to cost accounting in Wells [1978].

4 Paton and Littleton were also both members of the Executive Committee of the American Accounting Association which in 1936 produced *A Tentative Statement of Accounting Principles Underlying Corporate Financial Statements*. This was "one of the first major attempts to develop a framework which might be regarded as representing a structure of the fundamental principles of accounting" [Bedford and Ziegler, 1975, p. 438].

5 In their review of the influence of Littleton on accounting thought and practices, Bedford and Ziegler [1975] also identify the late 1930s as "the era to which the roots of much contemporary accounting practice may be traced" [p. 437]. Coincidentally, it was not until 1940 that the U.S. Securities and Exchange Commission brought together all of its various rules on the form and content of financial statements in one document — Regulation S-X [Zeff, 1972, p. 151].

6 Notice the similarity of symbolic generalizations, shared commitments and values to the conventions, doctrines and standards described by Gilman [1939], especially pp. 4, 41-43; 254; and 186, respectively.

7 "There is, it is believed, a corpus of principles of accounting which are generally accepted. It is true that they are not 'written law', they have not been codified; they must be sought in accounts and financial statements," [Sanders, Hatfield and Moore, 1938, p. 5]. For this reason, "the search for rules [is] both more difficult and less satisfying than the search for paradigms" [Kuhn, 1970, p. 43].

8 For examples of this kind of reaction, see Zeff [1972, pp. 119-140].

9 The first writer to pay particular attention to these conflicts, without resolving them, was Gilman [1939, pp. 128-130, 174, 235].

10 See, for example, the statement by the Inspectors of the Reid Murray Group of Companies, ". . . we believe that we are accustomed to the use of common sense, and common sense has compelled us to reject a number of accounting practices used in the group and, apparently regarded as acceptable by accountants," *Interim Report . . .* [1963, p. 107]. This case was commented upon by Stamp [1964]. This and similar comments by other inspectors provoked a Report by the General Council of the Australian Society of Accountants. See "Accounting Principles and Practices Discussed in Reports on Company Failures," *Members' Handbook*, Item 401 (January 1966). See also, Greer [1963]; "Unaccountable CPA.'s," [1966]; Louis [1968];

"Accounting—Profits Without Honor" [1970]; Raymon [1970]; Stamp and Marley [1970]; Birkett and Walker [1971]; Spacek [1969 and 1973]; de Jonquieres [1973]; and Bedford [1973].

11 See Zeff [1972], pp. 173-224] and the Australian Society of Accountants' Item 401, referred to above.

12 For further examples, including the switches to and from accelerated depreciation and to and from LIFO inventory values, see Chambers [1973, pp. 93-103].

13 For a useful summary and list of references, see [Hendriksen, 1970, Chapter 4].

14 Report of the Study Group on the Objectives of Financial Statements [the Trueblood Study] (1973). The study was commissioned in May 1971.

15 See the alternatives listed [Trueblood Study, 1973, p. 41]. Notice also Sterling's observation of the change in attitudes [1970, p. vii].

16 See Nelson [1973, p. 15] for a comment on the contribution of logic and other philosophical techniques to the accounting problem.

17 It is for the reason outlined here that Chambers was able to refer to Macdonald's book as a product of its time. See Chambers [1975]. The same comment might be made of May, Mueller and Williams [1975].

18 Notice that Dopuch and Revsine saw a similar result emerge at the Conference on Accounting Research held at the University of Illinois in 1971: "As is true in the literature, many contributors were quite convinced that their approach was correct but were unable to persuade those who disagreed" [Dopuch and Revsine, 1973, p. 34].

19 A fifth proposal—present value accounting—is not listed here. Although it has been argued cogently by Hansen [1966], it does not appear to have won support as an operational alternative. It has been discussed rather as an ideal against which alternatives might be evaluated. See for example, Solomons [1961] and Lemke [1966].

20 The following is an example of one attempt at identifying members of schools of thought in relation to generalized theories of accounting based on alternative asset measurement systems. Some people undoubtedly will want finer distinctions; some will object to being linked with others with whom they disagree in some respects; some will object to having been omitted. Nevertheless, at the risk of offending some or all of the people concerned, I would identify the following on the basis of their published work:

1. Price-Level-Adjusted: Jones [1956]; Mason [1971]
2. Replacement Cost: Edwards & Bell [1961]; Mathews [1965]; Gynther [1966]; Revsine [1973]
3. Deprival Value: Baxter [1967]; Wright [1970]; Stamp [1971]; Whittington [1974]
4. Continuously Contemporary (Net realizable value)
Chambers [1966]; Sterling [1970]; McKeown [1971]

For a slightly different version of these schools, see Sterling [1970, pp. 7-19].

21 Sterling and Harrison [1974, p. 144] draw attention to the universality of this factor in their comments on the Gonedes and Dopuch paper.

22 Compare Gynther [1966, pp 46-48] and Penman [1970, p. 338]: "Companies . . . just do not adapt": with Chambers [1966, p. 190].

REFERENCES

"Accounting: Profits Without Honor," *Time* (March 1970), p. 70.

American Accounting Association, "A Tentative Statement of Accounting Principles Affecting Corporate Reports," THE ACCOUNTING REVIEW (June 1936), pp. 87-91; reprinted as a Tentative Statement of Accounting Principles Underlying Corporate Financial Statements (1936).

Baxter, W.T., "Accounting Values: Sale Price Versus Replacement Cost," *Journal of Accounting Research* (Autumn 1967), pp. 208-214.

Bedford, Norton M., "The Need for an Evaluation of Accounting Research" in Dopuch and Revsine, eds., *Accounting Research 1960-1970: A Critical Evaluation*, Monograph 7 (Center for International Education and Research in Accounting, University of Illinois, 1973).

———, and Richard Ziegler, "The Contributions of A.C. Littleton to Accounting Thought and Practice," THE ACCOUNTING REVIEW (July 1975), pp. 435-443.

Birkett, W.P. and R.G. Walker, "Response of the Australian Accounting Profession to Company Failures in the 1960's," *Abacus* (December 1971), pp. 97-136.

Brief, Richard P., "The Accountants' Responsibility in Historical Perspective," THE ACCOUNTING REVIEW (April 1975), pp. 285-297.

Briloff, Abraham J., "Old Myths and New Realities in Accountancy," THE ACCOUNTING REVIEW (July 1966), pp. 485-495.

———, *Unaccountable Accounting* (Harper and Row, 1972).

Chambers, R.J., "Blueprint for a Theory of Accounting," *Accounting Research* (January 1955), pp. 17-25.

———, "Why Bother with Postulates?", *Journal of Accounting Research* (Spring 1963), pp. 3-15.

_____, *Accounting, Evaluation and Economic Behavior* (Prentice-Hall, 1966).

_____, "Methods of Accounting," Parts I-VI, *The Accountant* (February 1970), pp. 299-303; (March 1970), pp. 341-345; (March 1970), pp. 408-412; (April 1970), pp. 483-486; (April 1970), pp. 551-555; (April 1970), pp. 643-647.

_____, *Securities and Obscurities: A Case for the Reform of the Law of Company Accounts* (Gower Press, 1973).

_____, "Profit Measurement, Capital Maintenance and Service Potential: A Review Article," *Abacus* (June 1975), pp. 98-104.

Chatfield, Michael, *A History of Accounting Thought* (The Dryden Press, 1974).

de Jonquieres, Guy, "U.S. Firms Under Fire," *The Financial Times* (June 1973), p. 44.

Devine, Carl T., "Research Methodology and Accounting Theory Formation," THE ACCOUNTING REVIEW (July 1960), pp. 387-399.

Dopuch, Nicholas and Lawrence Revsine, eds., *Accounting Research 1960-1970: A Critical Evaluation*, Monograph 7 (Center for International Education and Research in Accounting, University of Illinois, 1973).

Edwards, Edgar O. and Philip W. Bell, *The Theory and Measurement of Business Income* (University of California Press, 1961).

Gilman, Stephen, *Accounting Concepts of Profit* (The Ronald Press, 1939; reprinted 1956).

Gonedes, Nicholas J. and Nicholas Dopuch, "Capital Market Equilibrium, Information Production and Selecting Accounting Techniques: Theoretical Framework and Review of Empirical Work," *Studies on Financial Accounting Objectives: 1974* (Supplement to Volume 12), *Journal of Accounting Research* (1974).

Greer, Howard C., "How to Succeed in Confusing People Without Really Trying," *The Journal of Accountancy* (March 1963), pp. 61-65.

Gynther, R.S., *Accounting for Price-Level Changes: Theory and Procedures* (Pergamon, 1966).

Hanna, John R., *Accounting Income Models: An Application and Evaluation* (The Society of Industrial Accountants of Canada, 1974).

Hansen, Palle, *The Accounting Concept of Profit* (North-Holland, 1966).

Hendriksen, Eldon S., *Accounting Theory* (Irwin, 1970).

Jones, Ralph Coughenour, *The Effects of Price Level Changes* (American Accounting Association, 1956).

Kuhn, Thomas S., *The Structure of Scientific Revolutions*, International Encyclopedia of Unified Science, 2nd enlarged edition (University of Chicago Press, 1970).

Lakatos, Imre and Alan Musgrave, eds., *Criticism and the Growth of Knowledge* (Cambridge University Press, 1974).

Lemke, Kenneth W., "Asset Valuation and Income Theory," THE ACCOUNTING REVIEW (January 1966), pp. 33-41.

Louis, Arthur M., "The Accountants are Changing the Rules," *Fortune* (June 1968), p. 177-9, 330, 336, 339, 346.

Macdonald, Graeme, *Profit Measurement: Alternatives to Historical Cost* (Accountancy Age, 1974).

MacNeal, Kenneth, *Truth in Accounting* (Ronald Press Co., 1939).

McDonald, Daniel L., *Comparative Accounting Theory* (Addison-Wesley, 1972).

McKeown, James C., "An Empirical Test of a Model Proposed by Chambers," THE ACCOUNTING REVIEW (January 1971), pp. 12-29.

Mason, Perry, *Price Level Changes and Financial Statements* (American Accounting Association, 1971).

Mattessich, Richard, "Toward a General and Axiomatic Foundation of Accountancy," *Accounting Research* (October 1957), pp. 328-356.

_____, Richard, *Accounting and Analytical Methods* (Irwin, 1964).

Mathews, R.L., "Price-Level Accounting and Useless Information," *Journal of Accounting Research* (Spring 1965), pp. 133-155.

May, Robert G., Gerhard G. Mueller and Thomas H. Williams, *A New Introduction to Financial Accounting* (Prentice-Hall, 1975)

Mueller, Gerhard G., ed., *A New Introduction to Accounting* (The Price Waterhouse Foundation, July 1971).

Nelson, Carl L., "A Priori Research in Accounting" in Dopuch and Revsine, eds., *Accounting Research 1960-1970: A Critical Evaluation*, Monograph 7 (Center for International Education and Research in Accounting, University of Illinois, 1973).

Paton, W.A., *Accounting Theory - with Special Reference to the Corporate Enterprise* (Ronald Press Co., 1922; reprinted, Accounting Studies Press, 1962).

_____, and A.C. Littleton, *An Introduction to Corporate Accounting Standards* (American Accounting Association, 1940, reprinted 1965).

Penman, Stephen H., "What Net Asset Value?—An Extension of a Familiar Debate," THE ACCOUNTING REVIEW (April 1970), pp. 333-346.

Raymon, R., "Is Conventional Accounting Obsolete?" *Accountancy* (June 1970), pp. 422-429.

Report of the Study Group on the Objectives of Financial Statements, *Objectives of Financial Statements* (American Institute of Certified Public Accountants, October 1973).

Revsine, Lawrence, *Replacement Cost Accounting* (Prentice-Hall, 1973).

Sanders, T.H., H.R. Hatfield, and U. Moore, *A Statement of Accounting Principles* (The American Institute of Accountants, 1938; reprinted 1959).

Shapere, Dudley, "The Structure of Scientific Revolutions," *Philosophical Review* (July 1964), pp. 383-394.

Solomons, David, "Economic and Accounting Concepts of Income," THE ACCOUNTING REVIEW (July 1961), pp.374-383.

Spacek, Leonard, *A Search for Fairness* (Arthur Andersen & Co., 1969 and 1973).

Sprouse, Robert T. and Maurice Moonitz, *A Tentative Set of Broad Accounting Principles for Business Enterprises*, Accounting Research Study No. 3 (American Institute of Certified Public Accountants, 1962).

Stamp, Edward, "The Reid Murray Affair," *Accountancy* (August 1964), pp. 685-690.

_____, "Income and Value Determination and Changing Price-Levels: An Essay Towards a Theory," *The Accountants' Magazine* (June 1971), pp. 277-292.

_____, and Christopher Marley, *Accounting Principles and the City Code* (Butterworth, 1970).

Sterling, Robert R., "On Theory Construction and Verification," THE ACCOUNTING REVIEW (July 1970), pp. 444-457.

_____, and William Harrison, "Discussion of Capital Market Equilibrium, Information Production, and Selecting Accounting Techniques: Theoretical Framework and Review of Empirial Work" in *Studies on Financial Objectives: 1974*, supplement to Vol. 12 of *Journal of Accounting Research*, pp. 142-157.

Sweeney, Henry W., *Stabilized Accounting* (Harper Bros., 1936; reprinted, Holt Rinehart & Winston, 1964).

"Unaccountable CPA's," *Forbes* (October 1966), p. 15.

Vatter, William J., "Postulates and Principles," *Journal of Accounting Research* (Autumn 1963), pp. 179-197.

Wells, M.C., *Accounting for Common Costs* (International Center for Education and Research in Accounting, University of Illinois, 1978).

Whittington, Geoffrey, "Asset Valuation, Income Measurement and Accounting Income," *Accounting and Business Research* (Spring 1974), pp. 96-101.

Wright, F.K., "A Theory of Financial Accounting," *Journal of Business Finance* (Autumn 1970), pp. 51-69.

_____, "Value to the Owner: A Clarification," *Abacus* (June 1971), pp 58-61.

Zeff, Stephen A., *Forging Accounting Principles in Five Countries* (Stipes Publishing Co., 1972).

_____, *Forging Accounting Principles in Australia* (Australian Society of Accountants, March 1973).

ON THE INTERACTION OF ACCOUNTING, ECONOMICS, AND FINANCE AND THE ECONOMIC CONSEQUENCES OF ACCOUNTING*

by Nils H. Hakansson

*Plenary address given at the Annual Meeting of the American Accounting Association; Honolulu, Hawaii August 21-25, 1979 (Berkeley, California: Institute of Business and Economic Research for the Professional Accounting Program).

THE subject matter of this paper does not associate itself naturally with a unique rubric. In fact, the chosen title could easily cause one to conclude that attention is equally divided between two separate and distinct topics, the interaction of accounting, economics, and finance on the one hand, and the economic consequences of accounting on the other. One purpose of this treatise is to argue that these two subjects are not really separable but are inextricably linked in such a way as to make a distinction pointless if not impossible. A second purpose is to characterize the nitty gritty of the economic consequences of accounting somewhat more completely than has hitherto been done. The paper begins by examining the interaction of accounting, economics, and finance, an approach that quickly leads us into the mire of economic consequences[1] that so occupies current discourse in accounting.

I do not wish to pretend that there is anything new about the notion that economics and finance are the closest of accounting's many sister disciplines. Current definitions of our field run something like:

> *Accounting* is concerned with the development and communication of *financial* information that is useful for *economic* decisions.

But earlier definitions, though cloaked in a different language that tended to emphasize the more mechanistic aspects of the accounting function, really were not substantively different. There are many other reminders of the close relationship between accounting, economics, and finance as well. For example, one of our classics, *The Nature of Capital and Income,* published in 1906, was written by Irving Fisher, an economist. Such well-known accountants as Henry Rand Hatfield, William Paton, Raymond Chambers, and the two most recent past presidents of the American Accounting Association (David Solomons and Maurice Moonitz) received their degrees in economics. The close association between accounting and finance, especially corporate finance, is also long and honorable although perhaps less conspicuous. In many of the Commonwealth countries, for example, accounting and finance frequently constitute a single department or school in the universities.

The plain fact is that the interdependence among accounting, economics, and finance is inevitable. As long as currency-based information about the various entities that compose a larger economy remains the cornerstone of what we call accounting, the links are going to be there whether we like it or not. The only issue is whether we should seek to strengthen or deemphasize these ties. The question is not an empty one in the sense that we should not expect the present linkage to remain intact if we made no conscious effort one way or the other. In other words, in the absence of a deliberate stance on our part, our ties to finance and economics would slip for the simple reason that finance and those parts of economics that are particularly relevant to us are currently undergoing rapid and profound changes, changes which are likely to continue for some time.

What this boils down to is that accounting as an academic discipline is currently at a crossroads, a crossroads that is exemplified by our relationship with economics and finance. We can make a sharp right or we can go straight on a road that curves to the left. The curving road would certainly not rock the boat. It would also permit the current makeshift approach to the forging of accounting principles to continue, unhampered by the presence of solid theoretical foundations. A few years downstream, some dissident ivory tower accounting academic, unhappy with the world's view of him, would likely be moved to write Part II of Hatfield's (1924) "Houn' dog" speech.

The road to the right, on the other hand, would rock the boat because it is bumpy. It is also mostly uphill, and full of speeding economists and finance people. But the view from the many crests is magnificent: the lay of the land shows rather clearly. Detailed surveys of the topography are frequently encountered. People are rather open about where they stand on inflation and other issues. After a while, they may even tell you why they are for or against inflation accounting, for or against replacement cost, for or against such and such a disclosure rule. Some even confide how much they see themselves gaining or losing from alternative accounting rules and various regulations designed to protect them from their less honorable fellows. Before too long, the FASB would begin to receive environmental impact studies that are comprehensive, factual, thorough, and surprising.

In the time that is left, I would like to focus on three questions. First, I would like to say a few words about the form that the links among accounting, finance and economics have taken in the last few years. Second, I want to take a closer look at the basic nature of this linkage. Finally, I would like to mention some of the problem areas in which a strong linkage, as opposed to a weak linkage, wold be helpful in moving toward a solution to the many accounting issues that face us.

RELATIONS BETWEEN ACCOUNTING, ECONOMICS AND FINANCE

One link among accounting, economics, and finance that is familiar to all of us is the present value formula under certainty. This formula has served as a minor cornerstone of all three fields for decades and continues to be both used and abused. Its applicability in accounting is more limited than a perusal of the accounting literature would suggest, but I shall not elaborate on that point here.

More recent interactions, however, tend to overshadow the durable chains that present values have forged. From the vantage point of accounting, some of these interactions have led to net inflows while others may be characterized as net outflows. Let's examine the net import side first.

Although empirical research in accounting is by no means new, its conduct on a significant scale goes back only a dozen years or so.[2] The enormous increase in such research that we have seen in the last few years is directly attributable to what is known as modern capital market theory in the field of finance. This theory, which is of recent origin, provides a characterization of the return structure one can expect to find in the financial market when that market is in equilibrium. It represents an important advance over traditional present value theory in that risk is explicitly taken into account. The two main components are usually referred to as the capital asset pricing model[3] and the option pricing model.[4] The phrase "market efficiency," which has never been adequately defined, is also implicitly connected with this theory but not in the rigid way usually suggested in the literature and in seminar conversations.

For our purposes, there are two points to be noted. First, capital market theory has been of direct value in a large number of accounting studies. Studies assessing the effects of changes in accounting methods on share prices provide an example. The evidence in this area, as most of you are aware, is, with some interesting exceptions,[5] consistent with the notion that share prices do not respond to changes in reporting methods that are merely cosmetic—i.e., that do not effect cash flows—but that prices do respond to switches between LIFO and FIFO, say, where tax effects are likely.[6] The second point is that modern capital market theory and other developments in finance appear to have served as catalysts in a great many of the accounting studies that did not directly employ constructs from finance. But this, of course, is precisely what we mean by interaction.

Turning now to economics, there are at least four subareas of that field that accounting researchers have found particularly valuable and stimulating. The first of these is the theory of decision, both at the individual level and at the collective or social level. Individual decision theory provides us with a somewhat idealistic definition of individual rationality, a definition which has long enjoyed a clear monopoly position due to a lack of serious challengers.[7] The theories on collective choice, on the other hand, are much more controversial.[8] As accountants, however, our needs for these staple import items are indisputable, for the simple reason that all of us make individual decisions while the sole business of the FASB and the SEC, for example, is to make social decisions.

A second necessity imported from economics is the theory of information. This theory also comes in two parts: the theory of private information and the theory of public information.[9] Like night and day, they have many things in common, yet are fundamentally different. Just what information is does not seem to be easy to answer. But it seems to be a capital rather than a consumer good, with the distinguishing feature that it, alone, is capable of revising probability assessments over future contingencies. These characteristics have far-reaching implications, the most important of which is the possibility of "market failure". That is, when it comes to the production and dissemination of information, Adam Smith's invisible hand does not work as well as one might like.[10] This definitely does *not* imply that regulatory intervention concerning accounting disclosure is automatically *justified*. But it does mean that regulatory intervention needs to be *considered*, in a framework that takes into account *all* costs, including the costs of the regulatory mechanism itself. In other words, whether we need an agency like the SEC is still an open, not a closed, question. This circumstance in turn suggests that the economics of regulation, a third subfield of economics, is of considerable relevance to accounting. Not surprisingly, a number of accounting researchers have indeed begun to recognize the potential of regulatory economics in addressing accounting questions at the policy level—that is, at the FASB, CASB, and SEC level.[11]

The fourth source of current imports from economics is the theory of incentives. Incentives, of course, are designed to motivate members of an organization to act in particular ways that they otherwise might not choose. Variance analysis reports, bonus plans, and executive stock options are examples of incentive schemes. Since many of these schemes are based on accounting measures, the relevance of incentive theory to accounting research *and* accounting practice is not difficult to fathom.[12]

What the preceding suggests is that even the most narrow, traditional, and pragmatic view of accounting cannot alter the fact that the accountant's work inevitably involves him in activities that are of intense interest to our two closest neighbor disciplines.

What about our academic exports to economics and finance? There can be no question that our exports in the recent past have been much smaller than our imports. This imbalance is not a surprising state of affairs, however, if one accepts the proposition that advances in finance and economics in particular are in the nature of a precondition for substantial progress in accounting. In other words, it is difficult to visualize an advanced theory of accounting that does not build on the theory of decision and information as well as full-blown theories of the financial market and of the firm under conditions of uncertainty.[13] Under that proposition we are seeing, in the areas just reviewed, just what we would expect to see, although perhaps on a somewhat smaller scale on the export side.

Accounting's export potential, as yet relatively undeveloped, seems to me to rest on two primary resources. One is the multidimensionality of the basic accounting model, and the second consists of the institutional richness of the environment accountants work in. Even current financial reports, aggregated as they are, provide measures along an impressive number of dimensions. This is in sharp contrast to finance, for example, where most models focus on a single dimension, wealth. And by our strategic location between the users and producers of financial information, with our finger virtually on the pulse of the decision-making process, we are in an enviable position to study and observe a number of empirical phenomena, including phenomena falling in the area of behavioral accounting.

There is some interesting evidence available on the value of the preceding resources. An advanced method for adaptive estimation of future security and portfolio risk that relies heavily on market as well as accounting descriptors has recently been developed by researchers in finance.[14] This method is based on the most powerful econometric methodology currently available and on an approach which, in effect, combines technical and fundamental analysis, with the data themselves providing the appropriate weighting, so to speak, that should be put on each. Accounting information of various types plays a strategic role in the model, which has been adopted by about fifty of our larger institutional investors via a commercial service.

In view of the important role played by published accounting information in the preceding study, two questions come to mind. First, why wasn't the research done by accountants?[15] Second, now that the research has been done, why do so few accountants seem to be aware of it? It is almost as if accounting research were an underdeveloped country, with foreigners developing, financing, and profiting handsomely from the country's main export industry and the populace reacting primarily with indifference. The time has clearly come for a more balanced interaction. But achieving that balance requires continued heavy investment in precisely those high-technology industries that link us to economics and finance.

ACCOUNTING AND ITS ECONOMIC CONSEQUENCES

Let me now leave the past and focus on some particular aspects of the relationship among accounting, economics, and finance. Consider a phrase that you have heard a lot recently—namely the expression "the economic consequences of accounting." As currently employed, the phrase is usually meant as a warning to standard setters that they should not impose new standards that may lead managements of companies to take actions that are in some sense "uneconomic".[16] But how do we decide whether the consequences are favorable or uneconomic?

Choices made by individuals on their own behalf presumably have favorable consequences to those individuals—this is really what we mean by individual rationality. Put differently, we expect people acting on their own behalf to act in their own interest. But actions taken by a company's management and by the FASB also have economic consequences, consequences that generally affect a great number of people as well as various economic entities. It is rare that these consequences are *uniformly* favorable or unfavorable to those affected. Virtually every (accounting policy) decision by corporate management and by bodies such as the FASB and SEC will make *some* individuals better off and *some* worse off. As a practical matter, there is perhaps no decision the FASB can make that will make everyone happy, including a decision to do nothing. This is an important point about mechanisms designed to make social choices, such as the FASB, that is not widely appreciated.

For example, it is often said that everyone loses from inflation. Not true, at least not in the short to intermediate run. Suppose the inflation rate is 1 percent, the rate paid on savings 3 percent, and that borrowers have to pay 5 percent. Someone in the 50 percent tax bracket would then earn a nominal rate of 1.5 percent and hence a real return of .5 percent after taxes, while a borrower in the same bracket would pay a real after-tax rate of interest of 1.5 percent. Tax-exempt investors would receive a real return of 2 percent. This is roughly what the situation was like in the United States some 20 years ago.

Let us now assume that the rate of inflation moves to 10 percent, that money market funds yield 10 percent and that borrowers pay 12 percent. Our 50 percent bracket saver now receives 5 percent *nominally* after taxes and thus an after-tax real return of *minus* 5 percent while his borrowing twin *pays* an after-tax, after inflation interest rate of *minus* 4 percent. The tax-exempt investor earns 0 percent in real terms.

For the taxable saver to get the same .5 percent after-tax return under 10 percent inflation as he did under 1 percent inflation, the nominal savings rate would have to go to 21 percent. By borrowing at 23 percent, the borrowing taxpayer would then also again be paying a 1.5 percent real after-tax rate of interest. But tax-exempt savers such as pension funds would now get 10 percent in *real* terms. The scramble for such enviable returns by the large tax-exempt institutional investors would drive interest rates down to near the levels we observe, saddling risk-averse investors (who tend to concentrate their savings in fixed income investments) with a clear loss from inflation and providing taxable borrowers with a hefty benefit, even *after* optimal adaptations have been made.[17]

We might trace the impact of inflation on interest rates further, to real estate for example, and its effect on capital formation, but I shall not do so here. The central point is that whatever other virtues, or lack thereof, that inflation has, its impact is clearly redistributive. There are *both* winners and losers. So a government policy to reduce inflation will not have general support from the populace. Neither will *any* proposal to move to some form of inflation accounting. One obvious reason for this is that adoption of such a proposal increases the chances that the tax system will then also be similarly changed, causing a redistribution of the tax burden in favor of the risk-averse and companies with a heavy investment in long-lived assets and low debt levels. And so it is with virtually every other proposal in the area of accounting measurement and disclosure: even after everyone has made an *optimal adaptation*, there will be those who gain from the implementation of any given change and there will be those who lose from it—at least in the shorter run.

In principle, there are four possible outcomes when a social choice is made, an example of which would be the adoption or abolishment of an accounting standard. First, it's possible that no one ends up worse off than without the change and that some end up better off.[18] Second, no one may gain even though some lose. Both of these situations presumably generate unanimous responses, but are rarely encountered in practice. Third, there may be no effect, to which the proper response would be indifference. Finally, we have the case which is by far the most common and which has already been alluded to in which, at least over the short run, there are both winners and losers.

Since, as noted, most accounting measurement and disclosure changes fall in the last category, there are two very important ramifications surrounding the work of bodies such as the FASB and the SEC. First, conflict between those affected is virtually inevitable.[19] Second, this conflict obscures the effect of the change in question on productive efficiency. Productive efficiency would be improved whenever aggregate consumption and investment over time would be positively affected in each contingency. Analogously, productive efficiency would be reduced if the effect on aggregate consumption and investment over time were uniformly negative. In between there are also a number of complex cases which I will ignore in the interest of brevity.[20]

The importance of separating the preceding effects cannot be over-emphasized. A productively efficient accounting change will generally cause everyone to benefit after a certain amount of time has passed. Similarly, a productively inefficient accounting change will typically cause everyone to be worse off in time. Unfortunately, the heat of the conflict generated by the immediate redistributive consequences tends to obscure these more lasting effects.

Implicit in these kinds of assessments, then, are the concepts of Pareto-efficiency and movements between and along Pareto surfaces.[21] These terms are merely a useful and succinct way of characterizing and describing economic consequences just as double entry accounting provides a useful and succinct way of describing the financial status and activities of a company. At a recent conference, I was dismayed to hear two leading accounting scholars dismiss the notion of Pareto-efficiency out of hand, as being irrelevant to a serious debate concerning accounting disclosure and measurement. Doing so is equivalent to dismissing double-entry accounting out of hand. A Pareto-efficient solution by itself may well be no more worthwhile than having a useless set of books that balance. But the concept of Pareto-efficiency, like the fundamental accounting equation, is an essential foundation for enlightened analysis. To pretend that economic consequences can be sensibly evaluated without reference to Pareto's criterion is equivalent to discarding double-entry accounting in favor of single-entry bookkeeping.

The economic consequences of accounting changes are there whether we ignore them or not. Those affected will respond by acting in their self-interest, adapting their decisions to minimize the damage inflicted on them or to maximize their new advantage. The repercussions of these actions will show up in the labor market, in the financial market, and in the market for consumer goods and capital assets via price changes and other adjustments. How can we possibly avoid what finance, in the form of portfolio and capital market theory, for example, and welfare economics have to offer in assessing the attendant consequences? Perhaps more to the point, how can we possibly *not* use knowledge and tools from finance and economics in accomplishing this task? Clearly we cannot. So the question is only whether we use primitive and outdated knowledge from these fields or whether we avail ourselves of the best models and findings those fields have to offer (which of course need not be the most recent).

Assessing the economic consequences of a given accounting standard or disclosure requirement is no small task. We can, of course, go on as we have and use the expression ''economic consequences'' as a mere catch-phrase. Or we can look at a few more associations between selected accounting variables and/or announcements or proposals and stock prices.[22] But that is not going to get us very far. Those who see their interests affected will continue to lobby for or against the proposal in question, in many cases carefully camouflaging the real reasons for their positions. It will continue to be a contest between narrow interests, with no one having a firm grasp of the overall economic consequences.

The alternative is to make a serious attempt at assessing the economic consequences of both current and proposed accounting practices. This means identifying both productive and redistributive effects. This step, in turn, must begin with an identification of the chief actors, as well as various subcategories. The most important of these, presumably, are management, financial analysts, subscribers to investment services, non-subscribing investors, accountants, attorneys, and financial market regulators. Recent developments in the theory of the firm under uncertainty, in capital market theory, in the economics of information, and in the theory of incentives, as well as various empirical findings, provide a solid basis for accounting scholars to model this interaction. Such a model should quickly reveal the self-interests of the various parties on any given issue. That is, it will be possible to characterize those who have vested interests in historical accounting, in slow reporting, and in minimum disclosure as well as those who would favor and oppose price-level accounting, various types of replacement cost disclosure, and other particular issues. These are things we don't seem to know much about at the present time,[23] and this knowledge gap alone no doubt causes hopeless proposals to be made by the rule-making bodies.

The preceding also implies that we need to take cognizance of our own self-interest. There can be no question but that the recent growth in mandatory requirements has boosted the employment opportunities available to us as accountants. The fact that many prominent accountants openly decry government regulation should not always be taken at face value. The same executives who speak out against government regulation often engage in intensive lobbying to prevent *de*regulation of their particular industry. The airline and trucking industries are recent cases in point. What I am saying, therefore, is that the effects of changes in mandatory accounting standards and other requirements on employment opportunities in accounting alone imply that the positions taken by various accounting subgroups may be quite far removed from considerations of overall productive efficiency. ''Promoting the efficiency of the capital market'' is an oft-heard phrase in this context, especially in arguments favoring increased disclosure requirements.[24] It is probably true that the capital market could be made more ''efficient'' if half of the population were engaged in accounting. But that need not be the best use of our resources in terms of aggregate output, for we would then have to rely on 10 percent of the people to actually produce the bulk of our food, our housing, our means of transportation, our health care, our entertainment, etc., assuming that another 20 percent worked for the government and 20 percent were engaged in the practice of law.

In the final analysis, then, what the productive efficiency question in accounting boils down to can be summarized in a single word: productivity. A certain amount of information about companies is going to reach investors with or without an SEC and with or without an FASB. If companies choose not to disclose, investors will simply use their own time or hire analysts to find out what's cooking. So the acid test is closely related to the *total* number of man hours per year spent in the generation and transmission of financial information about companies. The fact that analysts by the hundreds and by the thousands find it necessary to visit each of our larger companeis every year,[25] despite the presence of massive disclosure requirements, does not point to high productivity in accounting, broadly conceived. Either our present disclosure system omits important information or produces it too late or both. In a very real sense, then, the essence of the economic consequences of accounting question boils down to how many people it takes, with the help of space-age technology, to inform interested parties about the activities of our economic entities. In fact, from the perspective of economic efficiency a strong argument could be made to the effect that the sole responsibility of rule-making bodies such as the FASB and the SEC consists precisely in promoting the highest possible *overall* productivity in the generation and transmission of financial information.

Comprehensive models that capture the effects on aggregate output, on employment, and on the welfare of the parties affected will clearly not be simple to produce and to test. They will involve much hard work on the part of academic researchers and others, work that has numerous overlaps with economics and finance.. But as noted, this work should have useful payoffs to standard setters and others concerned with public policy. It would greatly assist in evaluating the productive and distributive effects of present practices and requirements and it should make it possible to accurately predict the redistributive and productive impact of proposed changes, as well as the lineup of supporters and antagonists that can be expected. The quality of the decisions made by the FASB, the SEC, and Congress, as in the case of personal decisions, can be no better than the accuracy with which the consequences of proposed alternatives have been assessed.

CONCLUDING COMMENTS

These, then, are some of the immediate implications of taking the bumpy, uphill road to the right. But they are not the only ones. For one thing, I don't think we would accept ideas from other fields as uncritically as we have in the past but that we would become much more discriminating. In addition, I believe it would, in time, gain the field of accounting a great deal of academic respectability. This benefit should extend well beyond a mere tickling of our vanity. It would give us an intellectual basis which other disciplines could learn and benefit from. Financial reporting data would then be something that could be placed in perspective, not merely dismissed as archaic and essentially useless and greatly biased. Members of the accounting profession, when called to testify before Congressional committees, would be able to provide inputs in conjunction with proposed tax reforms and measures designed to stimulate capital formation, say, that are firmly anchored in sound theory confirmed by observations. In other words, the increased respectability of academic accounting should quickly translate itself to increased respect for the professional accountant as well.

This kind of approach should have other beneficial fallout as well. Let me mention just three. Most of our current disclosure legislation appears, in some form or another, to spring from a concern that the public, and especially the small investor, needs to be "protected." But to be adversely affected by a fraudulent action on the part of any given company, say, the investor would have to have a relatively large position in that company. In other words, he would have to be undiversified. But the old adage, "never put all your eggs in one basket" and modern portfolio theory both offer the same advice to all investors: diversify. In practice, diversification is almost as available to small investors as to large ones. That is, the small investor's self-interest tells him to diversify anyway, and by so doing he automatically protects himself from misleading statements or fraudulent actions. Of course, his protection is not 100 percent since he may still suffer small losses. But the implementation of protective measures via legislation is also costly and it is unclear how much fraud, if any, such measures have eliminated. In a sense, it boils down to which approach is cheaper. The kind of analysis stimulated by the road to the right should therefore help us evaluate the productive effects, and hence the propriety, of current requirements founded on the "protect-the-small-investor" philosophy.

Closely related to the preceding question is the issue of how much auditing should be mandated, if any. In other words, what would be, for example, the redistributive and productive implications of removing the legal requirement of an audit? Since many of the services that auditors now perform are voluntarily purchased, there is no risk that auditing would go away. To help address questions like this (which may of course be independently raised in Congress anyway at any time), it would clearly be valuable to have a closer relationship with finance and economics rather than a more distant one.

Finally, the kind of approach I have outlined will help us avoid traps in the conduct of research as well. For example, it has been common to ask investors, via interviews or questionnaires, whether they would like such and such information publicly disclosed. But the self-interest of the respondent may cause him or her to give a false answer. For example, a financial analyst who regularly estimates certain quantities from unpublished data privately obtained by him and which he then sells to subscribers may see a positive answer as influencing the probability that public disclosure of that same information will be forthcoming on a *timely* basis, causing him, quite correctly, to view such a response as a threat to his income.

In summary, then, the junction just ahead is a crucial one, and I hope we will at least pause and not just go straight along the road that gradually curves to the left without at least noticing the road to the right. Our balance of payments vis à vis economics and finance has recently been substantially negative. Our currency on campus is still low and has, on balance, barely held its own even in the business school. Our self-confidence is still a bit shaky and our creativity less than what it could be. A right turn will not solve all these problems overnight. Our payments deficit would continue for some time but for a different reason. As a developing nation, the United States ran a consistent trade deficit during its period of greatest growth—namely, the late 1800s and the early 1900s. But as we grow in sophistication, others will become interested in our products, especially researchers in economics and finance. As academic accountants conversant with and recognized by modern economists, our institutional interests and background would cause us to be viewed as experts to be taken seriously. Accountants rather than economists would have reason to be called on as experts on the effects of inflation on corporate taxes and other matters of public financial policy. But most important of all, policy making bodies such as the FASB would have a stronger intellectual base to fall back on.

FOOTNOTES

[1] For a sampling of written material on the economic consequences of accounting, see, for example, Rappaport (1977), Swieringa (1977), Financial Accounting Standards Board (1978), Committee on the Social Consequences of Accounting Information (1978), Gellein (1978), and Zeff (1978).

[2] For a recent summary of this research, see Kaplan (1978).

[3] Due to Sharpe (1964).

[4] Due to Black and Scholes (1973): For a recent application to accounting, see Patell and Wolfson (1979).

[5] See, e.g., Ro (1978), Collins and Dent (1979), and Lev (1979). The two latter studies raise the possibility that cash flow changes may be *indirectly* induced by managerial and other contracts tied to specific accounting methods.

[6] See, e.g., Kaplan (1978).

[7] See, e.g., Savage (1954).

[8] See, e.g., Arrow (1951) and Sen (1970).

[9] The seminal paper here is usually attributed to Hirschleifer (1971).

[10] For a concise summary of some of these problems, see Beaver and Demski (1974).

[11] See, e.g., Buckley (1979).

[12] See, e.g., Demski and Feltham (1978) and Zimmerman (1979).

[13] For a more complete illustration of this point, see Hakansson (1978, pp. 21-23).

[14] See Rosenberg and Marathe (1975).

[15] Recall that the seminal study in this area is due to Beaver, Kettler, and Scholes (1970).

16 See, e.g., Gellein (1978, p. 77).
17 While such phenomena as investment tax credits, accelerated depreciation for tax purposes, and the LIFO inventory method offer means whereby the impact of inflation can be *imperfectly* offset, real-world financial markets offer no *perfect* hedges against inflation through which its effects can be neutralized.
18 Welloffness is generally measured by expected utility, the central concept in the modern theory of decision [see, e.g., Savage (1954)].
19 For descriptions of these conflicts, see, e.g., Horngren (1973), Moonitz (1974), and Watts and Zimmerman (1979).
20 For a more complete definition, see Hakansson (1977, pp. 410-411).
21 A Pareto-surface consists of the set of efficient allocations (in expected utility terms) of a given set of outputs. Movements along a Pareto-surface must therefore make some individuals worse off and some better off. A change in production plans will cause the surface to shift higher, lower, or a mixture of the two. Only shifts to higher Pareto-surfaces provide opportunities for Pareto-improvements—i.e., the opportunity for everyone to improve his lot.
22 While price effects are often of interest in their own right, they unfortunately do not provide reliable clues to the attendant impact on investor welfare. The relationship between prices and welfare is essentially random in this context.
23 For a beginning attempt, see Hakansson (1979).
24 For a recent example, see Financial Accounting Standards Board (1979, p. 2).
25 See, e.g., Axelson (1975, p. 45).

REFERENCES

Arrow, Kenneth. 1951. *Social Choice and Individual Values*. New York: John Wiley and Sons, Inc.

Axelson, Kenneth. 1975. "A Businessman's Views on Disclosure." *Journal of Accountancy* 140 (July): 42-46.

Beaver, William and Demski, Joel. 1974. "The Nature of Financial Accounting Objectives: A Summary and Synthesis. In *Studies on Financial Accounting Objectives,* Supplement to the *Journal of Accounting Research* 12: 654-682.

Beaver, William; Kettler, Paul; and Scholes, Myron. 1970. "The Association between Market-Determined and Accounting-Determined Risk Measures." *Accounting Review* 45 (October): 654-682.

Black, Fischer and Scholes, Myron. 1973. "The Pricing of Options and Corporate Liabilities." *Journal of Political Economy* 81 (May/June): 637-656.

Buckley, John. 1979. "Regulation and the Accounting Profession." Working Paper. Los Angeles: Graduate School of Management, University of California.

Collins, Daniel and Dent, Warren. 1979. "The Proposed Elimination of Full Cost Accounting in the Extractive Petroleum Industry: An Empirical Assessment of the Market Consequences." *Journal of Accounting and Economics* 1 (March): 3-44.

Committee on Social Consequences of Accounting Information. 1978. *Report of the Committee on the Social Consequences of Accounting Information.* Sarasota, Fla: American Accounting Association.

Demski, Joel and Feltham, Gerald. 1978: "Economic Incentives in Budgetary Control Systems" *Accounting Review* 53 (April): 336-359.

Financial Accounting Standards Board. 1978. Conference on the Economic Consequences of Financial Accounting Standards. Stamford, Conn..

_____. *Statement of Accounting Standards,* No. 33. 1979. Stamford: Conn.

Fisher, Irving. 1906. *The Nature of Capital and Income.* New York: Macmillan Co.

Gellein, Oscar. 1978. "The Task of the Standard Setter." *Journal of Accountancy* 146 (December): 75-79.

Hakansson, Nils. 1977. "Interim Disclosure and Forecasts: An Economic Analysis and a Framework for Choice." *Accounting Review* 52 (April): 396-416.

_____. 1978. "Information Needs for Portfolio Choice: Some Normative Aspects." In *Financial Information Requirements for Security Analysis.* Edited by Rashad Abdel-khalik and Thomas F. Keller. Durham, N.C.: Graduate School of Business Administration, Duke University.

_____. 1979. "On the Adversary Interests in Disclosure Alternatives and in the Selection of Accounting Methods." Working Paper..

Hatfield, Henry. 1924. "An Historical Defense of Bookkeeping." *Journal of Accountancy* 37 (April): 241-253.

Hirschleifer, Jack. 1971. "The Private and Social Value of Information and the Reward to Inventive Activity." *American Economic Review* 61 (September): 561-574.

Horngren, Charles. 1973. "The Marketing of Accounting Standards." *Journal of Accountancy* 136 (October): 61-66.

Kaplan, Robert. 1978. "The Information Content of Financial Accounting Numbers: A Survey of Empirical Evidence." In *The Impact of Accounting Research on Practice and Disclosure.* Edited by Rashad Abdel-khalik and Thomas Keller. Durham, N.C.: Duke University Press.

Lev, Baruch, 1979, "The Impact of Accounting Regulation on the Stock Market: The Case of Oil and Gas Companies." *Accounting Review* 54 (July): 485-503.

Moonitz, Maurice. 1974. *Obtaining Agreement on Standards in the Accounting Profession.* Sarasota, Fla.: American Accounting Association.

Patell, James and Wolfson, Mark. 1979. "Anticipated Information Releases Reflected in Call Option Prices." *Journal of Accounting and Economics* 1 (August): 117-140.

Rappaport, Alfred. 1977. "Economic Impact of Accounting Standards: Implications for the FASB." *Journal of Accountancy* 143 (May): 89-98.

Ro, Byung. 1978. "The Disclosure of Capitalized Lease Information and Stock Prices." *Journal of Accounting Research* 16 (Autumn): 315-340.

Rosenberg, Barr and Marathe, Vinay. 1975. "The Prediction of Investment Risk: Systematic and Residual Risk." *Proceedings of the Seminar on the Analysis of Security Prices.* University of Chicago (November).

Savage, Leonard. 1954. *The Foundations of Statistics.* New York: John Wiley and Sons, Inc..

Sen, Amartya. 1970. *Collective Choice and Social Welfare.* San Francisco: Holden-Day.

Sharpe, William. 1964. "Capital Asset Prices: A Theory of Market Equilibrium under Risk." *Journal of Finance* 19 (September): 425-442.

Swieringa, Robert. 1977. "Consequences of Financial Accounting Standards." *Accounting Forum* (May): 25-39.

Watts, Ross and Zimmerman, Jerold. 1979. "The Demand for and Supply of Accounting Theories: The Market for Excuses." *Accounting Review* 54 (April): 273-305.

Zeff, Stephen. 1978. "The Rise of 'Economic Consequences'." *Journal of Accountancy* 146 (December): 56-63.

Zimmerman, Jerold. 1979. "The Costs and Benefits of Cost Allocations." *Accounting Review* 54 (July): 504-521

> *The first mistake in public business is going into it.*
> *Benjamin Franklin*

WHERE WE ARE IN ACCOUNTING: A REVIEW OF "STATEMENT ON ACCOUNTING THEORY AND THEORY ACCEPTANCE"*

by Nils H. Hakansson

*Reprinted from *The Accounting Review* 53 (July 1978): 717-725

The author benefited from helpful discussions with Professor Maurice Moonitz.

BEGINNING with the 1930s, the American Accounting Association has endeavored to publish at least one comprehensive statement in the area of accounting theory each decade. Logistically, this enterprise has been carried out by a series of committees drawn from the Association's more prominent members.

The first four statements (1936, 1941, 1948, 1957) appear to have come quite close to general expectations in terms of both scope and specific issues addressed. Judged against this precedent, the 1966 statement was rather ambitious and reformist in character, but it still managed, despite a certain change in direction, to retain the basic thrust of its forerunners. The most recent document, *Statement on Accounting Theory and Theory Acceptance* (1977), however, reflects obvious disenchantment with the basic goals of its predecessors as well as its own committee charge. The result is a sharp turn to the left. The patient, thinking she had a foot problem, ended up with abdominal surgery. The surgeons' report, in essence, attempts to convince us that the surgery was necessary. The section containing the procedural description makes little effort to suppress the spilling of blood and reveals several infractions. While at times pompous in style, this part is also occasionally incisive. The findings section of the report, however, is simplistic and disappointing. I thought we all knew that even the feet derive most of their nutrition from processing activities centered in the digestive tract.

A SYNOPSIS OF THE STATEMENT

It may be useful to begin my elaboration of the above summary judgment by disclosing the contents of the 1977 Statement in synopsis form:

Chapter 1 quickly sets the tone by stating that " . . . this report does not attempt to develop a statement *of* universally accepted theory; instead ours is a statement *about* accounting theory and theory acceptance. . . . Theory *acceptance* would not be facilitated by this committee's attempting to impose theory closure

. . . There is currently an abundance of theories of external reporting'' (p. 1), which differ in the way they ''. . . view users and the preparer-user environments. . . . What we seek is a theory that is general enough to cope with this variety and specific enough to offer assistance to accounting policy makers'' (p. 3).

Chapter 2 classifies ''the dominant approaches that have evolved'' into three categories. The first of these is the ''classical ('true income' and inductive)'' approach, which has been used both by ''normative deductivists'' (Paton, Canning, Sweeney, MacNeal, Alexander, Edwards and Bell, Moonitz, and Sprouse) and by ''chiefly positive, inductive writers'' (Hatfield, Gilman, Littleton, and Ijiri) (pp. 5-10, 27-29). The second approach is identified as based on ''decision-usefulness'' and is also divided into two sub-categories: those which stress decision *models* (Chambers, the AAA 1966 statement, Sterling, etc.) and those which focus on decision *makers* (behavioral accounting and aggregate market-level research studies) (pp. 10-21). The third approach is labeled ''information economics,'' and a distinction is made between the ''single-individual case'' and the ''multi-individual case,'' with considerably greater emphasis given to the latter (pp. 21-25).

Chapter 3 goes on to examine the reasons ''. . . why no theoretical approach has yet achieved dominant acceptance within the accounting community'' (p. 31). The obstacles to acceptance of current accounting theories in general are identified and discussed under six headings: (1) the problem of relating theories to practice, (2) the allocation problem, (3) the difficulty with normative standards, (4) difficulties in interpreting security price-behavior research, (5) the problem of cost-benefit considerations in accounting theories, and (6) limitations of data expansion.

With this background, Chapter 4 provides an alternative attempt to ''. . . develop a plausible explanation for the lack of progress in achieving accounting theory consensus'' and suggests, by a detailed reference to Kuhn [1970], that what we have is ''. . . the existence of several competing paradigms,'' defined on pp. 41-42 as ''frameworks which 'provide models from which spring particular coherent traditions of scientific research'.'' It concludes that ''. . . defenders of a particular paradigm are forced to rely on persuasion rather than logic or empirics in attempting to defend a proposal'' (p. 48).

The final chapter summarizes the statement in the form of four ''messages,'' which I reproduce *verbatim*:

1. Theory closure cannot be dictated.
2. External reporting theory has a wider scope than that which has been generally perceived.
3. All theory approaches are flawed when viewed from the perspective of some alternative approach.
4. Until consensus paradigm acceptance occurs, the utility of accounting theories in aiding policy decisions is partial.

SCHOLARSHIP AND MARKET INTERVENTION

If we think of the members of the American Accounting Association as primarily concerned with teaching and research, one may legitimately wonder why the AAA has felt the need to publish five statements and 13 supplements on the subject of (financial) accounting principles, standards, and theory since 1936. During this same period, the Committee on Accounting Procedure, the Accounting Principles Board, and the Financial Accounting Standards Board, in turn, have formally represented the much larger practicing arm of the profession in its self-regulatory determination of standards governing accounting practice. It is clearly not that membership in academia and/or the AAA has precluded one from an active role in accounting rule making; professors of accounting have regularly been called on to serve in this capacity. A more likely reason is that the AAA, through its collective membership, is, from the inside at least, viewed as being in a unique position to give advice on ''practical'' accounting theory, whether that advice is solicited or not.[1] The FASB, say, may be thought of as having a harder time ignoring a statement published under the auspices of the AAA than any given collection of individual contributions.[2] In any case, it is worth noting that a similar situation does not exist in other disciplines. The American Finance Association, the American Economic Association, the American Marketing Association, and the American Psychological Association, to name a few, apparently do not feel the need to appoint committees to improve on, or add to, what individual scholars have to say about the state of knowledge in their respective fields. Recall that financial analysts, psychiatrists, and practicing psychologists are also, like CPAs, licensed practitioners.

As eloquently expressed by Chambers [1972] and seconded in the Statement (p. 49), appointed committees cannot conduct research. The very notion contains an antithetical element. Nobel Prizes will continue to be won by individuals and self-selected teams.

The remaining question, then, is whether the 1977 Committee succeeded in its ". . . role to survey the accounting theory literature" (p. 49), i.e., whether it did something that individuals and self-selected teams have not done or would not do—and is, in fact, needed. In other words, to demonstrate convincingly that a venture such as this one has been successful, it is necessary to establish (1) "market failure"[3] in the arena of accounting ideas, excluding efforts by appointed AAA *committees* (but not AAA-funded individual research studies), and (2) that there has been a successful repair of this "failure" by the appointed committee. More specifically, if the study were needed, could not the members voluntarily have formed a team, obtaining the requisite travel expenses from their respective departments or some other agency? Thus, in a sense which is consistent with the discussion on pp. 22-25 of the Statement, a necessary, but not sufficient, condition for this review to be laudable is that the free market in accounting ideas (excluding the AAA's publishing activities *via appointed committees*), with all its pecuniary and non-pecuniary incentives, has left us with a gap that a survey such as this, conducted by a solicited group of participants drawn from that same market, could fill (by having the committee members engage in limited interaction over a short period of time at AAA expense). That's a tall order, apparently taller than anything such a committee could reasonably hope to satisfy.

SCHOLARSHIP AND ACCOUNTING RULE-MAKING

Naturally any self-regulating profession looks to the accumulated body of knowledge relevant to its domain in setting standards and rules of practice. Accounting is no different. In this rule-making task, the applicable rule-making body needs two kinds of inputs: information about how the world works, especially that part of the world with which the profession rubs elbows, and information about what conclusions or implications follow from different sets of premises or assumptions. The first type is descriptive or positive knowledge, pure and simple, while the second may or may not be normative in character.[4] Only in the last 10 years has a serious *systematic* effort been under way to add to our (scant) stock of empirical knowledge. Most (though by no means all) of the earlier work done by accounting academics was normative in spirit although it often proceeded from unvalidated premises and rarely passed contemporary standards in other fields in coherence and reasoning, with the inevitable result that everyone has been left rather hanging, having gained little in incremental information.

There is still considerable confusion about the distinction between descriptive and normative knowledge in the accounting literature, the 1977 Statement included. For example, the Statement, on p. 33, reads: ". . . some theories of external reporting incorporate normatively *posited standards* that provide a basis for choosing information to be included in external reports" (emphasis added). The point is that *all the inputs (assumptions) to a normative (accounting) model are poisited* (i.e. the resources, the technological opportunities, the action space, the probability beliefs, and the preferences). It's impossible for them *not to be*. But they are *all* also subject to verification (via empirical research). Thus, the relationship between "standards" as a surrogate for preferences and utility functions as representations of preferences, for example, must be addressed by analysis. But as assumptions, both representations are empirically testable, at least in principle.

A second example occurs on p. 35, where the question is posed whether security price behavior studies should be interpreted ". . . as attempts to assess *consequences* or *desirability* of measurement method changes." This is an extreme case of confusion. An empirical study per se can only yield *descriptive* knowledge. Desirability, in the public policy sense, is a strictly logical proposition and can only be evaluated in a normative model with a full set of assumptions, including a posited criterion of "goodness"; different models typically give different rankings of accounting alternatives, but the "fit to reality" of each model's assumptions is again subject to empirical measurement.[5]

All decision makers (members of the FASB included) implicitly or explicitly employ normative decision models in making choices of a non-routine nature. The models used may be quite informal and erratically applied, but they do, nevertheless, have the properties of normative structures. These models are only altered or discarded by their users when new and (in their view, of course) better (descriptive or normative) information comes along. In capsule form, this is how accounting scholarship contributes to accounting practice. In particular, research that adds little or nothing will be ignored. As the 1977 Statement suggests (p. 9), the Paton-Littleton [1940] monograph is probably the single most influential work in the accounting literature—on theory as well as rule-making (there is a remarkably close correspondence between the "conclusions" in the monograph and the APB Opinions for example). But more recent writing most certainly appear to have had a negligible impact, with the possible exception of statistical sampling techniques in the area of audit planning and work in replacement cost accounting on the SEC disclosure requirements in that area. This is, at least, indirect evidence that, despite a high level of activity, the normative research of the last 35 years and our recently initiated formalization of empirical research have not yet led to any *major* advances in accounting knowledge.

To give the preceding assertion more precision, it may be useful to compare the situation in accounting to what has happened recently in our closest sister discipline, finance. There, no less than three recent *academic* contributions have profoundly affected financial practice in the last few years. The first of these concerns the measurement of portfolio risk, where techniques distinguishing between market-wide and firm-specific risk developed by academics in finance have left no significant area of investment management untouched. The resulting upheaval has been dubbed the *beta* revolution and as such may be characterized as swift and bloodless, although it certainly caused a great many bruised egos.

The second example is in the area of options. Trading in options has increased dramatically in the last few years with the opening of organized markets. While option markets have been likened to gambling casinos, they do, in fact, serve an important economic function as a part of our financial market system [Hakansson, 1978a]. Being relatively risky in isolation but also capable of reducing the investor's overall risk exposure when combined with other securities, options present a challenging valuation problem to investor and academic alike. A large number of market participants, including more than half of the market makers on the Chicago Board of Options Exchange, now utilize valuation models developed by Merton [1973] and Black and Scholes [1973], all academic searchers in the area of finance.

The third product of academic research in finance which is rapidly being adopted by our larger institutional investors is an advanced method for adaptive estimation of future security and portfolio risk [Rosenberg and Marathe, 1975]. It is based on the most powerful econometric methodology currently available and on an approach which in effect combines technical and fundamental analysis. It is surely one of the ironies of our time that almost no one in accounting is familiar with the underlying research, which reveals that ordinary accounting numbers possess an overwhelming (and reassuring) power to improve on estimates of future risk derived from past prices alone. Why, one must ask, wasn't the research itself done by a scholar in accounting? This question appears particularly pertinent in view of the fact that the seminal study in this area, analyzed on p. 20 of the Statement, was published in the accounting literature [Beaver, Kettler and Scholes, 1970].

PARADIGMS IN ACCOUNTING

The 1977 AAA Statement did not specifically concern itself with theory acceptance by *practitioners*, and in that sense, the preceding section may be viewed as a partial digression. One purpose of that digression is to provide additional background for the present section.

Kuhn's model (1970) of the behavior of scientists does offer an interesting perspective from which to view recent developments in accounting. While plausible, Kuhn's (descriptive) model has not, however, been systematically verified. For unexplained reasons, it seems to have received more attention among accountants than among other social scientists.

There is a cautious suggestion in the Statement that the three approaches summarized in Chapter 2 might ". . . each be treated as an alternative paradigm" (p. 43). I have considerable difficulty with this proposition.

If there is a paradigm in accounting, it would seem to me to have to be closely related with the structure of modern corporate accounting: a focus on assets, on claims to these assets, and on periodic changes in both, with each dimension associated with a *unique standardized number*. (This description is obviously similar (but not identical) to the "true income" approach described in the Statement.) One might argue that this paradigm took hold in the last century and reached its zenith in the 1930s, 40s, and 50s.

By the 1960s especially, considerable disenchantment had set in. The Statement attributes this to ". . . dissatisfaction with the prevailing matching-attaching paradigm" (p. 43). I am more inclined to interpret the problem more broadly, as caused primarily by the shortcomings of relying on the single-number (nominal currency point) estimates to which the double-entry system naturally leads us. (This property of the paradigm can also be viewed as directly responsible for "the allocation problem," which is discussed on pp. 32-33.) In trying to sort out the various anomalies, one group began to look to information and decision theory for help, another grew ever more uncomfortable with our utter lack of systematic knowledge of relevant empirical phenomena. Later, and more independently, a third group began to employ welfare-economic tools in searching for answers to certain accounting policy questions. Each of these approaches has had only modest success, and it seems much too early to think of them as alternative paradigms. The "old" one has not come close to being overthrown and may yet be repaired. For one thing, symptoms of narrow-mindedness should not be confused with paradigms. While scientists are not immune to tunnel vision, many recognize a much larger picture than the one they themselves are working on. In addition, the lessons from the failure of recent attempts to create a grand theory of accounting in one monograph have not been lost. For another thing, neither approach has much to show, for the effort expended, on which one might build a cohesive structure or theory.

There is one sentence in this context which I find particularly puzzling in the Statement: "Logic and empirics do not, therefore, provide a sufficient basis for selecting between competing paradigms" (p. 46). Why is a choice necessary, especially between such narrowly defined "paradigms" as the "decision-usefulness" and "information economics" approaches? Can't one be perfectly tolerant of, and learn from, both? Might not portfolio (diversification) theory apply here as well? In any case, what besides descriptive knowledge and logic does *anyone* have to work with in making choices?

GOODS AND BADS

Clearly the best part of the statement is the discussion of the "information economics" approach (pp. 21-25). This is also the area in which accountants have been the least active, by far. The main point is well stated; when it comes to information, there are indeed several reasons why a market system, guided by Adam Smith's invisible hand, does not work as well as one might like so that regulatory intervention (*e.g.*, with respect to accounting disclosure requirements) should be *considered*. But regulation is costly, so that whether it is actually the right remedy is generally unclear without empirical estimates of the impact (pp. 23, 25) and possibly even with such estimates. In this context, the cost benefit section on p. 37 is too negatively stated. The fact that a complete social ordering of (three or more) alternatives satisfying Arrow's criteria does not, in general, exist does not imply that we should throw up our hands. *Partial* orderings of the outcome distributions of accounting policy alternatives implementable at the social level can typically be obtained via Pareto's criterion [Hakansson, 1977]. That is, we may be able to assign grades (A, B, C, *etc.*) to categories of alternatives and conclude that the final choice should be drawn from the A category.

A related question, not considered in the Statement, is the welfare impact resulting from the licensing of public accountants. A recent (post-Statement) study suggests that licensed professions, under plausible assumptions, have incentives to generate monopoly rents by setting minimum professional standards on the high side [Leland, 1977].

I have no particular praise or criticism of the section on the "classical approach" to accounting theory (pp. 5-10) although I do not share the committee's confidence in the classification scheme used.

The section on decision models (pp. 10-17) is relatively lengthy and reflects accurately the lack of rigor in conceptualization and reasoning that characterizes so much of the work in the area.

The discussion of behavioral accounting research (pp. 17-19) is the second best in the Statement. The analysis of aggregate market-level research (pp. 19-21) is on the brief side and somewhat incomplete in its coverage; it profitably could have included reference to the interesting study by Collins [1975], for example.

The so-called "data expansion approach" to external reporting is, somewhat surprisingly, examined on pp. 37-39 rather than in Chapter 2. To claim that the "proponents of this approach argue that *more information is assuredly preferable to less*" (p. 37, emphasis in original) is surely an injustice. The cited paper by Sorter [1969] raises a simple but worthwhile point, namely that raw unaggregated data may well be better—within limits—than various aggregate summary measures (such as those provided by the current accounting model), the communication of which generally involves a clear loss of information.

THE STING

After reading the first four chapters of the 1977 statement (on which the preceding criticism is based), I confess that I was not quite ready for the final, summarizing chapter. Not that I hadn't been puzzled by the periodic allusion to "theory closure" (pp. 1 (twice), 25 (twice), 41, 47, and 49). But when I read "Our message is clear; *theory closure cannot be dictated*" (p. 49), I felt a definite letdown. Is that really what the Statement is about? Is that as far as an elite committee of the intellectual branch of accounting has managed to bring us in the year 1977? The committee apparently believes the rest of us equate theory closure (which I presume means a tendency for all concerned, in an environment of free inquiry, to agree on *a* theory) with some kind of utopia. The evidence, please. Furthermore, while utopia may be worth a visit, whoever said utopia was an interesting place to live?

The "second basic message" is that "external reporting theory has a wider scope than that which has been generally perceived" (p. 49): Perhaps this is news for those who were asleep when the ecology wave struck or who missed its point.

The "third basic message is that all theory approaches are flawed when viewed from the perspective of some alternative approach" (p. 50). This statement can be made both briefer and stronger. *All* models in the empirical sciences, being abstractions, or representations, or simplifications of some reality under study, necessarily cannot capture everything about that reality without themselves being complete reproductions of that reality. So the statement holds not only relatively but absolutely and trivially: All models are flawed.

The final "message . . . is that until consensus paradigm acceptance occurs, the utility of accounting theories in aiding policy decisions is partial" (p. 51). This statement errs by being too generous. As noted in the third section of this critique, the descriptive knowledge and the prescriptions provided by accounting research only have the *potential* of making policy makers aware of things they did not know before, even when a paradigm is in full bloom. It's what we genuinely learn from our research that counts.

EPILOGUE

As I indicated in the second section of this review, there are many reasons why I am far from convinced that the committee approach makes sense even in summarizing the state-of-the-art. There are few areas in which decentralized production decisions generated by self-interest can be surpassed, and scholarly activities is most likely not one of them. And when most of the members of a committee keep citing their own minor works, the effect is somehow more pronounced than when single or multiple authors do so.

In sum, the 1977 Statement, including the non-italicized part of Chapter 5, is clearly much better than the four (italicized) central messages discussed in the previous section. It does bring a number of seemingly disparate threads together in a way which is, on balance, helpful. It reflects faithfully the recent broadening of the accounting horizon and the gradual lifting of scholarly standards that is currently in motion. It suggests, if only indirectly, that careful attention to less ambitious slices of the accounting problem is essential to futher progress. But the accomplishments to date in accounting are on the whole overstated: recent developments in theory, frankly, have not moved us very far forward in the last 35 years in comparison with, say, recent developments in an area like finance. I have suggested elsewhere that advances in finance, economics, and behavioral science are in the nature of a pre-condition for substantial further progress in accounting [Hakansson, 1978b]. These developments are well on their way, and from this angle the next 10 years or so look exceedingly promising for accounting research.

FOOTNOTES

1 Recall that the pronouncements of the Committee on Accounting Procedure and of the Accounting Principles Board, before 1965, were not binding on the members of the American Institute of Certified Public Accountants; instead, their authority rested on their "general acceptability." Consequently, there existed, prior to the mid-sixties at least, a natural temptation for the American Accounting Association to step forward. In this context, it should also be noted that the 1966 and 1977 statements were prepared by *ad hoc* committees, while the 1936 and 1941 statements were issued by the Executive Committee and the 1948 and 1957 statements were developed by a standing committee.

2 It may be noted that a proposal to have the American Accounting Association take positions, as a body, on issues before the FASB was recently voted down by the membership.

3 "Market failure" is said to occur when a free market results in a situation which can be improved upon to everyone's advantage by deployment of non-market forces (market intervention) - one of the central results in economic theory is that this is never possible when the pre-conditions of a competitive market are met.

4 The methods employed in descriptive research include observation, examination of documents and artifacts, experimentation, the use of interviews and questionnaires, statistical analysis, and reasoning (both deductive and inductive). In contrast, there is but a single method available for the conduct of normative research—reasoning.

5 A few additional slips may also be noted:
   a. The word "normative" is either redundant or inappropriately used in a number of phrases: see e.g., "normative qualities" (p. 13), "normative standards" (pp. 15, 16, 33, 34), and "normative criterion" (pp. 23, 25, 32).
   b. On p. 48, there is a sentence which reads: "Each paradigm implicitly incorporates individual beliefs and premises that cannot be proved or disproved in a logical sense." Premises themselves can never be proved or disproved, although *conclusions* that are presumed to follow from premises can. On the other hand, premises (in an accounting model, say) are *empirically* verifiable, at least in principle.

REFERENCES

American Accounting Association Executive Committee, "Accounting Principles Underlying Corporate Financial Statements," THE ACCOUNTING REVIEW, June 1936, pp. 187-191; American Accounting Association Executive Committee, "Accounting Principles Underlying Corporate Financial Statements," THE ACCOUNTING REVIEW, June 1941, pp. 133-139; American Accounting Association Committee on Concepts and Standards Underlying Corporate Financial Statements, "Accounting Concepts and Standards Underlying Corporate Financial Statements," THE ACCOUNTING REVIEW, October 1948, pp. 339-344; American Accounting Association Committee on Concepts and Standards Underlying Corporate Financial Statements, 1957 Revision," THE ACCOUNTING REVIEW, October 1957, pp. 536-546.

American Accounting Association Committee to Prepare a Statement of Basic Accounting Theory, *A Statement of Basic Accounting Theory,* Sarasota, Florida: American Accounting Association, 1966.

American Accounting Association Committee on Concepts and Standards for External Financial Reports, *Statement on Accounting Theory and Theory Acceptance,* Sarasota, Florida: American Accounting Association, 1977.

Beaver, William, Paul Kettler, and Myron Scholes, "The Association Between Market Determined and Accounting Determined Risk Measures. THE ACCOUNTING REVIEW (October 1970), pp. 654-682.

Black, Fischer and Myron Scholes, "The Pricing of Options and Corporate Liabilities," *Journal of Political Economy* (May/June 1973), pp. 637-654.

Chambers, Raymond, "The Anguish of Accountants," *The Journal of Accountancy* (March 1972), pp. 69-70.

Collins, Daniel, "SEC Product Line Reporting and Market Efficiency," *Journal of Financial Economics* (June 1975), pp. 125-164.

Hakansson, Nils, "Interim Disclosure and Forecasts: An Economic Analysis and a Framework for Choice," THE ACCOUNTING REVIEW (April 1977), pp. 396-416.

————, "Welfare Aspects of Options and Supershares," *The Journal of Finance* (June 1978a), pp. 759-776.

————, "Information Needs for Portfolio Choice: Some Normative Aspects," *Financial Information Requirements for Security Analysis* (eds. Rashad Abdel-khalik and Thomas F. Keller), Graduate School of Business Administration, Duke University [1978b].

Kuhn, Thomas, *The Structure of Scientific Revolutions,* University of Chicago Press, 1970.

Leland, Hayne, "Quacks, Lemons, and Licensing: A Theory of Minimum Quality Standards," Finance Working Paper No. 60, Institute of Business and Economic Research, University of California, Berkeley, August, 1977.

Merton, Robert, "Rational Option Pricing," *Bell Journal of Economics and Management Science* (Spring 1973), pp. 141-183.

Rosenberg, Barr and Vinay Marathe, "The Prediction of Investment Risk: Systematic and Residual Risk," *Proceedings of the Seminar on the Analysis of Security Prices,* University of Chicago, November 1975.

Sorter, George, "An 'Events' Approach to Basic Accounting Theory," THE ACCOUNTING REVIEW (January 1969), pp 12-19.

Part III

POSITIVE VERSUS NORMATIVE ACCOUNTING THEORY AND STANDARD SETTING

WATTS and Zimmerman's battle-cry for a positive theory of accounting (as manifested by both of their articles, here reprinted) has reverberated throughout the American accounting community for the last half decade. Indeed, the response to this call to arms was not much short of the phenomenal. Articles praising the positivistic programme of these joint authors not only appeared in academic journals, but even in professional magazines;[1] scholars whose own approach is undeniably normative (though they may not want to admit it) felt compelled to proclaim that theirs is "a positive theory;" the *Collected Abstracts* of the 1982 Annual Meeting of the American Accounting Association lists no less than four papers under the two sections of "Positive Research in Accounting," and a fifth paper bearing the title, "Towards a Positive Theory of Information Evaluation," by A. Schepanski and W.C. Uecker. But what is most surprising is that all this enthusiasm occurs in accounting at a time when historians, epistemologists, natural scientists, and social scientists alike regard positivism as a naive, obsolete, and outmoded philosophy.[2] There can be little doubt that the call for a "positive theory" in our discipline filled a deep psychological need in many young academics trained in rigorous methods and influenced by the conservative Chicago school of economics. But one wonders whether all this fervour is not based on several misconceptions: first, many authors fail to comprehend "accounting in general" as an applied, hence conditionally prescriptive, discipline; second, they seem to underrate the limitations to which any positive theory concerned with human preferences is subjected; third, they do not fully grasp modern methodology and the reasons for the obsolescence of positivism; fourth, some of them even fail to realize that only a theory, but no research activity, can be free of value judgements; and, finally, they apply the term "theory" indiscriminately also to hypotheses, models, and standards.

Of particular importance is the distinction between *a theory of accounting measures*, on one side, and *a behavioural theory of accounting standard setting*, on the other. Unfortunately, some professional accountants and even many academics do not realize that only the latter theory is meant by "the positive theory of accounting." Most accountants assign a much more general or fundamental meaning to this expression. A theory studying bargaining and lobbying behaviour may well be carried out in a descriptive, i.e., positive, way. But, even here, its ultimate object of investigation is the purpose-directed action of people and groups searching and employing different means to attain various ends. And as long as these *means-end relationships* are not being analyzed, there will be no general accounting theory answering the most important questions posed by users and producers of accounting information. The manager, the investor, and the practicing accountant all want to know which set of accounting tools serve this purpose and which serve that. Of course, one might also want to know which accounting standards favour this group and which another. But, this becomes a major issue only in times when a fundamental overhaul in the accounting standards is contemplated. And since the FASB in the United States and the CICA in Canada are presently engaged in such an undertaking, it is understandable that this problem is currently magnified beyond its usual proportions.

Watts and Zimmerman illustrate their theory by means of a model capable of predicting which type of firms would be in favour of General Price Level Adjustments (GPLA, supplementary to the historical cost basis of presenting financial statements) and which would be against. The authors assert that such a change in accounting standards would affect the following factors: taxes, regulations, management compensation plans, bookkeeping costs, and political costs — all of which influence a firm's cash flow and present value. The model hinges on many assumptions, some of which might be considered as being tenuous; the study takes the *firm size* as the decisive criterion and predicts that larger firms will favour GPLA, while smaller firms will oppose it. This specific model is tested by means of a relatively small sample of submissions to the pertinent FASB discussion memorandum. Although there were exceptions, the prediction is within the range of statistical significance. But the significance of this article lies less in this particular model and its test than in the impact which the slogan "positive theory" has had on the accounting literature. Whatever one's reaction, there is little doubt that developing a general theory of accounting on the narrow basis of Watts and Zimmerman's "positive theory of accounting standard setting" resembles the unsuccessful attempt of Jacques Loeb (1859-1924 — the discoverer of biological phototropism and other tropisms) to develop a general theory of "mind" on the narrow basis of his "theory of tropism."

Watts and Zimmerman's second article, "The Demand for and Supply of Accounting Theories: The Market for Excuses," can be interpreted in different ways; but already the title suggests that traditional, nominal accounting theories (under subsequent reference to the theories of Paton, Edwards and Bell, Sprouse and Moonitz, Gordon and Chambers) are supplied by scholars on the demand of and financed by vested interests, who in turn exploit these theories as justifications for attaining their personal goals. Apart from the old truth that vested interests will use any means that fit their purposes, the authors' *implication* that, in general, accounting theoreticians are systematically bribed or tricked by research funds into providing convenient excuses for lobbying purposes must be rejected as counter-factual. Indeed, a recent historical collection edited by S. Zeff[3] (especially its last article, "The Breach of the Covenant," by M. Moonitz) illustrates vividly how strongly academic accountants have maintained their independent writing and publishing — even *against* the power of funding agencies or their constituents.

However, it may well have been the fault of academics that the above-mentioned hypothesis — or shall we say "accusation"? — could ever have been pronounced. Had academics been accustomed to present their normative theories in the way we have recommended, namely, as a general framework *together with a collection of various purpose-oriented models or interpretations*, Watts and Zimmerman's sail would have remained without wind. A theory which openly reveals that this and that accounting model serves this and that purpose, while further models serve other purposes, is no less objective than any positive theory, because the former openly reveals its ends or value judgements and thus is much less open to hidden abuse. This is confirmed by the following statement by Watts and Zimmerman: "While individuals [with vested interests] want a theory which prescribes procedures conducive to their own interest, they do *not* want a normative theory which has their self-interest as its stated objective." To *provide* models that do not reveal their *true* objectives might well be the *deadly sin of traditional, absolute-normative accounting theories* — something that is undoubtedly exposed in Watts and Zimmerman's article, though in a round-about fashion. To reveal those objectives, a *conditional-normative* accounting theory is required. Herein lies our disagreement with some other representatives of the normative camp (e.g., Chambers and Sterling) whose theories we regard as *absolute-normative*.

Christenson's article is an outspoken critique of Watts and Zimmerman's positive accounting approach and of the "Rochester School of Accounting" in general. He shows that the questions, which Michael C. Jensen[4] and other members of the "Rochester School" regard as *normative* questions, all refer to what we previously called "a theory of accounting measures," while those regarded as *positive* questions refer to the behaviour of accountants (or other users of accounting data), which Christenson regards as belonging not to questions about accounting entities, but to a *positive* meta-theory of accounting. Yet Christenson regards most accounting theorists as methodologists and thus as also belonging to the meta-theoretical camp, though to the *normative* one. In contrast to Watts and Zimmerman, whose plea for a positive theory of accounting seems to be rooted in a positivistic philosophy relying on *confirmation*, Christenson assumes a neo-rationalistic methodology and pleads for *falsification* and *corroboration*. He thus regards Watts and Zimmerman's hypothesis as insufficiently corroborated.

Bryant and Thornton's article goes beyond Watts and Zimmerman's work and aims at a *meta-theory of accounting* in which *expectations equilibria* (an idea derived from socio-biology and macro-economics but here referring to the fulfillment of *some* expectations concerning changes in accounting standards) as well as the notion of *institutional information* (based on more or less arbitrary institutional conventions)[5] play a prominent role. These authors, like Watts and Zimmerman, are strongly influenced by agency theory and exploit some of its basic ideas. By extending them to bond covenants, the authors regard institutional information parameters (e.g., a contractually required debt to owners' equity constraint of 2:1) as fulfilling a kind of "pricing function" between the firm and its bond-holders. It is then suggested that a change in the institutional information parameters, standards, and similar constraints will lead to a new equilibrium allocation and transfer of wealth among the parties who used the original parameters as a contractual basis. Since accounting standards are such parameters, the change of those standards may create considerable wealth transfers to be lobbied for or against, thus becoming a political issue. Hence Bryant and Thornton, in contrast to Watts and Zimmerman, seem to favour a *normative* approach when stating that "in our model, it is most definitely *not* the non-arbitrariness, the 'intrinsic correctness,' nor the 'economic reality' of these normative accounting theories that makes the institutional information based upon the theories useful or valuable but their *long-run endogeneity and logical consistency*." Bryant and Thornton also emphasize the importance of formulating a limited number of postulates or basic assumptions. Yet they fail to see that, between these assumptions and their ultimate application (which they unfortunately call "interpretation"), there are genuine *interpretations* that ought to be *part of the theory proper*, as repeatedly recommended by us.[6]

Further concerns of these authors are: (1) allowing for an *optimal transition period* in changing accounting standards; (2) the advocacy of different standards by different public accounting firms as being rooted in *product differentiation* rather than in the mere pandering to their clients' pecuniary advantages; and, (3) the deceptive couching of the *political* process of standard setting in *theoretical* terms. The last item seems to require clarification and resolution by openly recognizing the following: first, that accounting theory is a conditional *normative* framework that ought to provide different standards or models for different (political) goals; second, that the ultimate choice of a standard can never be an academic-theoretical one; lastly and most importantly, that the *matching* between model structure and goal, once theoretically confirmed, ought to offer sufficient public confidence and stability to supersede the kind of professional make-believe hinted at by these authors.[7]

Finally, Sunder and Haribhakti's short article analyzes the relation of the traditionally implied "truthfulness" of accounting statements to the facts of harsh reality, where standards are born under the pressure of vested interests. The authors regard this kind of "truthfulness" as being in the eyes of the beholder; they plead rather for an explicit recognition of the various conflicts and for a compromise that will be beneficial to society as a whole in the long run. They then discuss various means through which such a reasonable accounting policy may emerge, expressing the view that "strong technical standards, in absence of broad acceptance, carry seeds of their own ineffectiveness," and make a plea for reliance on market forces also in the standard setting process.[8] Sunder and Haribhakti finally argue in favour of standard setting bodies to specify "the economic conditions under which a particular accounting method would be the accounting standard." This comes close to the purpose-orientation of various accounting models previously suggested and nowadays materialized in the current value legislations of the United States and Canada.

R.M.

FOOTNOTES

[1] E.g., Sandra Felton, "Positive Thinking in Accounting Research," *CA Magazine* 115 (March 1982), pp. 60-64.

[2] Cf. R. Mattessich, *Instrumental Reasoning and Systems Methodology* (Dordrecht, Holland/Boston, Mass.: D. Reidel Co., 1978), pp. 260-299.

[3] *The Accounting Postulates and Principles Controversy of the 1960's* (New York: Garland Publishing, Inc., 1982).

[4] "Reflections on the State of Accounting Research and the Regulation of Accounting," *Price Waterhouse Lectures in Accounting* (Stanford University, 1976).

[5] Some twenty years ago, we expressed this idea in the following way: "Accounting and its effectivenes can be understood much better from a psychological than from a logical point of view. . . the effectiveness of traditional accounting lies not in the preciseness of information to management for maximizing profit or any other entrepreneurial goal, but in its authoritative character. The institution of control checks upon people and enables the depiction of the firm's financial structure in a simple and crude but overall model which constitutes a mighty bulwark against chaos." R. Mattessich, "Operations Research and Accounting: Competitors or Partners?" *The Quarterly Review of Economics and Business* (August 1962), pp. 7-14. Further remarks on *institutional facts as values* may be found in R. Mattessich, *Instrumental Reasoning and Systems Methodology* (Dordrecht, Holland/Boston, Mass.: D. Reidel Co., 1978/1980), pp. 48-52.

[6] E.g., R. Mattessich, "Methodological Preconditions and Problems of a General Theory of Accounting," *The Accounting Review* 47 (July 1972), pp. 469-487, especially pp. 471, 484-487.

[7] A related study by one of these authors, D.B. Thornton, *The Financial Reporting of Contingencies and Uncertainty: Theory and Practice,* ought to be mentioned in this connection; Vancouver: Canadian Certified General Accountants' Research Foundation, 1983.

[8] For further details on policy issues, see Lauren Kelly-Newton, *Accounting Policy Formulation — The Role of Corporate Management* (Reading, Mass.: Addison-Wesley Publ. Co., 1980).

We wish to thank members of the Finance Workshop at the University of Rochester, members of the Accounting Seminar at the University of Michigan and, in particular, George Benston, Ken Gaver, Nicholas Gonedes, Michael Jensen, Keith Leffler, Martin Geisel, Cliff Smith and an anonymous referee for their helpful suggestions.

ABSTRACT: This article provides the beginnings of a positive theory of accounting by exploring those factors influencing management's attitudes on accounting standards which are likely to affect corporate lobbying on accounting standards. Certain factors are expected to affect a firm's cashflows and in turn are affected by accounting standards. These factors are taxes, regulation, management compensation plans, bookkeeping costs, and political costs, and they are combined into a model which predicts that large firms which experience reduced earnings due to changed accounting standards favor the change. All other firms oppose the change if the additional bookkeeping costs justify the cost of lobbying. This prediction was tested using the corporate submissions to the FASB's Discussion Memorandum on General Price Level Adjustments. The empirical results are consistent with the theory.

TOWARDS A POSITIVE THEORY OF THE DETERMINATION OF ACCOUNTING STANDARDS*

*by Ross L. Watts
and Jerold L. Zimmerman*

ACCOUNTING standards in the United States have resulted from a complex interaction among numerous parties including agencies of the Federal government (notably the Securities and Exchange Commission and Treasury Department), state regulatory commissions, public accountants, quasi-public accounting standard-setting boards (the Committee on Accounting Procedures (CAP), the Accounting Principles Board (APB), and the Financial Accounting Standard Board (FASB)), and corporate managements. These parties have, in the past, and continue to expend resources to influence the setting of accounting standards. Moonitz [1974], Horngren [1973] and [1976], Armstrong [1976] and Zeff [1972] document the sometimes intense pressure exerted on the "private" accounting standard-setting bodies (i.e., CAP, APB,

*Reprinted from *The Accounting Review* 53 (January 1978): 112-134

FASB). These pressures have led to several reorganizations of the standard-setting boards.

Ultimately, we seek to develop a positive theory of the determination of accounting standards.[1] Such a theory will help us to understand better the source of the pressures driving the accounting standard-setting process, the effects of various accounting standards on different groups of individuals and the allocation of resources, and why various groups are willing to expend resources trying to affect the standard-setting process. This understanding is necessary to determine if prescriptions from normative theories (e.g., current cash equivalents) are feasible.

Watts [1974] and [1977] has started to develop such a theory. This paper expands on this initial work by focusing on the costs and benefits generated by accounting standards which accrue to managements, thereby contributing to our understanding of the incentives of management to oppose or support various standards. Management, we believe, plays a central role in the determination of standards. Moonitz supports this view:

> Management is central to any discussion of financial reporting, whether at the statutory or regulatory level, or at the level of official pronouncements of accounting bodies. [Moonitz, 1974, p. 64]

Hence, it seems appropriate that a precondition of a positive theory of standard-setting is understanding management's incentives.

The next section introduces those factors (e.g., tax, regulatory, political considerations) which economic theory leads us to believe are the underlying determinants affecting managements' welfare and, thereby, their decision to consume resources trying to affect the standard-setting process. Next, a model is presented incorporating these factors. The predictions of this model are then tested using the positions taken by corporations regarding the FASB's Discussion Memorandum on General Price Level Adjustments (GPLA). The last section contains the conclusions of the study.

FACTORS INFLUENCING MANAGEMENT ATTITUDES TOWARDS FINANCIAL ACCOUNTING STANDARDS

In this paper, we assume that individuals act to maximize their own utility. In doing so, they are resourceful and innovative.[2] The obvious implication of this assumption is that management lobbies on accounting standards based on its own self-interest. For simplicity, (since this is an early attempt to provide a positive theory) it could be argued that we should assume that management's self-interest on accounting standards is congruent with that of the shareholders. After all, that assumption has provided hypotheses consistent with the evidence in finance (e.g., the risk/return relationship of the various capital asset pricing models). However, one function of financial reporting is to constrain management to act in the shareholders' interest. (For example, see Benston [1975], Watts [1974], and Jensen and Meckling [1976a].) Consequently, assuming congruence of management and shareholder interests without further investigation may cause us to omit from our lobbying model important predictive variables. To reduce this possibility, we will examine next the effects of accounting standards on management's self-interest without the congruence assumption. The purpose of the examination is to identify factors which are likely to be important predictors of lobbying behavior so that we can include them in our formal model.

The assumption that management selects accounting procedures to maximize its own utility is used by Gordon [1964, p. 261] in an early attempt to derive a positive theory of accounting. There have been several attempts to test empirically Gordon's model, or variants of it, which we call the "smoothing" literature.[3] Problems in the specification of the empirical tests in the smoothing literature leave the Gordon model essentially unconfirmed.[4] Also, certain aspects of the Gordon model contribute to the model's lack of confirmation. Essentially, Gordon [1964] assumed that shareholder satisfaction (and, presumably, wealth) is solely a positive function of accounting income. This assumption avoids the conflict between shareholders and management by implying that increases in stock prices always accompany increases in accounting income. However, recent research casts serious doubt on the ability of management to manipulate directly share prices via changes in accounting procedures.[5]

We assume that management's utility is a positive function of the expected compensation in future periods (or wealth) and a negative function of the dispersion of future compensation (or wealth). The question is how do accounting standards affect management's wealth?[6] Management's total compensation from the firm consists of wages, incentive compensation (cash bonuses and stock or stock options), and nonpecuniary income, including perquisites (discussed in Jensen-Meckling, 1976a). Since it is unclear what role accounting standards play in the level of nonpecuniary income, we exclude it and focus on the first two forms of compensation. To the extent that management can increase either the level of incentive compensation or the firm's share price via its choice of accounting standards, they are made better off.

This analysis distinguishes between mechanisms which increase management's wealth: 1) via increases in share price (i.e., stock and stock options are more valuable) and 2) via increases in incentive cash bonuses. The choice of accounting standards can affect both of these forms of compensation indirectly through i) taxes, ii) regulatory procedures if the firm is regulated, iii) political costs, iv) information production costs, and directly via v) management compensation plans. The first four factors increase managerial wealth by increasing the cashflows and, hence, share price. The last factor can increase managerial wealth by altering the terms of the incentive compensation. Each of these five factors are discussed in turn.

FACTORS AFFECTING MANAGEMENT WEALTH[7]

Taxes. Tax laws are not directly tied to financial accounting standards except in a few cases (e.g., the last-in-first-out inventory valuation method). However, the indirect relationship is well documented Zeff [1972] and Moonitz [1974]. The adoption of a given procedure for financial accounting does not decrease the likelihood of that procedure's being adopted in future Internal Revenue codes, and more likely, will increase the chance of adoption. To the extent that management expects a proposed financial accounting procedure to influence future tax laws, their lobbying behavior is affected by the future tax law effects.

Regulation.[8] Most public utility commissions base their rate-setting formulas on accounting determined costs. A new accounting standard which reduces a utility's reported income may provide its management with an "excuse" to argue for increased rates. Whether the utility commission grants the increase depends on whether groups opposed to the rate increase (e.g., consumer groups) are able to exert political pressure on the commission.[9] This depends on such factors as information costs (to be discussed later). However, to the extent that there is some probability of a rate (and hence cashflow) increase (either temporary or permanent) as the result of an accounting standards change, utilities have an incentive to favor that change. Similarly, they have an incentive to oppose changes in accounting standards which might lead to a rate decrease.

Political Costs. The political sector has the power to effect wealth transfers between various groups. The corporate sector is especially vulnerable to these wealth redistributions. Certain groups of voters have an incentive to lobby for the nationalization, expropriation, break-up or regulation of an industry or corporation.[10] This in turn provides an incentive for elected officials to propose such actions. To counter these potential government intrusions, corporations employ a number of devices, such as social responsibility campaigns in the media, government lobbying and selection of accounting procedures to minimize reported earnings.[11] By avoiding the attention that "high" profits draw because of the public's association of high reported profits and monopoly rents, management can reduce the likelihood of adverse political actions and, thereby, reduce its expected costs (including the legal costs the firm would incur opposing the political actions). Included in political costs are the costs labor unions impose through increased demands generated by large reported profits.

The magnitude of the political costs is highly dependent on firm size.[12] Even as a percentage of total assets or sales, we would not expect a firm with sales of $100 million to generate the same political costs (as a percentage of sales) as a firm with $10 billion of sales. Casual empiricism suggests that Superior Oil Company (1974 sales of $333 million) incurs considerably less costs from anti-trust, "corporate responsibility," affirmative action, etc., than Exxon with sales of $42 billion.

Information Production (i.e., bookkeeping) Costs. Changes in accounting procedures are not costless to firms. Accounting standard changes which either increase disclosure or require corporations to change accounting methods increase the firms' bookkeeping costs (including any necessary increases in accountants' salaries to compensate for additional training).[13]

Management Compensation Plans. A major component of management compensation is incentive (bonus) plan income (Conference Board [1974]), and these plans are based on accounting income. Our survey of 52 firms in our sample indicates that the majority of the companies formally incorporate accounting income into the compensation plan.[14] Hence, a change in accounting standards which increase the firm's reported earnings would, *ceteris paribus*, lead to greater incentive income. But this would reduce the firm's cashflows and share prices would fall. As long as the per manager present value of the after tax incentive income is greater than the decline in each manager's portfolio, we would expect management to favor such an accounting change.[15] But this assumes that the shareholders and nonmanager directors do not oppose such an accounting change or do not adjust the compensation plans for the change in earnings.[16] In fact, the increased cashflows resulting from the political costs, regulatory process and tax effects of an accounting change assumes that various politicians/bureaucrats (i.e., the electorate) do not fully adjust for the change. A crucial assumption of our analysis is that the shareholders and nonmanaging directors have more incentive to adjust for and control increases in reported earnings due to changes in accounting standards than do politicians and bureaucrats.

INCENTIVES FOR VARIOUS GROUPS TO ADJUST FOR A CHANGE IN ACCOUNTING STANDARDS

An individual (whether a shareholder, nonmanaging director, or politician) will adjust a firm's accounting numbers for a change in accounting standards up to the point that the marginal cost of making the adjustment equals the marginal benefits. Consider the incentives of the outside directors to adjust bonus compensation plans due to a change in accounting standards. If these directors do not adjust the plans, management compensation rises and share price falls by the full discounted present value of the additional compensation.[17] Each outside director's wealth declines to the extent of his ownership in the firm and there is a greater chance of his removal from the board.[18]

If nonmanaging directors did not control management (including adjusting the compensation plans for changes in accounting standards), the decline in firm value offers incentives for an outsider or group to tender for control of the firm and install outside directors who will eliminate those managerial activities which are not in the best interest of the shareholders.[19] This group would then gain a proportionate share of the full capitalized value of the eliminated abuses (e.g., the present value of the incremental compensation resulting from the change in accounting standards). Therefore, the benefits for shareholders and nonmanaging directors to adjust compensation plans for changes in accounting standards are immediate and direct, if there is an efficient capital market for equity claims.

However, for the politicians and bureaucrats, our analysis suggests that the lack of a capital market which capitalizes the effects on the voters' future cashflows reduces the benefits accruing to the politicians of monitoring accounting standards, and the result is that they will perform less adjustments for changes in accounting standards.[20] For example, what are the benefits accruing to a utility regulator for adjusting a utility's accounting numbers for a change in standards? In the previous case of an outside director, the share price will fall by the discounted present value of the increased compensation resulting from an incomplete (or inaccurate) adjustment of the compensation plan. But if the regulator does not completely adjust for a change in accounting standards and allows the utility's rates to increase (resulting in a wealth transfer from consumers to the utility's owners), then the only cost the regulator is likely to incur is removal from office due to his incomplete adjustment. He incurs no direct wealth change. For small rate increases, the *per capita* coalition costs each consumer (or some group of consumers) would bear lobbying for the regulator's removal would vastly outweigh the small *per capita* benefits they would receive via lower regulated rates. Hence, rational consumers would not incur large monitoring costs of their regulators and other polticians (Downs [1957]; Alchian [1969]; and Alchian and Demsetz [1972]). Knowing this, it is not in the regulators' and politicians' interests as fully as if they were confronted with the same change in accounting standards to adjust changes in accounting standards in the role of outside directors or shareholders in the firm. The benefits of adjusting for changes in accounting standards are lower in the politcal sector than in the private sector.[21] Hence, there is a greater likelihood that a given accounting standard change will result in increased tax, regulatory, and political benefits than will the same change result in increased management compensation. For a given accounting standard change, managers should expect their own shareholders and outside directors to make a more complete adjustment than politicians.

Given this analysis, we predict that managers have greater incentives to choose accounting standards which report lower earnings (thereby increasing cashflows, firm value, and their welfare) due to tax, political, and regulatory considerations than to choose accounting standards which report higher earnings and, thereby, increase their incentive compensation. However, this prediction is conditional upon the firm being regulated or subject to political pressure. In small, (i.e., low political costs) unregulated firms, we would expect that managers do have incentives to select accounting standards which report higher earnings, if the expected gain in incentive compensation is greater than the foregone expected tax consequences. Finally, we expect management also to consider the accounting standard's impact on the firm's bookkeeping costs (and hence their own welfare).

The next section combines these five factors into a model of corporate lobbying standards.

A POSITIVE THEORY OF MANAGEMENT LOBBYING ON ACCOUNTING STANDARDS

Given a proposed accounting standard, management's position depends on the size of the firm (which affects the magnitude of the politcal costs) and whether the proposed standard increases or decreases the firm's reported earnings.[22] Figure 1 separates the standard's impact on earnings into decreases (1A) and increases (1B). The curve GB in Figure 1A (earnings decrease) denotes the proposed accounting standard's present value to management including the tax, regulatory, political, and compensation effects as a function of firm size. For small firms (below size E), not subject to much political pressure, these managers have an incentive to oppose the standard since their bonus compensation plans will have to be adjusted (a costly process), if their incomes are to remain unchanged by the new standard. Above size E, the political, regulatory, and tax benefits of reporting lower earnings due to the new standard are assumed to dominate the incentive compensation factor.

The benefits (costs) of a proposed accounting standard are expected to vary with the firm's size. This relationship can exist for two reasons: (1) the magnitude of the reported income change may be larger for larger firms and (2) for an income change of a given magnitude, the benefits (costs) vary with the firm size.[23] Hence, the present value of the stream of benefits (or costs) to the firm, GB, are an increasing function of firm size.[24]

Information production costs, curve IC, are also expected to vary to some extent with firm size due to the increased complexity and volume of the larger firm's accounting system. The difference

86

FIGURE 1

A Model of Firms' Submissions to the FASB

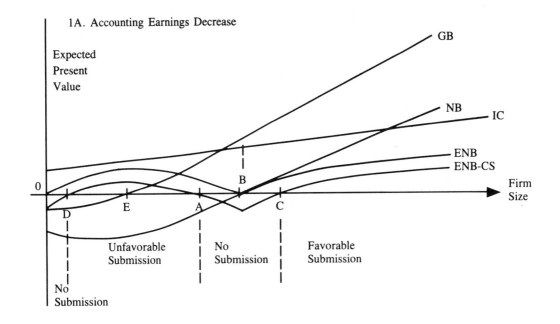

1A. Accounting Earnings Decrease

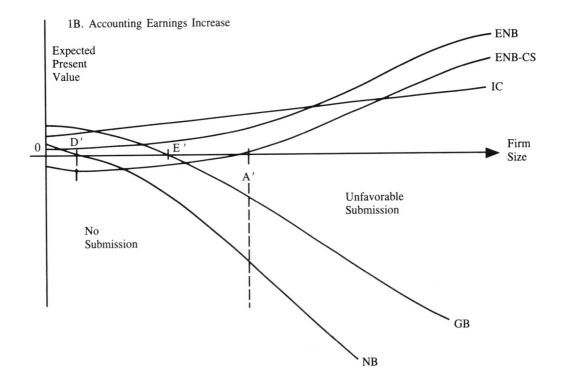

1B. Accounting Earnings Increase

between the gross benefits, GB, and the aditional information costs, IC, yields the net benefits curve, NB.

If the firm size is in the region OB, the net benefits curve, NB, is negative, and the firm will consider making an unfavorable submission to the FASB. Before the firm makes a submission, management holds beliefs regarding the likelihood the FASB will adopt the standard and the likelihood the FASB will adopt the standard if the firm makes an opposing submission.[25] The difference between these beliefs is the change in the adoption likelihood if management makes a negative submission. The product of this difference and the negative net benefits, NB, (i.e., the present value[26] of the cashflows arising from the five factors) is the expected present value of the net benefits curve, ENB. For example, a firm will incur negative net present value benefits of $100,000 if the standard is adopted. They believe the likelihood of adoption is .60. By making a negative submission to the FASB the likelihood falls to .59. The expected net present value of the benefits of the submission is then +$1000.

Firms larger than size B face positive net benefits if the standard is adopted. They will consider supporting the standard to the FASB, thereby increasing the standard's likelihood of adoption.[27] Hence, the expected net benefits curve is also positive beyond point B since it is the product of a positive net benefit and a positive change in the FASB's likelihood of adoption given a favorable submission.

If the cost of the submission is $CS, consisting primarily of the opportunity cost of the manager's time, then the total expected net benefits of a submission given the submission cost is a vertical downward shift in the ENB curve by the amount CS, ENB−CS. A firm will make a submission if ENB−CS is positive. This occurs in the regions DA, where opposing submissions occur, and beyond C, where favorable submissions are made. Between O and D and between A and C no submissions are made.

In *Figure 1B,* the proposed standard increases reported income. This case is similar to the previous one except the gross benefits are only positive for small firms where the management compensation plans are expected to dominate the tax, political, and regulatory factors. Beyond size E' gross benefits are negative since, for those firms, the income increases are expected to increase governmental interference (political costs), raise future tax payments, and lead the public utility commission to reduce the firm's revenues (if the firm is regulated). The net benefits curve is again the algebraic sum of GB (gross benefits) and IC (information costs) and the submission's expected net benefits less submission costs, ENB−CS, cuts the axis at A'. Accordingly, firms with asset sizes in the interval OA' make no submissions and firms of sizes beyond A' make unfavorable submissions.

When we consider the implications of both figures, we see that larger firms (firms larger than size C in *Figure 1*) will make favorable submissions if their incomes are decreased by the accounting standard, and unfavorable submissions if their incomes are increased. Smaller firms (firms smaller than size C in *Figure 1*) will either not submit or make unfavorable submissions.

While *Figures 1A* and *1B* reflect the general tendency of costs and benefits of an accounting standard to vary with firm size, there will be exceptions to this relationship. We have omitted variables, some of which we recognize. In particular, regulation costs borne by utilities depend not only on net income but also on operating earnings.[28] The effect of an accounting standard on operating earnings may vary with firm size.

The increment to a regulated firm's value of an accounting change which reduces operating earnings is increasing in firm size. Most public utility commissions set revenues according to the following type of equation:

$$\text{Revenues} = \text{Operating Expenses} + \text{Depreciation} + \text{Taxes} + r \cdot \text{Base} \quad (1)$$

where r is the accepted rate of return allowance on the investment base (usually the historic cost of net plant and working capital) [Haskins and Sells 1974.] Interest is not directly included in the rate-setting formula. The approach is to work on a return to total assets. Since all the terms on the right-hand side of equation (1) are highly correlated with firm size, any accounting standard that increases reported operating expenses, depreciation, or the recorded value of the asset base proportionally will, in general, result in an increase in the utility's revenues. And these increments to the utility's cashflows will, in general, be increasing in firm size.

When an accounting standard increases net income and decreases operating earnings of utilities, as does price-level adjustments [See Davidson and Weil, 1975b], we would not necessarily expect the relationship between management's attitude to the standard and firm size to be as we specified above (i.e., larger firms favoring or opposing the standard depending upon the effect on net income and smaller firms opposing the standard). As a consequence, we concentrate on testing that relationship for unregulated firms.

Another omitted variable is the political sensitivity of the firm's industry which clearly affects the political cost of an accounting standard change. We do not have a political theory which predicts which industries Congress singles out for wealth transfers. For example, why was the oil industry subject to intensive Congressional pressure in early 1974 and not the steel industry?[29] Consequently, we do not consider it formally in our model. As we shall see, political sensitivity has an impact on our results (only one steel company submitted on price-level accounting compared to seven oil companies submitting), but it does not eliminate the general relationship between firm size and management's accounting lobbying behavior.

EMPIRICAL TESTS

Data: On February 15, 1974, the FASB issued the discussion memorandum "Reporting the Effects of General Price-Level Changes in Financial Statements" and scheduled a public hearing on the topic for April 25, 1974. Public comments and position papers were solicited. One hundred thirty-three accounting firms, public corporations, industry organizations, and government agencies filed written comments.

We assume the submission indicates the position of corporate management. Clearly, this assumption could introduce some error into our tests. For example, some controllers of corporations may submit not because of corporate effects, but because they receive nonpecuniary income from the submission (e.g., if they are officers in their local chapter of the National Association of Accountants). However, we expect the error to be random. Ignoring this error biases our tests of management's attitudes on accounting standards towards rejecting the theory.

Almost all the corporations making submissions (49 out of 53) were New York Stock Exchange firms. Of the remaining four firms, one was listed on the American Stock Exchange, one was traded over the counter, and the other two were not traded. Of the 53 firms, 18 submitted opinions expressing favorable views on general price level adjustments whereas 34 expressed opinions ranging from strong objection to discussions of the merits of current costing to skepticism and feelings that GPLA was premature. These 34 were classified as opposing GPLA. For one firm, Transunion, an opinion could not be ascertained, and this firm was subsequently dropped from the sample. The firms making submissions and their position on the issue are listed in *Table 1*.

Once the sample of firms was identified from their submissions to the FASB, 1972 and 1973 financial data was obtained from the COMPUSTAT tape and the 1974 Moody Manuals. In addition, data on the existence of management incentive compensation plans was obtained by a questionnaire mailed to the chief financial officer of each firm. Missing data on the nonresponses (30 percent of the firms) was obtained from the firms' proxy statements and annual reports. If no mention of an incentive plan was found, we assumed the firm did not have one. Firms classified as having management incentive compensation plans based on accounting earnings[30] are denoted by an (M) in *Table 1*.

The precise impact of reported earnings on executive incentive compensation is difficult to estimate simply because the firm has such a plan. The most common procedure companies use is to take some fraction of reported earnings after deducting a return on invested capital as a pool out of which incentive compensation is paid. However, most companies do not pay out all of this pool each year. The important point, though, is that managers in firms with management compensation plans which report

Table I
Firms Making Submissions to the FASB on
General Price Level Adjustments*

Firms Advocating GPLA	Firms opposing GPLA
Regulated Firms	
AT&T	Aetna Life & Casualty (M)
Commonwealth Edison	Commerce Bank of Kansas City
Consumer Power (M)	Liberty Corporation (M)
Detroit Edison	Northeast Utilities
Duke Power	Peoples Gas
Indiana Telephone	Southern Natural Resources (M)
Iowa Illinois Gas & Electric	Pennzoil
Northwestern Telephone	Texas Eastern Transmission (M)
Southern Company	Texas Gas Transmission
Unregulated Firms	
Exxon (M)	Continental Oil (M)
Gulf Oil (M)	Standard Oil of Indiana (M)
Shell Oil (M)	Texaco (M)
Standard Oil of California (M)	Rockwell International (M)
Caterpillar Tractor	United Aircraft (M)
Dupont E. I. DeNemours (M)	Automated Building Components
General Motors (M)	Copeland Corporation (M)
Ford Motor Company (M)	General Electric (M)
Marcor (M)	General Mills (M)
	Gillette
	W.R. Grace (M)
	Harsco (M)
	Inland Steel (M)
	International Harvester (M)
	American Cyanamid (M)
	IT&T (M)
	Eli Lilly & Co. (M)
	Masonite (M)
	Merck (M)
	Owens-Illinois, Inc. (M)
	Reliance Electric (M)
	Seagrams Sons, Inc. (M)
	Sears Roebuck (M)
	Texas Instruments (M)
	Union Carbide (M)

*Transunion Corporation made a submission, but they did not state a position on GPLA. It made two technical comments.
M denotes the firm has a management compensation plan.

higher adjusted earnings will not suffer a decline in their incentive compensation and it may actually increase their compensation (depending on the monitoring by the outside directors).

Methodology

The FASB's General Price Level Adjustment (GPLA) standard would require supplementary price adjusted statements. Even though the supplementary statements will not replace conventional reports, users of the information will obviously make comparisons [See Ijiri, 1976] and if adjusted income is above (below) unadjusted income, we expect our previous reasoning to hold, and we assume the effect is the same as an increase (decrease) in reported income.

A price-level adjusted income figure does not exist for all firms in our sample. Since only a few firms voluntarily published GPLA statements, income proxies must be constructed. Fortunately, a previous series of studies by Davidson and Weil (1975a and 1975b) and Davidson, Stickney, and Weil (1976) developed an adjusting procedure which relies solely on published financial statements and GNP deflators. Using either their published figures for 1973 financial statements or using their procedures, we were able to obtain estimates of the direction of change in reported price-level income.[31]

In addition to using the Davidson and Weil results or procedures, we constructed proxy variables based on unadjusted depreciation and net monetary assets. Both of these variables have a direct negative impact on GPLA earnings (i.e., the larger depreciation or net monetary assets, the lower the adjusted income and the smaller or more negative the difference between GPLA adjusted income and unadjusted income). If we assume that our sample of firms has the same age distribution of depreciable property, then (cross-sectionally) depreciation and net monetary assets can serve as a surrogate for the effect of GPLA earnings.[32] Those numbers are readily available for our sample.

Davidson and Weil [1975c] also estimate the effect of GPLA on income for 1974 (which was in the future at the time of the submissions). Even though the adjustment procedure was slightly different, only two of our 19 firms in the combined samples reverse the direction of the income effect between 1973 and 1974. Similarly, all of the utilities (24), and 35 of the 50 other companies in their sample have income effects of the same sign in both years. Since the effects of income changes in the immediate future are less heavily discounted, these results suggest that the error introduced by our assumption of stationary income changes is not likely to be severe.

Tests of the Theory

In the reported tests, we use asset size as the surrogate for firm size.[33] Based on our model, we can make predictions about the relationship between asset size and firm submissions. We predict that firms whose earnings are increased by GPLA will oppose GPLA regardless of their size (i.e., there will be no association between size and submission). However, for firms whose earnings are decreased by GPLA, we predict that they will either support GPLA or will not make a submission depending on where asset size C (*Figure 1*) occurs in their industry. Since we cannot determine the asset size corresponding to point C, we are in a position analogous to being able to predict the sign of a regression coefficient but not its magnitude. Consequently, our test of the model does not include asset size C (analogous to the magnitude of the coefficient). The test is only of the prediction that there is a positive relationship between asset size and submission for firms with income decreases.

Firms making submissions were classified according to the direction of change in their net income and ranked by their asset size *(Table 2)*. Of the 26 firms with income decreases, eight voted yes and 18 no.[34] The eight yes votes came from the larger firms, thus supporting our prediction. To test the null hypothesis that the eight firms which voted yes are drawn from the same population of firms (with respect to size) as the 18 that voted no, we performed a Mann-Whitney U test. Our tables indicate that we can reject the null hypothesis at the .001 level.[35]

Of the eight firms with income increases or no changes in net income, seven voted no. Thus, the general tendency of these firms is to vote no as predicted by our model.

Table 2

Asset Size, Direction of Earnings Effect and Corporate Position on GPLA

Rank on Asset Size	Firm	Rank in Fortune 500 (1973)	Corporate Position, Classified by Earnings Change†	
			Increase or no change	Decrease
1	Exxon	1		Yes
2	General Motors	2		Yes
3	Texaco	3	No	
4	Ford	4		Yes
5	Sears Roebuck (Rank 1 in retail sales)	7		No
6	IT&T	8	No	
7	Gulf Oil	9		Yes
8	Standard Oil of California	10		Yes
9	General Electric	11	No	
10	Standard Oil of Indiana	12		No
11	Shell Oil	16		Yes
12	Dupont E.I. Nemours	18		Yes
13	Union Carbide	22		No
14	Continental Oil	26		No
15	Marcor (Rank 2 in retail firms)	33	Yes	
16	International Harvester	34		No
17	Caterpillar Tractor	47		Yes
18	Rockwell International	54	No	
19	W.R. Grace	55	No	
20	Owens-Illinois	80	No	
21	Inland Steel	85		No
22	American Cyanamid	92		No
23	United Aircraft	107		No
24	Seagrams Sons Inc.	108		No
25	Eli Lilly & Co.	135		No
26	Merck	143		No
27	General Mills	156	No	
28	Texas Instruments	164		No
29	Gillette	167		No
30	Reliance Electric	332		No
31	Harsco	368		No
32	Masonite	386		No
33	Automated Building Components	Not Ranked		No
34	Copeland Corporation	Not Ranked		No

Point C*———— (between rows 12 and 13)

* Point C in Figure 1 is determined by minimizing the number of misclassifications.
† Yes = Favored GPLA
  No = Opposed GPLA

The results in *Table 2* are consistent with the implications of our model including our assumption that the management compensation factor is dominated by political and tax considerations. Of the 31 unregulated firms with management compensation plans, eight had increases or no change in income and 23 had decreases in income as a result of price-level adjustments. If management compensation dominates tax and political factors, then firms with increases in income would be more likely to support price-level adjustments than firms with decreases. In fact, the reverse is true. The frequency of firms with income decreases which support price-level adjustment is seven out of 23 (30 percent) while the frequency of firms with income increases that support price-level adjustments is one out of eight (12.5 percent).

The above results support the relationship between management's attitudes on GPLA and firm size for the 23 unregulated firms. However, if we assume that firm size and the direction of the income change are indepedent (*Table 2* supports this assumption), then (if there is no size effect) the average size of firms supporting GPLA should be the same as the average size of firms opposing. Thus we can use the voting behavior of all 52 firms in our sample to test the size relationship.

Table 3 presents the median rank on asset size for both regulated and unregulated firms favoring and opposing GPLA. The median rank in the *Fortune* 500 of the nine unregulated firms supporting GPLA is 10. The median rank of the 25 unregulated firms opposing GPLA is 92.

TABLE 3

MEDIAN RANKS OF FIRM SIZE BY REGULATION AND
POSITION ON GPLA*

	Regulated (N = 18)		Unregulated (N = 34)	
	In Favor (9)	Against (9)	In Favor (9)	Against (25)
Median Rank	13	38	10	92

*Fortune [May and July, 1974].

For regulated firms, there also appears to be a relationship between size and management attitudes. The net incomes for all the utilities investigated by Davidson and Weil [1975b] are increased by GPLA suggesting none of the utilities should favor GPLA. However, as noted in the preceding section, operating earnings are relevant to rate determination. Those earnings fall for all the utilities investigated by Davidson and Weil [1975b] and this could explain why relatively larger regulated firms favor GPLA.

If we assume our model is correct and that asset size C is the same for all industries, we can estimate C by minimizing the number of prediction errors (analogous to estimating a regression coefficient by minimizing the sum of squared errors). This estimate provides information on the relative importance of political and/or tax costs for different size firms. Given the data, C is between the 18th and 22nd largest firms in the *Fortune* 500 in 1973 (see *Table 2*). This suggests that reduced political and/or tax costs outweigh information production and/or management compensation factors in determining management's position on GPLA only for very large firms. For most other firms, information production costs dominate.

Are the major benefits of reporting lower adjusted incomes derived from tax or political considerations? It is very difficult to differentiate between these two factors, but one possible way is the following. Is the change in adjusted income proportional to firm size? If it is, then both the tax and political factors may be operating. But if there is no association between firm size and the magnitude of the income change, then the tax effect cannot explain why larger firms favor GPLA. Therefore, this result could only be due to political costs. We can obtain estimates of the income effect of GPLA for 11 of the firms whose incomes would be reduced by GPLA (six supporting, five opposing).[36] The average reduction in income for the six firms which supported GPLA is $177.7 million, while the average reduction for the five which opposed GPLA is $38.5 million. Thus, it appears that the income change does vary with size and the preceding results are consistent with both the tax and political costs affecting management's attitudes.

The preceding results test only whether the size effect exists for firms which did submit to the FASB. It is interesting to examine the effect of GPLA on firms which did not submit. In particular, the firms of asset size above our estimated C which did not submit are of interest since our model predicts they would submit on the basis of the income effect. Dupont is the last firm above asset size C in *Table 2* to vote. It is ranked 18th in the *Fortune* 500 in 1973. There are seven firms ranked higher than 18th which did not make a submission to the FASB. They are IBM (ranked 5th), General Telephone (6th), Mobil Oil (7th), U.S. Steel (13th), Chrysler (14th), Tenneco (15th), and Atlantic Richfield (17th).

The size of the income change is crucial to determining why these seven firms did not submit. If changes are not associated with firm size, the expected benefits of a submission could be very small and may not exceed the submission costs. Unfortunately, Davidson and Weil only estimated the change in earnings in 1973 for three of these seven firms: IBM, U.S. Steel, and Chrysler. All three have income reductions with GPLA and their average reduction is $88 million. This is less than the average reduction for the six firms with income reductions which did submit ($177 million), but it is not trivial. Further, the reductions for two of the three nonsubmissions (IBM and General Telephone) exceed the reductions for four of the six submissions. Consequently, it is difficult to attribute the fact that the three firms did not submit to the lack of an income effect.[37]

In summary, these tests confirm the relationship between size and management attitudes on GPLA. Political costs and, perhaps, tax effects influence management's attitudes on accounting standards. Although we are not able to explain some of the notable nonsubmitting firms' decisions, we would point out that most of the firms submitting are large, and the likelihood of submission increases with asset size (12 of the 18 firms ranked 1-18 in the Fortune 500 submitted, four of the 18 firms ranked 19-36 submitted, two of the 18 firms ranked 37-54 submitted, one of the 18 firms ranked 55-72 submitted, etc.).

Discriminant Analysis

The preceding tests were based on the direction of the earnings change, not the magnitude of the change. A discriminant analysis is conducted including management compensation, depreciation, and net monetary assets as independent variables, and using data on 49 of the 53 firms making submissions to ensure consistency of the Davidson and Weil procedures.

The change in price-adjusted income is correlated with the magnitudes of depreciation and net monetary assets. The larger both of these variables in unadjusted terms, the larger will be the decline (in absolute dollars) in adjusted net income. We do not perform an actual price-level adjustment, but rely on the unadjusted magnitude of depreciation and net monetary assets.

The general form of the discriminant function we estimate is[38]

$$P_i = \alpha_1 + \alpha_2 \frac{DEP_i}{MKTVL_i} + \alpha_2 \frac{NMA_i}{MKTVL_i} + \alpha_3 (SALES_i) CHG_i$$

$$+ \alpha_4 \left(\frac{SALES_i}{TSALES_i} \right) CHG_i + \alpha_5 MCOMP_i + \alpha_6 REG_i$$

where

$$p_i = \begin{cases} \dfrac{\text{Number of opposing firms}}{\text{Total firms in sample}} & \text{if the } i^{th} \text{ firm favored GPLA} \\[2ex] \dfrac{\textit{Number of supporting firms}}{\textit{Total firms in sample}} & \textit{if the } i^{th} \textit{ firm opposed GPLA} \end{cases}$$

$MKTVL_i$ = the market value of the firm's equity (number of common shares outstanding $\times$ average share price)

$$REG_i = \begin{cases} 1 & \text{if the } i^{th} \text{ firm was regulated} \\ 0 & \text{otherwise} \end{cases}$$

$$MCOMP_i = \begin{cases} 1 & \text{if the } i^{th} \text{ firm had a management incentive scheme} \\ 0 & \text{otherwise} \end{cases}$$

DEP_i = unadjusted depreciation expense in 1973 for the ith firm

NMA_i = net monetary asset position in 1973 for the ith firm

$$CHG_i = \begin{cases} +1 & \text{if price-level adjusted income is below unadjusted income or if the firm is regulated} \\ -1 & \text{if price-level adjusted income is above unadjusted income} \\ 0 & \text{otherwise} \end{cases}$$

$SALES_i$ = Sales of the ith firm

$TSALES_i$ = Total sales of the Compustat firms with the same SIC code as firm i.

$\dfrac{SALES_i}{TSALES_i}$ = a proxy variable for market share

Table 4 presents the results of various functional forms of equation (2) fitted over various subsets of the data.[39] The first two terms,

$$\frac{NMA}{MKTVL} \text{ and } \frac{DEP}{MKTVL},$$

normalize the unadjusted figures by the market value of the equity[40] and the estimated coefficients measure the extent to which an increase in relative depreciation or net monetary assets affect voting

Table 4

Discriminant Analysis

Coefficients (t-statistics)

Model Number	N	Sample	Constant	DEP/ MKTVL	NMA/ MKTVL	SALES × CHG	SALES TSALES × CHG	MCOMP	REG	R^2	Yates Adjusted Chi Square*
1	49	total sample	−.0241 (−.12)	122.6 (.60)	−38.9 (−1.62)	.000044 (3.67)	−.4131 (−1.11)	−.2355 (−1.42)	−.3443 (−1.29)	.358	9.25
2	49	total sample	−.0855 (−.44)	160.4 (.79)	−14.2 (−.98)	.000043 (3.53)	−.4381 (−1.17)	−.1619 (−1.03)		.332	9.25
3	49	total sample	−.0973 (−.50)	143.0 (.70)	−15.6 (−1.07)	.000034 (3.58)		−.1601 (−1.02)		.311	9.25
4	34	unregulated firms	.0431 (.19)	74.0 (.27)	−36.5 (−1.06)	.000044 (3.58)	−.3271 (−.89)	−.2186 (−.89)		.366	19.96
5	34	unregulated firms	.0412 (.18)	86.2 (.32)	−35.3 (−1.03)	.000038 (3.73)		−.2335 (−.96)		.347	13.16
6	49	total sample	−.0079 (−.04)	215.3 (1.09)		.000033 (3.44)		−.2365 (−1.39)	.0077 (.05)	.293	11.74
7	49	total sample	−.0662 (−1.03)			.000033 (3.44)				.201	5.98

* The Yates correction for continuity is useful in estabishing a lower bound on the χ^2 statistic.

behavior. These coefficients, which should capture the tax effects, are predicted to be positive under that hypothesis (the larger the depreciation and net monetary assets the greater the decline in adjusted income and the greater the tax benefits).

The sign on normalized depreciation is as predicted, but normalized net monetary assets is of the wrong sign. One of the following three hypotheses explain this result: the tax effect is only operating via depreciation;[41] depreciation and net monetary assets, being inversely related (correlation coefficient ranging from $-.41$ to $-.55$), are entering the regression with opposite signs; or the tax effect is not an explanatory factor. Since our sample is very small, it is not possible to use a holdout subset to distinguish between these hypotheses.

The next two variables,

$$(\text{SALES}) \text{ CHG and } \left(\frac{\text{SALES}}{\text{TSALES}}\right) \text{CHG},$$

are proxies for political costs. These two variables assume that political costs are symmetric for both earnings increases and decreases. The multiplicative dummy, CHG, is positive if earnings decline (based on the Davidson-Weil [1975a] results) or if the firm is regulated.[42]

The sign on SALES × CHG is as predicted, positive, and in addition has the highest t-statistic of all the independent variables. In addition, the coefficient on SALES × CHG is the most stable coefficient across various realizations and subsamples which leads us to conclude that firm size is the most important variable. The sign of

$$\frac{\text{SALES}}{\text{TSALES}} \times \text{CHG}$$

is of the wrong sign. But this is probably due to the crude metric of market share,

$$\frac{\text{SALES}}{\text{TSALES}},$$

this variable is attempting to measure.[43] When the market share proxy is eliminated, the model's predictive ability is not impaired.

MCOMP, a dummy variable for management compensation schemes is expected to have a negative sign regardless of the change in earnings. Prior research indicates that executive compensation is more highly associated with operating income (which includes depreciation) than net income (which includes gains/losses on monetary assets).[44] Therefore, MCOMP is not multiplied by CHG. The sign of MCOMP being negative is consistent with our predictions.

If the firm is regulated, the dummy variable, REG, is one. Regulated firms' price-level adjusted operating incomes decline, unambiguously, and therefore these firms should tend to favor GPLA if the regulatory factor is operating. Yet, the sign of the coefficient of REG is negative in Model 1. This sign is negative because REG is inversely related to

$$\text{MCOMP and } \frac{\text{NMA}}{\text{MKTVL}}$$

(correlation coefficients of $-.60$ and $-.86$ respectively). When

$$\frac{\text{NMA}}{\text{MKTVL}}$$

is deleted from the model (Model 6), the sign of REG reverses, the importance of

$$\frac{DEP}{MKTVL}$$

increases, and the discriminatory power of the model improves from a Chi-Square of 9.25 to 11.74. However, the multicolinearity between

$$REG, MCOMP, \text{ and } \frac{NMA}{MKTVL}$$

precludes our drawing any conclusions regarding the impact of management compensation or regulation on lobbying behavior.

Models 4 and 5 are fitted using only the unregulated firms (N=34). REG and then

$$\frac{SALES}{TSALES} \times CHG$$

have been deleted. The R^2 statistic still remains high and the Yates adjusted Chi Square is significant at the 1 percent level. In fact, Model 4 correctly classifies the voting behavior for 32 out of the 34 firms.

The constant should be capturing the partial effect of information production costs after controlling for the other factors. When the total sample is used in the estimation, the constant is negative as expected. When the regulated firms are exluded, the constant is positive. But in all models the constant is close to zero.

The estimated discriminant functions are consistent with the tests of the theory. All of the discriminant functions are statistically significant and the intervening variable driving these findings is firm size. In fact, firm size explains over half the explained variance in voting behavior (Model 7).

These results are consistent with those using the Davidson and Weil findings. The discriminant functions indicate that the political cost factor is more important than the tax factor in affecting management's attitudes.

The major empirical problem in the discriminant analysis is the rather small sample size which precludes using a holdout sample and, furthermore, does not allow more sophisticated econometric techniques to control for the multicolinearity. Hence, it is difficult to control for the interaction between the underlying factors. However, these preliminary results are encouraging and suggest that additional research in this area is warranted.

SUMMARY AND CONCLUSIONS

We have focused in this paper on the question of why firms would expend resources trying to influence the determination of accounting standards. The histories of the Committee on Accounting Procedures, the Accounting Principles Board, and FASB are replete with examples of managements and industries exerting political pressure on the standard-setting bodies.

A possible answer to this question is provided by the government intervention argument, namely, that firms having contact (actual or potential) with governments, directly through regulation (public utility commissions, Interstate Commerce Commission, Civil Aeronautics Board, etc.) or procurement, or indirectly through possible governmental intervention (antitrust, price controls, etc.), can affect their future cashflows by discouraging government action through the reporting of lower net incomes. The empirical evidence with respect to the position 52 firms took before the FASB on price level restatements is consistent with respect to this hypothesis.

The single most important factor explaining managerial voting behavior on General Price Level Accounting is firm size (after controlling for the direction of change in earnings). The larger firms, *ceteris paribus*, are more likely to favor GPLA (if earnings decline). This finding is consistent with our government intervention argument since the larger firms are more likely to be subjected to governmental interference and, hence, have more to lose than smaller corporations.

The existence of costs generated by government intervention may have more fundamental and important effects on the firm's decisions than just its lobbying behavior on financial accounting standards. Not only would we expect the firm to manage its reported earnings, but also to alter its investment-production decisions if the potential costs of government interference become large. For example, government intervention costs may lead the firm to select less risky investments in order to eliminate the chance of high returns which then increase the likelihood of government intervention. If the total risk of these less risky investments tends to be positively correlated with the systematic risk of the firm, then we would expect the beta (the estimate of the covariance between the return on the stock and the market return normalized by the variance of the market) on the common stock to be significantly below one (average risk) for those firms facing large government intervention costs. The evidence from the sample of firms making submissions to the FASB on GPLA is consistent with this hypothesis. The average β is .67. Furthermore, firms favoring GPLA tend to have lower betas than the firms in opposition.[45]

Our findings, in a preliminary extension of these results, tend to confirm the decline in systematic risk as firm size increases and as government intervention costs rise. These tentative findings are suggestive of fertile research possibilities of examining the effects of politically motivated factors on the maximizing behavior of firms' managements and shareholders.

We believe that the general findings in this paper, if confirmed by other studies, have important implications for the setting of financial accounting standards in a mixed economy. As long as financial accounting standards have potential effects on the firm's future cashflows, standard setting by bodies such as the Accounting Principles Board, the Financial Accounting Standards Board, or the Securities and Exchange Commission will be met by corporate lobbying. The Committee on Accounting Procedures and the Accounting Principles Board could not withstand the pressure. The former Chairman of the FASB also has complained of the political lobbying, and the FASB has been forced to defer the controversial GPLA topic. The SEC has, until recently, avoided direct involvement in the setting of accounting standards. One could hypothesize that this was in their own interest. By letting the American Institute of Certified Public Accountants be the scapegoat, the Securities and Exchange Commission could maintain their "credibility" with Capitol Hill and the public.

FOOTNOTES

[1] See Jensen [1976] and Horngren [1976].

[2] Many economic models assume a rather limited version of economic man. In particular, they assume that man maximizes his own welfare when he is constrained to play by certain rules and in certain institutional settings, ignoring his incentives to avoid or change the rules, setting, etc. Meckling [1976] analyzes this issue.

[3] Ball and Watts [1972]; Barefield and Comiskey [1972]; Barnea, Ronen and Sadan [1975]; Beidleman [1973]; Copeland [1968]; Cushing [1969]; Dasher and Malcom [1970]; Gordon [1964]; Gordon, Horwitz and Meyers [1966].

[4] For these defects see Ball and Watts [1972], Gonedes [1972] and Gonedes and Dopuch [1974].

[5] Fama [1970] and Gonedes and Dopuch [1974]. Further, the results of studies by Kaplan and Roll [1972], Ball [1972] and Sunder [1975] which address the specific issue support the hypothesis that the stock market can discriminate between real events and changes in accounting procedures. Given that the market can on average discriminate, then it must be concluded that managers (on average) expect the market to discriminate. Obviously, managers do and will attempt to influence their share price by direct accounting manipulation, but if these attempts consume resources, then incentives exist to eliminate these inefficient allocations.

[6] For earlier discussions of this question see Watts [1974] and Gonedes [1976].

[7] We have purposefully excluded from the set of factors being examined the information content effect of an accounting standard on stock prices. We have done this because at present the economic theories of informa-

tion and capital market equilibrium are not sufficiently developed to allow predictions to be made regarding the influence of an accounting standard on the capital market's assessment of the distributions of returns (see Gonedes and Dopuch, 1974). We believe that a theory of the determination of accounting standards can be developed and tested ignoring the information content factor. If at some future date, the information content factor can be specified and included in the theory, then the predictions and our understanding of the process will be improved. But we see no reason to delay the development of a theory until information content is specified.

8   We deal in this paper with public utility regulation and the forms of rate regulation employed. Other industries (e.g., banking and insurance) are regulated differently and these industries are ignored in this paper to simplify the analysis.

9   For the economic theory of regulation upon which this discussion is based see Stigler [1971], Posner [1974] and Peltzman [1975]. Also, Horngren [1976].

10 Stigler [1971], Peltzman [1975], and Jensen and Meckling [1976b]. An example of an industry facing such action is the oil industry.

11 For an alleged example of this, see Jack Anderson, Syndicated Column, United Features (New York, April 10, 1976).

12 Several studies document the association between size and anti-trust [Siegfried 1975]. In proposed anti-trust legislation, size *per se* has been mentioned specifically as a criterion for action against corporations. See the "Curse of Bigness," *Barron's*, June 30, 1969, pp. 1 and 8. Also see a bill introduced into the Senate by Senator Bayh (U.S. Congress, Senate, Subcommittee on Anti-trust and Monopoly (1975), pp. 5-13) would require divestiture for oil firms with annual production and/or sales above certain absolute numbers. In the hearings on that bill, Professor Mencke of Tufts University argued that absolute and not relative accounting profits are the relevant variable for explaining political action against corporations.

   Mencke said, "Nevertheless, precisely because the actions of large firms are so visible, the American public has always equated absolute size with monopoly power. The major oil companies are among the very largest and most visible companies doing business in the United States.

   Huge accounting profits, but not high profit rates, are an inevitable corollary of large absolute firm size. This makes these companies obvious targets for public criticism." (U.S. Congress, Senate, Subcommittee on Anti-trust and Monopoly (1976), p. 1893).

13 We are assuming that any change in accounting standards does not reduce the firm's information production costs. Although there may be cases where a firm is using a costly procedure which is eliminated by a simpler, cheaper procedure, information production costs in this case may decline, but we expect these situations to be rare.

14 The frequency is 69 percent.

15 At this early stage in the development of the theory, we assume that management of the firm is composed of homogeneous (i.e., identical) individuals to simplify the problem.

16 Our examination of the description of 16 management compensation plans indicated that all the plans were administered by the nonmanaging directors.

17 Likewise, we would expect the outside directors to adjust the incentive compensation targets in those circumstances when it is in the shareholders' interest to report lower earnings (e.g., LIFO), thereby not reducing the managers' incentive via bonus earnings to adopt LIFO.

18 Our analysis indicates that outside (nonmanaging) directors are "efficient" monitors of management. Watts [1977]. If this were not the case, the capital market would quickly discount the presence of outside directors. As far as we can determine, firms are not required by the New York Stock Exchange listing requirements or Federal regulations to have outside directors. Paragraph 2495G of Commerce Clearing House, Volume 2, New York Stock Exchange encourages listed firms to appoint outside directors. "Full disclosure of corporate affairs for the information of the investing public is, of course, normal and usual procedure for listed companies. Many companies have found this procedure has been greatly aided by having at least two outside directors whose functions on the board would include particular attention to such matters." This listing statement is consistent with our observation that outside directors provide monitoring benefits.

19 This assumes, of course, that such takeovers earn a fair rate of return net of transactions costs.

20 See Zimmerman [1977] and Watts [1977] for further discussion of this issue.

21 It could also be argued that politicians and regulators have a higher marginal cost of adjusting than do shareholders, nonmanaging directors, and other capital market participants since the former group does not necessarily have a comparative advantage of adjusting financial statements, whereas, existing capital market participants probably have a comparative advantage at such activities.

22 The expected effect of an accounting standard could vary over time (i.e., it could increase current reported income and decrease some future reported income). In that case, the analysis is slightly more complex, but the criterion is still the same (i.e., the effect on the manager's wealth). However, for simplicity, the remainder of the paper refers to standards increasing or decreasing reported income as though the whole time series of future income shifts up or down.

23 Whether the magnitude of the income change does vary with firm size depends on the particular accounting

standard in question. For certain accounting standards (e.g., requiring all firms to report depreciation based on current replacement costs) it is apparent *a priori* that there will be a correlation between the income change and firm size. For other standards (e.g., general price level accounting) *a priori*, it is not obvious that a relationship will exist (e.g., net monetary gains may offset depreciation in larger firms). However, since political costs depend on firm size then we expect the benefits (costs) of standard changes to vary with firm size. For example, if all firms' earnings decline by $1 million (due to a standards change) then we would expect larger firms to incur larger benefits since the likelihood of anti-trust actions are expected to be associated with firm size.

[24] We would expect firms in different industries to be subject to different political pressures, tax structures, and regulation. Hence, Figure 1 is developed for firms in the same industry that only differ by size.

[25] In this situation, it is possible that management will lobby on an accounting standard because of secondary (or gaming) effects (i.e., vote trading thereby influencing subsequent FASB pronouncements). We chose not to introduce gaming because it complicates the model and such complication is only justified if it improves or is likely to improve the empirical results. We are able to predict corporate behavior without considering gaming, and we do not consider it likely to improve these results.

[26] The firm is discounting the future cashflows with the appropriate, risk-adjusted discount rate. Furthermore, we are assuming that this discount rate is not increasing in firm size which is consistent with the available evidence.

[27] We are assuming that the likelihood of the FASB adopting the standard, if the firm makes a submission is independent of firm size. This is unrealistic since large firms, we expect, would have more influence with the Board. However, inclusion of this additional dependency does not change the results: in fact, it strengthens the predictions.

[28] Operating earnings, although explicitly defined by each public utility commission, are generally, utility revenues less operating expenses, including depreciation but excluding interest and taxes. We assume that the adoption of GPLA would mean that price-adjusted depreciation would affect operating earnings while the gain or loss on monetary assets would be treated like interest and would only affect net income.

[29] This does not mean we do not have any ideas as to which variables are important. For example, in the case of consumer goods industries, we suspect that the relative price change of the product is important.

[30] If the firm had an incentive plan, but it was not tied to reported earnings then this firm was coded as not having an incentive plan (Gillette).

[31] 1973 was a period of high inflation. If firms based their FASB lobbying position on the price adjustments produced by high unexpected inflation without considering more "typical" years, then this would introduce errors into the data and finding a statisically significant result becomes more difficult. If these errors are systematic with respect to firm size, then our results could be biased. We do not expect this to be the case. To control partially for this, statistical tests are performed which are independent of the magnitude of the price change. Net monetary assets in 1973 may still be abnormally small (large) due to the high rate of inflation, but these preliminary tests suggest that our results are not dependent upon 1973 being atypical.

[32] The assumption that the age distribution of depreciable property is the same across our firms is reasonable. The firms who submitted to the FASB on the GPLA issue, generally, were large, capital-intensive and long-established firms. Moreover, the results using these surrogates are consistent with the results using Davidson and Weil's estimates.

[33] In this case, firm size is measured by the firm's *Fortune* 500 rank in assets. The results are identical when rank in sales is used. Furthermore, the intent of government intervention depends on the metric used by the courts, legislators, and regulators. Market share, concentration and size are among the commonly used indicators. Absolute size is important in explaining government regulation for both theoretical and empirical reasons. An implication of Peltzman's (1975, p. 30) theory of regulation is that the amount of wealth redistributed from firms by government intervention is a positive function of economies of scale. Since we expect large firm size to indicate the presence of economies of scale, implication of Peltzman's theory is that government intervention will be greater for larger firms. Empirically, we observe numerous cases of politicians and regulators echoing the conventional wisdom of certain segments in society, that big business is inherently bad. (See, "Curse of Big Business," *Barron's* June 16, 1969 and footnote 12).

[34] We use the term "vote" to mean responding to a discussion memorandum by issuing a corporate opinion.

[35] Siegel [1956], p. 274. Even after any reasonable adjustment for the degrees of freedom lost due to previous statistical analysis, this result is still significant.

An intuitive idea of the strength of the relationship between management's attitude and firm size can be obtained by considering an analogy. Suppose we put 26 balls in an urn representing the firms with earnings decreases; eight red balls representing the firms that voted yes; and 18 black balls, representing the firms that voted no. Now, we randomly draw 13 balls out of the urn without replacement representing the largest 13 firms (out of the 26). The probability that we draw eight red balls (analogous to the probability of the eight firms voting yes being the "large" firms if the null hypothesis of no association between votes and size is correct) is .001. If the votes of firms are not independent, as in the case of gaming, this analogy is inappropriate. But we do not have any evidence of vote dependence (via gaming or otherwise).

[36] This test was performed on 11 firms with income decreases which Davidson and Weil reported 1973 adjusted earnings. Firms which were manually adjusted by us for Table 2 were excluded from this test since only the sign of the earnings change was calculated.

[37] A more likely explanation of U.S. Steel's failure to submit is the fact that the steel industry was not as politically sensitive as the oil industry (for example) at the time. In other words, a given earnings effect has less political cost or benefit. This possibility is not included in our model. This could also explain Chrysler's failure to submit. As number three after General Motors and Ford they may be subject to less political pressure (and hence cost). In addition, the "free rider" effect may explain some of these nonsubmissions.

While we can only expect a positive theory to hold on average, the failure of IBM to submit is puzzling. That firm has anti-trust suits outstanding and some economists allege that it earns monopoly profits. For a discussion of one of these suits and statements by economists that IBM earns monopoly profits, see "The Breakup of IBM" *Datamation,* October 1975, pp. 95-99.

[38] Northwestern Telephone, Commerce Bank of Kansas City, and Indiana Telephone were dropped from the sample due to a lack of data.

[39] The discriminant function is estimated using ordinary least squares. t-statistics on the coefficients are reported. The usual t-tests cannot be performed since the dependent variable is not normally distributed nor can asymptotic properties of large samples be used. However, the t-statistic is still useful as an index of the relative importance of the independent variable.

[40] Normalizing by the market value of the common stock introduces some error since we are not including the market value of the debt or preferred stock. However, since the market value of the common is highly correlated with total market value of the firm, we do not expect serious problems except that there may be some systematic, negative understatement of normalized net monetary assets.

[41] That is, this sample of firms does not expect the tax laws to be changed to include in taxable income gains/losses on net monetary assets.

[42] Since the regulatory commission bases rates on depreciation, net monetary assets are not expected to be an important consideration, hence operating earnings decline for regulated firms.

[43] Our measure of industry sales does not include firms in the industry not on the COMPUSTAT tape and furthermore all the firm's sales are assumed to be in the firm's dominant SIC category.

[44] Our examination of management compensation plans indicates that although the minimum and maximum amounts transferred to the bonus pool depend on the final net income number, we find that the actual bonus paid is most highly associated with operating or current income (depreciation is included, but extraordinary gains and losses are excluded). We correlated the change in management incentive compensation expense for 271 COMPUSTAT firms with changes in operating income and changes in net income after extraordinary items. The correlation coefficient for changes in operating income exceeded that for changes in net income after extraordinary items for over two-thirds of the firms. Gains or losses on monetary assets are not included in operating income. Consequently, only adjusted depreciation (ignoring inventory adjustments) are expected to affect management compensation and the effect is to reduce management pay.

[45] The average betas of various subclasses are:

	Regulated	Unregulated	Combined
Firms opposing GPLA	.67	.72	.71
Firms favoring GPLA	.50	.65	.59
Combined	.59	.70	.67

Note that as a firm grows via diversification its beta should tend to one.

REFERENCES

Alchian, A.A., "Corporate Management and Property Rights," in *Economic Policy and the Regulation of Corporate Securities* (H. Manne, ed.). (American Enterprise Institute, 1969).

_____ and H. Demsetz, "Production, Information Costs and Economic Organization," *American Economic Review* (December 1972), pp. 777-795.

Armstrong, Marshall S., "The Politics of Establishing Accounting Standards," A speech before the Third Annual Securities Regulation Institute in San Diego, California, January 16, 1976, as reported in Arthur Andersen & Co., *Executive News Briefs* (February 1976), p. 1.

Ball, R., "Changes in Accounting Techniques and Stock Prices," *Empirical Research in Accounting: Selected Studies, 1972.* Supplement to *Journal of Accounting Research* (1972), pp. 1-38.

_____ and Ross Watts, "Some Time Series Properties of Accounting Income," *Journal of Finance* (June 1972), pp. 663-82.

Barefield, R.M., and E.E. Comiskey, "The Smoothing Hypothesis: An Alternative Test," THE ACCOUNTING REVIEW (April 1972), pp. 291-298.

Barnea, A., J. Ronen, and S. Sadan, "The Implementation of Accounting Objectives—An Application to Extraordinary Items," THE ACCOUNTING REVIEW (January 1975), pp. 58-68.

Beidleman, C.R., "Income Smoothing: The Role of Management," THE ACCOUNTING REVIEW (October 1973), pp. 653-667.

Benston, George J., "Accountants Integrity and Financial Reporting," *Financial Executive* (August 1975), pp. 10-14.

The Conference Board, *Top Executive Compensation* (Conference Board, 1974).

Copeland, Ronald M., "Income Smoothing," *Empirical Research in Accounting: Selected Studies.* Supplement to *Journal of Accounting Research* 1968, pp. 101-116.

Cushing, B.E., "An Empirical Study of Changes in Accounting Policy," *Journal of Accounting Research* (Autumn 1969), pp. 196-203.

Dasher, B.E. and R.E. Malcom, "A Note on Income Smoothing in the Chemical Industry," *Journal of Accounting Research* (Autumn 1970), pp. 253-259.

Davidson, Sidney, Clyde P. Stickney and Roman L. Weil, *Inflation Accounting* (McGraw-Hill, 1976).

_____ and Roman L. Weil, "Inflation Accounting: What Will General Price Level Adjusted Income Statements Show?" *Financial Analysts Journal* (January-February 1975a) pp. 27-31; 70-81.

_____ and Roman L. Weil, "Inflation Accounting: Public Utilities," *Financial Analysts Journal* (May-June 1975b), pp. 30-34; 62.

_____ and Roman L. Weil, "Inflation Accounting: Some 1974 Income Measures," *Financial Analysts Journal* (September-October 1975c), pp. 42-54.

Downs, A., *An Economic Theory of Deomocracy"* (Harper and Row, 1957).

Fama, Eugene F., "Efficient Capital Markets: A Review of Theory and Empirical Work," *Journal of Finance* (May 1970), pp. 383-417.

Gonedes, N., "Income-smoothing Behavior Under Selected Stochastic Processes," *Journal of Business* (October 1972), pp. 570-584.

_____, "Class Discussion Notes: Section 8," unpublished manuscript, University of Chicago (January 1976).

_____ and N. Dopuch, "Capital Market Equilibrium, Information Production, and Selecting Accounting Techniques: Theoretical Framework and Review of Empirical Work," *Studies on Financial Accounting Objectives: 1974.* Supplement to *Journal of Accounting Research* (1974).

Gordon, M.J., "Postulates, Principles and Research in Accounting," THE ACCOUNTING REVIEW (April 1964), pp. 251-263.

_____, B.N. Horwitz, and P.T. Meyers, "Accounting Measurements and Normal Growth of the Firm," *Research in Accounting Measurement,* eds. Jaedicke, Ijiri and Nielsen (American Accounting Association, 1966), pp. 221-231.

Haskins and Sells. *Public Utilities Manual* (New York, 1974).

Horngren, Charles T., "The Marketing of Accounting Standards," *Journal of Accountancy* (October 1973), pp. 61-66.

_____, "Setting Accounting Standards in 1980," unpublished speech before the Arthur Young Professors Roundtable (March 30-31, 1976).

Ijiri, Yuji, "The Price-Level Restatement and its Dual Interpretation," THE ACCOUNTING REVIEW (April 1976), pp. 227-243.

Jensen, Michael C., "Reflections on the State of Accounting Research and the Regulation of Accounting," Presented at the Stanford Lectures in Accounting, May 21, 1976.

_____, and William H. Meckling, "Theory of the Firm: Managerial Behavior, Agency Costs and Ownership Structure," *Journal of Financial Economics* (October 1976a), pp. 305-360.

_____, and William H. Meckling, "Can the Corporation Survive?" Public Policy Working Paper Series, PPS76-4, Graduate School of Management, University of Rochester (April, 1976b).

Kaplan, R.S., and R. Roll, "Investor Evaluation of Accounting Information: Some Empirical Evidence," *Journal of Business* (April 1972), pp. 225-57.

Meckling, William H., "Values and the Choice of the Model of the Individual in Social Sciences," *Revue Suisse d' Economic Politique et de Statistique* (December 1976).

Moonitz, Maurice, *Obtaining Agreement on Standards.* Studies in Accounting Research No. 8 (Sarasota, Florida: American Accounting Association, 1974).

Peltzman, S., "Toward a More General Theory of Regulation," *Journal of Law and Economics* (August 1976), pp. 221-240.

Posner, Richard A., "Theories of Economic Regulation," *The Bell Journal of Economics and Management Science* (Autumn 1974), pp. 335-358.

Siegel, Sidney, *Nonparametric Statistics* (McGraw-Hill, 1956).

Siegfried, John, "Determinants of Antitrust Activity," *Journal of Law and Economics* (October 1975), pp. 559-581.

Stigler, G.J., "The Theory of Economic Regulation," *The Bell Journal of Economics and Management Science* (Spring 1971), pp. 3-21.

Sunder, S., "Empirical Analysis of Stock Price and Risk as They Relate to Accounting Changes in Inventory Valuation," THE ACCOUNTING REVIEW (April 1975), pp. 305-315.

U.S. Congress, Senate, Subcommittee on Antitrust and Monopoly of the Committee on the Judiciary, *Hearings, The Petroleum Industry,* Part I, 9th Congress, 1st Session, 1975.

U.S. Congress, Senate, Subcommittee on Antitrust and Monopoly of the Committee on the Judiciary, *Hearings, The Petroleum Industry,* Part III, 9th Congress, 1st Session, 1976.

Watts, Ross, "Accounting Objectives," Working Paper Series No. 7408, Graduate School of Management, University of Rochester (April 1974).

Watts, Ross, "Corporate Financial Statements: Product of the Market and Political Processes," *Australian Journal of Management* (April 1977), pp. 53-75.

Zeff, Stephen, *Forging Accounting Principles in Five Countries: A History and an Analysis of Trends,* Arthur Andersen Lecture Series (Stipes Publishing Company, 1972) pp. 110-268.

Zimmerman, Jerold, "The Municipal Accounting Maze: An Analysis of Political Incentives," Supplement to the *Journal of Accounting Research* (1977).

This research was supported by the Center for Research in Government Policy and Business, Graduate School of Management, University of Rochester. The authors wish to acknowledge the suggestions of Ray Ball, George Benston, Richard Brief, Nicholas Dopuch, Nicholas Gonedes, David Henderson, Robert Holthausen, Michael Jensen, Melvin Krasney, Richard Leftwich, Janice Maquire, William Meckling, Philip Meyers, Katherine Schipper, William Schwert, Clifford Smith, and Jerold Warner. We also acknowldge the suggestions received on an earlier version of this paper presented at the Stanford Summer Research Colloquium, August 2, 1977, and the comments of the anonymous reviewers.

THE DEMAND FOR AND SUPPLY OF ACCOUNTING THEORIES: THE MARKET FOR EXCUSES*

by Ross L. Watts and Jerold L. Zimmerman

ABSTRACT: This paper addresses the questions of why accounting theories are predominantly normative and why no single theory is generally accepted. Accounting theories are analyzed as economic goods, produced in response to the demand for theories. The nature of the demand is examined, first in an unregulated, then in a regulated economy.

Government regulation creates incentives for individuals to lobby on proposed accounting procedures, and accounting theories are useful justifications in the political lobbying. Further, government intervention produces a demand for a variety of theories, because each group affected by an accounting change demands a theory that supports its position. The diversity of positions prevents general agreement on a theory of accounting, and accounting theories are normative because they are used as excuses for political action (i.e., the political process creates a demand for theories which prescribe, rather than describe, the world).

The implications of the authors' theory for the changes in the accounting literature as a result of major changes in the institutional environment are compared with observed phenomena.

THE literature we commonly call financial accounting theory is predominantly prescriptive[1]. Most writers are concerned with what the contents of published financial statements should be; that is, how firms should

*Reprinted from The Accounting Review 54
(April 1979): 273-305

account. Yet, it is generally concluded that financial accounting theory has had little substantive, direct impact on accounting practice or policy formulation despite half a century of research. Often the lack of impact is attributed to basic methodological weaknesses in the research. Or, the prescriptions offered are based on explicit or implicit objectives which frequently differ among writers.[2] Not only are the researchers unable to agree on the objectives of financial statements, but they also disagree over the methods of deriving the prescriptions from the objectives.[3]

One characteristic common to the the prescriptions and proposed accounting methodologies, however, is their failure to satisfy all practicing accountants and to be accepted generally by accounting standard-setting bodies. A committee of the American Accounting Association recently concluded that ''a single universally accepted basic accounting theory does not exist at this time.''[4]

The preceding observations lead us to pose the following question: What is the role of accounting theory in determining accounting practice? Our objective in this paper is to begin building a theory of the determinants of accounting theory. This theory is intended to be a positive theory, that is, a theory capable of explaining the factors determining the extant accounting literature, predicting how research will change as the underlying factors change, and explaining the role of theories in the determination of accounting standards.[5] It is *not* normative or prescriptive.[6]

Other writers have examined the relationship between accounting theory and practice. For example, Zeff [1974, p.177] examines the historical relationship and concludes:

> A study of the U.S. experience clearly shows that the academic literature has had remarkably little impact on the writings of practitioners and upon the accounting policies of the American Institute and the SEC. *Too often, accounting theory is invoked more as a tactic to buttress one's preconceived notions, rather than as a genuine arbiter of contending views* (emphasis added).

Horngren [1973, p.61] goes further and suggests an explanation for accounting theory's limited impact on the setting of accounting standards:[7]

> My hypothesis is that the setting of accounting standards is as much a product of political action as of flawless logic or empirical findings.

Our tentative theory is consistent with both Zeff's and Horngren's observations. It predicts that accounting theory will be used to ''buttress preconceived notions'' and further, it explains why. Our contribution to Zeff's and Horngren's ideas is to give them more structure so that we can make additional predictions about accounting theory. The source of that structure is economics. We view accounting theory as an economic good and examine the nature of the demand for and the supply of that good.

Understanding why accounting theories are as they are requires a theory of the political process. We model that process as competition among individuals for the use of the coercive power of government to achieve wealth transfers. Because accounting procedures[8] are one means of effecting such transfers, individuals competing in the political process demand theories which prescribe the accounting procedures conducive to their desired wealth transfers. Further, because individual interests differ, a variety of accounting prescriptions, hence a variety of accounting theories, is demanded on any one issue. We argue that it is this diversity of interest which prevents general agreement on accounting theory.

While individuals want a theory which prescribes procedures conducive to their own interest, they do *not* want a normative theory which has their self-interest as its stated objective. The reason is that information is costly to obtain. Some voters will not obtain information on political issues personally. Those voters are not likely to support political actions which have as their stated objective the self-interest of others. The most useful theories for persuading uninformed voters are theories with stated objectives appealing to those voters, *e.g.*, the ''public interest.'' As a result, individuals demand normative accounting theories which make prescriptions based on the ''public interest.'' In other words, the demand is for rationales or excuses. Because it arises from the political process, the demand for normative, ''public interest''-oriented accounting theories depends on the extent of the government's role in the economy.

Section II analyzes the demand for financial accounting and accounting theory first in an unregulated economy, in which the only role of government is to enforce contracts, and then in a regulated economy. In Section III, we examine the nature of the supply of accounting theories. Because of the diverse demands for prescriptions, we expect to observe a variety of normative theories. Further, we expect theories to change over time as government intervention changes. In Section IV we examine the effect of government intervention on extant accounting theory during the last century. Section V summarizes the issues and presents our conclusions.

THE DEMAND FOR ACCOUNTING THEORIES

This section analyzes the demand for accounting theories in an unregulated economy (Part A) and the additional demands generated by government intervention (Part B).

The Demand for Accounting Theories in an Unregulated Economy

Accounting in an Unregulated Economy. Audited corporate financial statements were voluntarily produced prior to government mandate.[9] Watts [1977] concludes that the original promoters of corporations or, subsequently, corporate managers have incentives to contract to supply audited financial statements. Agreements to supply financial statements were included in articles of incorporations (or by-laws) and in private lending contracts between corporations and creditors.[10] These contracts increase the welfare of the promoter or manager (who is raising the new capital) because they reduce the *agency costs*[11] which he bears.

Agency costs arise because the manager's (the agent's) interests do not necessarily coincide with the interests of shareholders or bondholders (the principals). For example, the manager (if he owns shares) has incentives to convert assets of the corporation into dividends, thus leaving the bondholders with the "shell" of the corporation. Similarly, the manager has incentives to transfer wealth to himself at the expense of both the shareholders and bondholders (*e.g.*, via perquisites).

Bondholders and shareholders anticipate the manager's behavior and appropriately discount the price of the bonds or shares at the time of issue. Hence, the promoter (or manager) of a new corporation receives less for the shares and bonds he sells than he would if he could guarantee that he would continue to act as he did when he owned the firm (*i.e.*, when there were no outside shareholders or bondholders). This difference in the market value of the securities is part of the cost of an agency relationship, it is part of agency costs, and is borne by the promoter (or manager).[12] Jensen and Meckling [1976, p. 308] call it the "residual loss."

Because he bears the residual loss, the manager has incentives to make expenditures to guarantee that he will not take certain actions which harm the principal's interest or that he will compensate the principal if he does. These are "bonding" and "monitoring" expenditures and are additional elements of agency costs. Examples of such expenditures include contracting to restrict dividend payments and expenditures to monitor such dividend covenants.

The final element of agency costs is the utility of the increase in perquisites, wealth transfers, *etc.*, the manager receives because of his actions as an agent. An equilibrium occurs when the net costs of an agency relationship, the agency costs, are minimized by trading-off the decreases in the promoter's (or manager's) utility due to the residual loss, the monitoring and bonding expenditures, and the increased utility due to increased perquisites. The promoter or manager will write contracts for monitoring and bonding as long as the marginal benefits of these contracts (*e.g.*, reduction of the residual loss) are greater than the marginal costs (*e.g.*, the costs of contracting and the utility of any perquisites foregone). Moreover, since he bears the agency costs, the manager or promoter will try to write the contracts and perform the bonding or monitoring at minimum cost. In fact, the Jensen and Meckling analysis suggests that the equilibrium set of contractual devices is the one which minimizes the agency costs associated with the separation of management and control and with the conflict of interests associated with the different classes of investors.

Promoters and managers voluntarily included bonding covenants in corporate articles and by-laws in the nineteenth century. Dividend covenants were voluntarily included in company charters as early as 1620.[13]

Watts's [1977] analysis of agency relationships suggests that the function of audited financial statements in an unregulated economy is to reduce agency costs. This theory predicts that accounting practices (*i.e.*, the form, content, frequency, *etc.*, of external reporting) would vary across corporations in an unregulated economy depending on the nature and magnitude of the agency costs. Agency costs, in turn, are, among other things, a function of the amount of corporate debt outstanding and of the relative share of equity owned by the manager.[14] These variables affect the manager's incentive to take actions which conflict with the interests of shareholders and bondholders. Agency costs also vary with the costs of monitoring managers, which, in turn, depend on the physical size, dispersion, and complexity of the firm. Further, the practices underlying financial statements will vary across firms because an accounting practice which minimizes agency costs in one industry may not minimize those costs in another.

As an example of the association between agency costs and accounting procedures, consider management compensation schemes in the nineteenth century. Some management compensation schemes in the nineteenth century were included in corporate articles. Those schemes tied management compensation to the firms' "profits" [Matheson, 1893, pp. vii-viii] to reduce the divergence between the interests of the managers and shareholders.[15] At that time "profits" were effectively operating cash flows, since accrual accounting was not used. [Litherland, 1968, pp. 171-172]. However, a cash flow "profit" index is susceptible to shortrun manager manipulation. The manager can reduce repairs and maintenance expenditures and increase cash flows and "profits,"[16] which would increase the manager's compensation.[17] In addition, reduced maintenance increases the ability of the corporation to pay current dividends. Such dividends could reduce the value of the creditors' claims and increase the shareholders' wealth.[18]

To reduce these agency costs of equity and debt, several contractual devices were used to decrease the likelihood that managers and shareholders would run down the value of the capital stock.

 i) Dividends were restricted to a fixed proportion of profits, thereby creating a buffer.[19]
 ii) Reserve funds of fixed amounts had to be maintained if dividends were to be paid.[20]
 iii) Fixed assets were treated as merchandise accounts with changes in value (usually not called depreciation) closed to profits prior to dividend distribution.[21]

In the latter procedure, depreciation was treated as a valuation technique which had to be estimated only in profitable years, since dividends were paid only in these years. A typical company charter requiring depreciation is:

> The directors shall, before recommending any dividend, set aside out of the profits of the company, but subject to the sanction of the company in general meeting, such sum as they think proper as a reserve fund, for maintenance, repairs, depreciation and renewals.[22]

The court interpreted this article and the term "proper reserve" as a mechanism to account for declines in the capital stock.[23] Thus, the existence of a depreciation covenant (and hence the presence of depreciation in the financial statement) or other restrictions on dividends was a function of the amount of fixed assets and the nature and magnitude of the agency costs of debt.

Capital market participants contract to supply capital. Managers and owners seeking capital have incentives to enter into contracts which limit the agency costs they incur. But these contracts must then be monitored and enforced since managers have incentives to circumvent the contracts. For example, the promoter or manager of a corporation may contract to restrict dividends to, or base management compensation on, profits after a deduction for depreciation because such a covenant enables him to sell bonds and shares at a higher price. However, *after* the contract is written the manager has incentives to minimize that depreciation charge, thereby leading to increased profits (and potentially increased management compensation) and dividends which transfer wealth from bondholders to shareholders (including management). Thus, contracts will reduce agency costs only if they include provisions for monitoring. Since audited financial statements are useful devices to monitor these voluntary agreements between owners and managers, these statements serve a useful role in the capital markets and owner-managers will agree to provide them in advance.

The Function of Accounting Theories

The preceding analysis suggests that accounting theories will serve three overlapping functions in an unregulated economy.

i) Pedagogic demand. Accounting procedures are devised in order to reduce agency costs of contracts. Since these costs vary across firms, accounting procedures will vary, giving rise to diversity of techniques, formats, *etc.*[24] However, diversity in accounting procedures increases the difficulty of teaching the practice of accounting. Consequently, accounting teachers develop pedagogic devices (rules-of-thumb) to assist learning and to structure the variation found in practice. Theorists examine existing systems of accounts and summarize differences and similarities. These descriptions of practice highlight the tendencies of firms with particular attributes to follow certain accounting procedures.

Nineteenth century accounting texts and articles indicate that accounting theorists recognized the diversity of practice and attempted to distill general tendencies from the diversity. For example:

> No fixed rules, or rates of depreciation can be established for general use, because not only do trades and processes of manufacture differ, but numerous secondary circumstances have to be considered in determining the proper course. It may, however, be possible to lay down some general principles which will always apply, or which, at any rate, may with advantage be held in view in deciding particular cases.[Matheson, 1893,p. 1]

Similarly, Dicksee and Tillyard's [1906] treatise describes current accounting practice for goodwill and the relevant court cases. Based on this description, the authors "enunciate general business principles and explain their practical application" [Dicksee and Tillyard, 1906, p. vii].

ii) Information Demand. In an unregulated economy there is a demand for writers to do more than just describe variations in accounting practice. There is a demand for predictions of the effects of accounting procedures on both the manager's and auditor's welfare via exposure to law suits. The auditor contracts with the shareholders (and creditors) to monitor management, and he is legally liable if he fails to report breaches of covenants in the corporation's articles or by-laws.[25] Furthermore, the demand for a given auditor's services is a function of the auditor's efficiency in monitoring management.[26] Hence, the auditor again has an incentive to understand how management's choice of accounting procedures affects agency costs.

Auditors would value information in the form of theories predicting how agency costs vary with accounting procedures. In particular, auditors would like to know how managers' actions and hence agency costs would be affected by alternative accounting procedures.

iii) Justification Demand. Early accounting textbooks warned that managers would use accounting to serve their own interests at the expense of shareholders. The second edition of Matheson [1893] contains examples of such warnings. Matheson provides illustrations of how managers can take advantage of deficiencies in the definition of depreciation, repairs, and maintenance charges to increase "profits" and their own compensation at the expense of shareholders and/or bondholders. For example, on page 5 he writes:

> The temptation to treat as Profit the Surplus of Income over Expenditure, without sufficient allowance for Deterioration, appears to be often irresistible. Thus, in the case of a Tramway undertaking in its first years of working, a dividend may be possible only by writing off little or nothing from the capital value of the cars, the harness, and the horses. This, of course, cannot last without the introduction of new capital, but in undertakings long established there yet may be epochs of fictitious profits due to various causes. For instance there may be neglect of repairs, which, when the necessity for them becomes evident, will involve a heavy outlay for renewals; or it may arise from actual fraud in postponing expenditure, so as to show large profits, which will raise the value of shares for stock-jobbing purposes. There are railways where the dividend income and the corresponding value of the shares have fluctuated considerably, not according to alterations in the real earnings, but according to alternate neglect and attention in regard to plant.

Accounting texts (and theories) which detail how managers seek to manipulate profits and the consequent effects of those manipulations on shareholders and bondholders not only improve the auditor's ability to monitor such behavior, but also provide the auditor with ready-made arguments to use against such practices in discussions with management. It is clear that Matheson's work fulfilled this role. William Jackson, a member of the Council of the Institute of Chartered Accountants in England and Wales, stated that he used Matheson's book in that fashion:

> To those who honestly and from conviction treat the subject on the only sound basis, it may seem superfluous to urge due consideration of the arguments so convincingly set out in these pages; but Auditors, and especially those who have to deal with joint-stock or other concerns where the remuneration of the management is made wholly or partly dependent upon declared Profits, know in what varied forms resistance to an adequate Charge against Profits for Depreciation is presented.
>
> The fallacies underlying these objections present themselves again and again with the modifications caused by the lack of apprehension in some, or the ingenuity of others. *Mr. Matheson's work provides the Auditor with true antidotes to these fallacies, and it has been in past times used by the writer with satisfactory effect, where his own less-reasoned arguments have failed to convince.*
>
> He therefore recommends it afresh to the notice and for the support, where necessary, of members of his own profession, and of those who, untrained in the practice of Auditing, are confronted with unfamiliar and specious pretexts for avoiding the unwelcome charge against Profits [Matheson, 1893, pp. vii-viii] (emphasis added).

The Demand for Accounting Theories in a Regulated Economy

This section extends the previous analysis of the demand for theories to include the effects of government. We assume that private citizens, bureaucrats, and politicians have incentives to employ the powers of the state to make themselves better off and to coalesce for that purpose. One way by which coalitions of individuals are made better off is by legislation that redistributes (i.e., confiscates) wealth.

Accounting And The Political Process.

Farm subsidies, tariffs, welfare, social security, even regulatory commissions[27] are examples of special interest legislation which transfer wealth. The business sector is both the source (via taxes, anti-trust, affirmative action, *etc.*) and the recipient of many of these wealth transfers (via tax credits, tariffs, subsidies, *etc.*).

Financial accounting statements perform a central role in these wealth transfers and are affected both directly and indirectly by the political process. The Securities and Exchange Commission (SEC) regulates the contents of financial statements directly (upward asset revaluations are not allowed, statements of changes in financial position must be prepared, *etc.*). The Federal Revenue Acts also affect the contents of financial statements directly (*e.g.*, LIFO). In addition, regulatory commission (*e.g.*, state public utility boards, various banking and insurance commissions, the Interstate Commerce Commission, the Federal Trade Commission) often affect the contents of financial statements.

Besides these more direct effects, there are indirect effects. Government commissions often use the contents of financial statements in the regulatory process (rate setting, antitrust, *etc.*). Further, Congress often bases legislative actions on these statements.[28] This, in turn, provides management with incentives to select accounting procedures which either reduce the costs they bear or increase the benefits they receive as a result of the actions of government regulators and legislators.[29]

Since public utilities have incentives to propose accounting procedures for rate making purposes which increase the market value of the firm, their arguments are assisted if accounting standard-setting bodies such as the Financial Accounting Standards Board (FASB) mandate the same accounting procedures for financial reporting.[30] Consequently, managers of utilities and other regulated industries (*e.g.*, insurance, bank and transportation) lobby on accounting standards not only with their regulatory commissions but also with the Accounting Principles Board (APB) and the FASB.

Moonitz [1974 a and b] and Horngren [1973 and 1977] document instances of regulated firms seeking or opposing accounting procedures which affect the value of the firm via direct and indirect wealth transfers. Examples of other firms lobbying on accounting standards exist. Most of the major U.S. oil companies made submissions regarding the FASB's Discussion Memorandum on General Price level Adjustments [Watts and Zimmerman, 1978].

The Effect Of Government Intervention On The Demand For Accounting Theories.

The rules and regulations which result from government regulation of business increase the pedagogic and information demands for accounting theories. Even beginning accounting textbooks report the income tax requirements of LIFO, depreciation, *etc.* Practitioners demand detailed texts explaining SEC requirements (*e.g.*, Rappaport [1972]), tax codes, and other government regulations.

The justification demand for theories also expands with regulation. The political process in the U.S. is characterized as an advocacy proceeding. Proponents and opponents of special interest legislation (or petitioners before regulatory and administrative committees) must give arguments for the positions they advocate. If these positions include changes in accounting procedures, accounting theories which serve as justifications (*i.e.*, excuses) are useful. These advocacy positions (including theories) will tend to be based on contentions that the political action is in the public interest,[31] that everyone is made better off, that most are made better off and no one is harmed, or that the action is "fair," since those contentions are likely to generate less opposition than arguments based on self-interest. Often, those public interest arguments rely upon the notion that the unregulated market solution is inefficient. The typical argument is that there is a market failure which can only be remedied by government intervention.

Politicians and bureaucrats charged with the responsibility for promoting the general welfare demand public interest testimony not only to inform them of the trade-offs but also for use in justifying their actions to the press and their constituencies. Consequently, when politicians support (or oppose) legislation, they tend to adopt the public interest arguments advanced by the special interests who promote (oppose) the legislation.

i) Examples of Public Interest or Market Failure Justifications. The reported objective of the Securities Exchange Act of 1934 and of required disclosure is stated by Mundheim [1964, p. 647]:

> The theory of the Securities Act is that if investors are provided with sufficient information to permit them to make a reasoned decision concerning the investment merits of securities offered to them, investor interests can be adequately protected without unduly restricting the ability of business ventures to raise capital.

This objective stresses economic efficiency. The statement suggests that required disclosure can increase investors' welfare at virtually zero cost (*i.e.*, that there is a market failure).

Examples of "public interest" justifications of accounting procedures are observed in rate-setting hearings for public utilities. For example, Public Systems, an organization that represents municipalities and rural electrification agencies, applied for a hearing on the Federal Power Commission's (FPC) Order 530 which allowed the use of income tax allocation in setting rates.[32] Order 530 increases the cash flow of electric utilities "at the expense of customes using electricity" and hence harms the interests of Public Systems. But, Public Systems did not argue that is is in its self-interest to oppose Order 530. Instead it argued that "normalization [income tax allocation] represents an *inefficient* means of subsidizing the public utility industry" [U.S. Congress, Senate, 1976, p.683] (emphasis added).

Bureaucrats also use public interest arguments to justify their actions.[33] For example, the former SEC Chief Accountant, John Burton, a bureacrat, justified the disclosure regulations imposed during his term in office by arguing:

> In a broad sense we hope [that disclosure regulations] will contribute to a more efficient capital market. . . . The way in which we hope that will be achieved is first by giving investors more confidence that they are getting the whole story and second by encouraging the development of better tools of analysis and more responsibility on the part of the professional analyst to understand what's going on. We think that by giving them better data we can encourage them in the direction of doing a better job, thus leading, we hope, to more effective [sic] capital markets [Burton, 1975, p.21].

Government regulation creates a demand for normative accounting theories employing public interest arguments, that is, for theories purporting to demonstrate that certain accounting procedures *should* be used because they lead to better decisions by investors, more efficient capital markets, *etc.* Further, the demand is not for *one* theory, but rather for diverse prescriptions. On any political issue such as utility rate determination, there will be at least two sides. In the FPC Order 530 example, Coopers & Lybrand, who opposed Public Systems, wanted a theory which prescribed income tax allocation, while Public Systems wanted a theory which did not. When we consider that accounting methods are relevant to taxes, antitrust cases, union negotiations, disclosure regulations, *etc.*, as well as utility rate-setting, we expect a demand for a multitude of prescriptions.

With increased government intervention in business, the demand for theories which justify particular accounting procedures (proposed in the self-interest of various parties) has come to eclipse the demand for theories which fulfill the pedagogic and information roles. We present evidence to support this proposition in Section V.

ii) Rationality or "Theory Illusion." Until recently, it had been popular in the economics literature to assume that politicians elected officials, bureacrats, *etc.*, acted in the "public interest" (the public interest assumption).[34] In order to determine which actions are in the public interest, politicians require theories which predict the consequences of alternative actions. "Rational," "public interest"-oriented politicians/bureaucrats would tend to use the theories which best predict (*i.e.*, the "best" theories)[35] and hence those theories would predominate. Leading articles in the accounting literature are implicitly based on the public interest premise (AAA [1966, p. 5], AICPA [1973, p. 17], Gonedes and Dopuch [1974, pp. 48-49 and pp. 114-118], Beaver and Demski [1974, p. 185]) that the "best" theories prevail.

In recent years, however, economists have questioned whether the public interest assumption is consistent with observed phenomena.[36] They have proposed an alternative assumption—that individuals involved in the political process act in their own interest (the self-interest assumption). This assumption yields implications which are more consistent with observed phenomena than those based on the public interest assumption.[37]

The costs and benefits to voters of becoming informed, of lobbying, of forming coalitions, and of monitoring their representatives' actions are of central importance in a self-interest model of the political process. Downs [1957] suggests that the expected effect of one individual's vote on the outcome of an elections is trivial, and, hence, the individual voter has very little incentive to incur the costs of becoming informed on political issues. On the other hand, individual voters do have incentives to act as groups in the political process. Economies of scale in political action encourage group participation. When several voters have similar interests on particular issues (*e.g.*, members of a trade union), those voters can share the "fixed" costs of becoming informed and moreover can increase the likelihood of affecting the outcome of an election by voting as a bloc.[38]

The costs of political action also depend on the existing political institutions (*e.g.*, whether political decisions are made by referendum or a vote of elected representatives) [Leffler and Zimmerman, 1977]. If we call the sum of the costs of political action the "transactions costs" of political decisions, the crucial question is "what is the magnitude of these transactions costs?" If the transactions costs of political decisions are high, self-interest motivated government servants will not always act in the public interest; if they are zero, they will.[39] Hence, if the transactions costs of the political process are high, government officials will not use the "best" theory available; if they are zero, they will.

As an example of the importance of positive political transactions costs, consider the manager of a utility advocating deferred tax accounting because of its effects on utility rates. The manage will argue that recognizing deferred taxes as current operating costs is in the public interest. The official responsible for allowing or not allowing this practice has a greater incentive to resist the lobbying efforts of the utlity manager if other individuals (*e.g.*, consumer advocates) lobby against the procedure. Whether those individuals lobby depends on the costs of consumers being informed about the effects of the accounting procedures on their welfare (which requires human capital), the costs of forming groups to oppose the procedure, *etc.* The manager's public interest theory (which is an "excuse" to cover a self-interest motive and need not be valid) increases the costs of others being informed and will tend to be accepted by the public official *if* the transactions costs are large enough.

We assume that political transactions costs are large enough to cause the acceptance of "invalid" theories, that the competition among excuses does not always lead to acceptance of the "best" theory. The usefulness of that assumption depends on the empirical cosistency of its implications. It is an empirical question. The work by Posner [1974], Stigler [1971], and Peltzman [1976] supports the assumption.

The assumption that the transactions costs of the political process are non-zero is analogous to the assumption of non-zero transactions costs in capital markets.[40] In capital market theory it is typically assumed that transactions costs are zero despite the fact they obviously are not, because that assumption yields empirically confirmed hypotheses. Why then, should political transactions costs be sufficiently more important than capital market transactions costs to warrant their inclusion in a political theory?

We suggest that there is an important difference between capital markets and the political process which make transactions costs important in the latter case. There is, in the capital markets, a direct market for control. If the manager of a corporation is not maximizing the market value of the corporations's shares, then an individual can, by buying its shares, acquire control of the corporation in the capital markets and, therefore, obtain the right to make the decisions. That individual can change the corporation's decisions and reap for himself the capital gain from the increase in the value of the corporation's stock. If the Chairman of the Securities and Exchange Commission were not making decisions in the public interest, an individual could not directly buy the right to make those decisions and capture the benefits of the changed decision. Because direct payments to elected officials are illegal and payments in kind are generally more expensive, it is costlier to bribe Congressmen, Senators, *etc.*, than to purchase a controlling interest in a corporation. It is also costly to establish indirect ways of achieving the same result.[41]

Notice that in our model of the political process everyone is rational. No one is being "fooled" by accounting theories; they are not "fooled" by "theory illusion."[42] If people do not investigate the validity of theories, it is because they do not expect such investigation to be worthwhile. If the expected benefits of investigation to an individual are small, he will make only a limited investigation.

Our assumption of high political costs is crucial to our theory. As we shall see in the next section, the assumption enables us to discriminate between the empirical implications of our theory and the implications of an alternative theory. This allows empirical testing. Ultimately, the test of the political cost assumption is whether the implications of the theory based on the assumption are confirmed or not by empirical tests. Thus, the merit of an assumption is judged by the predictions it generates. Those accounting researchers who build theories on the assumption that information is a pure public good (*e.g.*, Gonedes and Dopuch [1974] and Beaver [1976]) often assert that information is a pure public good. Yet, no tests of these theories have been provided. In Section IV we argue that implications of our theory are consistent with the evidence.

THE SUPPLY OF ACCOUNTING THEORIES

Accounting theorists often view themselves as expert critics or defenders of accounting prescriptions (*e.g.*, replacement cost, historical costs, *etc.*). They argue that accounting theory should be used to determine accounting practice and standards.[43] The ideal state of affairs to them is one in which theorists logically and objectively determine the merits of alternative procedures.[44] For example, Hendriksen [1977, p.1] writes: " . . . the most important goal of accounting theory should be to provide a coherent set of logical principles that form the general frame of reference for the evaluation and development of sound accounting practices." Theorists tend to bemoan the fact that this ideal state does not exist and that corporate managers, auditors, and politicians do not allow them to determine accounting standards.[45]

Most theorists probably believe that an objective of their research and the reason they supply theories is to provide knowledge which will ultimately improve accounting practice. They would not regard themselves as supplying "excuses". But we suggest that the predominant contemporary demand for accounting theories (the demand for accounting in a regulated economy) is the demand for justifications—"excuses." If that empirical proposition is correct, the question is: How responsive is the supply side (accounting research) to changes in the nature and quantity of the economic good being demanded?

As long as there exists a large number of individuals who are able to supply a wide diveristy of theories (*i.e.*, as long as numerous close substitutes exist) at relatively low cost, then supply will be very responsive to demand. Stigler's observation succinctly summarizes this point:

> . . . consumers generally determine what will be produced, and producers make profits by discovering more precisely what consumers want and producing it more cheaply. Some may entertain a tinge of doubt about this proposition, thanks to the energy and skill of Professor Galbraith, but even his large talents hardly raise a faint thought that I live in a house rather than a tent because of the comparative advertising outlays of the two industries. This Cambridge eccentricity aside, then, *it is useful to say that consumers direct production—and therefore, do they not direct the production of the words and ideas of intellectuals, rather than, as in the first view, vice-versa?* [Stigler, 1976, p.347] (emphasis added).

The consumers ("vested interests") determine the production of accounting research through the incentives they provide for accounting theorists. The greater the prestige and articulation skills of an accounting researcher, the more likely practitioners, regulators and other academics will know his work and the greater the flow of both students and funds to his university. Researchers have non-pecuniary incentives to be well-known, and this reputation is rewarded by a higher salary and a plenitude of research funds.[46] Practitioners, regulators, and those teaching future practitioners are more likely to read or hear of the output of an accounting researcher if it bears on topics of current interest. As a result, the researcher who is motivated by pecuniary and non-pecuniary factors (e.g., "free" trips to conferences) will tend to write on the current controversies in accounting. Therein lies the connection to the demands of vested interests. Controversies arise in accounting when vested interests disagree over accounting standards. For example, the LIFO controversy arose when the Supreme Court outlawed the base stock method of valuing inventory for tax purposes and the American Petroleum Institute recommended LIFO to replace it, thereby reducing the present value of its members' taxes. The Internal Revenue Servie resisted because of the effect on revenues. The parties demanded pro and con LIFO theories which were eventually produced [Moonitz, 1974, pp. 33-34].

Accounting researchers often include a set of policy recommendations as part of their research project.[47] Those recommendations, made on the basis of some objective assumed by the researcher, may never have been intended to serve as an "excuse" for the corporate manager, practitioner or politician who prefers the recommended procedure for self-interest reasons. Nevertheless, the research findings will be favorably quoted by those with vested interests.[48] The more readable the research, the more frequently it is quoted, the more researcher's fame increases. Similarly, criticisms of alternative accounting practices will be quoted by vested interests and will also increase the researcher's reputation.

The link between suppliers of accounting theory and consumers goes further than mere quotation. Partners in accounting firms, bureaucrats in government agencies and corporate managers will seek out accounting researchers who have eloquently and cosistently advocated a particular practice which happens to be in the practitioner's, bureacrat's, or manager's self-interest and will appoint the researcher as a consultant, or expert witness, or commission him to conduct a study of that accounting problem. Consistency in the researcher's work allows the party commissioning the work to predict more accurately the ultimate conclusions. Thus, research and consulting funds will tend to flow to the most eloquent and consistent advocates of accounting practices where there are vested interests who benefit by the adoption or rejection of these accounting practices.

The tendency of vested interests to seek out researchers who support their position produces a survival bias.[49] The bias is introduced by the vested interests. We do not mean to impugn the motives of accounting researchers who advocate particular practices. In fact, the more consistent the positions of the researcher and the greater his integrity, the more support he lends to the vested interest's position.

Given the rewards for supplying theories on controversial issues, we expect to observe competition in the supply of accounting theories related to those issues. The prescriptions for an issue are likely to be as diverse as the positions of vested interests. But despite this diversity, we do not necessarily expect accounting researchers to be inconsistent from issue to issue. Academic evaluation and criticism create incentives for each researcher to be consistent. However, the rationales given for observed accounting standards may well be inconsistent across issues and different sections of the same accounting standard.

Rationales differ (and are inconsistent) across accounting standards because a standard is the result of political action. The outcome depends on the relative costs which the various involved parties are willing to incur to achieve their goals. And these costs will vary with the expected benefits. The rationale given for a standard will be the successful party's rationale; and if it is a compromise, such as APB Opinion 16 on business combinations, mixtures of rationales will be used.[50] The same party is not successful in every issue; indeed many are not even involved in every issue. Further, vested interests (*e.g.*, an insurance company) are less constrained to give consistent rationales across issues. Hence, we observe a party supporting historical cost evaluation in some cases and market valuation in others.[51]

If political transactions costs are high so that there is a demand for excuses which are useful weapons in the political arena, if the demand for accounting theory is dominated by that demand for excuses, and if demand determines production, accounting theories will be generated by, not generate, political debates. We will observe the nature of accounting theory changing as political issues change. Accounting theory will change *contemporaneously* with or *lag* political issues. We will *not* observe accounting theory generally *leading* political action.

Contrast the preceding predictions to what we would expect under alternative theories of accounting theory. The only alternative theory which we can even partially specify is that theories in the accounting literature are used to further the "public interest" (*i.e.*, they assist politicians or bureacrats in producing regulations to further the "public interest"). In order for politicians or bureaucrats to use that literature we would have to observe the theories appearing in the literature before or, at best, at the same time as the relevant regulation. The appearance of the theories in the literature could not *lag* the regulation. Thus, we can discriminate between our theory and the alternative public interest theory if the appearance of theories in the literature tends to lead or lag regulation. If it tends to lead, the public interest hypothesis is supported. If it lags, our theory is supported. On the other hand, if the literature and regulation are contemporaneous we cannot discriminate between the two hypotheses.

It is important to remember that we are attempting to explain accounting theory as it is represented in the accounting literature (see footnote 1). It is conceivable that an accounting theory could be produced and used in the political process to institute a regulation, but not appear until later in the accounting literature. In other words, the "public interest" could, in fact, motivate the theory and the regulation, but the publication of the theory nonetheless, could, lag legislation. In that case, neither the public interest theory nor our theory could explain the accounting literature. In essence, we would be left without a theory of the literature. However, those who would argue such a scenario must then produce another explanation for, or theory of, the accounting literature.

In Section IV we compare the timing of general movements in the accounting literature to the timing of regulation to see if *a priori* the evidence supports our theory or the public interest theory. We do not present any formal tests which discriminate between the two theories, although we believe such tests could be performed (*e.g.*, by using citation tests). However, the serious problem in doing a formal test is that the public interest theory, like other alternative theories, is poorly specified. Hopefully, this paper will cause others to specify the public interest theory better or specify alternative theories of the accounting literature so that testing is facilitated.

One or two papers dicussing a topic prior to the time the topic becomes politically active is not sufficient to reject our theory, just as one or two "heads" is not sufficient to reject the hypothesis that a given coin is "fair." It is important to remember that as in all empirical theories we are concerned with *general* trends. Our predictions are for the accounting literature in general. We are not purporting to have a theory that explains the bahavior of all accounting researchers or the acceptance, or lack of acceptance, of every published paper. There are many interesting phenomena that this theory, at this stage of development, cannot yet explain. But this does not *ipso facto* destroy the value of the theory.

Our analysis suggests that the accounting literature is not the simple accumulation of knowledge and consequent development of techniques. It is not a literature in which, as Littleton suggests,[52] concepts become better understood and consequently leads to "better" accounting practices. Instead it is a literature in which the concepts are altered to permit accounting practices to adapt to changes in political issues and institutions.

In this section, the existence of close substitute suppliers of theories was shown to make the supply of accounting "excuses" very responsive to the demand. In the next section we argue that the evidence we have gathered is consistent with the proposition that the market for accounting research is the market for "excuses" and suggests that the theory will be confirmed in formal testing.

THE EMPIRICAL RELATIONSHIP BETWEEN GOVERNMENT INTERVENTION AND ACCOUNTING THEORY

If the demand for "excuses" is important in determining the output of accounting theorists, we expect to observe changes in accounting theory when a new law is passed which impinges on accounting practice. This section examines how accounting practice and theories were affected by several major types of legislation. We have selected three types of legislation which we believe have had a pronounced impact on accounting theory: the laws regulating railroads, the income tax laws, and the securites acts.

In this section we do not purport to present an exhaustive list of legislation which has created a demand for accounting "excuses" or to present a complete analysis of each type of legislation. Our objective is merely to present *prima facie* support for the hypothesis that accounting theory has changed *after* the introduction of government regulation.

When dealing with historical events such as government regulation, the "evidence" presented is always subject to interpretation and the *ex post* selection bias of the researchers. Critics can always charge that "strategic sampling" of references produced the results. In fact, much of the economic theory of regulation suffers from this *ex post* rationalization. However, at this early stage in the development of the theory, an *ex post* case study approach has yielded insights [Posner, 1974] and appears to be the logical and necessary precursor to a general theory of regulation. We are aware of these methodological problems. Even though the evidence we present is somewhat "casual," and not as "rigorous" as we would like, it is, nonetheless, evidence.[53] Furthermore, we have endeavored to choose the references from the standard, classical accounting literature. Undoubtedly, conflicting citations and references exist. Critics can, will and should raise these conflicting citations, keeping in mind the statistical fallacies of drawing inferences based on sample sizes of one. We do not contend that all issues are settled, but rather encourage others to pursue, correct, and extend our analysis.

Railroad Legislation.

The growth of railroads is considered by many accountants to have been very importnat in the development of accounting theory. Hendriksen [1977, p. 40] lists it as one of the main influences on accounting theory in the period from 1800 to 1930. Littleton [1933, pp. 239-241] is more specific; he ascribes the development of depreciation accounting and the concern with depreciation in the literature in the nineteenth century to the growth of railroads.

There is no doubt that the development of railroads both in the U.S. and the U.K. affected tha accounting literature on the nature of depreciation, including the question of charging depreciation as an expense [Pollins, 1956; and Boockholdt, 1977]. Holmes [1975, p. 18] writes:

> Depreciation was a knotty problem for these early railroad accountants. They argued over
> it, scorned it, denied it, anatomized it, and misused their own concepts. But in the end it

was from the very ashes of their disagreements that our modern concepts of depreciaiton rose Phoenix-like fifty years later.

This literature existed at least by 1841 in the U.K. [*The Railway Times*, October 30, 1841, quoted in Pollins, 1956] and by 1850 in the U.S. [Dionysius Lardner's book quoted in Pollins, 1956]. Although the debate did not result in depreciation being treated as an expense in either the U.S. or U.K.,[54] theories of depreciation were enunciated. Consequently, given our theory, we have to answer two questions: (1) why did this depreciation debate arise with the railroads (*i.e.*, was there some government regulation or political action present in the case of the railroads that was not present for earlier corporations); and if so, (2) did that government regulation or political action precede the literature?

(1) *The reason for the debate* was investigated by Littleton [1933]. He asserts that two conditions were necessary to the development of depreciation accounting—corporations with limited liability and long-lived assets. He suggests that limited liability was a necessary condition, because it led to covenants restricting dividends to profits and thereby created the demand for financial statements which report profits (see Section II). Long-lived assets were important because, if they had not existed, there would have been no necessity to calculate depreciation to determine profits.

We think that Littleton's analysis is incomplete. *First*, agency costs of debt and equity exist whether or not a corporation has legally limited liability. Limited liability merely shifts some of the risk [Jensen and Meckling, 1976, pp. 331-332]. Given that the function of dividend covenants is to reduce the agency costs of debt, it is not surprising to obesrve them existing as early as 1620 for U.K. companies, long before limited liability was generally recognized for companies. We can easily amend Littleton's argument for this defect; for the first condition of limited liability, we substitute the existence of dividend covenants.

Second, dividend covenants and long-lived assets would not necessarily lead to depreciation being treated as an *expense*. The dividend covenants put a lower bound on the equity participation of shareholders. As long as sufficient earnings have been retained in the past to cover the depreciation of fixed assets to the current time, there would be no necessity to deduct depreciation systematically each year. We do not observe depreciation being treated as an expense prior to this century. Instead it was treated as an allocation of profits.

This suggests that Littleton's analysis has not been supported empirically. Observation of his two conditions would not necessarily be accompanied by depreciation being treated as an expense. Littleton's two conditions existed in the seventeenth and eighteenth centuries (dividend covenants can be observed as early as 1620 and were included in company charters as a general practice in the eighteenth century). Limited liability for U.K. companies existed *de facto* at least by the 1730s and was explicitly recognized by 1784.[55] The U.K. trading companies of the seventeenth and eighteenth centuries certainly had long-lived assets—forts and ships. Yet, we do not observe any real concern with depreciation expense until the nineteenth century.

Littleton recognized that his analysis was inconsistent with observed phenomena and that some other variable was necessary to explain the absense of concern about depreciation expense in both accounting theory and practice. He eloquently expresses the inconsistency [Littleton, 1933, p. 240]:

> The simultaneous appearance of these two elements—active, long-lived assets and a special need for the careful calculation of net profit—seems to be essential to the recognition of the importance of depreciation. Before these two are joined depreciation is incidental to the profit calculation; afterward it becomes indispensable. First in the trading companies, later in the railroads, these two elements were united and the foundations for depreciation accounting were laid. But, so far as could be learned, the depreciation of ships and forts did not receive consideration in the trading companies' bookkeeping, while the railroads, as has been seen, did give considerable attention to the problem of wear and tear of roadway and equipment. *Apparently some third element was also needed, which was present in the case of the railroads* but not earlier (emphasis added).

Littleton [1933, p. 240] suggests that the missing variable is knowledge, that it took 200 years for the nature of the corporation to become known. We suggest that a more plausible explanation is that, in the case of railroads, fares and rates were regulated by government on the basis of "profits."

Both in the U.S. and the U.K., some transportation prices were regulated before the existence of railroads. For example, the rates of the Fort Point Ferry (U.S.), incorporated in 1807, were, according to its charter, to be fixed by the court. [Dodd, 1954, p. 258]. However, railroad rates came to be tied to profits. The early U.S. railroad charters often had provisions for the adjustment of their rates based on profits. For example, the charter of the Franklin Railroad Company, incorporated in Massachusetts in 1830, included the following provision:

> If at any time after the expiration of four years from the completion of the Road, the net income shall have amounted to more than ten percent per annum, from the date of the completion aforesaid, upon the actual cost of said Road, the Legislature may take measures to alter and reduce the rates of toll and income, in such manner as to take off the overplus for the next four years, calculating the amount of transporation and income to be the same as the four preceding years; and, at the expiration of every four years thereafter the same proceeding may be had [Dodd, 1954, p. 260].

The charters of three other railroads incorporated in Massachusetts in the same year included a similar provision. [Dodd, 1954, p. 261].

The private acts of parliament incorporating the early U.K. railroads typically fixed the maximum rates explicitly; but, in one notable exception, the Liverpool and Manchester Railway Act in 1826 limited the company's dividends to ten percent of the capital and required that its rates by reduced by five percent for each one percent of dividend above ten percent [Pollins, 1956, pp. 337-338]. Parliament soon began regulating railroad profits. In 1836, James Morrison sought to have Parliament restrict the profits of all railways. Clauses in Gladston's 1844 Bill,

> authorized the Board of Trade to consider the position and profits of any railway which had a charter for fifteen years and to decide whether to buy it up on prescribed terms or, alternatively, to revise all its charges if it had made a profit of more than ten percent on its capital for three consecutive years [Cooke, 1950, p. 135].

Though these clauses were weakened in the actual Railways Regulation Act of 1844, a principle was established. Cooke [1950, p. 136] explains,

> The Act therefore fell short of the designs of Gladstone's committee and it is notable not for any reform it accomplished but rather for the principle embodied in it, that railway companies were one example of a class of company which was formed under special parliamentary sanction to carry on an undertaking of a special public nature. Since for this purpose it had special powers, it should therefore be subject to special scrutiny and (if necessary) control by the State on behalf of the public.

The question of railroad profits and the public interest was raised in the political process in both the U.S. and the U.K. in the nineteenth century. Hence, it is not suprising that questions of calculating profits and whether depreciation should be charged as an expense were raised. The accounting methods of treating capital additions, depreciation, repairs and renewals, *etc.*, could affect reported profits and hence the rates and market values of railroads. Thus, there was a demand for rationalizations of alternative procedures.

The political issue of railroad profits led several U.S. states (Virginia (1837), New Hampshire and Rhode Island (1841), New York (1855), Massachusetts (1869) and Illinois (1869)) to pass legislation which in some way regulated railroads, usually by "controlling extortionate rates." [Boockholdt, 1977, p. 13; Johnson, 1965, p. 218; and Nash, 1947, p. 2]. According to Nash [1947, p. 3], "Several of the early state laws called for statements of provision for depreciation in annual reports but without definition as to what such provisions should be." Arguments for depreciation are expected to follow such regulations. Finally, in 1887 federal legislation established the Interstate Commerce Commission to prohibit unreasonable rates and price discrimination, control mergers, and prescribe a uniform system of accounts. The Interstate Commerce Commission adopted an accounting policy of charging "repairs or renewals of ties, rails, roadway, locomotives and cars under the classification 'operating expenses' [which typically results in higher reported expenses than depreciation] but did not mention depreciation" [Littleton, 1933, p. 236].

Although railroads were the prime target of regulation, the rates of other public utilities were also regulated in the nineteenth century. A Gas Commission was established in Massachusetts in 1885 and two years later was expanded to regulate electric companies. Later, it was given control over capitalization and rates [Nash, 1947, p. 3]. Municipalities regulated water company rates (*Spring Valley Water Works v. Schottler* (1833)) [Clay, 1932, p. 33] and such regulation led to legal disputes over whether depreciation should be considered in determining rates (*San Diego Water Co, v. San Diego*) [Riggs, 1922, pp. 155-157]. In addition, states regulated the charges for grain elevators (*Munn v. Illinois* (1877)) [Clay, 1932, p. 30].

It is our hypothesis that rate regulation (primarily of the railroads) created a demand for theories rationalizing depreciation as an expense. Furthermore, we expect that the more popular of these theories would stress that it is in the "public interest" for depreciation to be treated as an expense. Without regulation there was no necessity for depreciation to be a charge, systematically deducted each year in determining net income. However, because rate regulation was justified in terms of restricting the economic profits of monopolists (or eliminating "ruinous" competition), regulation created a demand for justifications arguing for depreciation to be treated as an annual charge to profits. Furthermore, because regulatory legislation was often based on economic arguments, theories of depreciation came to be couched in terms of economic costs.

(2) *The timing of the debate* appears to confirm our hypothesis that political action generated accounting theory, not vice-versa. As we have seen, the early U.S. railroad charters in the 1830s included provisions for regulation of profits. Those charters *precede* the debates observed in the accounting literature. The move by Morrison to have Parliament regulate the profits of U.K. railroads also *precedes* the debates.

Income Tax Acts.

The influence of the income tax laws on financial reporting *practice* is well known and much lamented by academics.[56] That influence is very obvious in the practice of charging depreciation to net income, rather than treating it as an allocation of profit. Saliers [1939, pp. 17-18] describes the effect of the 1909 Excise Tax Law, the forerunner of the 1913 Income Tax Law:

> "Financial looseness" describes the accounting practices of industries in general at that time. The company bookkeepers, when closing their books, based the amount of the depreciation charge on the amount of profit earned in that year. A lean year caused the property to receive little or no charge for depreciation, while a prosperous year caused a liberal allowance to be made. The authorities had reason for either action at their fingertips, shifting one side to the other as conditions warranted. But after the year 1909 the shift was to the side of larger depreciation charges, for in that year the Corporation Excise Tax Law was enacted. Ths law levied a 1% tax on net income of corporations in excess of $5,000. This net income was said to be the figure resulting after deducting ordinary and necessary expenses and all losses, including an allowance for depreciation, from gross profit. Depreciation expense was made an allowable deduction and was universally deducted by those corporations affected by the act. The effect of this act on the growth of the use of the depreciation charge cannot be overemphasized. *It was the first instance in which the writing off of depreciation as expense was definitely advantageous. That fact alone insured its general application* (emphasis added).

The influence of tax laws on accounting theory appears to be as dramatic as Saliers' description of the U.S. tax laws' effect on accounting practice, particularly with respect to depreciation. Concern with depreciation as an expense existed only in the *railroad* accounting literature until the 1880s. In that decade we observe a spate of U.K. journal articles and textbooks on the question of depreciation for corporations in *general*. We do not observe the same concern in the U.S. at that time. This raises the question of why the sudden concern with depreciation in the U.K., not just for public utilities, but for all corporations. Further, why did such a concern with depreciation for all corporations not manifest itself in the U.S.?

Brief [1976, p. 737] suggests that the U.K. literature was motivated by a concern with "paying dividends out of capital" and that "accountants sought first of all to clarify theory, and second, to understand their responsiblity in these matters. However, they were offered little assistance from judicial and statutory authority which failed to specify rules of accounting behavior." Although the accounting authors of the time may have suggested that was the problem, we think it is a very unsatisfactory answer to the question of what really motivated the literature for two reasons. First, we have already noted that the "profits available for dividends" question had existed for 260 years. Second, there was no uncertainty in the law as to when depreciation should or should not be deducted before determining "profits available for dividends." The legal decisions were consistent: if the corporate articles required a provision for depreciation, it had to be taken; if not it did not. As Litherland [1968, p. 171] states, "the question of depreciation was a matter of internal management with which the law had nothing to do. The Articles of the given company were to govern."

We suggest that the reason a general concern with the depreciation for all corporations (and not just railroads) appeared in the U.K. literature in the 1880s and not before is that, prior to 1878, the U.K. tax laws made no allowance for depreciation. "In 1878 the law was modified to permit the deduction of a reasonable amount for the diminished value of machinery and plant resulting from wear and tear. Depreciation was not mentioned in the law and no amount was permitted for obsolescence" [Saliers, 1939, p. 255]. Now there was an additional reason for arguing over the concept of annual depreciation and its level—taxes [Leake, 1912, p. 180].

The income tax explanation for the late nineteenth century depreciation debate also explains the absence of that debate in the U.S. Brief's hypothesis does not. The first effective U.S. corporate income tax law was the Excise Tax Act of 1909 (which went into effect before it was declared unconstitutional).[57] Thus, in 1880 there was no federal tax motivation driving a debate over depreciation. There was in the U.S. in 1880 the problem of determining "profits available for dividends."

The tax laws affected not only the timing of depreciation discussions, but also the resulting concepts of depreciation and of accounting income. In the legal cases on "dividends out of profits," depreciation was regarded as a valuation procedure (see p. 169). Whether the amount of depreciation taken was sufficient would be decided in the event of a dispute. Administering the tax laws is less costly if the periodic valuation is replaced by an arbitrary proportion of historical cost. This saving was recognized in the early literature [Matheson, 1893, p. 15] and was the likely reason that both U.S. and U.K. income tax allowances for depreciation were based on historical cost. The demand for a rationalization of this procedure and other accruals under the tax law eventually resulted in the concept of income based on matching and the realization concept. Storey [1959, p. 232] reports this effect of the tax law as follows:

> [The realization concept] probably did not exist at all before the First World War, and at least one writer states that the first official statement of the concept was made in 1932 in the correspondence between the Special Committee on Cooperation with Stock Exchanges of the American Institute of Accountants and the Stock List Committee of the New York Stock Exchange. The letter referred to rejects the method of determining income by the inventorying of assets at the beginning and end of each period in favor of the recognition of profit at the time of sale. This concept of profit was gradually taking form during the period after the First World War and had become dominant in the field of accounting determination of net income by the late 1930s. *That it was influenced by the concept of income laid down by the Supreme Court in early income tax litigation is obvious* (emphasis added).

The timing of the depreciation debates in the U.K. also appears to confirm our hypothesis that political action caused the observed change in accounting theory. The tax allowance of the depreciation deduction (1878) *precedes* the 1880s debates.

It might appear that the development of the profession could explain the difference in the timing of the concern with depreciation in the U.K. and U.S. The professional bodies did not really develop until the 1870s in the U.K. and until the 1890s in the U.S. [Edwards, 1968a, pp. 197-199]. Hence, we could not observe depreciation debates in either country until those times. However, this alternative hypothesis is unsatisfactory on several counts. *First*, while the first professional society was not formed un the U.K. until 1854, Littleton [1933, p. 265] reports evidence of individuals (primarily lawyers) practicing accounting in the U.K. in the eighteenth century and suggests it is highly likely that accounting was practiced by lawyers in earlier times also. Similarly, there were public accountants in the U.S. at least as early as 1866 [Edwards, 1968a, p. 198]. *Second*, the lack of a *formal* accounting profession did not prevent the appearance of the railroad depreciation literature in both the U.S. and U.K. in the 1840s and 1850s. *Third*, the formation of professional societies, itself, is likely to be due, at least partly, to political action. Accountants have incentives to lobby on government prescription of accounting practices. Given some economies of scale in lobbying, government intervention in accounting would be expected to produce professional bodies.

Securities Acts

There appear to be at least two major effects of the U.S. Securites Acts of 1933-34 on the accounting literature: they caused the objective of accounting to shift to what we call the "information objective"; and they stimulated a search for accounting principles. Both *follow* the Securities Acts.

(1) The Information Objective. Prior to the Securites Acts accounting theorists tended to describe and base their prescriptions on the multiple objectives of accounting, and they listed the numerous users. Consistent with our analysis of accounting in an unregulated economy, the control, or stewardship role, was frequently stressed. For example, Leake [1912, pp. 1-2] includes as reasons for calculating profit and loss:

1. the stewardship role of management to "uphold the value of the capital investment and to ascertain and distribute the annual profits with due regard to the differential rights" of the various classes of capital;
2. profit sharing schemes between capital and labor;
3. income taxes; and
4. public utility regulation.

Daines [1929, p. 94] describes the "orthodox" or dominant objective of accounting as being "to reflect that income which is legally available for dividends." Sweeney [1936, p. 248] states that "the fundamental purpose of accounting should consist of an attempt to distinguish between capital and income."

In his book based on his doctoral dissertation, Sweeney adds other functions to the stewardship role:

> Business management guides the affairs of business. For its own guidance it depends heavily on reports submitted to it by its employees. Periodically it renders reports of its stewardship to the owners of the business. From time to time it also renders reports to bankers who have lent money to the business, to federal and state governments that tax or regulate business, and to the general financial public.
>   The whole system of business, therefore, depends upon reports. Reports are made up largely of accounting statements [Sweeney, 1936, p. xi].

Managers were frequently cited as important users of accounting. Paton [1924, p. 1] defines accounting as a

> mechanism and body of principles by means of which the financial data of the particular concern are recorded, classified, and periodically presented and interpreted, with a view, thereby, to the *rational administration of the enterprise* (emphasis added).

After the Securites Acts the providing of information to investors and creditors in order to aid them in making rational investment choices became the dominant objective in the literature. We call this the information objective. One of the earliest documents which illustrates this new emphasis on the investor's decision is the AAA's 1936 "Tentative Statement on Accounting Principles." A number of "unsatisfactory" accounting procedures are discussed, including upward asset revaluations:

> Occasional uncoordinated "appraisals" produce in the average financial statement a hodgepodge of unrelated values of no explicable significance to *the ordinary investor*, if indeed they have any to the managements of the enterprises affected [American Accounting Association, 1936, p. 189] (emphasis added).

Notice the emphasis given to investors. Hendricksen [1977, p. 54] also supports our contention that the objective changed "from presenting financial information to management and creditors to that of providing financial information to investors and stockholders." In a more recent example, *A Statement of Basic Accounting Theory* [American Accounting Association, 1966, p. 4], the information objective is listed first among four objectives of accounting. The objectives are:

1. to provide information for decisions concerning limited resources by "individuals acting in their own behalf, such as the stockholders or creditors of a firm, by agents serving in fiduciary capacities, or by individuals or groups in business firms, in government, in not-for-profit organizations and elsewhere" [p.4].
2. to effectively direct and control an organization's human and material resources,
3. to maintain and report on the custodianship of resources,
4. "to facilitate the operations of an organized society for the welfare of all" [p. 5].

Recent writers no longer even list management as a principal user of financial statements. The dichotomy of internal and external accounting has become complete. The recent statement on accounting objectives, the FASB's Conceptual Framework Study [1976], also excludes management:

> Financial statements of business enterprises should provide information, within the limits of financial accounting, that is useful to present and potential investors and creditors in making rational investment and credit decisions [FASB, 1976, p. 10].

The dominance of the information objective arose, we suspect, as a public interest justification consistent with and in support of the *raison d'*être of the Securities Acts. The SEC was justified in terms of, and charged with, maintaining the orderly functioning of the capital markets. In particular the SEC was to protect the public from another stock market crash. That crash was alleged to have been caused in part by inadequate corporate disclosure, although very little evidence exists to support this claim.[58]

Although the SEC delegated the power to determine accounting standards for corporate disclosure to the accounting profession, there is evidence that it still exercised control over that determination. According to Horngren [1973] and Zeff [1972, pp. 150-160] the SEC managed by exception, threatening to intervene, or actually intervening in the standard-setting process whenever the Committee on Accounting Procedure (CAP) or the APB proposed a standard of which it did not approve. Consequently, proponents advocating particular accounting procedures would justify those procedures in terms of the SEC's stated objective—the public interest (which "requires" the information objective).

The hypothesis that the dominance of the information objective was caused by the Securities Acts is supported not only by the tendency of modern writers to cite the public interest as an objective along with the information objective [*e.g.*, the fourth objective of *A Statement of Basic Accounting Theory* listed above], but by the tendency to argue that fulfillment of the information objective is necessary to the "public interest." An example of that latter tendency is provided by the FASB [1976, p. 3]:

> Financial accounting and reporting is an important source of information on which investment, lending, and related decisions are based. Confidence in financial information is vital not only to ensure that individual decisions result in an equitable allocation of capital but to ensure continuing public support of the free enterprise system as a whole.

The close relationship between the information objective and the "public interest" is exemplified by the argument recently raised in the literature that information provided in accounting reports is a public good and that as a consequence, there may be an under production of information from society's viewpoint (*i.e.*, there may be a market failure). If there is a market failure, the argument proceeds, the "public interest" may require disclosure laws requiring the provision of information to investors [Beaver, 1976, p. 66].

(2) The Search for Accounting Principles. Before the Securities Acts most of the accounting literature did not stray far from practice, and prescriptions were usually based on rationalizations of practice (*e.g.*, the matching concept). Even Sweeney's price-level accounting proposals of the 1920s were based on practice. According to the author [Sweeney, 1936, p. xii] the work "has its roots in methods that were developed in Germany and France during the late inflation periods in those countries." There was, with the notable exceptions of Paton [1922] and Canning [1929], little effort devoted to establishing a theory of accounting.[59] Indeed, Chambers [1955a, p. 18] claims that except for Paton [1922] the word theory was not attached to any work in the accounting literature until after World War II.

Taggart describes the general situation in 1922 as follows:

> Some of the writers on theory, notably Sprague and Hatfield, not satisfied merely to describe practice, had earnestly addressed themselves to exposition of pure theory; but the textbook writers, for the most part, had quite naturally concerned themselves primarily with practice and with not much more than an occasional nod toward theory, where it seemed to bolster practice. Paton's *Accounting Theory* is concerned only with theory; it touches on practice only for illustration or contrast; and it is quite the opposite of an apologia for practice [Foreword in the 1962 re-issue of Paton, 1922, p. v.].

Canning [1929, p. 160] himself wrote, "accountants have no complete philosophical system of thought about income; *nor is there evidence that they have ever greatly felt the need for one*"[60] (emphasis added).

A potential explanation for the two famous departures from the orthodox accounting thought of the 1920s [Canning, 1929; and Paton, 1922] is that both were based on doctoral dissertations written in economics departments [Zeff, 1978, p. 16]. Undoubtedly, both authors were influenced heavily by economists as well as accountants. Canning himself writes, "I need not declare my obligation to Professor [Irving] Fisher for the influence of his writings upon my thought—that obligation appears throughout the whole book" [Canning, 1929, p. iv].

If Paton and Canning were harbingers of a change in accounting thought, we would expect to observe a shift in the orthodox accounting view during the 20s, following publication of their books. Alternatively, if Canning's and Paton's views were outliers or aberrations due to their economics training, we would expect to observe them modifying their views towards the orthodox position to ensure their survival as accounting academics.

Zeff [1978] presents evidence that Paton's views, at least, moved more towards the orthodox view during the 1920s and 1930s, than the orthodox view moved towards Paton's. Thus, it is difficult to argue that Paton and Canning were representative of a change in the accounting literature which influenced the passage of the Securities Acts. Instead, we suspect that much of the attention which Paton's and Canning's views received after the Securities Acts was a result of the Acts themselves.

The literature's concern with practice before the Securites Acts is not surprising (given our theory). Prescriptions based on rationalizations of practice are to be expected in an economy in which corporate reporting is not regulated. Theorists would base their prescriptions for individual firms on the current institutional arrangements determining practice (*i.e.*, in the terms of the agency or stewardship relationships, utility regulation, taxes, *etc.*). Hence, theory would be very concerned with practice. Further, because the advantages are to the individual firms, the theorist would not *require* all firms to follow his prescriptions, but expect his prescriptions to be adopted because of self-interest. The theorist would not try to specify accounting principles which all firms *should* adopt.

As we have noted, the Securites Acts were based on the argument that required disclosure is necessary to the "public interest." The idea was that without required disclosure capital markets would be less efficient. We do not observe this theory being generally advanced in the accounting literature prior to the Securities Acts.[61]

The justification for required disclosure is that the private incentives to adopt accounting prescriptions are insufficient. Hence, current accounting practice cannot serve as a basis for prescriptions. This justification sets accounting theory free from practice. It makes it possible to "build up a theory of accounting without reference to the practice of accounting" [Chambers, 1955a, p. 19]. Further, the justification caused the SEC to demand such theories. Because they were to reform existing accounting practice, the SEC commissioners could not base regulations on practice; they required a theory or a set of accounting principles to justify their rulings.

Zeff [1972, pp. 133-173] documents the AICPA's initial search for accounting principles and the SEC's passing the responsibility for the determination of principles to the profession in SEC Accounting Series Release No. 4 [U.S. SEC, ASR 4].[62] Zeff also documents the search for accounting principles (or standards) by the succession of standard-setting bodies established by the profession. As noted, the SEC exercised control over the standard-setting bodies' search for accounting principles. Thus, we expect these bodies (like the SEC) to search for or demand accounting principles which do *not* describe existing practice.

We expect accounting theorists, who are accustomed to developing rules based on practice, to be perplexed by a demand for accounting principles not based on practice. *After* the SEC's call (in ASR 4) for accounting principles for which there is substantial authoritative support [1938], the accounting literature begins to discuss the nature of principles [Scott, 1941; Wilcox and Hassler, 1941; and Kester, 1942].[63] Further, as theorists come to observe less emphasis being placed on the practicality of their approach, we observe philosophical works becoming far removed from practice such as Chambers [1955a, 1955b, 1966], Mattessich [1957] and Edwards and Bell[1961].

It is instructive to compare the search for accounting principles in the U.S. to that in the U.K. where there has not been a government regulatory body with the statutory power to prescribe accounting procedures [Benston, 1976, pp. 14-30; Zeff, 1972, pp. 1-69].[64] Until recently there has been considerably less "progress" in the U.K. in the search for accounting principles [Zeff, 1972, p. 310 and Shackleton, 1977, pp. 17-21] and further, "the English began late" [Zeff, 1972, p. 310]. The evidence suggests that the U.K. search for principles is also a response to government pressure which arose out of various financial crises [Zeff, 1972, pp. 39-40; Benston, 1976, pp. 15-17; and Shackleton, 1977, pp. 17-21].

The difference in the timing of the search for principles in the two countries is reminiscent of the 30-year difference in the timing of the general depreciation debates in the U.K. and the U.S. That 30-year difference also coincides with a difference in the timing of government regulation (*i.e.*, corporate income tax laws allowing depreciation as a deduction). The difference in timing cannot be explained *per se* by the fact that we are comparing two different countries. In the depreciation debates, the U.K. led, while the U.S. led in the search for principles.

The discussion in this section has suggested that much of accounting theory (*e.g.*, the concepts of depreciation, accrual accounting, the application of the concept of economic income, and the idea that the objective of financial statements is generally to provide information to investors rather than to control agency costs), *follows* government intervention. Thus, the evidence is consistent with our hypothesis that much of accounting theory is the product of government intervention and that accounting theory satisfies the demand for excuses. The evidence appears to be inconsistent with what we have called the "public interest" hypothesis. Undoubtedly there are alternative theories which can also explain the timing of the accounting literature. The challenge is to those who would support those alternative theories to specify them and show that they are more consistent with the evidence than ours.

CONCLUSIONS

In our view, accounting theories have had an important role in determining the content of financial statements—although it might not be the role envisioned by the theorists. Instead of providing "an underlying framework" for the promulgation of "sound" financial reporting practices by standard-setting boards, accounting theory has proven a useful "tactic to buttress one's preconceived notions" [Zeff, 1974, p. 177]. While accounting theories have always served a justification role in addition to information and pedagogic roles, government intervention has expanded the justification role. The predominant function of accounting theories is now to supply excuses which satisfy the demand created by the political process; consequently accounting theories have become increasingly normative.

We are not offering any judgments on the desirability of accounting theories fulfilling an excuse role. What we are arguing, however, is that *given* the existing economic and political institutions and the incentives of voters, politicians, managers, investors, *etc.* to become involved in the process by which accounting standards are determined, the only accounting theory that will provide a set of predictions that are consistent with observed phenomena is one based on self-interest. No other theory, *no normative theory currently in the accounting literature*, (e.g., *current value theories*) *can explain or will be used to justify all accounting standards*, because:

1. accounting standards are justified using the theory (excuse) of the vested interest group which is benefitted by the standard;
2. vested interest groups use different theories (excuses) for different issues; and
3. different vested interest groups prevail on different issues.

While a self-interest theory can explain accounting standards, such a theory will not be used to justify accounting standards because self-interest theories are politically unpalatable. As a consequence, *not only is there no generally accepted accounting theory to justify accounting standards, there will never be one.*

FOOTNOTES

[1] For example, see Canning [1929], Paton [1922], Edwards and Bell [1961], Sprouse and Moonitz [1962], Gordon [1964], Chambers [1966], and American Accounting Association [1966]. We would prefer to reserve the term "theory" for principles advanced to explain a set of phenomena, in particular for sets of hypotheses which have been confirmed. However, such a definition of theory would exclude much of the prescriptive literature and generate a semantic debate. To avoid that consequence, in this paper (unless qualified) we use the word "theory" as a generic term for the existing accounting literature.

[2] For example, Chambers [1966, Chapters 9-11] apparently adopts economic efficiency as an objective while the American Institute of Certified Public Accountants (AICPA) Study Group on the Objectives of Financial statements [1973, p. 17] decided that "financial statements should meet the needs of those with the least ability to obtain information. . . ."

[3] Some writers (*e.g.*, Chambers [1966]) make assumptions about the world without regard to *formal* empirical evidence and derive their prescriptions using those assumptions. Others (*e.g.*, Gonedes and Dopuch [1974]) argue that prescriptions to achieve any given objective must be based on hypotheses which have been subjected to formal statistical tests and confirmed.

[4] American Accounting Association [1977, p.1]. This report also reviews the major accounting theories.

[5] The Committee on Concepts and Standards for External Reports, American Accounting Association [1977] examines many of these same questions, and the interested reader should refer to this committee report for an alternative explanation of these phenomena, specifically Chapter 4.

[6] The terms "normative" and "prescriptive" are used interchangeably. See Mautz and Gray [1970] for an example of prescriptions to "improve" accounting research and hence its impact on practice.

[7] See Sterling [1974, pp. 180-181] for Horngren's response to Zeff's initial remark.

[8] Accounting "procedures," "techniques," and "practices" are defined as any computational algorithm used or suggested in the preparation of financial accounting statements. "Accounting standards" are those "procedures" sanctioned or recommended by an "authoritative" body such as the APB, FASB, SEC, ICC, *etc.*

[9] Benston [1969a] reports that as of 1926 all firms listed on the New York Stock Exchange published a balance sheet, 55 percent disclosed sales, 45 percent disclosed cost of goods sold, 71 percent disclosed depreciation, 100 percent disclosed net income, and 82 percent were audited by a CPA.

[10] In the period 1862-1900, many U.K. companies voluntarily adopted the optional articles included in Table A of the 1862 U.K. Companies Act. See Edey [1968], Edey and Panitpakdi [1956] and Watts [1977]. Examples of private contracts can be found today in any note or bond indenture agreement.

[11] Jensen and Meckling [1976, p. 308] define an agency relationship as "a contract under which one or more persons (the principal(s)) engage another person (the agent) to perform some service on their behalf which involves delegating some decision making authority to the agent." There are at least two agency relationships which cause corporate promoters and managers to bear agency costs. The first is the relationship between shareholders (the principals) and the manager (the agent) and the second is the relationship between the bondholders (the principals) and the manager (the agent).

[12] See Jensen and Meckling [1976] for a formal proof that he bears this cost.

[13] See Kehl [1941, p.4].

[14] Agency costs are also a function of the tastes of managers for non-pecuniary income, the extent of managerial competition, the degree to which the capital markets and the legal system are able to reduce agency costs, *etc.* See Jensen and Meckling [1976, pp. 328-330].

[15] The terms "shareholders" and "stockholders" are used interchangeably.

[16] See Matheson [1893, p.5] for a report that managers did in fact adopt this tactic in the nineteenth century.

[17] See Matheson [1893, p.vii] for a statement that managers did in fact resist depreciation charges because of the effect on their compensation.

18 See Smith [1976, p. 42]. Also, we find labor managed firms in socialist countries faced with the same agency problem. Labor has less incentive to maintain physical capital than an owner-manager. Jensen and Meckling [1977].

19 For example, the General Bank of India had a provision in its charter limiting dividends to not more than ⅔ of net (cash) profits [DuBois, 1938, p. 365].

20 The Phoenix Insurance Company, 1781, required a reserve fund of £52,000 before any dividends could be paid. *Ibid.*

21 See Littleton [1933, pp. 223-227].

22 *Dent v. London Tramways Company,* 1880, in Brief [1976, p. 193].

23 "Take the case of a warehouse: supposing a warehouse keeper, having a new warehouse, should find at the end of the year that he had no occasion to expend money in repairs, but thought that, by reason of the usual wear and tear of the warehouse, it was 1,000*l.* worse than it was at the beginning of the year, he would set aside 1,000*l.* for a repair or renewal or depreciation fund, before he estimated any profits; because, although that sum is not required to be paid in that year, it is still the sum of money which is lost, so to say, out of capital, and which must be replaced." *Ibid.*

24 Prior to the creation of the Securities and Exchange Commission (SEC) in 1934, much variation existed in accounting procedures. See Blough [1937, p. 7]. In an unregulated economy, the market itself regulates the amount of diversity of accounting procedures. There are economies associated with using existing practices and terminology. If the firm adopts previously unknown accounting practices, then the users of the statements (*i.e.,* creditors monitoring shareholders and shareholders monitoring management) will incur costs in learning the new accounting procedures. If creditors and shareholders have alternative uses of their capital (*i.e.,* capital markets are competitive) the costs of the new procedures are ultimately borne by the shareholders and managers. Hence, new procedures (and increased diversity) will be implemented only if their added benefits offset the added costs they impose.

25 See the *Leeds Estate Building Company* case in Edwards [1968b, p. 148].

26 Share prices are unbiased estimates of the extent to which the auditor monitors management and reduces agency costs (see Fama [1970] and Gonedes and Dopuch [1974] for a review of the evidence on market efficiency). The larger the reduction in agency costs effected by an auditor (net of the auditor's fees), the higher the value of the corporation's shares and bonds and, *ceteris paribus*, the greater the demand for that auditor's services. If the market observes the auditor failing to monitor management, it will adjust downwards the share price of all firms who engage this auditor (to the extent to which the auditor does not reduce agency costs), and this will reduce the demand for his services.

27 See Stigler [1971], Posner [1974], and Peltzman [1976].

28 The reported profits of U.S. oil companies during the Arab oil embargo were used to justify bills to break up these large firms.

29 See Watts and Zimmerman [1978] for a test of this proposition. Also, see Prakash and Rappaport [1977] for further discussion of these feedback effects. See a bill introduced into the Senate by Senator Bayh (U.S. Congress, Senate, Subcommittee on Anti-trust and Monopoly [1975, pp. 5-13] and [1976, p. 1893]). Note that it is absolute size and profits which are used as a justification. On this point, see the "Curse of Bigness" *Barron's* [June 30, 1969, pp. 1 and 8]. Also see Alchian and Kessel [1962, p. 162].

30 The Interstate Commerce Commission based its decision to allow tax deferral accounting on APB Opinion No. 11. See Interstate Commerce Commission, *Accounting for Federal Income Taxes,* 318 I.C.C. 803.

31 Other writers have also recognized the tendency for advocates to use public interest arguments. For example, Pichler [1974, pp. 64-65] concludes that the accounting profession has increased its economic power via control over entry "through legislation justified as protecting the public interest" (p. 64). "In most cases, *public rather than professional interest was cited as the primary reason for* [the legislation]" (p. 65) (emphasis added).

32 U.S. Congress, Senate [1976, p. 59]. "Metcalf Staff Report."

33 McGraw [1975, p. 162]. Also, see U.S. Securities and Exchange Commission [1945, pp. 1-10].

34 For a summary of this literature see Posner [1974] and McGraw [1975].

35 By "best" theory, we mean the theory most consistent with observed phenomena. Such theories allow public officials to predict the outcomes of their actions, thereby helping them select actions which increase social welfare.

36 See Posner [1974].

37 For analyses of the political process based on this assumption see Downs [1957], Jensen [1976], Meckling [1976a and b], Mueller [1976], Niskanen [1971], Peltzman [1976], Stigler [1971], and Leffler and Zimmerman [1977].

38 Stigler [1971] attempts to explain the regulation of an industry on the basis of variation of coalition costs, free-rider costs, *etc.,* with such variables as group size, homogeneity of interests, *etc.*

39 The social choice literature (see Mueller [1976]) discusses the conditions which guarantee Pareto-efficient decisions by regulators.

40 See Fama [1976] for a review of capital market theory.

41 See Zimmerman [1977] for further discussion of this issue. Essentially, the reason it is costlier to purchase "control" of the political system (via a system of bribes, payoffs, *etc.*) is that the legal system does not enforce these contracts to the same extent that the state enforces the property rights of residual claimants in corporations. Hence, more (costly) monitoring is required to enforce contracts between politicians/bureaucrats and other parties.

42 Buchanan and Wagner [1977, pp. 128-130] introduce the concept of "fiscal illusion" as a systematic bias in individuals' perceptions of the differential effects of alternative taxing procedures. They hypothesize "that complex and indirect payment structures create a fiscal illusion that will systematically produce higher levels of public outlay than those that would be observed under simple-payment structures." (p. 129) It could be argued that individuals also suffer from "theory illusion" (*i.e.*, that more complex theories obscure political behavior). We do not subscribe to this phenomenon, but offer it as an alternative explanation.

43 Mautz [1966, p. 6] and Sterling [1973, p. 49].

44 Ijiri [1971, p. 26] states, "Accounting theorists are scientific observers of accounting practices and their surrounding environment. Their theories are required to have the highest degree of objectivity."

45 Moonitz [1974b] does not believe that accounting research should be the sole source for setting practice, but that it should have a role, "Almost everyone agrees that research is an essential component of the process of establishing accounting standards" (p. 58). He goes on to suggest that "accountants must curb the power of the management" (p. 68).

46 Even though we have argued the existence of close substitutes, all researchers will not be earning the same compensation. Higher compensation will accrue to the most prolific, articulate, and creative advocates—to those who are able to establish early property rights in a topic and thus must be cited by later theorists.

47 See Beaver [1973] for an example of policy prescriptions based on accounting research.

48 An interesting case in point is the work of Ijiri [1967 and 1975]. Ijiri claims to be a positivist—". . . the purpose [of this book] is a better understanding of the foundations of accounting as it is and not as someone thinks it ought to be." [1967, p. x] He states that his work "is not intended to be pro-establishment or to promote the maintenance of the status quo. The purpose of such an exercise is to highlight where changes are most needed and where they are feasible." [1975, p. 28] But, then, in the same monograph (pp. 85-90), Ijiri presents a defense of historical costs, saying, "Our defense of historical cost should not, however, be interpreted to mean that historical cost is without any flaw" (p. 85). Ijiri concludes this defense with a statement, "We should in fact try to improve the accounting system based on historical cost not by abandoning it, but by modifying it (*e.g.*, through price level adjustments) and supplementing it with data based on other valuation methods" (p. 90). Despite being a professed positivist, Ijiri is making a strong normative statement. No wonder the AAA [1977, p. 10] committee when summarizing Ijiri [1975] concludes, "[he] defends historical cost against the criticism of current-cost and current value. . . ." At least part of the "market" views Ijiri as a defender of the status quo.

49 Just as in any market, those who produce what is demanded have a better chance of survival than those who do not.

50 See Zeff [1972, pp. 212-216] for an account of this compromise.

51 Ernst & Ernst [1976] has proposed that replacement cost be used for depreciable assets while historical costs be continued for other assets.

52 "There is little evidence of fresh ideas regarding depreciation until the middle of the nineteenth century. The appearance of steam railroads at that time directed attention as never before to fixed assets and their associated problems of maintenance, renewal and improvement. Out of the discussion and experience which followed, new ideas about depreciation took form and the ground was prepared for a better comprehension of the real nature of depreciation itself" [Littleton 1933, p. 227].

53 It is tempting to suggest citation tests of the theory (*i.e.*, the frequency of articles on a subject increases with regulation). Besides the obvious cost of such a test, it suffers from the interpretation bias of the researchers. Also, how should changes in terminology be controlled? We would welcome anyone who can overcome these methodological difficulties to perform the tests.

54 The general practice in both countries came to be the writing-off of the value of fixed assets at the time of retirement of the asset.

55 See DuBois [1938, pp. 94-95] for a report on the incorporation proceedings of the Albion Flour Mill in 1784. In those proceedings, the Attorney General gave an opinion on limited liability which caused DuBois to conclude that, "for England at any rate, the fact of incorporation either by the Crown or by Parliament came to be the criterion for the extent of limited liability" (p. 96). Note, however, that it was theoretically possible for shareholders of insolvent companies to be made subject to calls. (See DuBois, pp. 98-103). DuBois (p. 95) recognized that *de facto* limited liability existed in the 1730s and 1740s: "it should be noted that through the financial tribulations of the Charitable Corporation, the York Buildings Company, and the Royal African Company, which in the thirties and forties were making life miserable for their creditors, there was no suggestion of any attempt to proceed against the personal estates of the members of the corporations."

56 Hendriksen [1977, p. 49] states, "The effect on accounting theory of taxation of business incomes in the United States and in other countries has been considerable, but it has been primarily indirect in nature. . . .

While the revenue acts did hasten the adoption of good accounting practices and thus brought about a more critical analysis of accepted accounting procedures and concepts, they have also been a deterrent to experimentation and the acceptance of good theory.''

[57] An increase in the effective corporate tax rate from less than 1 percent in 1909 to over 7 percent in 1918 further stimulated the concern for depreciation in the U.S. (Source: *Historical Survey of the United States*, U.S. Department of Commerce [1975, p. 1109]).

[58] See Benston [1969a and b]. The U.S. Securities and Exchange Commission [1945, pp. 1-3 and Part X] makes this claim, although Sanders [1946, pp. 9-10] disputes much of their argument.

[59] The Federal Reserve Board published a 1917 bulletin (*Uniform Accounting*) written by Price, Waterhouse & Co. in response to the Federal Trade Commission threatening to establish a federal accountant's register, but the bulletin ''consisted of mainly audit procedures'' [Carey, 1969, pp. 1:129-135].

[60] Canning's principal intentions were not to reform existing practice or to construct a general theory but rather to make ''the work of the professional accountant more fully intelligible to those in other branches of learning'' [1929, p. iii].

[61] The theory does appear in *The Journal of Accountancy* in October, 1930 (see Hoxsey [1930]), but the author is not an accounting theorist; instead he is an employee of the New York Stock Exchange. The theory also appears in the writings of Ripley in the popular financial literature in the 1920s (*e.g.*, Ripley [1926]). However, Ripley is also not representative of the financial literature.

[62] ASR 4 stated that ''financial statements filed with this Commission . . . [which] are prepared in accordance with accounting principles for which there is *no substantial authoritative support*, . . . will be presumed to be misleading or inaccurate'' (emphasis added). ASR 4 created a demand for some procedure or device to provide ''substantial authoritative'' support.

[63] Storey [1964, p. 3] supports our contention that the Securities Acts were ''landmark events'' and directly related to the search for accounting principles.

[64] See Sanders [1946] for an overview of the different prevailing attitudes in the U.S. and U.K. in the 1940s.

REFERENCES

Accounting Principles Board, *Opinion 16: Business Combinations,* (American Institute of Certified Public Accountants, 1970).

Alchian, Armen and Reuben Kessel, ''Competition, Monopoly and the Pursuit of Money,'' in *Aspects of Labor Economics* (Princeton University Press: N.B.E.R., 1962), pp. 157-175.

American Accounting Association, ''A Tentative Statement of Accounting Principles Affecting Corporate Reports,'' THE ACCOUNTING REVIEW (June 1936), pp. 187-191.

————, Committee on Basic Accounting Theory, *A Statement of Basic Accounting Theory* (American Accounting Association, 1966).

————, Committee on Concepts and Standards for External Reports, *Statement on Accounting Theory and Theory Acceptance* (American Accounting Association, 1977).

American Institute of Certified Public Accountants, *Objectives of Financial Statements,* (Trueblood) Report of the Study Group on the Objectives of Financial Statements (American Institute of Certified Public Accountants, 1973).

Beaver, William H., ''What Should Be the FASB's Objectives?'', *Journal of Accountancy* (August, 1973), pp. 49-56.

————, ''The Implications of Security Price Research for Disclosure Policy and the Analyst Community,'' in A.R. Abdel-khalik and T.F. Keller (eds.), *Financial Information Requirements for Security Analysis*, Duke Second Accounting Symposium, Duke University (December 1976), pp. 65-81.

———— and Joel S. Demski, ''The Nature of Financial Accounting Objectives: A Summary and Synthesis,'' *Studies on Financial Accounting Objectives,* supplement to the *Journal of Accounting Research* (1974), pp. 170-187.

Benston, George J., ''The Value of the SEC's Accounting Disclosure Requirements,'' THE ACCOUNTING REVIEW (July 1969a), pp. 515-532.

————, ''The Effectiveness and Effects of the SEC's Accounting Disclosure Requirements,'' in Henry G. Manne (ed.), *Economic Policy and the Regulation of Corporate Securities* (American Enterprise Institute, 1969b), pp. 23-79.

————, *Corporate Financial Disclosure in the UK and the USA* (Saxon House, 1976).

Blough, Carman G., ''Some Accounting Problems of the Securities and Exchange Commission,'' *The New York Certified Public Accountant* (April 1937), pp. 3-14.

Boockholdt, James L., "Influence of Nineteenth and Early Twentieth Century Railroad Accounting on Development of Modern Accounting Theory," unpublished working paper 31, University of Alabama (July 1977).

Brief, Richard P. (ed.), *The Late Nineteenth Century Debate Over Depreciation, Capital and Income* (Arno Press, 1976).

Buchanan, James M. and Richard E. Wagner, *Democracy in Deficit: The Political Legacy of Lord Keynes* (Academic Press, 1977).

Burton, John C., "An Interview with John C. Burton," *Management Accounting* (May, 1975), pp. 19-23.

Canning, John B., *The Economics of Accountancy* (Ronald Press, 1929).

Carey, John L., *The Rise of the Accounting Profession*, Vols. 1 & 2 (American Institute of Certified Public Accountants, 1969-70).

Chambers, Raymond J., "Blueprint for a Theory of Accounting," *Accounting Research* (January 1955a), pp. 17-25.

_____, "A Scientific Pattern for Accounting Theory," *Australian Accountant* (October 1955b), pp. 428-434.

_____, *Accounting, Evaluation and Economic Behavior* (Prentice-Hall, 1966).

Clay, Cassius M., *Regulation of Public Utilities* (Henry Holt and Company, 1932).

Cooke, C.A., *Corporation, Trust and Company* (Manchester University Press, 1950).

"Curse of Bigness," *Barron's* (June 30, 1969), pp. 1 and 8.

Daines, H.C., "The Changing Objectives of Accounting," THE ACCOUNTING REVIEW (June 1929), pp. 94-110.

Dicksee, Lawrence, *Depreciation, Reserves and Reserve Funds* (1903), reprinted by Arno Press, 1976.

Dodd, Edwin M., *American Business Corporations Until 1860* (Harvard University Press, 1954).

Downs, Anthony, *An Economic Theory of Democracy* (Harper and Row, 1957).

DuBois, Armand B., *The English Business Company After the Bubble Act 1720-1800* (The Commonwealth Fund, 1938).

Edey, Harold C., "Company Accounting in the Nineteenth and Twentieth Centuries," reprinted in Michael Chatfield (ed.), *Contemporary Studies in the Evolution of Accounting Thought* (Dickenson Publishing Co. Inc., 1968), pp. 135-143.

_____ and Prot Panitpakdi, "British Company Accounting and the Law 1844-1900," in A.C. Littleton and B.S. Yamey (eds.), *Studies in the History of Accounting* (Richard D. Irwin, Inc., 1956), pp. 356-379.

Edwards, Edgar O. and Philip W. Bell, *The Theory and Measurement of Business Income* (University of California Press, 1961).

Edwards, James D., "Some Significant Developments of Public Accounting in the United States," *Business History Review* (June 1956), reprinted in Michael Chatfield (ed.), *Contemporary Studies in the Evolution of Accounting Thought* (Dickenson Publishing Co., 1968a), pp. 196-209.

_____, "The Antecedents of American Public Accounting," *Accounting Research* (January 1956), reprinted in Michael Chatfield (ed.), *Contemporary Studies in the Evolution of Accounting Thought* (Dickenson Publishing Co., 1968b), pp. 144-166.

Ernst & Ernst, *Accounting Under Inflationary Conditions* (Ernst & Ernst, 1976).

Fama, Eugene F., "Efficient Capital Markets: A Review of Theory and Empirical Work," *Journal of Finance* (May 1970), pp. 381-417.

_____, *Foundations of Finance* (Basic Books, Inc., 1976).

Financial Accounting Standards Board, *An Analysis of Issues Related to Conceptual Framework for Financial Accounting and Reporting: Elements of Financial Statements and Their Measurement* (FASB, 1976).

Gonedes, Nicholas and Nicholas Dopuch, "Capital Market Equilibrium, Information Production and Selecting Accounting Techniques: Theoretical Framework and Review of Empirical Work," *Studies on Financial Accounting Objectives,* supplement to the *Journal of Accounting Research* (1974), pp. 48-129.

Gordon, Myron J., "Postulates, Principles and Research in Accounting," THE ACCOUNTING REVIEW (April 1964), pp. 251-263.

Hendriksen, Eldon, *Accounting Theory*, 3rd Edition (Richard D. Irwin, Inc., 1977).

Holmes, William, "Accounting and Accountants in Massachusetts," *Massachusetts CPA Review* (May-June 1975), pp. 18-21.

Horngren, Charles T., "The Marketing of Accounting Standards," *Journal of Accountancy* (October 1973), pp. 61-66.

_____, "Setting Accounting Standards in the 1980's," in Norton Bedford (ed.), *Accountancy in the 1980's— Some Issues* (The Council of Arthur Young Professors, 1977).

Hoxsey, J.M.B., "Accounting for Investors," *Journal of Accountancy* (October 1930), pp. 251-284.

Ijiri, Yuji, *The Foundations of Accounting Measurement* (Prentice-Hall Inc., 1967).

_____, "Logic and Functions in Accounting," in Robert Sterling and William Bentz (eds.), *Accounting in Perspective* (South-Western Publishing Co., 1971).

_____, *Theory of Accounting Measurement* (American Accounting Association, 1975).

Interstate Commerce Commission, *Accounting for Federal Income Taxes*, 318, I.C.C. 803, U.S. Government Printing Office.

128

Jensen, Michael C., "Towards a Theory of the Press," unpublished paper, Graduate School of Management, University of Rochester, June 1976.

_____ and William H. Meckling, "Theory of the Firm: Managerial Behavior, Agency Costs and Ownership Structure," *Journal of Financial Economics* (October 1976), pp. 305-360.

_____, and William H. Meckling, "On 'The Labor Managed' Firm and the Codetermination Movement," Public Policy Working Paper Series GPB 77-2, Center for Research in Government Policy and Business, Graduate School of Management, University of Rochester, February, 1977.

Johnson, Arthur M., *Government-Business Relations* (Charles E. Merrill Books, 1965).

Kehl, Donald, *Corporate Dividends* (The Ronald Press Company, 1941).

Kester, Roy B., "Sources of Accounting Principles," *Journal of Accountancy* (December 1942), pp. 531-535.

Leake, P.D., *Depreciation and Wasting Assets and Their Treatment in Assessing Annual Profit and Loss* (1912), reprinted by Arno Press, 1976.

Leffler, Keith and Jerold Zimmerman, "A Theory of Municipal Government Agency Costs, Organizational Form, and Scale," working paper, Graduate School of Management, University of Rochester (July 1977).

Litherland, D.A., "Fixed Asset Replacement a Half Century Ago," reprinted in Michael Chatfield (ed.), *Contemporary Studies in the Evolution of Accounting Thought* (Dickenson Publishing Co., Inc., 1968), pp. 167-175.

Littleton, A.C., *Accounting Evolution to 1900* (1933), reprinted by Russell & Russell, 1966.

Matheson, Ewing, *The Depreciation of Factories, Mines and Industrial Undertakings and Their Valuation* (1893), reprinted by Arno Press, 1976.

Mattessich, Richard, "Towards a General and Axiomatic Foundation of Accountancy; with an Introduction to the Matrix Formulation of Accounting Systems," *Accounting Research* (October 1957), pp. 328-355.

Mautz, Robert K., "The Role of the American Accounting Association in Accounting Research," *Research in Accounting Measurement*, Robert Jaedicke, Yuji Ijiri and Oswald Nielsen (eds.), (American Accounting Association, 1966).

_____ and Jack Gray, "Some Thoughts on Research Needs in Accounting," *The Journal of Accountancy* (September 1970), pp. 54-62.

McGraw, Thomas K., "Regulation in America: A Review Article," *Business History Review* (Summer 1975), pp. 159-183.

Meckling, William H., "Towards a Theory of Representative Government," presented at the Third Annual Conference on Analysis and Ideology, Interlaken, Switzerland, June 4, 1976 (1976a).

_____, "Values and the Choice of the Model of the Individual in the Social Sciences," *Revue Suisse d'Economic Politique et de Statistique* (December 1976b), pp. 545-560.

Moonitz, Maurice, "Accounting Principles—How They are Developed," in Robert Sterling (ed.), *Institutional Issues in Public Accounting* (Scholars Book Company, 1974a), pp. 143-171.

_____, *Obtaining Agreement on Standards in the Accounting Profession* (American Accounting Association, 1974b).

Mueller, Dennis C., "Public Choice: A Survey," *The Journal of Economic Literature* (June 1976), pp. 395-433.

Mundheim, Robert H., "Foreword, Symposium on Securities Regulation," *Law and Contemporary Problems* (Summer 1964), pp. 647-652.

Nash, Luther R., *Anatomy of Depreciation* (Public Utilities Reports, Inc. 1947).

Niskanen, William A., *Bureaucracy and Representative Government* (Aldine-Atherton, 1971).

Paton, William A., *Accounting Theory—With Special Reference to the Corporate Enterprise* (New York: The Ronald Press Company, 1922). Re-issued in 1962 by A.S.P. Accounting Studies Press, Ltd. Reprinted by Scholars Book Co., 1973.

_____, *Accounting* (Macmillan Company, 1924).

_____ and A.C. Littleton, *An Introduction to Corporate Accounting Standards* (American Accounting Association, 1940).

Peltzman, Sam, "Towards a More General Theory of Regulation," *Journal of Law and Economics* (August 1976), pp. 211-240.

Pichler, Joseph A., "An Economic Analysis of Accounting Power," in Robert Sterling (ed.), *Institutional Issues in Public Accounting* (Scholars Book Co., 1974), pp. 45-73.

Pollins, Harold, "Aspects of Railway Accounting Before 1868," reprinted in A. Littleton and B. Yamey (eds.), *Studies in the History of Accounting* (Richard D. Irwin, Inc., 1956), pp. 332-355.

Posner, Richard A., "Theories of Economic Regulation," *Bell Journal of Economics and Management Science* (Autumn 1974), pp. 335-358.

Prakash, Prem and Alfred Rappaport, "Information Inductance and Its Significance for Accounting," *Accounting, Organizations and Society*, Vol. 2, No. 1 (1977), pp. 29-38.

Rappaport, Louis H., *SEC Accounting Practice and Procedure*, Third Edition (Ronald Press, 1972).

Riggs, Henry E., *Depreciation of Public Utility Properties* (McGraw Hill Book Co., 1922).

Ripley, William Z., "Stop, Look, Listen!", *The Atlantic Monthly* (September, 1926), pp. 380-399.

Saliers, Earl A., *Depreciation: Principles and Applications*, Third Edition (Ronald Press Company, 1939).

Sanders, Thomas H., "A Review of Reviews of Accounting Progress," *Journal of Accountancy* (January 1946), pp. 9-26.

_____, Henry R. Hatfield, and Underhill Moore, *A Statement of Accounting Principles* (American Institute of Accountants, 1938).

Scott, D.R., "The Basis for Accounting Principles," THE ACCOUNTING REVIEW (December 1941), pp. 341-349.

Shackleton, Ken, "Government Involvement in Developing Accounting Standards: The Framework," *Management Accounting* (U.K.), (January 1977), pp. 17-21.

Smith, Clifford, "On the Theory of Lending," unpublished paper, Working Paper Series No. 7635, Graduate School of Management, University of Rochester, 1976.

Sprouse, Robert T. and Maurice Moonitz, "A Tentative Set of Broad Accounting Principles for Business Enterprises," *Accounting Research Study No. 3* (American Institute of Certified Public Accountants, 1962).

Sterling, Robert R., "Accounting Research, Education and Practice," *Journal of Accountancy* (September 1973), pp. 44-52.

_____ (ed.), *Institutional Issues in Public Accounting* (Scholars Book Co. 1974).

Stigler, George J., "The Theory of Economic Regulation," *Bell Journal of Economics and Management Science* (Spring 1971), pp. 3-21.

_____, "Do Economists Matter?", *Southern Economic Journal* (January 1976), pp. 347-363.

Storey, Reed K., "Revenue Realization, Going Concern and Measurement of Income," THE ACCOUNTING REVIEW (April 1959), pp. 232-238.

_____, *The Search for Accounting Principles* (American Institute of Certified Public Accountants, 1964).

Sweeney, Henry W., *Stabilized Accounting* (Harper & Bros. Publishers, 1936).

U.S. Congress, Senate, Subcommittee on Antitrust and Monopoly of the Committee on the Judiciary, Hearings, *The Petroleum Industry,* Part I, 94th Congress, 1st Session, 1975.

U.S. Congress, Senate, Subcommittee on Reports, Accounting and Management of the Committee on Government Operations, *The Accounting Establishment: A Staff Study* (Metcalf Staff Report), 94th Congress, 2nd Session, 1976.

U.S. Department of Commerce, Bureau of the Census, *Historical Statistics of the United States, Colonial Times to 1970* (U.S. Government Printing Office, 1975).

U.S. Securities and Exchange Commission, "Administrative Policy on Financial Statements," *Accounting Series Release No. 4,* (April 25, 1938).

U.S. Securities and Exchange Commission, *Tenth Annual Report of the Securities and Exchange Commission: Fiscal Year Ended June 30, 1944* (1945).

Watts, Ross L., "Accounting Objectives," working paper series no. 7408, Graduate School of Management, Unviersity of Rochester, April 1974.

_____, "Corporate Financial Statements, A Product of the Market and Political Processes, " *Australian Journal of Management* (April 1977), pp. 53-75.

_____, and Jerold L. Zimmerman, "Towards a Positive Theory of the Determination of Accounting Standards," THE ACCOUNTING REVIEW (January 1978), pp. 112-134.

Wilcox, E.B. and R.H. Hassler, "A Foundation for Accounting Principles," *Journal of Accountancy* (October 1941), pp. 308-314.

Zeff, Stephen A., *Forging Accounting Principles in Five Countries: A History and an Analysis of Trends,* Arthur Andersen Lecture Series (Stipes Publishing Co., 1972).

_____, "Comments on 'Accounting Principles—How They are Developed'," in Robert R. Sterling (ed.), *Institutional Issues in Public Accounting* (Scholars Book Co., 1974), pp 172-178.

_____, "Paton on the Effects of Changing Prices on Accounting: 1916-1955," unpublished manuscript (March 1978).

Zimmerman, Jerold L., "The Municipal Accounting Maze: An Analysis of Political Incentives," *Studies on Measurement and Evaluation of the Economic Efficiency of Public and Private Nonprofit Institutions,* supplement to the *Journal of Accounting Research* (1977), pp. 107-144.

THE METHODOLOGY OF POSITIVE ACCOUNTING*

by Charles Christenson

Research supported by the Division of Research, Harvard University Graduate School of Business Administration, out of funds provided by the Associates of the Harvard Business School. For comments on earlier drafts of this article, I am indebted to Rashad Abdel-khalik, Robert Anthony, W.W. Cooper, Anthony Hopwood, Robert Jaedicke, Spiro J. Latsis, E.A. Lowe, Richard Mattessich, Merton Miller, Joseph G. San Miguel, Edward Stamp, Robert Sterling, Tony Tinker, Richard Vancil, H. Martin Weingartner, and two anonymous reviewers. I have also benefited from the comments of the participants in the Seminar in Financial Accounting and Financial Analysis at the Harvard Business School; the Workshop in Accounting at the Sloan School of Management, Massachusetts Institute of Technology; and the Workshop in Methodology and Accounting of the European Institute for Advanced Studies in Management.

HERALDING an "emerging Rochester School of Accounting," Jensen [1976] charged that "research in accounting has been (with one or two notable exceptions) unscientific . . . [b]ecause the focus of this research has been overwhelmingly normative and definitional" [p. 11]. In accounting, he said, "'theory' has come to mean normative proposition. The so-called accounting theory texts are almost entirely devoted to the examination of questions of a 'what ought to be done' nature" [p. 11]. Jensen called for "[t]he development of a positive theory of accounting [which] will explain why accounting is what it is, why accountants do what they do, and what effects these phenomena have on people and resource utilization" [p. 13]. Without such "positive theory," he said, "neither academics nor professionals will make significant progress in obtaining answers to the normative questions they continue to ask . . ." [p. 12].

Subsequently, Jensen's colleagues Watts and Zimmerman have carried the banner of Positive Accounting forward in a series of articles which repeat several of Jensen's themes. Watts [1977, p. 54], for example, calls the traditional financial accounting literature "unscientific" because it "concentrates on prescriptions" and gives "[v]ery little attention . . . to develop-

*Reprinted from *The Accounting Review* 58 (January 1983): 1-22

ing a theory . . . to explain why financial statements take their current form.'' Watts and Zimmerman [1978, pp. 112-113] argue that ''a positive theory of the determination of accounting standards'' is necessary ''to determine if prescriptions from normative theories . . . are feasible.'' In a later paper, while continuing to distinguish between ''positive'' and ''normative'' theories, they make it clear that they award the honorific ''theory'' to the normative accounting literature only to avoid ''semantic debate''; they ''would prefer to reserve the term 'theory' for principles advanced to explain a set of phenomena'' [Watts and Zimmerman, 1979, p. 273 n. 1]. Zimmerman [1980, pp. 107-108] says that ''positive research seeks to develop a theory that can explain observed phenomena.'' Watts and Zimmerman, then, appear to be the principal members of the ''Rochester School'' announced by Jensen.

Each of the two articles coauthored by Watts and Zimerman cited above won the AICPA's award for a Notable Contribution to the Accounting Literature in its year of publication, and an article by Zimmerman [1979] seeking to develop a ''positive'' explanation of cost allocation won the Competitive Manuscript Award of the AAA. That these articles are considered ''top of the heap'' is, I shall argue, a sad commentary on the standards used in evaluating contemporary accounting research. This is a reflection, I would say, of the fact that accounting researchers today are well trained in research methods but hardly at all in *methodology*.[1] Machlup [1963] distinguishes the two:

> Methodology, in the sense in which literate people use the word, is a branch of philosophy or of logic . . . Semiliterates adopt the word when they are concerned neither with philosophy nor with logic, but simply with methods. Instead of ''statistical techniques'' they would say ''statistical methodology,'' and instead of ''research methods'' they love to say ''research methodology.''

''The methodology of a science,'' as Blaug [1980, p. 47] says, ''is its rationale for accepting or rejecting its theories or hypotheses.'' Thus, methodology is normative, and for that reason it would presumably be called unscientific by Jensen and Watts.[2] Yet, obviously no science can exist without making methodological commitments. Hayek [1952, p. 37] even asserts that science as a whole is normative: ''Its concern is not what men think about the world and how they consquently behave, but *what they ought to think*'' [emphasis supplied].

Like other normative judgments, methodological ones may be made with varying degrees of self-consciousness. In the more established sciences, which have a research tradition of proven fruitfulness to follow, awareness of methodological issues among what Kuhn [1970] calls ''normal scientists'' may be low. But as Friedman [1953, p. 40] argues, ''more than other scientists, social scientists need to be self-conscious about their methodology.'' Samuelson [1962, p. 21] for once agrees: ''Paradoxically, the soft sciences that are still akin to an art benefit more from an explicit awareness of the canons of scientific method . . . than do the hard sciences, where doing what comes naturally will protect even a fool from gross methodological error.''

In the interests of consciousness-raising among accounting researchers, therefore, I will examine in this article the following questions raised by the methodology of the Rochester School. What should be the domain of accounting theory? What, if anything, is a ''positive'' theory? How can scientific theories be used in explanation, prediction, and prescription? How should scientific theories be appraised?

THE DOMAIN OF ACCOUNTING THEORY

''To have a science of anything,'' according to Caws [1972, p. 72], ''is first to have recognized a domain and a set of phenomena in that domain, and second to have devised a theory whose inputs *and outputs* are [descriptions of] phenomena in the domain (the first observations, the second predictions) and whose terms may describe the underlying reality of the domain.''[3]

To illustrate the distinction between ''normative'' and ''positive'' research questions, Jensen [1976, pp. 11-12] presents two lists of examples, reproduced as Figure 1. The most obvious difference between the two lists—as Jensen intended—is that each question on the "normative" list contains the world "should" and each question on the "positive" list contains the words "why," "what," or "how."

There is a second, more subtle difference between the two lists. Every question on the first list is about the description of *accounting entities* [Kohler, 1975, p. 14]. Every question on the second list, in contrast, is about the description and explanation of the behavior of accountants, i.e., those persons responsible in some way for the description of accounting entities.

Thus, in his attempt to illustrate the positive-normative distinction, Jensen has managed to confound it with another—that between phenomenal domains at two different levels. Jensen's confusion is of exactly the type warned against by Popper [1972, pp. 176-177], who points out that the problem of understanding the behavior of a problem-solver is on a higher level than the problem which concerns the problem-solver:

> The problem of understanding is a *metaproblem* . . . Accordingly, the theory designed to solve the problem of understanding is a *metatheory* . . . We have to distinguish clearly between the metaproblems and metatheories of the historian of science . . . and the problems and theories of the scientists . . . It is only too easy to mix these two up . . .

To clarify matters, I propose a three-way classification of accounting problems rather than the one-way, positive-normative classification suggested by Jensen. With respect to a given problem, the first question to be asked is whether it is, in Popper's terms, a problem or a metaproblem. To use an accounting example, are we concerned with the problem faced by General Electric's management in deciding what to present in the company's financial statements for 1981? Or are we concerned with the metaproblem of understanding why management made the choices it did?

FIGURE 1

EXAMPLES OF "NORMATIVE" AND "POSITIVE QUESTIONS
[Jensen, 1976, pp. 11-12]

"Normative" Questions	"Positive" Questions
1) How should leases be treated on the balance sheet? 2) Should replacement (or liquidation) values be used in the balance sheet and income statements? 3) How should changing price levels be accounted for? 4) How should changes in foreign exchange rates be accounted for by firms with foreign interests? 5) How should inventories be valued? 6) What should be reported in annual financial statements? 7) Should interim financial statements be audited? 8) How should minority interests in subsidiaries be treated in consolidated statements?	1) There is much discussion in the literature regarding the "needs" of those using accounting reports. Why is there little or no attention paid to the "needs" of the suppliers of accounting reports? What are the supply-side forces, and what impact do they have on accounting practices? 2) Why do most firms continue to allocate overhead charges to performance centers? 3.) Why do firms change accounting techniques? 4) Why do firms change auditors? 5) Why has the accounting profession been cursed with a strong authoritative bias—resulting in the establishment of professional bodies such as the CAP, APB, and FASB to rule on "generally accepted accounting techniques?" 6) How have court regulation and rulings influenced accounting practice? 7) Why do firms continue to use historical cost depreciation for other than tax purposes? 8) Why are public accounting firms organized as partnerships? 9) Why is fund accounting so different from corporate accounting? 10) What impact has the CPA certification procedure had on the practice of accounting and on research in accounting? 11) What have been the effects on the focus of research of accounting educational programs which require faculty to expend substantial effort teaching institutionally oriented material aimed at the CPA exam? 12) Why does the accounting field place an emphsis on "professionalism" and "professional ethics?"

For reasons to be stated in Section II, I wish to avoid use of the term "positive." As an alternative to the positive-normative distinction, therefore, I will use what Popper [1966, vol. ii, p. 383] has referred to as the dualism of "propositions, which state facts, and proposals, which propose policies, including principles or standards of policy." Questions on Jensen's first list call for proposals in response; those on his second list call for propositions. The second question to be asked in classifying research problems, then, is whether our problem is to be resolved with a *proposition* or *proposal*. Do we want to know what method GE uses for inventory valuation? Or are we instead concerned with what method they should use?

In Section II I will show that propositions—statements of fact—are of two distinct logical forms: observational and theoretical. If the research problem we are classifying is to be resolved by a proposition, then a third question must be aked: Is the required proposition *observational* or *theoretical*?

Figure 2 shows how this classification scheme would apply to various kinds of accounting-related problems. In each cell of the figure, I have indicated the actors who would be concerned with the accounting problems falling in that cell.

FIGURE 2

A TAXONOMY OF ACCOUNTING PROBLEMS

| | Character of Problem Resolution | | |
| | Proposition | | |
Problem Level	Observational	Theoretical	Proposal
Primary (Accounting Entities)	Practicing accountants	Some accounting theorists	Entity managers
Meta [Accountants, managers, and users)	Historians, economists, and sociologists of accounting (such as Rochester School)		Accounting methodologists (most accounting "theorists")

The first row of the table is concerned with problems at the primary level, about the state or behavior of accounting entities. The financial statements of an accounting entity have the character of observational propositions. Therefore, practicing accountants, who are concerned with constructing (or "verifying") these statements on the basis of analyses of the entity's actual transactions, belong in the first cell of this row.

It has been suggested [FASB, 1978] that an objective of financial reporting for an entity is to enable the prediction of its future cash flows. In Section III, I will show that predictions require not only observational propositions, such as financial statements, but also primary-level theories. The second cell of the first row would be the concern of those who are interested in constructing predictive theories of this kind.

The managers of an accounting entity are concerned with what the transactions of the entity (as distinct from their accounting representation) ought to be. These problems fall in the rightmost cell of the first row.

The problems considered in the traditional "accounting theory" literature criticized by the Rochester School are concerned with how practicing accountants ought to describe accounting entities. They are metaproblems whose solutions are proposals, and therefore they belong in the rightmost cell of the bottom row. I have said above that financial statements of an accounting entity have the character of observational hypotheses. I would therefore call those who are concerned with the rationale for accepting or rejecting these descriptions "methodologists" rather than "theorists."

The program of the Rochester School is concerned with describing, predicting, and explaining the behavior of accountants and managers, not that of accounting entities. Therefore it also belongs on the metalevel, but in the leftmost cell. (I have not shown the division of this cell into "observational" and "theoretical.") The discipline of the Rochester School might be called "history of accounting" or "economics of accounting," since it uses concepts and methods from both history and economics. I prefer to call it "sociology of accounting," using "sociology" in the inclusive sense of Pareto [1935, p. 3]: "Human society is the subject of many researches . . . . To the synthesis of them all, which aims at studying human society in general, we may give the name of *sociology*."[4]

Having sorted matters out as shown in Figure 2, I will now make a few observations. First, the problems addressed by both the traditional accounting literature and the program of the Rochester School occur at the metalevel. For this reason, I would argue that neither the traditional literature nor the Rochester School is directly concerned with what should properly be called "accounting theory." Such theory belongs to the primary level. This is consistent with usage in the established sciences: Chemical theory consists of propositions about the behavior of chemical entities (molecules and atoms), not about the behavior of chemists.[5]

Second, I agree with the Rochester School that a scientific theory should be useful in predicting and explaining the phenomena that occur in its domain. However, it is "positive" theory at the primary level that is required to predict the behavior of accounting entities, not theory at the metalevel where the Rochester School has directed its attention. Moreover, as I have already argued, the development of good "positive" theory at the primary level requires sound "normative" theory—methodology— at the metalevel.

It is as if Jensen had advised his fellow financial economists to cease their "unscientific" interest in "normative and definitional" questions such as "How should market efficiency be defined?", and to turn their attention instead to trying to explain the behavior of other financial economists. The latter would be a fascinating investigation, and useful for some purposes, but it would hardly have improved our understanding of financial markets.

THE CONCEPT OF "POSITIVE" THEORY

The reader will have observed that, except in direct quotation from the Rochester School, I have generally enclosed the word "positive" in quotation marks. In this usage, I am following the example of Einstein [1944, p. 281], who wrote that "just as on the part of a real philosopher, quotation-marks are used here to introduce an illegitimate concept, which the reader is asked to permit for the moment, although the concept is suspect in the eyes of the philosophical police."

In this section, I will present the grounds the "philosophical police" have for suspecting the concept of "'positive' theory." As is appropriate when legitimacy has been questioned, I will begin by discussing ancestry. Then I will show the deficiencies of the concept from a methodological perspective.

Ancestry of the Concept

The Rochester School has drawn its concept of "'positive' theory" from that guru of the Chicago School of Economics, Milton Friedman.[6] Zimmerman [1980, p. 107] cites a well-known essay in which Friedman [1953] argued "for distinguishing positive economics sharply from normative economics" [pp. 6-7]. It was Friedman's judgment that "a consensus on 'correct' economic policy depends much less on the progress of normative economics proper than on the progress of a positive economics yielding conclusions that are, and deserve to be, widely accepted" [p. 6]. Friedman does not use the term "positive theory," but he does say that "the ultimate goal of a positive science is the development of a 'theory' or 'hypothesis' that yields valid and meaningful (i.e., not truistic) predictions about phenomena not yet observed'' [p. 7]. The echoes of Friedman in the program of the Rochester School are clear.

Friedman credits his distinction between "positive" and "normative" science to J.N. Keynes, who wrote [1891, pp. 34-35]:[7]

> [A] *positive science* may be defined as a body of systematized knowledge concerning what is; a *normative* or *regulative science* as a body of systematized knowledge relating to criteria of what ought to be, and concerned therefore with the ideal as distinguished from the actual . . .

The concept of "positive science" was popular throughout the nineteenth century. It was associated with a philosophical school called "positivism," which held that only the methods of the natural sciences provide "positive knowledge" of "what is."

As a philosophy of science, positivism is no longer taken seriously. Passmore [1967, p. 56], for example, says that "logical positivism [the last vestige of positivism] is dead, or as dead as a philosphical movement ever becomes."

Part of what killed logical positivism was the failure of its program to establish the traditional positivist dogma that the propositions of the established sciences such as physics, chemistry, and biology refer only to the actual, i.e., to "what is." These sciences use theories. Theoretical propositions, as I will show, are neither positive nor normative in Keynes's sense, neither statements of the *actual* nor of the *ideal*. Rather, they are statements of the *possible*.

The Rochester School's concept of " 'positive' theory" is philosophically suspect, then, because it reflects the erroneous belief that a scientific theory constitutes "systematized knowledge concerning what is." A theory is no such thing. Moreover, the Keynes-Friedman-Rochester concept of " 'positive' science" is also philosophically suspect, since, to the extent that science is theoretical, science is not concerned solely with "what is."

Both terms—" 'positive' science" and " 'positive' theory"—are misleading and ought to be abandoned. There is a perfectly good substitute for the term "positive" to refer to sciences that are concerned with propositions—matters of fact—rather than with proposals—questions of value. It is the term "empirical," which I will use henceforth.

Besides, why should anyone want to stand next to a dead philosophical movement?

Product vs. Process Views of Science

Empirical science can be viewed either as a *product* (a body of systematizd knowledge, in Keynes's terms) or as a *process* (the human activity producing the knowledge). Positivists have emphasized the product view of science, as exemplified by Keynes's definition and by the logical positivists' preoccupation with the formal structure of empirical propositions. The newer philosophy of science emphasizes the process view. An early exponent of this view, Popper, proposed that "empirical science should be characterized by its methods: by our manner of dealing with scientific systems: by what we do with them and what we do to them," and not "merely by the formal or logical structure of its statements" [Popper, 1959, p. 50].

Popper argues, on the other hand, that the first step in understanding *any* process should be an examination of its product [Popper, 1972, p. 114]. This should be the case whether our interest is empirical, in which case we start with an actual product and seek to explain it in terms of the process that produced it; or normative, in which case we start with an ideal product and seek to design a process that will produce it.[8]

Since Popper's concern is with methodology—the normative theory of science—he is led to analyze what a body of empirical knowledge ideally ought to be, including its logical structure.[9] He starts from the premise that the aim of science is to explain observed phenomena, although he observes that a body of knowledge that is explanatory will also be useful as an instrument for prediction and for technological application. So far, it will be seen, the Rochester School's concept of science is consistent with Popper's, although some differences will appear later.

I will summarize Popper's concept of an empirical theory in the remainder of this section. Then, in Section III, I will show what we may do *with* such a theory, by way of explanation, prediction, and prescription. Finally, in Section IV, I will discuss what we should do *to* an empirical theory before we accept it, and show that these norms are violated by the Rochester School.

Empirical Propositions

Popper agrees with the logical positivists in considering empirical science, as a body of knowledge, to be a collection of propositions. He also agrees with the positivists in accepting " 'the fundamental thesis of empiricism'—the thesis that experience alone can decide upon the truth or falsity of scientific statements . . . '' [Popper, 1959, p. 42]. On the other hand, Popper also accepts Hume's proof [1739 (1888), p. 139] that experience can never conclusively establish the truth of any statement.[10] He is thus led to ask whether it is possible to save the fundamental thesis by demanding only one-sided decidability; by requiring, that is, that only the falsity of scientific statements be decidable by experience.

Popper concludes that one-sided decidability—falsifiability—is possible, *but only if scientists follow certain methodological norms*. What preserves the empirical character of science as a body of knowledge are these norms, and not the logical form of its propositions. It is this conclusion, of course, that drives Popper to the process view of science.

From a strictly logical point of view, a proposition is falsified not by experience but only by the acceptance of another proposition with which it is logically inconsistent.[11] Accordingly, Popper defines a proposition as *falsifiable* (and hence potentially belonging to the body of empirical knowledge) if and only if there is at least one observational proposition (or basic statement, in Popper's own terminology) with which it is logically inconsistent.

An observational proposition asserts that an observable event is occurring in a specified individual .region of space and time. The requirements that the event be "observable" in a "specified individual" region are necessary to insure that observational propositions are themselves falsifiable[12] [Popper, 1959, Section 28]. Whether a proposition is an observational proposition is partly a matter of fact. Whether certain events are observable may depend, for example, on the state of the art of scientific instrumentation and may thus change over time, whereas logical form is immutable.

Falsification must be distinguished from falsifiability. A proposition is *falsified* if and only if an observational proposition is accepted with which it is logically inconsistent. Falsification involves not only a logical element, the inconsistency of two propositions, but also a nonlogical element, the decision to accept the falsifying observational proposition. Logic alone cannot compel one to accept a falsifying observational proposition. It is the nonlogical element which enables theories to evade even falsification by experience unless methodological safeguards are adopted.

Thus, Popper [1959, p. 54] is led to lay down a "supreme rule . . . which says that the other rules of scientific procedure must be designed in such a way that they do not protect any statement in science against falsification.'' An important subsidiary rule is that a proposition should be accepted into the body of empirical knowledge only if it has been corroborated, meaning that it has survived serious attempts to refute it. Corroboration, like falsifiability and observability, is not a matter of strict logic; a proposition once corroborated may be falsified by later evidence. Thus the acceptance of a proposition into the body of empirical science is always tentative.

Logical Form of Observational Propositions and Theoretical Propositions

As noted above, an observational proposition asserts that an observable event is occurring in a specified individual region of space and time. The logical form of an observational proposition is exemplified by the paradigm:

$$\text{There is an occurrence of the event } S \text{ in the region } K. \qquad (1)$$

The region K may also be interpreted as an event. It is, however, a *singular* event since it contains at most one occurrence.[13] The event S, on the other hand, has no restriction on the number of occurrences it might have and so is called *universal*.

The *joint event* AB is defined as the event that includes all those occurrences that are occurrrences of both the event A and the event B. Using this concept we can rewrite (1) as:

There is an occurrence of the event *SK*. (2)

The event *SK* contains at most one occurrence and is therefore singular.

The two preceding paragraphs may be summarized by saying that *the logical form of an observational proposition is that of a singular existential proposition:* singular, because it refers to a singular event; and existential, because it asserts that an occurrence of that event exists.

The *complementary event* $\bar{A}$ is defined as the event that includes all those occurrences that are not occurrences of *A*. As an example of the use of this concept, consider the proposition:

There is an occurrence of the event $\bar{S}K$. (3)

This is a singular existential proposition and therefore an observational proposition. Moreover, its acceptance would falsify (2), since *SK* and $\bar{S}K$ are logically incompatible events; if any event is occurring in the region *K*, it is either *S* or $\bar{S}$, not both.

Next consider the proposition:

There is no occurrence of the event *S*. (4)

This proposition is neither singular (it refers only to the universal event *S*) nor existential (it denies, rather than asserts, the existence of occurrences of a certain kind). Yet it is falsifiable![14] It is falsified by the acceptance of (2), which asserts the existence of an occurrence of *S* in a singular region. Therefore, according to Popper's proposal, (4) must be counted as an empirical proposition—although it certainly is not a statement of "what is."

Proposition (4) can be called a *law* since, like the laws passed by legislative bodies, it prohibits the occurrence of certain events.[15] It is also the paradigm of a theoretical proposition. Thus, we can conclude that *the logical form of a theoretical proposition, or law, is that of a strictly universal negative-existential proposition.*

As shown in Figure 3, theoretical propositions, or laws, are distinguished from observational propositions in two ways. First, theoretical propositions are *negative* existential; observational propositions are *positive* existential. Second, theoretical propositions are *strictly universal*; observational propositions are *singular*. Observational propositions assert *what is.* Theoretical propositions assert *what is not*, anywhere in spacetime.

FIGURE 3

OBSERVATIONAL PROPOSITIONS AND LAWS DISTINGUISHED

Range of Applicability	Existential Import	
	Positive	Negative
Singular	Observational Proposition	Not Falsifiable
Strictly Universal	Not Falsifiable	Empirical Law

To have an empirical theory of a phenomenal domain, then, means to have:

(1) A collection of logically possible events, including some elementary events plus all the self-consistent compound events that can be constructed from the elementary ones by the operations of forming complements and intersections; and
(2) One or more empirical laws, each of which prohibits at least one observable event.

Thus, of the class of *logically* possible events recognized by a theory, the theory asserts that only members of a proper subclass are *empirically* possible.

THE UNIVERSAL CONDITIONAL FORMS OF LAWS

Some empirical laws have, besides the negative existential form already discussed, two logically-equivalent alternate forms. Most methodologists have focused their attention on these alternate forms, or even on only one of them. This has been a source of a considerable amount of confusion about the relationship of laws to empirical evidence.[16]

The laws in question are those that prohibit the joint occurence of two or more events. An example might be:

$$\text{There is no occurrence of the event } R\bar{S}. \tag{5}$$

This asserts that the events R and $\bar{S}$ never occur in conjunction with each other.

From the definition of the complementary event, it is obviously equivalent to assert:

$$\text{All occurrences of the event } R \text{ are occurrences of the event } S. \tag{6}$$

To use a familiar example, "All men are mortal" is logically equivalent to "There is no immortal man."

In modern mathematical logic, (6) is further analyzed into:

$$\text{For all } x: \text{ If } x \text{ is an occurrence of the event } R \text{ then } x \text{ is an occurrence of the event } S. \tag{7}$$

The logical form of (7) is that of a *universal conditional* proposition: universal because of the prefixed phrase "for all x" (called the "universal quantifier" in logic), and conditional because of the "if . . . then . . ." clause. The sentence following the "if," "x is an occurrence of the event R, is called the *antecedent* of the conditional; and the sentence following the "then," "x is an occurrence of the event S," is called its consequent.

Thus, every empirical law that prohibits the joint occurrence of two or more events can be stated in the form of a universal conditional proposition.[17]

By a kind of optical illusion, the universal conditional form has misled many methodologists into thinking that a law such as (7) has positive import and is "confirmed" by an observation of the event RS. ("The evidence is consistent with the theory," they would say.) Hempel [1946] has pointed out that this view leads to a paradox.[18] For, it can be seen that (5) is also logically equivalent to:

$$\text{For all } x: \text{ If } x \text{ is an occurrence of the event } \bar{S} \text{ then } x \text{ is an occurrence of the event } \bar{R}, \tag{8}$$

The logical form of (8) is called the *contrapositive*, but it is obviously just another version of the universal conditional form.

Here is the paradox: If observation of an instance of RS "confirms" (7), then observation of an instance of $\bar{R}\bar{S}$ "confirms" (8) and therefore, by virtue of the logical equivalence, it also "confirms" (7). To be concrete, the law "All crows are black" is equally confirmed by observing a black crow and a nonblack noncrow—such as a green vase. In fact, almost anything one might observe is consistent with a law and therefore "confirms" it!

FIGURE 4

HOW SEVERAL KINDS OF INFORMATION ARE COMBINED IN PREDICTION

(Shaded areas represent events excluded in region K)

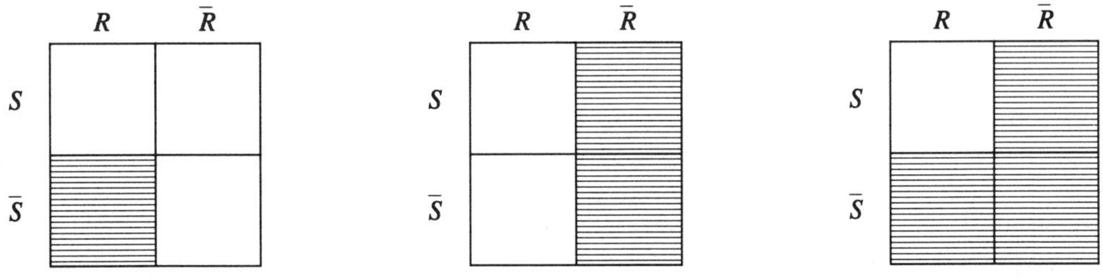

(a) Law   (b) Initial Conditions   (c) Prediction

The paradox arises because the universal conditional forms (7) and (8) make it appear that a law says something positive, i.e., that it asserts that something is the case. It is then natural to think that positive evidence supports or "confirms" the law. The paradox disappears with the recognition that both (7) and (8) reduce to the canonical form (5), which does not assert anything positive. The law "There are no nonblack crows" is refuted by the observation of a nonblack crow, but it is not "confirmed" by anything [Quine, 1974].

PREDICTIVE, EXPLANATORY, AND NORMATIVE REASONING

The Rochester School demands that what they call a "positive" theory ought "to predict" [Watts and Zimmerman, 1979, p. 174], "to explain a set of phenomena" [Watts and Zimmerman, 1979, p. 273, n. 1], and to enable one "to determine if prescriptions from normative theories . . . are feasible" [Watts and Zimmerman, 1978, pp. 112-113].

I will now show how an empirical theory of the "negative" form discussed in the preceding section can be used in predictive, explanatory and normative reasoning. (Since exactly the same kind of theory is used in all three kinds of reasoning, I find it more appropriate to distinguish kinds of reasoning rather than kinds of theories.)

Predictive Reasoning

A prediction is, for present purposes, simply one or more observational propositions that refer to as yet unobserved occurrences, whether these occurrences are in the future or in the past.

Since a theory states only what is empirically possible, not what is actually the case, in general no positive prediction can be derived from a theory alone. Suppose, for example, that we are given a theory consisting of a single law, "There is no occurrence of the event, $R\bar{S}$." From this law we can deduce "negative" predictions of the form, "The event $R\bar{S}$ is not occurring in the spacetime region K." Except for $R\bar{S}$, however, any event might be occurring in the region K. Each of the atomic events R, $\bar{R}$, S, and $\bar{S}$ is empirically possible, for example, as well as all the joint events that can be constructed from them except $R\bar{S}$ (see Figure 4(a)).

A definite prediction *can* be derived with the right kind of additional information. Suppose we are given the observational proposition, "The event R is occurring in the spacetime region K." As shown in Figure 4(b), this sentence rules out the occurrence in that region of the event $\bar{R}$. Combining this information with that contained in the law, we can conclude (see Figure 4(c)) that all possibilities are excluded except RS, the joint occurrence of R and S. Thus, we can derive the prediction, "The event S is occurring in the spacetime region K."

An observational proposition used in deriving a prediction is called a *statement of initial conditions* [Popper, 1959, p. 59]. Thus, in order to deduce a positive prediction, one needs in general *both* an empirical theory (one or more laws) *and* one or more statements of initial conditions. In terms of Caws's characterization of a theory (quoted at the beginning of Section I), the inputs to a theory are statements of initial conditions, the outputs are predictions. Both inputs and outputs are descriptions of occurrences in the phenomenal domain. This may be represented by the following schema:

Given: $\begin{cases} L_1, L_2, \ldots, L_n & \text{(Laws)} \\ C_1, C_2, \ldots, C_m & \text{(Initial Conditions)} \end{cases}$

To Find; $\therefore P$ (Prediction)

To give an accounting example, suppose we are interested in predicting the future cash flows of an accounting entity. In Section I, I suggested that the financial statements of an accounting entity have the character of observational propositions. For purposes of prediction they would constitute the statements of initial conditions. The schema shows that, in addition to these statements, we would need an empirical theory governing the behaviour of the entity (a primary-level theory, in terms of Section I).

Explanatory Reasoning

From a purely logical perspective, the explanation of a singluar occurrence is the mirror image of prediction. In the case of prediction, we are given an empirical theory and some inputs (statements of initial conditions); we seek to derive a proposition describing an as-yet-unobserved occurrence. In the case of explanation, we are given an observed occurrence; we seek both an explanatory theory and some statements of initial conditions (the *explicans*) from which we can derive a sentence (the *explicandum*) describing the observed occurrence. This process may be represented by the following schema:

$$
\begin{array}{lll}
\text{To Find:} & \left.\begin{array}{l} L_1, L_2, \ldots, L_n \\ C_1, C_2, \ldots, C_m \end{array}\right\} & \begin{array}{l}\text{(Laws)} \\ \text{(Initial Conditions)}\end{array} \Big\} \text{ (Explicans)} \\
\text{Given:} & \therefore E & \text{(Explicandum)}
\end{array}
$$

In some cases, characteristic of what Kuhn [1970] calls "normal science," we may already have a set of well-corroborated laws, so that the process of finding an explanation reduces to finding a set of initial conditions. Where we do not have such laws but must discover them, finding an appropriate description of the explicandum becomes a necessary part of the process of explaining it. Since, in a scientific system, occurrences are described in terms of events, finding an appropriate description of the explicandum means finding an appropriate event structure (or "conceptual framework") for the phenomenal domain.

NORMATIVE REASONING

Empirical theories can be used as guides to action in two different ways, corresponding respectively to predictive and explanatory reasoning. To distinguish the two ways, Popper [1957, p. 43] has called the predictions yielded by predictive reasoning *prophecies* and has pointed out that predictions of a completely different kind, which he calls *technological predictions*, can be derived by a process analogous to explanatory reasoning. In the case of a prophecy, according to Popper, "we are told about an event which we can do nothing to prevent. Its practical value lies in one being warned of the predicted event, so that we can side-step it or meet it prepared." Technological predictions, in contrast, "form a basis of *engineering*. They are, so to speak, constructive, intimating the steps open to us *if* we want to achieve certain results." I will refer to the derivation of technological predictions as "normative reasoning."

As an example of a technological prediction, one can calculate with the aid of Newton's theory of gravitation the force that would have to be applied to a given mass on the earth's surface in order to place it in orbit. It is interesting that Newton himself anticipated this technological application of his theory [Newton, 1729, p. 551]. Of course, a test of this particular prediction was not technologically feasible for nearly a quarter of a millenium! But it could not be derived at all from earlier theories which lacked the dynamical concepts of mass and force.

Two points may be observed from this example. First, technological predictions require the explanatory concepts of the theory ("mass" and "force" in the example.) Second, they require that at least some of these explanatory concepts correspond to controllable events, since it is through manipulation of these events that the desired outcome is obtained.

Normative reasoning, the derivation of technological predictions, follows this schema:[19]

$$
\begin{array}{lll}
\text{To Find:} & \left\{\begin{array}{l} L_1, L_2, \ldots, L_n \\ C_1, C_2, \ldots, C_m \end{array}\right. & \begin{array}{l}\text{(Empirical Laws)} \\ \text{(Controllable Initial Conditions)}\end{array} \\
\text{Given:} & \therefore S & \text{(Desired Final State)}
\end{array}
$$

When there is a well-established empirical science applying to his problem, the technological predictor may find the relevant laws within that body of knowledge rather than having to develop them from scratch. The modern mechanical engineer, for example, applies the laws of the science of mechanics. Before there is such a science, however, the practitioner faces exactly the same logical problem as a scientist searching for an explanatory theory [Christenson, 1976].

Analysis and Synthesis

Note that there is a close formal resemblance between the schema for normative reasoning and that for explanatory reasoning. In each case we are given the conclusion of a deductive argument, and we seek to find the premises from which it can be deduced. In other words, we reason in the reverse of the deductive direction. There is this difference: In explanatory reasoning, we accept the explicandum as true on the basis of observation; we terminate reverse reasoning when we have found laws and initial conditions that we likewise accept as true on the basis of observation. In normative reasoning, we desire that the description of a certain final state be true; we terminate reverse reasoning when we have found laws that we accept as true and controllable initial conditions that we can make true by our actions.[20]

In ancient Greek geometry, forward or deductive reasoning, which was used in "proofs," was known as the "method of synthesis," since in it a number of conditions are combined or synthesized to produce a single result. Reverse reasoning, which seeks to discover the necessary conditions, was known as the "method of analysis." The two methods are discussed by Polya [1945, pp. 141-154]. See also Hintikka and Remes [1974, Chapter IX].

THE APPRAISAL OF THEORIES

My purpose in this section is not to appraise the theories of the Rochester School but rather to criticize the standards by which they think a theory ought to be appraised, that is to say, their methodology. It is not possible, of course, to draw a clean line between these two purposes. The essence of my criticism of the Rochester School's methodology is that they use it to defend their theories against what would be appropriate criticism.

Instrumentalism vs. Realism

In Section III it was noted that, from a purely logical point of view, explanation is prediction in reverse. There are two divergent methodological interpretations of this state of affairs, and they lead to different conclusions regarding the appraisal of theories.

According to one methodological view, called *instrumentalism*, explanation is *nothing but* prediction in reverse, or, to put it a little differently, a theory is *nothing but* an instrument for prediction. The credo of instrumentalism has been characterized as follows: In explanatory reasoning, both the statements of initial conditions and the explicandum describe aspects of reality, to-wit, occurrences in the phenomenal domain. In contrast, the theory itself does not describe any aspect of reality. Reality, according to the instrumentalist, consists of *nothing but* occurrences of events [Popper, 1965, p. 108].

Instrumentalism, it may be noted, is a slightly liberalized version of positivism. Positivism awards scientific status only to statements of "what is." Instrumentalism differs from strict positivism in admitting that theories, although they cannot be reduced to statements of "what is," are nevertheless needed in science. It claims, however, that their utility is only as instruments for prediction, and not as descriptions of reality. Positivism and instrumentalism both agree that only observational propositions describe reality.

An alternative methodological view, called *realism*, agrees that explanation is (logically speaking) prediction in reverse and that, therefore, a theory that explains can also be used as an instrument for prediction. Realism also admits that *some* theories may be *nothing but* instruments for prediction. Realism holds, however, that for a theory to be considered *explanatory*, it must be *more than* an instrument for prediction. It must also be interpretible as a description of a deeper reality that underlies the surface reality of the phenomenal domain of occurrences.

A theory known to be false can still yield predictions that are highly accurate, or at least sufficiently accurate for many practical purposes. Newton's gravitational theory, and even the Ptolemaic theory, are still adequate for many astronomical predictions. On the other hand, *an explanation that is false is no explanation at all*. An explanatory theory is supposed to answer the question "why," and a false answer to the question is certainly unsatisfactory. For this reason, Einstein's theory has replaced Newton's as an explanation. An explanatory theory, in short, ought to be true (or at least not be known to be false), a merely predictive theory need not be [Popper, 1972, p. 192].

Although the Rochester School claims to base its positivist methodology on Friedman [1953], they diverge from him on the issue of instrumentalism vs. realism. Friedman puts great stress on the predictive function of theory and downplays the explanatory function. By my count, he uses the words "explain" or "explanation" only four times in a 40-page essay. Each time, he encloses the word in quotation marks (as if to signify he is using an illegitimate concept) and makes clear that what he really means by the terms is correct prediction.

Friedman's position is avowedly instrumentalist [Boland, 1979]. He says, for example, that "the *only* [my emphasis] relevant test of the *validity* [his emphasis] of a hypothesis is comparison of its predictions with experience" [1953, pp. 8-9]. It is notable that, in addition to insisting that its instrumental value is the *only* relevant test of a theory, Friedman also speaks of the *validity* of a theory rather than its truth. Friedman goes so far as to say [1953, p. 14] that "truly important and significant hypotheses will be found to have 'assumptions' that are wildly inaccurate descriptive representations of reality [i.e., are false], and, in general, the more significant the theory, the more unrealistic the assumptions (in this sense)."[21]

In my opinion, instrumentalism is a mistaken philosophy of science. It results, I think, from confusing an empirical law, in its universal conditional form, with a rule of logical inference.[22] Rules of inference may be said to be valid or invalid, but empirical laws are true or false. Also, instrumentalism has the effect (and, in Friedman's case, the intent) of shielding some of the propositions of a theoretical system from falsification. As I indicated in Section III, this robs these propositions of any claim to belong to empirical science. (Perhaps that's why Friedman prefers the term " 'positive' science.") Finally, instrumentalism is incompatible with the method of analysis since, in that method, we terminate reverse reasoning only when we have discovered premises that are *both* sufficient to predict observed occurrences *and* are "already known or admittedly true," or at least not known to be false. For essentially the same reason, theories that have only an instrumental interpretation are useless in normative reasoning as described in Section III; only theories that are at least a good approximation to the truth are acceptable for this purpose.

The Rochester School, however, is immune to any criticism of instrumentalism, since it abandons (perhaps unselfconsciously) that part of Friedman's methodology. It places the greater stress on theories that describe and explain, and it mentions prediction relatively infrequently, usually in a context where the testing of a theory through its predictions rather than its instrumental use is the issue. Jensen's list of "positive" questions (Figure 1) illustrates this emphasis on explanation rather than prediction. And Watts and Zimmerman [1979, p. 274] proudly claim that their theory not only "predicts that accounting theory will be used to 'buttress preconceived notions'" but also that "it explains why."

If someone questions the realism of part of Friedman's theories, he can fall back behind his instrumentalist ramparts and argue that the criticism is irrelevant; the theories with which he is concerned do not purport to explain but only to predict, and so long as they predict correctly they are adequate. The same defense is not available to the Rochester School. The Rochester School's theories must either be realistic or they must be rejected as explanations.

Appraisal of an Explanatory Theory

The Rochester School appears to believe that the only way one can test the truth of a theory is to derive predictions from it. They also appear to believe that correct predictions make a theory more acceptable. [Watts and Zimmerman, 1978, p. 125; 1979, p. 283; Zimmerman, 1980, p. 122]. (As a matter of fact, as I will show later, Watts and Zimmerman claim that their theories should be accepted even though predictions derived from them are false.)

Popper [1972, p. 353], however, calls the notion that an *explicans* is corroborated[23] by drawing correct predictions from it "incorrect and grossly misleading." He points out that "A true prediction may easily have been validly deduced from an *explicans* that is false." As we have seen in Section II, a theory as a collection of laws has no positive import, and almost all observations will be consistent with (i.e., will not contradict) even a false theory. Therefore, we cannot infer the truth of a theory from the truth of predictions drawn from it. In short, the Rochester School's notion that an explanatory theory is made acceptable merely by successful prediction is logically fallacious.

On the other hand, a false conclusion to an argument does entail the falsity of its premises. If, therefore, a prediction derived from an explanatory argument turns out to be false, we can be sure that the *explicans* is also false. "This means," as Popper [1972, p. 353] says, "that a prediction can be used to corroborate a theory only if its comparison with observations might be regarded as a serious attempt at testing the *explicans*—a serious attempt at refuting it. A 'risky' prediction of this kind may be called 'relevant to a test of the theory.'"

Since an *explicans* consists of at least two premises—a law and a statement of initial conditions—the fact that the falsity of the conclusion implies the falsity of the *explicans* does not determine how this falsity is to be distributed over the terms of the *explicans*. That is, the falsity of the *explicans* may mean that the law(s) are true and the initial conditions false; that the law(s) are false and the initial conditions true; or that both are false.

The fact that a prediction permits a test only of the *explicans* as a whole leads to the methodological norm that an *explicans* should be considered satisfactory prior to testing only if its terms are *independently* testable. That is to say, if a prediction intended as a test of an *explican* fails, we can determine which of the premises is (are) responsible for the failure only if we can test each of them independently of the others.

But, as Zimmerman [1980, p. 122] has acknowledged, he and Watts in their several articles have made "simplifying assumptions regarding (unobservable) *relative costs*," assumptions that at times "appear arbitrary and ex post." Zimmerman attempts to excuse the use of untestable assumptions by saying that "if they yield testable implications that are consistent with the evidence in replications, then progress towards a positive theory of accounting is achieved." This flies in the face of the logical fact that the truth of an *explicandum* does not entail the truth of its *explicans*.

There is a way in which a theory can be tested without introducing initial conditions. Although initial conditions are required to make a *positive* prediction, a theory *negatively* predicts, without initial conditions, that certain logically possible events will not occur. If one is seriously interested in testing a theory, then, rather than an entire *explicans*, one could specify what these prohibited events are and where, in the light perhaps of background knowledge, they would be most likely to occur; and one would then do one's damndest to find these prohibited occurrences. *That* would be the kind of severe test Popper calls "relevant." The search for correct predictions engaged in by the Rochester School is simply not "relevant."

The Issue of "Exceptions"

The fact that the Rochester School only weakly tests its theories becomes less significant, perhaps, when we observe that their theories fail even these weak tests. That is, their theories yield false predictions, which are then excused away.

Watts and Zimmerman [1978, p. 118, n. 24] tell us, for example, that their theory of corporate lobbying on accounting standards "is developed for firms in the same industry that only differ by size.'' In testing the theory, therefore, a control by industry should clearly be used. Instead, Watts and Zimmerman pool their data across industries. This tends to obscure the fact that the two firms in the retail industry behave in exactly the opposite way to that predicted. We also observe a contrary-to-prediction rank reversal in the responses of the oil industry. Finally, as the authors themselves note, at least three firms who were predicted to submit to the FASB did not submit.[24]

Since this article is a critique of the Rochester School's methodology rather than of their theories, my concern is less with the fact that the Rochester School's ''explanations'' were falsified at the first attempt to test them, than with the rationalizations used by Watts and Zimmerman to ''explain'' these falsifications. We are told, for example, that ''we can only expect a positive theory to hold on average'' [Watts and Zimmerman, 1978, p. 127, n. 37]. We are also advised ''to remember that as in all empirical theories we are concerned with *general* trends'' [Watts and Zimmerman, 1979, pp. 288-289], where ''general'' is used in the weak sense of ''true or applicable in most instances but not all'' rather than in the strong sense of ''relating to, concerned with, or applicable to every member of a class'' [*American Heritage Dictionary*, 1969, p. 548]. In other words, we are told without any evidence or argument that since *all* empirical theories admit exceptions we needn't worry about the exceptions to the Rochester School's theory.

In responding to this argument, I will again follow Jensen's advice and consult Pareto, who tells us:

> A 'law' that has exceptions, that is to say, a uniformity which is not uniform, is an expression devoid of meaning. . . . If one grants to a person who is stating a law that his law may have its exceptions, he can always meet every fact that is adduced against him with the excuse that it is an ''exception,'' and he will never be caught in the wrong. And that is exactly what literary economists, moralists, and metaphysicists do [Pareto, 1935, Section 1689, no. 3].

And that, of course, is also exactly what Watts and Zimmerman do!

If astronomers were interested only in general trends, the assertion that the heavenly bodies move uniformly from east to west would be a satisfactory theory, since only a handful of pesky bodies (planets and comets) behave exceptionally. Almost the entire history of astronomy, however, consists of attempts to explain these exceptions rather than to excuse them.[25] Even the Ptolemaic astronomers had the good sense to add another epicycle or equant when needed!

Pareto concluded the statement quoted above by saying, ''A law [that admits exceptions] has no significance, and knowledge of it is not of the slightest use.'' By arguing that their theories admit exceptions, Watts and Zimmerman condemn them as insignificant and useless. I agree.

Watts and Zimmerman [1979, p. 288] also attempt to deal with the problem of exceptions by drawing an irrelevant analogy with the toss of a coin: They say that ''one or two 'heads' is not sufficient to reject the hypothesis that a given coin is 'fair'.'' The analogy is irrelevant because, in the case of a fair coin, we are dealing with a stochastic law, which asserts that events occur with specifically stated numerical probabilities derived from symmetry considerations. There is nothing remotely comparable to such a law in the theories of the Rochester School.[26]

As Blaug [1976, p. 173] has written, ''Much empirical work in economics is like 'playing tennis with the net down': instead of attempting to refute testable predictions, economists spend much of their time showing that the real world bears out their predictions, thus replacing falsification, which is difficult, with confirmation, which is easy.'' The work of the Rochester School is certainly no exception to this ''general trend.''

SUMMARY AND CONCLUSION

The main criticisms of the methodology of Positive Accounting advanced in this article are the following:

1. The Rochester School's assertion that the kind of ''positive'' research they are undertaking is a prerequisite for normative accounting theory is based on a con-

fusion of phenomenal domains at two different levels (accounting entities vs. accountants), and is mistaken.

2. The concept of "'positive' theory" is drawn from an obsolete philosophy of science and is in any case a misnomer, because the theories of empirical science make no positive statement of "what is."

3. Although a theory may be used merely for prediction even if it is known to be false, an explanatory theory of the type sought by the Rochester School, or one that is to be used to test normative proposals, ought not to be known to be false. The method of analysis, which reasons backward from the phenomena to premises which are acceptable on the basis of independent evidence, is the appropriate method for constructing explanatory theories.

4. Contrary to the empirical method of subjecting theories to severe attempts to falsify them, the Rochester School introduces *ad hoc* arguments to excuse the failures of their theories. This tactic is a violation of the norms which, according to Popper [1959, Section 20], must be followed if a system of propositions is to be considered "scientific."

Of course, Watts and Zimmerman [1979, p. 290] do say, "We do not contend that all issues are settled, but rather encourage others to pursue, correct, and extend our analysis."

This encouragement is a trap for the unwary. As the authors point out earlier in the same article [p. 286], "Researchers have non-pecuniary incentives to be well-known, and this reputation is rewarded by a higher salary and a plenitude of research funds." A footnote adds that "Higher compensation will accrue to the most prolific, articulate, and creative advocates—to those who are able to establish early property rights in a topic and thus must be cited by later theorists" [p. 286, n. 46].

In other words, the Rochester School is inviting other researchers to repair the deficiencies in their program, while acknowledging that they will be the main beneficiaries of this activity.

The Rochester School ought to put its own program in order before it asks others to take that program seriously. A useful first step would be for them to stick with one set of phenomena until they have understood it well and satisfactorily explained it, rather than leaping to a different phenomenal domain in each new article in an effort to establish squatters' rights.[27] They should follow the advice of Newton, who said (quoted by Guerlac [1973, p. 385]):

> But if without deriving the properties of things from Phaenomena you feign Hypotheses and think by them to explain all nature you may make a plausible systeme of Philosophy for getting your self a name, but your systeme will be little better than a Romance. To explain all nature is too difficult a task for any one man or even for any one age. Tis much better to do a little with certainty and leave the rest for others that come after you than to explain all things by conjecture without making sure of anything.

Newton himself set an appropriate example, refraining from publishing his lunar theory for nearly twenty years while he attempted to resolve discrepancies between its predictions and observational data. As Lakatos [1978, vol. i, p. 216] observes, "The first dozen [versions of Newton's theory] ended up in Newton's wastepaper-basket." In a footnote, Lakatos explains:

> 'Wastepaper-baskets' were containers used in the seventeenth century for the disposal of some first versions of manuscripts which self-criticism—or private criticism of learned friends— ruled out on the first reading. In our age of publication explosion most people have no time to read their manuscripts, and the function of wastepaper-baskets has now been taken over by scientific journals.

The old ways have much to recommend them.

FOOTNOTES

1 Zimmerman, [1980, p. 120] asserts that the time is now propitious for positive research in accounting because accounting researchers are becoming increasingly well trained in economic theory and research methods. If Blaug [1980, p. xiii] is to be believed, however, this is no cause for complacency. He says that "the average modern economist has little use for methodological inquiries" and that, "to be perfectly frank, economic methodology has little place in the training of modern economists."

2 It is not surprising that positivists such as Jensen and Watts hold methodology in low esteem. As Popper [1959, p. 51] observes, it is a characteristically positivist dogma to deride methodology as "unscientific" and "meaningless": "The positivist dislikes the idea that there should be meaningful problems outside the field of 'positive' empirical science. . . . He dislikes the idea that there should be a genuine theory of knowledge, an epistemology or a methodology." This dogma does not enable positivists to avoid methodological commitments but only makes it less likely that they will be self-conscious about the commitments they make.

3 I have interpolated the two bracketed words into Caws's statement in anticipation of a point to be developed later in this article.

4 Jensen [1976, p.15] disdains "sociological" explanation as too narrow, advocating instead a model of "resourceful, evaluative, maximizing man (REMM)." See also Meckling [1976]. Pareto [1935] argues, on the other hand, that the standard economic assumption that people act in accordance with their perceived self-interest is inadequate to explain observed social phenomena and he therefore advocates augmenting this assumption with sociological premises. Jensen [1976, p. 14] advises accounting researchers to become more familiar with Pareto's ideas. Perhaps he should follow his own advice!

5 A special problem in the social sciences is that the social scientist, as a human being, is also a social entity—and every human being is at least an amateur social scientist. This makes it much more difficult to distinguish between primary and meta levels, but it does not make it any less important.

6 Significantly, both Jensen and Watts earned their Ph.D.s at the University of Chicago, and, of 17 persons acknowledged by Watts and Zimmerman [1979, p. 273], at least eight (including Jensen) did graduate work at Chicago and three others have taught there.

7 From the final clause of this quotation I infer that Keynes believed that "positive science" is concerned with "the actual." I shall criticize this notion later in this section. Friedman, incidentally, does not quote this clause. Nor does Zimmerman [1980, p. 107], who apparently did not consult the original source. Perhaps that is why he misattributes the quotation to "J.M. Keynes," confusing Neville Keynes with his son Maynard.

8 As Popper says [1972, p. 115], "In all sciences, the ordinary approach is from the effects [products] to the causes [processes]."

9 This has led many of Popper's critics to miss the point that his ultimate concern is with the process of science rather than with its product, and to assume that he has proposed only some minor improvements to the logical positivist program, such as replacing its verificationist criterion of meaning with a falsificationist one. For one such critic who eventually saw the light—"it came to me as a revelation"—see Bar-Hillel [1974, p. 333].

10 Russell [1946, p. 673], an empiricist himself, somewhat despairingly refers to this as "Hume's destruction of empiricism" and says that its natural sequel has been "the growth of unreason throughout the nineteenth century and what has passed of the twentieth."

11 Cf. Einstein [1944, p. 287], who refers to "the gulf—logically unbridgeable—which separates the world of sensory experiences from the world of concepts and propositions."

12 Popper, whose concern is primarily with the physical sciences, uses only the method of spacetime coordination to individuate occurrences. In the biological and social sciences other methods of individuation may be requried; e.g., the numerical tagging of biological specimens.

13 As stated at note 12, the singularity is necessary to make an observational sentence falsifiable.

14 It is not effectively verifiable, since all of spacetime would have to be searched to prove that there is no counterexample. Nor is it "confirmable" in the sense of being rendered more probable by favorable evidence. The essence of Hume's anti-inductivist argument is that no amount of favorable evidence to a proposition such as (4) can preclude the possibility of a counterexample.

15 "Not for nothing do we call the laws of nature 'laws,'" as Popper [1959, p. 41] says. "The more they prohibit the more they say."

16 For example, Nagel [1963, p. 215] has suggested that Friedman's [1953, p. 14] argument that the "assumptions" of a theory need not be "realistic" is based on the erroneous notion that the antecedent of a universal conditional proposition is an assumption of a theory. Another example of a confusion, to be discussed shortly, is Hempel's paradox of confirmation.

17 Zimmerman [1980, p. 108] says, "A positive theory is of the form, 'If A then B', that is capable of being refuted." This represents some progress over the statement by Watts and Zimmerman [1979, p. 273]: "We would prefer to reserve the term 'theory' . . . for sets of hypotheses which have been confirmed [sic]." Yet Zimmerman commits three technical errors in his short sentence: (1) he omits reference to universal

148

quantification over a free variable, (2) he omits the restriction of the conditional form to those laws which prohibit a joint event, and (3) he calls the conditional "positive" when in fact it has only negative import.

[18] Hempel's "paradox of confirmation" is discussed by Ijiri [1975, pp. 165-167]. Since I consider Hempel's paradox to be a *reductio ad absurdum* of the concept of confirmation, I do not agree with Ijiri's analysis.

[19] As Simon [1965] points out, the initial conditions and the description of the desired final state in this schema will not be observational propositions but rather what he calls *commands* and what I have earlier called *proposals*. With a couple of restrictions, however, these commands can be treated for logical purposes as if they were observational propositions. The following analogy may be enlightening. In a linear programming problem, the constraint set and the objective function usually define what is empirically possible, and thus correspond to the set of empirical laws. The command "maximize the objective function" characterizes the desired final state. The values of the variables appearing in the constraints and the objective function are the controllable initial conditions.

[20] Reverse reasoning is, of course, the method used in reasoning from a product to the process that produces it, as discussed in Section III of this article.

[21] Friedman's instrumentalism may be contrasted with the realism of Galileo [1967, p. 341], who said approvingly that Copernicus "very well understood that although the celestial appearances might be saved by means of assumptions essentially false in nature, it would be very much better if he could derive them from true suppositions." Galileo could have avoided trial by the Inquisition by accepting Cardinal Bellarmino's suggestion that he adopt an instrumentalist interpretation of the Copernican Theory.

[22] Popper himself acknowledges [1959, p. 76] that at the time he wrote the original German version of his book he was confused about the distinction between a conditional proposition and a rule of logical inference.

[23] As indicated in Section II above, Popper considers a theory to be corroborated only if it has survived serious attempts to refute it. His reasons for preferring the term "corroboration" to the "confirmation" are given in [1959, pp. 251-252, n.*1].

[24] The three firms are identified at one point as IBM, U.S. Steel, and Chrysler; later in the same paragraph two of the three are identified as IBM and General Telephone. No explanation is given of this obvious inconsistency [Watts and Zimmerman, 1978, p. 127].

[25] Cf. Holton and Brush [1973, p. 430].

[26] Because their theories are not formulated in stochastic terms, I have not discussed in this article the nature of stochastic laws and the particular problems involved in testing them. Popper [1959, Chapter VIII] discusses these problems in detail.

[27] Watts and Zimmerman [1978], for example, deals with the behavior of practicing financial accountants and managers; Watts and Zimmerman [1979], with that of academic accountants; and Zimmerman [1979], with that of cost accountants.

REFERENCES

American Heritage Dictionary (1969) (Houghton Mifflin Co., 1969).

Bar-Hillel, Y. (1974), "Popper's Theory of Corroboration," in Paul A. Schilpp (ed.), *The Philosophy of Karl Popper* (Open Court, 1974), pp. 332-348.

Blaug, Mark (1976), "Kuhn versus Lakatos, *or* Paradigms versus research programmes in the history of economics," in S.J. Latsis (ed.), *Method and Appraisal in Economics* (Cambridge University Press, 1976), pp. 149-180.

_____ (1980), *The Methodology of Economics* (Cambirdge University Press, 1980).

Boland, L.A. (1979), "A Critique of Friedman's Critics," *Journal of Economic Literature* (June 1979), pp. 503-522.

Caws, Peter (1972), "Accounting Research—Science or Methodology?", in R.R. Sterling (ed.), *Research Methodology in Accounting* (Scholars Book Co., 1972), pp. 71-73.

Christenson, Charles (1976), "Proposals for a Program of Empirical Research Into the Properties of Triangles." *Decision Sciences* (October 1976), pp. 631-648.

Einstein, Albert (1944), "Remarks on Bertrand Russell's Theory of Knowledge," in Paul A. Schilpp (ed)., *The Philosophy of Bertrand Russell* (Open Court, 1944), pp. 277-291.

Financial Accounting Standards Board (1978), "Objectives of Financial Reporting by Business Enterprises," *Statement of Financial Accounting Concepts No. 1* (FASB, 1978).

Friedman, Milton (1953), "The Methodology of Positive Economics," in *Essays in Positive Economics* (University of Chicago Press, 1953), pp. 3-43.

Galilei, Galileo (1967), *Dialogue Concerning the Two Chief World Systems* (University of California Press, 1967; translation from the 1632 Italian version by Stillman Drake).

Guerlac, Henry (1973), "Newton and the Method of Analysis" in *Dictionary of the History of Ideas* (Charles Scribner's Sons, 1973), pp. 378-391).

Hayek, F.A. (1952), *The Counter-Revolution of Science* (Free Press, 1952).

Hempel, Carl G. (1946), "A Note on the Paradoxes of Confirmation," *Mind* (January, 1946), pp. 79-82.

Hintikka, Jaakko, and Unto Remes (1974), *The Method of Analysis* (D. Reidel, 1974).

Holton, Gerald, and S.G. Brush (1973), *Introduction to Concepts and Theories in Physical Science* (Addison-Wesley, 1973).

Hume, David (1739), *A Treatise of Human Nature* (Oxford, 1888; reprinted from the original 1739 edition and edited by L.A. Selby-Bigge).

Ijiri, Yuji, (1975), *Theory of Accounting Measurement*. Studies in Accounting Research #10 (American Accounting Association, 1975).

Jensen, M.C. (1976), "Reflections on the State of Accounting Research and the Regulation of Accounting," *Stanford Lectures in Accounting 1976* (Graduate School of Business, Stanford University, 1976), pp. 11-19.

Keynes, J.N. (1891), *The Scope and Method of Political Economy* (Macmillan, 1891).

Kohler, Eric L. (1975), *A Dictionary for Accountants* (Prentice-Hall, 1975).

Kuhn, T.S. (1970), *The Structure of Scientific Revolutions* (University of Chicago Press, 1970).

Lakatos, Imre, (1978), *Philosophical Papers* (2 vols.) (Cambridge University Press, 1978).

Machlup, Fritz (1963), "Introductory Remarks," *American Economic Review* (May 1963), p. 204.

Meckling, W.H. (1976), "Values and the Choice of the Model of the Individual in the Social Sciences," *Revue Suisse d'Economie Politique et de Statistique* (December, 1976), pp. 545-560.

Nagel, Ernest (1963), "Assumptions in Economic Theory," *American Economic Review* (May 1963), pp. 211-219.

Newton, Isaac (1729), *Principia* (University of California Press, 1934; reprinted from the English translation of 1729).

Pareto, Vilfredo (1935), *Treatise on General Sociology* (Harcourt, Brace & Co., 1935; translated by Andrew Bongiorno and Arthur Livingston from the 1923 Italian edition).

Passmore, John (1967), "Logical Positivism," in *The Encyclopedia of Philosophy* (Collier-Macmillan, 1967), pp. 52-57.

Polya, George (1945), *How to Solve It* (Princeton University Press, 1945).

Popper, K.R. (1957), *The Poverty of Historicism* (Routledge and Kegan Paul, 1957).

_____ (1959), *The Logic of Scientific Discovery* (Basic Books, 1959).

_____ (1965), *Conjectures and Refutations* (Harper & Row, 1965).

_____ (1966), *The Open Society and Its Enemies* (Princeton Univesity Press, 1966).

_____ (1972), *Objective Knowledge* (Oxford, 1972).

Quine, W.V.O. (1974), "On Popper's Negative Methodology," in Paul A. Schilpp (ed.), *The Philosophy of Karl Popper* (Open Court, 1974), pp. 218-220.

Russell, Bertrand (1946), *A History of Western Philosophy* (Simon & Shuster, 1946).

Samuelson, P.A. (1962), *Problems of the American Economy* (Stamp Memorial Lecture, 1962).

Simon, H.A. (1965), "The Logic of Rational Decision," *British Journal for the Philosophy of Science* (November, 1965), pp. 169-186.

Watts, R.L. (1977), "Corporate Financial Statements, A Product of the Market and Political Processes," *Australian Journal of Management* (April 1977), pp. 53-75.

Watts, R.L. and J.L. Zimmerman (1978), "Towards a Positive Theory of Determination of Accounting Standards," THE ACCOUNTING REVIEW (January 1978), pp. 112-134.

_____ (1979), "The Demand for and Supply of Accounting Theories: The Market for Excuses," THE ACCOUNTING REVIEW (April 1979), pp. 273-305.

Zimmerman, J.L. (1979), "The Costs and Benefits of Cost Allocations," THE ACCOUNTING REVIEW (July 1979), pp. 504-521.

_____ (1980), "Positive Research in Accounting," in R.D. Nair and T.H. Williams (eds.), *Perspectives on Research* (Graduate School of Business, University of Wisconsin, 1980), pp. 107-128.

PUBLIC CHOICE OF CORPORATE ACCOUNTING STANDARDS*

by Murray J. Bryant and Daniel B. Thornton

*This hitherto unpublished paper was presented in Spring 1981 at the Annual Conference of the Canadian Academic Accounting Association, in Halifax, N. S. We gratefully acknowledge the helpful comments of John Butterworth, John Waterhouse, Bob Scapens, Chris Robinson, and Brian Galvin. We must bear the responsibility for misinterpreting any of their excellent suggestions, however.

WATTS and Zimmerman [1979], in their discussion of the historical development of accounting theory, assert that

> . . . the evidence is consistent with our hypothesis that much of accounting theory is the product of government intervention and that accounting theory satisfies the demand for excuses . . . Undoubtedly there are alternative theories which can also explain the timing of the accounting literature. The challenge is to those who would support those alternative theories to specify them and show that they are more consistent with the evidence than ours. (p. 300).

In the present paper, we do not pick up that particular gauntlet: indeed, we agree with their assertion to a considerable extent. Our concern is that it does not go far enough. Our objective is to present a meta-theory of accounting theories that derives the Watts and Zimmerman theory of the market for excuses as a particular consequence, yet is general enough to offer new insights into the financial accounting standard setting process and the development of theories used to justify the standards.

The motivation for the paper is that, in our opinion, the existing literature on standard setting examines only parts of the framework developed here. Though our model of the process is not complete, we maintain that it contains substantially more endogeneity than other models proposed to date, and consequently much more explanatory power.[1]

As a point of departure, we review briefly two theories of behavior that have, in our opinion, extremely important implications for deductive and empirical research in accounting: a theory of expectations equilibria and a theory of institutional information. Neither has received much attention in accounting literature to date.[2]

THEORIES OF EXPECTATIONS EQUILIBRIA AND INSTITUTIONAL INFORMATION

Theories of expectations equilibria (henceforth, EE) appear to have developed independently in two major fields: socio-biology and macro-economics. Socio-biologists [e.g.

Dawkins 1978] have used the theory of "evolutionarily stable strategies" to explain the equlibrium ratios of numbers of species with certain traits that seem to persist. Equilibrium occurs in such a system when, on average, an organism's expectation of the probability of a certain sort of behavior by rivals is equal to the proportion of genes in the rival's gene-pool that foster such behavior. Macro-economists have used the theory of "rational expectations equilibria" to explain why the customary Keynesian remedies for inflation and unemployment seem not to be working [See Poole 1976 for a review of the literature]. The explanation is that people make plans based on anticipated economic parameters (such as the rate of inflation) and on anticipated government policies directed at controlling them. If people generally form *rational expectations* concerning a government policy and its effect, they will simply arrange their affairs *ex ante* to neutralize the policy.

We maintain that expectations concerning the corporate accounting standard setting process are of paramount importance. People whose behavior is monitored by accounting data (e.g. managers, debtors, etc.) make contracts with one another using existing accounting standards *and* the *expected* changes in those standards as an information base that is verifiable by public accountants. They revise their expectations as information becomes available regarding the direction and possible extent of changes in the standards. As an example of what we mean by "direction and extent" of changes, consider pension accounting. If pension accounting were under consideration by the standard setting body, one *direction* that could be taken by standard setters would be to increase the number of actuarial components of the firm's pension obligations that would be classified as liabilities. The *extent* of such a change would depend on such decisions as how much recognition were given to past service costs and whether the related charge were made to income or retained earnings. These changes would alter the way in which accounting information could be used in a variety of contracts between the firm and outsiders.

An EE occurs in our model when people's expectations concerning the direction and extent of changes in the accounting standards *relevant to their situations* are, on average, correct. Not everyone must have rational expectations concerning all accounting issues of the day in order for an EE to occur. It should be noted in passing that Hayek [1948] alludes to a similar idea: not everyone needs to know the price of every commodity for an equilibrium in the real goods market. As academics, for instance, we do not need to know the price of a Rolls when shopping for a car.

Theories of institutional information have a long and perhaps apocryphal pedigree. Individualist philosophers (represented most recently in the work of Hayek [1948] and Popper [1966]) have all stressed at times the virtue of an arbitrary set of rules, constraints, or institutions (e.g. go on green, stop on red) to which individuals *voluntarily* submit, even though they know the rules are arbitrary and unenforceable. Veblen [1899] broadened the notion of institutions to include any widely practised custom, such as the forty-hour work week. Newman [1976] and Thornton [1979] discuss at length the concept of "institutional information" (II). The most important feature of such information is that it is voluntarily taken as given by individuals in the short run, even though each individual knows that the basis for the II must be arbitrary.[3] The II is then used by those individuals to make explicit or implicit agreements. Two such agreements are monitoring and bonding contracts to reduce agency costs of equity, and debt indentures to specify rights and obligations of security holders and management [Jensen and Meckling 1976, Smith and Warner 1979].

A central notion in any theory of institutional information is that it is more costly for individuals to reform or revise the existing set of II than to alter their behavior to conform with it. Recently, two explanations for this idea have developed independently in the law and economics literature on the one hand, and in the management accounting literature on the other, though neither specifically mentions II. Shavell [1980] addresses the question: Why are contracts incomplete, in the sense that they do not specify what is to be done by the parties to contracts in every conceivable contingent future state of the world? The answer that is apparent from a review of previous literature in economics is that (a) it would be too costly to negotiate a complete contract, *ex ante*, because the number of payoff-relevant states is potentially infinite; and (b) it may be extremely costly or even impossible to verify that a state has occurred, *ex post* [Arrow 1974]. Moreover, verification becomes more difficult as the states specified become more numerous. As a result, the law has specified certain standard remedies for breach (e.g. damages, specific performance) that may motivate the parties to contracts to behave almost as if they were complete. In the context of our model, these standard remedies may be viewed as II.

Demski and Feltham [1976] use the concept of completeness in a management accounting setting. A complete model is a decision model that would be used by a decision maker if specification and analysis of decision problems were costless. Such a model would specify unambiguously what the decision maker should do, given his or her tastes, beliefs and endowment, and given the alternative actions open to him or her. Because specification and analysis are costly, however, individuals necessarily rely on incomplete decision models just as contractors rely on incomplete contracts. Some arbitrary simplifications are made so that a model can specify a preferred action for the decision maker, though he or she may not in fact undertake that action: the output of an incomplete model is information that the decision maker may use to make a decision, though it may not actually *be* the decision.

The implication of these theories is that we do not observe complete contracts or complete decision models in either a managerial or financial accounting setting. Rather, the majority of contracts focus upon measured outcomes specified in terms of accounting numbers, where the numbers are derived according to a particular set of II at the time of the contract and expectations of changes in II over the life of the contract. Though completeness is sacrificed, rewards and penalties are relatively easy to assess *ex post*, and *ex ante* contracting costs are much lower than they would be if the parties had to bargain for and pay for a tailor-made information system as well as the terms of the contract. The role of both generally accepted accounting principles (GAAP) and generally accepted auditing standards (GAAS) in our framework is that they form a set of II that is used to deal with incompleteness in contracts and decision models in the capital market. In a managerial accounting context internal accounting policy manuals rather than GAAP serve as the appropriate II. Nonetheless, GAAP still influences management accounting procedures, by supplying certain fundamental rules such as matching and realization whose implementation can be audited by public accountants.

THE NEGOTIATION OF II-PRICES

The theories of EE and II are utilized in *Figure 1*. At the center of the diagram is management of business firms, who play a crucial role as conduits of II and establishers of EE, as will be explained below. We begin our analysis by adding an accounting profession to the picture, which arises initially to supply an arbitrary set of II that can be used to reduce the costs of transacting both in the capital market and within firms. Any set of II with the same fineness [Ng 1978] will do as well as any other, initially. However, once contracts have been negotiated based on this II, any future changes in II may impact differently on different interest groups.

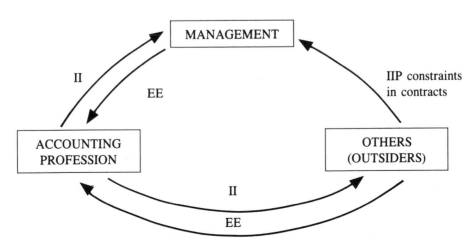

Figure I: Institutional Information, Expectations Equilibria, and II-Prices.

The profession imposes arbitrary measurement and disclosure standards on managers, and managers voluntarily accept them initially, since they are aware of the benefits of II. Future changes in II do not come as a surprise to managers: they form expectations concerning the pronouncement process which depend not only on their understanding of the process, but also on their ability to influence it through the exposure draft process, service on professional committees, or their association with public accounting firms that can advocate their positions indirectly. We assume, however, that no single corporation is powerful enough to alter II specifically to suit its own contracting purposes: General Motors cannot write the *CICA Handbook*, even though it may have a significant influence upon some of its contents.

Management uses II (perhaps in modified form) in contracts such as management incentive contracts and bond covenants. The precise terms of such contracts will be adjusted to conform to the set of II currently in use and to management's expectations of how II may change in the future. Bond covenants, for example, often rely on audited accounting data in order to monitor many of the firm's production, investment and financing activities.[4] A bond covenant might contain a 2:1 debt/equity constraint based on historic cost II or a 1:1 ratio based on current cost II. The point to note here is that the debt/equity constraint is *a parameter that is specific to the II that is being used*. It is determined as the competitive outcome of the bargaining that occurs between the firm and outsiders. It is an endogenously determined parameter, along with the interest rate on the bonds, the price of the firm's common stock, etc. In fact, it shares many, if not all the characteristics of price itself in neo-classical economics. Because of this, we refer to these parameters as II-prices (IIP's). Readers who object to this label may use the term II-parameter whenever we refer to IIP without changing the thrust of our theory, however.

Generally, parties to contracts will find it easier to use the II currently in use in financial accounting handbooks than to negotiate both an information system and IIP's simultaneously. If very few bond indentures contain IIP's based on current value accounting, we maintain the reason is that the parties to the covenant can obtain much the same result merely by very carefully negotiating IIP's based on historic cost II.

In management incentive contracts, we suggest that the parties agree upon II; then, given the II, they negotiate an IIP relating management compensation to conditional outcomes measured in terms of the II (e.g. "5% of profits based on GAAP"). The IIP agreed upon will take into account not only the intentions and bargaining power of the parties, but also the attributes of II itself, such as the fineness of the partitioning of contingent states and the bias of the system. For example, if the chosen II understates depreciation relative to other possible measurement systems, the IIP will be lower than it would have been if one of these other systems had been used (e.g. "4% of profits" under the chosen system; "5%" under the other systems).

In his characterization of the principal-agent problem, Ng [1978] argues that the parties agree on a reward payment schedule and then agree upon a system to measure performance. This seems to fail to capture the *simultaneity* in the selection of the IIP along with the II. For instance, if II is coarser, favoring the agent *ceteris paribus*, the IIP may be lower, favoring the principal. Therefore, coarseness in II *per se* cannot be said to favor the agent. Similarly, upward bias in II cannot be said to favor the agent, since the upward bias could be counteracted by downward pressure on the IIP in the incentive contract.

An analogous though not identical idea finds expression in the Coase Theorem [Coase 1960]. One statement of this theorem is that no allocation of property rights among individuals will prevent an efficient allocation of resources. Individuals will simply take the rights as given, then establish market clearing prices by bargaining around them. Each allocation of rights will give a different equilibrium distribution of wealth among them, but all such distributions will be Pareto-efficient. Similarly, we suggest that, given the set of IIP's currently in existence, each change in II will give a different equilibrium allocation of wealth among those who have used the II for contracting. The reason is that each change in II alters the explicit constraints imposed by IIP's. This logically leads to a transfer of wealth, to transaction costs of renegotiation, or to the costs of "keeping two sets of books" (see Thornton [1982] for a list of costs).

Except for the costs of learning the new rules, a single change in II should *not* affect the constraints imposed in *future* contracts, because contractors can adjust IIP's accordingly. But, if II changes too often, it will be used less in contracting than if it were more stable. This will impose higher costs of contracting on parties because they will have to bargain over many details of the information system to be used in the contract as well as the IIP's.

It follows that standard setters, by choosing one set of standards over another, are implicitly and perhaps even unconsciously choosing one wealth distribution over another. May and Sundem [1976] argue that because of this, standard setting can be best understood as a political process. In this political process interested parties can lobby in favor of or against particular standards and influence the "problem issues" placed on the agenda by the standard setting body. Not surprisingly, a recurring question by some authors [e.g. Rappaport 1977] is the issue of legitimacy of the standard setting body. In some respects in our framework the issue of legitimacy is determined by the acceptance of the II by the contracting parties. If the II promulgated by the standard setters is not employed in contracts, then the institution itself may be replaced by an alternative institution whose II is accepted as a rational basis for reducing the costs of transacting. That is, the legitimacy of the institution is assessed primarily in terms of the demand for its outputs and its ability to satisfy this demand. In this context, the general acceptance of accounting principles becomes *primus inter pares* in the list of desirable attributes of II. Butterworth, Gibbins and King [1982] arrive at a very similar conclusion via a different route.

Market Forces and Accounting Standard Setting. Watts and Zimmerman [1979] hypothesize that a "market for excuses" exists in the promulgation of normative accounting theories. In our framework, their hypothesis is consistent with the simple observation that management and other parties with interests in II (because of the IIP's that constrain them) may demand justification or rationalization of existing II in order to preserve the integrity of their IIP's. The normative accounting theories, then, are *endogenous* to the system. Our model logically implies that when managers and others understand the theories used to derive II, they will be able to predict how II will be applied in non-standard situations not explicitly covered in accounting handbooks, and how II may be changed by the standard setting body in the future. It is this predictability that gives II its value for long term contracting.[5] We wish to emphasize here that, in our model, it is most definitely *not* the non-arbitrariness, the intrinsic "correctness," nor the "economic reality" of these normative accounting theories that makes the II based upon the theories useful or valuable, but their *long-run endogeneity and logical consistency*. II based on modern portfolio theory may be less valuable to managers than II based upon what appear to be totally arbitrary matching and realization theories, for the logic of portfolio theory may be largely exogenous to the concerns facing managers and the parties with whom they wish to contract at the level of the firm.

Similarly, the standard setting *process* can have profound effects on the expectations of users of II. If we compare the "family compact" sort of standard setting in Canada with the more open, participative process in the United States, we note that, whatever may be said of the processes themselves, there should be relatively fewer surprises in Canada, since the group that sets the standards is a homophilous one with easy-to-understand biases. The introduction of an economist into this group might result in a very grave upset in user's expectations for II. Paradoxically, standard setters who pursue (vainly) the notion of economic reality can imbue II with very desirable properties, because as long as users understand the accountants' theories, EE's are easily formed. The fact that many users find the theories somehow "intrinsically objectionable" is not relevant in our model.

We hasten to point out that our meta-theory is founded on the philosophical basis of *instrumentalism*.[6] II is seen merely as an instrument for facilitating economic interaction by allowing the low cost negotiation of IIP's. Normative accounting theories are just instruments for generating II and for helping individuals form EE's about how II might change in the future. In this context Thomas' [1969 and 1974] observations that allocations are arbitrary and incorrigible, based on *deductive* arguments alone, are irrelevant to our meta-theory. In an instrumentalist framework, allocations are meant not to partition reality, but to create arbitrary partitions that can be used by individuals in bargaining for IIP's, which create a reality of their own.

Another outsider with whom the firm in *Figure 1* transacts is government. The government collects taxes based on sales and income, using II as the basis for defining these items. Then, based on the II, a tax rate is established to levy sufficient revenues to accomplish the government's fiscal objectives. The tax rate in our framework is viewed as merely another IIP. If II changed, provisions of the tax law would be modified too, but in our model even the wording of the tax law itself may be viewed as merely a very complex IIP that is endogenous to the system.

Our framework also offers some insight into the familiar debate over whether accounting standards ought to be set by the government or by an independent profession. A traditional argument [Rappaport 1977] is that the government lacks the competence to establish accounting standards because of the complex nature of accounting itself as a subject. The profession possesses the competence, but not the social legitimacy to establish standards that alter the allocation of wealth in society. It is logical, therefore, for governments to delegate standard setting authority to the profession. We find this argument unsatisfactory, for the government has ample resources to purchase whatever expertise it needs. A complete explanation for the government's role in accounting standard setting lies in a subtle interpretation of the forces at work in our framework. First, the government is generally seen to alter not II, but IIP's such as tax rates, investment tax credits, allowable depreciation write-offs, etc. The reason is that the government realizes that if it were to alter II continually to accomplish its own objectives, it would be destroying the integrity of II in a wide range of human interaction totally unrelated to its own endeavors. Arguably, if II is seen to vary capriciously and unexpectedly, it will have no value whatever as a basis for establishing IIP's in bond covenants, incentive contracts and the like. Because governments are immune (at least, in the short run) to market pressures that could lead to an EE for corporate II, it is more efficient to leave standard setting to the private sector.

Second, government announcements of IIP's through budget speeches, proclamations, or legislation are almost invariably done quickly, at discrete intervals, in order to attempt to prevent insiders from capitalizing on their knowledge of the precise effect of government subsidies. Accounting standards, in contract, are established only after painstaking exposure drafts on which all affected parties have ample opportunity to comment. This standard setting process has always recognized, at least implicitly, that during the process opportunities may arise for one interest group to profit at the expense of others. Again, because the government is immune to many market based influences, it logically eschews any formal association with the formation of specific accounting standards.

It appears that in well-disciplined auction markets such as the New York Stock Exchange, changes in II *per se* have no measurable effect on security returns (see Foster [1978] for a review of research supporting this assertion). On the other hand, researchers have been able to detect changes in security returns that result *indirectly* from changes in II. For instance, if a change in II upsets existing bond covenants, share prices may react (see for example Thornton [1982], Leftwich [1978]). These reactions do not necessarily imply any inefficiency in the capital market: they may be simply the *efficient results* of contracts predicated on a former EE whose meaning is changed later when uncertainty surrounding the pronouncement process is resolved, either once and for all or gradually, as the pronouncement process unfolds.[7]

Prakash and Rappaport [1977] observe that sometimes managerial behavior seems to change when II changes. For example, new rules for accounting for foreign currency lead to increased amounts of hedging by financial managers. Shank, Dillard and Murdock [1979], in particular, do find evidence of such actions. Prakash and Rappaport explain such behavior as an "information inductance" effect: management hedges in the foreign exchange market in order to smooth the firm's reported earnings, to prevent a misconception by readers of financial statements that something unfavorable has happened to the firm. In our framework, however, these apparently dysfunctional hedging actions could in fact be based on logical maximizing behavior. All that is required for this to be so is that it be less costly to incur the real costs of hedging in the foreign exchange market than to incur the costs of renegotiating the relevant IIP's.

A final outsider in *Figure 1* that we shall discuss is an information intermediary, such as a rating agency. Often, managers voluntarily pay to have their firms rated in some way. Once ratings are established, they may by publicly available as institutional information (e.g. bond ratings) or may be sold privately (e.g. credit ratings). A question that arises is why this information is not provided in financial statements along with other II. One plausible answer is that financial statements do not provide a communication medium that is timely enough to disseminate this information efficiently. Another explanation is that rating signals summarize an extremely complex array of IIP's which would be too cumbersome to report in financial statements because of the sheer number of covenants in existence for most firms, and because of the lack of consistency in the IIP's relating to a particular kind of covenant across firms.

It has come to our attention that when bond covenants are being drafted it is common practice for representatives of rating agencies to be present at the negotiations, advising management of the trade-off between IIP's and the consequent rating that would be given to the firm's bonds for each set of IIP's. For instance, a bond might be rated Aaa if the times-interest-earned constraint were 10:1 based on II: but Aa if it were 5:1. Again, the IIP's are seen to have substantial endogeneity in the framework we propose.

EQUILIBRIUM FOR THE ACCOUNTING PROFESSION

An EE for the profession involves rational expectations about the sort of II that it will be required to attest to in the foreseeable future. This, in turn, gives rise to a mandated education and training program for incoming students, continuing education for existing members of the profession, and the promulgation and enforcement of professional standards of conduct. Members must form expectations concerning the theory that can be used to guide accounting practice in situations in which professional judgment is required. Once again, the chief virtue of the theory in our framework is its very *endogeneity*, not its correspondence with some exogenous economic theory of the firm developed in another discipline such as Economics or Finance. The impetus for changing the theory is the observation by professional accountants that the IIP's are somehow failing to achieve efficient allocation, or that the II is so irrelevant to the needs of contracting parties as to make the IIP's ambiguous and difficult to negotiate.

The mechanism for changing II and the conceptual framework on which it is based is then required to be one that can balance the virtues of stability of II against its responsiveness to demands from various quarters to change it. For instance, one interest group may argue that II would better serve the needs of investors if it aided them in predicting future cash flows. Our framework makes clear that this interest group is a very small subset of users of II and there is no *a priori* reason to believe that it is the most important one. In fact, the theories that might logically provide guidance to the profession in implementing such disclosures are in large measure exogenous to the concerns of many other parties who have a direct interest in the firm and who have used the present set of II to negotiate IIP's.

The profession is indirectly responsible to users of its II through governments. In most jurisdictions, government gives a licence to a specific group or to specific groups of accountants to perform public accounting ("who does it") and decides on the definitions of II that is to be within the purview of the profession ("what they do"). By changing either the definition of public accounting or the scope of the licence, the government can alter II. This is especially true when there is more than one group of accountants who could be licensed. Consequently, an EE for the profession must involve rational expectations concerning government policy directed at the regulation of public accounting.

IMPLICATIONS FOR FINANCIAL ACCOUNTING STANDARD SETTING

In this section we review briefly some immediate applications of the framework and show that it has considerable explanatory power. The list of issues reviewed is far from exhaustive, and is meant only to illustrate how the framework may be applied.

THE ROLE OF ABSTRACTION AND BASIC ASSUMPTIONS IN OBTAINING AGREEMENT.

One of the conventional threads in the accounting literature is that accounting rules ought to be based on a set of postulates or basic assumptions, few in number, common to all accounting systems [e.g. as by Mattessich 1964/77, ch. 2 and 1979, pp. 343- 348).[8] Then, a deductive logical structure can be used to generate all of the specific rules of accounting. We suggest that the parsimony that is sometimes suggested in the establishment of the postulates is directed not so much at achieving elegance or rigor in accounting theory, but agreement, so that an EE is more easily achieved. The higher the level of abstraction in the postulates, the greater is the chance of obtaining consensus among the various interest groups as to the validity of the postulates. On the other hand, when the postulates at the foundation of the theory decline in number or specificity, the deductive structure of the theory logically generates a higher variance in the actual application of II, since different interpretations of the meaning of the postulates become reasonable in different circumstances.

As the level of abstraction in the postulates increases, the incentive to use II in contracts declines, for contractors see the statement of postulates as non-operational. Because different interpretations of the postulates are possible, individuals will feel the need to specify more precisely the information base that is to be used in monitoring and bonding contracts. This increases the level of transaction costs in society. Moreover, the pedagogic demand for theories [Watts and Zimmerman 1979] is for pegs on which to hang procedures in accounting, essentially. The higher the level of abstraction in the postulates, the lower their value in satisfying the pedagogic demand for theories in accounting, and the higher the cost of training accountants.

THE ROLE OF TIME IN ESTABLISHING ACCOUNTING STANDARDS.

The longer the time involved in the establishment of a new standard, the more likely it is that individuals affected by the standard or affecting the standard process will be able to form rational expectations concerning the eventual form of the new II. This will also mean that they will have the time to alter their affairs so as to adapt to the changes in standards in advance of the change.[9] For instance, if it took 20 years to establish a new standard relating to foreign currency accounting, and if multinational firms had ample opportunity to participate in the exposure draft process, we suggest that by the time the standard was put in place there would be no bond covenants whose meaning would be altered appreciably by the change, since over the twenty year period all new covenants would be negotiated taking the change into account. Unless firms had perpetual bonds outstanding, the change in standards would become less and less relevant as the discussion period became longer and longer.[10]

THE AGENDA EFFECT IN STANDARD SETTING.

The variance rate of II depends jointly on the time allowed for discussion of a proposed change, and on the proportion of standards in the professional handbook whose possible change is being discussed. We define the variance rate as

$$\text{var (II)} = \lim_{\Delta t \to 0} \frac{\text{number of items being discussed}}{\text{time over which they are discussed and resolved.}}$$

Imagine a situation in which the standard setting body announces that all accounting principles in existence will be changed precisely five years from now, all at once, to conform with a new conceptual framework for accounting. Then II is useless except in very short term contracts (less than 5 years). We suggest that this effect helps to explain why standard changes are generally done piecemeal. We do not expect to see sweeping changes proposed of a wide variety of accounting principles on the same agenda. In the same vein, we do not expect to see a conceptual framework adopted quickly that departs radically from the one implicit in current standards, for such a change would not augur well for contracts with IIP's based upon the old conceptual structure.

If the proportion of standards on the agenda is held constant, then the variance rate of II depends on the time allowed for comment, lobbying and adaptation by the various interest groups, as was suggested above. When the time allowed is too short, individuals do not have time to form EE's. In the limit, as the time approaches zero (capricious changes, day by day in standards), the variance rate of II becomes so high that it is useless for contracting. On the other hand, as the time allowed approaches infinity, II lacks responsiveness to exogenous economic events such as new volatility in foreign exchange rates, double digit inflation, or the advent of new kinds of financial instruments that need to be accounted for. Then the variance rate becomes zero, but II again may become irrelevant for many kinds of contracts, since it may ignore some important contingent states of the world. That is, II may be perfectly predictable and understandable when it is perfectly stable, but the cost of this stability is irrelevant to many contractors and other users of accounting information. Thus, it is possible to imagine an optimal variance rate for II, or an optimal half-life for a professional handbook (this idea is developed by Thornton [1983], ch. 1).

WHY ARE PUBLIC ACCOUNTING FIRMS ADVOCATES OF PARTICULAR STANDARDS?

One of the standard notions of the role of public accounting (henceforth PA) firms is that they must be independent of the standard setting process, and act merely as arbiters of the use of the standards that are prescribed by the standard setting body. Yet, we observe examples of particular firms advocating specific standards: for instance, Arthur Andersen has advocated the successful efforts method of accounting for drilling and exploration costs; Deloitte, Haskins and Sells has supported full cost; Price Waterhouse has pressed for the adoption of price level accounting in preference to current cost accounting. The allegation has been made (e.g. by the Metcalf Committee) that large firms advocate standards that are on balance favorable to their clients. It is tempting to conclude that the firms are sensitive to the same IIP's as their clients: if a proposed change in II upsets the integrity of the IIP's in their clients' contracts, the firms would be expected to oppose it either openly or by pressing for the adoption of an alternative standard that is less inimical to those contracts.

We suggest that this analysis is too facile. Our hypothesis is that the advocacy of standards by particular PA firms plays the role of product differentiation in the market for public accounting services.

The auditing profession is able to extract higher aggregate fees from clients when there is this product differentiation, for the same reason that product differentiation can lead to higher aggregate profits in the market for real goods.

This analysis implies that PA firms state their views on various accounting issues, and this statement provides information that serves to differentiate them from other PA firms. Clients then select PA firms whose views suit them, given the IIP's that constrain them at the present time. Once this self-selection has occurred, the PA firms must get involved in the standard setting process in order to preserve the differentiation that they have instigated. This lobbying activity is expensive, and requires considerable expertise: we suggest that only the large PA firms can afford to rent the specialized skills required to perform it. When the volume of clients involved is large, there is a high return to activities that preserve the differentiation. Clients, for their part, stand to benefit from having a large firm as their advocate, since a large firm has resources at its disposal to mount a more persuasive campaign than a small one. Moreover, the advocacy activities of large PA firms do much to keep the differentiated product that they provide before the public, and this exposure increases their ability to attract new clients who wish to press for a particular interpretation of II.

WHY DO STANDARD SETTERS NOT OPENLY ADMIT THAT THE PROCESS IS POLITICAL?

Given the analysis in the paper, it seems obvious that the standard setting process is a political one that strives for acceptance of standards by several interest groups. Why, then, do standard setters persist in saying that they select accounting standards on the basis of accounting theory rather than the self-interest of people that provide input to the process? The Watts and Zimmerman [1979] explanation is that the theories serve as excuses for self-interest arguments that might seem to be socially unpalatable. We agree with this assessment, but feel that it stops considerably short of providing a complete explanation of why standard setting arguments are couched in terms of accounting theories such as matching and realization. We suggest, rather, that when standard setters state publicly that reform of II will be based on such theories, they eliminate an infinity of possible suggestions for the reform of II, with good reason: such statements serve to keep II more stable than it would be in the absence of this arbitrary discipline, *and* to facilitate the formation of an EE.

We conclude that even if standard setters are well aware that the standard setting process is a political one, they will quite rationally lie to everyone — including themselves if necessary — in order to preserve the stability of II. If everyone assumes that future changes in II will conform to the constraints of "economic reality" in terms of accrual accounting, EE's will form much more easily and more quickly than they would in the absence of this arbitrary discipline, and II can be more valuable in a wide range of human interaction.

EXPECTATIONS AND THE WATTS-ZIMMERMAN MODEL.

Watts and Zimmerman [1978, pp. 118-119] advance the theory that managers of firms whose reported income would decrease if a particular standard were adopted would lobby against it, providing that their potential costs of renegotiating contracts (IIP's) exceeded their potential political costs. In our view, this would be a special case — one in which the IIP's had been negotiated assuming the proposed change in accounting standards would *not* be adopted. If, on the other hand, the IIP's had been negotiated assuming that the standard *would* be adopted, the managers would be expected to lobby *for* it to avoid renegotiation costs. Without modeling expectations in a specific case, we would be unable to predict whether firms' managers would lobby for or against a proposed new standard.[11]

CONCLUSIONS

Our model of institutional information with expectations equilibria appears to offer interesting explanations of how financial accounting standards are determined and how changes in the standards affect users of accounting information. The model also shows promise in explaining many management accounting phenomena, though space in the present paper does not permit a full exposition of this extension.

We suggest that our model may aid also in the development of testable hypotheses in studies of the economic consequences of changes in accounting principles. This will involve very careful explicit consideration of how the parties involved in the change fit into the framework in *Figure 1*: What IIP's existed at the time of the change and how will the new II alter their restrictiveness? How will the government use the new II in its fiscal policies and what will be the result for the cash flows accruing to the firm? To what extent were the theoretical underpinnings of the new II understood by the parties affected by the change or endogenous to the discussion of the change? Did the firms affected by the change have time to renegotiate their IIP's or to arrange their affairs so as to neutralize the effect of the change? When were the expectations of security holders concerning the change "rational"?

Only if these questions (among others) can be answered will economic consequences studies have interesting results. Even if they can be answered, however, it may still be impossible to distinguish between observed consequences that are due to "surprises" from the standard-setter on the one hand, and consequences that are the efficient results of the rational use of old II in incomplete contracts on the other hand. We believe that the construction of empirical studies based upon these considerations will be one of the most important methodological challenges facing accounting researchers in future years, with the most important implications for the public choice of corporate accounting standards.

FOOTNOTES

[1] See, for instance, Beaver [1973, !978]; Bryant and Mahaney [1981]; Demski [1973]; Prakash and Rappaport [1977]; Thornton [1979]; and Watts and Zimmerman [1978, 1979].

[2] Exceptions are papers by Thornton [1979] and by Bryant and Mahaney [1981], which do consider these theories, at least implicitly.

[3] As Thornton [1979] points out, the only II that can be justified to each and every individual is II that is imposed upon them by a dictator. The paradox of such ultra-rationalism is that it can lead only to totalitarianism.

[4] See Smith and Warner [1979] or Thornton [1980] for a review of these covenants.

[5] Watts and Zimmerman [1979] discuss a "pedagogic demand" for normative accounting theories that partially fulfills this requirement. But without EE's such theories can never be completely satisfactory.

[6] Boland [1979] presents an excellent exposition of the use of instrumentalism in the history of economic thought by Milton Friedman, among others.

[7] By "efficient," we mean that the resolution of uncertainty is not a surprise: It is like getting a head after tossing a fair coin.

[8] For further discussion see also Hendriksen [1982, chapters 1- 3].

[9] Foster [1978] points out the difficulty in defining "the" economic event caused by a change in accounting principles. Since expectations are continually being revised, such definition may be impossible, even if EE's exist at each moment in time. It may be impossible to distinguish security price changes that are efficient results of prior EE's from those that are caused by random shocks.

[10] Note, too, that many contracts are in the n ature of *options*, which logically entail the freedom to choose a time for exercising. For instance, stock options may be exercised by managers at times that would render a change in II irrelevant to them: it all depends on whether the managers have rational expectations of the standard setting process. If they do, they will exercise such options and negotiate IIP's to neutralize any changes in II that they feel will be detrimental to their interests.

[11] If the firm did not utilize GAAP in its contracts, we would expect no lobbying, unless the firm were subject to significant political costs.

REFERENCES

Arrow, K. J. [1963]. *Social Choice and Individual Values*. Yale University Press.

Arrow, K. J. [1974]. "Limited Knowledge and Economic Analysis." *American Economic Review* 64: 1-10.

Beaver, W. H. [1973]. "What Should Be the FASB's Objectives?" *Journal of Accountancy* (August):49-56.

Beaver, W. H. [1978]. "Current Trends in Corporate Disclosure." *Journal of Accountancy* (January):44-52.

Boland, L. A. [1979]. "A Critique of Friedman's Critics." *Journal of Economic Literature* XVII:503-522.

Bryant, M. J., and Mahaney, M. C. [1981]. "The Politics of Standard Setting." *Management Accounting* (March):26-33.

Butterworth, J. E., Gibbins, M., and King, R. [1982]. "The Structure of Accounting Theory: Some Basic Conceptual and Methodological Issues," Chapter 1 in *Research to Support Standard Setting in Financial Accounting: A Canadian Perspective*. Clarkson, Gordon Foundation.

Coase, R. H. [1937]. "The Nature of the Firm." *Economica* NS 4:1-20.

Dawkins, R. [1978]. *The Selfish Gene*. Penguin.

Demski, J. S. [1973]. "The General Impossibility of Normative Accounting Standards." *Accounting Review* (October):718-723.

Demski, J. S., and Feltham, G. A. [1976] *Cost Determination: A Conceptual Approach*. Iowa State University Press.

Foster, G. [1978]. *Financial Statement Analysis*. Prentice-Hall.

Hayek, F. A. [1948]. *Individualism and Economic Order*. University of Chicago Press.

Hendriksen, E. S. [1982]. *Accounting Theory*. 4th edition. Richard D. Irwin, Inc.

Jensen, M., and Meckling, W. H. [1976]. "Theory of the Firm: Managerial Behavior, Agency Costs and Ownership Structure." *Journal of Financial Economics:305-360*.

Leftwich, R. W. [1978]. "Accounting Numbers and Bond Indentures: The Impact on Stockholders Wealth of Changes in Generally Accepted Accounting Principles." Unpublished manuscript, Graduate School of Management, University of Rochester.

Mattessich, R. [1964/1977]. *Accounting and Analytical Methods*. Richard D. Irwin, Inc./Scholars Book Co.

Mattessich, R. [1979]. "Instrumental Aspects of Accounting," in *Accounting for a Simplified Firm Owning Depreciable Assets: Seventeen Essays and a Synthesis Based on a Common Case*, pp. 335-351. Ed. by R. R. Sterling and A. L. Thomas. Scholars Book Co.

May, R. G., and Sundem, G. [1976]. "Research for Accounting Policy: An Overview." *Accounting Review* (October):747-763.

Newman, G. [1976]. "An Institutional Perspective on Information." *International Social Science Journal* 28:466-492.

Ng, D. S. [1978]. "An Information Economics Analysis of Financial Reporting and External Auditing." *Accounting Review* (October):910-920.

Poole, W. [1976]. "Rational Expectations in the Macro Model." *Brookings Papers on Economic Activity* 2:463-505.

Popper, K. R. [1966]. *The Open Society and Its Enemies*. Routledge and Kegan-Paul.

Prakash, P., and Rappaport, A. [1977]. "Information Inductance and Its Significance for Accounting." *Accounting, Organizations and Society:29-38*.

Rappaport, A. [1977]. "Economic Impact of Accounting Standards — Implications for the FASB." *Journal of Accountancy* (May):89-98.

Shank, J. K., Dillard, J. F., and Murdock, R. J. [1979]. *Assessing the Economic Impact of FASB No. 8*. Financial Executives Institute.

Shavell, S. [1980]. "Damage Measures for Breach of Contract." *Bell Journal of Economics* 11:466-490.

Smith, C. W., and Warner, J. [1979]. "On Financial Contracting: An Analysis of Bond Covenants." *Journal of Financial Economics* :117-162.

Thomas, A. L. [1969]. *The Allocation Problem in Financial Accounting Theory*. AAA.

Thomas, A. L. [1974]. *The Allocation Problem: Part Two*. AAA.

Thornton, D. B. [1979]. "Information and Institutions in the Capital Market." *Accounting, Organizations and Society:211-234*.

Thornton, D. B. [1980]. "Law and Economics of Unanticipated Changes in Generally Accepted Accounting Principles: A Canadian Perspective." *Law and Economics Workshop Series* WS 111-7. University of Toronto.

Thornton, D. B. [1982]. "Economic Consequences of Lease Capitalization in Canada: Implications for Standard Setting," Chapter 6 in *Research to Support Standard Setting in Financial Accounting: A Canadian Perspective*. Clarkson, Gordon Foundation.

Thornton, D. B. [1983]. *The Financial Reporting of Contingencies and Uncertainties: Theory and Practice*. CGA Research Foundation.

United States Senate Subcommittee on Reports, Accounting, and Management [1976]. *The Accounting Establishment*. "The Metcalf Report." United States Government Printing Office.

Veblen, T. [1899]. *The Theory of the Leisure Class*. Vanguard.

Watts, R. L., and Zimmerman, J. L. [1978]. ''Towards a Positive Theory of the Determination of Accounting Standards.'' *Accounting Review* (January):112-134.

Watts, R. L., and Zimmerman, J. L. [1979]. ''The Demand for and Supply of Accounting Theories: The Market for Excuses.'' *Accounting Review* (April):273-305.

ECONOMIC INTEREST AND ACCOUNTING STANDARDS

by Shyam Sunder and Shailesh Haribhakti

THE last twenty years have seen a great deal of change in accounting standards, mechanisms for setting them, and the accountant's understanding of standards. Heated controversies have raised new questions and doubts in the minds of professional accountants and managers about the nature and socio-economic function of standardization in accounting practices, about how it affects their work and economic welfare and about how they should react to proposals for new or modified standards.

ECONOMIC INTEREST

Accountants think of accounting standards as being rooted in a set of basic assumptions, (e.g., economic entity, going concern, monetary unit, periodicity, etc.) and basic principles (e.g., historical cost, realization, matching, consistency, full disclosure and verifiability) modified by considerations of materiality and conservatism. Education, training and the traditions of the accounting profession promote the premise that accounting standards enhance the socio-economic relevance of accounting by providing "true and fair" financial statements using uniform practices, and by helping the auditors and financial executives meet their ethical obligation. Accountants are keenly aware of the influence standards have on accounting policy choices, on interactions between the auditors and auditees and, most importantly on their own behavior.

The premise that financial accounts are expected to present a true and fair picture of the firm and its operations is widely accepted. If the balance sheet and income statement could not be relied upon to be truthful, they will cease to serve the function expected of them. The shareholders will no longer have the assurance that their capital is well managed; the creditors will be uncertain as to the value of the collateral and the government will receive little assurance from audited financial statements that taxes due have been paid. Truthfulness of financial statements seems to provide the very basis of their perceived value. Everything done to preserve and enhance the truthfulness of financial statements, therefore, seems desirable.

Truthfulness of financial statements, it is often argued, should be the key criterion for choices made among alternative accounting methods by firms and by bodies entrusted with the setting of accounting standards.

Yet, the day-to-day practice of accounting and the reporting of accounting issues in the financial press, etc., clearly indicate that these same standards and practices appear to be shaped by the pressures exerted by conflicting economic interests. The accountant can hardly fail to recognize considerations that sometimes lead his clients to adopt accounting policies that he finds unacceptable or highly objectionable; nor is he unaware of the influence accounting standards can have on his own economic survival and prosperity. The interplay among conflicting economic interests provides a relatively general, practical and even fascinating interpretation of accounting phenomena. Accounting practice, when looked at this way, appears as a compromise solution which balances the economic interests of various groups such as the investors, creditors, managers, auditors and the government. Each group seeks to advance its own economic advantage and therefore, attempts to install a system of accounting that seems to be better for itself. These economic interests may be incorporated into accounting standards through three different processes (to be explained later in the article in greater detail): direct negotiation, political process and the market. If all interested parties agree to a solution, in absence of evidence to the contrary, we must conclude that such a solution is more desirable from the point of view of the society as a whole.

EXTERNALLY DEFINED CRITERIA

In traditional accounting theory, externally defined characteristics of accounting methods and statements such as verifiability, relevance, truthfulness, etc., have been all important.[1] However, when we look at accounting from the perspective of economic interest, we find that while such externally defined criteria may be useful for determining individual choices, they are not useful for determining the social choice (except in the trivial case when all groups have the same choice).

Verifiability, for example, may serve the interests of the auditors in the form of lower costs or risks and therefore, they can be expected to advocate the use of accounting methods, and standards are more easily verifiable. The economic interests of financial executives (showing the entity they represent in the most favorable light consistent with the desire to limit tax liabilities) may be served by a less verifiable method of accounting, which they would favor. Thus, the utility of verifiable methods/accounting standards in the broader context of society is not determinable merely on the basis of the principle that "a more verifiable accounting method/standard is better." It may well be that the cost or damage inflicted by the use of a relatively verifiable method of accounting on one group is far in excess of the benefits conferred on other groups. The socially desirable solution may well be to adopt the less verifiable method of accounting.

Similarly truthfulness or representational faithfulness, cannot be used as a criterion for social choice. Accountants trained to use approximations of quantities and prices know too well that truthfulness of accounting numbers in representing assets and liabilities of a firm is itself a matter of judgement. A few accounting numbers are no more able to provide a "truthful" representation of a complex organization than a photograph can provide of an object, or a map can provide of a piece of land. Even an excellent photograph can only be an acceptable representation of an object for certain purposes. A map can at so best be designed to serve limited purposes. Financial statements similarly convey a limited idea about a firm and can hardly be expected to serve all or even most purposes. "Truth" is in the eye of the beholder. The same fact may be "truthful" for one party and "untruthful" for another. An external criterion, such as verifiability or truthfulness, may be desirable for some interest groups and undesirable for other. It is generally difficult to establish a connection between a specific accounting policy or standard and the external criteria that it satisfies.

ECONOMIC INTEREST AND INDIVIDUAL BEHAVIOR

One may argue that without the fetters of technically determined standards, which rely exclusively on external criteria such as truth, verifiability, relevance, etc., individuals are likely to behave in a narrow, selfish and shortsighted manner. Individuals may just as likely behave in a farsighted and socially responsible manner, realizing that their own welfare in the long run may be better served by standards opposite to those that may serve them well in the short run. An explicit recognition of the conflicts of economic interest inherent in the choice of accounting methods and standards is likely to clear the way for more stable and widely accepted standards.

ECONOMIC INTEREST AND INTERACTIVE PROCESSES

The economic interest of various groups and individuals may get incorporated into accounting standards and policies through a variety of mechanisms. We shall confine our attention to three major parts: direct negotiation among the parties, the political process and the market process.

DIRECT NEGOTIATION

External auditors and the financial executives of a firm are continually in touch with each other on the matters of accounting policy. When differences arise between them, discussion and negotiation are used to resolve them. Little data are available on the nature of these negotiations, especially those that conclude successfully. However, when occasionally the negotiating process breaks down leading to the resignation of the auditors, enough information becomes available to suggest that it is the economic self interest as perceived by the negotiating parties that plays the key role in the process. Auditors weigh the risk of law suits, damage to their reputation with other clients and their standing in the profession, potential revenues and ability of their partners to negotiate with management of other firms in the future. Managers are often driven by considerations of the effect their financial statements may have on the stock market, relationship with the bankers, government, unions and on their own job security and compensation. Accounting policies and standards are in part, the result of such private negotiations among managers and auditors driven by economic interest as perceived by them.

THE POLITICAL PROCESS

The effects of economic interest on accounting practice and standards through the political process are manifested less frequently but are no less profound. It was through the congressional initiative and support of the executive branch of the government that independent audit of publicly held firms became a legal requirement in the U.S. in 1933-34. CPA profession lobbied for its economic interest and won the right to conduct such audits by successfully persuading the lawmakers that they can do the job better than the government auditors. Creation of the SEC itself, with its profound effect on accounting and auditing practice was a decision taken at the political level to meet the various economic pressures brought to bear on the government at the time.

Direct intervention of the Congress or the executive branches of government in the matters of accounting and audit practice is infrequent, but not unknown. In 1971, the government decision on accounting for investment tax credit led to a restructuring of the accounting rule-making mechanism in force since 1959. In the midseventies, the Metcalfe and Moss Committees in the U.S. Congress induced much rethinking in the accounting circles and led to the creation of Public Oversight Board and the Peer Review System in public accounting.

Appointments to key government positions such as the membership of the SEC and its chief accountant are yet another means by which economic interests are brought to bear on the accounting environment through the political process. Appointments to such positions reflect the political philosophy of those in power and influence the choice of accounting standards and policies in their administration.

THE MARKET PROCESS

Finally and most profoundly, accounting policy and standards are affected by economic interests brought to bear on them through the operation of various markets. The effect is not discussed as often as others merely because it operates more slowly but at a very pervasive level. Slow response of the markets makes it more difficult to establish the correlation between the activity in various markets and accounting policy.

The first market we consider is the one through which capital resources are obtained for the enterprise. In arriving at the supply function of capital to a firm, or class of firms, such suppliers will assess the perceived risks and rewards of the proposed investment in the light of the information available to them currently and promised to them in the future. Promise of prompt, accurate and reliable information about the firm in the future forms an important consideration for investors. Other things being equal firms which operate a more satisfactory accounting system, and this depends to a great extent on the firms' accounting and auditing policy, will be able to raise capital at a lower cost. The firm will thus, enjoy a competitive advantage over other firms unless the additional cost of such an accounting system outweighs the savings in the cost of raising capital. On the margin, operation of the capital market will tend to push the accounting and audit policy towards a point where the marginal reduction in the cost of raising capital is balanced by the marginal increase in the cost of operating an accounting system.

The market for managerial skills is the second market that affects accounting policy. In determining the supply function of managerial labor, the potential entrants to this market weigh the total package of rewards, obligations and risks of their jobs. More onerous accounting and reporting requirements may subject them to a level of risk they are either unwilling to take or for which they demand additional compensation greater than the additional benefits conferred by such reporting on other parties. Thus, on the margin, accounting standards and policy must strike a balance between the demands of managers on one hand and the investors and government, etc., on the other.

The third important market to be considered is the market for audit services. If a change in accounting/auditing policy or standard places the burden of higher risks without compensating rewards on the auditors, they will shift their supply function until their economic interest is optimized in the altered environment. Like the managerial labor, operation of the market for audit services ensures an equilibrium between the demand and supply of audit services through adjustment of accounting/auditing policy on the one hand and the number of people willing to work as auditors on the other.

The speed with which these three markets respond to changes is not equal. Because the cost of adjustments in the capital markets are relatively small, the investors can adjust readily, and at relatively low-cost to the new environment and do not have to rely on either direct negotiations or on the political process to protect this economic interest. On the other hand, the costs of adjustment for managers and auditors being large, the response of these markets to changing conditions is sluggish and, of necessity, they resort to greater reliance on direct negotiation and on the political process to protect their own economic interest with respect to accounting. In the long run, however, even the presence and availability of direct negotiation and political mechanism cannot keep the supply and demand of auditors and managers from moving towards a point where they are in equilibrium with the accounting/auditing methods and standards in force.

IMPLICATIONS FOR STANDARD SETTING

Those who find the economic interest a useful instrument of comprehending accounting phenomena will be inclined to ask: What are its implications for setting accounting standards? In the present section we discuss some of these implications.

MARKET BASED VS. TECHNICAL STANDARDS

Effectiveness of standards depends on the breadth of their acceptance among various economic interests. This is the reason why standards which find broad acceptance are likely to be those which make only marginal adjustments to interests of various groups, thus enabling the standard setting body to anticipate the adjustment in their behavior in response to the standard more accurately. In contrast, standards which confer big advantages or impose large costs on some parties are likely to induce drastic changes in behavior of parties when they are enforced, thus making it difficult for the standard setters to anticipate the effect of the standard. Accounting standards for leases (SFAS 13) and foreign currency translation (SFAS 8) are two examples of standards, enforced on purely technical grounds which in absence of broad acceptability were rendered ineffective by altered behavior of certain parties. Note that the point here is not that the power of enforcement of the FASB should be enhanced because the FASB had virtually all support of the government on these matters. The point is that the absence of broad acceptability of a standard itself renders it ineffective when economic interests alter the behavior of interest groups in response to the standard.

It is easy to be lulled into thinking that given enough enforcement power and statutory backing, a technically desirable standard can be made effective. But, as in civil or criminal law, once you set the rules, people choose their own behavior which they find optimal in the new environment. If a particular standard places a burden of bearing extra risk on auditors, they will either demand adequate extra compensation or, failing to receive it, will cease to perform the function. No matter what the power of enforcement, it is fallacious to think that a standard can be enforced merely because it is technically sound.

Given the ethical terms in which discussions of these matters are usually couched, the stronger the economic consequences of a standard the more difficult it is for the standard setting body to learn how people will change their behavior in response. Thus, strong technical standards, in absence of broad acceptance carry seeds of their own ineffectiveness.

Emphasis on general acceptability of standards, a criterion which does not even appear in the list of qualitative characteristics produced by the FASB (1980) recently, leads directly to greater reliance on the "market" for choosing accounting standards and less reliance on standards based on technical research or posing brand new solutions to accounting issues. Accounting methods already in the market place have received broad exposure, provided an opportunity to a variety of economic interests to understand their consequences for themselves and to adjust their own behavior to them. The effects of market based standards can, therefore, be anticipated more easily than the effects of brand new technical solutions which take time to be understood and to be adjusted to. Considerable amount of turbulence in the reactions to financial accounting standards in recent years seems to have been caused by an inadequate appreciation of this difference between our ability to measure the economic consequences of accounting standards derived from the market and from technical research.

Emphasis on market based standards rather than those based purely on technical research will mean fewer big or revolutionary changes in accounting systems. It will disappoint those who may regard such changes per se, as a measure of progress in accounting. However, for those whom the progress of a social system like accounting implies movement towards a stable solution which is satisfactory to a larger and larger number of participants, will find that a greater reliance on the market for accounting methods will result in progress.

Excessive reliance on technical research in formulating accounting standards leads to pronouncements which are not generally accepted, require frequent revisions or even recissions, and finally create more chaos in accounting and create an unstable image for the concept of accounting standards.[2] Frequent changes in accounting standards defeat the purpose of standarization itself. A primary task of the standard setting bodies is to find the right balance between the speed of adjustment and the frequency of errors.

SUNSET STANDARDS FOR CHANGING ENVIRONMENT

Demands for change in accounting standards are largely based on observed changes in environment such as inflation, new tax laws (investment tax credit) or new business practices (leasing). It follows that an accounting standard which is satisfactory in one environment may not be satisfactory in another. The changing environment should be reflected in changing standards.

Instead of specifying one or more methods of accounting in the light of the environment prevailing at the time of setting the standard, it would be desirable to specify a class of accounting methods of which a particular member is recommended as standard for a specific environment. Thus, for example, there would be no need for the FASB to choose between the historical cost and replacement cost accounting in general, it could have specified the economic conditions under which a particular accounting method would be the accounting standard. Given the amount ot time and effort necessary to develop new standards, a changed environment results in a tremendous waste when it necessitates search for a new standard. Choosing accounting standards for a class of specified environments may be a useful way to conserve on the standard setting efforts.

There is also the opposite problem of accounting standards which linger on books beyond time and environment for which they were chosen. Specification of the environment to which they are applicable, as we have suggested above, will help remove obsolete standards with less effort. Alternatively standards formulated to meet transient environmental phenomena could be formulated with specific sunset provisions to self distinct after a stated period of time. The standard setting body could, of course, reenact them in case their continuation is deemed desirable.

COMPOSITION OF STANDARD SETTING BODIES

If people behave to promote their economic interests, we should expect that the standard setting body will be criticized by those who see their interest as being hurt by their action. If the body does its job reasonably well, its every action will end up upsetting somebody or the other. If any single group makes the mistake of allowing itself a larger representation on the standards setting body, it will end up being the target of all blame and accusations by the aggrieved parties. FASB which in the U.S. started out insisting on a majority representation of public accountants has realized the mistake and has been settling down to a more equitable distribution of seats in recent years. In the international bodies such as IFAC, IASC, etc., such change has not yet occured. In bodies whose effectiveness depends largely on consensus, equal representation of numerous interests is more likely to yield effective results.

CONCLUDING REMARKS

Economics provides a new window on accounting issues. The perspective from this window does not make other, more familiar perspectives invalid or obsolete; it simply adds to our understanding of accounting. Recent years have seen much discussion of economic consequences of accounting standards. If we accept that accounting standards have knowable, or unknowable economic consequences, we are driven to the conclusion that once these standards are enforced, people will change their behavior and thus limit the effectiveness of such standards. What can a standard setting body do in a world full of economically motivated people? Tread slowly, carefully and very softly.

FOOTNOTES

1 See Financial Accounting Standards Board [1980] and Canadian Institute of Chartered Accountants [1980].
2 The theoretical foundation for such a purpose-oriented approach have been developed and presented by R. Mattessich [1964/1977, 1972, 1978].

REFERENCES

Canadian Institute of Chartered Accountants, Corporate Reportings: *Its Future Evolution,* Toronto: CICA, 1980.
Financial Accounting Standards Board, *Statement of Financial Accounting Concepts No. 2: Qualitative Characteristics of Accounting Information,* Stamford, Conn.: FASB, 1980.
Mattessich, Richard, *Accounting and Analytical Methods.* Homewood, Ill.: R.D. Irwin, Inc. 1964; reprinted in "Accounting Classics Series," Houston, Tex.: Scholars Book Co., 1977.
idem. "Methodological Preconditions and Problems of A General Theory of Accounting" The Accounting Review 47 (July 1972), pp. 469-487.
idem. "Instrumental Aspects of Accounting" *Accounting for a Simplified Firm Owning Depreciable Assets* ed. by R.R. Sterling and A.L. Thomas, Houston, Tex.: Scholars Book Co., 1978; pp. 335-351.

Part IV

AGENCY THEORY AND INFORMATION ECONOMICS

WE regard the current Part as the very core of this book and, perhaps, the key to a future theory of accounting. Unfortunately, it is also the most difficult one to digest and requires some concentration on the part of the reader. Analytical methods have assumed an increasing importance in accounting since the publication of the first books in this area almost twenty years ago.[1] This approach has become highly sophisticated and has attained its apex in a combination of information economics and agency theory, and in its application to accounting.

Information economics is a natural extension of statistical decision theory in which an individual makes a choice according to the rank ordering of expected values (i.e. the sums of state-contingent utilities weighted by the probability of each state). Information economics enriches this simple decision theoretic model in many ways, the most important of which is the formulation of each expected value as conditioned on the receipt of some information. This not only preserves the basic decision-theoretic features, but also provides an analytical framework for assigning definite expected values to alternative information systems from which the one with the highest expected value can be chosen. But the emphasis is on *conceptualization* rather than on actual calculations which are feasible only for relatively simple situations.

Agency theory, on the other hand, focuses on situations in which one party (principal) delegates authority, through a contractual relationship, to another party (agent) to accomplish some task. The principal, however, may not always be able to obtain the most desirable outcome via the agent's action. This failure to achieve the so-called "first best" solution is due to two factors, at least: first, the agent's objective (or utility function) is different from that of the principal, and second, the agent's action itself, or the ensuing outcome, is not observable. For example, if the agent is risk-averse and the principal is risk-neutral and, in addition, the agent's action is not observable (directly or indirectly through the outcome), then the agent's optimization behaviour (of maximizing his expected utility) may not result in maximizing the principal's objective function (e.g., expected profits). In such a situation, information on the outcome, or on the action of the agent, becomes an important tool for the principal's decision making. Often, a third party is required to collect necessary information as a monitor or auditor. Such information can be used as a basis for maintaining the contractual relationship between the principal and the agent.

Accounting information may thus fulfill an indispensable function, not only in monitoring the agent's activity, but also in providing a contractual basis for sharing the risks and the fruits of a common endeavour. The basic agency theory[2] has been greatly enriched through a fusion with information theory and might more appropriately be called *agency-information theory*.

The first paper is by Feltham, one of the leading accounting researchers in the area of information economics. The essay is a comprehensive survey of various developments in information economics and its significance for financial accounting research. Its primary focus is on the implications of information economics "for understanding the impact of and demand for alternative external financial reporting systems." Information contained in financial reports is used by managers, investors, financial analysts, and others for various purposes (e.g., to make investment and allocation decisions, to draw up contracts, and to enforce them). To the extent that information is not fully revealed or inferable from other sources, (verified) accounting reports have been proved useful in providing a basis for decision making; hence the need for a satisfactory information system. But it is no easy or straightforward task to determine how satisfactory an accounting system actually is. Out of this need for evaluating information systems arose the analytical framework of information economics, created by Jacob Marschak and others.[3]

Feltham's rich and rewarding paper consists of eight sections beginning with (I) an historical perspective reviewing models of rational choice under uncertainty for a *single person*. The remaining sections (except the last) deal with *multi-person* models: (II) general comments; (III) cooperative models of information choice; (IV) market models of public pre-decision information; (V) market models of public post-decision information; (VI) market models of private investor information; (VII) market models of private management information. Lastly, some concluding remarks are presented in Section VIII. Multi-person models vary in a number of important dimensions. In particular, some of the dimensions are: (1) the number of individuals involved (competitive vs. monopolistic pricing of information); (2) the tranferability of claims (transferable vs. nontransferable); (3) the variety of transferable claims (complete vs. incomplete); (4) the alternative model types (exchange model vs. production model vs. agency model); (5) the action preferences in agency models (no preference for action, only for outcome vs. preference for action as well); (6) the degree of similarity of action preferences between principal and agent (independent vs. identical vs. opposite vs. mixed); (7) the degree of enforceability of commitments; (8) the similarity of prior beliefs (homogeneous vs. heterogeneous); (9) the timing of information distribution (pre-commitment vs. pre-decision); (10) the extent of information distribution (public vs. private vs. private before public).

In each section, the author carefully examines major aspects of the literature on information economics (including statistical decision theory, game theory, signaling, and agency theory) and attempts to relate some of the results to accounting. For example, if we are to address ourselves to accounting issues, we need to look at multi-period models; but, in this setting, the distinction between pre- or post-decision becomes less interesting.

In general, information economics confirms that investors prefer (at least in a weak sense and under *ceteris paribus* conditions) a more informative public reporting system. Thus the incremental cost of acquiring more information should be weighed against the incremental benefits. Information can be considered as a production factor like labour or capital. However, the problem is not quite straightforward, because information often creates externalities and often is a public good, thus resulting in a "free-rider" problem. In such a situation, we may encounter a market failure. Even if information is private, the individual possessing the information may reveal it by his action (or the outcome of his actions, e.g., by prices) or may have an incentive to reveal it voluntarily. Sometimes, private and public information may be regarded as substitutes for each other or as complements.

In the next essay, Butterworth, Gibbins, and King provide a programmatic overview of various issues relevant to the further development of accounting theory. Their basic position is that accounting ought to respond to the market demand for information. We interpret this as conforming to our own claim that means of information must be provided which satisfy specific ends or needs manifesting themselves in our economy. The paper is divided into six sections: (I) introduction; (II) historical perspectives of the standard setting process; (III) agency framework as a basis for developing accounting theory; (IV) methodological issues in accounting research; (V) review of recent accounting research; and (VI) summary and future directions.

The authors believe that the basic difficulty in the past has been the lack of an *economic* theory suitable for accounting, taking into consideration the important role of information. Above all, they discuss the use of accounting information within the framework of agency theory. Corporations are viewed as legal artifacts designed to provide a contractual focus for their activities in the market place. In such a setting, information is indispensable in providing a contractual basis for sharing risks and providing incentives. Although accounting information is useful for predictive as well as retrospective purposes, the authors emphasize that it is this *contractual use* that is the principal objective of accounting information (they consider the historical cost approach as being consistent with this contractual purpose).

Thus the most interesting and perhaps surprising aspect of this second essay is that *accounting theory has come full circle back to the stewardship function as the major goal of accounting practice.* For decades, leading theoreticians tried to convince us that, unless financial accounting serves the shareholders in *their investment decisions*, it has little raison d'être. Yet, more recently, the efficient market hypotheses and the pertinent empirical evidence have revealed that financial statements are of relatively little use for investment decisions and that investors, indeed, rely on those statements to a limited extent only. The agency theory reinstates the stewardship function and illuminates it from an entirely novel and more sophisticated perspective.

The three major usages of information (predictive, contractual, and retrospective) are further divided by these authors into a total of seven finer categories. In terms of the *predictive* usage, information is useful by reducing uncertainty with respect to future events for (1) management and (2) investors. Furthermore, information is useful for *contractual* purposes by providing (3) a basis for efficient risk-sharing, (4) a basis for efficient sharing of beliefs with respect to the relative likelihood of future economic events, (5) a basis for incentives designed to encourage efficient execution of contracts within the corporation, and (6) a basis for the above incentives between the investors and managers of the corporation. And lastly, information is used for (7) *retrospective purposes*, i.e., to comprehend past actions and events. In short, information is deemed useful if it serves any of these seven objectives effectively. However, the four uses for contractual purposes have only recently attracted much attention in modern accounting. Financial information is indispensable for risk sharing or for the provision of incentives; without it, there is no basis for contracts. Of course, for an information system to be useful, it has to be "objective," "reliable,"and "adequate."

In the section dealing with methodological issues, theoretical vs. empirical research, and normative vs. positive theories, are contrasted and discussed. Later, recent results of accounting research are surveyed and classified into five categories, based on the responses to accounting information by individuals, groups, the market, firms, and various economic agents and entities. While most research work has focused on the predictive and retrospective uses of information, future research needs to place more emphasis on the use of contractual information in a general equilibrium context.

Abdel-khalik[4] has criticized the fact that the authors regard various accounting objectives as competing with each other, while they are actually complementary; he further points out that the authors' thesis has a normative rather than the claimed positive foundation and that the use of the "historical cost basis and nothing else . . . is a step backwards into the 1940s." (pp. 86-87)

The next article, by Stanley Baiman, is the link to Part VI and could have been incorporated there, as it is a careful effort to put the ever growing literature on agency theory into a managerial accounting perspective. If managerial accounting has advocated the use of certain procedures (such as overhead allocation, standard costing, etc.) without offering well-developed justifications, the agency approach may overcome this deficiency and, furthermore, provides useful insights into the design of managerial accounting systems. More specifically, the purpose of this article is fourfold: (1) to survey and synthesize the agency literature (the overlap with the preceding article by Feltham is minimal, because this preceding contribution was specifically written for our book and hence with Baiman's article in mind); (2) to develop some of the positive implications of agency research for managerial accounting problems; (3) to provide a basis for evaluating the agency model for normative implications in managerial accounting; and (4) to identify some unanswered managerial accounting questions that can be analyzed within the agency framework.

The article is divided into five major sections: (I) introduction; (II) a survey of non-agency models relevant for managerial accounting; (III) the agency model; (IV) a critical review of the agency literature; and (V) summary and conclusion.

In agency theory, the firm is viewed as an overlapping set of contracts among principal(s) and agent(s), each of whom is motivated solely by self-interest. Each individual chooses his/her actions optimally based on available information and agreed-upon contracts. Thus, managerial accounting information is regarded as an integral and, possibly, as the most important part of the agency model.

In order to highlight the agency framework, Baiman first briefly surveys (Section II) non-agency models that have previously been suggested as analytical frameworks for managerial accounting problems. These include the Decision Theory model, the Theory of Syndicate, the Information Evaluation-Decision Maker model, the Team Theory and the Demand Revelation model. These models treat information as an exogenous variable in the decision making process and can neither take into consideration the revision of beliefs about future events nor the evaluation of performance. The agency model, in contrast, is capable of incorporating satisfactorily both belief revisions and performance evaluations. These two information functions appear to play crucial roles in optimization. Although self-interest is the prime motivation for each agent, this does not preclude the possibility of Pareto improvement (making one party better off, but none worse) through mutual cooperation; the nature and the degree of "cooperation" are determined by the contractual relationships which exist among the involved parties. Cooperative solutions may not be obtainable when appropriate information is unavailable in the following two situations: the case of moral hazard (due to the conflict of interests and lack of contract enforceability) and/or the case of adverse selection (due to asymmetry in information between agent and principal). The discussion of the agency model starts with a simple example, followed by a description and a mathematical formulation of the so-called "basic agency model." This model deals with situations involving a single agent, exogenous labour markets, and a single period.

A further section offers an extensive survey and an evaluation of the agency literature. In doing so, the value of information and its optimal use are emphasized. A particular information system is preferred when its usage in designing incentive contracts (payment schedules) can achieve a Pareto improvement. Results in the literature as to conditions under which a Pareto improvement is achievable are carefully reviewed with detailed discussion on each of the major articles as well as intuitive interpretation for managerial accounting. The literature investigates situations with costless information, costly information, imperfect information (all in post-decision settings) and asymmetric information (in pre-decision settings). Although there appears to be much room for further research, especially on pre-decision cases (where belief revision is the major issue), Baiman concludes that the agency approach has clarified our thinking and has provided much-needed insights into managerial accounting issues. Furthermore, he asserts that "the agency model has the potential to serve as the basis for a useful normative theory of managerial accounting."

Finally, the author examines the agency approach as a positive model (but serving ultimately a normative theory) of managerial accounting by comparing commonly-used managerial accounting procedures with those derived from the agency model. The procedures studied are: responsibility accounting, budgets, variance analysis, cost allocation, participative budgeting, and standards. It is found that a number of practices are consistent with the agency perspective (e.g., budgets, variance analysis, and participative budgeting). At the end of the article, Baiman offers an optimistic summary by stating that "the agency model will be a fruitful tool for future research in managerial accounting and may, indeed, provide a framework from which a useful theory of managerial accounting can be derived." In this connection, we should like to draw attention to the work of Leibenstein,[5] which is somewhat related to agency theory but which illuminates the extremely important concept of *non-allocative effi-*

ciency ("X-efficiency" in his terminology and dealing with all inefficiencies *beyond* those due to in-optimal resource *allocation*) which until recently was completely neglected in the economic literature because of the exclusive concern for allocative efficiency.

Before closing this commentary, a word about shifting and recurring trends. In the commentary to Part II, we hinted at a rejuvenation of the *principle of conservatism* by transferring or extending it from historical cost accounting to current value accounting. In the commentary to the current Part IV (discussing the paper by Butterworth, Gibbins, and King), we indicated a subtle return to the *steward-ship principle* via agency theory. And now we have to point out that the application of information economics and other forces might *reestablish the predominance of the balance sheet over the income statement or, at least, the equality between the two.*

When Schmalenbach, some sixty years ago in his *Dynamic Accounting*,[6] made the income state-ment the centre of attention, relegating the balance sheet to the secondary position of collecting residuals, it seemed that the symmetry between the two financial statements was broken forever. But recently, the status of the balance sheet as an equal or even superior partner has made itself felt in several ways. The problems of pension fund obligations, of financial overextensions, reduced cash flows, and illiquidity are practical issues concerning the balance sheet and the flow of funds statement (which during the seventies even seemed to steal the glory from the income statement[7]). On the theoretical side, it was Fritz Schmidt, the originator of a systematic current value theory,[8] who from the very beginning opposed Schmalenbach's view and pleaded for a realistic valuation in and balanced treat-ment of the two major financial statements. With the recent legislative introduction of current value accounting in several countries, the realistic (i.e., current) evaluation not only of cost of goods sold, depreciation, etc., but also of assets and equities seems automatically secured. But there exists a more ominous theoretical aspect that threatens the income notion.

Since the early forties, when Hicks chastised income as a bad tool that breaks in our hands,[9] some micro and financial economists have accepted the maximization of the value of the firm, rather than short-run profit maximization, as the firm's objective (e.g., Lutz and Lutz).[10] This shift made the income concept less visible but could not eliminate it totally. It rather substituted a long-run and aperiodic income notion for the conventional short-run and periodic one. As a consequence, some accountants began to question the usefulness of both the traditional income notion as well as the income statement, thus putting more emphasis on cash flows and the balance sheet. In this we have a further illustration that history follows the principle of the pendulum. And it may be consoling to know that accounting too pivots upon the golden middle, confirming the saying of Lampedusa's "Leopard" that "the more things change, the more they remain the same."

M. Darrough and R. Mattessich

FOOTNOTES

[1] See R. Mattessich, *Accounting and Analytical Methods — Measurement and Projection of Income and Wealth in the Micro- and Macro-Economy* (Homewood, Ill.: R.D. Irwin, 1964; reprinted in the "Accounting Classics Series," Houston: Scholars Book Co., 1977); and its companion volume: *idem, Simulation of the Firm through a Budget Computer Program* (Homewood, Ill.: R.D. Irwin, 1964; reprinted in facsimile in Ann Arbor, Mich.: University Microfilms International, 1979); see also T.H. Williams and C.H. Griffin, *The Mathematical Dimension of Accounting* (Cincinnati: South-Western Publishing Co., 1964); and Yuji Ijiri, *Management Goals and Accounting for Control* (Chicago: Rand McNally, 1965).

[2] As originally formulated in A.A. Alchian and H. Demsetz' "Production, Information Costs, and Economic Organization," *American Economic Review* 62 (December 1972), pp. 777-795; and in M.C. Jensen and W.H. Meckling's "Theory of the Firm: Managerial Behavior, Agency Costs and Ownership Structure," *Journal of Financial Economics* 3 (October 1976), pp. 306-360.

[3] See, for example, Jacob Marschak, *Economic Information, Decision and Prediction — Selected Essays*, Vol. II/Part II (Dordrecht, Holland/Boston, Mass.: D. Reidel Co., 1974).

[4] "Discussant's Comments" in *Research to Support Standard Setting in Financial Accounting: A Canadian Perspective*, ed. by Sanjoy Basu and J. Alex Milburn (Toronto: Clarkson, Gordon Foundation, 1982), pp. 82-87.

[5] Harvey Leibenstein, *Beyond Economic Man — A New Foundation for Microeconomics*, 2nd ed. (Cambridge, Mass.: Harvard Univ. Press, 1980); and *idem*, "Microeconomics and X-Efficiency Theory," in *The Crisis in Economic Theory*, ed. by Daniel Bell and Irving Kristol (New York: Basic Books, Inc., 1981), pp. 97-110.

[6] *Dynamische Bilanz*, 11th ed. (Leipzig: Glocker, 1953; 1st ed. 1919); English translation by G.W. Murphy and K.S. Most, *Dynamic Accounting* (London: Gee & Co., 1959).

[7] Mainly under the impact of Arthur L. Thomas' thorough and influential studies: *The Allocation Problem in Financial Accounting* (Sarasota, Fla.: AAA, 1969); and *The Allocation Problem: Part Two* (Sarasota, Fla.: AAA, 1975); and also the book by R.K. Jaedicke and R.T. Sprouse, *Accounting Flows: Income, Funds and Cash* (Englewood Cliffs, N.J.: Prentice-Hall, Inc., 1965).

[8] See *Die Organische Tageswertbilanz* (Wiesbaden: Gabler, 1953; 1st ed. 1921, 3rd ed. 1929 by Gloeckner of Leipzig); and R. Mattessich, "On the Evolution of Inflation Accounting — with a Comparison of Seven Major Models," *Economia Aziendale* 1/3 (December 1983), pp. 349-381; and *idem*, "Fritz Schmidt and His Pioneering Work — Six Decades of Current Value Accounting" (Pisa: Congress of Accounting Historians, forthcoming 1984).

[9] See R. Hicks, *Value and Capital*, 2nd ed. (Oxford: Clarendon Press, 1946), p. 177.

[10] Friedrich Lutz and Vera Lutz, *The Theory of Investment of the Firm* (Princeton, N.J.: Princeton University Press, 1951).

FINANCIAL ACCOUNTING RESEARCH: CONTRIBUTIONS OF INFORMATION ECONOMICS AND AGENCY THEORY†

by Gerald A. Feltham

†Helpful comments on an earlier draft of this paper were provided by Amin Amershi, John Butterworth, Pat Hughes, Dan Simunic, and Shyam Sunder, as well as other participants of the accounting research workshop at the University of British Columbia.

SEVERAL significant changes in accounting research began in the sixties. The role of accounting reports in decision making was being stressed, and there was a general call to make accounting reports more relevant to decision makers (e.g. American Accounting Association [1966]). From this call arose three areas of research that have explored the decision-informativeness role of accounting. One area developed from research in *finance* and explored the impact of accounting reports on investor decisions as reflected in changes in stock market prices. The research in this area has been primarily *empirical*, using publicly available data about past events (such as those recorded on the stock market data tapes developed at the University of Chicago). A second area developed from research in *psychology* and explored the impact of information on individual decisions. The research in this area has been primarily *experimental*, examining how judgments or decisions of individuals acting in an artificially constructed context are influenced by variations in the information they receive. The third area developed from research in *information economics*. The research in this area has been primarily *analytical*, examining the impact of alternative information systems on hypothetical, rational decision makers in hypothetical decision contexts.

Information economics is the term given to research that analyzes the economic impact of and demand for alternative information systems. If we view accounting systems as information systems, then information economics must be viewed as a fundamental discipline in accounting research. Much of the information economic research has been conducted by researchers who have no particular interest in accounting, but their research often has implications for accounting. Furthermore, a number of accounting researchers have conducted information economic research.

This paper focuses on information economic research that potentially has implications for understanding the impact of and demand for alternative financial accounting systems (i.e., systems that provide investors with financial reports about a firm). Other surveys that have a similar focus are found in Atkinson and Feltham [1982] and Verrecchia [1982].[1]

Baiman [1982] provides an excellent survey of recent information economics research that has implications for understanding the impact of and demand for alternative managerial accounting systems (i.e., systems that provide managers with reports about a firm's operations); his survey is reproduced in this volume. Baiman gives particular attention to information economic analyses that utilize the recent developments in agency theory, since principal/agent relationships are a central part of managing a firm. This paper considers agency theory issues that arise in the contracting between management and investors, but much of the research reviewed here does not involve agency theory.

Section I provides an historical perspective by very briefly reviewing early information economic research that used single-person models. These models are embedded in the multi-person models that have dominated recent information economic research. As a lead into the discussion of specific multi-person models, section II outlines some of their important dimensions. Two of these dimensions are the number of persons considered and the degree of cooperation among them. Section III discusses models involving a "small" number of individuals, who make cooperative agreements with respect to sharing risks and the selection of actions and information systems. The remaining sections discuss settings in which there are a large number of individuals who interact through a competitive market. Section IV examines the impact of public information on investor preferences, market trading and market prices. In these models, ownership of all assets is assumed to be publicly tradeable and production decisions are either taken as given or firm managers are assumed to maximize the market value of the firm. Section V relaxes these assumptions by recognizing that assets cannot be traded unless claims to their output can be implemented and by recognizing that managers select actions on the basis of their personal preferences. This gives rise to a demand for information that can be used as a basis for enforcing risk sharing and management incentive contracts. The next two sections consider the impact of private information, including the extent to which informed individuals are motivated to publicly reveal their information and the means by which they do this. Section VI considers private information that is obtained by investors, while section VII considers private information that is obtained by managers. Section VIII contains some brief concluding remarks.

Prior to beginning our review, some comments on the criteria for evaluating information economic research are in order. As stated above, this research is primarily analytical -- models are constructed in which assumptions are made about the nature of the decision makers, the decision contexts they face, and the systems that provide them with information, then the model is analyzed to derive conclusions regarding the decision makers' demand for information and the impact of alternative information systems. Therefore, there are two key elements in the research, the assumptions made and the the the analyses performed.

The *assumptions* are the foundation of the model. They may be explicitly stated or implicit in the analysis. The *explicit assumptions* are easy to recognize, but the implicit assumptions are often overlooked. Many *implicit assumptions* are not mentioned because they are so common that the researcher assumes that the reader is familiar with them. On the other hand, the researcher may at times fail to recognize that his analysis only holds if some unstated condition is assumed to hold; that is, either his analysis must be viewed as incorrect or his list of assumptions must be viewed as incomplete.

The assumptions of a model give it structure and determine the context to which it applies. In specifying his assumptions the researcher is typically concerned with both *tractability* and *representiveness*. If the model is to be analytically tractable, then its structure must be relatively simple and specific. Consequently, it must be an abstraction of the contexts to which it is presumed to apply. The models do not reflect all factors that are relevant in a particular context, but they should reflect the dominant factors. Moreover, any one piece of research must be viewed in the context of the entire research in the area. Many papers analyze but one piece of a larger puzzle, and hence they often assume away other important factors in order to assess more clearly the impact of the particular factor of interest. Of course, if this research is to make an effective contribution to our understanding of the larger puzzle, care must be taken in the way in which the other important factors are assumed away.

The insights provided by a model are obtained through *analysis*. It is important, of course, that any analysis be *logically consistent,* otherwise false conclusions may be drawn. As indicated above, the assumptions must be clearly specified if the logical consistency of a particular analysis is to be ascertained. Another aspect of analysis is the *interest in the results obtained.* The researcher should seek to obtain results that provide new insights into the phenomenon being examined. These results largely depend on the assumptions that are made, but the method and extent of the analysis are also determining factors.

Most models can be viewed from either a *normative* or a *positive perspective.* The decision makers are assumed to make choices that they believe are optimal, and the analyses can be viewed as *determining* the information and strategies they *should use* in a given context. This perspective is prevelant in the early single-person information economics research. However, if rational choice models provide reasonable approximations to the choices made by decision makers, then the analyses can be viewed as *explaining or predicting* the information and strategies they *do or will use* in a given context. This latter perspective has been more prevalent in the recent multi-person information economics research. In fact, the assumptions and analysis of these models are often evaluated in terms of whether the predicted choices and consequences are confirmed by observed choices and consequences, either in the form of anecdotal evidence or formal empirical studies.

An effective positive model provides *new,* or at least *clearer, understanding of observed phenomena,* perhaps by serving as a basis for more effective experimental or empirical research. Some experimental research has been motivated by information economic analyses. Most of this research focuses on single-person models (e.g., Uecker [1978], and Hilton and Swieringa [1981]), but some recent experimental research has examined the impact of information in a market setting (e.g., Plott and Sunder [1982]). Future experimental research based on information economic analyses may provide insights into the role and impact of alternative financial accounting systems, but it is extremely difficult to construct experiments which reflect the important factors that influence the use of accounting information. The use of information economic analyses to generate empirically testable hypotheses is likely to provide more significant results. The link between information economic and empirical research has been rather limited to date, but I believe that this will develop more fully in the future. Some links between these two areas of research are discussed during the following review.

There are many sources of information in an economy and accounting systems are but one potential source. Most information economic analyses treat information at a very general level and do not consider specific forms of information. Consequently, while information economic analyses may identify conditions under which information has value to decision makers, it does not necessarily follow that accounting information has value under those conditions. Some information economic research is directly applicable to accounting because accounting reports appear to fulfill the role of the information being considered, other research is indirectly applicable because it considers information that potentially affects the impact of accounting information, but still other information economic research appears to have neither direct nor indirect applicability to accounting. Unfortunately, very few studies to date consider information that has many of the important structural properties of accounting information. This is largely because there have been very few multi-period models and much of the structure of accounting information results from the necessity to report on economic activity prior to the full realization of the consequences of that activity. However, some multi-period models have been developed and this is likely to be a significant area of research in the near future. Furthermore, a thorough understanding of the role of information in single-period contexts provides a firm foundation for future research, as well as providing immediate insights into the role of accounting information in our economy.

SINGLE-PERSON MODELS: AN HISTORICAL PERSPECTIVE

If an individual is uncertain about the consequences of a set of alternative actions, then he is likely to value information that reduces his uncertainty about those consequences. To formally explore the nature of that demand for information we must have a model of choice under uncertainty. Consequently, the development of models of *rational choice under uncertainty* by such pioneers as von

Neumann and Morgenstern [1944] can be viewed as the starting point of information economics. They demonstrated that if an individual's choice behavior satisfies a few rather basic "consistency" axioms, then his behavior can be represented as the maximization of his expected utility for the consequences of the actions available to him.[2]

The expected utility model serves as the base for *statistical decision theory*. In this theory, an individual is assumed to process information in accordance with his prior beliefs and the rules of probability calculus. The key theorem in probability calculus is due to Bayes, and the use of prior beliefs in deriving posterior beliefs from observed events is termed Bayesian statistics (in contrast to classical statistical inference which ignores prior beliefs). Statistical decision theory, which combines the expected utility model and Bayesian statistics, is often referred to as *Bayesian decision theory*.

From the perspective of information economics, the most important theorem from Bayesian decision theory was proven by Blackwell [1951, 1953]. Blackwell defines one information system to be *more informative*[3] than another if it is *never less valuable* (i.e., there is no single-person decision context in which it is less valuable). He then proves that one system is more informative than another *if, and only if,* the signals from the latter can be viewed as providing more *"garbled"* information about the state than do the signals from the former (the state consists of all uncertain events that influence the consequences of actions).[4] The original theorem is couched in terms of experiments, but various authors have explored its implications for comparing information systems (e.g., Marschak and Miyasawa [1968], Marschak [1971], Marschak and Radner [1972], and McGuire [1972].

Jacob Marschak is generally viewed as the father of *information economics*. Beginning in the mid-fifties he produced a number of papers that examined the impact of alternative information structures. Many of these papers focused on a single decision maker and used the techniques of statistical decision theory (e.g., Marschak [1959, 1963, 1971]). However, he was also interested in the role of information in organizations with many decision makers, and this led to his work with Roy Radner on the theory of teams (e.g., Marschak [1955], Radner [1962], and Marschak and Radner [1972]).

Information economic research in accounting began in the mid-sixties with three Ph.D. dissertations at the University of California. Butterworth [1972] and Feltham [1968, 1972] characterized the choice of accounting systems in terms of the preferences of the decision makers who would use the reports from those systems. They provided a precise interpretation of relevance, aggregation, timeliness, and accuracy,[5] analyzed the impact of these system characteristics on the value of an information system, and identified their relationship to Blackwell's informativeness concept. Mock [1969], on the other hand, used a business game to conduct experiments which assessed the relationship between the theoretical value of more timely information and its observed value.

These initial studies, and several that followed, were primarily concerned with management accounting systems. They focused on a *single decision maker* who selects both the optimal information system and the optimal action given the signal provided by that system. There was no attempt to consider the issues that arise when the actions and well-being of more than one decision maker are influenced by the information system that is used. For a summary of a number of the insights provided by single-person information economic analyses see Hilton [1979, 1981].

A variation on the basic single person model was proposed by Feltham and Demski [1970]. They adopted the perspective of a *rational information evaluator* who predicts the actions that will result from each of the possible signals that may be generated. Unlike the basic single person model, these actions need not be optimal from the information evaluator's perspective. This may be because the actions are selected by a decision maker who has different preferences and beliefs, or because the identification of the optimal action is too costly and hence simplified decision rules are used. This latter perspective provided a useful means for examining the nature of optimal cost determination for management decisions (see Demski and Feltham [1976]).

MULTI-PERSON MODELS: SOME GENERAL COMMENTS

During the seventies the focus of information economic research shifted from single-person models to multi-person models. This shift resulted from a recognition of the short-comings of single-person analyses in many contexts and the development during the sixties and seventies of a variety of models of multi-person decision making under uncertainty. The rational decision maker of statistical decision theory is still a key element in these models, but now a number of multi-person issues are considered.

Multi-person models vary in a number of important dimensions and Table 1 lists several that significantly influence information economic analyses. These dimensions are outlined here and are discussed in more detail during our review of the current literature.

First, the *number of individuals* considered *may be small or large.* Game theory is often used to examine the *personal* bargaining and competition that occurs when the number of individuals is small, whereas market equilibrium analysis is used to examine the *impersonal* trading and competition that occurs when the number of individuals is large. Second, *claims to outcomes may or may not be transferable;* such transfers are often desirable because they permit individuals to make mutually acceptable agreements as to the actions they will take and the way in which they will share the outcomes from those actions. However, such agreements may not be feasible either because they are illegal (e.g., to preclude collusion by competitors) or because there are no means of enforcing them. Third, in those models in which claims are transferable, there are *differences in the variety of claims that are available for transfer.* The set of transferable claims (e.g., the set of securities traded in the capital market) is termed *complete* if its components are sufficiently varied to permit any set of individuals to share outcomes in the way they would find most beneficial, otherwise the set is termed incomplete. In many analyses the set of transferable claims is *exogenously specified*[6] and the specified set may be either complete or *incomplete.* If the set of transferable claims is *endogenously determined,* then incompleteness can occur if there is *insufficient information* available to enforce a complete set. This latter form of incompleteness appears to create a significant demand for accounting information.

TABLE 1

DIMENSIONS OF MULTI-PERSON INFORMATION ECONOMIC MODELS

1. NUMBER OF INDIVIDUALS
   - Small
   - Large

2. TRANSFERABILITY OF CLAIMS TO OUTCOMES
   - Transferable
   - Non-transferable

3. VARIETY OF TRANSFERABLE CLAIMS AVAILABLE
   - Complete
   - Incomplete due to exogeneous restrictions
   - Incomplete due to insufficient information

4. ALTERNATIVE ACTIONS IN TRANSFERABLE CLAIMS MODELS
   - Pure exchange models - no choice
   - Production models - collective choice
   - Agency models - individual choice

5. DIRECT PREFERENCES FOR ACTIONS IN AGENCY MODELS
   - None
   - Disutility for more productive actions

6. SIMILARITY OF PREFERENCES FOR ACTIONS IN NON-TRANSFERABLE CLAIMS MODELS
- Strictly independent
- Strictly identical
- Strictly opposite
- Mixed

7. ACTION COMMITMENTS IN NON-TRANSFERABLE CLAIMS MODELS
- None feasible
- All feasible
- Some feasible

8. SIMILARITY OF PRIOR BELIEFS
- Homogeneous
- Heterogeneous

9. TIMING OF INFORMATION DISTRIBUTION
- Pre-commitment
- Pre-decision
- Post-decision

10. EXTENT OF INFORMATION DISTRIBUTION
- Public report
- Private acquisition
- Private acquisition prior to public report

11. EXTENT TO WHICH PRIVATE INFORMATION IS REVEALED
- None revealed
- Fully revealed
- Partially revealed

12. SELECTION OF INFORMATION SYSTEMS
- Exogeneous
- Endogeneous

13. NUMBER OF PERIODS
- Single period
- Multiple periods

The fourth through seventh dimensions refer to the actions that can be taken. Models that assume that outcome claims are transferable vary as to the *alternative actions available, the mechanism for choosing actions,* and the *direct preferences for actions.* In *pure exchange models* there is *no choice,* the actions are exogenously specified and are not influenced by any information that is produced; information can only influence the exchange of outcome claims. In *production models* there are alternative actions and the *choice* of specific actions is *determined collectively;* this may be done by explicitly considering the individuals' collective choice or by assuming that managers choose actions in the best interest of a firm's owners (e.g., if there is a complete set of tradeable claims they maximize the firm's market value). In agency models there are also alternative actions, but now actions are determined by individual choice (e.g., a manager selects actions in accordance with his own interests). In some *agency models* managers have no *direct preferences for* the *actions* they select,[7] but in many models they are assumed to have *greater disutility for more productive actions* (e.g., a disutility for effort). In agency models, and particularly in those in which agents have a disutility for productive actions, accounting information plays a significant role in motivating managers.

Models that assume that outcome claims are *not* transferable vary as to the *similarity of preferences for alternative actions* and the *enforceability of action commitments*. Individuals select their actions in accordance with their own preferences, and the preferences with respect to each others' actions may be *strictly independent, strictly identical, strictly opposite, or mixed*. If preferences are mixed, then the individuals often prefer to make binding commitments as to the actions they will take; *non-cooperative models* assume that *all commitments are infeasible, pure cooperative models* assume that *all commitments are feasible*, while *mixed models* assume that only *some commitments are feasible*.

The eighth through twelfth dimensions refer to the individuals' beliefs and the information that influences those beliefs. *Prior beliefs* are those that individuals hold before the receipt of any information that is explicitly considered in the analysis; those beliefs may be *homogeneous* (i.e., identical) *or heterogeneous* (i.e., different). Analyses that permit heterogeneous beliefs implicitly assume that the source of that heterogeneity, such as differences in prior experiences and information, is of no interest to the individuals considered. This assumption may not be appropriate if that heterogeneity leads to "side-betting" on the outcomes that may occur.

The information produced varies as to the *timing of its distribution*, the *extent to which it is distributed*, the *extent to which it is revealed* by those who receive it, and the *means by which it is selected*. Pre-commitment information is received prior to any commitments or exchange of claims, *pre-decision information* (for a given period) is received prior to at least some actions or exchange of claims, and *post-decision information* (for a given period) is received after all actions and exchanges have occurred. In some models all information is assumed to be *publicly reported*, in others all information is *privately acquired*, and in still others information is *privately acquired prior to its public release*. We are primarily interested in publicly released accounting information, but the impact of that information depends on the extent to which there is private information acquisition and the extent to which that private information is publicly revealed. Some models of private information acquisition assume that there is no *public revelation* of private information, but in most models private information is either *fully or partially revealed*. Ideally, the information produced and acquired in a given context is *endogenously determined* by the model, but this would make many models too complex and hence most analyses *exogenously* specify the information systems and examine the impact of varying those systems.

The thirteenth dimension is the *number of periods* considered. Most models to date have been *single-period models*, but there has been some analysis of *multi-period models*. Single-period models are an important first step, but, as indicated earlier, multi-period models are required in the analysis of many accounting issues.

In the next section we focus on the impact of public information on a "small" number of individuals who have either strictly independent, strictly identical or mixed interests and who can enforce any commitment that is desirable. Other variations are discussed in subsequent sections.

COOPERATIVE MODELS OF INFORMATION CHOICE

In a single-person model there is, of course, no communication or commitment among individuals. The decision maker's information comes from either an exogenously specified system or from a system which he selects. In these models a system cannot have value unless it provides *state-informative, pre-decision information*, i.e., information that influences the decision maker's beliefs about the state and is received prior to the selection of some action. In general, the relative value of two systems depends on the decision maker's set of alternative actions, preferences, and prior beliefs, but we know that one system is never less valuable than another if it provides pre-decision information that is *more state-informative* (in the Blackwell sense).

In a multi-person model with *strictly independent interests* the actions of one individual do not affect the outcomes of another (which implies, for example, that outcome claims are non-transferable). Consequently, this model is essentially a set of single-person models. It becomes a multi-person model if the individuals obtain their information from a *public information system.* This type of model is considered in the accounting literature by Marshall [1972] and Demski [1973a]. A fundamental point made in these two papers is that, in general, different individuals have different preferences with respect to alternative information systems. Consequently, it is not always possible to select a system (or accounting standards) that is preferred by all users. However, the Blackwell theorem implies that the users prefer more disclosure, more accuracy, and more timely reporting if increasing the informativeness of the system does not increase the cost to them.

In a multi-person model with *strictly identical interests* the individuals have a common goal and essentially operate as one individual, although each may receive different information and take different actions. This is the perspective adopted in the previously mentioned *theory of teams;* all team members have the same preferences and prior beliefs with respect to the team's outcome. Since the team operates much as a single individual it is not surprising that Blackwell's theorem also applies in this context.[8]

While interesting from an historical perspective, the models of strictly independent and strictly identical interests are of little current interest. In most situations individuals are concerned about their personal consumption, and an individual's consumption is usually influenced by his own actions, the actions of others, and any agreements he makes regarding the sharing of the outcomes from those actions (if outcome claims are transferable). In these contexts the individuals usually have *mixed interests* and are motivated to negotiate agreements as to the actions they will take and, if possible, the way in which they will share the outcomes from those actions. *Cooperative game theory* is used to analyze those contexts in which *agreements* can be *costlessly enforced.*[9] In the contexts considered here, enforcement of the most preferred agreement often requires that the information system provide verified public reports of the actions taken and the outcomes that occur, and that externally imposed penalties (e.g., by the legal system) deter any deviation from these agreements. The most preferred agreement is termed the *first best* agreement; information and enforcement costs may induce individuals to accept some *second best* agreement in order to avoid some of these costs.

The agreements that are negotiated are influenced by the preferences, beliefs, and opportunities of each individual. An individual will *block* (i.e., reject) any agreement that he believes makes him worse-off than if he acted independently. Similarly, an agreement will be blocked by a *coalition* of individuals if they can independently implement another agreement that would make all members of the coalition at least as-well-off and some better-off. Any agreement that is not blocked is in the *core* of the game. Except where a large number of players result in a competitive equilibrium, there are usually many agreements in the core.[10]

Any agreement in the core is *Pareto efficient,* i.e., there is no other agreement that will make all individuals at least as-well-off and some better-off (otherwise it would be blocked). Many analyses of cooperative games seek to identify necessary conditions for an agreement to be Pareto efficient. These conditions do not fully characterize the core, but they often provide interesting insights into the general nature of agreements we would expect to observe in situations represented by the models.

A cooperative game termed a *syndicate* has received some attention in the accounting literature, and the analyses of syndicates provides a foundation for the analysis of several other multi-person models.[11] A syndicate consists of a set of individuals whose preferences depend on their personal income and who have agreed to share the uncertain aggregate money-outcome from their actions (or some collective act). For example, the syndicate members could be partners in a firm, diversified investors in several firms, or members of a mutual insurance company. Necessary characteristics of Pareto efficient sharing rules (which specify how the aggregate outcome is to be divided) have been identified, as well as conditions under which these sharing rules induce the individuals to have identical preferences with respect to the alternative actions available to the syndicate. From an accounting perspective it is important to note that a Pareto efficient contract among the syndicate members is only enforceable if there is a *verified public report of the aggregate outcome.*[12] If conditions are such that the Pareto optimal sharing rules induce identical preferences with respect to the alternative actions, then the contract is self-enforcing with respect to the action choice. If these conditions do not hold, enforcement of a Pareto efficient contract may require a verified report of individual actions.

Reports of the outcome and individual actions are post-decision information. Additional post-decision information has no value to the sydicate members unless they have heterogeneous beliefs about the likelihood of particular signals, in which case the report can provide a basis for side-betting (e.g., betting on verified reports of football scores).[13] This is an unlikely role for accounting information!

If a syndicate has alternative actions it can take, then *public pre-decision information* that is state informative may have value to the syndicate members. Furthermore, if beliefs are homogeneous, then a system that is more state-informative (in the Blackwell sense) is never less valuable. That is, an agreement (with respect to sharing rules and decision strategies) based on one system can always be at least weakly Pareto dominated[14] by an agreement based on a more informative system (if it is no more costly). It is important to note that *the value of these systems is derived from the benefits of improved decisions; pre-decision information cannot provide any improvement in risk sharing.*[15]

Public pre-commitment information also can improve decisions, but it can have a *negative impact on risk sharing.*[16] Therefore, an informative pre-commitment information system can have negative value to a syndicate. This implies that syndicate members always prefer to make their agreements before obtaining public information.

MARKET MODELS OF PUBLIC PRE-DECISION INFORMATION

A large body of empirical research in accounting and finance focuses on the impact of public information in capital markets. A number of information economics papers have also examined this area, including several papers in accounting. The empirical research has based most of it analyses on the capital asset pricing model developed in finance, whereas the information economics research has based most of its analyses on the state-contingent model developed in economics. The state-contingent model does not lend itself to empirical testing unless a number of additional assumptions are introduced and, hence, the connections between the two areas of research have been limited.

The basic model in the information economics literature is a single-period model in which investors are endowed with some quantity of a current consumption good and the ownership of tradeable claims to an end-of-period consumption good (or wealth). A claim is often contingent on some uncertain event, such as the output produced by a firm, and hence these analyses implicitly assume that at the end of the period there will be a *verified public report of each event upon which the claims are based.* This report is essential to the legal enforcement of the claim.

Several analyses focus on *pure exchange economies* in which the production activities are taken as given. The current consumption good and the claims to end-of-period consumption are traded at competitively determined prices that equate supply and demand. Each investor selects a current consumption level and a portfolio of claims that maximizes his expected utility subject to a budget constraint (the market value of his current consumption and portfolio of claims cannot exceed the market value of his endowment). The resulting equilibrium is termed *fully Pareto efficient* (FPE) if there is no state-contingent agreement among the ''syndicate'' of all investors that would Pareto dominate the competitive equilibrium. And full Pareto efficiency is achieved if the *set of tradeable claims is complete or investors are sufficiently similar.*[17]

The first analysis of information issues using this type of model is provided by Hirshleifer [1971], and it is introduced into the accounting literature by Demski [1974]. Several papers use specific versions of the model to explore the impact of public information that is received either before any trades are made or between two rounds of trades.[18] The studies by Rubinstein [1975], Hakansson, Kunkel and Ohlson [1982], Ohlson [1980, 1980a], Ohlson and Buckman [1980, 1981] and Amershi [1982] provide the most general analyses.

The most important result is that *in a pure exchange economy, public information has no impact on investor trades* (and hence investor well-being) if it is received when the *economy is in equilibrium* (perhaps because there was a prior round of trading), *investor beliefs about the information are homogeneous, investor utility functions are additive over time,* and the *prior equilibrium is fully Pareto efficient.* If the economy is not in equilibrium, then it is the same as a syndicate receiving public pre-commitment information — the receipt of the information removes the opportunity to insure against some risks and can therefore make investors worse-off than if no public information was received. However, if the market is constantly adjusting to information and other changes in market conditions, the impact of information in a nonequilibrium situation would not appear to be an important issue.

In a *pure exchange economy* there are three reasons why public information may have *social value* (i.e., make all investors at least as-well-off and some better-off) if it is received when the market is in equilibrium but prior to a final round of trading. First, it can provide a basis for *additional side-betting if investor beliefs* about the information are *heterogeneous.* As indicated above, this does not appear to provide a significant role for accounting information. Second, public information can assist investors in *more efficiently choosing between current consumption and claims to future consumption.* This may be an important role for accounting information, particularly if the information influences the aggregate allocation of current resources between consumption and investment. However, in a pure exchange economy the aggregate allocation is taken as given and an investor can only increase his current consumption if some other investors decrease theirs. This may occur *if investor utility functions are not additive over time.*[19] Third, public information may *improve the efficiency with which risks are shared if the market is incomplete* and this incompleteness has resulted in an equilibrium that is not full Pareto efficient. A key point that should be recognized is that market incompleteness is due to an isufficient variety of tradeable claims, but the post-decision information assumed in these models is sufficient to provide the basis for a complete set of tradeable claims. Therefore, issuing additional claims may be more effective than producing more information.

Another important result from this literature is that while *public information* may have no impact on investor trades it *does affect market prices* if it changes investor beliefs. This implies that *price changes* can *indicate* that a report has *information content* with respect to the returns provided by tradeable claims, but that does not imply that implementing the reporting system will change the investors' *ex ante* expected utility. Ohlson [1980a] suggests that if we are interested in the impact of information on the investors' well being, then these results imply that empirical research should examine trading volume instead of price changes (as Beaver [1968] had suggested in an early empirical study). If we ignore other factors that can affect an investors' desire to trade, trading volume will be zero if information has no value and it will be nonzero if any of the previously mentioned result in the information having social value.[20]

The analysis of production economies has been limited, but it is here that we find a significant role for public pre-decision information. The basic production economy has the same structure as the basic pure exchange model except that the tradeable claims represent direct claims against the output from firms whose production activities are endogenously determined. Each firm is operated by a manager who selects the production activity that maximizes the net market value of the claims to the firm's output.[21] This production activity can vary with respect to the amount of input used and possibly the way that it is used. The firms and investors are endowed with a current good that may either be consumed or used in production, and the owners receive or provide the difference between a firm's endowment and usage.

Hirshleifer [1971] provided the initial analysis of public information in this type of model, and Kunkel [1982] provides an analysis that is the production analogue to the pure exchange analysis of Hakansson, Kunkel, and Ohlson [1982]. These analyses demonstrate that if the market is in equilibrium prior to the release of public information, then that information can have social value even if beliefs are homogeneous, investor utility functions are additive, and markets are complete. The information can have value for three basic reasons. First the information may permit each manager to *more effectively utilize* the *inputs* into his firm (if there are alternative projects). Second, the information may induce a *more effective allocation of inputs across firms.* Third, the information may permit investors to *more effectively allocate* their *resources between consumption and investment* (both at the individual and aggregate level).

As in the pure exchange economy, it is important that the market be in equilibrium when public information is released. Otherwise, some investors may be adversely affected by the information. Similarly, to ensure that a *more state-informative system* is at least weakly preferred by all investors, the market must either allow signal contingent trades prior to release of the information (similar to the syndicate agreements discussed earlier) *or* the market must be in equilibrium with respect to the signal from the less informative system prior to release of the signal from the more informative system.

Single-period models identify some key factors that affect the impact of public information, but multi-period models are required if we are to address accounting issues. To date, there have been very few multi-period market models in the accounting literature,[22] and only a limited number in the broader information economics literature.[23] However, multi-period market models under uncertainty are analyzed in the economics literature, and these provide a base from which future information economics research is likely to develop.

A key issue in the analysis of multi-period market models is the nature of the markets that are assumed to exist. There are two basic approaches. First, one can assume that tradeable claims can be written contingent on any information that will be available at the time the claim is to be exercised. That is, the market is complete with respect to the information that will be available. Under these conditions the initial market equilibrium for a given information structure[24] determines which claims each investor holds for the duration of the economy. Trading can occur in the future, but there will be no incentive for investors to trade at those times. One information structure is *at least as informative* as another if at each point in time it will provide at least as much information about the events that have occurred.[25] And if the market is in equilibrium with respect to some information structure, then no investor will oppose the introduction of another structure that is at least as informative. This is a straight-forward extension of the informativeness result for the single-period model.

The second approach is to consider a set of exogenously specified tradeable claims that do not provide a complete market with respect to the anticipated information. At any given point in time there are a set of claims that are being traded and there are equilibrium prices for those claims. However, this is only a *temporary equilibrium* in that the release of information over time will result in new trades. This is a more realistic approach, but it is difficult to analyze because now one must specify investor and manager behavior in terms of both *current* information and prices and their *expectations* with respect to *future* prices. Deriving equilibrium rational expectations is a non-trivial task, much less assessing the impact of alternative information structures.

Kanodia [1980] provides a "simple" but interesting information economic model of the second type. He considers a single type of investor and a single type of firm with a very specific form of production function. The firm's output is influenced by two types of uncontrollable factors: transitory and long-lasting. A public reporting system (such as an accounting system) that reports the factors influencing a firm's output, instead of just the total output, results in a more efficient allocation of the output between consumption (dividends) and investment.[26]

In general, information economic analyses indicate that investors at least weakly prefer a more informative public reporting system if it is not more costly. However, most information economic analyses do not model the process by which public reporting choices (that consider reporting costs) are made. Ideally, models would include information production as an object of choice for at least some individuals (such as the managers of firms) and would include access to the information produced as a "good" that can be sold or freely distributed.[27] Conceptually there is no difficulty in modelling this, but information production and use generally have properties that preclude the application of traditional methods for analyzing economic equilibria. For example, users may have different preference orderings over the alternative information systems, the private use of information can have a detrimental effect on others (i.e., there can be externalities), and use by one individual does not preclude its use by others (i.e., it is to some extent a "public good" and this can create a "free-rider" problem).

Gonedes [1975] provides one of the few models of endogenous information choice in a market setting, but it involves some very restrictive assumptions.[28] He assumes that firms provide constant stochastic returns to investment, and this avoids the externality problem (since this gives the investors *strictly independent interests*). The problems created by different preference orderings are avoided by assuming that such differences do not exist; this is in part achieved by assuming that all alternative information about a particular attribute of the uncontrollable events can be ordered on the basis of informativeness. The free-rider problem is avoided by analyzing the production and sale of information as a market *game* in which *coalitions* of investors and information producers can agree to share the returns form the information produced and can *restrict the use of their information* to coalition members. Gonedes demonstrates that under these conditions the implemented information structure (and the allocation of information costs) is *Pareto efficient,* with different users paying different amounts for the same public information.

An important issue is whether Pareto efficiency is achieved under less restrictive assumptions, or do externalities and free-rider problems result in "market failures". This has been a subject of debate in the literature, and the assumption of market failure appears to implicitly underlie much of the regulation of public reporting.[29] That literature is not explored here because most of it does not involve explicit modelling of the economic system. Furthermore, to understand the impact of reporting regulations we must understand the consequences of different "levels" of regulation. This requires a much richer modelling of *individual incentives to produce, use and distribute information* than is found in the models of public information reviewed above. Research in this area is reviewed in subsequent sections.

MARKET MODELS OF PUBLIC POST-DECISION INFORMATION

The initial modelling of information in multi-person contexts focused on pre-decision information. This was natural given that in single-person models only pre-decision information can have value. However, in a multi-person context cooperation among individuals creates a demand for post-decision information that can be used as a basis for enforcing agreements. This provides a significant source of demand for auditied accounting information.

In the models that focus on pre-decision information, the post-decision information is taken as given. In particular, it is common to assume that each firm's output is publicly reported and hence claims against that output can be publicly traded. However, if output reports are costly, then the output would not be reported unless such reporting is exogenously imposed or individuals are motivated to incur the reporting costs.

The simplest context in which there is a demand for output reporting occurs in a *pure exchange economy* in which an individual owns an asset (e.g., a firm or a house) that provides him with an uncertain level of output (consumption). If the output is not publicly reported then the owner cannot issue claims against it (e.g., issue shares in the firm or buy house insurance) and hence he must bear the risk associated with that output.[30] However, he may be able to at least partially offset that risk by making appropriate investments in the claims that are publicly traded.[31] Therefore, the completeness of the existing set of tradeable claims is an important factor in determining whether an individual is motivated to pay to publicly report his output as a basis for issuing tradeable claims. In particular, he would *not* be motivated to pay for the report if *the existing set of tradeable claims is complete with respect to the uncontrollable events that influence his output*.[32] Conversely, issuing a claim conditioned on a report of his output would have value to an individual if his output is influenced by *asset specific events.*

If full, accurate reporting of the output is costly, then the individual may consider *incomplete or imperfect reporting.* Insurance claims often involve a form of *incomplete reporting* in that the insuree usually reports only those outcomes that involve losses that exceed an agreed deductible. Townsend [1979] demonstrates that this is an optimal strategy if output verification is costly and these costs need not be incurred until the insuree has observed his output and issued instructions to have it verified.

Evans [1980] applies this type of analysis to an auditing context. In both analyses *all* risks are implicitly assumed to be asset specific.

Imperfect reporting may arise if it is less costly to estimate the output on the basis of imperfect observations of the output or observations of events that are correlated with the output. Atkinson and Feltham [1982a] and Gjesdal [1982] explore the value of imperfect reporting. They demonstrate that if existing tradeable claims do not permit an individual to efficiently share his risks with others, then a post decision report is *valuable if, and only if, the report and the firm specific variations in the output are not independent.* Furthermore, one reporting system is *more valuable* than another *if* its reports are *more insurance-informative* (i.e., more informative about the firm specific variations in output).[33] This informativeness relationship is very similar to Blackwell's state-informativeness for pre-decision information, but now the focus is on those elements of the state that affect the output of a particular asset.

In a pure exchange economy the investors are only concerned with risk-sharing and hence they are only willing to pay for post-decision reports that are insurance-informative with respect to their personal risks. However, there is a demand for additional post-decision information in a *production economy in which managers are motivated to select production activities in accordance with their personal interests.* Unlike the production economy literature that focuses on pre-decision information, the post-decision information literature treats the manager's motivation as endogenous. In particular, the manager's motivation depends on his utility for end-of-period consumption, the claims he holds for end-of-period consumption (in the form of compensation contracts and personal investments in tradeable claims), and any direct utility he has for the actions he takes (e.g., his utility for perquisites or disutility for effort).

The manager is an agent of all investors whose claims are influenced by his actions. Hence, the recent literature on agency theory is relevant to this problem. Baiman [1982] provides an extensive review of this literature, with particular emphasis on how it relates to management accounting. Consequently, the comments here are brief and focus on external reporting issues for a manager who can invest in the market and whose principals are diversified investors.

The simplest case to consider is one in which an individual seeks to share his risks with others and the output from his asset is influenced by his actions. If the individual is an entrepreneur, he may also seek to obtain capital from investors. As in the pure exchange case, *post-decision reporting has no value* to the owner of the asset *if the existing set of tradeable claims is complete with respect to the uncontrollable events that influence the asset's output* (and if the owner can *obtain* any desired *capital by issuing riskless debt*, i.e., investors believe there is no chance of bankruptcy). However, post-decision reporting can have value to the owner of the asset if there are asset specific risks. In particular, a reporting system has *value* to him *if, and only if, the report and the asset specific variations in output are not independent.* Furthermore, one reporting system is more valuable than another if its report is *more insurance-incentive-informative* (i.e., more informative about the asset specific variations in output *and* the owner's actions that influence that output).[34] Observe that whereas in the pure exchange case only information about the output is valuable, now information about the owner's actions are also valuable (but there must be at least some information about the output).

Similar results are obtained if the firm is owned by diversified investors who do not manage it. They must hire a manager and their contract with him determines his motivation. Consequently, an incentive-informative report will be valuable to them, and the more incentive-informative it is the more valuable it will be. The owners do not seek to share risks with the manager (since they are diversified), but they will still value a verified report of the output. A report of the output is incentive-informative, particularly if the manager could otherwise retain the output for his own use, and a report of the output would be a key element in the risk sharing agreement that exists among the owners.

There are many variations on the basic principal/agent model, and most of these are reviewed by Baiman elsewhere in this volume. Two seem particularly crucial if we are to gain further insight into the demand for financial accounting information. First, the basic model considers a single period, but most accounting issues involve interrelationships between the actions and events in one period and the results in subsequent periods. *Multi-period models* are considerably more complex than the basic model and only a limited amount of analysis has been done on them.[35] Observe that in a multi-period context the distinction between post-decision and pre-decision information becomes blurred, since post-decision information for one period becomes pre-decision information for all subsequent periods. This implies that planned production of additional public information at a particualr point in time has value to a decision maker if it can be used either to enforce better prior contracts or to make better subsequent decisions. *Informativeness with respect to the state* (which includes all events that influence aggregate output and asset specific variations in output) *and agent actions* are likely to be important information characteristics in multi-period contexts, but now inter-period relationships must be considered in defining them.

A second important variation in the basic model is the recognition of *contracts with creditors*, such as banks and bondholders. Creditors often share risks with the managers and owners of a firm because, while their contracts may call for fixed payments, these amounts cannot be collected if the firm goes bankrupt. Management actions can influence the probability of bankruptcy, and an action that increases the value of the common stock can sometimes increase the probability of bankruptcy. Creditors recognize this and the prices of the funds they provide depend on their beliefs about the actions that will be taken. In order to obtain a favorable price the owners of a firm may be motivated to restrict the actions taken by management. Post-decision accounting information is often an important means of implementing those restrictions, e.g., bond indentures often impose restrictions on a firm's status and activities as stated in the firm's accounting reports. The finance and accounting literature have discussed this role of accounting reports, and there have been several empirical tests of the impact of changes in accounting methods based on this role.[36] However, there has been little explicit analysis of the consequences of reporting changes in an equilibrium setting. Further analysis in this area may provide additional insights into the motivation for changes in accounting methods and a basis for improving empirical tests of the impact of those changes.

Before concluding this section, some brief comments on auditing are warranted. Most multi-person models implicitly assume the existence of an auditor who truthfully reports the events he is hired to observe. Antle [1981, 1981a] provides a model in which the auditor's motivation is endogenous to the analysis. This is a simple three person model (principal, agent, and auditor) that may provide some insight into the motivation of internal auditors, but it does not reflect some of the important characteristics of external auditors. In particular, it does not reflect the importance of the "profession" as an enforcement agency and the importance of "reputation" to an auditing firm that seeks to maintain and expand its set of clients over a prolonged period of time.[37] Exploration of the role of these factors may provide useful insights in the future.

MARKET MODELS OF PRIVATE INVESTOR INFORMATION

Public information is provided by a variety of sources for a variety of reasons. The news media provide, at little or no charge, both verified and unverified reports of events that are of interest to large numbers of individuals. News reports attract the attention of consumers and this allows profit oriented firms to sell advertising "space" to suppliers of consumer goods and services. In addition, many public and private organizations provide reports of events for little or no charge. These reports may be provided because they are required by statute or contract, or because management believes that it is in their best interests to provide them. Some private organizations seek to earn profits from their information gathering activities by selling the "timely" use of the information they acquire (although exclusion of "free-riders" is a problem). Finally, some public information may be *inferred* from the observed or reported consequences of actions taken by individuals who have acquired private information and seek to use it to their personal advantage.

To understand the role of accounting reports as *public pre-decision information,* we must determine the extent to which these reports contain information that is not provided by other sources and the extent to which this information changes individual beliefs and decisions. Furthermore, to understand the impact of disclosure laws and reporting standards we must determine how alternative laws and standards influence the reporting choices of management and the information acquisition activities of investors.

These issues have been of considerable interest to accounting researchers who are involved in empirical research. Information economics research into these issues has been more limited, but there are several areas of analysis that have provided interesting insights. In particular, there are a number of studies in economics, finance and accounting that analyze the preferences and choices of individuals who are or can become privately informed. Theses individuals may seek to privately use their information (and possibly reveal it by their actions) or they may be motivated to publicly reveal their information. We first consider privately informed investors and then privately informed managers.

The models discussed in the previous sections assume that all investors have the same prior information and all receive any subsequent information.[38] Subsequent information is likely to result in price changes, but it might not have any social value (particularly in a pure exchange economy). However, that information can be *valuable to an investor if he can acquire it and make trades prior to its public release.* Of course, to take advantage of early information acquisition, the investor's actions *must not fully reveal his information.* Analyses in this area vary in three important dimensions: the information content of prices, the role of public reporting, and the strategic behavior of informed investors.

The first dimension, the *information content of prices,* refers to the extent to which the actions of informed investors reveal their information. The investors' actions are not directly observed, but their actions may influence prices and prices are observed by all individuals. Some analyses, such as Hirshleifer [1975, 1977] and Verrecchia [1980], assume that the *uninformed make no attempt to infer information from prices.* Within these models, information could be inferred from prices, but the non-inference assumption can be viewed as a substitute for making the model more complex by introducing other uncertain factors that influence prices and thereby make such inferences difficult.

Other analyses recognize that information can be at least partially inferred from prices. Some analyses do this in an ad hoc manner, such as Hakansson [1977a], but most of the recent analyses assume that uninformed investors develop *rational expectations* from observed prices. That is, they develop beliefs that are consistent with their knowledge of the economic system and the way in which equilibrium prices are influenced by the signals received by informed investors. Grossman [1981] provides an excellent introduction and review of this approach. Most of these analyses use simple models with very specific structures. If the models are such that private information is the only cause of variations in prices, then, in general, *prices fully reveal private information.*[39] However, there is no incentive to acquire private information if it is going to be fully revealed before it can be used (at least, in a pure excange economy that can achieve full Pareto efficiency).[40] Consequently, most analyses assume that there are other uncertain factors (i.e., *noise*) that also cause variations in prices and, hence, *prices only partially reveal private information* (e.g., Grossman [1977], Hellwig [1980], Diamond and Verrecchia [1981], and Verrecchia [1982a]). These models are used to analyze the factors that affect the extent to which costly private information is acquired and the extent to which it is publicly revealed. For example, these models indicate that:

- A decrease in the cost of acquiring private information induces more investors to acquire private information and increases the information content of prices;
- An increase in the noise influencing prices induces more investors to acquire private information, but decreases the information content of prices;
- An increase in the informativeness of private information increases the information content of prices, but may induce either more or fewer investors to acquire private information;
- In a "large" economy, prices only convey information that is common to a "large" number of privately informed investors, and does not convey individual variations in information.

The second dimension in the analysis of private information is the *role of public reporting.* Some analyses ignore public reporting, others focus on the impact of using private information prior to its public release, and a couple consider the impact of publicly disclosing information before it can be used privately.

Most analyses that *ignore public reporting* focus on the *extent to which* private information is reflected in or communicated by prices. These analyses have been stimulated by the considerable discussion of *market efficiency* in the finance and accounting literature (e.g., see Fama [1970], Rubinstein [1975], and Beaver [1981]. For example, much of the previously mentioned rational expectations literature has been concerned with whether a rational, uninformed investor could infer private information from the equilibrium prices of a simple economy. In general, these analyses demonstrate that private information is partially revealed by prices, and it is fully revealed only if there are no other uncertain factors (noise) influencing prices. Another form of analysis ignores the information content of prices and seeks to identify conditions under which the trading of informed and uninformed investors results in prices that are the same as those that would occur if all private information was made public. There are conditions under which this occurs, as demonstrated by Verrecchia [1979, 1980a], but the conditions are very restrictive. In effect, private information must be widely dispersed and result in investor beliefs that are randomly distributed around the *consensus beliefs* that would result from public release of all private information.

Analyses that focus on the *impact of using private information prior to its public release* assume that there are at least two rounds of trading. *Pre-release trading* occurs after private information has been acquired but prior to its public release, whereas *post-release trading* occurs after the private information has been publicly reported. If pre-release prices differ from post-release prices, then an informed investor can gain from his information. This occurs in the analyses by Hakansson [1977a], Hirshleifer [1975, 1977], and Verrecchia [1980]; they assume that all privately informed investors receive the same information and pre-release prices do not convey that information to the uninformed. On the other hand, Tirole [1982] argues that rational expectations with respect to pre-release prices eliminates these gains; but he ignores the possibility of noise affecting prices.

Gains to private information no doubt occur as long as prices do not fully reveal that information. These gains are made at the expense of the uninformed investors and this has led to *insider trading laws*. These laws preclude the private use of firm specific information by those who have priviledged access to it. Of course, by reducing the incentives to acquire private information, these laws may also reduce the public information that is available and thereby reduce the allocative efficiency of the economy.

Disclosure laws can also affect the incentives to acquire private information. The potential impact of disclosure laws has been analyzed using models that assume that *public reports* are *released before private information can be used*. Gonedes [1980] identifies a number of issues using a rather loosely constructed partial equilibrium model, whereas Verrecchia [1982a] provides a more narrow analysis using a simple rational expectations equilibrium model. These analyses indicate that increased disclosure reduces the incentives to privately acquire information and hence more disclosure by firms may largely result in a shift in the source of information with little increase in the total public information.

The third dimension in the analysis of private information is the *strategic behavior of informed investors*. Most analyses assume that informed investors act as *myopic price takers;* that is, they invest as if their trades have no impact on prices and as if there will be no future trading. in the rational expectations analyses informed investors influence prices, but, as Hellwig [1980] demonstrates, the price taking assumption is reasonable in a large economy, since prices only reflect information that is common to many investors and does not reflect individual variations in information.

Prices prior to the public release of private information generally differ from post-release prices (provided that prices do not fully reveal private information). As Hakanssen [1977a] and Verrecchia [1980] demonstrate, an informed investor can gain from his private information even if he ignores the fact that there will be a post-release round of trading. However, he can obtain even greater gains if he trades to a *speculative position* during pre-release trading and then trades to a *consumptive position* during post-release trading.[41] Hirshleifer [1975,1977] analyzes the optimal trading strategy in this case.

Many of the empirical studies into the information content of accounting reports can be interpreted as determining whether the early private acquisition of accounting reports would permit an informed investor to gain from this information. Ohlson [1979] explores this interpretation of these studies.[42]

The analyses discussed in this section demonstrate that there are strong incentives to acquire private information either as a substitute for public reports or in anticipation of public reports. If these incentives result in information acquisition by a large number of investors, then public reports have a limited impact on prices unless they contain hitherto highly confidential and unanticipated information. Empirical evidence suggests that most of the information contained in accounting reports has been previously disseminated through other sources. An interesting question is whether that information would continue to be disseminated if the issuance of verified public reports were to cease.

MODELS OF PRIVATE MANAGEMENT INFORMATION

The preceding section has considered the incentives for investors to acquire private information and the extent to which prices might reveal that information to others. The analyses in that area assume that the actions of informed investors cannot be directly observed by uninformed investors. If these actions could be observed, then they might reveal private information more fully than do prices. The assumption that actions are not observable is reasonable in the context of impersonal trading among diversified investors, but it is not reasonable in many contexts involving the activities of the informed management of firms.

In the process of operating a firm, management is likely to acquire considerable private information about the factors that affect the outcomes of the firm's activities. Some of that private information is ultimately revealed by required and voluntary public reports, and some may be revealed by observed management actions (e.g., product prices, investment projects undertaken, dividends declared, securities issued, etc.). To understand the information content of accounting reports and the reporting choices made by management, we must understand the market forces that create incentives for management to acquire and then reveal or disguise private information.

Many types of individuals are potentially interested in management's private information. These include current and potential investors, creditors, suppliers, employees, customers, competitors, and regulators. Management has a primarily *cooperative* relationship with some, but with others the relationship is primarily *non-cooperative*. Therefore, both cooperative and non-cooperative game theory provide analyses that are relevant to understanding management's choices. Furthermore, since there are many individuals and firms competing for the economy's resources, analyses that explicitly recognize the impact of competitive market forces are particularly relevant.

To achieve tractability, existing information economic analyses typically focus on only one or two dimensions of the forces that influence management's choices. For example, there are analyses that consider firms competing in the same markets, investors in the firm's securities, and employees to whom decisions are delegated, *but* each of these analyses focuses on only one of the groups and ignores the other two. The discussion that follows briefly reviews the analyses that consider competitive firms and investors.

In the classical economic model of competitive markets all information is assumed to be freely available to all members of the economy. No firm has an advantage due to private information. However, management is likely to have private information about its own operations (e.g., the marginal costs of producing various products) and may have private information about production opportunities and the demand for various products (e.g., as a result of product and market research). The classical economic model cannot be used to analyze the demand for and impact of this type of private information. Consequently, many analyses in this area are based on *non-cooperative game theory* and only consider the competing firms (individual consumers and investors are not explicitly included).[43]

Non-cooperative game theory deals with games in which the players cannot implement cooperative agreements and have either strictly opposite or mixed interests. Each player acts independently and selects a strategy that is optimal *given* the strategies that the other rational players select. A strategy vector (with one strategy for each player) that satisfies this rationality condition is termed a *Nash equilibrium*.

From an information economic perspective, the most interesting aspect of these games is that Blackwell's theorem holds for private pre-decision information if there are strictly opposite interests, but does not always hold if there are mixed interests. In particular, if players have *strictly opposite interests* (which only occurs in *two-person constant-sum games*), then costless *private pre-decision information always has non-negative value* to the informed players. Furthermore, a *more state-informative* system is *more valuable* (see, for example, Ponssard [1976]). On the other hand, in a non-cooperative game *with mixed interests* a player *may prefer a more informative private pre-decison information system* in some circumstances (e.g., see Ponssard [1979] and Novshek and Sonnenschein [1982]), and *prefer a less informative system* in other circumstances (e.g., see Baiman [1975], Ponssard [1976], and Palfrey [1982]). The latter can occur if a ''competitor''knows that a player has a superior information system and selects a ''defensive'' strategy which makes both players worse off than with the less informative system. This raises the possibility, as Magee [1978] illustrates, that in a competitive bidding situation a more precise cost accounting system may be preferred under one set of conditions and not preferred under slightly different conditions.

There is a vast game theory literature dealing with the nature of equilibrium strategies in a wide variety of contexts, including contexts in which the players receive different information. No attempt is made to review that literature here since, except for some of the papers referred to above, these analyses have had very little impact on the accounting literature (see Baiman [1977] for a review). However, the interest in information issues in the game theory literature has increased significantly in recent years. These analyses are likely to be of interest to accounting researchers in that they help us to understand how the structure of competitive markets influences management's acquisition of private information and its revelation of that information through its actions.

The structure of a competitive market may be an important factor in determining the information acquired and revealed by management, but management's cooperative agreements may be even more significant. The importance of management information in cooperative agreements is illustrated by the fact that the market value of a firm's securities and the terms of credit a firm can obtain are influenced by the information that investors and creditors receive from management. And the complexity of the process is illustrated by the fact that management is motivated to reveal ''good news'' and to withhold or lie about ''bad news'', but the investors and creditors are fully aware of this and will act accordingly.

The importance and complexity of the communication of private information in a variety of cooperative contexts has led to considerable analysis in the past few years. In the discussion that follows the *manager* is a *privately informed* individual and, hence, he is the potential sender of messages about that information. The *uninformed* individuals are the *receivers* of any messages sent; they could be investors, creditors, governmental agents, or any others whose actions can affect the well-being of the manager.

As a starting point for discussing some of the important concepts and variations in these analyses, consider the following simple context. A single sender obtains information about the state (uncertain, uncontrollable events) and transmits a message about his information to the receiver who then takes an action which, with the state, determines both the sender's and receiver's outcomes (outcome claims are non-transferable). One form of analysis of this basic problem (see Green [1982] and Green and Stokey [1981] assumes that, prior to communication by the sender. the *receiver makes an irrevocable commitment* as to which actions he will take given each of the messages he may receive. An interesting aspect of all analyses that involve pre-commitment by the receiver is that the receiver's optimal action rule *always induces the sender to truthfully reveal all of his information.*[44] This is termed the *revelation principle* (Myerson [1979]). It is important to note that in order to induce truthtelling the receiver must often agree to not select the action he would most prefer given the information received; hence, the irrevocability of his commitment is vital. Interestingly, in this basic context a more informative system can make both the sender and receiver better-off, both worse-off, or one better-off and the other worse-off (see Green [1982]).

Receiver pre-commitment is an important assumption in a number of different types of analyses. These include analyses of the basic sender/receiver model, principal/agent models, and some competitive market models.[45]

The *principal/agent models* assume that outcome claims are transferable and the principal's action rule includes a specification of the compensation to be paid to the agent. The agent has other opportunities so that the compensation must be sufficient to induce him to fulfill his duties as an agent. A fixed payment would impose no risk on the agent and would induce him to truthfully report his information (he would have no incentive to lie). However, such a trivial solution does not arise because the agent also provides actions that influence the principal's outcome and to induce the desired actions the agent's compensation often must vary with the outcome (or any other incentive-relevant information available). In this context, the compensation function that would most efficiently induce the agent's action (given truthful reporting) would not induce truthful reporting. Consequently, in selecting a compensation function, the principal must consider the motivation of both the agent's actions and his reports. The private information can assist the agent in selecting a "better" action, but a "better" action for the agent may not be a "better" action for the principal. Hence, private agent information can make the principal better-off in some situations and worse-off in others (see Christensen [1981]),[46] but in either case, the revelation principle implies that the principal's optimal strategy is to induce the agent to fully reveal his information.

If a manager acts as an agent for individuals external to the firm, then contracts may induce him to reveal private information to those individuals and this may result in information becoming public knowledge. For example, *compensation contracts* may induce the manager to reveal private information to the firm's owners and *sales contracts* may induce the manager to reveal private information to the firm's customers (e.g., cost-plus contracts).[47] This information may be kept private if ownership is closely held and only a small number of customers are informed. However, the information is likely to become public knowledge if there are a large number of owners (e.g., the firm's stock is listed on a stock exchange) or a large number of customers are informed.

Another form of analysis in which receiver pre-commitment is often assumed is that associated with *market signalling and screening*. In these analyses there are a large number of privately informed individuals seeking either to insure risks or to sell some good, service, or investment opportunity. There are also a large number of uninformed insurers, customers, and investors and, hence, there is competition on both sides of the market. In many of these analyses it is assumed that each receiver pre-commits by offering a set of contracts from which any sender can choose (e.g., insurance companies offer alternative insurance contracts). A set of contracts constitutes an *equilibrium* if no *receiver* is motivated to withdraw a contract or offer some alternative contract.[48] If senders with different private information select different contracts, then the equilibrium is termed a *separating equilibrium* (i.e., private information is fully revealed). If all senders select the same contracts, then it is a *pooling equilibrium* (no private information is revealed). Between these two extremes are *partitioning equilibria* which reveal some private information but not all of it.[49]

In the simplest screening context the senders are identical except that some have good news while others have bad news (e.g., worker skill, product quality, or expected return on investment is high for some senders and low for others).[50] There are two types of contracts that can be used to distinguish senders with good news from those with bad news (see Spence [1976]). The first type requires a sender to *confirm his good news by taking some costly action* that is less costly for him than for a sender with bad news. For example, highly skilled individuals may be required to confirm (and possibly enhance) their skills by successfully completing additional education (e.g., see Spence [1974, 1976a]). The second type requires a sender to *confirm* his *good news by accepting outcome contingent compensation* that is "too risky" for those with bad news. For example, highly skilled individuals may be required to confirm their skills by having a significant portion of their compensation depend on the sales they make or the profits earned by their division.

From a financial accounting perspective, the most important area of signalling and screening is the communication of private information to potential investors by the owners or managers of firms. In general, owners and managers are motivated to communicate good news (and thereby increase the market value of their firm), but they would prefer to disguise bad news. The potential investors, on the other hand, would like to know the bad news. Several papers have explored signalling in this environment and most assume that the resulting equilibrium fully reveals the private information (i.e., a separating equilibrium).[51] All papers in this area assume that contingent contracts are used to signal private information, but the form of those contracts vary. Some papers, such as Leland and Pyle [1977] and Downes and Heinkel [1982], demonstrate that an owner can signal good news by *retaining a significant portion of his firm's shares;* this exposes him to more firm specific risk than would otherwise be optimal. Others, such as Ross [1977, 1978] and Feltham and Hughes [1982], demonstrate the signalling of private management information through contracts that make *management compensation contingent on firm performance;* except in special cases, these compensation contracts must impose more firm specific risk on the manager with good news than would otherwise be optimal.[52] The level of dividends paid is another possible signal; Bhattacharya [1979] explores this by assuming that the *commitment to pay an end-of-period dividend* is less costly to owners if there is good news than if there is bad news (he assumes that if dividends are paid then costs are incurred in obtaining additional investment capital).

Although many analyses implicitly or explicitly assume that the receiver initiates any pre-commitments he makes, there are many situations where this is not the case. In these contexts a receiver merely responds to the observed actions of the senders by selecting an action he perceives to be optimal, given the information communicated by the senders' actions. Observe that *the revelation principal does not hold* in this context — if a receiver knows the full truth he will use it to his full advantage. Of course, a sender may choose to fully disclose his private information (as in a separating equilibrium), but he may choose to at least partially disguise it (as in a partitioning equilibrium).

The basic sender/receiver model has been analyzed from the persepective that the sender and receiver make an "agreement" as to the sender's communication procedure and the receiver's action response (see Crawford and Sobel [1982] and Green and Stokey [1980]). The implemented agreement is not binding, but it constitutes a *Nash equilibrium* (neither is motiviated to deviate as long as he believes that the other will not deviate). In most situations of this type a *partitioning equilibrium* results, i.e., the sender partially reveals his information.

Some of the market signalling literature can be viewed as analyzing the action choices of senders and the responses of receivers. In particular, each sender offers a contract which the receivers accept or reject; in equilibrium all contracts offered are accepted and no sender is motivated to offer a different contract.[53] This appears to be a more realistic view of management's signalling activity — it is the manager who initiates a signal not the investors. Feltham and Hughes [1982] adopt this approach and assume that if an owner or manager wishes to communicate good news, then he offers securities that leave him with an outcome contingent return that would be too risky if he had bad news. On the other hand, if convincing investors that he has good news is too costly, then the manager offers the same securities whether he has good news or bad news (the securities will be underpriced if he has good news and over priced if he has bad news).

Feltham and Hughes [1982] also point out that from an ex ante perspective a *manager prefers to make* his *contracts* with investors *prior to observing* his *private information* (and thereby not eliminate risk sharing opportunities). In fact, as in the analysis of public information, *private information has zero or negative ex ante value* to the manager *in a pure exchange context. It can only have positive value if it helps him to make better production decisions,* and then to ensure that it has positive value he must contract with investors prior to obtaining the information.

In some situations it appears that managers send messages about their private information without taking any action designed to confirm the validity of what they are saying. For example, management often makes *unverified* financial forecasts as well as less formal statements about their firm's prospects. The extent to which these statements have information content and the process by which investors have confidence in these statements is not well understood. it has been discussed in the accounting literature (e.g., Gonedes [1978] and Gonedes and Dopuch [1978]), but the analyses in these studies is generally incomplete. Additional analytical and empirical research is required if we are to understand the *extent* to which managers communicate private information outside of the financial reports, their *motivation* for doing so, and the *process* by which it is accomplished.

CONCLUDING REMARKS

Information economic research has grown significantly during the past decade. This paper has reviewed some of the major elements of that research which are relevant to understanding the economic impact of and demand for externally reported accounting information. The review is not exhaustive. While the list of references is lengthy, it omits many papers, particularly in the economics literature.[54]

External accounting reports are usually made public and hence the most relevant literature is that which seeks to assess the impact of publicly reported information. The analyses to date examine two potential roles for public information.

The first is the *decision-informativeness* role. To fulfill this role external accounting reports must provide, to decision makers external to the firm, information that has not been obtained from other sources and which reduces the decision makers' uncertainty about the consequences of their actions. Investors and creditors are the most obvious potential users of accounting reports, and accounting reports are likely to be an important source of firm specific information if the firm is relatively small and of interest to only a limited number of investors and creditors. However, if the securities of a firm are extensively traded, then it is quite possible that much of the information relevant to assessing the consequences of investing in that firm will have been disseminated through private information acquisition activities prior to its disclosure in accounting reports.

It is this latter possibility that makes research into the demand for and release of private information of interest to accounting researchers. This research has established that there is a strong incentive to privately acquire information prior to its public release. However, there is no clear indication of the potential impact on private information acquisition activities of changes in regularly reported accounting information. For example, would private information acquisition activities increase or decrease if there was to be no public report?

Recent research has clarified the role of public information in a pure exchange economy, and the general conclusion must be that public pre-decision information is of little value in this context. The primary benefit of pre-decision information must come from the more efficient allocation of resources among firms and between current and future consumption. Future research must move from focusing on pure change economies to focusing on production economies (or, more preferably, agency economies).

As stated earlier, existing research analyzes the impact of information at a very general level and does not give specific consideration to accounting reports. To assess the impact of accounting alternatives future research must more specifically model some of the structural elements of accounting information. In particular, additional insights could be provided by the analysis of multi-period models that explicitly recognize that the actions and events of one period influence the outcomes of both the current and future periods. It is the numerous aspects of this phenomenon that gives rise to many accounting issues. Furthermore, additional insights could be provided by analyzing models that explicitly recognize that some uncertain events are primarily firm specific while others influence the outcomes of many firms. Any unanticipated information that is contained in accounting reports is likely to be firm specific (or perhaps industry specific). The literature dealing with pre-decision information in capital markets has not explicitly considered firm specific information.

The second role of public information is the *contract-implementation role*. To fulfill this role accounting reports must provide information which can be used as a basis for enforcing contracts that permit individuals to make mutually acceptable agreements as to the actions each will take and the sharing of the outcomes from those actions. Reports that provide information with respect to actions are termed incentive-informative and those that provide information with respect to outcomes are termed insurance-informative. Accounting reports have both of these characteristics, and verification by an independent third party, the auditor, reduces managements' opportunities to manipulate this information. Consequently, accounting reports are key elements in the agreements made among managers, investors, and creditors.

As with the first role, existing research analyzes the impact of contract-implementation information at a very general level. It contains some elements that relate it more closely to accounting than does the decsion-informativeness research, but there is still a need to introduce more of the structure of accounting information. In particular, while firm specific factors have received explicit recognition, additional insights could be provided by the analysis of multi-period models and models that recognize the role of accounting reports in contracts with creditors. In addition, analysis of the extent to which management reveals its private information through required or voluntary accounting reports (including profit forecasts) may provide important insights.

Ideally, information economic research will develop in three complementary directions. Much of the research to date is "fundamental" research in that it focuses on the general characteristics of the impact of and demand for information and it seeks to overcome a number of the technical problems involved in analyzing information issues. Additional research of this type is essential to the development of the field, and accountants as well as economists should be encouraged to continue this type of analysis. However, if information economics research is to make a significant contribution to our understanding of the impact of and demand for external accounting reports, then it is essential that analyses be undertaken that explicitly recognize some of the structural elements of accounting information. Some of these analyses are likely to be quite complex, making them difficult to understand by those not involved in such analyses. This creates barriers between those who conduct analytical research and those who conduct empirical research. Greater understanding is likely to be achieved if these two areas of research are more closely linked. Consequently, significant contributions can be made by utilizing developments in information economics to generate empirically testable hypotheses, perhaps by using specific models that have more easily understood structures than do more general models. The results of the empirical tests can then provide a basis for improving the representativeness of the analytical models.

FOOTNOTES

[1] For a recent review of information economics research from an economics perspective see Hirshleifer and Riley [1979].

[2] The expected utility is computed by assigning utility numbers, based on the individual's preferences, to each of the possible consequences and by assigning probability numbers, based on the individual's beliefs, to each of the consequences for each of the possible actions.

[3] The term "more informative" is used although it would be more precise to refer to the system as "at least as informative".

[4] For a more precise statement of this theorem in its various forms see, for example, Marschak and Miyasawa [1968].

[5] Relevance, timeliness, and accuracy had been proposed in the accounting literature (e.g., American Accounting Association [1966] and Snavely [1967] as desirable characteristics of an accounting system.

[6] Issuance of additional transferable claims is implicitly assumed to be too costly.

[7] Of course, they do have preferences with respect to the compensation earned from their actions.

[8] If communication within the team is costless, then it does not matter who receives the information. On the other hand, if communication is costly, then to guarantee that one system is at least as valuable as another, the information received by each individual must be at least as informative as the information he receives under the alternative system.

[9] There are three major types of cooperative game theory models: games with side-payments, games with transferable output claims, and games without either side-payments or transferable output claims. The first is of no interest here because it assumes that the side-payments are measurable in units of utility that are common to all individuals. The second is of primary interest because if cooperative agreements are legal then it is likely that transferable output claims are legal. The third would be applicable if all measures of output are too costly to implement.

10 Various criteria have been suggested for identifying a particular agreement within the core (for a review of some of these see Shubik [1981]. However, there has been little interest in these criteria in the information economics literature.

11 The initial analysis of syndicates is by Wilson [1968] and Raiffa [1968], and they make use of the basic results on risk sharing by Borch [1962]. Rosing [1970] and Kobayashi [1980] introduce bargaining issues, and Amershi and Stoeckenius [1981] generalize Wilson's results. Explicit analysis of syndicates in the accounting literature is provided by Demski [1973] and Verrecchia [1978].

12 To achieve Pareto efficiency the report must also distinguish between states that yield the same outcome *if* the players' have heterogeneous beliefs with respect to those states *given* the outcome. See Hakansson [1977] and Amershi [1982].

13 See Milgrom and Stokey [1982] and Amershi [1982].

14 That is, all individuals are at least as-well-off and some may be better-off.

15 If beliefs are heterogenous, then pre-decision information (like post-decision information) can be used as a basis for side-betting, as well as improving decisions.

16 For example, mutual insurance agreements cannot be made *after* the losses are known.

17 The market is complete if the tradeable claims are sufficiently varied to permit the implementation of any possible state-contingent agreement. (See Hakansson [1977] and Amershi [1982] for discussion of the achievement of FPE with less than a complete set of claims.) Of course, FPE is achieved no matter what the market is like if all investors are identical (and hence there are no trades). And FPE can be achieved with two or more claims if one is risk free, the investors' beliefs are homogeneous, their utility functions are additive, and their utility for end-of-period consumption is of the same HARA-class with identical risk cautiousness.

18 These papers include Fama and Laffer [1971], Marshall [1974], Ng [1975, 1977] and Demski and Feltham [1976].

19 An investor's utility function is not additive if his initial consumption level influences his *marginal utility* for end-of-period consumption.

20 Verrecchia [1981] makes a similar point, but he fails to recognize that market completeness is sufficient to result in no trading in the context he analyzes.

21 These basic models do not discuss the motivation of the manager. The objective of maximizing net market value is used because under some standard assumptions from the economics literature this is what all owners prefer and it results in a Pareto efficient allocation of risk and resources. Problems arise, however, if markets are not sufficiently complete, because now the manager cannot be viewed strictly as a price taker and the owners may not agree on which productive activity is most preferred. See Radner [1974] for a discussion of some of these issues.

22 Some multi-period market models considered by accountants include Gonedes and Dopuch [1974] and Kanodia [1980].

23 Radner [1968, 1970, 1974, 1982] provides an early discussion and recent review of multi-period issues in information economics.

24 The state describes all uncontrollable events that occur over all periods and an information structure defines a partition on the set of possible states at each point in time.

25 One system provides at least as much information at a given point in time as another system if the partition it defines is at least as fine.

26 This occurs in Kanodia's model even though in both cases the manager knows the factors causing this output. However, he is assumed to make his production decision on the basis of maximizing the market value of the firm, and this depends on what the investors know.

27 The producer does not sell a specific signal but instead sells the right to use whatever signal he produces.

28 This model also underlies the multi-period model outlined in Gonedes and Dopuch [1974] and an analysis of disclosure in Gonedes [1980].

29 Discussion of this issue is provided by Arrow [1962], Demsetz [1969], Hirshleifer [1971], and Leftwich [1980].

30 The asset is assumed to be nontradeable, or at least nondivisible. For example, the firm is managed by the owner and he controls the output. He might shift the risk by selling the firm to someone else, but now the new owner/manager must bear the risk. And if someone acquired ownership of many firms he would lose control of the output to those hired to manage the firms.

31 Mayers [1972], for example, illustrates this in his discussion of the impact of nontradeable assets on the capital asset pricing equilibirum.

32 The state consists of all uncontrollable events that influence the output of any asset or claim. A market is *complete with respect to a given partition of the state* (defined by particular events) if for each conceivable partition-contingent claim there is a portfolio of claims that can provide it.

33 One system is *more insurance-informative* than another if the insurance-relevant aspects of the second system's reports are a garbling of the insurance-relevant aspects of the first system's reports. See Atkinson and Feltham [1982a].

[34] See Atkinson and Feltham [1982a] and Gjesdal [1981, 1982] for further discussion of these concepts.

[35] See, for example, Lambert [1981] and Radner [1981]. Fama [1980] discusses some general issues that arise in a multi-period context. Selten [1975] and Kreps and Wilson [1982] provide important insights into the nature of equilibria in sequential decision contexts.

[36] Jensen and Meckling [1976] brought this issue to the fore, and Smith and Warner [1979] analyze it from a finance perspective. Accounting studies in this area include Holthausen [1981] and Leftwich [1981], among many others.

[37] Recently there have been several theoretical analyses of the role of reputation as a determinant of individual behavior. See, for example, Kreps and Wilson [1982a].

[38] These models often allow the investors to have heterogeneous beliefs and these can be viewed as arising from differences in information. However, investors in these models make no attempt to determine the source of their differences, implying that knowledge of the source would not change their beliefs.

[39] Radner [1979] proves that, under suitable regularity conditions, a fully revealing rational expectations equilibrium almost always exists. For illustrations of this in more specific models see Grossman [1976, 1981] and Tirole [1982].

[40] However, as Radner [1982] suggests, the process by which an equilibrium is achieved may provide opportunities for gain. Almost all analyses ignore this process and merely identify the equilibrium.

[41] The pre-release position is termed speculative because it is not the position he would take if there was no further trading. The latter is termed his consumptive position.

[42] These are usually referred to as API studies because of the use of what is termed the abnormal performance index. Other information economic analyses of these studies are provided by Marshall [1975] and Patell [1979].

[43] See Shotter and Schwodiauer [1980] and Shubik [1981] for a recent survey of the use of game theory in economics.

[44] More accurately, for any optimal action rule there is always a rule that provides the *same expected utility* and that *does not induce the sender to lie*. If a sender is indifferent between telling the truth or lying, then he is assumed to tell the truth.

[45] Laffont and Maskin [1981] provide an excellent review and synthesis of analyses that assume receiver precommitment. Many of these deal with public choice problems which are not considered here.

[46] In these models the agent does not gain or lose *ex ante* because he receives a compensation scheme designed to be just sufficient to induce him to serve as agent (i.e., he is paid the market price for his services). In designing the compensation scheme the principal must consider whether the agent has the opportunity to withdraw his services after observing the information, or perhaps has already observed the information at the time the contract is offered. See, for example, Baiman and Evans [1981] for an analysis of this type of setting.

[47] Discussion of contracts between managers and investors is provided by Barnea, Haugen, and Senbet [1980] and Feltham and Hughes [1982]. Discussion of cost-plus contracts is provided by Cummins [1977] and Weitzman [1980].

[48] The conditions under which a contract would be withdrawn or offered depends on the type of foresight a receiver has regarding the impact of any changes he might consider. Alternative assumptions are discussed in Riley [1979, 1979a] and Wilson [1977, 1980].

[49] Of course, if the receiver has pre-committed to the offered contracts then the revelation principle applies. The sender can safely reveal his information after the contract is signed and the receiver cannot take advantage of it.

[50] Milgrom [1981] provides a formal discussion of the good news/bad news distinction.

[51] A more general approach is to let the extent of information revelation be endogenous to the analysis. See Feltham and Hughes [1982] for a discussion of this approach.

[52] The special cases include those in which the agent is risk neutral and those in which there is some outcome that could not possibly occur if the manager had good news but could occur if he had bad news. In the latter case, severe penalties for "impossible" outcomes deter the manager from lying.

[53] The differences between a sender initiated equilibrium and the receiver-initiated equilibria mentioned earlier are rather subtle and are not discussed here. See Feltham and Hughes [1982].

[54] A more extensive categorized list of references can be obtained from the author. Also see Hirshleifer and Riley [1979] and Radner [1982] for a list of references from the economics literature.

REFERENCES

American Accounting Association. *A Statement of Basic Accounting Theory*. Sarasota, Florida: American Accounting Association [1966].

Amershi, A. "Necessary and Sufficient Conditions for Pareto-Efficient Risk Sharing in Incomplete Markets", Working Paper, Stanford University [1982].

Amershi, A.H. and J. Stoeckenius. "A Unified Theory of Syndicates, Aggregation and Separation in Financial Markets", Working Paper, Stanford University [1981].

Antle, R. "An Agency Model of Auditing", Working Paper, University of Chicago [1981].

Antle, R. "Auditor Independence", Working Paper, University of Chicago [1981a].

Arrow, K.J. "Economic Welfare and the Allocation of Resources for Inventions," *The Rate and Direction of Inventive Activity* [1962], pp. 609-625.

Atkinson, A.A. and G.A. Feltham. "Agency Theory Research and Financial Accounting Standards", *Research to Support Standard Setting in Financial Accounting: A Canadian Perspective*, S. Basu and J.A. Milburn (eds.) Toronto: Clarkson Gordon Foundation [1982], pp. 259-289.

Baiman, S. "The Evaluation and Choice of Internal Information Systems Within a Multiperson World", *Journal of Accounting Research* [Spring 1975], pp. 1-15.

Baiman, S. "Information Economics in a Multiperson Context: A Survey", Working Paper, Carnegie-Mellon University, [1977].

Baiman, S. "Agency Research in Managerial Accounting: A Survey", *Journal of Accounting Literature* [1982].

Baiman, S. and J.H. Evans. "Decentralization and the Role of Pre-Decision Information", Working Paper, University of Pittsburg [1981].

Barnea, A., R.A. Haugen, and L.W. Senbet. "An Agency Theoretic Analysis of the Incentive to Advance Accounting", Working Paper, University of Wisconsin-Madison [1980].

Beaver, W.H. "The Information Content of Annual Earnings Announcements - Empirical Research in Accounting", *Journal of Accounting Research* (Supplement 1968), pp. 67-92.

Beaver, W.H. "Market Efficiency", *Accounting Review* [January 1981], pp. 23-37.

Bhattacharya, S. "Imperfect Information, Dividend Policy, and 'The Bird in the Hand' Fallacy", *Bell Journal of Economics* [Spring 1979], pp. 259-270.

Blackwell, D. "Comparison of Experiments", *Proceedings of the Second Berkeley Symposium on Mathematical Statistics and Probability*. Berkeley: University of California Press [1951], pp. 93-102.

Blackwell, D. "Equivalent Comparisons of Experiments", *Annals of Mathematical Statistics* [1953], pp. 267-272.

Borch, K. "Equilibrium in a Reinsurance Market", *Econometrica* [July 1962], pp. 424-444.

Butterworth, J. "The Accounting System as an Information Function", *Journal of Accounting Research* [Spring 1972], pp. 1-27.

Christensen, J. "Communication in Agencies", *Bell Journal of Economics* [Autumn 1981], pp. 661-674.

Crawford, V.P. and J. Sobel. "Strategic Information Transmission", *Econometrica* [November 1982], pp. 1431-1451.

Cummins, J.M. "Incentive Contracting for National Defence: A Problem of Optimal Risk Sharing", *Bell Journal of Economics* [Spring 1977], pp. 168-185.

Demsetz, H. "Information and Efficiency: Another Viewpoint", *Journal of Law and Economics* [April 1969], pp. 1-22.

Demski, J.S. "Rational Choice of Accounting Method for a Class of Partnerships", *Journal of Accounting Research* [Autumn, 1973], pp. 176-190.

Demski, J.S. "The General Impossibility of Normative Accounting Standards", *Accounting Review* [October 1973a], pp. 718-723.

Demski, J.S. "Choice Among Financial Reporting Alternatives", *Accounting Review* [April 1974], pp. 221-232.

Demski, J.S. and G.A. Feltham, *Cost Determination: A Conceptual Approach*, Ames, Iowa: Iowa State University Press [1976].

Diamond, D.W. and R.E. Verrecchia. "Information Aggregation in a Noisy Rational Expectations Economy", *Journal of Financial Economics* [1981], pp. 221-235.

Downes, D.H. and R. Heinkel. "Signaling and the Valuation of Unseasoned New Issues", *Journal of Finance* [March 1982], pp. 1-10.

Evans, J.H. III. "Optimal Contracts with Costly Conditional Auditing", *Studies on Economic Consequences of Financial and Managerial Accounting: Effects on Corporate Incentives and Decisions, Journal of Accounting Research* [Supplement 1980], pp. 108-128.

Fama, E.F. "Efficient Capital Markets: A Review of Theory and Empirical Work", *Journal of Finance* [May 1970], pp. 383-417.

Fama, E.F. "Agency Problems and the Theory of the Firm", *Journal of Political Economy* [April 1980], pp. 288-307.

204

Fama, E.F. and A.B. Laffer "Information and Capital Markets", *The Journal of Business* [July 1971], pp. 289-298.

Feltham, G.A. "The Value of Information", *Accounting Review* [October 1968], pp. 684-696.

Feltham, G.A. *Information Evaluation: Studies in Accounting Research #5*. Sarasota, Florida: American Accounting Association [1972].

Feltham, G.A. and J.S. Demski. "The Use of Models in Information Evaluation", *Accounting Review* [October 1970], pp. 623-640.

Feltham, G.A. and J.S. Hughes. "Communication of Private Information in Capital Markets: Contingent Contracts and Verified Public Reports", Working Paper, University of British Columbia [1982].

Gjesdal, F. "Accounting for Stewardship", *Journal of Accounting Research* [Spring 1981], pp. 208-231.

Gjesdal, F. "Information and Incentives: The Agency Information Problem", *Review of Economic Studies* [1982], pp. 373-390.

Gonedes, N.J. "Information-Production and Capital Market Equilibrium", *Journal of Finance* [June 1975], pp. 841-864.

Gonedes, N.J. "Corporate Signaling, External Accounting, and Capital Market Equilibrium: Evidence on Dividends, Income, and Extraordinary Items", *Journal of Accounting Research* [Spring 1978], pp. 26-79.

Gonedes, N.J. "Public Disclosure Rules, Private Information-Production Decisions, and Capital Market Equilibrium", *Journal of Accounting Research* [Autumn 1980], pp. 441-476.

Gonedes, N.J. and N. Dopuch. "Capital Market Equilibrium, Information Production, and Selecting Accounting Techniques: Theoretical Framework and Review of Empirical Work", Studies on Financial Accounting Objectives, *Journal of Accounting Research* [Supplement 1974], pp. 48-129.

Gonedes, N.J. and N. Dopuch. "Signaling and Screening: Implications for Accounting Numbers and Capital Market Equilibrium", Teaching Note, University of Chicago [1978].

Green, J. "Statistical Decision Theory Requiring Incentives for Information Transfer", *The Economics of Information and Uncertainty,* J.J. McCall (ed.) University of Chicago Press [1982], pp. 77-96.

Green, J.R. and N.L. Stokey. "A Two-Person Game of Information Transmission", Working Paper, Northwestern University [1980].

Green, J.R. and N.L. Stokey. "The Value of Information in the Delegation Problem", Working Paper, Harvard University [1981].

Grossman, S. "On the Efficiency of Competitive Stock Markets Where Traders have Diverse Information", *Journal of Finance* [May 1976], pp. 573-585.

Grossman, S.J. "The Existence of Future Markets, Noisy Rational Expectations and Informational Externalities", *Review of Economic Studies* [October 1977], pp. 431-450.

Grossman, S.J. "An Introduction to the Theory of Rational Expectations Under Asymmetric Information", *Review of Economic Studies* [October 1981], pp. 541-559.

Hakansson, N. "The Superfund: Efficient Paths Toward Efficient Capital Markets in Large and Small Countries", *Financial Decision Making Under Uncertainty,* H. Levy and M. Sarnat (eds.) New York: Academic Press [1977], pp. 165-201.

Hakansson, N.H. "Interim Disclosure and Public Forecasts: An Economic Analysis and a Framework for Choice", *Accounting Review* [April 1977a], pp. 396-416.

Hakansson, N.H., J.G. Kunkel, and J.A. Ohlson. "Sufficient and Necessary Conditions for Information to Have Social Value in Pure Exchange", *Journal of Finance* (December 1982).

Hellwig, M.F. "On the Aggregation of Information in Capital Markets", *Journal of Economic Theory* [June 1980], pp. 477-498.

Hilton, R.W. "The Determinants of Cost Information Value: An Illustrative Analysis", *Journal of Accounting Research* [Autumn 1979], pp. 411-435.

Hilton, R.W. "The Determinants of Information Value: Synthesizing Some General Results", *Management Science,* [January 1981], pp. 57-64.

Hilton, R.W. and R.J. Swieringa. "Perception of Initial Uncertainty as a Determinant of Information Value", *Journal of Accounting Research* [Spring 1981], pp. 109-119.

Hirshleifer, J. "The Private and Social Value of Information and the Reward to Inventive Activity", *American Economic Review,* [September 1971], pp. 561-574.

Hirshleifer, J. "Speculation and Equilibrium: Information, Risk, and Markets", *Quarterly Journal of Economics* [November 1975], pp. 519-542.

Hirshleifer, J. "The Theory of Speculation Under Alternative Regimes of Markets", *Journal of Finance* [September 1977], pp. 975-999.

Hirshleifer, J. and J.G. Riley. "The Analytics of Uncertainty and Information - An Expository Survey", *Journal of Economic Literature* [December 1979], pp. 1375-1421.

Holthausen, R.W. "Evidence on the Effect of Bond Covenants and Management Compensation Contracts on the Choice of Accounting Techniques", *Journal of Accounting and Economics* [March 1981], pp. 73-109.

Jensen, M.C. and W.M. Meckling. "Theory of the Firm: Managerial Behavior, Agency Costs, and Ownership Structure", *Journal of Financial Economics* [October 1976], pp. 305-360.

Kanodia, C. "Effects of Shareholder Information on Corporate Decisions and Capital Market Equilibrium", *Econometrica* [May 1980], pp. 923-953.

Kobayashi, T. "Equilibrium Contracts for Syndicates with Differential Information", *Econometrica* [November 1980], pp. 1635-1665.

Kreps, D.M. and R. Wilson. "Sequential Equilibria", *Econometrica* [July 1982], pp. 863-894.

Kreps, D.M. and R. Wilson. "Reputation and Imperfect Information", *Journal of Economic Theory* [1982a], pp. 253-279.

Kunkel, J.G. "Sufficient Conditions for Public Information to Have Social Value in a Production and Exchange Economy", *Journal of Finance* (September 1982).

Laffont, J.-J. and E. Maskin. "The Theory of Incentives: An Overview", Economic Theory Discussion Paper, University of Cambridge [1981].

Lambert, R.A. *Managerial Incentives in Multiperiod Agency Relationships*, Unpublished Dissertation, Stanford University [1981].

Leftwich, R. "Market Failure Fallacies and Accounting Information", *Journal of Accounting and Economics* [December 1980], pp. 193-212.

Leftwich, R. "Evidence on the Impact of Mandatory Changes in Accounting Principles in Corporate Loan Agreements", *Journal of Accounting and Economics* [March 1981], pp. 37-71.

Leland, H.E. and D.H. Pyle. "Informational Asymmetries, Financial Structure, and Financial Intermediation", *Journal of Finance* [May 1977], pp. 371-387.

McGuire, C.B. "Comparison of Information Structures", *Decision and Organization*, C.B. McGuire and R. Radner (eds.). New York: North-Holland [1972], pp. 101-130.

Magee, R.P. "The Demand for Cost Information in a Competitive Bidding Environment", Working Paper, Northwestern University [1978].

Marschak, J. "Elements for a Theory of Teams", *Management Science* [January 1955], pp. 127-137.

Marschak, J. "Remarks on the Economics of Information", *Contributions to Scientific Research in Management Science*, Los Angeles: University of California Press [1959], pp. 79-98.

Marschak, J. "The Payoff-Relevant Description of States and Acts", *Econometrica* [October 1963], pp. 719-725.

Marschak, J. "Economics of Information Systems", *Journal of the American Statistical Association* [March 1971], pp. 192-219.

Marschak, J. and K. Miyasawa. "Economic Comparability of Information Systems", *International Economic Review* [June 1968], pp. 137-174.

Marschak, J. and R. Radner. *Economic Theory of Teams*. Yale University Press [1972].

Marshall, J.M. "Private Incentives and Public Information", *American Economic Review* [June 1974], pp. 373-390.

Marshall, R. "Determining an Optimal Accounting System for an Unidentified User", *Journal of Accounting Research* [Autumn 1972], pp. 286-307.

Marshall, R. "Interpreting the API", *Accounting Review* [January 1975], pp. 99-111.

Mayers, D. "Nonmarketable Assets and Capital Market Equilibrium Under Uncertainty", *Studies in the Theory of Capital Markets*, M.C. Jensen (ed.) New York: Praeger [1972], pp. 223-248.

Milgrom, P.R. "Good News and Bad News: Representation Theorems and Applications", *Bell Journal of Economics* [Autumn 1981], pp. 380-391.

Milgrom, P. and Stokey, N. "Information, Trade, and Common Knowledge", *Journal of Economic Theory* (February 1982), pp. 17-27.

Mock, T.J. "Comparative Values of Information Structures", *Empirical Research in Accounting: Selected Studies, 1969*, Journal of Accounting Research [1969], pp. 124-159.

Myerson, R.B. "Incentive Compatability and the Bargaining Problem", *Econometrica* [January 1979], pp. 61-74.

Ng, David. "Information Accuracy and Social Welfare Under Homogeneous Beliefs", *Journal of Financial Economics* [March 1975], pp. 53-70.

Ng, David. "Pareto-Optimality of Authentic Information", *Journal of Finance* [December 1977], pp. 1717-1728.

Novshek, W. and H. Sonnenschein. "Fulfilled Expectations Cournot Duopoly with Information Acquisition and Release", *Bell Journal of Economics* [Spring 1982], pp. 214-218.

Ohlson, J.A. "Residual (API) Analysis and the Private Value of Information", *Journal of Accounting Research* [Autumn 1979], pp. 506-527.

Ohlson, J.A. "Efficiency and the Social Value of Public Information in Exchange Economies", Working Paper, University of California, Berkeley [1980].

Ohlson, J.A. "Asset-Price Behavior and Socially Useful (Useless) Information", Working Paper, University of California, Berkeley [1980a].

Ohlson, J.A. and A.G. Buckman. "Toward a Theory of Financial Accounting", *Journal of Finance* [May 1980], pp. 537-547.

Ohlson, J.A. and G. Buckman. "Toward a Theory of Financial Accounting: Welfare and Public Information", *Journal of Accounting Research* [Autumn 1981], pp. 399-433.

Palfrey, T.R. "Risk Advantages and Information Acquisition", *Bell Journal of Economics* [Spring 1982], pp. 219-224.

206

Patell, J.M. "The API and the Design of Experiments", *Journal of Accounting Research* [Autumn 1979], pp. 528-549.

Plott, C.R. and S. Sunder. "Efficiency of Experimental Security Markets with Insider Information: An Application of Rational-Expectations Models", *Journal of Political Economy* [Autumn 1982], pp. 663-698.

Ponssard, J. "On the Concept of the Value of Information in Competitive Situations", *Management Science* [March 1976], pp. 739-747.

Ponssard, J. "The Strategic Role of Information on the Demand Function in an Oligopolistic Market", *Management Science* [March 1979], pp. 243-250.

Ponssard, J.P. *Competitive Strategies,* New York: North-Holland [1981].

Radner, R. "Team Decision Problems", *Annals of Mathematical Statistics* [September 1962], pp. 857-881.

Radner, R. "Competitive Equilibrium Under Uncertainty", *Econometrica* [January 1968], pp. 31-58.

Radner, R. "Problems in the Theory of Markets Under Uncertainty", *American Economic Review* [May 1970] pp. 454-460.

Radner, R. "Market Equilibrium and Uncertainty: Concepts and Problems", *Frontiers of Quantitative Economics,* Volume II. M.D. Intriligator and D.A. Kendrick (eds.) New York: North-Holland [1974], pp. 43-90.

Radner, R. "Rational Expectations Equilibrium: Generic Existence and the Information Revealed by Prices", *Econometrica* [May 1979], pp. 655-677.

Radner, R. "Monotoring Cooperative Agreements in a Repeated Principal-Agent Relationship", *Econometrica* [September 1981], pp. 1127-1148.

Radner, R. "Equilibrium Under Uncertainty", *Handbook of Mathematical Economics* Volume II, K.J. Arrow and M.D. Intriligator (eds.) New York: North-Holland [1982] pp. 923-1006.

Raiffa, Howard. *Decision Analysis: Introductory Lectures on Choices Under Uncertainty.* Reading, Mass.: Addison-Wesley [1968].

Riley, J.G. "Noncooperative Equilibrium and Market Signalling", *American Economic Review* [May 1979] pp. 303-307.

Riley, J.G. "Informational Equilibrium", *Econometrica* [March 1979a], pp. 331-359.

Rosing, J. "The Formation of Groups for Cooperative Decision Making Under Uncertainty", *Econometrica* [May 1970], pp. 430-448.

Ross, S.A. "The Determination of Financial Structure: The Incentive Signalling Approach", *Bell Journal of Economics* [Spring 1977], pp. 23-40.

Ross, S.A. "Some Notes on Financial Incentive-Signalling Models, Activity Choice and Risk Preferences", *Journal of Finance* [June 1978], pp. 777-792.

Rubinstein, M. "Securities Market Efficiency in an Arrow-Debreu Economy", *American Economic Review* [December 1975], pp. 812-824.

Schotter, A. And G. Schwodiauer. "Economics and the Theory of Games: A Survey", *Journal of Economic Literature* [June 1980], pp. 479-527.

Selten, R. "Reexamination of the Perfectness Concept for Equilibrium Points in Extensive Games", *International Journal of Game Theory* [1975], pp. 25-55.

Shubik, M. "Game Theory Models and Methods in Political Economy", *Handbook of Mathematical Economics,* Volume I. K.J. Arrow and M.D. Intriligator (eds.) New York: North-Holland [1981], pp. 285-330.

Smith, C.W. and J.B. Warner. "On Financial Contracting: An Analysis of Bond Covenants", *Journal of Financial Economics* [June 1979], pp. 117-161.

Snavely, H.J. "Accounting Information Criteria", *Accounting Review* [April 1967], pp. 223-232.

Spence, A.M. *Market Signaling: Information Transfer in Hiring and Related Screening Processes,* Harvard University Press [1974].

Spence, A.M. "Informational Aspects of Market Structure: An Introduction", *Quarterly Journal of Economics* [November 1976], pp. 591-597.

Spence, A.M. "Competition in Salaries, Credentials, and Signaling Prerequisites for Jobs", *Quarterly Journal of Economics* [February 1976a], pp. 51-74.

Tirole, J. "On the Possibility of Speculation Under Rational Expectations", *Econometrica* [September 1982], pp. 1163-1181.

Townsend, R.M. "Optimal Contracts and Competitive Markets with Costly State Verification", *Journal of Economic Theory* [October 1979], pp. 265-293.

Uecker, W.C. "A Behavioral Study of Information Choice", *Journal of Accounting Research* [Spring 1978], pp. 169-189.

Verrecchia, R.E. "On the Choice of Accounting Method for Partnerships", *Journal of Accounting Research* [Spring 1978], pp. 150-168.

Verrecchia, R.E. "On the Theory of Market Information Efficiency", *Journal of Accounting and Economics* [March 1979], pp. 77-90.

Verrecchia, R.E. "The Rapidity of Price Adjustments to Information", *Journal of Accounting and Economics* [March 1980], pp. 63-92.

Verrecchia, R.E. "Consensus Beliefs, Information Acquisition, and Market Information Efficiency", *American Economic Review* [December 1980a], pp. 874-884.

Verrecchia, R.E. "On the Relationship Between Volume Reaction and Consensus of Investors: Implications for Interpreting Tests of Information Content", *Journal of Accounting Research* [Spring 1981], pp. 271-283.

Verrecchia, R.E. "The Use of Mathematical Models in Financial Accounting", Current Research Methodologies in Accounting: A Critical Evaluation, *Journal of Accounting Research* [Supplement 1982].

Verrecchia, R.E. "Information Acquisition in a Noisy Rational Expectations Economy", *Econometrica* [November 1982a], pp. 1415-1430.

Von Neumann, J. and O. Morgenstern. *Theory of Games and Economic Behavior.* Princeton University Press [1944].

Weitzman, M.L. "Efficient Incentive Contracts", *Quarterly Journal of Economics* [June 1980], pp. 719-730.

Wilson, C. "A Model of Insurance Markets with Incomplete Information", *Journal of Economic Theory* [December 1977], pp. 167-207.

Wilson, C. "The Nature of Equilibrium in Markets with Adverse Selection", *Bell Journal of Economics* [Spring 1980], pp. 108-130.

Wilson, R. "The Theory of Syndicates", *Econometrica* [January 1968], pp. 119-132.

The authors gratefully acknowledge the detailed criticisms of earlier drafts by Jerry Feltham and Alex Milburn.

THE STRUCTURE OF ACCOUNTING THEORY: SOME BASIC CONCEPTUAL AND METHODOLOGICAL ISSUES*

by John E. Butterworth, Michael Gibbins and Raymond D. King

*Reprinted from The Clarkson, Gordon Foundation, *Research to Support Standard Setting in Financial Accounting: A Canadian Perspective, Proceedings of the 1981 Research Symposium*, ed. Sanjoy Basu and J. Alex Milburn (Toronto: Clarkson, Gordon Foundation, © 1982), pp. 1-65.

WE are concerned with the problem of constructing and testing theories designed to help us choose appropriate accounting rules. It is evident to the most casual observer that there is absolutely no agreed theoretical basis at the present time for this choice. We observe a variety of competing and generally fragmentary hypotheses, each supported by arguments of questionable validity and reflecting the special interests of its proponents.

Not only is there widespread disagreement with respect to the possible content of a theory of accounting information choice, there is even profound disagreement about the proper methodological approach to the problem. As the Research Study, *Corporate Reporting: Its Future Evolution.* [1980] has pointed out, accounting is variously regarded as an art, as an extension of the legal process, as a deductive science, as an empirical science, and as a language. It would not be difficult to add to this list. There is also disagreement with respect to the relative importance of the various potential uses of accounting information, which is compounded by a surprising degree of ignorance about what those uses are.

The accounting profession has taken pains to encourage the consistent application of specific reporting rules based amost exclusively on acquisition cost, yet has been unable to provide an adequate rational support for this policy. Therefore, choices are made according to principles that seem inconsistent with many competing hypotheses. The profession seeks the rational justification that it believes, as a matter of faith, must exist for the rules it chooses, and resists arguments in support of valuation methods that are not based on actual market transactions.

The contrast between the disarray at the level of theory and the consistency of practice is extraordinary and seems to have no contemporary parallel. It has existed for so long that it is taken for granted by all but a few single-minded proponents of alternative valuation methods. Our objective is to study the theory underlying accounting choices, and it is clear that we must provide at least a tentative explanation for this paradox. How can any theory of accounting choice achieve even modest credibility if it is at variance with six hundred years of accounting practice, and no satisfactory explanation is provided? It is too simplistic to dismiss the differences between observed practice and various proposed alternatives as the result of inertia or political pressures. If there are market opportunities, market agents will take advantage of them. If there is political pressure, it usually has an economic motivation. We will suggest that political activity associated with the development of generally accepted accounting principles (GAAP) is a consequence of underlying market forces. If the nature of these forces were understood and their consequences predicted, this would constitute a long stride forward in the development of a theory of accounting

Much of this paper, therefore, is concerned with providing a rational explanation for the observed preferences of accounting practitioners and their representative bodies such as the Accounting Research Committee (ARC) of the Canadian Institute of Chartered Accountants (CICA) and the U.S. Financial Accounting Standards Board (FASB). This problem has been studied by many other researchers. Our analysis takes as a point of departure the work of Jensen and Meckling [1976], Watts [1977], and Watts and Zimmerman [1978, 1979], who explain the standard-setting process as determined, essentially, by the opposing self-interests of the market agents who are affected by the proposed alternatives. Because they emphasize the political process, rather than its underlying economic causes, their analysis of the economic factors that might give rise to conflicts of interest, and hence to political action, is limited. In contrast to their approach, we suggest that political action is a consequence of market pressures. An understanding of this relationship is fundamentally important in the development of future accounting theories, since it seems naive to presume that changes can be made in the information supplied without reference to the nature of the market demand.

If, therefore, we can improve our ability to predict the economic consequences of alternative accounting rules, we can use this knowledge to predict the political processes to which they may give rise. Moreover, an understanding of the economic forces that affect accounting choices provides insight into the reasons underlying the widespread appeal of familiar concepts such as objectivity, verifiability, freedom from bias, price aggregation, market exchange, and cost and revenue matching. Our aim is to provide a framework in which such basic concepts are consequences of more fundamental economic relationships.

We view the primary role of GAAP as descriptive of effective current practices rather than as prescribing new and hitherto little used principles on the basis of a priori arguments. As with the English language, a generally accepted usage of today may become the anachronism of tomorrow. We shall suggest that the criterion of preference is simply market efficiency: the principles that survive are those that prove the fittest to survive in a given economic environment.

In the next section, we provide a brief historical perspective of the standard-setting process. In Section III, we relate this perspective to developments in modern economic and financial theory, which suggest an explanation of the observed response to the various attempts to define accounting principles and postulates, as well as a basis for explaining the general acceptance of historical cost accounting. In Section IV, we discuss methodological issues and some difficulties which must inevitably be confronted in constructing and testing theories of accounting. In Section V, we review the results of some recent reseach and relate them to our earlier findings. Finally, in Section VI, we discuss the implications of our ideas and suggest some tentative priorities for the course of future accounting research.

STANDARDS AND PRINCIPLES: A PERSPECTIVE

It is only in the present century that the emphasis in the sparse accounting literature began to shift from the recording of current practice to the analysis of overall philosophy. The general approach taken by modern authors has been to assume some basic (but often incompletely specified) referential economic framework and then to analyse alternative accounting rules within the context of their chosen framework. The more aggressive writers have asserted that current practice would be improved if it were made consistent with their assumed conceptual framework. The more cautious writers have admitted the possibility that there might be good reasons for the discrepancy between the alternatives suggested by their criteria and those observed to be the prevalent practice, and have attempted to provide those reasons. Since the assumed economic framework is different in each case, it is not surprising that the conclusions of the various authors have been significantly different.

A basic difficulty has been that the economic concepts and theories available to modern accounting researchers have been quite inadequate for the task in hand. The accounting problem requires an economic theory of information in a financial market setting, and most authors have drawn upon concepts which ignore both information and market issues. It is not surprising that their conclusions have been contradictory, and have generally been treated with some scepticism by practitioners.

At the same time, the accounting profession has long been under considerable pressure to provide a better conceptual foundation for its chosen policies. This pressure appears to have first had a recognizable focus in 1933, when several events of some significance to the profession occurred. In that year, the New York Stock Exchange announced that audited financial statements would henceforth be required from all its member firms, the Securities Act became law, and a committee of the New York Stock Exchange asked the Special Committee on Cooperation with Stock Exchanges of the American Institute of Accountants (later the American Institute of Certified Public Accountants (AICPA)) to form a new committee to identify the basic principles of accounting.[1] In 1934, the Securities Exchange Act became law and empowered the Securities and Exchange Commission (SEC), which it created, to regulate the form and content of financial reports.

So began the long and continuing search for a consistent and rational basis for the choice of accounting standards.[2] We do not wish to attempt a detailed review of the history of this search,[3] but it is instructive to observe the changes that have taken place in the approach to the problem over the past fifty years.

The first collective response to the demand for a set of consistent accounting principles was published by the American Accounting Association (AAA) [1936]. ''A Tentative Statement of Accounting Principles Underlying Corporate Financial Statements,'' as it was entitled, strikes a surprisingly authoritative note. For example:

> The purpose of the statements is the expression, in financial terms, of the utilization of the economic resources of the enterprise and the resultant changes in and position of the interests of creditors and investors. Accounting is *thus not essentially a process of valuation, but the allocation of historical costs and revenues to the current and succeeding fiscal periods.* Each of the following propositions embodies a corollary of this fundamental axiom. [p. 61: emphasis added]

Notice the unequivocal statement of the stewardship viewpoint,[4] followed by the assertion that the use of historical cost is the only possible consequence of this assumption. It is, perhaps, the strongest statement exclusively supporting historical cost that has ever appeared in a document bearing the imprimatur of a recognized accounting body. Although we shall see later that this position is supported by a substantial amount of recent economic research, it must have been difficult to sustain in 1936. Perhaps for this reason, it was watered down considerably in subsequent revisions. By 1941, after a lapse of only five years, we read:

> The purpose of periodic financial statements of a corporation is to furnish information that is necessary for the formulation of dependable judgments. A knowledge of the origin and expiration of the economic resources of a company and the resulting changes in the interests of its creditors and investors is essential for this purpose. [AAA, 1941, p. 52]

And later, after historical cost has been stated to be the valuation basis:

> The cost principle stated above, together with the examples of its application, is sufficiently definite to provide a common basis for statement procedure. It should be applied with enough flexibility to meet business and financial needs under all ordinary circumstances. A marked change in the value of money might impair the usefulness of cost records; however, such

changes in price levels as have occurred in this country during the last half century have afforded insufficient reason for the adjustment of asset values. [p. 54]

In these paragraphs, we can observe the appearance of discretionary terms such as "dependable judgments," "enough flexibility," "business and financial needs," "ordinary circumstances," and "marked change," which are so typical of subsequent attempts to state generally applicable accounting principles. We assert that most such attempts are, essentially, generalizations designed to permit all the preferred current accounting practices, as well as the modifications to them which have some significant current support among practitioners or theoreticians. None has any sound theoretical basis, for no such basis exists. Therefore, the authors had no alternative but to provide a summary of what they believed to be the best features of existing practice.

During the 1950s accounting thought began to be influenced by the emphasis of contemporary economic research upon anticipated cash flows as the primary criterion for informed business decisions. By 1957, the American Accounting Association had entirely abandoned its axiomatic dependence upon historic cost and then stated:

> The value of an asset is the money-equivalent of its service potentials. Conceptually, this is the sum of the future market prices of all streams of service to be derived, discounted by probabilities and interest factors to their present worths. However, this conception of value is an abstraction which yields but limited practical basis for quantification. Consequently, the measurement of assets is commonly made by other *more feasible methods*. [AAA, 1957, p.4: emphasis added]

Here, the use of historical cost was justified because it provided an objectively determinable approximation to another concept of value, not because it had essential properties which made its choice inevitable.

Up to this time, the AICPA had concentrated upon the standardization of procedures, and had made no attempt to identify the underlying principles. But in 1959 its new Accounting Principles Board (APB) commissioned *The Basic Postulates of Accounting* [Moonitz, 1961] and *A Tentative Set of Broad Accounting Principles for Business Enterprises* [Sprouse and Moonitz, 1962]. The principles expressed in this latter document represented a radical departure from the then current practice, and included the use of replacement and exit prices in the valuation of inventories and fixed assets. There was an immediate and vehement reaction from the profession. The APB took the unprecedented step of issuing a disclaimer which accompanied every copy of Sprouse and Moonitz [1962] and which stated, *inter alia:*

> Accounting principles and practices should be adapted to meet changing times and conditions, and, therefore, there should be experimentation with new principles and new forms of reporting to meet those conditions. The Board believes, however, that while these studies are a valuable contribution to accounting thinking, they are too radically different from present generally accepted accounting principles for acceptance at this time.

It is probably fair to say that the views expressed by the APB were representative of those held by the vast majority of practitioners at that time. It is interesting to speculate upon the reasons for the existence of such a consensus, when the arguments on both sides rested upon flimsy foundations. As was pointed out by many critics, the principles supposedly developed by Sprouse and Moonitz from their basic postulates did not flow in a logical manner from them. The postulates could quite reasonably have been used to support a wide variety of alternative propositions.

The proposals of Sprouse and Moonitz rested heavily, if implicitly, upon a proprietary view of accounting, in which assets are valued by their future economic services and profit is the amount of the increase in the owners' equity, which is the residual interest in the assets after deducting liabilties (obligations). Their proposals were immediately rejected by the profession, as we have seen.[5] The consistency of the adverse reaction can only be explained, we believe, by the existence of compelling but little-understood market forces. It is difficult to understand why there would not have been more open discussion by the profession of the possible merits of Sprouse and Moonitz' proposals unless the practitioners at least *believed* that they would incur significant economic costs by adopting its ideas. So we question whether there is, in fact, a rational basis for that belief. The answer to this question will be the central focus of the next section.

Since 1962, the American Accounting Association has made two more attempts to formulate basic principles [AAA, 1966, 1977a]. The Accounting Principles Board prepared *Basic Concepts and Accounting Principles Underlying Financial Statements of Business Enterprises*, Statement No. 4 [AICPA, 1970], before being dissolved in 1973. Its successor, the FASB, has released Statements of Financial Accounting Concepts No. 1 [1978] and Nos. 2, 3 and 4 [1980a, 1980b, 1980c] as part of a much more ambitious project, the so-called "conceptual framework." In Canada, the CICA has just released *Corporate Reporting: Its Future Evolution* [*Corporate Reporting*, 1980]. In all of these documents, the authors have avoided stating propositions that imply radical changes from current accounting practice. Rather, the trend has been to use undefined terms such as "information useful to investors and creditors" [AICPA, 1973] and "relevance to users' needs" [*Corporate Reporting, 1980*]. This allows a welcome freedom to emphasize, from time to time, the perceived needs of different user groups. As one might expect, none of these studies has had any discernible effect on actual accounting practice.

The major points we wished to make, in this brief outline are:
1. All attempts to provide a sound rational basis for *any* set of accounting principles have so far failed.
2. All attempts to introduce changes in valuation methods that depart radically from historical cost have been resisted, and have succeeded only in economies suffering significant inflation.
3. Accounting practice has continued to follow its own course, being unaccountably resistant to innovation or experiment.

Next, we turn to an explanation of these phenomena.

AGENCY: A BASIS FOR ACCOUNTING THEORY

(A) Information usefulness: some alternative concepts

The corporation was once described in a legal judgment as an "artificial person." In this section, we will concentrate our attention on this particular form of business entity, since it exemplifies the problems we wish to analyse and is central to the accounting principles debate.

As an "artificial person," the corporation enjoys many of the legal rights of a real person. Most important, it has the right to make contracts with other persons, both artificial and real. Since the corporation itself is an artificial person, all such contracts must be agreed to by real persons who are empowered to act on its behalf. This power is based on the consent of the stockholders of the corporation, and is constrained by law and by the corporate charter. Therefore, the corporation can be thought of as a legal artefact designed to provide a contractual focus for its activities in the market place, whose contracts are entered into by corporate officers who act as agents of the stockholders.

In a large corporation, the variety of contracts in process of negotiation or performance is extraordinarily broad. They typically include contracts for the acquisition of goods and services from external suppliers, for the sale of the firm's output, labor contracts with the work force; management compensation contracts, and financial contracts encompassing a broad range of monetary obligations to the firm's creditors. Since almost all of these contracts involve the exchange of money or monetary obligations for goods and services, information about market transactions is a natural component of the firm's information system

As has already been pointed out, a popular criterion for accounting information choice is usefulness to investors, creditors, or others. It is, therefore, necessary to consider the purposes information serves, which are much broader than is generally recognized. Frequently, researchers fix upon a particular end use of information and argue as though that were the sole relevant use. This has been a source of much confusion, and clarification of this issue is essential.

In any economic situation involving a business enterprise, there are several distinct, but not mutually exclusive, uses of information. They are as follows:

1. Reduction of management uncertainty with respect to future economic events, e.g., future market demands and operating costs.
2. Reduction of investor uncertainty with respect to future economic events, e.g., future market prices of securities and commodities.
3. The provision of a contractual basis for the efficient sharing of risk among economic agents, e.g., among the managers, creditors, and owners.
4. The provision of a contractual basis for the efficient sharing of beliefs with respect to the relative likelihood of future economic events.
5. The provision of a contractual basis for incentives designed to encourage efficient execution of contracts between the managers of a corporation and their subordinates (management control information).
6. The provision of a contractual basis for incentives designed to encourage efficient execution of contracts between the investors and managers of a corporation (managerial performance evaluation information).
7. Retrospective understanding, i.e., making sense of past actions and events.

The distinction between these alternative uses is important, and will now be discussed in some detail.

1. REDUCTION OF MANAGEMENT UNCERTAINTY WITH RESPECT TO FUTURE ECONOMIC EVENTS

It may not be generally realized that almost the entire body of economic knowledge regarding the impact of uncertainty on individual, group, and market decisions is less than thirty-five years old. Classical economics assumes a world of certainty, and hence cannot provide an adequate basis for the analysis of accounting problems. All seven information uses share at least one common characteristic: they all reduce individual uncertainty with respect to either past or future events. Once we assume that there is no uncertainty to reduce, there is no role for an information system. Paradoxically, most of the debates about accounting standards have virtually ignored this rather obvious fact.

The utility theory originated by Von Neumann and Morgenstern [1953] provided the first comprehensive and rigorous conceptualization of individual rationality in a form which made possible the analysis of problems of individual decision making under uncertainty. This provided the basis for the development of an economic theory of information which, essentially, analyses the relationship between an individual's information system and the decisions it induces. While "information economics" in its original form has provided some useful insights into the manager's information problems, the range of problems to which it is relevant is really quite narrow. Initially, it was an individual theory, which cannot be applied directly to multi-person situations. Unfortunately, even at the managerial level most interesting accounting problems involve interaction between individuals. While the theory was extended to the multi-person context by Marschak and Radner [1974], the theory of teams (as it was called) applies only to groups of identical individuals and is unable to deal with the basic problems caused by conflicts of interest. Extensions of information-economic ideas to group and market environments have begun only in the last ten years.

Later, we will discuss the methodological issues in more detail. But we should point out here a recurring methodological fallacy. *We cannot assume that a theory that has been fully developed only at the individual level is necessarily valid for an aggregation of individuals.* The theory of the small may be neither valid nor appropriate in the large. We cannot assume that a theory of individual behavior, whether based on economics or on psychology, provides sufficient basis for accounting choice in an aggregate group or market setting. This is, perhaps, the most pervasive fallacy in the whole accounting literature. In the absence of convincing theories of aggregate behavior, it is tempting to seize upon particular theories of individual behavior and to extrapolate them to the market or group. Most competing hypotheses of accounting choices owe their existence to this fallacy, which has been expressed in a wide variety of forms.

2. REDUCTION OF INVESTOR UNCERTAINTY WITH RESPECT TO FUTURE ECONOMIC EVENTS

The criterion of investor usefulness seems to have more appeal than any other accounting objective, and has been given prominence in every recent statement of accounting concepts. There is, however, no explanatory theory that can be used to assess the relative usefulness of alternative information choices. There are not even convincing conjectures that might be used as a basis for such a theory. So we find ourselves in the position of supporting an admittedly desirable objective without any real agreement or understanding as to how it might be implemented. We simply do not know, in any systematic sense, what sources of information are used by investors or how they process the information they use.

Consequently, most of the research studies that have attempted to assess the usefulness of accounting reports to the investor have treated the information relationships as a black box whose mechanism is unspecified. The studies simply seek to identify statistically significant relationships between information choices and security returns that are consistent with somewhat *ad hoc* conjectures about investor responses. The whole field of empirical accounting research would be strengthened if it could be based upon a viable theory of investor information. We shall have more to say about these issues in the next section.

The extensive literature of capital market research exemplifies the fallacy of composition referred to above. For example, in Dopuch and Gonedes [1974] and Foster [1978], it is assumed very explicitly that the role of information is to provide a basis for the investor to improve his assessment of the probability distributions of future security returns. Somewhere, at the end of the rainbow, there is a "true" distribution of returns, and superior information is that which leads to investor estimates that are "closer" to the "true" distribution. As will be described in more detail in the next section, one of the effects of a change in market information is to change the expectations of market agents. This, in turn, leads to changes in the behavior of managers and hence to changes in the distribution of security returns.

In summary, we have described a class of information we will call *predictive information*, which has been identified as important to the problem of accounting choice. However, the ways in which particular rules might prove useful to investors are little understood, and the empirical work based on these ideas presently rests on rather weak foundations.

3. THE PROVISION OF A CONTRACTUAL BASIS FOR THE EFFICIENT SHARING OF RISKS AMONG ECONOMIC AGENTS

The first six of our seven information uses are listed in approximately the chronological order in which attention has been given them in economic research. The theory of risk sharing originated with the work of Borch [1962] and was substantially generalized by Wilson [1968]. It is concerned with the problem of dividing a risky return among several agents in such a manner that no other sharing rule can be found that will improve the welfare of any one agent except at the expense of another. It has many applications and has provided, for example, a basis for much of the modern theory of insurance and reinsurance.

Even when beliefs about future events are identical (which we assume here), the form of an efficient sharing rule depends critically on the risk attitudes of the participating agents. If, for example, there is even one risk neutral[6] agent in the group, he will absorb all the risk, while all other (risk averse) agents will receive a constant fee.

Clearly, this theory is important in understanding the behavior of investors with differing risk attitudes, and in analysing the properties of securities markets. Information systems or signals intended to facilitate efficient risk sharing need not improve probability assessments of future events. They simply provide an adequate basis for the contractual sharing of amounts or commodities resulting from actually realized events. However, it is frequently the case that an information system provides signals that serve both predictive and contractual purposes. There is no intention here to suggest that a particular system has only one end use, and it should be clear that the same system may be used in many different ways.

Accounting systems are no exception, and it is certain that their uses are manifold. It is equally certain that the conclusions of the theory of risk sharing extend to the problem of risk sharing among the stockholders, bondholders, and other creditors of a corporation. Without information about the economic outcome (in a sense still to be determined), they cannot share the mutual risk in an efficient manner. Hence all financial contracts between a corporation and its stockholders and creditors must be based on a report which is "sufficiently detailed" to allow efficient sharing of the mutual risk, after taking into account the reporting costs. Without such a report, the mutually beneficial sharing of risk cannot be efficient. Hence, an adequate cost-efficient description of economic outcomes is an essential ingredient of all financial contracts. In this context, the term "outcome" is ambiguous, and no one statistic is a natural candidate to fill this role. We shall return to this issue later.

4. THE PROVISION OF A CONTRACTUAL BASIS FOR THE EFFICIENT SHARING OF BELIEFS WITH RESPECT TO THE RELATIVE LIKELIHOOD OF FUTURE ECONOMIC EVENTS

The fourth information use relates to the efficient sharing of beliefs. When individuals assess the likelihood of future events in an identical fashion, they may all benefit by sharing the mutual risk. When their assessment of the relative likelihood of those events differs, they may wish to improve their welfare by trading on those differences in beliefs. Markets exist for this purpose (among others), and individuals may trade their beliefs with respect to the future price of gold, silver, the US dollar, orange juice, and a variety of other commodities. In a more subtle way, contracts between individuals may, implicitly, incorporate the effects of differences in beliefs. A contractor may accept a larger penalty for non-performance as his assessment of the likelihood of that eventuality becomes smaller. A developer may seek to accept a larger share of the profit from a real estate sale in a price range that he thinks is more likely relative to his partners' beliefs. In general, therefore, efficient sharing of beliefs requires a cost-efficient report that is "sufficiently detailed" to provide an adequate description of those events about which there may be probabilistic disagreement.

In most real situations, the efficient sharing of risk is difficult to separate from the efficient sharing of beliefs. However, in theorectical analysis of such situations, the aggregate efficient sharing rule can be separated into a pure risk sharing rule based on homogeneous beliefs, and a side-bet (as it is often called) that reflects a gamble on the outcome, depending on the relative likelihood of an event for the contracting individuals.

Some theoreticians are unhappy with the situation described here, and argue that heterogeneous beliefs can only result from differences in the available information. If all information is exchanged (they argue), this will ultimately lead to homogeneous beliefs. Often, co-operating individuals will attempt to arrive at similar probability assessments by a systematic process of communication, and competing individuals will seek to infer the information received by others through observation of their actions. Ultimately, however, there may be a residual difference that cannot be affected by further communication, and that may depend on fundamental differences in the life experience of the individuals concerned. It is this residual difference with which we are concerned here, and which is the basis for the side-bet to which we referred above. The side-bet depends *only* on residual differences in probability assessments, and not at all on risk attitudes.

5. THE PROVISION OF A CONTRACTUAL BASIS FOR INCENTIVES DESIGNED TO ENCOURAGE EFFICIENT EXECUTION OF CONTRACTS BETWEEN THE MANAGERS OF A CORPORATION AND THEIR SUBORDINATES

The third of the information uses introduces a concept whose importance as a determinant of contractual behavior has only begun to be realized in economics in the past ten years. Where two or more individuals contract to share a mutual benefit, they must certainly take into account their relative risk attitudes and beliefs. But this is not sufficient. One or more of the individuals in the group may realize that by violating his contractual agreement, he may obtain an advantage for himself. For example, a worker who is paid by the hour may abrogate any responsibility for the production of output. A company director who is paid an annual fee may choose not to attend board meetings. A manager who is paid only a monthly salary may choose to ignore his budget targets. In all of these examples the individual will receive his contractual reward without the sacrifice that was originally contemplated by the other contracting parties. Thus we observe the so-called problem of *moral hazard*, which can arise in any situation in which the probability of specific economic outcomes or the way in which they are reported can be influenced by the unilateral action of one of the contracting parties. The problem of moral hazard has been studied most thoroughly in the context of insurance contracts, where the difficulties it causes are immediately obvious. Indeed, there are many insurance contracts for which the insured can, by his actions, increase the probability of maximum loss to one hundred percent. He may, for example, burn down his house or his business and then claim the full amount of the loss.[7]

The modern economic theory of agency considers the changes in the form of efficient sharing rules when an economic agent must be provided with an incentive designed to induce co-operative behavior. The problem was first analysed by Mirlees [1971] and Spence and Zeckhauser [1971], and these articles stimulated an extensive literature, which also includes Harris and Raviv [1979], Holmström [1979] and Shavell [1979]. The only difference between an agency (incentive) contract and a pure risk-sharing contract is that an incentive contract must satisfy the self-interest of the contracting parties. In other words, any departure from the agreed action must make an individual worse off than if he adheres to the originally agreed action. Hence, he will execute the contract as agreed, since it suits his interest to do so.

Of course, if the actions of the individuals can be observed, there is a contract which produces exactly the same results as a pure risk sharing contract. It will penalize severely all actions that are not those agreed. If the penalty is sufficiently large, the agreed action will be taken, the risks will be efficiently shared, and the threat of a large penalty will be sufficient to ensure that no penalty is imposed. However, monitoring individual actions is generally not cost-effective, and the typical efficient contract is the result of a trade-off between the amount of costly information obtained and the losses imposed on the contracting parties by actions that are different from those agreed.

The basic agency model has many potential applications at the microeconomic level. For example, the budgetary planning and control problem seems to be most naturally expressed in an agency framework. The operating budget can be viewed as a contract whose agreed actions are implied by the preferred outcomes. Incentive arrangements are sought which will induce the contracting agents to take those actions through self-interest. The resulting compensation arrangements reflect both the incentive and the risk sharing effects.

6. THE PROVISION OF A CONTRACTUAL BASIS FOR INCENTIVES DESIGNED TO ENCOURAGE EFFICIENT EXECUTION OF CONTRACTS BETWEEN THE INVESTORS AND MANAGERS OF A CORPORATION

The theoretical basis for the study of this class of information use is less complete than one would wish. Primarily, this is due to the present lack of a comprehensive and rigorously developed general model of the multi-person agency situation. Besides this, we need some better insights into the more specific problems of financial markets and the role of information in this context, as was pointed out earlier. In spite of these deficiencies, we believe that there is now enough evidence to suggest that this particular information use is a major driving force underlying the process of accounting standard selection. Here, we shall briefly review some earlier developments, and our subsequent analysis will occupy the remainder of this section.

In a seminal article, Jensen and Meckling [1976] viewed the relationships between a firm, its managers, and its bondholders in an agency framework. They took the contractual view of the firm that we shall espouse, stating:

> It is important to recognize that most organizations are simply legal fictions which serve as a nexus for a set of contracting relationships among individuals. [p. 310]

(Of course, this view of the firm is not new, and may also be found, for example, in Alchian and Demsetz [1972]).

Jensen and Meckling point out that the behavior of a manager who is also the owner of a firm will not be the same if he sells off a large portion of his equity to outside interests. In this situation, the new bondholders and shareholders of the firm will be faced with exactly the problem we described earlier. The manager's preferences may not be the same as those of the bondholders and shareholders, and imperfect monitoring of his actions will allow the manager's actions to be different from those preferred by the bondholders and shareholders. Jensen and Meckling suggest that in this situation an efficient contract involves a trade-off among three classes of agency costs. The monitoring of the manager's activities is costly and is one such cost. The manager may voluntarily choose to enter into covenants that constrain his activities in areas of importance to investors. (He may, for example, agree not to undertake commercial or industrial actions outside the scope of some specified set, or to limit the debt/equity ratio.) Such covenants constitute a second class of agency cost, since they exclude potentially more profitable alternatives. Finally, any deviation of the manager's actions from those preferred by holders of financial interests imposes the third class of agency costs. The efficient contract is that which reduces the *total* welfare costs imposed on the group to a minimum, and involves a trade-off among the three costs already described. Much of Jensen and Meckling's analysis is concerned with the issue of who bears these agency costs, but this is not a question that can be easily analyzed without reference to aggregate market effects.

7. RETROSPECTIVE UNDERSTANDING, i.e., MAKING SENSE OF PAST ACTIONS AND EVENTS

Information is also used to understand the past as well as to report it for contracting purposes. Such an understanding may have a specific application to one of the other uses, such as in revising beliefs or enabling prediction of contractual consequences on the basis of past patterns, but it also plays a role in accumulating general wisdom that may "come in handy" at some indefinte future time.

We shall make reference to several aspects of this retrospective role of information. First, the role spans a wide range of conscious and unconscious effects. Classical learning theory, cybernetics, information theory, and psychological communication theory do not assume that the decision maker is conscious of his own learning, though he may be. In recent years, however, several conceptions of conscious, retrospective sense making have appeared, such as attribution theory [Nisbett and Wilson, 1977] and retrospective rationality [Weick, 1979]. A major function of this paper is to make conscious sense out of the history of accounting and accounting research!

Second, people's experiences differ and so do their accumulated learnings. A crucial role of information about the past is to provide evidence upon which people may reduce these differences where such reduction is desirable. For example, agreement to a forward contract will be assisted by evidence which produces a consensus about typical action-outcome relationships or about how the incentive measure (e.g., accounting income) performs.

Third, people's generalized background beliefs, whether or not consciously held, affect substantially their learning from more immediate, ongoing events. Some psychologists have suggested that this prevents people from adjusting their prior beliefs sufficiently to use new evidence properly in predictions (e.g. Kahneman and Tversky, [1979]; Tversky and Kahneman [1974]). March [1978] argued that people may actually wish to make their learning ambiguous in order to prevent over-commitment to any particular interpretation. It has been suggested that organizations need information both about ongoing events and prior beliefs, and that a preponderance of the former will produce a tendency to disordered actions, and of the latter will produce stagnation or inaction [Weick, 1979].

Fourth, people's actions are part of the ongoing events and affect future outcomes and future contracts. Therefore, if people act on the basis of particular beliefs, their own actions may give those beliefs greater or less subsequent verity. If all contracts are drawn on the basis that accounting numbers will be computed by some particular method, it will later be found that the computed numbers correlate with outcomes. It may even become so highly correlated (in "reality" or by convergence of beliefs) with the outcomes that it can stand as a useful proxy for those outcomes. If we are unwilling to wait to find out which companies will go bankrupt, but are convinced from past events that bankruptcy is related to low accounting income, we will respond to low accounting income as a close proxy to bankruptcy and may well call loans or take other actions to precipitate that very outcome.

Observe that the seven uses of information that we have identified here fall into three natural groups. For convenience, we shall refer to the first two uses as *predictive* information, to the next four (3-6) as *contractual* information, and to the last (7) as *retrospective* information. In the remainder of this seciton, we focus on contractual information and its apparently close relationship to accounting information.

CONTRACTUAL INFORMATION AND ACCOUNTING RULES

The preceding discussion has drawn some important distinctions among the several classes of information. These are important because the predictive, contractual and retrospective uses of information are fundamentally different and imply correspondingly different research approaches. As we pointed out earlier, research in information economics was focused almost exclusively on predictive uses until quite recently.

Of course, we do not mean to imply that the accountability role of historical cost accounting has passed unobserved. It has been noticed by many writers, but has not always been deemed useful. Ijiri [1981], for example, perhaps the staunchest defender of historical cost accounting today, gives the following Socratic exchange:

> [Person A:] Let me first examine the accountability function of historical cost accounting, since this is a function of accounting that is totally different from the issue of usefulness of reported information.
> [Person B:] I thought usefulness of information is the sole purpose of accounting. At least, this is the way accounting is defined in many official pronouncements. [p. 27]

Here, we will take a rather different point of view. We suggest that accounting is useful if it effectively serves *any* of the seven information uses that were defined above. Statements like Ijiri's have been made by many authors, and are due to the emphasis upon predictive uses. This exclusive view of information usefulness is at the root of many apparent contradictions, such as the supposed conflict between objectivity and relevance, to name one example. The conflict exists only if we deny that information is a useful and necessary adjunct to the contractual process. Once we admit this, our conclusions may be quite different. The major point we wish to make is that, while the concept of accountability has existed for centuries, and is closely related to the stewardship role of accounting, its precise economic motivation is only now becoming understood.

Recent research has recognized some of these issues, but does not yet appear to have come to grips with the essential problem. For example, Watts [1977], and Watts and Zimmerman [1978, 1979] recognize some of the costs apparently imposed on firms by changes in accounting standards. They suggest that such changes affect taxes, regulation, management compensation, bookkeeping costs, and political costs, which, in turn, have an impact upon the firm's cash flows. The perceived impact may then give rise to political activity, which, in their view, is the ultimate determinant of accounting standards. They say, for example:

> Rationales differ (and are inconsistent) across accounting standards because a standard is the result of political action. The outcome depends on the relative costs which the various involved parties are willing to incur to achieve their goals. And these costs will vary with the expected benefits. [Watts and Zimmerman, 1979, p. 287]

These authors also state that "accounting procedures are devised in order to reduce the agency costs of contract," which is a very explicit recognition of the contractual role of accounting information. Their consideration of specific agency costs includes only a narrow class, however, and virtually ignores the costs imposed on economic agents outside the firm. In addition, it is often apparent that the relative costs actually imposed by the financial markets on the shareholders, bondholders, and managers of a firm may be quite different from those originally anticipated. In other words, we cannot assume that the managers of a firm are, necessarily, competent predictors of agency costs. While the political activity observed by Watts and Zimmerman undeniably exists, it is difficult to avoid the conclusion that it is motivated by other economic forces besides those they describe. Certainly these provide no basis for explaining why accounting standards take the particular form we observe.

In the remainder of this section, therefore, we shall analyse the contractual uses of information in more detail, and argue that the use of financial reports based on historical cost is a natural consequence of the incentive contract point of view.

To understand how the perceived use of information affects its form, it is necessary to summarize some of the known properties of information in a contractual setting, and in the presence of moral hazard, which is a pervasive economic phenomenon.

In this setting, the ideal contract has, essentially, three components. There must be agreement with respect to the actions to be taken by the contracting parties. There must be agreement with respect to the way in which these actions and their economic consequences will be observed and reported (which implies some form of generally accepted information principles). And there must be agreement with respect to how the reported information will be used to determine the parties' relative shares in the ultimate outcome. Here, we are especially interested in the role of information.

If the contract does not provide for *any* feedback information we know [Atkinson and Feltham, 1981] that financial contracts between investors and managers can be based only on a fixed fee (interest only). While this is obviously an extreme case, it does draw attention to the vital role played by feedback information for this type of contract. *If there is to be any sharing of risk, or incentive to perform, it must have some information base.* Unless it is prohibitively expensive, feedback information provides a basis for an efficient contract. (Here and throughout this paper we use the word efficient in its usual economic sense. In this context, an efficient contract has the property that a move to any alternative contract must involve a loss for at least one of the contracting parties. Observe that there may be many contracts with this property. Selection of a particular efficient contract involves normative issues, which we wish to avoid.)

To share financial risk efficiently, we should, ideally, be able to contract with each other on the basis of all anticipated economic events. For example, a bond contract should enable the bondholder to predict the amounts he will receive in all economic eventualities, and not just some. This suggests an obvious but important observation: the manager or entrepreneur who enters into financial contracts with investors or creditors will, in that process, transfer a share in the firm's risk to them[8], in various proportions, according to their relative risk attitudes.

In this situation, it is clear that the nature of the contract offered by the manager or entrepreneur plays a vital role in determining the amounts that will be contributed by the various ownership categories, since it specifies their relative shares under all eventualities *as well as the reporting method*. Thus, the contracting parties must decide how economic events will be observed and reported, and incorporate this into their financial contract.

This brings us to a related and vital issue. The detailed observation of economic events is very costly, and it is clearly cost-effective for the firm and its managers to collect and report such information to all interested parties, rather than have each operate his own (costly) information system. Now the problem of moral hazard appears in a new form, since there may well be a temptation for the manager to report information that increases his own relative share at the expense of others. As well, he may operate the firm in ways that conflict with his explicit agreements with the owners, and which therefore lead to inefficient sharing of the ultimate economic benefits. Of course, *rational* investors may anticipate this, and the market will reflect their expectations.

The essential question seems to be: what characteristics of a contract can most effectively minimize the kinds of difficulties we have described? An optimal contract between a manager or entrepreneur and the investors or creditors of the entity he manages involves a basic trade-off between efficient sharing of economic consequences and efficient motivation of proper contractual performance. The trade-off exists because such motivation has both explicit and implicit costs. The explicit cost is that of operating an information system that generates contractually useful information. The implicit cost is the result of choosing a contract that in the absence of moral hazard is not efficient. In other words, a contract constructed in such a manner as to provide incentives for proper performance is necessarily worse for at least one contracting party than an alternative contract based on assumptions of complete trust. If sufficiently reliable and detailed information about the manager's activities is generated, presumably at a very great cost, we know that he can be motivated efficiently so that there will be no residual implicit cost. On the other hand, if we make no attempt to acquire reliable information about his activities, the implicit costs of the manager's deviant performance may be correspondingly great. So a middle ground must be found, and the result is a contract in which some (and perhaps all) parties will find themselves worse off than in a situation of absolute trust, i.e., without moral hazard. Recollect from our earlier discussion that there is no simple way of predicting just how these costs will be shared among the contracting parties.

We return to the essential question and consider now the attributes a contractual information system must possess for the contract which uses its output to be efficient. The first and most fundamental requirement is that the basic properties of the information system be common knowledge among the contracting parties. If this condition is violated and there are competing sources of information, or differing perceptions with respect to the properties of a system, contracting becomes difficult or impossible. The problems are described by Milgrom and Stokey, who say:

> If agents' prior beliefs about the state of the world differ because each has access to private information, each will scrutinize the actions of others (as reflected in prices and/or trades) to make inferences about what they know. A Pandora's box of possibilites opens up when agents acquire information during trading, since it may matter not only whether 'Agent 1 knows fact A', but also whether 'Agent 2 knows that 1 knows A,' whether '1 knows that 2 knows that 1 knows A,' etc. Many conclusions in general equilibrium settings are very sensitive to the assumptions made about the initial data given to each agent and to the assumptions made about what agents observe during trading. [Milgrom and Stokey, 1979, p. 2]

The difficulties they describe are only overcome if the information system exhibits what they term the property of *statistical information*. This means that, given a particular economic event, everyone is agreed with respect to the probability of the various possible messages that the information system might generate. As well, it is clear from our earlier discussion that the output of the information system must be verifiable by all the contracting parties. Relative shares cannot be based on unobservable events. The players generally put down their cards face upwards at the end of a hand of poker!

While these properties have been deduced from a priori economic analysis, it is obvious that they accord very well with the stated views of many accountants. They seem to correspond quite closely with the concept of objectivity as defined by Moonitz:

> The term "objective" is used ... to mean "unbiased; subject to verification by another competent investigator." In this usage, an estimate or forecast can be objective, along with completed events of the past. [Moonitz, 1961, p. 42]

Observe that the critical issue here is not just that the "competent investigator" should have access to the system output. He must also be able to satisfy himself that the *process* by which the information was generated corresponds to what we termed common knowledge with respect to that process. But in the context of financial reporting this is nothing else but the set of generally accepted accounting principles (GAAP). These provide a basis for common agreement with respect to the information rules to be followed, given a particular set of business circumstances ("state of the world") without being precise enough to enable prediction of the specific form of a report from knowledge of all these circumstances. Hence, economic analysis has provided a basis for deducing the properties of objectivity, verifiability, and lack of bias from prior assumptions. We no longer need to call these concepts "postulates."

Notice also that the concept of statistical information provides, as Milgrom and Stokey pointed out, the essential foundation for all scientific experiment. We may not be able to predict the outcome of a scientific experiment in advance, and the prior predictions of different individuals will vary. But, if all are agreed on the experimental process, repetitions of an experiment will ultimately result in the convergence of individual beliefs. The basic intuition here is that statistical information will influence beliefs in a uniform manner, while information systems without this property may produce inconsistent or unpredictable changes in individual beliefs.

In conformity with accounting usage, we shall call the property of statistical information *objectivity*, a substitution which seems justified by their approximate equivalence. Objectivity alone, however, is not sufficient to guarantee informational efficiency. Information may be objective but unreliable, and may not adequately disclose the detail of economic events. We shall term a system *reliable* if a given set of events can generate only a narrow range of alternative messages. Thus, reliability reflects the quality of internal control. Again, an objective and reliable system may not be efficient, since it may objectively report aggregate data which fails to reveal the underlying events. (Total assets could be objectively and reliably reported, but would tell us little about operations.) Hence, adequate disclosure of relevant events is the final criterion of informational efficiency.

Economic analysis, therefore, has shown that it is desirable for efficient contractual information to have the properties of objectivity, reliability, and adequate disclosure. The last requirement dodges the question of what we will accept as adequate and this raises some thorny issues peculiar to accounting information systems. The main difficulty is that there is no obvious collection of economic statistics that can serve as a benchmark of adequacy. This is so because the concept of adequacy has meaning only in the context of a particular business environment. Information is adequate when the revelation of additional detail will cause no changes in the form of proposed contracts. Without a more complete theory of contractual information, the relative adequacy of disclosure must remain a matter of judgment. It is precisely this problem that has caused the frequent appeals to "economic reality" in the current accounting literature, as well as the introduction of the term "representational faithfulness" in FASB [1980a]. It seems clear that the concept of economic reality, while seemingly absolute, is really used in an incremental sense. When it is asserted that a particular accounting method "does not reflect economic reality," the writer generally means that it fails to discriminate among economic events when discrimination is essential for market efficiency. Similarly, the concepts of reliability and adequate disclosure we have described seem to approximate the concept of "respresentational faithfulness," which is defined as follows:

> Representational faithfulness is correspondence or agreement between a measure or description and the phenomenon it purports to represent. In accounting, the phenomena to be represented are economic resources and obligations and the transactions and events that change those resources and obligations. [FASB, 1980a, p. 27]

Hence, our use of the term *objectivity* seems to comprehend jointly the concepts of representational faithfulness and verifiability in FASB [1980a] and embraces also the criterion of adequate disclosure of economic reality.

The criterion of objectivity forces us to base contractual reporting on objective data. One possible source of such data is the firm's cash flows and balances. But this turns out to be unsatisfactory, since a firm's cash balance and net cash receipts clearly cannot provide an adequate basis for the assessment of risk, which depends on the firm's total resources and not on just one of them. So the criterion of disclosure is not satisfied. To the investor, risk is a function of the total resources exchangeable for money as well as the money itself.

If we wish to report information about the firm's resources, one obvious source of objective data is the set of contracts to which the firm is a party, and which involves economic exchanges between the firm and other economic entities. Let us look a little more closely at the form of a typical exchange contract. Most often, it involves the following stages or transactions:

1. A contingent contract is agreed which provides for the future exchange of goods or services for money, or, more commonly, for the substitution of the exchange contract by a financial contract.
2. The goods or services are transferred, and the contingent amount of money or financial obligation becomes known.
3. Any remaining financial contingencies are determined, and an appropriate amount of cash is transferred, thus completing execution of the original contract.

The essential point here is that virtually all exchange contracts are contingent upon future economic events, of which the most important is the recognition by the contracting parties of the precise nature of the exchanged goods or services. For example, the value of the goods transferred will typically depend on their quality and quantity, as well as the actual date and time of the transfer.[9] Hence, we assert that the form of the resources exchanged by an entity is not known with certainty to either buyer or seller until the actual transfer has occurred. At that time, the contingent form of the exchanged goods or services is agreed by the parties involved, and a financial contract whose amount was originally dependent upon agreed contingencies is then determined.

Of course, the financial contract may itself depend on still other contingencies such as the payment date or dates, the inflation rate, and the market rate of interest. And there may be residual commodity contingencies that depend on the existence of express or implied warranties with respect to the goods exchanged. But most of the sources of uncertainty have been removed and, most important of all, the exchange for money or for a financial obligation enforceable at law provides prima facie evidence of the impact of the exchange upon the ultimate total income of the firm. Moreover, the evidence is verifiable by reference to the other contracting party, and to the documents recording the details of his contractual obligations.

Here, we observe the underlying reasons for the use of actual exchange transactions as a basis for the accounting record. For transactions are simply verifiable stages in the performance of contracts, verifiable because they involve both another contracting party and events that have already taken place. They provide a natural source of information with respect to the interaction between the firm and its economic environment. Moreover, the fact that all these exchanges are measured in terms of money, or financial obligations with readily ascertainable money values, provides a natural choice for the aggregation of these contractual effects.[10]

These arguments lead us to assert that the widely used accounting principles (or postulates) of verifiability, objectivity, exchange, and money as the aggregation device are all a natural consequence of the contractual nature of accounting information. In other words, they are principles that flow naturally from the acceptance of the incentive and risk sharing uses of information as the primary driving force underlying the choice of accounting principles and rules. The fact that there are, without question, other uses of information does not invalidate our argument. If accounting in its present form did not exist, something very like it would have to be invented.

So far, we have argued that economic exchanges provide a source of information that satisfies some of the criteria arising from the assumed contractual purpose of accounting. But this is not sufficient to explain why the accountant processes the aggregates of market transactions in the conventional ways to which we are accustomed. In particular, it is useful to try to understand how we arrived at the empirically vague principle of cost and revenue matching.

To this end, let us now focus upon the set of financial contracts. Some of these originated as exchange contracts in the manner described above. But there are others for which the financial contract is an end in itself, and where the exchange of money is the only exchange contemplated. Included in this category are bank loans, notes payable, mortgages, bonds, and the various classes of shares. Each of these involves a class of investor with different consumption preferences and risk attitudes, and the risk and agency theory to which we referred earlier provides a basis for predicting how the risk facing the firm will efficiently be shared among the investors in these circumstances. For example, it would be inefficient for a risk averse, short-term investor to purchase a long-term bond, thereby assuming a risk he could easily avoid. In general, the presence of a fixed interest security suggests a difference in risk attitudes among the holders of the financial interests in the firm.

No investor can fully diversify risk caused by moral hazard. The unscrupulous manager has the power to change the relative risks faced by the holders of the various classes of financial contracts, as well as to influence the aggregate risk through his operating policies. For example, the manager whose compensation is tied to the welfare of the common shareholders may be tempted to improve the welfare of the common shareholder at the expense of others. He can do this by, for example, distributing excessive dividends, thereby increasing the risk exposure of all other classes of investor. The common shareholder can recognize and appropriately price this risk only to the extent that he can rationally anticipate it.

We have stated that the basic property of objectivity is desirable for contractual efficiency. This requires that all economic agents assess the likelihood of alternative messages in the same manner, given a particular set of economic circumstances. In addition, adequate disclosure of all relevant events is desirable, where adequacy is defined to be achieved when the disclosure of additional detail would not result in changes in the contracts preferred by rational agents. Roughly speaking, therefore, a given information system acts as a constraint upon the ability of market agents to contract efficiently with one another. As the degree of costly disclosure increases, there are potential benefits to all the contracting parties, until the point of adequate disclosure is reached, beyond which (by definition) there can be no further improvements.

So far, we have suggested that objectivity dictates the choice of transactions as the basis for accounting information, where a transaction was defined to be a stage in the performance of an exchange contract, measurable in terms of money, and representing a legally enforceable right. Any other form of economic data raises moral hazard difficulties since market exchanges that are not consummated cannot be verified, and therefore do not meet the objectivity criterion. But this is only the first stage of the accounting process, and leads us to the crucial issue of the choice of an aggregation method. We must now bear in mind the ultimate assumed purpose of contractual information, which is to provide a conditional basis for the sharing of mutually owned economic resources.

In the simplest kind of situation, which is a joint venture, there is no real difficulty. The venture will terminate with the liquidation of all assets and liabilities, and those participating need only know the residue available for distribution. However, in the more typical business situation this amount (called *ultimate total income* by Canning [1929]) cannot be known until the end of the life of an enterprise. In the mean time, holders of the various financial interests will expect to receive a return based on some tentative measure of enterprise performance. The efficient sharing of risk requires that such a measure exist, for without it there can be no basis for assessment of the relative shares to which the holders of the relative interests are entitled, and, therefore, no basis for a contract between them.

Since the rights of bondholders and lenders are fixed by their financial contracts, it is natural to focus upon the rights of the shareholders, since they assume the residual risk. It also follows from our earlier discussion that whatever rights are exercisable by the shareholders must be capable of prediction by the various holders of financial interests for any given set of economic conditions. (This does not imply, of course, that they must share the same views as to what those future economic consequences might be.)

These observations enable us to suggest some desirable properties of accounting information. In particular, the concept of *earnings* serves the purpose of providing an objectively predictable basis for assessing the total money value to be shared for some period of time. We postulate, therefore, that earnings should be:

(1) objective;
(2) time additive;
(3) enterprise additive;
(4) irrevocable;
(5) risk-constraining; and
(6) cash convergent.

The first of these desiderata has already been discussed in detail, and we now explain the other five.

We want earnings to be *time additive* so that, for example, the earnings of four quarters should equal the earnings for the year. While additivity is a fundamental property of all numerical measurement systems, observe that it is not satisfied by some of the proposed current value reporting methods. We also want earnings to be *enterprise additive*, which means that consolidated earnings of two or more independent firms should be equal to the sum of their separate earnings. By independent we imply that they have no mutual contractual relationship. It is interesting to observe here that mutual contracts are precisely those eliminated in consolidation procedures. This is perfectly consistent with our criterion of objectivity, since, in this situation, a mutual contract becomes subject to moral hazard, and can no longer provide a suitable basis for contracting with outside parties. Without the additivity property, we cannot meaningfully aggregate earnings across firms and time, a property that we often take for granted.

Earnings should also be irrevocable. They represent a constraint on amounts distributable to the residual owners and provide a basis for financial contracts between the managers and the holders of the various classes of financial interest in the firm. Since the distribution of assets to the shareholders is, for all practical purposes, a legally irrevocable action, it makes sense to treat the information that constrains this action as irrevocable also. A change in the basis for a past and irrevocable action can serve no useful contractual purpose. However, the same underlying economic events may well require current recognition, and may modify the amount of resources considered currently distributable. This reasoning supports the observed reluctance of standard-setting bodies to permit retrospective adjustments to prior years' earnings. The property of irrevocability also induces a reluctance to make earnings dependent upon future events, since the eventual outcome may suggest a revision which cannot be useful at that time.

The *risk constraint* criterion is desired because of the effect of resource distributions (dividends) on the *relative* risks faced by the various classes of investors in the firm. As an extreme example, the holder of a bond cannot rationally assess the default risk he faces unless he can predict the dividend and investment policy the firm will follow, as well as their future operating results. *Ceteris paribus*, the larger the dividend, the greater his default risk. Presumably, if the firm continues to reinvest at a rate sufficient to maintain its mean return and restricts its investments to a similar risk class, amounts in excess of that reinvestment rate can be distributed without impairing the bondholder's default risk. The income number appears to act as an overriding constraint on dividend policy, in a manner that protects the default risk of the holders of senior securities. This concept is neglected in most discussions of capital maintenance, which focus upon the mean return, without regard either to risk or the effects of distributions to investors. Often, financial contracts contain other provisions that reinforce the general earnings constraint. This is the purpose of most bond covenants, for example, which allow some control over the actions of management in such areas as new financing and dividend distribution, and which may convey much broader powers if the default risk of the bondholders increases significantly.[11] Obviously, all such contractual arrangements must be based on objective information, and the earnings amount is an important component of that information.

Finally, earnings should be *cash convergent*: in the long run, the cumulative total earnings should converge to the excess of operating cash inflows over operating cash outflows. This is merely a common-sense requirement, since this is all that can be distributed or reinvested in the long run.

These six criteria have some clear implications for the selection of transaction aggregation rules. The criteria of objectivity, additivity, and irrevocability together suggest the use of the money amount of actual transactions as the aggregation basis, and will discourage the use of any current value technique which is not based on some objective device such as an agreed time series. The same criteria also have implications with respect to the form of the aggregation process.

To begin with, in order to satisfy the criterion of objectivity, the process of aggregation must be well understood, capable of verification, and outside the control of the manager (or any other of the contracting parties). This again implies some form of GAAP, or agreed rules for aggregating the underlying transactions. We pointed out earlier that the exclusive use of cash exchanges does not satisfy the risk-constraint criterion, since it is an inadequate measure of financial resources. In addition, although cash flow is sometimes regarded as the ultimate in objective measures, this is not really the case. In fact, cash flow is very sensitive to moral hazard problems, and can easily be manipulated by the unscrupulous. As an example, all of the so-called pyramid schemes actually rely on cash flow as a means of deception.

Another obvious aggregation alternative is simply to add the exchange value of all transactions in a period. This provides a measure akin to that of net funds changes and at least has the advantage of taking into account all monetary commitments, and not just those which have already been exchanged for cash. However, it is a short-run rather than a long-run concept. It is affected by the random (or deliberately chosen) occurrence of large transactions, which may occasionally cluster and thereby signal risk changes that are more apparent than real. Therefore, this aggregation concept is subject to moral hazard. If this number is used as a risk measure, the manager of the firm may be tempted to distribute funds really needed for capital maintenance or to invest excessively with the object of depriving shareholders of amounts to which they would be entitled. Whatever the results, the amount on which the distributions depend is capable of manipulation.

So, faced with this dilemma, and insisting on reports that satisfy our six criteria, we are driven inexorably toward an aggregation method that eliminates the problem of moral hazard by averaging major expenditures over the periods that benefit from them. Ideally, the earnings number should be unaffected by the timing of non-recurring transactions such as the purchase or sale of major capital items. Thus some form of cost and revenue matching seems to be a natural response to the need to write financial contracts on a basis that takes full account of moral hazard issues. This latter point certainly necessitates the use of objective data, but the objectivity criterion must extend also to the aggregation process itself, as we have already stated. This is not only the driving force behind the need for generally accepted accounting principles, but it also explains the need for a cost-effective verification by the auditor, which can then be relied upon by all the contracting parties, and which removes the need for costly individual verification. Of course, without GAAP, the auditor would be unable to fulfill this role.

It is worth noting here that our concept of earnings and the criteria underlying it are not at all consistent with some alternative concepts of income. In Beaver and Demski [1979], for example, income is postulated to represent a preference ordering on a firm's production plans. They then show that, in a complete market (i.e., a market with adequate disclosure for risk contracting) such an income number has no role. In an incomplete market it may not exist. The moral hazard difficulties are not considered, nor are the problems of financial contracting included in their model. We have suggested that the role of income is fundamentally different from that postulated by Beaver and Demski: it is *retrospective* rather than predictive.

It is no simple matter to trace the consequences of these hypotheses to the specific form of particular rules, and we will not attempt this task here. It is interesting to note, however, how a change in the economic environment such as an increase in the inflation rate might change the choice among rules. History shows that the interest in alternative transaction measures, such as replacement cost, has generally varied with the rate of inflation. The framework we have developed helps to explain why, for we can observe the obvious trade-off between the greater risk of moral hazard and the improved protection of, for example, bondholders resulting from the sacrifice of objectivity in this context. How that trade-off should be resolved is a question which requires research into problems we have only begun to explore.

In this section, we have suggested that financial reporting has arisen in response to a market demand for information required by considerations of contractual market efficiency. We have also suggested that this seems to be the primary use of accounting information. If this premise is accepted, much of the conventional approach to accounting seems to have a very rational basis. In particular, we have asserted that the contractual approach helps to explain the universal appeal of the criteria of objectivity, verifiability, market exchange, and price aggregation. It also seems to provide a reasonable basis for understanding the process of cost and revenue matching.

But, it is important not to throw out the baby with the bathwater and to suppose that the sole purpose of accounting information is to provide for contractual efficiency. This is far from being the case. Nothing we have said has suggested that accounting information is not useful in the more usual sense intended, i.e., for the resolution of uncertainty with respect to future economic events. The results of empirical research bear out this statement, as we will report in detail later. Rather, we have been suggesting that it is the contractual uses of information that provide the primary economic impetus for the directions taken by conventional accounting principles. If accounting information has other uses, it is incidental to the motivation we have suggested. These other uses are also served by sources of information which have no connection whatsoever with accounting. What information sources should be used for the purpose of resolving uncertainty above future economic events is a question of market efficiency which we cannot explore further here. Suffice it to say that there is no a priori reason why we should consider accounting information to be the major source of such information.

In the next section, we will investigate some methodological issues of great importance in the study of accounting theory.

METHODOLOGICAL ISSUES

Many accounting researchers wish to construct and test theories that will help in choosing accounting information rules appropriate to a particular economic context. In this section we shall provide some methodological perspective, evaluate the current status of relevant research, and try to spell out some of the difficulties that must be overcome before accounting choice can have a sound theoretical basis. Because of the shortcomings in our theoretical knowledge of accounting, accounting policy is formed almost independently of it; we proceed by trial and error and a "kind of patch-work and tinkering," as Canning [1929] called it. Disagreements about the *desirability* of proposed changes are ofen confused with disagreements about the *effects* of those changes. This situation can only be improved, in the long run, by a program of research designed to provide answers to some very fundamental questions. Our task is to identify these questions and to explain the nature of the research needed to address them.

Since the scope of this problem is very broad, we begin by mildly restricting the range of our analysis. First, we shall be concerned only with the choice of accounting rules relating to the external financial statements of an enterprise (as opposed to internal, managerial information), without in any way restricting the scope of that choice to some particular class of accounting rules, e.g., historical cost, accrual, current value, etc. Second, in much of what follows we consider only financial market agents, including investors, creditors, and financial analysts, thus ignoring for the moment the demands of, for example, government, labor unions, and regulatory bodies. However, insofar as these latter groups have explicit or implicit contractual relationships with the firm, the basic contracting framework we have introduced is still appropriate for them. We emphasize, however, that these restrictions in the scope of our inquiry are not intended to preclude the analysis of individual decision makers rather than market (i.e., price) effects.

In any discussion of research methodology certain terms must have an agreed-upon definition. We must first make the obvious and important distinction between *theoretical* research based on a priori reasoning from assumed first principles, and *empirical* research based on comparisons of hypothesized relationships with observed phenomena. This methodological difference has important implications for the process of research validation, as is well known.

We recognize, however, that many research efforts in accounting are directed at simply looking for relationships or trying to understand the world. By the strict definition given above, these do not qualify as empirical research since they are "theoryless" and without hypotheses. They may, however, be an important step in the formulation of the assumed principles which precede the development of theory. Disagreement concerning which must come first is akin to the chicken-egg debate and may generate more heat than light. For purposes of this study we shall think of theoryless empirical research as pre-theory study and admit that in a relatively new discipline, which the rigorous analysis of accounting information definitely is, such study may have important contributions to make.

Another important methodological distinction we shall need to make clear is between *normative* (or prescriptive) and *positive* (or predictive) theories. Both involve the use of deductive logic[12] from a priori assumptions. But positive theories are concerned with the prediction of observable phenomena, while normative theories are concerned with means-ends statements, i.e., statements of the general form: "if the relevant attributes of your problem can be represented by model X, and you wish to achieve B, then do A." The significance of the distinction lies in the fact that normative statements are not empirically falsifiable. Although this is quite well known, one still sees authors of accounting research studies attempting to draw normative conclusions from empirical analysis.

Of course, if a viable theory to guide accounting standard setters can be constructed, it is clear that it must take a normative form. That is, accounting standard setters are required to formulate principles (or rules) that dictate the *preferred* choice for reporting in a variety of economic contexts. Since their choices will necessarily benefit some individuals at the expense of others, the fundamental problem facing standard setters is in deciding which results are most desirable. Positive theories which help us understand the *consequences* of accounting choices, and which are empirically falsifiable, can make the choice problem clearer by reducing the confusion between consequences and their desirability, but these positive theories and the empirical evidence supporting them cannot in any sense indicate which consequences are most desirable. This point must be kept in mind when standard setters commission or examine research. No research results can eliminate the social choice problems inherent in the standard-setting process. Research can only predict or validate consequences on the basis of which the normative choices are to be made.

The failure of empirical tests for normative theory is not due to any minor technical or practical difficulty. Recollect that we are faced with the problem of falsifying a statement of the form: "if the relevant attributes of your problem can be represented by model X, and you wish to achieve B, then do A." The fundamental dilemma arises from the prescription that one should do A to achieve B. But specifying A as the (only) appropriate action to achieve B implies that the model (descriptor) X of the system is sufficiently complete so that A can be compared with alternative actions and judged as "best" by some criteria. However, there can be no absolutely sufficient description X of the model at issue. If we do A and C occurs, this does not absolutely falsify the prescription because we cannot know whether descriptor X was a sufficient basis for action. The prescription *given* X may have been fine but perhaps X was not an adequate descriptor in the circumstances. And if we consider alternative system descriptors $X_1, X_2, ..., X_k$ selected from the multitude of possibilities, each may indicate a different action prescription. The alternative prescribed actions resulting from the different descriptions may each be true for *some* of the system states that the given descriptor inadequately represents. So, to resolve the dilemma, we may seek a more comprehensive descriptor Y from which the whole set of descriptors $X_1, X_2, ..., X_k$ can be deduced. Then Y suggests an unequivocal action choice. But Y is, in its turn, only one of many alternative, albeit richer, system descriptors. So we are again faced with the same dilemma, and find ourselves at the threshold of an infinite regress, from which there is no escape. While there is no way around this ultimate dilemma, the preceding discussion does have some positive aspects. Although no system descriptor can be completely adequate, a more complete system representation will generally reduce the frequency of error, at the expense of analytical complexity. This basic trade-off was very well described by Boulding [1956] who said:

> We always pay for generality by sacrificing content, and all we can say about practically everything is almost nothing. Somewhere, however, between the specific that has no meaning and the general that has no content, there must be, for each purpose and at each level of abstraction, an optimum degree of generality. [p. 198]

Figure 1: Our Taxonomy of Research

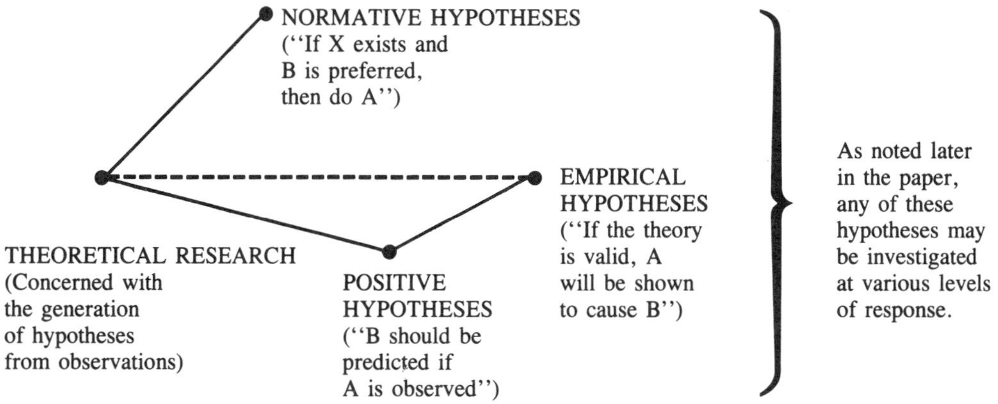

NORMATIVE HYPOTHESES
("If X exists and
B is preferred,
then do A")

**EMPIRICAL
HYPOTHESES**
("If the theory
is valid, A
will be shown
to cause B")

THEORETICAL RESEARCH
(Concerned with
the generation
of hypotheses
from observations)

**POSITIVE
HYPOTHESES**
("B should be
predicted if
A is observed")

As noted later
in the paper,
any of these
hypotheses may
be investigated
at various levels
of response.

To summarize at this point. We have defined a research classification according to methodological approach (normative theory, positive theory). In addition, we have drawn a distinction between theoretical and empirical research. Figure 1 illustrates our methodological framework. We have not attempted to relate these two classification approaches directly since the distinction between normative and positive theory is sometimes subtle, and it is not at all unusual to see the same theoretical constructs interpreted as either normative or positive depending on the researcher's specific needs. In other words, a theory is not inherently normative or positive but can be either depending on the way in which the theory is used. For example, if asked to classify the neo classical theory of the firm as normative or positive, many respond "normative," having in mind the kind of statement it generates (e.g., "to maximize profits, set marginal cost equal to marginal revenue"). But Friedman [1953] treats it as a positive theory, whose value (to him) depends on its ability to predict the response of a firm in the marketplace to alternative demand/supply schedules.

In the previous section, we postulated certain hypotheses concerning the process of choosing among accounting alternatives. Essentially, our methodological approach was positive, since we were attempting to explain the observed preference of the market for particular classes of accounting rules. But, while our arguments may have provided a rather loosely specified rational justification for the choices we observe, our efforts fell very far short of the positive *theory* which must, necessarily, be constructed and tested in order to justify properly the statements we have made, as well as to provide them with a more concrete form. Ideally, we want a theory that will enable us not only to predict the economic consequences of accounting rules but also to order preferences among them.

However, as we have already noted, such a theory must ultimately involve normative issues. The criterion to which we have appealed throughout the preceding discussion is that of efficiency in the market[13]. That is, efficient solutions to accounting choice problems are those which suppliers and users of accounting information have settled upon as satisfactory for their purposes considering their costs and benefits and considering that no alternative solution can be identified that makes some market participants better off without making any market participants worse off. However, this Pareto efficiency criterion is not sufficient to enable us to identify a specific preferred choice; it gives no guidance with respect to choice among efficient solutions, of which there may be many.

For example, a change in an accounting rule *may* well result in an increase in bondholder wealth at the expense of the holders of residual equity. The new *market equilibrium*[14] might still be efficient. But it would be different, and, clearly, those who were made worse off would object. Whether they *should* be worse off is a normative question, which involves much the same issues as, say, a decision on the size of a minimum wage, or the level of unemployment compensation.

However, a positive (descriptive) theory that was sufficiently detailed to predict the new efficient market equilibrium that would result from a specific proposed change in accounting rules would be of enourmous help to the accounting community, for it would permit the choice to be made on the basis of the ultimate welfare consequences of the change. At present, the arguments tend to involve much disagreement about what those consequences might be, and this really obscures the normative issues.

In the next section, we shall discuss accounting research, some of which has attempted to develop and test predictions concerning the effects of accounting policies on certain individuals or groups in society.

REVIEW OF RECENT ACCOUNTING RESEARCH

Our discussion of methodologies in accounting research requires an organization framework. To provide a basis for analysis, we have classified the response to accounting information and hence to accounting standards choices into five levels. Each of the levels is naturally identified with a particular stage in a sequence of economic events.

1. Individual investors, creditors, managers and employees are affected and they react to the choice of standard or the information it implies.
2. Various groups are affected and react collectively, e.g, the accounting profession, financial analysts, industrial trade associations, etc. The reactions may involve political activity.
3. These individual and group responses aggregate into market price effects for all goods and services including securities.
4. Business firms (and their managers) respond to market changes through their production, investment and financing decisions.
5. Finally, these altered actions of firms affect the individuals, groups and aggregate markets noted above, and engender additional responsive behavior which may cause additional adjustments by the firm and so on until an equilibrium is reached.

Though the five levels of response will provide an adequate framework for developing accounting research insights relevant to the agency perspective we have used in this paper, this framework is not sufficient to include all of the financial accounting research we wish to review. Much accounting research has been concerned with the properties of accounting information itself, apart from how people might respond to it. Examples of such research are "time series" studies of accounting numbers' changes over time, income smoothing studies, some studies of accounting measurement postulates, simulations of effects of various proposals for price-level adjustments to accounting statements, analyses of apparent information loss through summarization, and comparison of pension accounting methods to actuarial assumptions. Some of this research is presented against an explicit (or implicit) information use background, but we believe it will be more helpful to review it as a separate category rather than to arbitrarily force it into our "levels of response" framework. This sixth category will precede the other five in our review and will be referred to as "pre-response" research.

We emphasize that, while the levels of response were described above in generally economic terms, research questions clearly may be stated in economic or behavioral terms. Also, the process outlined in the five levels listed above is essentially the development of a new economic equilibrium (in which the distribution of resources has shifted, to the benefit of some and to the detriment of others). Whether this shift is desirable or not is a normative question. While research can shed light on *outcomes* of policy decisions it cannot, as explained earlier, support one outcome as better than another.

Our agency hypothesis focuses on contracting between various individuals and groups and the firm. These include, of course, investors, creditors, managers, employees and customers. The five levels of response to accounting policies are broad enough to allow for effects due to this contract-basis function of accounting as well as the alternative uses of accounting information listed in Section III.

The positive agency hypothesis of accounting set forth in this study is still insufficiently developed to yield very much in the way of predictions of consequences of the sort policy makers would undoubtedly like to have. Our present lack of knowledge is deplorable, but some progress has been made. For example, we now know a good deal about the role of information in an equilibrium risk-sharing market, albeit under somewhat restrictive market assumptions [Ohlson, 1980].[15] However, we know very little about the effect of moral hazard on that equilibrium. If our hypotheses are correct, this will be a vitally important area of research. In addition, since accounting is but one of many sources of information about the firm, it would be helpful to know more about those other sources and about the relationship between accounting and other, possibly more efficient (cheaper and/or more timely), information sources.

To summarize to this point. We have left aside for the moment the normative questions and focused on the prediction of consequences. We have specified several obviously interrelated levels that are influenced by policy choices, and have indicated the paucity of knowledge regarding the consequences to be expected from information. Of course, predicting consequences is an extremely complex undertaking. Research aimed at predicting or detecting responses at one level probably must ignore or make simplifying assumptions about the responses at the other levels. It is, for example, common for research to be directed at responses of individual investors, creditors, or managers while ignoring aggregate market effects. Equally common is research on market effects that makes simplified (and apparently simplistic) assumptions concerning individual and group reactions and ignores the potential effects on the operating decisions of firms.

One other limitation with which a good deal of the analytic research concerning the effects of accounting information is burdened involves the static nature of the analysis. In most cases there is no learning or adaptive behavior allowed in the modelling. While simplifications are necessary for tractable analysis, this particular simplification causes considerable difficulty when one attempts to analyse practical standard-setting issues.

Before we turn to discussing research methodologies and results, we should note that researchers' approaches are highly colored by their own training and by what is generally accepted in various research disciplines. Drawing inferences for the notions developed in one discipline from research carried out in another is difficult because the phenomena of principal interest in one discipline are often largely ignored in the other. This paper's analysis provides an example of the difficulty. We wish to review accounting research and relate it to our agency-contracting structure, and included in that research are numerous behavioral studies. The agency structure comes from economics and has an integrated foundation in the economic theory of choice. That theory develops complex formulations of choice behavior and aggregate (e.g., market) effects from relatively few axioms and assumptions. Behavioral research is almost opposite on these dimensions. It is atomistic. Behavioral theories of choice are numerous and behavioral researchers put little priority on integrating them. It is non-axiomatic. Behavioral researchers tend to question and test the assumptions themselves. For example, some behavioral research in decision making does not take for granted that a decision precedes behavior [Cohen and March, 1974; Nisbett and Wilson, 1977; Weick, 1979]. Behavioral research is generally not oriented to the kinds of policy-making issues that are of concern in financial accounting. Those psychological researchers who have tried to study decision making have even been advised recently to leave that field to others and return to the study of more fundamental psychological processes such as memory, retention, internal cognitive organization, and perceptual processing [Einhorn and Hogarth, 1981].

Behavioral accounting research is still a young field: not much research has yet been done in most areas. Because its foundation disciplines (especially cognitive and social psychology) are jumbled, atomistic, and contradictory, and because research methods and priorities seem ill suited to the policy issues of interest to researchers whose background is in economics or finance, it is fair to say that many accounting academics see the connection between behavioral accounting research and important financial accounting issues as very tenuous indeed. For more complete reviews of behavioral accounting research than we provide, the reader is referred to Dyckman, Gibbins, and Swieringa [1978], AAA [1976], Gibbins [1977a], AAA [1977b], Libby and Lewis [1977], and Gibbins and Brennan [1981].

The following discussion reviews briefly what we have called "pre-response" research and will attempt, within the "five levels of response" framework, to look at existing accounting research and to point out potential areas of interest for future study. While we have argued that existing reporting practices may be understood in terms of information being used for contracting purposes, it does not follow that other uses of information are unimportant. Most research has assumed other uses of information. e.g., reduction in uncertainty regarding future events, provision of a contractual basis for risk sharing, and retrospective rationalization (sense making). We shall thus be referring to research having different assumptions regarding the use of information.

(A) Pre-response Research

This category of research includes studies sharing an interest in the behavior of accounting information but differing in methodology, objectives and sophistication. Many can be viewed as providing a generalized understanding of accounting itself which is helpful to understanding accounting's contribution to the five levels of response we discuss later and which is similar to the "sense-making" use of information. For example, a study of the time series properties of accounting information might provide evidence that would assist a group in reaching a consensus about an appropriate collective stance and thus indirectly be relevant to group-level response (2). But it may also affect individuals' responses (level (1)) and firms' responses (level (4)). Indeed, causality is likely to be the other way around. The properties of accounting numbers are a result of responses at all levels and therefore an *understanding* of those properties cannot, in our view, be divorced from an understanding of the response levels and the economic forces behind those responses. However, accounting does produce numbers whose *descriptive* or *deduced* properties can be presented without explicit reference to such economic forces, and we do not quarrel with the many researchers who have felt that setting out such properties will contribute to, or provide data for, more complete analysis.

The research relevant to this category falls into five groups: general accounting measurement research, logical and simulation analyses of alternative accounting methods, communication-theory investigations of the quality of accounting signals, attempts to define accounting concepts empirically, and empirical studies of how accounting numbers behave over time.

General accounting measurement research was most popular from the early sixties to the mid-seventies, under the impetus of Ijiri [1967, 1975], Mock [1976], Mattessich [1964, 1972], Sterling [1970], Vickery [1970], and many others. These writings were associated with an increasing concern about logical and empirical support for accounting's way of representing underlying phenomena and the apparent intrinsic meaningfulness of accounting numbers. That concern is reflected in quite recent attempts to clarify accounting's conceptual foundations [FASB, 1980a; *Corporate Reporting*, 1980]. Spirited debates were plentiful, and everyone became more aware of the varying assumptions that may underlie accounting numbers, of concepts such as reliability, objectivity, and bias, and of the necessity for theory construction and verification in accounting.

Logical and simulation analyses of alternative accounting methods have also been plentiful, for example the AICPA's recent study of four ways to account for changing prices [AICPA, 1979]. Such analyses can suggest general cost-benefit evaluations, particularly if the costs to prepare accounting numbers under various methods appear to differ more than do the resulting numbers.

Communication-theory investigations enjoyed a brief flurry of popularity in the early seventies (e.g. Nakano [1972]). Dyckman, Gibbins, and Swieringa [1978] reported several studies on entropy (loss of information through aggregation), but such research has not continued in financial accounting, probably because researchers have in recent years been less inclined to try to separate *how* accounting information is communicated from *what* is communicated. Recent research, mostly behavioral, on communication effectiveness is concerned with individuals' responses and is therefore included under the first response level below.

Attempts to define accounting concepts empirically have arisen from measurement and communication concerns and from accounting researchers' observation of how other disciplines deal with the definition of empirically elusive concepts such as intelligence, test fairness, judicial fairness, and so on. For example, Ashton [1977] suggested defining objectivity by using a multi-rule, multi-measure consensus approach borrowed from psychometrics. These efforts are still rudimentary and are likely to be elaborated through the study of individual or group responses [Belkaoui, 1980].

One other area of research in financial accounting that has received considerable attention is modelling the behavior of accounting numbers, particularly earnings, across time. Called time series analysis, this sort of research is not new but has achieved a new popularity in the past decade with the application of new statistical techniques.

Time series researchers have concerned themselves primarily with two approaches. First, they have been interested in evidence of intentional income smoothing on the part of managers. While some smoothing is an inherent part of accrual accounting, many researchers have maintained that additional smoothing is inappropriate and that it fools or otherwise harms investors. The second area of interest has been the prediction of future earnings numbers. If one can describe how accounting earnings behave over time, one may be able to make superior predictions about future earnings.

Justifying in a rigorous way the interest in the patterns of accounting numbers over time has proved difficult. The following arguments have been advanced to provide some rationale for the curiosity about time series relationships [Chope, 1980]. Beginning with the primitive issues of wealth and consumption, investors may be assumed to be interested in future cash flows of the firm and in information concerning those flows. The interesting characteristics of those cash flows include both the expected amounts and the variability around those expectations. Knowledge of the relationship between accounting earnings and the actual cash flows or other economic events, combined with an understanding of the process followed by the accounting earnings, would provide information useful to investors.

The research in modelling the time series behavior of accounting numbers has examined annual and quarterly earnings, portfolios of firms and individual firms, and various earnings measures. The results are neither strong nor consistent. The only general conclusions which appear warranted at present are that no universal model of earnings for all firms has so far been found, and that individual firm models do not appear to be consistently superior to very general naive models, e.g., income this year is the best estimate of income next year. Chope [1980] provides a good review of the time series work.

(B) Levels of Response to Accounting Information

1. Individual-level response
Most existing research on individual responses uses behavioral methods. However, some of the research into the problems of agency relationships may be considered as directed at the individual level in the sense of predicting the response of the individual agent to particular contractual forms [Harris and Raviv, 1979; Holmstrom, 1979; Shavell, 1979].

Several research methods are common in behavioral studies of this level: controlled experiments (usually using the approaches and theoretical concepts of social or cognitive psychology), detailed tracking of individuals' apparent decision processes, interviews, and questionnaire surveys. In few topics have there been enough studies to enable an empirically sound understanding of individuals' response to accounting information to emerge. Research approaches have been fragmentary; most studies do not build on other accounting studies but instead draw on research disciplines beyond accounting, and few of these are followed up in accounting beyond the initial study or two.

The agency framework we have outlined in this paper requires a fairly rich characterization of the economic forces and people in accounting settings. Under what circumstances would study of individuals' responses be of interest given this framework? There seem to be three possibilities:

(1) findings at the individual level may translate to the aggregate market levels contemplated by our earlier arguments; or

(2) certain individuals may be so important that their responses noticeably affect the aggregate; or

(3) understanding individual responses may contribute to a general descriptive understanding of accounting (much as was mentioned regarding accounting measurement research earlier).

At the present state of knowledge and research, the first two possiblities have to be dismissed. As we have already mentioned, and as have been pointed out by a variety of researchers (e.g., Milgram and Toch [1969, pp. 507-510], Beaver [1972], Schelling [1978]), aggregate behaviour is likely to have properties not fully deductible from individual actions. In addition, while we do not yet have a good descriptive understanding of how individual responses are aggregated into, for example, stock market behavior, it is obvious that many important influences exist to prevent straightforward extrapolation of individual-level findings. For example, suppose it were shown that investors have difficulty processing enough information to be anywhere near "rational" in their choices (see, for instance, Simon [1979]); this does not imply the market is not rational, for market analysts, securities commissions, and others clearly play a role in translating individual actions into market effects. Regarding the second possibility, it may be that certain individuals do directly affect the market but to our knowledge no accounting research has been done on such individuals.

The value of research to date on individuals' response to accounting information must therefore lie in its descriptive elaboration of likely accounting users and use settings. From that perspective, we have drawn the following conclusions from individual-level research (some of it conducted in associated disciplines such as behavioral decision theory as well as in accounting directly):

1. Research on presumed users such as analysts, investors, and financial managers has produced inconclusive but often negative findings [Dyckman, Gibbin, and Swieringa, 1978]. For every study claiming that investors do use financial statements in investment decisions (e.g., Most and Chang, [1979]), there is a study claiming they do not (e.g., Epstein [1975]). The various studies differ widely in the questions they ask and many are relatively unsophisticated surveys. Researchers have had some difficulty demonstrating that anyone actually uses financial statements in particular decisions (except bankers, about whom we will comment later). However, there is not much evidence of the actual process of investment decision making. Since accounting information does seem to affect aggregate behavior, perhaps the inconclusive results at the individual level suggest that behavioral accounting researchers have not yet asked the right questions. Our earlier comments suggest potential uses of financial accounting information that have not yet been addressed in individual-level research: monitoring of contract specifications, revisions to contracts or writing new ones, and general sense making and learning.

2. People's decision making in general is very poorly understood. Serious difficulties have been encountered in testing the predictive ability of decision models popular in economics (especially the subjective expected utility and Bayesian probability evaluation models). There is much debate about this research area, but the results have led several respected researchers [Simon, 1979; Hogarth, 1975; Kahneman and Tversky, 1979; Shafer, 1978] to claim that those decision models are invalid as positive theories of individual decision making. Attempts are still being made to connect the economic models and behavioral findings [Mock and Vasarhelyi, 1978; Hilton, 1980; Einhorn and Hogarth, 1981], but the prognosis for successful connections is not strong.

3. Out of the attempts to model people's decision behavior have arisen three robust and general findings. First, people, even experts, have little awareness of their own cognitive processes [Lichtenstein and Fischoff, 1977; Nisbett and Wilson, 1977; Gray, 1979]. This finding suggests that survey results, even if adjusted for all their other problems of incomplete responses, untruthfulness, misunderstandings, etc., will be poor indicators of people's real decision processes or information preferences. Second, simple statistical models tend to provide better predictions of people's decisions than do complex ones, and than do the people themselves [Meehl, 1954; Slovic, Fischoff, and Lichtenstein, 1977, p. 12; Ogilvie and Schmitt, 1979; Abdel-khalik and El-Sheshai, 1980], but see, for example, Libby [1976] and Libby and Blashfield [1978] for contrary findings. The models' superior performance is an empirically strong finding [Dawes, 1979], though the research settings may be unfamiliar or confusing enough to bias the results in favor of the statistical models. Third, people have difficulty coping with their information load, and evidence is accumulating that when faced with complex, repetitive, or unfamiliar decision-making tasks, people use various simplifications (e.g., rules of thumb or "heuristics"), refuse to recognize some aspects of the setting or even ignore changing information. One behavior of the latter sort that has received considerable attention in accounting research is the "functional fixation hypothesis": the notion that people will retain decision methods even if changing circumstances make those methods inappropriate. The hypothesis has received considerable support in individual-level accounting research [Ashton, 1976; Chang and Birnberg, 1977; Abdel-khalik and Keller, 1979; Swieringa, Dyckman and Hoskin, 1979].

4. There seems to be little enthusiasm among presumed users of financial statements for any substantive changes in accounting. Such improvements in communication as confidence interval financial statements do not appear useful to decision makers [Birnberg and Slevin, 1976; Keys, 1978; Collins and Yeakel, 1979] and while statements in the form of human faces [Jensen, 1976; Moriarity, 1979] may seem intriguing, there appears to be no demand for them. Several studies have reported a lack of interest in alternatives to historical cost financial statements that would adjust for inflation [Dyckman, Gibbins, and Swieringa, 1978; Eyes and Tabb, 1978; Benston and Krasney, 1978] or provide social or human resources information [Flamholtz and Cook, 1978; Buzby and Falk, 1979]. Accounting information is used together with other information, so the value (and costs) of changes in accounting must be measured against other sources of information the decision maker may already have. Most accounting use settings are not well enough specified yet to permit an adequate marginal usefulness analysis or to give the decision maker a realistic information choice.

2. Group-level response

This intermediate level has not been studied extensively and results are sparse. Positive economics studies have tried to analyse the reactions of specific interest groups to proposed accounting changes. (Watts and Zimmerman [1978] examined the proposed adjustment for general price-level changes). Also, some economic research has been done concerning the institutional structure of government licensed professions [Leland, 1979]. Essentially, this research explores the economic demand for and the results of certain institutional structures. It is likely that a complete characterization of the effects of accounting policy choices must take into account the profession and its collective interests and influences. Some recent research in auditing takes this tack [Simunic, 1980; Dopuch and Simunic, 1980]. While research at this level is only beginning to be integrated into the accounting literature, it appears to have promise, particularly when considered in conjunction with the reactions of firms to policies and to individual and group actions. For example, the responses of interest groups such as accounting practictioners to a policy choice, such as foreign currency translation, may very well influence the behavior of firms in regard to their hedging and financing activites in foreign currencies.

Behavioral studies bearing directly on group responses have been few, but two kinds of studies appear indirectly relevant: surveys comparing apparent preferences of various groups with respect to accounting issues, and studies of the information use of particular groups of users.

Surveys of groups' preferences were plentiful ten years ago but are rare now. Dyckman, Gibbins, and Swieringa [1978, p. 82 ff.] review a number of reasons for questioning the usefulness of many accounting surveys; perhaps also higher standards for publication in academic and professional journals are responsible for the decline. A fairly typical comparative result is that reported from an extensive international survey by Chang and Most [1979]: financial analysts were more interested in annual financial accounting reports than were institutional investors, who in turn were more interested than individual investors. Comparative surveys usually seem to confirm rather than challenge one's expectations of groups' responses. If that is the case, such surveys may play a role similar to that of authoritative pronouncements: providing evidence on which a group consensus may be built [Schelling, 1971].

Bankers are the principal user group whose actual information use has been studied. Bankers and loan officers' decision-making processes have been modelled and analysed in many studies, usually experimental ones [Kennedy, 1975; Libby, 1975, 1979; Eyes and Tabb, 1978; Estes and Reimer, 1977; Abdel-khalik and El-Sheshai, 1980; Casey, 1980; Zimmer, 1980]. Because the studies have varied substantially in their tasks and information sets, no particular picture of bankers' responses as a group has emerged, except that they are sensitive to information related to credit risk and seem to use relatively few pieces of information in making judgments.

3. Aggregate market response level

Much of both analytical and empirical research on accounting information in the financial economics literature is directed at the level of aggregate market response. While these responses would be reflected in the prices of all goods and services, the finance and accounting research in this area has focused on security prices, implicitly assuming that the prices of a firm's securities reflect the effects on the firm of changes in prices of other goods and services.

Empirical research over the past fifteen years has shown that securities markets do not respond blindly to accounting numbers or attend only to accounting information. Apparently accounting is but one of numerous information sources utilized by investors in financial markets. This body of empirical research was spawned by advances in theories from finance and economics. These theories are "partial equilibrium" theories, specifically portfolio[16] and asset pricing theories.[17] They form the theoretical basis for considerable research in accounting and finance. In this research, accounting information is assumed to be used primarily to reduce uncertainty about the future. While in a few cases accounting information is used as a basis for efficient risk sharing, there is almost no empirical research that considers the moral hazard issue, i.e., the use of information as a contractual incentive. The motivation for the existing market research in accounting will be briefly developed in the following paragraphs.

At a primitive level, individuals are concerned with their consumption and welfare. These concerns are closely related to wealth and changes in wealth. For investors in firms (security holders), wealth is partially determined by the value of their holdings or claims on the firm. Therefore, individuals may be assumed to be concerned with those values and desire information reflecting those values and changes thereto. Since individuals are concerned about their wealth and consumption, they are concerned with future cash flows to themselves. In turn, since the firm may be viewed as a cash conduit, the investors are concerned with the future cash flows into and out of the firm. Under uncertainty the amounts of future cash flows are variable and investors are assumed to be interested in not only the expected cash flow (average) but also the riskiness (variability and distribution) of the cash flows.

Finally, following portfolio theory,[18] rational investors would diversify in so far as this would reduce the total variability of their cash flows. Under the above-stated assumptions, portfolio theory indicates investors will be concerned not with the riskiness of cash flows from a single firm but with the effect that the risky flow from each firm has on the variance of a diversified (market) portfolio.

Under these assumptions, accounting policy decisions might be expected to affect one or more of the following factors in the economy (see Foster [1980]):

1. The expected cash flows of individual firms may be altered. This would occur, for example, if the accounting policy causes the firm's managers to change the production or investment activites of the firm. Assertions of this reaction have been made in regard to hedging activites of firms under alternative foreign currency translation policies.
2. The covariance (comovement) of the cash flows of individual firms and the market may be altered. An accounting policy that increased debtholder wealth at the expense of shareholders could make highly leveraged firms more "risky" relative to the market.
3. The risk and return relationship for the entire market may be changed. Only a policy choice with substantial and pervasive effects on the economy would be likely to have such an impact. While major political changes could, it is difficult to think of accounting policy decisions that would have this effect.
4. Finally, the information sources used by market participants (investors, creditors, etc.) may be affected. Certain policy changes may very well make accounting information more or less available, timely, or costly, relative to alternative sources. Such an effect certainly has importance to accounting.

Virtually no research in accounting has attempted to address the latter two effects. They are generally ignored or more charitably, assumed to be unaffected by whatever phenomena are under examination. Most empirical work in accounting assumes that the effect of the item under study is on the expected cash flows of a firm, i.e., effect (1) above. This level has received the most attention because of the existence of partial equilibrium theories (e.g., the two-parameter pricing model)[19] that specify what the expected return on a security would have been had nothing altered the equilibrium. Given some event which is hypothesized to change the expected return, researchers have compared the actual security returns to the returns indicated by the model and attempted to draw some conclusions as to whether the event being examined (an accounting change, for example) had any effect. While these studies have been subject to criticism on both theoretical and methodological bases, they have consistently concluded that securities markets are not systematically fooled or misled by accounting practices or alternative treatments. Beaver and Dukes [1973], for example, found that the market, in pricing firms' securites, appears to adjust for the use of alternative depreciation methods.

Many different research studies have been undertaken to test associations between accounting information and market prices. In an early study, Ball and Brown [1968] found that "unexpected" increases (decreases) in reported annual earnings were associated with above average increases (decreases) in the market prices of securities. This appears to support contentions of information content in accounting earnings reports. However, the study also found that the annual accounting report was not "timely" in that the market price changes *preceded* it. Subsequent research has examined accounting-market associations for a wide variety of announcements and events including quarterly earnings announcements, dividend announcements, earnings forecasts, accounting changes, etc. Generally, the results have been consistent with the hypothesis that accounting reports do contain information similar to that used by market participants in pricing securities, but that the investors apparently have other sources as well, since market reactions tend to precede accounting reports. Excellent reviews of this research may be found in Foster [1978] and Dyckman, Downs, and Magee [1975] and will not be attempted here.

No equilibrium theory of the behavior of the covariance of firm and market cash flows (the risk of the firm in a portfolio) equivalent to the two-parameter model exists; and therefore, in the smaller group of studies addressing the effects of accounting policies on risk, i.e., effect (2) above, some assumptions are always made regarding what the risk would have been in the absense of the phenomena under study. Not only are there fewer of these studies, but the results are less strong and less consistent perhaps because we lack theories connecting accounting and market risk/return relationships. In one recent empirical study, which does find some connection, Bowman [1980] hypothesized that accounting risk measures that consider long-term leases as equivalent to debt would be more highly correlated with market risk than would accounting risk measures ignoring leases. His results support this intuitively appealing hypothesis. Foster [1978] also reviews this research.

We should note at this point the severe narrowing of scope we can observe when examining existing research at the level of aggregate market responses. Beginning with the fundamental problem of selecting among alternative accounting policies, we have described the inability of research to answer the social choice question of what should be the desired outcomes. Once restricted to positive research we see that the studies generally examine the potential responses at only one level. Finally, even when focusing on market reactions we see that of at least four potential effects, studies have ignored two (market changes and information changes) almost completely. And when the other two (changes in return and changes in risk) are examined, they are generally examined separately with the one not under examination assumed not to change.

In light of the impossibility, noted previously, of drawing policy implications from empirical research, it is of interest to survey the literature to observe what claims have been made by accounting researchers regarding the implications of their studies. Using the bibliographies of Foster [1978] and a review of major accounting journals for more recent works, we conducted a fairly broad but certainly not exhaustive survey of empirical financial accounting research for the past twelve to fifteen years. This survey resulted in the striking, but not wholly unexpected, conclusion that empirical researchers make relatively few claims for their work. The most common claims were that the study tested the "information content" of some event or announcement or that associations were detected between market and accounting numbers. For example, Patell [1976] claimed to "test the hypothesized information content of management forecasts" and found a statistically significant price change during the week of the forecast. Also, a significant number of studies claimed to provide evidence on the relative predictive ability of various accounting and non-accounting models. For example, Beaver [1968], Altman [1968] and Deakin [1972] used statistical techniques and accounting numbers and ratios to predict business failure. In addition, studies such as Beaver, Kettler, and Scholes [1970] and Eskew [1979] claimed to show that accounting risk measures may be used to form predictions of future market risk measures which are superior to predictions using only market data. Finally, many of the studies appear to be concerned with providing guidance for future empirical researchers on various technical issues including statistical properties and sample selection biases. For example Gonedes [1973] examined the statistical properties of accounting numbers with one stated purpose being the improvement of research on the predictive ability of accounting numbers.

It was rare to find overt normative claims for empirical findings. This indicates a broad recognition of the limitations of empirical research in this regard. However, a case could also be made (and has been, Ohlson [1980]) that the generally modest claims for the empirical financial accounting research may indicate that a good deal of what has been done is difficult to justify on any basis broader than simply describing observed associations in the economic environment. The difficulty is, of course, to justify why we should care about these associations. That is, what can we learn of importance to accounting policy makers from a knowledge of market reactions to accounting disclosures?

We have previously discussed the limitations inherent in this type of research, e.g., the focus on one level of response while assuming other levels are unaffected. Given these limitations, so-called market research has a definite role in *predicting and verifying the consequences* of various accounting methods and disclosures. The focus on consequences is, of course, the appropriate role for positive research. The legitimate criticisms of the market-effects research are not, therefore, concerned with whether the analysis of economic consequences is important. That is accepted. The criticisms are, rather, concerned with whether the research methodologies used focus on the appropriate consequences and whether empirical measures of these consequences really capture the actual effects. For example, knowledge of wealth transfer effects of an accounting change is important, but one may still question whether security price changes adequately measure the impact on wealth and further, whether the statistical methodologies used really isolate the security price effect. Recent work by Ohlson [1979, 1980] and Patell [1979] indicates that given certain rather technical conditions and assumptions, the measures of association and wealth effects that have been used are appropriate in that these measures reflect the value of information (accounting) either to individuals or to society. The private and social values of alternative disclosures or methods are the very sort of consequences at which this research has been aimed. In addition, much attention has been given recently to the design of empirical research so that experiments will actually capture the intended effect [Foster, 1980].

While research on market effects is still subject to criticism and while a portion of this research has been poorly executed or poorly justified, this type of research has dramatically expanded and changed the way accounting information is viewed in the investment and academic communities [Beaver, 1981]. Our earlier assertions that accounting practice has evolved only slowly should not obscure this changed outlook nor the great increase in general disclosure (e.g., footnotes) which has characterized financial reporting over the past fifteen years.

Parenthetically, it is interesting to note the relationship between the construction of positive theories (analytical research) and the testing of these theories (empirical research). Advances in equilibrium models in financial economics (e.g., the portfolio theory and two-parameter pricing model referred to earlier) precipitated a substantial burst in accounting research directed at examining associations between accounting numbers and market prices. Some of the issues addressed and claims made for this research went well beyond the existing theoretical base. More recently, theoretical developments in the economics of information have provided additional support for some of the empirical research completed earlier. This teeter-totter relationship appears to us to be a healthy phenomenon so long as empirical work is not too far removed from a theoretical basis, or theory development does not completely ignore the empirical observations gathered in the "real world."

The research surveyed in this discussion of market-level responses has assumed that accounting information is used for reducing future uncertainty or for risk sharing. Very little has been done to examine the effects of accounting information when it is used as a basis for contracting. Such research is likely to be difficult since it must examine who is helped and who is hurt by certain alterations in information. Further, specifying these wealth effects will require very general models of equilibrium in which information system choice is part of (endogenous to) the model. Atkinson and Feltham [1981] provide a step in this direction. They are able to specify the types of contracts that will be observed under various assumptions about the available information.

Another important step will be to broaden the research focus from a single level of response to the interaction of the several levels. While most research has attempted to identify responses at only one of the five levels, Kanodia [1980] provides a notable exception. He shows that the information available to shareholders will affect the firm-level responses and different equilibria will result from different information sets. This is an important result. Most of the studies on the market effects of accounting information have assumed that firms' production policies are constant. Upon finding that markets appear to reflect new information rapidly, some researchers have asserted that the only use of accounting information is in helping to predict future risk and return parameters. But, when it is recognized that future risk and return depend, through firms' responses, on the information system, the circularity of the reasoning and the weakness of focusing on a single response level become apparent. Kanodia's work is a first step toward generally integrating the responses at various levels into our analysis of informational effects.

4. Firm actions response level

The influences of accounting policies upon the actions of firms and their managers, and their subsequent effects on individuals and groups, is possibly one of the most interesting and promising areas of research. As was mentioned previously, much existing research ignores this level, although it has received considerable attention recently.

One way to study the responses of firms is to focus on the incentives of the managers and to analyse the effects of accounting information on those incentives. This is one aspect of the agency theory approach. Agency theory, of course, can address broader issues than simply owner/manager interactions. In a general sense agency theory is concerned with contracting and any contractual relationship can be analysed, at least conceptually, in agency terms. For accounting we have argued that one use of accounting information is in providing a basis for contracting among the firm, its managers, creditors, and owners. Some elements of this informational role, which is related to the stewardship concept, have been used in defense of historical cost based accounting for many years [Ijiri, 1971]. Since the mid 1970s this agency emphasis has been generalized and its supporting theory extended. A growing body of literature uses this framework in developing a "positive theory" of accounting [Zimmerman, 1977; Watts and Zimmerman, 1978, 1979]. This work has attempted to explain existing accounting alternatives and the development of accounting rules in terms of political interactions that reflect the economic interests of various groups. Our tentative hypotheses in the early parts of this paper are a generalization and an extension of these ideas. While in developing the agency-related positive hypotheses these authors cite some casual evidence in support of their theory (as we have), rigorous empirical tests of hypotheses running directly from this agency perspective are very sparse. To date the studies known to us have focused on bond covenants and loan agreements [Holthausen, 1979; Leftwich, 1979; Mikkelson, 1979; Thornton, 1980]. Essentially, these studies have hypothesized that bond covenants provide some measure of control by creditors (principals) over the actions of management (agents). The tests have attempted to detect whether the presence of such covenants results in different firm reactions or market reactions than would result in the absence of the covenants. The results of the empirical studies to date have not consistently supported the agency hypothesis. The problem may well be that the tests so far devised have not been able to separate the effects of the covenants from other effects. This is a pervasive problem in empirical research. It is extremely difficult to be certain that a market or firm reaction is caused by event X when one cannot hold all other influences constant. Various empirical methodologies have been developed to reduce the problem, but they cannot eliminate it.

A recent research approach in economics that appears to have potential for addressing some accounting issues concerns firms' signalling certain information to outsiders through voluntary actions. That is, a firm may take an action (for example, a stock repurchase [Vermaelen, 1981]) that is costly to the managers in order to signal that their estimates of future prospects are above average. Managers whose expectations are less optimistic would be unwilling to bear the cost of the (false) signal. Therefore, the fact that the signal is costly and that it is more costly to signal falsely than truthfully reduces the moral hazard of "false advertising." In finance the potential role of signalling in such areas as capital structure [Ross, 1977] and dividend policy [Bhattacharya, 1979] have been explored.

Firms may choose from among several alternative accounting methods for inventories, depreciation, installment sales, franchising, etc. In many of these cases the choice of method will have some fairly predictable effects on the pattern of earnings and other accounting numbers. For example, the full cost method of accounting for petroleum exploration costs is usually assumed to smooth income. Since firms select from amoung the various generally accepted methods and one can hypothesize costs associated with unexpected reductions in reported income or liquidity, the actual choices of a firm may indeed serve as signals reflecting management's outlook or plans for the future. While some recent accounting research has recognized the importance of firms' ability to select among accounting methods for such items as inventory valuation [Ricks, 1980] and petroleum exploration costs [Collins, Rozeff and Dhaliwal, 1980], no attention has yet been given to the possibility that the choice of accounting methods may be an intentional signal. One possible policy implication which follows from the signalling hypothesis is that, if accounting method choices are signals, then reducing the available alternatives (e.g., eliminating full costing for oil exploration) may, among other effects, reduce the information flowing from the firm to outsiders.

Much ferment currently exists in behavioral theories about organizations' decision-making activities. New concepts with strange names are gaining considerable support, such as the "organizational failures framework" [Williamson, 1975], the "garbage can model" and "organized anarchy" [Cohen and March, 1974; March and Olsen, 1976]. An awareness is growing that organizations' decisions are often coincidental (i.e., capitalizing on opportunities as they turn up), probably not explicitly goal-directed or oriented to clear means-ends relationships, and generally subtle. This awareness has cast into doubt many of the traditional ideas of purposive organizational planning, directing, and acting.

There has been little connection between financial accounting research and organization theory (though managers have appeared often enough among groups surveyed, interviewed, and experimented upon), and therefore the ferment in organization theory has had no effect on the research we have reviewed.

Occasional glimmers appear, such as the "information inductance" notion of information affecting managerial behavior [Prakash and Rappaport, 1977] or the finding by Shank, Dillard, and Murdock [1980] that in spite of an apparent lack of stock market reaction to the FASB's Statement of Financial Accounting Standards No. 8 [FASB, 1975] on foreign currency translation, financial managers undertook costly and risky actions in order to preserve "desired" relationships in accounting numbers.

Various "income-smoothing" studies in the mid-seventies included assertions about corporate responses to accounting numbers [Moore, 1973; Barnea, Ronen, and Sadan, 1976; Gibbins, 1977b]. Though these could have been followed up with organization-level behavioral studies, they have not been.

In summary, firm-level responses to accounting are receiving increasing attention. Certainly more work is needed, but we are beginning, at least, to recognize that firm responses to accounting information and to investor activities are an integral element of the overall impact of accounting information on society.

5. Second and higher order response levels

Responses at this level would be of an interactive nature where firms respond to actions by individuals, groups, and the market and then the other levels respond in turn to the firms' actions. Most economic models of equilibrium do not consider this interaction since they describe an equilibrium that has been reached rather than explaining how it is achieved. None the less, while little attention has been given to this level, the actual dynamics by which equilibria are reached could well be important in accounting policy choices. For example, an equilibrium could be effecient in the sense of reflecting all available information in prices, but the process of reaching that equilibrium could have involved unequal access to information which results in some individuals being able to improve their position at the expense of others. Research which addresses this issue of *equity* and *efficiency* in reaching an equilibrium would possibly reveal consequences in which policy makers would be interested. This is one of the areas where behavioral research methods may be joined with economic modelling to provide a richer understanding. Behavioral research is entirely consistent with this view of a highly interactive organizational and information use setting. However, the factors that influence how accounting information is used are likely to interact so substantially that a general behavioral theory of financial accounting will remain elusive.

SUMMARY AND FUTURE DIRECTIONS

We began this paper with some observations about the anomalous nature of the relationship between current accounting theory and practice and we suggested that an explanation of some apparent contradictions was essential to an informed understanding of accounting research. We then provided a tentative explanation of these phenomena, which was based on an extension of the classical entity view of accounting. More specifically, we distinguished among the predictive, contractual, and retrospective uses of information, and conjectured that the anomalies rested upon the widespread presumption that the primary use of accounting information was to reduce uncertainty with respect to future events.

In contrast, we have hypothesized that the principal role of accounting information is contractual, and that its focus is on *past* events. We provided a detailed explanation of the nature of the market demand for contractual information, and of the kinds of properties it must possess. The most fundamental of these properties was that of objectivity, defined in terms of homogeneity of beliefs with respect to the structure of the information system. This property, derived from economic models, was observed to be virtually synonymous with the conventional accounting view of objectivity, and with the basic requirements of scientific experimentation. The other basic property was adequate disclosure, defined as the degree of disclosure beyond which the form of financial contracts would remain unchanged. Thus, accounting (we supposed) primarily provides information about past events, and only incidentally about future events.

Building on our agency-contracting foundation, we have shown how this past-oriented view of accounting information seems completely consistent with the observed preferences of accounting standard setters, and with the conventional process of cost and revenue matching, as well as providing a basis for explaining the historical resistance by practitioners to innovative current value methods of accounting. Moreover, the contractual view of accounting information seems to provide a basis for deducing from the underlying economic phenomena postulates besides objectivity, such as verifiability, freedom from bias, money exchange, and continuity.

Our review and analysis of existing accounting research lead us to the conclusion that much of this work assumes the use of accounting information to be something other than the contractual role, which has primacy in our framework. In capital market research the role of information is assumed to lie in improving predictions concerning future returns and risks. Critics have long noted that historical cost-based accounting information appears to be singularly unsuited to this predictive role. Indeed, some concepts that characterize conventional historical cost accounting may, in fact, reduce predictive ability (e.g. conservatism, cost basis, transactions basis, objectivity, stable dollar basis).

Over the past fifteen years, there has been increased emphasis on disclosure, particularly footnote and parenthetical disclosure, but the basic format of financial statements has been little changed. Beaver [1973] maintains that disclosure has a pre-emptive role in preventing abnormal returns to those with superior access to information. Further, he argues that for any item of information, opponents of disclosure must justify why it should not be reported rather than advocates of disclosure justifying reporting it. In fact the "revolution" in financial reporting referred to by Beaver [1981] has been in this supplementary disclosure area.

Our definition of "adequate disclosure" in Section III states that disclosure is adequate when increased disclosure will not lead to different contracts. (Of course, this neglects costs of disclosure which in practice may suggest acceptance of less efficient contracts.) The disclosure revolution to which we referred above results from concern with prediction as well as contracting. Therefore, we might well expect to observe supplemental disclosure that exceeds what is necessary for efficient contracting. If the disclosure were aimed at prediction it need not necessarily possess the characteristics that we argued would be required for a contracting information system. Increased demand for this type of supplemental information may, in fact, be interpreted as evidence of the predictive uses of accounting information while retaining objective information for efficient contracting.

In our paper, we constructed a taxonomy of research methodology based on the distinctions between theoretical and empirical research, and between normative and positive hypotheses. We further classified the research studies on the basis of their domain of interest into the five levels of individual, group, market, firm, and feedback (interaction) response and a sixth pre-response level. In view of the anomaly originally observed, it is scarcely surprising that the survey of research in these categories finds that the research almost exclusively assumes the predictive and retrospective forms of information. If the *practice* of accounting is driven by contractual forces, we can expect to observe these contradictions between theory and practice. The accounting profession must respond to market demands, which may be translated into political pressures. And, if these market demands are ignored or misinterpreted by researchers, a conflict between their proposals and the choices of the profession becomes inevitable.

Of course, there is also another side to the coin. If researchers presume that the market demand is for predictive accounting information, when in fact it is for contractual information, they are likely to have difficulties in explaining the results of market tests based on predictive hypotheses. This, in fact, appears to be the case. As we have observed, the claims of researchers in this area are generally modest, and their methodology limited to associative tests. There is a tendency to identify an apparent association between, say, abnormal returns and the choice of an accounting method, and then to provide conjectural explanations of the observed association. Presumably, this approach is due to the absence of a theory of market information on which to base viable hypotheses.

If our conjectures are correct, they suggest that the entire range of market research that utilizes predictive power as a primary criterion of preference for accounting rules is misdirected. If we accept the primacy of contractual forces, it is not the capability to predict but the capability for being predicted which is critical. Indirectly, then, we can interpret Ball and Brown [1968] and the related studies cited earlier as providing evidence of the contractual efficacy of accounting information. These results have consistently shown the ability of the market to predict earnings effectively in advance of the earnings announcement. This phenomenon may be easily be explained by the availability of independent non-accounting market sources of information about individual firms and their economic environment. To the extent that this information is public knowledge, and the accounting system objective, we would expect to observe a uniform prediction of the accounting numbers. If accounting information did not possess the desirable contractual properties, we would expect more variability in the predictability of earnings than seems to be the case. Paradoxically, if accounting earnings were focused entirely on the future, and were based, for example, on management predictions of the change in the present worth of estimated future cash flows, the ability of the market to predict earnings would undoubtedly decline.

The preceding discussion suggests that some shifts in research emphasis are desirable if accounting research and practice are to enjoy a more symbiotic relationship than seems to have been the case in the past. We should put more emphasis on contractual information uses, and, in particular, on the criteria of predictability and disclosure. What does this imply with respect to the kinds of research that seem worth while using the ideas developed in this paper? At the individual and group levels, we need a richer theoretical model, which will help us to predict better the properties of (efficient) contracts in a wider variety of settings than is now the case. Fortunately, there is a good deal of interest among economists and accountants in this class of problem, and it seems likely that research will proceed in this direction.

We also need to incorporate the notions of contractual information and moral hazard into the structure of general equilibrium models in order to get better insights into the nature of the wealth transfer effects which might result from the choice of specific information rules. At the present time, our knowledge in this area is limited to the risk-sharing and beliefs-sharing aspects of contractual information: the incentive component has not been studied in any general equilibrium setting. On the other hand, there are partial equilibrium models that comprehend the problems of moral hazard, of which Atkinson and Feltham [1981] is one of the very few examples. As the construction of general equilibrium models including moral hazard as well as the other contractual uses of information is likely to prove extremely difficult, the expansion of analysis using partial equilibrium methods seems necessary.

We pointed out earlier that there is a temptation for the theoretical economics researcher to isolate individuals or groups from the economic phenomenon they help to determine. Recently, a method of economic analysis generally referred to as *rational expectations equilibrium analysis*, has been utilized to avoid such isolation. Its applications are now much broader than investment and include, for example, analysis of the impact of monetary policy on inflation. This analysis has some features in common with the popular "cognitive balance" theories in social psychology and attitude research.

Roughly, the key difference in this economic approach as compared to previous ones lies in the view of the individual as a rational information processor, whose beliefs must depend on all information available to him through the market, including the information conveyed by market prices. In this view, the ultimate market equilibrium will exist only when individual beliefs are consistent with that equilibrium, when each is acting to maximize his own self-interest. The available information plays a key role in reaching such an equilibrium. At the time of writing, Kanodia [1980] is the sole example of research in this area that is specifically directed at the problems of accounting. Much more work is needed in the future if we are to overcome the present inability to analyse the reciprocal impact of economic phenomena exemplified by our "five levels" analysis.

All of the above fall under the general heading of *positive theoretical* research, designed to provide a convincing basis for positive hypotheses with repect to the properties of accounting information. Of course, this has implications too for the empirical research that might be used to test hypotheses arising from this analysis. Most of the preceding arguments were based on economic concepts that are difficult to define and use empirically, such as contractual efficiency, equilibrium, rationality, and beliefs congruence. While some components (e.g., rationality) are not as important positively as they are normatively, and so may not matter much in empirical research to test our hypotheses, others (e.g., efficiency) require credible empirical analogues if any testing of the overall theory is to be conducted. (We believe tests of individual components will not be as useful as overall tests, if the empirical measurement problem can be solved.)

We believe that behavioral and market-based research aimed at contracting uses of accounting information will be useful in developing empirical measures, and in providing insights to refine the positive hypotheses. However, the empirical task is great and it is not likely to be accomplished any more quickly than is the task of developing the theory we referred to above. In the meantime, we hope our ideas will generate further insights and will encourage researchers to take seriously the development of positive (and ultimately empirical) theory to explain how accounting actually *works* and how accounting standards themselves work. Such an approach may develop a theory of financial accounting, a theory of how people make use of information prepared under general rules set by "authoritative" bodies, how people act if the rules are not what they would have wished, and how the rules themselves evolve.

We have challenged some of the premises upon which much of the research on market reactions to accounting disclosure is based. That is, we have argued that the development of accounting practice is inconsistent with the use of accounting information primarily to predict the future. This challenge has implications for research aimed at predicting and detecting consequences of accounting changes. For example, under our framework, accounting changes may be as likely to affect debt values as equity values, and in the same direction or opposite directions depending on the effects on the costs which are being traded off, e.g., costs of moral hazard and costs of inefficient contracting.

Research on the consequences of accounting policies must take a much wider view of potential effects than simply looking at stock price changes. Similarly, changes in stock prices may be the result of more complex effects than simply changes in assessments of stable future return distributions, as is often assumed. Research concerning consequences of accounting policies is important. Policy makers will certainly wish to understand the potential effects of their decisions. What is at issue is whether the changes in security prices adequately capture those effects.

In summary, this paper develops a framework that we believe explains financial reporting practices remarkably well. In additon, our categorization of existing research by its assumptions concerning the use of information provides some insights into the reasons for the dichotomy between reporting practice and the associated financial accounting research. Our analysis leads to hypotheses reinterpreting past research as well as suggesting a different thrust and focus for new research. In essence, we argue that accounting researchers cannot ignore the market-determinded development of financial reporting practices. This is not to argue for the *status quo* in accounting policies, but for an improved understanding of the evolution of existing practices, which should provide a better basis for research and for choosing accounting principles to reach desired ends.

FOOTNOTES

[1] Such a committee was formed, but appears not to have produced any results. It was later disbanded and replaced by the Committee on Accounting Procedures in 1939. This was, in its turn, disbanded and replaced by the Accounting Principles Board in 1959, which was itself replaced by the Financial Accounting Standards Board in 1973.

[2] In fact, Paton [1922] contains the first attempt to formulate general principles of accounting. But it remained the only attempt until American Accounting Association (AAA) [1936], which leaned heavily on Paton's ideas.

[3] See, for example, Moonitz [1974] for a detailed historical analysis.

4   See Gilman [1939] for an excellent and comprehensive summary of the stewardship (or entity) and proprietorship concepts.

5   It may be argued that some of these proposals have since been accepted. For example, replacement cost is now a widely used and even required valuation basis. However, it is still provided as *supplementary* information, and has not displaced historical cost as the primary basis for financial statement values in most countries.

6   A risk neutral individual is one who is indifferent between all risks with the same expected value, regardless of their form. Risk, in this context, can be viewed as the dispersion around the expected value.

7   Perhaps the most spectacular recent example of moral hazard in insurance was that of the Liberian tanker that was allegedly scuttled off the African coast after the illegal sale of its cargo in South Africa. An insurance claim was filed for US $84 million, the full value of the ship and its cargo.

8   Risk resulting from moral hazard cannot be "diversified away" in the same way as firm-specific risk. Firm-specific risk can be eliminated by efficient diversification because the actual outcomes are simply random drawings from an assumed stable distribution of possible outcomes, and a large number of draws must move an investor's outcomes asymptotically to an average market result. However, if there is moral hazard, the outcome distribution may not be stable because outcomes are partly a result of unobservable behavior on the part of one of the economic actors, and therefore increasing the number of drawings from these non-stable distributions will not insure the investor against the risks of moral hazard. Only if the possibility of moral hazard is confined to a very small proportion of an investor's holdings can diversification help, and then only because as the number of holdings increases, the impact of any single security approaches zero.

9   Because of this, economists often use the term contingent commodities to emphasize the dependence of the eventual form of the commodity upon as yet unrealized contingencies.

10 Exchanges that are *not* ultimately consummated in money or money equivalents give a good deal of trouble to standard setters. Examples include the acquisition of subsidiary corporations in exchange for shares, and the compensation of managers by the issue of rights to purchase shares at fixed rates.

11 See Thornton [1980] for a more detailed discussion of specific kinds of bond covenants.

12 See Mattessich [1978] for an extensive discussion of these methodological distinctions and their implications (especially, Chapter 4).

13 We do not explicitly address the issue of insufficient information production in a social sense due to "free rider" problems. We do not consider this to be a major shortcoming in our analysis since the existing institutional and rule-making structures would allow the groups that would be benefited by additional information disclosure to lobby for this disclosure. That is, if the benefits resulting from new contracts were to exceed *all* the costs of the information necessary to form those contracts, it is likely that the benefited groups would bring this to the attention of the standard setters. At that point if the proposed movement were toward the Pareto surface, there would be no opposition and the change could easily be made. If the movement were along a Pareto surface, then we would be back to the familiar social choice problem previously discussed.

14 A *market equilibrium* is a theoretical construct used to describe an economic condition where all producers and consumers have adjusted to existing production technologies and uncontrollable conditions. In such a situation, and under competition, producers and consumers will compete for sales and purchases so that the market clears. This is the point of intersection of the supply and demand curves in a simple two-good economy diagram. Where all goods in the economy and all tastes of participants are considered this may be called a *general equilibrium*. However, in much economic analysis the general equilibrium is such a broad concept that, as was mentioned above, few useful implications can be drawn. In most cases *partial equilibrium* analysis is a useful narrowing of the concept. In a partial equilibrium analysis some factors are taken as fixed (exogenous) and the analysis investigates the effects of changes in the remaining (endogenous) factors. We will explore in detail later as an example the analysis of accounting policies in terms of their effect on investors while assuming the production decisions of the firms are unchanged.

15 Analytical research on the economics of information must inevitably trade realism for tractability. Typically, simplifications include, among others, assuming individuals in the economy are homogeneous in their beliefs and/or their access to the information, restricting the time horizon to a limited number of periods, and restricting the number of commodities considered. These assumptions are necessary to examine fundamental economic issues but obviously they are simplifications. The important question is, of course, how well do the theories predict in the real world? This is an empirical question and must be addressed by comparing the theories' predictions with actual outcomes.

16 Portfolio theory dates from the work of Markowitz [1952] and the extensions and simplifications of Sharpe [1963]. Essentially, the important point is that the risk and return relationship that is of interest to investors is not the risk and return for an individual security but rather that of a grouping or portfolio of securities. The impact on finance and accounting is that under portfolio theory, security analysis would be directed at determining the effect of an individual security upon a portfolio rather than its risk and return merits alone.

17 The most important asset-pricing (valuation) theory has been the two-parameter pricing model (also called the capital asset-pricing model) of Sharpe [1964], Lintner [1965] and Mossin [1966]. The model is a statement about security pricing in a world with informed, rational, and risk averse investors. All portfolios may be characterized by two parameters, their risk and their return. Under certain assumptions the risk can be

completely captured by the variance of the return. For an individual security only its contribution to the portfolio risk and return is important. The two-parameter model is an extension of portfolio theory in that it focuses on the securities market as a whole rather than on a single investor. The model has provided the equilibrium value against which many kinds of market reactions to accounting numbers or events have been compared.

[18] See note 16.
[19] See note 17.

REFERENCES

AAA (American Accounting Association), "A Tentative Statement of Accounting Principles Underlying Corporate Financial Statements," *The Accounting Review* (June 1936).

_____, "Accounting Principles Underlying Corporate Financial Statements," *The Accounting Review* (June 1941).

_____, *Accounting and Reporting Standards for Corporate Financial Statements: 1957 Revision* (AAA, 1957).

_____, *A Statement of Basic Accounting Theory* (AAA, 1966).

_____, Committee on Concepts and Standards - Management Planning and Control, "Managerial Accounting Literature Abstracts," AAA, (October 1976).

_____, Committee on Concepts and Standards for External Financial Reports. *Statement on Accounting Theory and Theory Acceptance* (AAA, 1977a).

_____, Committee on Human Information Processing, "Report of the 1976-77 Committee on Human Information Processing," AAA (1977b).

Abdef-khalik, A.R. and El-Sheshai, K., "Information Choice and Utilization in an Experiment on Default Prediction," *Journal of Accounting Research* (Autumn 1980).

Abdel-khalik, A.R. and Keller, T.F., *Earnings or Cash Flow: An Experiment on Functional Fixation and the Valuation of the Firm,* Studies in Accounting Research No. 16 (AAA, 1979).

Acland, D., "The Effects of Behavioral Indicators on Investor Decisions: An Exploratory Study," *Accounting, Organizations and Society* 1 (2-3) (1976).

AICPA (American Institute of Certified Public Accountants), *Basic Concepts and Accounting Principles Underlying Financial Statements of Business Enterprises.* Statement of the Accounting Principles Board No. 4 (New York: AICPA. October 1970).

_____, Study Group on the Objectives of Financial Statements, *Objectives of Financial Statements* (New York: AICPA, 1973).

_____, Task Force on a Conceptual Framework for Accounting and Reporting. *The Accounting Response to Changing Prices: Experimentation with Four Models* (New York: AICPA, 1979).

Alchian, A. and Demsetz, H., "Production, Information Costs, and Economic Organization," *American Economic Review* (December 1972).

Altman, E.I., "Financial Ratios, Discriminant Analysis and the Prediction of Corporate Bankruptcy," *The Journal of Finance* (September 1968).

Atkinson, A.A. and Feltham, G.A., "Information in Capital Markets: An Agency Theory Perspective," Working Paper, the University of British Columbia (January 1981).

_____, "Agency Theory Research and Financial Accounting Standards," The Clarkson, Gordon Foundation, *Proceedings of the 1981 Research Symposium*, pp. 257-289 (Toronto: Clarkson, Gordon Foundation, 1982).

Ashton, R.H., "Cognitive Changes Induced by Accounting Changes: Experimental Evidence on the Functional Fixation Hypothesis," *Studies on Human Information Processing in Accounting,* Supplement to *Journal of Accounting Research* (1976).

_____, "Objectivity of Accounting Measures: A Multirule-Multimeasure Approach. *The Accounting Review* (July 1977).

Ball, R. and Brown, P., "An Empirical Evaluation of Accounting Income Numbers." *Journal of Accounting Research* (Autumn 1968).

Barnea, A., Ronen, J., and Sadan, S., "Classifactory Smoothing of Income with Extraordinary Items," *The Accounting Review* (January 1976).

Beaver, W.H., "Alternative Accounting Measures as Predictors of Failure," *The Accounting Review* (January 1968).

_____, "The Behavior of Security Prices and Its Implications for Accounting Research Methods," in *Report of the Committee on Research Methodology in Accounting,* Supplement to *The Accounting Review* (1972).

_____, "What Should be the FASB's Objectives?", *Journal of Accountancy* (August 1973).

_____, *Financial Reporting: An Accounting Revolution* (Englewood Cliffs, New Jersey: Prentice Hall, 1981).

Beaver, W.H., and Demski, J.S., "The Nature of Income Measurement," *The Accounting Review* (January 1979).

Beaver, W.H. and Dukes, R.E., "Interperiod Tax Allocation and Depreciation Methods: Some Empirical Results," *The Accounting Review* (July 1973).

Beaver, W.H. and Kettler, P., and Scholes, M., "The Association Between Market-Determined and Accounting-Determined Risk Measures," The Accounting Review (October 1970).

Belkaoui, A., "Linguistic Relativity in Accounting," *Accounting, Organizations and Society 3* (2) (1978).

_____, "The Interprofessional Linguistic Communication of Accounting Concepts: An Experiment in Sociolinguistics," *Journal of Accounting Research* (Autumn 1980).

Benston, G.J. and Krasney, M.A., "DAAM: The Demand for Alternative Accounting Measurements," *Journal of Accounting Research* 16, Supplement (1978).

Bhattacharya, S., "Imperfect Information, Dividend Policy, and 'The Bird in the Hand' Fallacy," *Bell Journal of Economics* (Spring 1979).

Birnberg, J.G. and Slevin, D., "A Note on the Use of Confidence Interval Statements in Financial Reporting," *Journal of Accounting Research* (Spring 1976).

Borch, K., "Equilibrium in a Reinsurance Market," *Econometrica* (July 1962).

Boulding, K., "General Systems Theory - The Skeleton of Science," *Management Science* (April 1956).

Bowman, R.G., "The Debt Equivalence of Leases: An Empirical Investigation," *The Accounting Review* (April 1980).

Buzby, S.L. and Falk, H., "Demand for Social Responsibility Information by University Investors," *The Accounting Review* (January 1979).

Canning, J.B., *The Economics of Accountancy* (New York: Ronald Press, 1929).

Casey, C.J., Jr., "Variation in Accounting Information Load: The Effect on Loan Officers' Predictions of Bankruptcy," *The Accounting Review* (January 1980).

Chang, D.S. and Birnberg, J.G., "Functional Fixation in Accounting Research: Perspective and New Data," *Journal of Accounting Research* (Autumn 1977).

Chang, L.S. and Most, K.S., "Financial Statements and Investment Decisions," Florida International University (1979).

Chope, R.A., "Market and Industry Factors, Accounting Policy, and the Time Series Properties of Accounting Earnings," Dissertation Proposal, University of Oregon (November 1980).

Cohen, M.D. and March, J.G., *Leadership and Ambiguity: The American College President,* A Report Prepared for the Carnegie Commission on Higher Education (New York: McGraw-Hill, 1974).

Collins, D.W., Rozeff, M.S., and Dhaliwal, D.S., "The Economic Determinants of Market Reaction to Proposed Mandatory Accounting Changes in the Oil and Gas Industry: A Cross-Sectional Analysis," *Journal of Accounting and Economics 3* (1981).

Collins, F. and Yeakel, J.A., "Range Estimates in Financial Statements: Help or Hindrance?" *Journal of Accountancy* (July 1979).

Corporate Reporting: Its Future Evolution (Toronto: CICA, 1980).

Dawes, R.M., "The Robust Beauty of Improper Linear Models in Decision Making," *American Psychologist 34* (7) (July 1979).

Deakin, E.B., "A Discriminant Analysis of Predictors of Business Failure." *Journal of Accounting Research* (Spring 1972).

Dopuch, N. and Gonedes, N., "Capital Market Equilibrium, Information Production, and Selecting Accounting Techniques: Theoretical Framework and Review of Empirical Work," in *Studies on Financial Accounting Objectives* (Graduate School of Business, University of Chicago, 1974).

Dopuch, N. and Simunic, D., "Competition in Auditing: An Assessment," *Symposium on Research Auditing IV*, 1980 (University of Illinos at Urbana-Champaign, forthcoming).

Dyckman, T.R., Downes, D., and Magee, R.R., *Efficient Capital Markets and Accounting: A Critical Analysis* (Englewood Cliffs, New Jersey: Prentice-Hall, 1975).

Dyckman, T.R., Gibbins, M., and Swieringa, R.J., "Experimental and Survey Research in Financial Accounting: A Review and Evaluation," in *The Impact of Accounting Research on Practice and Disclosure*, ed. A.R. Abdel-khalik and T.F. Keller (Durham, N.C.: Duke University Press, 1978).

Einhorn, H.J. and Hogarth, R.M., "Behavioral Decision Theory: Processes of Judgement and Choice," *Annual Review of Psychology 32* (1981).

Epstein, M.J., *The Usefulness of Annual Reports to Corporate Shareholders* (Bureau of Business and Economics Research, California State University, Los Angeles, 1975).

Eskew, R.K., "The Forecasting Ability of Accounting Risk Measures: Some Additional Evidence," *The Accounting Review* (January 1979).

Estes, R. and Reimer, M., "A Study of the Effect of Qualified Auditors' Opinions on Bankers' Lending Decisions," *Accounting and Business Research* (Autumn 1977).

Eyes, A.D. and Tabb, B., "Bank Managers' Use of Financial Statements," *The Accountants' Journal* (April 1978).

FASB (Financial Accounting Standards Board), *Accounting for the Translation of Foreign Currency Transac-*

tions and Foreign Currency Financial Statements. Statement of Financial Accounting Standards No. 8 (Stamford, Conn: FASB, October 1975).

_____, *Objectives of Financial Reporting by Business Enterprises,* Statement of Financial Accounting Concepts No. 1 (Stamford, Conn: FASB, November 1978).

_____, *Qualitative Characteristics of Accounting Information,* Statement of Financial Accounting Concepts No. 2 (Stamford, Conn: FASB, May 1980a).

_____, *Elements of Financial Statements of Business Enterprises,* Statement of Financial Accounting Concepts No. 3 (Stamford, Conn: FASB, December 1980b).

_____, *Objectives of Financial Reporting by Nonbusiness Organizations,* Statement of Financial Accounting Concepts No. 4 (Stamford, Conn: FASB, December 1980c).

Flamholtz, E. and Cook, E., "Connotative Meaning and Its Role in Accounting Change: A Field Study," *Accounting, Organizations and Society 3* (2))1978).

Foster, G., *Financial Statement Analysis* (Englewood Cliffs, New Jersey: Prentice-Hall, Inc. 1978).

_____, "Accounting Policy Decisions and Capital Market Research," *Journal of Accounting and Economics* (March 1980).

Friedman, M., "The Methodology of Positive Economics," *Essays in Positive Economics* (Chicago: University of Chicago Press, 1953).

Gibbins, M., "A Behavioral Approach to Auditing Research," *Symposium on Auditing Research II,* November 1976 (University of Illinois at Urbana-Champaign, 1977a).

_____, "Classifactory Smoothing of Income with Extraordinary Items: Research Implications," *The Accounting Review* (April 1977b).

Gibbins, M., and Brennan, P., "Behavioral Accounting Research and Financial Accounting Standards: A Research Review and Hypotheses About Connections," University of British Columbia, March 1981. (This paper will be a chapter in a study being directed by P.A. Griffin for the FASB.)

Gilman, S., *Accounting Concepts of Profit* (New York: Ronald Press, 1939).

Gonedes, N., "Properties of Accounting Numbers: Models and Tests," *Journal of Accounting Research* (Autumn 1973).

Gray, C.W., "Ingredients of Intuitive Regression," *Organizational Behavior and Human Performance* 23 (1979).

Harris, M. and Raviv, A., "Optimal Incentive Contracts with Imperfect Information," *Journal of Economic Theory* 23 (April 1979).

Hilton, R.W., "Integrating Normative and Descriptive Theories of Information Processing," *Journal of Accounting Research* (Autumn 1980).

Hogarth, R.M., "Cognitive Processes and the Assessment of Subjective Probability Distributions," *Journal of the American Statistical Associaiton 70* (1975).

Holmström B., "Moral Hazard and Observability," *Bell Journal of Economics* (Spring 1979).

Holthausen, R.W., "Bond Covenants and the Choice of Accounting Techniques: The Case of Alternative Depreciation Methods," Working Paper, University of Rochester (1979).

Ijiri, Y., *The Foundations of Accounting Measurement (Englewood Cliffs, N.J.: Prentice-Hall, 1967).*

_____, *"A Defense for Historical Cost Accounting, in Asset Valuation and Income Determination* ed. R.R. Sterling (Lawrence, Kansas: Scholars Book Co., 1971).

_____, *Theory of Accounting Measurement,* Studies in Accounting Research No. 10 (AAA, 1975).

_____, *Historical Cost Accounting and Its Rationality.* Research Monograph No. 1 (Vancouver: Canadian Certified General Accountants Association, 1981).

Jensen, M.C. and Meckling, W.H., "The Theory of the Firm: Managerial Behavior, Agency Costs, and Ownership Structure," *Journal of Financial Economics* (October 1976).

Jensen, R.E., *Phantasmagoric Accounting: Research and Analysis of Economic, Social and Environmental Impact of Business,* Studies in Accounting Research No. 11 (AAA, 1976).

Kahneman, D. and Tversky, A., "Prospect Theory: An Analysis of Decision Under Risk," *Econometrica* (March 1979).

Kanodia, C., "Effects of Shareholder Information on Corporate Decisions and Capital Market Equilibrium." *Econometrica* (May 1980).

Kennedy, H.A., "A Behavioral Study of the Usefulness of Four Financial Ratios," *Journal of Accounting Research* (Spring 1975).

Keys, D.E., "Confidence Interval Financial Statements: An Empirical Investigation," *Journal of Accounting Research* (Autumn 1978).

Leftwich, R., "The Impact of Mandatory Changes in Accounting Principles on Corporate Loan Agreements," Working Paper, University of Rochester (1979).

Leland, H.E., "Quacks, Lemons and Licensing," *Journal of Political Economy* (December 1979).

Libby, R., "Accounting Ratios and the Prediction of Failure: Some Behavioral Evidence." *Journal of Accounting Research* (Spring 1975).

_____, "Man Versus Model of Man: Some Conflicting Evidence," *Organizational Behavior and Human Performance* (June 1976).

_____, "The Impact of Uncertainty Reporting on the Loan Decision," *Journal of Accounting Research,* 17 Supplement, (1979).

Libby, R. and Blashfield, R.K., "Performance of a Composite as a Function of the Number of Judges," *Organizational Behavior and Human Performance* 21 (1978).

Libby, R. and Lewis, B.L., "Human Information Processing Research in Accounting: The State of the Art," *Accounting, Organizations and Society,* 2 (3) (1977).

Lichtenstein, S. and Fischoff, B., "Do Those Who Know More Also Know More about How Much They Know?" *Organizational Behavior and Human Performance* 20 (1977).

Lintner, J., "The Valuation of Risky Assets and the Selection of Risky Investments in Stock Portfolios and Capital Budgets," *Review of Economics and Statistics* (February 1965).

March, J.G., "Bounded Rationality, Ambiguity and the Engineering of Choice," *Bell Journal of Economics* (Autumn 1978).

March, J.G., and Olsen, J.P., *Ambiguity and Choice in Organizations* (Bergen, Norway: Universitetsforlaget, 1976).

Markowitz, H., "Portfolio Selection," *The Journal of Finance* (March 1952).

Marschak, J. and Radner, R., *The Economic Theory of Teams* (New Haven, Conn: Yale University Press, 1974).

Mattessich, R., *Accounting and Analytical Methods,* (Homewood, Ill: Richard D. Irwin, 1964).

_____, "Methodological Preconditions and Problems of a General Theory of Accounting," *The Accounting Review* (July 1972).

_____, *Instrumental Reasoning and Systems Methodology: An Epistemology of the Applied and Social Sciences* (Dordrecht, Holland and Boston: D. Riedel Publishing Co., 1978).

Meehl, P.E., *Clinical vs. Statistical Prediction: A Theoretical Analysis and a Review of the Evidence* (Minneapolis: University of Minnesota Press, 1954).

Mikkelson, W., "Convertible Security Calls and Securityholder Returns: Evidence on Agency Costs, Effects of Capital Structure Change, and Supply Effects," Working Paper, University of Oregon (1979).

Milgram, S. and Toch, H., "Collective Behavior: Crowds and Social Movements," in *The Handbook of Social Psychology* 2nd ed., Vol. 4 *Group Psychology and Phenomena of Interaction* ed. Gardner Lindzey and Elliott Aronson (Reading, Mass.: Addison-Wesley, 1969).

Milgrom, P. and Stokey, N., "Information Trade and Common Knowledge," Discussion Paper No. 377, Northwestern University Graduate School of Management (April 1979).

Mirlees, J., "An Exploration in the Theory of Income Taxation," *Review of Economic Studies* (April 1971).

Mock, T.J., *Measurement and Accounting Information Criteria,* Studies in Accounting Research No. 13 (AAA, 1976).

Mock, T.J. and Vasarhelyi, M.A., "A Synthesis of the Information Economics and Lens Models," *Journal of Accounting Research* (Autumn 1978).

Moonitz, M., *The Basic Postulates of Accounting,* Accounting Research Study No. 1 (New York: AICPA, 1961).

_____, *Obtaining Agreement on Standards in the Accounting Profession,* Studies in Accounting Research No. 8 (AAA, 1974).

Moore, M.L., "Management Changes and Discretionary Accounting Decisions," *Journal of Accounting Research* (Spring 1973).

Moriarity, S., "Communicating Financial Information Through Multidimensional Graphics," *Journal of Accounting Research* (Spring 1979).

Mossin, J., "Equilibrium in a Capital Asset Market," *Econometrica* (October 1966).

Most, K.S. and Chang, L.S., "How Useful are Annual Reports to Investors?" *Journal of Accountancy* (September 1979).

Nakano, I., "Noise and Redundancy in Accounting Communications," *The Accounting Review* (October 1972).

Nisbett, R.E. and Wilson, T.D., "Telling More Than We Can Know: Verbal Reports on Mental Processes," *Psychological Review* (May 1977).

Ogilvie, J.R. and Schmitt, N., "Situational Influences on Linear and Nonlinear Uses of Information," *Organizational Behavior and Human Performance* 23 (1979).

Ohlson, J.A., "Residual (API) Analysis and the Private Value of Information," *Journal of Accounting Research* (Autumn 1979).

_____, "Asset-Price Behavior and Socially Useful (Useless) Information," Working Paper, University of California, Berkeley (July 1980).

Patell, J.M., "Corporate Forecasts of Earnings per Share and Share Price Behavior: Empirical Tests," *Journal of Accounting Research* (Autumn 1976).

_____, "The API Analysis and the Private Value of Information," *Journal of Accounting Research* (Autumn 1979).

Paton, W.A., *Accounting Theory* (New York: Ronald Press, 1922).

Prakash, P. and Rappaport, A., "Information Inductance and Its Significance for Accounting," *Accounting, Organizations and Society* 2 (1) 1977.

Ricks, W., "The Market's Response to the 1974 LIFO Switch," PhD Dissertation, University of California, Berkeley (1980).

Ross, S.A., "The Determination of Financial Structure: The Incentive Signalling Approach," *Bell Journal of Economics* (Spring 1977).

Schelling, T.C., "On the Ecology of Micromotives," Public Interest 25 (1971).

_____, *Micromotives and Macrobehavior* (New York: Norton, 1978).

Shafer, G., "Two Theories of Probabilities," Paper presented to the Philosophy of Science Association Convention, San Francisco, October, 1978, (Shafer is at the Department of Mathemetics, University of Kansas, Lawrence, Kansas).

Shank, J.K., Dillard, J.F., and Murdock, R.J., "FASB No. 8 and the Decision-Makers," *Financial Executive* (February 1980).

Sharpe, W.F., "A Simplified Model for Portfolio Analysis," *Management Science* (January 1963).

_____, "Capital Asset Prices: A Theory of Market Equilibrium under Conditions of Risk," *The Journal of Finance* (September 1964).

Shavell, S., "Risk Sharing and Incentives in the Principal and Agent Relationship," *Bell Journal of Economics* (Spring 1979).

Simon, H.A., "Rational Decision Making in Business Organizations," *American Economic Review* (September 1979).

Simunic, D.A., "The Pricing of Audit Services: Theory and Evidence," *Journal of Accounting Research* (Spring 1980).

Slovic, P., Fischoff, B., and Lichtenstein, S., "Behavioral Decision Theory," *Annual Review of Psychology* (1977).

Spence, A.M. and Zeckhauser, S., "Insurance, Information and Individual Action," *American Economic Review* (May 1971).

Sprouse, R.T. and Moonitz, M., *A Tentative Set of Broad Accounting Principles for Business Enterprises*, Accounting Research Study No. 3 (New York: AICPA, 1962).

Sterling, R.R. *Theory of the Measurement of Enterprise Income* (University Press of Kansas, 1970).

Swieringa, R.J., Dyckman, T.R., and Hoskin, R.E., "Empirical Evidence About the Effects of an Accounting Change on Information Processing," *Behavioral Experiments in Accounting II*, Proceedings of the October 13-14, 1978 Symposium, ed. Thomas J. Burns (College of Administrative Science, The Ohio State University, 1979).

Thornton, D.B., "Law and Economics of Unanticipated Changes in Generally Accepted Accounting Principles: A Canadian Perspective," Working Paper, University of Toronto (November 1980).

Tversky, A. and Kahneman, D., "Judgment Under Uncertainty: Heuristics and Biases," *Science* 185 (1974).

Vermaelen, T.J., "Issue Tender Offers and Market Signalling: Theory and Evidence," *Journal of Financial Economics* (1981).

Vickrey, D.W., "Is Accounting a Measurement Discipline?" *The Accounting Review* (October 1970).

Von Neumann, J. and Morgensten, O., *The Theory of Games and Economic Behavior* (Princeton: Princeton University Press, 1953).

Watts, R.L., "Corporate Financial Statements, A Product of the Market and Political Processes," *Australian Journal of Management* 2 (2) (April 1977).

Watts, R.L., and Zimmerman, J.L., "Towards a Positive Theory of the Determination of Accounting Standards," *The Accounting Review* (January 1978).

_____, "The Demand for and the Supply of Accounting Theories: The Market for Excuses," *The Accounting Review* (April 1979).

Weick, K., *The Social Psychology of Organizing*, 2nd ed. (Reading, Mass.: Addison-Wesley, 1979).

Williamson, O.E., *Markets and Hierarchies: Analysis and Antitrust Implications* (New York: Free Press, 1975).

Wilson, R., "The Theory of Syndicates," *Econometrica* (January 1968).

Zimmer, I., "A Lens Study of the Prediction of Corporate Failure by Bank Loan Officers, *Journal of Accounting Research* (Autumn 1980).

Zimmerman, J.L., "The Municipal Accounting Maze: An Analysis of Political Incentives," in *Studies on Measurement and Evaluation of the Economic Efficiency of Public and Private Nonprofit Institutions.* Supplement to *Journal of Accounting Research* (1977).

This paper would not have been possible without the continuing intellectual stimulation provided by Joel Demski. Harry Evans and James M. Patton made significant improvements to this paper as a result of their comments and criticisms. The comments of Barry Lewis, Katherine Schipper, the Editor and an anonymous referee also significantly improved this paper. Finally, Bob Kaplan made numerous helpful suggestions on an earlier draft of this paper.

AGENCY RESEARCH IN MANAGERIAL ACCOUNTING: A SURVEY*

by Stanley Baiman

MANAGERIAL accounting texts advocate the use of several different types of procedures including overhead allocation, flexible budgeting, standard costing, and cost-volume-profit analysis. Managerial accounting texts also advocate a cost-benefit approach toward the choice, design, and implementation of such procedures. (See, for example, [Horngren, 1977, p. 7]). Until recently, however, managerial accounting research has not attempted to assess formally the value of these procedures by applying this cost-benefit philosophy to them. Rather, managerial accounting research has tended to assume their usefulness and value and has concentrated on (a) studying the attributes of specific ways or techniques of implementing these procedures, (b) generalizing the standard techniques, and (c) generating new variations of the standard techniques. For example, the recent game theoretic overhead allocation literature has suggested new methods of overhead allocation and new criteria for evaluating different procedures (see [Moriarity, 1975] and [Hamlen, et. al., 1977]). Dopuch, et. al. [1967] and Demski [1967] generalized variance computations. However, in none of the cited studies is there a formal demonstration of the value of the standard procedure or of the extensions advocated by the authors.

Cost-benefit analysis has not been rigorously applied to these procedures because the fundamental economic analysis on which such cost-benefit computations must be based has only recently been attempted in a systematic manner. Horngren [1977] implicitly admits this when he states: "Admittedly the measurement of these cost and benefits is an imposing,

*Reprinted from *The Journal of Accounting Literature* 1 (Spring 1982): 154-213

complex undertaking that may often be infeasible.'' [Horngren, 1977, p. 7]. ''The cost-benefit way of thinking is widely applicable even if the costs and benefits defy precise measurement.'' [Horngren, 1977, p. 7, fn. 2]. One reason for this absence of fundamental economic analysis of managerial accounting procedures has been the lack of a well-defined, useful model of individual behavior within an organization. Both ''well-defined'' and ''useful'' are important characteristics which have been absent from models of human behavior previously suggested as frameworks for evaluating managerial accounting procedures. For example, Ronen and Livingstone [1975] suggested the expectancy model as a basis for the design of budgets. Hayes [1977] suggested contingency theory as a framework for managerial accounting. Both these behavioral models are so loosely defined that few precise and unambiguous implications have been derived from them. At the opposite extreme, models of the firm based on mathematical programming formulations have been suggested (see [Hamlen, 1980]), but these models are so complex and intractable that few managerial implications have been derived from them. Because managerial accounting information is produced and used by individuals within a multiperson organizational setting, the benefit and cost of installing a managerial accounting procedure depends upon how people react to and use its output in that setting. The agency model of the firm is based on a description of individual behavior within a multiperson organization. Analysis of the managerial accounting function based on this model has recently begun. The purpose of this paper is to survey and synthesize the subset of agency literature that has implications for managerial accounting.

Agency theory research focuses on the optimal contractual relationships among members of the firm, where each member is assumed to be motivated solely by self-interest. (The concepts of optimality, rationality, and efficiency used in agency research are discussed later in the paper). In the agency model of the firm, one or more individuals (the principal(s)) hire one or more persons (the agent(s)) for the purpose of delegating responsibilities to the latter. The rights and responsibilities of the members of the firm are specified in the firm's mutually agreed upon employment contracts. Agency research examines the relationship between the firm's information systems, its employment contracts, and the welfare of its members. In the agency model, the firm's employment contracts are optimal functions of the information supplied by the firm's managerial accounting information system. Further, in the agency model each individual chooses his actions optimally (in his own self-interest) based upon his own information (in part supplied by the firm's managerial accounting information system) and the chosen employment contracts. Agency theory therefore provides a model from which uses of managerial accounting information can be derived and studied.

In agency theory the firm is viewed not as an individual, but merely as an overlapping set of contracts among principals and agents, each of whom is assumed to be motivated solely by self-interest. Therefore the behavior of the firm is the outcome of the process that brings into equilibrium, via the agreed upon contracts, the (possibly) conflicting self-interests of the principals and agents. In fact, much of the early agency research was devoted to analyzing the reasons for the existence of the firm as an alternative to strictly market-mediated transactions [Alchian and Demsetz, 1972, Williamson, et. al. 1975]. While this early research was insightful and must be credited with developing the agency perspective (along with Jensen and Meckling [1976]), most of its results were based on casual rather than rigorous analysis.[1] The literature surveyed in this essay builds upon these early studies by specifying the agency model more carefully and analyzing it more rigorously.

This survey concentrates on those papers whose analyses have implications for managerial accounting. Results that are basically methodological are discussed only briefly. The survey does, however, critically analyze possible limitations of the agency model. Because of space limitations, the survey is limited to only the formal analytical agency research within nonprice (nonmarket) mediated settings.

> The multiperson information economics literature studies the use and value of information in both small groups and in competitive markets. The latter generally studies the existence and characteristics of market equilibria in the presence of unequally distributed information. For example, see [Hakansson, 1977; Ng. 1975; Gonedes and Dopuch, 1974; Grossman and Stiglitz, 1976; Amershi, 1980b; and Riley 1979]. Atkinson and Feltham [1981] examine the agency problem within a capital market setting. While this literature is certainly important for understanding the efficient functioning of the economy, questions of market equilibrium are of tangential interest to the managerial accountant faced with choosing an information

system. As a result, in this paper only the literature dealing with a small number of participants is surveyed. In addition, the literature dealing with behavioral experiments to measure the effects of different information systems is not surveyed in this paper. Schelling [1960] has been the source of many of the hypotheses tested. Harnett and Hamner [1973] survey some of this literature and provide their own results. Further, since members of a firm can always base their employment contracts on the chosen accounting system, this paper does not consider the literature that assumes a fixed contractual relationship and hence is more suitable to an analysis of the role of information in oligopolies (see, for example, [Baiman, 1975; and Ponssard and Zamir, 1973]).

This survey is potentially valuable for four reasons. First, because the area of agency research is new, the literature contains different perspectives, emphases, and sets of assumptions. A paper that classifies the existing work, pointing out similarities and differences, would be most helpful to future research. Second, the paper develops some positive implications of the agency research for commonly used managerial accounting procedures and for the philosophy on which they are based. That is, one purpose of this survey will be to analyze the extent to which the use of some familiar managerial accounting procedures is consistent with the agency model of the firm. Third, surveying the results of recent agency research will provide a basis for evaluating the potential of the agency model as the foundation for a rigorous normative theory of managerial accounting. Finally, the paper identifies some unanswered managerial accounting questions that may be amenable to the type of analysis discussed here.

> In the social sciences a theory may be evaluated as either a normative theory or positive theory or both. A normative theory would describe how managerial accounting procedures should be designed. A positive theory would predict how people would react to given procedures as well as predict the form and use of observed procedures. The second purpose for the survey, as stated above, is to evaluate the agency model as a basis for a positive theory. The third purpose is to see whether a fruitful normative theory of managerial accounting can be based on the agency model. These two purposes are complementary since the degree to which we can have confidence that our normative suggestions will lead to the desired outcomes depends upon how well we understand (can predict) how people behave within an organizational setting. Further, a finding that the results of agency research are consistent with observed managerial accounting procedures (a positive statement) does not eliminate the usefulness of the agency model as a basis for a normative theory of managerial accounting. The agency model only describes the current equilibrium solution. New technology will bring down monitoring costs and make new monitoring alternatives available. The agency model in its normative role can help to evaluate these new alternatives and to attain the new equilibrium point more efficiently than might be possible without the formal agency model guiding our analysis.

In order to put the agency model in perspective, the second section discusses some other analytical models that have been suggested as possible frameworks for a theory of managerial accounting and compares them to the agency model. The third section contains a more formal description and discussion of the agency model. The fourth section contains the survey together with the classification scheme used to organize the literature. The fifth section provides the summary and conclusions.

NONAGENCY ANALYTICAL MODELS SUGGESTED AS FRAMEWORKS FOR A THEORY OF MANAGERIAL ACCOUNTING

In order to emphasize the distinctive features of the agency model, it will be helpful to first discuss briefly other analytical models that have been suggested as frameworks for the managerial accounting and control process. These include the Decision Theory model, the Syndicate Theory model, the Information Evaluator-Decision Maker model, the Team Theory model, and the Demand Revelation model. In each of these frameworks, a model of the firm (including a model of individual behavior within the firm) is described and then used to derive the demands for (i.e., uses of) managerial accounting information implied by that model. Each model can then be analyzed to determine how the managerial accounting information system should be designed in order to supply the kinds of information demanded.

> The uses of managerial accounting information shoud be a derivable implication of the model rather than an assumption of the model. A model may lack internal consistency if it merely assumes the demand for an accounting procedure. For example, in the game-theoretic cost allocation literature, the demand for cost allocations is assumed to exist. This literature then analyzes different allocation procedures in terms of various criteria. But the analyses invariably take place within the context of a model in which a strict improvement could be achieved (according to the chosen criteria) by not allocating costs. The assumed demand for the allocation of costs is inconsistent with the model in which the different allocation procedures are evaluated (see [Baiman, 1981] and [Demski, 1981] for critiques of this literature). This internal inconsistency leaves the model's implications suspect.

One test of the usefulness of any proposed model is whether its derived demands for information include those uses of managerial accounting information that are observed. This is a reasonable test because a model of the managerial accounting process whose derived demands for information do not include uses that are observed is probably based on an overly restrictive view of the managerial accounting process and therefore is likely to lead to the choice of suboptimal managerial accounting information systems and procedures. In this section these alternative analytical models are evaluated by comparing each of their derived demands for managerial accounting information to three observed uses, which are described next.

Managerial accounting information has at least three observed uses. The first use is to improve a manager's *ex ante* assessment of the production environment in order to improve his production decisions. This is the *belief revision* use of managerial accounting information. For example, a plant manager may base his make versus buy decision on a forecasted incremental cost analysis, which is an output of the managerial accounting system. The manager revises his beliefs about the production environment based on this incremental cost analysis. (This belief revision use of information is comparable to the problem-solving use discussed in [Simon, et. al. 1954].) The second use is to help supervisors *motivate* subordinates. The third use is to facilitate the *allocation*—among members of the firm—*of the risk* inherent in operating in an uncertain production environment. These *motivational* and *risk-sharing* uses of information are interrelated in that a subordinate's motivation can be influenced by the amount of financial risk imposed on him. For example, a plant manager's compensation may depend upon a comparison between his plant's actual production cost and its cost budget, both of which are outputs from the same managerial accounting system as the previously mentioned incremental cost analysis. The financial *risk* to the manager (the uncertainty with respect to his compensation) will differ according to whether his cost budget is fixed or flexible. As a result, the plant manager's *motivation* to cut discretionary costs such as repair and maintenance will differ according to whether he is evaluated relative to a fixed or a flexible budget. Thus, the plant manager's motivation is affected by the financial risk that is imposed on him, and both motivation and risk are affected by the managerial accounting information that is collected and how it is used. Since the *risk-sharing* and *motivational* uses of information are interrelated, hereafter they will be jointly referred to as the *performance evaluation* use of managerial accounting information. (The performance evaluation use of information includes the scorekeeping use discussed in [Simon, et. al., 1954].)

Assume that one's preference ordering over a set of information systems when the signals of each are to be used only for belief revision purposes is different from one's preference ordering over the same set of information systems when the signals of each are to be used only for performance evaluation purposes. If this assumption is true,[2] then any model whose derived demands for information do not include *both* the belief revision and the performance evaluation uses will, in general, lead to incorrect managerial accounting information system choices because one use of the system's output is ignored. For each of the alternative models, its derived uses of information are compared to the observed uses of belief revision and performance evaluation.

The Decision Theory model [Feltham, 1968] was the first model in management accounting in which the demand for information was formally derived rather than assumed. In the Decision Theory model the firm is viewed as a single individual who is playing a game against nature. Prior to his own action choice, the individual may gather information, which he can use to revise his beliefs about nature's chosen action. While this model derives the belief revision use of managerial accounting information, it ignores the performance evaluation use because performance evaluation is meaningful only in a multiperson firm.

Syndicate Theory [Wilson, 1968; Demski and Swieringa, 1974; and Demski, 1976] models multiperson firms. In the Syndicate Theory model several individuals jointly choose a set of actions and a method for sharing the resulting uncertain outcome (the sharing rule). Each individual is interested in maximizing his own expected utility through the choice of the action and the sharing rule. The belief revision demand for information can again be derived. In addition, the choice of the action and the sharing rule will have an important effect on the total risk borne by the Syndicate and how that risk is allocated among its members. Since the sharing rule can be based only on jointly observed information, the Syndicate Theory model can be used to derive the risk-sharing use of information. The motivational use of information is still ignored because all motivational problems are assumed away. In particular, all information is assumed to be publicly available and the action is assumed to be jointly chosen and implemented.

The multiperson context is preserved in the Information Evaluator-Decision Maker literature [Demski and Feltham, 1977] and the Mathematical Programming literature [Bailey and Boe, 1976; Hamlen, 1980]. These models include an owner who delegates the action choices to one or more agents. The owner or information evaluator is assumed to act in his own best interest. Each agent however, is assumed to act in a *exogenously specified* manner. No model of individual behavior is provided to explain why the firm's agents act in the assumed manner.[3] Assuming rather than deriving the agent's decision rule creates difficulties if the agent is assumed to act contrary to his own best interest. Since these models do not explicitly state the agent's utility function, the reader does not know whether the agent is assumed to act in his own best interest. Therefore, any motivational implications derived from these models are suspect.[4]

In the Team Theory model [Marschak and Radner, 1972], as in the Syndicate Theory model, several individuals come together to choose a set of actions and share the resulting payoff. Unlike the Information Evaluator-Decision Maker model, each individual is assumed to act in his own best interest. Further, unlike the Syndicate Theory model, in a Team setting the individual action choices are delegated to *different* individuals who may separately acquire private information on which each can base his decision. Each individual bases his action choice only on the information available to him. But the welfare of the team depends upon the successful coordination of the individual action choices. The problem for the team is to choose the individual decision rules in order to maximize the team's welfare in the presence of decentralized information. Clearly, the belief revision use of information can be derived from the Team model, but there is no motivational role for information in the Team model since all individuals are assumed to have the same preferences. Each team member will therefore implement whichever decision rule is given to him. Further, the assumption of identical preferences implies that technological constraints are the only impediments to the full sharing and utilization of the privately acquired information. That is, when information can be transmitted in a Team setting, it is assumed to be transmitted honestly. In a more realistic setting, self-interest as well as technology may prevent the full and honest communication of information within a firm.

The Demand Revelation model [Loeb, 1975; Groves, 1975; Groves and Loeb, 1979] is the same as the Team Theory model *without* the assumption of identical preferences. The issue of interest is how to induce (motivate) the agents to reveal their private information honestly and to use the information to maximize the profits of the firm. Thus both a belief revision and motivational use for information is derived in the Demand Revelation model. Since the objective is to maximize the firm's profit, *unadjusted* for the compensation paid to the agents rather than the owner's residual claim to the firm's profits after compensating the agents, the Demand Revelation model is more appropriate for analyzing worker cooperatives than capitalist firms. (See [Groves and Ledyard, 1976] for a discussion of other problems with the Demand Revelation model).

In summary, the nonagency analytical models proposed as frameworks for the managerial accounting process all have drawbacks. The use of information for performance evaluation (specifically motivational) purposes is either (1) ignored (the Decision Theory, Syndicate Theory, and Team Theory models) or (2) constrained by the use of *assumed* rather than derived decision rules for subordinates (the Information Evaluator-Decision Maker and Mathematical Programming models) or alternatively (3) the model of the firm is inappropriate (the Demand Revelation literature). These problems are all avoided by the agency model. The agency model represents the firm as an overlapping set of contracts between self-interested individuals. Further, there is an owner of the firm who is interested in his *residual* claim (after compensating the agents) to the firm's income. Therefore the agency model is based on a reasonable representation of the capitalist firm. In addition, because the firm's employment contracts are optimal functions of the information produced by the firm's managerial accounting information system and because each individual acts in his own best interest based on his own information (some of which he receives from the firm's managerial accounting information system) and his employment contract, the performance evaluation and belief revision uses of information observed in practice can be derived from the agency model.

THE AGENCY MODEL

In this section the agency model is discussed in more detail and an example of what will be called the basic agency problem is offered. This basic agency problem is then formulated mathematically and the formulation is discussed and criticized. Finally, generalizations of this basic agency problem are discussed.

The Sources of Conflict and Cooperation in the Agency Model

Although the agency model assumes that all individuals (whether principals or agents) are motivated by self-interest, this does not preclude there being a common interest among the members of the firm. As Fama [1980, p.289] notes: "In effect, the firm is viewed as a team of individuals whose members act from self-interest but realize that their destinies depend to some extent on the survival of the team in its competition with other teams."

In Fama's description of the firm, self-interest motivates each individual so that the potential for intrafirm conflict is recognized. However, since each individual's welfare is dependent upon the success of the firm, increased cooperation among the members of the firm might result in an increase in the welfare of some members without a decrease in the welfare of any of the others—i.e., in a Pareto improvement.[5] The contractual relationships agreed upon by the members of the firm determine the extent to which self-interested and cooperative behavior diverge; hence the interest of agency research in optimal contractual relationships.

If individuals are motivated by self-interest and if engaging in cooperative behavior would increase the welfare of some individuals but not decrease the welfare of any individuals, why would the individuals not engage in cooperative behavior? That is, why may there be a divergence between self-interested and cooperative behavior? To explain this phenomenon it is first necessary to explain more fully what is meant by cooperative behavior.

The behavior of the members of the firm is defined to be cooperative when:

(1) all members honestly share all information.
(2) all members act in the manner agreed upon; that is each member implements the action rule he is assigned (see (3) below).
(3) all members agree on a set of individual action rules and a method of sharing the uncertain outcome resulting from their individual actions such that no one can be made better off without making someone worse off. That is, they agree to a *Pareto optimal* set of action rules and sharing rules.

A cooperative solution is obtained when all members engage in the agreed upon cooperative behavior. For any situation, there may be many possible cooperative solutions since there may be many alternative Pareto optimal sets of action rules and sharing rules. *But the cooperative solution ignores motivational problems.* The Pareto optimal sharing rules agreed to in Rule (3) are not necessarily such that it is in each member's *self-interest* to reveal his information honestly (as *assumed* in Rule (1)) and to implement the action rule he is assigned (as *assumed* in Rule (2)). That is, if all other members of the firm behave cooperatively, it may still be in the self-interest of one member, *given his sharing rule*, to act in a manner different from that agreed to. If this is true for one or more members of the firm and if they are motivated by self-interest, then each will *not* act cooperatively but rather act differently—in a purely self-interested manner—possibly making *all* members worse off than if they had acted cooperatively. The problem is that the cooperative behavior agreed upon may not be *enforceable* (may not be in the self-interest of each member to implement) given the cooperative sharing rules agreed upon. More generally, the environment in which the firm operates may be such that there exists *no* set of sharing rules and action rules based on cooperative behavior such that it is in the self-interest of each member to reveal his information honestly and to implement his assigned action rule. Thus cooperative behavior need not be enforceable (i.e., achievable) for the self-interested individuals who make up the firm. Again, agency research focuses on the design of employment contracts to mitigate the divergence (i.e., conflict) between the cooperative behavior that will maximize the welfare of the individuals and the self-interested behavior that is achievable.

This divergence between self-interested and cooperative behavior may arise for either of two reasons. Both reasons result from the principal hiring the agent to perform some duties but not being able to *motivate* the agent appropriately to perform those duties. The principal hires an agent in order to delegate to him the responsibilities for providing inputs to the firm's production process and possibly for gathering and processing information for decision-making purposes. First, assume that the agent is hired only to provide inputs to the firm's production process. If the inputs supplied by the agent are observed by the principal, then the amount supplied can be used as the basis for contracting between the principal and agent. In this case, the agent can be appropriately motivated to supply the inputs since he is paid only for inputs he actually supplies. However, some variable other than the agent's actual input may have to serve as the basis for contracting between the principal and agent, as when the principal cannot observe the input supplied by the agent. The use of this surrogate as the basis for contracting between the principal and agent may result in a reduction of the agent's incentive to supply the input (it may increase his incentive to shirk) and result in a loss of welfare for *both* the principal and the agent. This resulting reduction in the welfare of *both* individuals indicates a divergence between self-interested and cooperative behavior; that is it indicates imperfectly resolved conflicts between the two individuals. When motivational problems and conflicts arise as a result of basing contracts on imperfect surrogates of behavior, the problem of *moral hazard*[6] is said to arise.

The second possible reason for the divergence between cooperative and self-interested behavior may arise even if the principal can verify the amount of input supplied by the agent and can base the agent's employment contract on his input. For if the agent bases his input supply decision on private information that cannot be verified by the principal, then the principal cannot determine whether the observed input was the appropriate choice given the action rule that the principal wants the agent to use and given the agent's actual private information. This situation arises in decentralized firms in which subordinates are typically *better informed* about the production environment or the marketing environment than are their supervisors. If the agent is motivated to misrepresent his private information in order to successfully implement an input action rule different from that desired by the principal (again, possibly in order to shirk) then the problem of *adverse selection* is said to arise.

Both moral hazard and adverse selection are information-based problems. If the principal's information system accurately reports the agent's input choice and private information, moral hazard and adverse selection can be eliminated. For example, the principal and agent would agree on the desired input decision rule and payment due to the agent for implementing that decision rule. Since the principal can observe both the agent's input and information, he can verify whether the agent has in fact fulfilled his contract. If the agent has fulfilled his contract, the principal pays the agent the agreed upon amount; if the agent has not, the principal pays a smaller amount. This is termed a forcing contract. In this situation the principal and agent's relationship is effectively reduced to a market-mediated transaction. Agency theory's concern with the welfare of the firm's members leads to its interest in the use of information in contracts to mitigate the welfare-reducing problems of moral hazard and adverse selection.

An Example of an Agency-Type Problem

In this section an example of an agency-type problem that is representative of the types of problems analyzed in much of the extant agency literature is presented. This example should make clearer to the reader the kinds of problems amenable to an agency-type analysis. Further, the more detailed description of the agency model and the survey of the agency literature that follow in later sections will be made more concrete by discussing them in terms of the simple agency-type problem presented next.

The firm consists of two individuals, a principal and an agent, and operates in a single-period world. One person (the principal) owns a fully automated machine that lasts only one period. The principal hires a second person (the agent) to perform preventive maintenance on the machine. This preventive maintenance is to be performed at the start of the period. The agent is hired solely for his labor. Any information that the agent has about the machine is also known by the principal. If the machine breaks down during the period, it remains down for the duration of the single period. The agent cannot repair the machine once it breaks. The market for the machine's output is competitive with a known price per unit. The sales value of the machine's output (x) is a random variable that is a function of the amount of preventive maintenance supplied by the agent (e) and the machine's realized breakdown parameter (θ, the state realization), where x = x(e,θ). For a given state realization, the more preventive maintenance supplied by the agent, the longer the machine will run before it breaks down and therfore the greater the sales value of the machine's output during the single period. Likewise, for a given amount of preventive maintenance, the greater the state realization, the greater will be the sales value of the machine's output during the single period.

The agent receives no additonal information about the machine's breakdown parameter between the time when he is hired and the time when he performs the preventive maintenance. The principal cannot directly verify the amount of preventive maintenance provided by the agent, nor can he directly verify the machine's realized breakdown parameter. The principal is assumed to sell the output of the machine himself and therefore to observe directly the machine's sales output (x). In additon, the firm has an information system, (η), which reports a signal (y ϵ Y) at the *end* of the period to both the principal and the agent. This *public post-decision* information system (η, hereafter also referred to as the *monitoring system*) produces signals that may convey information about the amount of preventive maintenance actually supplied by the agent (e) and/or about the realized breakdown parameter (θ). Thus, depending on the form of monitoring system, the agent may not learn the machine's sales output.

The principal values only his residual claim on the firm's cash flow, the difference between the firm's sales output (x) and the amount paid to the agent (I($\cdot$)[7]). The agent values his income (I($\cdot$)) but dislikes providing preventive maintenance. Both individuals are expected utility maximizers. The principal's decision problem is to choose the agent's payment schedule (I($\cdot$)) and the monitoring system (η) so as to maximize his own expected utility subject to inducing the agent to work for him. The agent's problem is to supply that amount of preventive maintenance (e) that will maximize his own expected utility given the chosen payment schedule and monitoring system. In evaluating any payment schedule-monitoring system repair, the principal must consider what level of preventive maintenance the agent (acting in his own best interest) will be induced to supply given that repair.

In this simple example a moral hazard problem may arise because the principal cannot directly verify the amount of preventive maintenance activity supplied by the agent and therefore may have to contract with the agent based on some surrogate measure of his preventive maintenance activity. No adverse selection problem can arise because the principal has access to all the information on which the agent bases his preventive maintenance decision.

Before this problem can be analyzed within an agency context, the environment in which the firm operates and the assumptions underlying agency analysis must be discussed more fully. For example, what restrictions are there on the kinds of contracts into which the principal and agent can enter? What are the characteristics of the agency solution concept? This more thorough discussion of the agency model, within the context of the preventive-maintenance problem outlined here, is presented next.

Description of the Basic Agency Problem

The agency model of the firm is distinguished from other models by its description of the individual members of the firm and of the world in which they operate. The preventive maintenance example given above and its description are representative of the class of problems, hereafter referred to as the *basic agency problem*, which is the focus of much of agency research. In this section, the description of the basic agency problem will be illustrated within the context of the preventive-maintenance example. Criticisms and generalizations of this basic agency problem will be discussed later.

The description of the basic agency problem can be divided into three major categories. The first category ((a) and (b) below) consists of the description of the principals and agents, their relationship, preferences, and belief. The second category ((c) through (i) below) includes the description of the production, informational, and legal environment in which the firm operates. The final category ((j) through (1) below) consists of the specification of the solution concept used in the agency literature. The basic agency problem, consists of the following:

(a) Description of the two individuals:

> i) The principal or residual claimant of the firm who supplies the production process (the machine, in the preventive maintenance example).
> ii) The agent who is hired by the principal and to whom is delegated the responsibility for supplying productive inputs (preventive maintenance, in the example) and possibly information (for example, knowlege about the machine's breakdown parameter). In the basic agency problem and preventive maintenance example, the agent is *not* hired to gather or process information.

Both individuals subscribe to the expected utility hypothesis. That is, they both exhibit rationality and can perform all necessary computations costlessly. The principal values only consumption and is risk averse. His utility function for income is assumed to be $G(x - I(\bullet))$. The agent also values consumption and is assumed to be strictly risk-averse. Further, the agent gets disutility from providing preventive maintenance services, i.e. he dislikes the task. His utility function for income and preventive maintenance services is assumed to be $U(I(\bullet), e)$.

The principal hires the agent to perform the preventive maintenance task, and it is assumed that the principal cannot directly observe the service provided by the agent. The principal can influence the agent's actions only to the extent that he can control the agent's payment schedule $(I(\bullet))$ and the monitoring system (η) and hence can influence the agent's *motivation* to provide the preventive maintenance.

(b) Description of the initial distribution of information and beliefs.

In the basic agency problem and in the preventive maintenance example, prior to the formation of the firm the principal and agent possess exactly the same information and beliefs about the stochastic process generating the machine's realized breakdown parameter and about the characteristics of each feasible information system.[8] That is, neither individual has *private pre-contract* information. Alternatively stated, there is no *asymmetry* of pre-contract information. The principal is assumed to know the agent's preferences and beliefs.

(c) Description of the number of periods.

The basic agency problem assumes a one-period world.

(d) Description of the firm's production function.

The firm's production function relates the following to the machine's sales output (x):

> i) the amount of capital supplied by the principal (the machine)
> ii) the agent's level of preventive maintenance, e and
> iii) an exogenously determined uncertain state realization (the machine's breakdown parameter, θ).

(e) Description of the feasible set of actions from which the agent chooses.

In the basic agency problem it is assumed that the level of preventive maintenance supplied by the agent can be represented as a nonnegative, bounded scalar.

(f) Description of the labor and capital markets.

Each individual has access to a market in which he can sell his labor or capital for a given expected utility. The agent's opportunity cost of joining the firm is foregoing an expected utility of K by selling his services in the labor market. The principal's opportunity cost of devoting his machine to the firm is foregoing an expected utility of C by selling the use of his machine in the market.

(g) Description of the feasible set of information system.

Information can be acquired by the principal or agent at any of three times. Each may acquire pre-contract information prior to joining the firm. As was stated earlier, in the basic agency problem it is assumed that the principal and agent join the firm with the same information and beliefs; that is, they have symmetric *pre-contract* information and beliefs. Once the principal and agent join the firm they may jointly or separately acquire information at either or both of two times.

Before the agent makes his preventive maintenance decision, the firm's *predecision* information system may provide a signal with information about the machine's realized breakdown parameter, say as a result of conducting a test of the machine. The signal may be observed by both individuals or only by one of them. In the basic agency problem and the preventive maintenance example it is assumed that the firm has *no* pre-decision information system. The information on which the agent bases his maintenance decision is therefore merely his pre-contract information, which was assumed to be identical to the principal's pre-contract information.

Subsequent to the agent supplying his maintenance services, the firm's post-decision information system (i.e., the monitoring system) supplies a signal, y, with information about one or more of the following: the machine's sales output, the realized breakdown parameter, or the amount of maintenance supplied by the agent. This signal is reported *publicly* (i.e. to *both* the principal and the agent). The principal is assumed to sell the machine's output personally and therefore is assumed always to observe the sales output (x) directly. Since the agent is not involved in selling the machine's output, he is not assumed to observe directly the sales output (x). Therefore, the signal produced by the monitoring system is the *only* jointly observed signal produced within the firm. That is, while the principal's post-decision information consists of (x,y), the agent's consists only of (y). The monitoring system (η) is the only information system that is a choice variable (rather than a given) in the basic agency problem. (As will be discussed in later sections, the basic agency model can be expanded to include those situations in which the pre-decision information system is a choice variable as well.) Further, in the basic agency problem it is assumed that for each feasible monitoring system ($\eta \epsilon \Xi$), both individuals agree on the probability distribution of x and y given e (as represented by $\phi(x,y|e,\eta)$).

(h) Description of the legal system

The central focus of agency theory is the employment contract (which includes the agent's payment schedule and the monitoring system). Contracts are enforced by legal insitutions.[9] The decision of legal institutions as to whether an employment contract has been honored or violated depends upon the evidence that can be submitted by the contracting parties to the legal enforcement mechanism. The legal system specifies what is admissible evidence. This specification clearly influences the set of contract types that would be considered by the contracting parties. For example, the agent would never agree to an employment contract in which the agent's payment schedule was a function of inadmissible data. In the basic agency problem it is assumed that only *jointly* observed data can serve as the basis of contracting, i.e. are admissible data. The monitoring signal (y) is the only jointly observed piece of data and therefore that signal is the only piece of data on which the principal and agent can contract. If the monitoring signal (y) does not include the amount of preventive maintenance supplied by the agent, the potential for moral hazard arises.

The legal system also specifies the types of behavior that can be legally enforced. For example, can the agent credibly commit himself *now* to perform some act *in the future* from which *neither* principal nor agent would *then* benefit, if the pricipal does not now agree to the agent's most desired employment contract? If the agent can, then he can engage in such strategic or threatening behavior in order to improve his bargaining position with respect to his payment schedule and the monitoring system.[10] The agent makes such threats credible if he can use the legal system to put himself into a position in which he *has* to carry out his threat if his demands are not met by the principal. In the basic agency problem, it is assumed that the legal system does not give the agent the option of committing himself to engage at some future time in behavior that would not *then* be in his self-interest. Thus, it is assumed that the agent cannot crediby engage in strategic behavior in order to influence the principal's choice of the employment contract.

> For example, can the agent commit himself to destroy the principal's machine if the principal does not agree to the agent's most desired contract? If the agent would go to jail for this act, he might not go through with such a plan even if the principal did not agree to the agent's most desired contract. In this case the threat is not credible. If the agent had already hired an arsonist to destroy the machine if the principal did not agree to the desired contract and if the agent has no way of subsequently communicating with the arsonist but the arsonist can independently observe the contract to which the principal and agent have agreed, then the threat is enforceable and credible and may cause the principal to capitulate, thereby assuring that the threat would never be carried out.

(i) Description of the feasible set of payment schedules.

In the basic agency model, the principal chooses the payment schedule and the monitoring system to reward and motivate the agent. The information and legal restrictions on the feasible set of payment schedules were discussed earlier. It is important to emphasize the relationship between the chosen monitoring system and the feasible set of payment schedules. If a certain type of information is not publicly reported by the chosen monitoring system (say the sales value of the output (x)), then any contract based on that information is not enforceable and thus not feasible. Finally, there may also be technical restrictions on the set of feasible payment schedules. In the basic agency problem these restrictions are quite weak. For example, the payment schedule is not even required to be a continuous or differentiable function.

> The usual assumption is that the payment schedule must be chosen from the set of bounded and measurable functions. An experiment is a set S of elements or outcomes τ. Events are subsets of S to which probabilities are assigned. Let A and B be events and A^c be the complement of A. A field F is a nonempty class of sets such that:
>   i) if $A \epsilon F$, then $A^c \epsilon F$
>   ii) if $A \epsilon F$ and $B \epsilon F$, then $A \cup B \epsilon F$
> A real-valued function whose domain is in the space S such that the set $\{x \leq \bar{x}\}$ is an event for any real number $\bar{x}$ is called measurable in the field F. See [Papoulis, 1965].

(j) Description of the solution to the basic agency model.

The solution to the basic agency problem consists of:

>   i) the employment contract, which incorporates:
>   1. the payment schedule for the agent;
>   2. the information system choices ($\eta \epsilon \Xi$ for the basic agency problem);
>   3. specification of how the agent *promises* to act;
>   ii) the agent's actual action

Since the payment schedule and information system choices that are implemented are jointly observable and admissible data, the agreed upon payment schedule and information system choices are legally enforceable. That is, it can be assumed that the principal and agent legally commit themselves to the agreed upon payment schedule and information system choices. However, if the agent's action choice is not jointly observable, the agent cannot credibly commit himself to any action that is not in his best interest to implement.

The remaining descriptions relate to the assumed behavior of the principal and the agent and to the solution concept employed in agency research. These specifications are the essential defining characteristics of the agency framework and are common to all agency work, not just those dealing with the basic agency problem.

(k) The role of self-interest.

Each individual acts in his own best interest. That is, each individual's choices are endogenously derived (rather than assumed) and are based only on his own self-interest. Further, each individual expects all other individuals to act solely in their own best interests, and therefore each chooses his own action based on that expectation. Each individual's expectations about the choices made by the other must therefore be in equilibrium. Thus, the principal chooses the payment schedule and monitoring system that best exploits (based on the principal's own interest) the agent's self-interested behavior. In short, agency theory exploits the power of self-interest as a stabilizing and predictive force.

(l) The solution concept and the nature of optimality.

While each individual acts in his own best interest (according to expected utility maximization) based on the expectation that all others will act in their own best interest, the nature of this expectational equilibrium must be further specified. To do so, the forces of self-interest and shared interest must be reconciled.

Agency theorists have accomplished this reconciliation by using the intersection of two game-theoretic solution concepts. *First*, agency theory restricts the set of feasible employment contracts to those that are self-enforcing as defined by the *Perfect Nash solution concept*, which has the following assumptions:

> (i) It is assumed that the agent cannot engage in credible strategic or threatening behavior in order to influence the principal's choice of the employment contract. This follows from the assumed legal environmnet discussed in (h), above. Therefore, it is assumed that the agent will always choose to supply that level of preventive maintenance service that maximizes his expected utility *given* the chosen employment contract and his own information.
>
> (ii) It is assumed that the principal restricts his choice of the employment contract to be from that set of contracts such that the agent actually supplies (i.e. finds it in his own best interest to supply) the level of preventive maintenance that he *promised* to supply when he agreed to the contract.[11]

The self-enforcing aspect of the Perfect Nash solution concept comes from the fact that the chosen payment schedule-monitoring system pair is such that the agent does (i.e. from Part (i) finds it in his own best interest to do so at the time that he must act) what the principal expects him to do (from Part (ii)). We call such a $(\eta, I(\bullet),e)$ triple a self-enforcing triple or a self-enforcing contract.

Second, from this set of Perfect Nash self-enforcing employment contracts, it is assumed that all contracts that are Pareto-inferior to at least one other contract in the set of self-enforcing contracts are eliminated from consideration. The employment contract chosen will be selected from the subset of contracts remaining after these two stages.

It may be helpful to illustrate the use of this agency theory solution concept within the context of the preventive maintenance example. For a given feasible monitoring system, η_1, the principal enumerates *all* feasible payment schedules and the agent's optimal preventive maintenance response to *each* monitoring system-payment schedule pair. Each triple $(\eta_1, I(\bullet),e)$, will generate a pair of expected utility points, one for the principal, one for the agent. From this set the principal eliminates all those triples that produce Pareto inferior expected utility pairs. The principal is then left with the Pareto frontier for the given monitoring system, η_1. The principal then repeats this exercise for each feasible monitoring system. If the Pareto frontier for any monitoring system is everywhere dominated by the Pareto frontier of any other system (the frontier of the first is everywhere to the left of the frontier of the second), the dominated one is eliminated. If one Pareto frontier remains, then that is the Pareto optimal monitoring system and the principal and agent bargain over the particular feasible payment schedule (or a randomization over payment schedules if the frontier is not concave).[12] If there is more than one Pareto frontier left (for example, two or more frontiers cross) then the principal and agent must bargain over randomizations of payment schedule-monitoring information system pairs in order to produce an overall concave Pareto frontier. In summary then, all Pareto comparisons between information systems are comparisons between Pareto frontiers, not between individual expected utility pairs.

Both the cooperative solution concept and the agency solution concept arrive at a solution by applying the Pareto criterion to a set of contracts, i.e. $(\eta, I(\cdot), e)$ triples. The cooperative solution is arrived at by applying the Pareto criterion to all possible combinations of η, $I(\cdot)$ and e subject only to $I(\cdot)$ being feasible given η (as was indicated in the discussion of the relationship between the set of feasible payment schedules and the monitoring system). The agency solution is arrived at by applying the Pareto criterion to all possible combinations of η, $I(\cdot)$ and e subject to: (1) $I(\cdot)$ being feasible given η *and* (2) e being the agent's optimal response to η and $I(\cdot)$. It is this additional second constraint imposed by the agency solution concept that captures the idea of self-interested behavior and that causes the divergence between the cooperative solution and the self-interested, agency solution discussed above. The cooperative solution ignores motivational considerations while the agency solution concept considers them (via this second constraint).

The use of the Pareto criterion in the agency solution concept defines the notion of firm efficiency; efficiency is defined in terms of the expected utilities of the principal and agent. The utility of the principal is a function of the probability distribution of his residual claim (x - I(y)), while the utility of the agent is a function both of his preventive maintenance activity (e) and of the probability distribution of his payment (I(y)). Therefore, not only is the firm's probability distribution of sales output an important consideration of the chosen employment contract, but also the payment schedule I(y)), which specifies how the risk of this sales output probability distribution will be shared is important. The choice of the firm's employment contract most often is the result of a trade-off between its productive efficiency (the distribution of x induced by the contract via its effect on the agent's incentive to provide preventive maintenance) and its risk-sharing efficiency. For example, if the agent is paid a flat fee, he has no motivation to provide preventive maintenance and bears no financial risk. In order to achieve a more preferred sales output probability distribution, the principal may have to increase the agent's incentive to provide preventive maintenance by increasing the agent's financial risk. The agent's motivation to provide preventive maintenance will be maximized if he pays a flat fee for the use of the machine and keeps the balance of the sales output for himself. Such an arrangement greatly increases the financial risk that the agent must bear. Because the agent is risk averse, this latter arrangement might not be Pareto optimal either. In short, the agency solution requires a trade-off between productive efficiency and risk-sharing efficiency.

Finally, it should be noted that the optimal agency employment contract is *ex ante* efficient, but not necessarily *ex post* efficient. After the agent has chosen his preventive maintenance level, both individuals might be made better off by renegotiating the chosen payment schedule and monitoring system. But since the original agreement is assumed to be legally enforceable, they are prohibited from renegotiating. If the agent knew that they would renegotiate the employment contract after his action was implemented, his original action choice would no longer be optimal. Both individuals are made better off, *ex ante* by being prohibited from renegotiating the contract, *ex post*.

The Mathematical Formulation of the Basic Agency Model

The principal and agent must agree on a contract that is Pareto optimal as of the time that the firm is formed. Therefore the efficiency of any contract must be evaluated based on the information possessed by each at the time that the firm is formed. In addition, the efficiency of the contract is constrained by the fact that the level of preventive maintenance implemented will be the one that maximizes the agent's expected utility given the employment contract and his information.

Any Pareto optimal contract can be represented as one that maximizes one person's expected utility subject to the other person receiving no less than some specified level of expected utililiy.[13] Thus, an optimal contract for the preventive maintenance example is one that maximizes the principal's expected utility subject to the agent receiving at least some specified level of expected utility and also subject to the level of preventive maintenance activity being chosen so as to maximize the agent's expected utility given the chosen contract and his own information. In the agency literature it is usually assumed that the principal is the dominant bargainer and therefore that the agent's minimum specified level of expected utility is the expected utility he could receive by selling his services to the market, K.[14] The following is therefore the standard agency formulation of the preventive maintenance example and, more generally, of the basic agency problem:[15]

$$\max_{\substack{\eta \epsilon \Xi \\ I(\cdot)\epsilon I \\ e\epsilon E}} \iint G(x-I(y))\phi(x,y|e,\eta) \; dxdy \tag{1}$$

Subject to:
$$\int U(I(y),e)\phi(y|e,\eta)dy \geq K \tag{2}$$
$$e\epsilon \; \text{Argmax}_{e'\epsilon E} \left[\int U(I(y),e')\phi(y|e',\eta)dy \right] \tag{3}$$

The only jointly observed information signal is y; therefore the monitoring signal y is the only argument on which the payment schedule, I($\cdot$), can be based.[16] Second, all individuals are assumed to have the same beliefs at the time that the firm is formed. They also share these same beliefs at the time that the preventive maintenance level is chosen. This is reflected in the mathematical formulation by having all individuals use the same probability distribution $\phi(\cdot)$.

The preceding mathematical program represents the principal's problem of choosing a Pareto optimal employment contract. His problem is to choose that employment contract that maximizes his own expected utility (Expression (1)) subject to the agent finding it in his own best interest to work for the firm (Expression (2)) and subject to the agent choosing that preventive maintenance activity that maximizes his own expected utility (Expression (3)). It will be easiest to explain the above mathematical formulation by explaining the meaning of each expression starting first with (3).

Expression (3), referred to as the agent's action self-selection constraint, represents the agent's preventive maintenance decision rule. It specifies that the agent will choose that preventive maintenance activity that maximizes his expected utility, taking the principal's choice of the payment schedule and monitoring system as given. The agent does not try to influence the principal's choice of I($\cdot$) and η with threats (the Perfect Nash solution). It is Expression (3) that restricts the principal's attention to only the self-enforcing triples $(\eta,I(\cdot),e)$. The agent bases his decision on his beliefs (represented by $\phi(y|e, \eta)$), which are the same as those held by the agent and principal at the time that the firm was formed. No new information is revealed between the time that the firm is formed and when the agent chooses e. If, at optimality, Expression (3) were not a binding constraint and therefore could be dropped,[17] then the cooperative solution would be attained since the problem of motivating the agent represented by Expression (3) could then be ignored.

The agent will not join the firm unless his expected utility from doing so is at least as great as his expected utility from selling his services in the labor market. Since the principal knows the agent's preferences and beliefs, the principal is able to evaluate each $(\eta,I(\cdot))$ and *induced* e combination from the agent's point of view. The principal can then restrict his search to those self-enforcing triples $(\eta,I(\cdot),e)$ for which the agent would agree to work for the firm. This restriction is reflected in Expression (2).

Expression (1) indicates that the monitoring system and payment schedule are chosen to maximize the principal's expected utility. Of course, the value to the principal of any monitoring system — payment schedule pair depends upon the level of preventive maintenance that it will induce the agent to take. Again, the principal is assumed to know the agent's preferences and information. Therefore, for each feasible employment contract the principal can solve the agent's choice problem (Expression (3)) in order to determine the preventive maintenance activity that the agent would be induced to provide given that contract. Thus the solution to Expression (3) is an argument in the principal's objective function, Expression (1). If the solution to Expression (3) for any given pair $(\eta,I(\cdot))$ is unique, then that preventive maintenance activity which the agent is induced to provide by $(\eta,I(\cdot))$ is used in Expression (1) to evaluate that pair $(\eta, I(\cdot))$. Thus only self-enforcing triples $(\eta, I(\cdot), e)$ are evaluated by the principal. If, however, for any given pair $(\eta, I(\cdot))$ the solution to Expression (3) is not unique, it is assumed that the agent will pick from the set of maintenance levels that satisfies Expression (3) the maintenance level most preferred by the principal (as implied by the Pareto criterion). This accounts for the presence of the preventive maintenance activity as a decision variable in the principal's objective function.

Criticisms and Extensions of the Basic Agency Problem

The basic agency problem described earlier can be criticized along at least two dimensions. First, its assumptions would seem to limit its descriptive validity to a very small set of problems. Second, even if we accept the intrinsic interest of this small set of problems, the standard mathematical formulation of the basic agency problem can be criticized. Because most of the agency research has been based on the basic agency problem using the formulation as given above, it is necessary to consider the severity of these two types of criticisms in order to evaluate the potential of the agency model as a foundation for a positive as well as normative theory of managerial accounting. The criticisms of the standard mathematical formulation are discussed first.

Some Criticism of the Basic Agency Formulation

(a) The Class of Payment Schedules

In Expression (1), the principal restricts his choice of payment schedules to the class of pure, nonrandomized payment schedules. This seems intuitively reasonable since the agent and (usually) the principal are risk averse and therefore introducing any additional uncertainty by means of randomized payment schedules could only reduce utility. Accordingly, almost all of the agency research starts by implicitly restricting the payment schedule to be nonrandomized. (Myerson [1979; 1980; 1981] is the exception). However, if the Pareto efficient frontier is not concave, then randomized payment schedules may be Pareto superior to nonrandomized ones (see [Raiffa, 1968] for a graphical illustration of this point). The idea here is that if the Pareto surface is not concave it can be made concave by randomizing the payment schedule.

A problem therefore arises in that the results of much of the basic agency research may be based on suboptimal payment schedules. However, Gjesdal [1981] showed that a sufficient condition for the Pareto optimality of pure payment schedules is that the agent's utility in wealth and effort be additively separable (i.e., $U(I,e) = H(I) - V(e)$). But that is the assumed form of the agent's utility function in most of the extant agency literature. Further, the condition that the agent's utility function be additively separable is a sufficient condition, not a necessary condition. Therefore, the Pareto optimality of pure payment schedules *may* hold for an even larger class of utility functions, as well. Thus the severity of the criticism cannot be determined until the entire class of utility functions for which pure payment schedules are Pareto superior to randomized ones is established. This remains an open question.

(b) Formulation of the Agent's Problem

The formulation of the basic agency problem (Equations (1), (2), and (3)) allows for the situation in which the agent's optimal maintenance choice is not unique. However, the problem is almost always analyzed using a solution approach which requires that the optimal preventive maintenance level exist, that it be *unique*, and that it satisfy a *stronger* condition than Expression (3), namely the stationarity condition:

$$\frac{\partial}{\partial e'} \left[\int U(I(y),e')\phi(y|e',\eta)dy \right]_{e' \,=\, e} = 0 \tag{3'}$$

which is comparable to a first-order condition in the calculus.

> The uniqueness of the optimal maintenance activity is required because the agency problem is usually formulated as an optimal control problem with η and $I(\cdot)$ as the decision variables and e as the state variable. In optimal control problems the path of the state variable must always be uniquely defined by the state equation (Expression (3) or (3')).

Expression (3') is more restrictive than Expression (3) in that Expression (3) is the necessary and sufficient condition for optimality, for the agent's choice problem for *all* situations, while Expression (3') is the necessary and sufficient condition for optimality for only a subset of situations. Therefore, most of the basic agency results hold only for the class of problems for which, at the optimal $I(\cdot)$ and η, the agent's optimal preventive maintenance level exists, is unique and satisfies Expression (3'). Does such a class of problems exist? Can the class be characterized? These questions are addressed next.

Grossman and Hart [1980] found examples for which, at the optimal $I(\cdot)$ and η, the agent's optimal action choice was not unique. Mirrlees [1974] and Gjesdal [1976] found a class of problems for which the agent's optimal action did not exist. This latter class of problems, however, does not appear to be very large or interesting, since it essentially assumes that the principal can inflict arbitrarily large penalities on the agent.

Mirrlees [1979], however, found conditions under which the agent's optimal action choice exists and is unique and for which Expression (3') is a necessary and sufficient condition. The conditions found by Mirrlees [1979] do not appear to be overly restrictive and are consistent with Gjesdal's [1981] sufficient condition for the optimality of pure payment schedules. Further, by employing a formulation of the basic agency problem different from Expressions (1), (2), and (3'), Grossman and Hart [1980] were able to use a less restrictive solution approach than that used in previous agency research. Their formulation and solution approach allowed for the situation in which the agent's optimal maintenance level choice is not unique. Most of the results derived by Grossman and Hart [1980] were consistent with results derived from the more usual formulation (Expressions (1), (2) and (3')).

Thus Mirrlees [1979] showed that the class of problems for which the usual agency formulation (Expressions (1), (2), and (3')) is appropriate is both large and interesting. Further, Grossman and Hart [1980] showed that many of the results derived from the usual agency formulation also hold for classes of problems that cannot be so formulated.

In summary, the generality of the basic agency results seems to withstand both of these technical criticisms. The basic agency problem still analyzes a highly simplified organizational context, however. To what extent can the model be generalized? This issue is addressed below.

Extensions of the Basic Agency Problem

The basic agency problem includes a number of restrictive assumptions. In this section the implications of some of these assumptions are discussed. What will *not* be discussed in this section is whether the assumptions are realistic or not. Rather an instrumentalist approach [Friedman, 1953; Boland, 1979] will be taken; this approach judges a theory by its implications, not by its assumptions. From an instrumentalist veiwpoint the falsity of a theory's assumptions does not matter if its predictions are correct. This section studies the sensitivity of the results derived from the basic agency problem to changes in its underlying assumptions. Among the most restrictive assumptions imposed by the basic agency problem are: a single agent, exogenous labor markets, and a single period. Almost all of the results that will be discussed later were derived from models incorporating these three assumptions; therefore it is important to analyze the implications of these assumptions before discussing the results.

(a) Multiple Agents

While the agency problem as formulated can be expanded to the case of more than two people, most results are based on the two-person case. The results from a two-person analysis may not necessarily extend to a larger firm for several reasons. First, the subtle and difficult problems associated with coalition formation among the members in a firm of three or more persons are suppressed in a two-person firm. Allowing for collusive behavior among the firm's members may give rise to substantially different employment contracts and managerial accounting procedures than in a two-person firm. In additon, admitting coalitions implies that the self-enforcing notion discussed earlier must be broadened to incorporate coalition formation. That is, not only must the contract be such that each agent acting on his own finds it in his best interest to act as promised, but each agent acting in concert with any subset of the firm's members finds it in his own best interest to act as promised (see [Amershi and Butterworth, 1979] on this point). Second a two-person firm ignores the full hierarchical nature of the firm. Admitting multilevel firms may give rise to results that are also different from those to be presented later. Finally, in a firm with several agents, an agent could engage in a simultaneous play game against the other agents and therefore find it optimal to engage in randomized behavior.[18] In the basic agency problem, the agent plays a sequential-play game with the only other person involved (the principal), and therefore a pure action strategy is optimal.

The extent to which allowing for multiple agents will qualitatively change the two-person agency results or reduce the tractability of the agency model must await further research. However, there appear to be no *conceptual* problems in expanding the agency model to incorporate more people.

(b) Exogenous Labor Market

Because the agent's minimum expected utility is given and independent of the decisions taken by both the agent and the principal, the analysis of the basic agency problem is a partial equilibrium analysis. Interesting issues such as the effect of introducing new monitoring technologies on the labor market cannot be addressed within the model as formulated. Again, there appear to be no conceptual or technical problems in expanding the basic agency model to incorporate an endogenous labor market. In addition, the result should not be qualitatively different with this change since the effect is merely to enlarge the range of rewards and penalities that the agent can incur.

(c) Single Period

By limiting the model to a single period, many interesting issues are suppressed. Certain observed phenomena such as downward wage rigidity and the importance of trust and reputation in market exchanges are all meaningless in a single-period world but can be shown to be optimal responses in multiperiod settings. (See [Townsend, 1980], [Dye, 1980], [Holmstrom, 1981b], [Milgrom and Roberts, 1980] and the implicit contract theory literature separately surveyed by Azariadis [1980]). By expanding the basic agency model to multiple periods one may also be able to address rigorously the issue of short-run vs. long-run maximization by management (see [Lambert, 1981]). Further, combining a multiperiod model with an endogenous labor market constraint may greatly reduce the problem of moral hazard by increasing the cost to the agent of diverging from the cooperative action choice. Fama [1980] has argued that moral hazard will be completely eliminated in this case. Townsend [1980] and Radner [1980] found restrictive conditions under which moral hazard can be eliminated when one goes to an *infinite* period problem.

In addition, two weaknesses in the Perfect Nash solution concept arise when the agency model is expanded to include multiple periods and asymmetric information. First the rationality implied by the Perfect Nash solution concept may not be applicable at all decision points. Second the incompleteness of information may not be dealt with satisfactorily by the Perfect Nash solution concept. As a result, within a multiperiod setting, the solution concept may lead to results that do not conform to a priori notions of optimality. (See [Kreps and Wilson, 1981]).

For a multiperiod setting, the definition of a Perfect Nash solution needs to be stated more formally than it was earlier for a single-period setting. A strategy is Perfect Nash for a game if for every proper subgame, the strategy restricted to that subgame constitutes a Nash equilibrium for that subgame. Given this definition, two problems may arise. First, at any information set on the game tree, what is optimal behavior depends on one's beliefs as to which node within that information set one is occupying. But these beliefs may depend on which strategies were previously implemented. The Perfect Nash solution concept does not allow for the complete incorporation of this dependence within one's beliefs. Second, in a game with asymmetric information, not every decision node is the start of a proper subgame. Therefore, the Perfect Nach solution concept does not require its rationality assumption to hold at any decision node that is not the start of a proper subgame.

Kreps and Wilson [1981] overcome these problems by generalizing the Perfect Nash solution concept to what they call a sequential equilibrium solution concept. A sequential equilibrium requires that the decision taken by each player at *each* information set must be part of the equilibrium strategy from that point forward given his beliefs about the evolution of the game to that point. His beliefs must be consistent with Bayesian updating based on the hypothesis that the equilibrium strategy has been used to date and will be used in the future.

Thus, the Kreps and Wilson [1981] analysis provides the techniques with which to expand the basic agency problem to a multiperiod setting. The few results based on the analyses that have been done within the context of a finite-lived agency model are not qualitatively different from results based on a single-period model (see [Lambert, 1981] and [Townsend, 1980]).

In summary, then, it appears that the three basic agency problem assumptions discussed here can each be relaxed without raising major conceptual or technical problems. Whether relaxing one or more of these assumptions will result in qualitatively different findings must await further analysis. However, at this time, while it appears that relaxing the labor market and single-period assumptions will result in richer findings, it does not appear that such relaxations will result in findings that are qualitatively different from those derived from the basic agency problem. More analysis of multiagent problems is needed before we can determine the effect of relaxing the single-agent assumption.

This completes the preparatory explanation of the agency model, its objectives and assumptions. Given this previous discussion, we can next proceed to the survey and evaluate the results of the agency literature.

SURVEY OF THE AGENCY LITERATURE

Classification Scheme for the Survey

The agency theory literature is concerned with two interrelated issues: the *ex ante* value of information and how that information should be used in contracts. These issues are interrelated since the value of information depends upon its use. These issues are also crucial to the managerial accountant in his work. In designing the firm's managerial accounting system, the accountant must decide which information to collect regularly and which to collect on an *ad hoc* basis. In short, he must have a way of assessing the *ex ante* value of information. The managerial accountant is also concerned with the use of the information collected. For example, simultaneous with deciding whether and how to measure the cost of a maintenance department, the managerial accountant must decide how to use that information in evaluating the performance of the maintenance department as well as the production departments that use the services of the maintenance department.

Can agency theory help the managerial accountant to assess the *ex ante* value of information and to design procedures to use that information? The agency literature is surveyed here with this question in mind. The literature dealing with the *ex ante* value of information is broken down into parts. The value of the public post-decision information system (the monitoring system) in the basic agency problem is studied first. Thereafter, the value of information in the presence of pre-contract information asymmetry and in the presence of pre-decision information asymmetry is studied. The discussion may be more technical than some readers require. Therefore, each of these parts starts with a summary of the issues addressed and the results derived by the literature surveyed in that section. The section on the Value of Information is concerned only with necessary and sufficient conditions for information to have *ex ante* positive value, assuming that the information is used optimally. The normative aspects of agency results (when *should* information be collected) are therefore stressed.

The literature dealing with the optimal use of information is surveyed next. The concept of responsibility accounting is often used as a framework when designing managerial accounting information systems and procedures. The responsibility accounting concept is evaluated in light of recent agency results. The question of interest here is whether the results of agency research are consistent with the implications of responsibility accounting. The remainder of this section discusses agency theory results relevant to managerial accounting tools such as budgets, conditional variance investigation policies, cost allocation procedures, participative budgeting, and standards. The focus is whether the observed use and form of each of these managerial accounting procedures is consistent with an agency view of the firm. Thus, discussion of the positive implications of agency results is stressed.

As noted earlier, managerial accounting information is used for two purposes: belief revision and performance evaluation. Performance evaluation involves risk-sharing and motivation. These three uses of information are often in conflict. By using information to reduce the risk borne by the agent one may reduce his motivation. By providing pre-decision information to the agent for belief revision purposes one may make it less risky for the agent to shirk and thereby reduce his motivation. These examples suggest that with incomplete information, moral hazard and adverse selection problems (that is, motivational problems) are often mitigated by inefficient risk-sharing (relative to when motivation is not an issue). Therefore, to understand the value and uses of information fully, it is important to study it in situations in which both state uncertainty (and therefore, risk-sharing) and motivational issues are present. For this reason, this survey will concentrate on the literature in which both risk-sharing and motivational considerations are important to the value and use of information. Table 1 presents a classificaton of the agency literature based on the previous discussion.

Table 1. Classification of Agency Literature

Motivational Issues (Moral Hazard and/or Adverse Selection)

	Suppressed	Allowed
Suppressed		Alchian and Demsetz [1972], Holmstrom [1981[a]]
Allowed *State Information Symmetry*	Arrow [1973], Raviv [1979], Demski [1976], Wilson [1968], Demski-Swieringa [1974]	Harris and Raviv [1979], Demski and Feltham [1978], Gjesdal [1976], Feltham [1977], Mirrlees [1974, 1975, 1979], Shavell [1979], Holmstrom [1979], Baiman and Demski [1980a, 1980b], Fama [1980], Lambert [1981], Lewis [1980], Radner [1980], Townsend [1980], Grossmann and Hart [1980]
State Uncertainty *Pre-Contract State Information Asymmetry*		Harris and Townsend [1981], Myerson [1979, 1980, 1981], Sappington [1979], Demski and Feltham [1978]
Pre-Decision State Information Asymmetry		Harris and Raviv [1979], Christensen [1979; 1980a; 1980b], Holmstrom [1979], Groves [1975], Groves and Loeb [1979], Loeb [1975], Magee [1980], Atkinson [1978; 1979], Baiman and Evans [1981] Kanodia [1980], Baron and Holmstrom [1980], Ramakrishnan [1980], Sappington [1979]
Post-Decision Information Asymmetry	Townsend [1979][a]	Gjesdal [1981], Holmstrom [1981a], Evans [1980][a], Ng and Stockenius [1979][a]

[a]These papers concern auditing and will not be discussed in this survey.

The Value of Information

The uses of information were discussed in the previous sections. This section addresses the determinants of the value of information. Given the basic agency model in which the only information system to be manipulated is the post-decision information system producing signal y (i.e., the monitoring system), what changes in that system can make both principal and agent unambiguously better off? The literature addressing this issue is surveyed first; the literature dealing with pre-contract information is addressed next; and that concerned with pre-decision information is addressed last.

The Value of Post-Decision Information in the Basic Agency Problem

Should a division's income be measured on the basis of historical cost, price-level adjusted historical cost, or current cost? Should a division's fixed assets be measured on the basis of historical gross book value, historical net book value, or current cost? These and comparable questions are addressed in the managerial accounting literature but have not yet been satisfactorily resolved [Solomons, 1965;

Anthony and Dearden, 1976]. Each of these questions is asking for a preference ordering over a set of public post-decision information systems. These questions are specific examples of the more general issue concerning the conditions under which one public post-decision information system (i.e. monitoring system) is strictly Pareto superior to another, independent of the preferences and beliefs of the individuals involved. (All comparison with respect to information systems are comparisons between their *Pareto frontiers*: η_1 is Pareto superior to η means that the Pareto frontier of η_1 is everywhere to the right (northeast) of the Pareto frontier of η.) The fact that a preference ordering over information systems is independent of the preferences and beliefs of the individuals involved is important since it reduces the amount of information required to correctly apply the ordering.

In this section, the agency literature that addresses this general issue is surveyed. Any guidelines this literature can offer to help the managerial accountant assess the relative values of different public post-decision information systems should be of great benefit.

The most general result in this area is due to Holmstrom (1981a]. His analysis concerns the relative evaluation of any two costless[19] public post-decision information systems such that the signal produced by the second system is a deterministic transformation (independent of the state realization and the agents' actions) of the signal produced by the first system. An example of such a comparison would be between one monitoring system whose signal is (x,e) and a second system whose signal is (x). His result states that the first costless public post-decision information system is *strictly* Pareto superior to the second, regardless of the preferences and beliefs of the principal and agents, *if and only* if the signals of the first system convey more information about the actions chosen by the agents than do the signals of the second system. The idea of more information as used here is that implied by the concept of statistical insufficiency as defined in statistics and decision theory. While the *if* part of this result may seem intuitive or even tautological, recall that the measure of more information is a technical condition derived from a single-person setting in which there are no problems of risk-sharing or motivation. But yet Holmstrom's result shows that this measure is still useful in a multiperson setting in which risk-sharing and motivational considerations are important. The *only if* part of Holmstrom's result is important in its restrictiveness. In order to evaluate the usefulness of this result for managerial accounting, it is first necessary to determine which, if any, pairs of managerial accounting reporting systems satisfy the information system relationship assumed by Holmstrom [1981a]. That is, which pairs are such that the signal of one is a deterministic transformation of the signal of the other. If the traditional reporting alternatives are found to satisfy the relationship between the information systems assumed by Holmstrom [1981a] *and* are comparable on the basis of his informativeness condition, then the sufficiency (*if* part) of Holmstrom's [1981a] result provides the managerial accountant with a way of choosing among alternative public post-decision information systems independent of the beliefs and preferences of the principal and agent involved. If the traditional reporting systems can be paired such that the signal of the second system is a deterministic transformation of the signal of the first but the first signal does not convey more information than the second, Holmstrom's [1981a] result says that the ranking of the two monitoring systems *cannot* be done independent of which principal and agent are to use the system. Finally, if the alernative monitoring systems with which the managerial accountant is concerned are such that the signal of one is not a deterministic transformation of the signal of any of the others, then Holmstrom's [1981a] result is of no direct help. Analysis of which of these three situations describes the managerial accountant's choice problem has not yet been addressed. But at least Holmstrom's [1981a] result helps us to know what to look for first in analyzing the managerial accountant's monitoring system choice problem.

In the basic agency problem, on which the research to be surveyed is based, there is (i) homogeneity of opinions, (ii) symmetric pre-decision information, (iii) symmetric pre-contract information, (iv) a single agent, and (v) the post-decision information system alternatives are costless. Asymmetry of information arises only after the single agent chooses his preventive maintenance as a result of the principal privately observing the output, x. This part of the survey of the agency literature is concerned with the value of public post-decision information systems and is organized and discussed in order of increasing generality of the information system comparisons.

Comparing a Nonnull Public Post-Decision Information System With a Null System

The least general comparison between public post-decision information systems is between one that produces a signal y ϵ Y and one that produces no signal at all (the null system). When would receiving the costless public post-decision signal y, be strictly Pareto superior to receiving no public post-decision signal? In other words, when can any constant payment schedule [20] be strictly Pareto dominated by a payment schedule based on y ϵ Y?[21] Clearly it can never be Pareto inferior to observe y jointly and costlessly because both individuals can always agree on a payment schedule that ignores y. However, when can *strict* gains be made by jointly and costlessly observing y? Shavell [1979] showed that the principal and agent can both be made strictly better off (a strict Pareto improvement can be made) by installing a costless information system that publicly reports y = x. Gjesdal [1981] generalized Shavell's result by showing that as long as y is correlated with x,[22] a strict Pareto improvement can be made by installing the information system and using its signal as an argument in the payment schedule. The reasoning behind both results is that by jointly observing y versus no signal, a contract with improved motivational effects [Shavell, 1979] and/or improved risk-sharing effects [Gjesdal, 1981] can be achieved, resulting in a strict Pareto improvement.

Comparing a Public Post-Decision Information System That Produces Signal y With One that Produces Signal y' = (y,e)

Assume that the principal and the agent have previously agreed on an employment contract that incorporates the costless public post-decision information system, η, whose signal is y ϵ Y. Under what conditions can a strict Pareto improvement be made by substituting a new costless post-decision information system, η', whose signal y' ϵ Y' reports both the signal from the previous system η and the agent's actual preventive maintenance activity e, i.e., y' = (y,e)? Again this question can be restated as: When can any payment schedule based solely on y ϵ Y be strictly Pareto dominated by a payment schedule based solely on y' = (y,e)?

> Clearly a necessary condition for η' to be strictly preferred to η is that the cooperative solution cannot be achieved with a payment schedule based only on y. Otherwise, reporting the maintenance level can have no value. Demski and Feltham [1978] and more generally Harris and Raviv [1979] showed that neither party can be made better off by expanding the public post-decision information systems to η' (i.e. substituting a payment schedule based on y' for one based on y) if either:
>
>   (i) y = x and the agent is risk neutral
>
> or
>
>   (ii) y = (x,θ)
>
> That is, if either (i) or (ii) holds, the cooperative solution can be achieved with a payment schedule based only on y and hence there can be no value to publicly reporting the agent's chosen preventive maintenance level, e. In the first case, efficient risk sharing implies that the agent should bear all the risk by paying the principal a flat fee. (This assumes that the agent will not go bankrupt and be unable to pay the fee.) The agent bears all the cost of his maintenance decision, thereby eliminating the motivational (moral hazard) problem by internalizing it. In the second case, knowing θ and x(e,θ) allows the principal effectively to infer ex post the agent's maintenance decision. Since the principal is work indifferent, all he needs to know is whether, given the realized breakdown parameter (θ), the payoff would have been generated by his desired e*, if it had been chosen. If we view (x(e,θ),θ) as an imperfect monitor of e we see that the probability of a Type II error (concluding that the agent chose e $\neq$ e* when, in fact, he chose e*) is zero. Thus the negation of (i) and (ii) provides a necessary condition for the cooperative solution to be unattainable with a payment schedule based only on signal y and hence provides a necessary condition for the managerial accountant to collect information on the agent's maintenance activity, such as by installing time clocks, or supervisory monitoring. This necessary condition is simple to apply and, thus, may be useful to the managerial accountant who is assessing the value of expanding his public post-decision information system.

Is the negation of (i) and (ii) also a sufficient condition for the strict Pareto superiority of publicly, costlessly, and perfectly monitoring the agent's maintenance activity? That is, does the negation of (i) and (ii) imply that any payment schedule based only on signal y can be strictly Pareto dominated by a payment schedule based on signal y' = (y,e)? Harris and Raviv [1979] assert that given that y = x, the negation of (i) and (ii) is a sufficient condition. If this analysis held under general conditions, it would represent a very useful result for the managerial accountant. The Harris and Raviv [1979] proof is based on the calculus of variations and therefore holds only for those situations for which the optimal payment schedule exists, is unbounded, and is differentiable. How, general, then, is their sufficiency condition?

Mirrlees [1974] provides an example in which no optimal solution exists when one allows for unbounded payment schedules or an unbounded utility function for the agent. In this case a contract based solely on x can approximate arbitrarily closely one based on x and e. Further, Gjesdal [1976] and Feltham [1977] point out a class of problems for which the optimal payment schedules do exist but are neither differentiable nor continuous. For example, if the firm's production function is such that the minimum possible firm payoff is increasing in e

(i.e. $\dfrac{\partial}{\partial e}\left\{\min_\theta x(e,\theta)\right\} > \theta$)

and there are sufficient penalties available, then the optimal sharing rule based on y = x will be discontinuous, and either the cooperative solution is attained or it can be approximated arbitrarily closely.[23] Therefore, in neither of these cases would the agent or principal pay to report the level of maintenance. Notice that the assumption which drives the Gjesdal [1976] and Feltham [1977] results is that the production function is such that by using x as an imperfect monitor of e, one can construct a monitoring system with a zero probability of a Type II error. Thus the restrictions underlying Harris and Raviv's [1979] sufficiency result reduces its generality and usefulness for managerial accounting.

Noting these problems with the Harris and Raviv [1979] result, Holmstrom [1979] formulated the agency problem differently. He restricted the optimal payment schedule to be bounded but allowed it to be nondifferentiable. Holmstrom [1979] showed that if the set of x's (the set of sales values of the machine's output) which have a positive probability of occurring is independent of e,[24] if x is increasing in e, and if the agent is strictly work averse, then the cooperative solution is not attainable with a contract based solely on x. These conditions eliminate the situation in which x can be used as an imperfect monitor of e but one whose probability of a Type II error of zero, such as the production functions studied by Gjesdal [1976] and Feltham [1977]. Because the cooperative solution can be achieved with a contract based solely on y' = (x,e),[25] and because his assumptions do not appear overly restrictive, Holmstrom [1979] has defined a large class of problems in which both the principal and agent can be made strictly better off by expanding the accounting system to costlessly and perfectly monitor the agent's maintenance decision.

In summary, recent agency results provide the managerial accountant with conditions as to when a strict Pareto improvement can be achieved by expanding the public post-decision information system to costlessly and perfectly report the agent's preventive maintenance activity (e). Costlessly expanding the monitoring system to report e has *no* value if either (i) the agent is risk-neutral and x is already being reported or (ii) x and θ are already being reported [Harris and Raviv, 1979; Demski and Feltham, 1978]. Under either of these two conditions the cooperative solution is achievable with a contract based only on x and (x,θ), respectively. Therefore reporting the agent's preventive maintenance activity (e) cannot result in a strict Pareto improvement. Further if x is currently being reported, if the principal can inflict arbitrarily large penalties on the agent and if the firm's production function is such that using x as a monitor of e results in a zero probability of a Type II error (concluding that the agent chose e $\neq$ e* when in fact he chose e* for any e* ϵ E), then again reporting e cannot result in a strict Pareto improvement [Gjesdal, 1976; Feltham, 1977]. Thus, the negation of the above conditions is a necessary condition for monitoring the agent's activity to have strictly positive value. Finally, Holmstrom [1979] found a *sufficient* condition for a strict Pareto improvement to result from costlessly expanding the monitoring system from one that reports x to one that reports x and e. This sufficient condition is essentially the previously mentioned necessary condition. This sufficient condition seems to be consistent with a large class of problems. A drawback of these necessary results and sufficiency results is that they relate to the issue of costlessly expanding the public post-decision information system to include the perfect reporting of the agent's preventive maintenance activity. However, this is an alternative that the managerial accountant rarely has available. More often the accountant must decide whether to expand the accounting system to include an *imperfect* monitor of the agent's activity. This type of information system comparison is discussed next.

Comparing a Public Post-Decision Information System Which Produces Signal y With One that Produces Signal y' = (y,z) Where z Is An Imperfect Monitor

The question now becomes: When can a strict Pareto improvement be made by costlessly expanding the public post-decision information system from reporting $y = x$ to reporting $y' = (x,z)$, where z is an *imperfect* monitor of θ and/or e?[26] The answer is not intuitively obvious. For even if there are gains to the *perfect* monitoring of e, this may not imply that a strict Pareto improvement can be achieved with *imperfect* monitoring of e. While the imperfect monitoring of e may reinforce the agent's work incentive, the additional uncertainty introduced by the imperfect monitor may decrease the welfare of the risk-averse principal and agent more than enough to compensate for the first effect.

> With this in mind Harris and Raviv [1979] found conditions under which any contract based solely on signals $y = x$ can be Pareto dominated by one based solely on signals $y' = (x,z)$. However, the criticisms made earlier of the Harris and Raviv [1979] analysis also hold here. Harris and Raviv [1979] restricted their analysis to public post-decision information systems such that $z = e + \delta$ where the distribution of δ is independent of e and θ and the range of δ is independent of e. With unbounded payment schedules and this type of monitoring system, one can use the Gjesdal [1976] analysis to show that one can either attain the cooperative solution or come arbitrarily close to it. Since such monitoring systems are therefore essentially perfect, they are of limited interest.
>
> Gjesdal [1976] and to a greater extent Shavell [1979] and Holmstrom [1979] generalized the imperfect monitoring results of Harris and Raviv [1979]. Holmstrom [1979] defined a signal, $y' = (x,z)$ to be informative relative to the signal $y = x$, with respect to action e, if $y = x$ is not sufficient for $y' = (x,z)$ with respect to e, in the sense of statistical sufficiency. That is, the signal $y' = (x,z)$ is informative relative to the signal $y = x$ with respect to e if z conveys information about e not already conveyed by x alone. Assuming that both information systems are costless, Holmstrom [1979] proved that, regardless of the preferences and beliefs of the principal and agent, a payment scheduled based on signal $y = x$ can be strictly Pareto dominated by one based on signal $y' = (x,z)$ if and only if $y' = (x,z)$ is informative relative to $y = x$, with respect to action e. Note that since x is reported by both information systems compared by Holmstrom [1979] and the principal and agent have homogeneous opinions, this informativeness condition assigns no purely risk-sharing value to the additional signal z. The value of reporting z derives solely from its motivational influence on the agent.
>
> The analyses of Holmstrom [1979], Gjesdal [1976], and Shavell [1979] differ in a number of assumptions. Holmstrom [1979] assumed that the agent's utility function is separable in money and effort. Gjesdal [1976] proved the sufficiency part of Holmstrom's [1979] result for the same utility assumption as Holmstrom [1979] but for signals that are independent of the realized breakdown parameter (the state). Shavell [1979] proved the sufficiency part for a more general agent's utility function, one that is increasing and concave in money and decreasing in effort but not separable. Shavell [1979] assumed that a pure payment schedule is Pareto superior to a randomized one (see earlier comments on this issue in the third section). Also Gjesdal [1976] and Shavell [1979] assumed that their problems were such that the cooperative solution could not be attained or approximated arbitrarily closely with a contract based only on x, whereas Holmstrom [1979] proved this. Finally, Holmstrom's [1979] result should be carefully applied since technically it holds only for those production function-information system pairs for which

$$\frac{\phi_e(x,z|e)}{\phi(x,z|e)} = g(x|e)$$

> for either all e or no e. That is, he uses a global (for all e) definition of nonsufficiency. Those distributions $\phi(\bullet|\bullet)$ for which the above holds for some but not all preventive maintenance levels are excluded from Holstrom's [1979] analysis. The size of the class of distributions thus excluded has not yet been established.

In summary, even when the managerial accountant is faced with a decision of whether to expand costlessly his managerial accounting system from one that currently reports only the firm's sales output to one that *also* reports an imperfect monitor of the agent's activity, the results of agency theory provide the managerial accountant with a theoretically correct method of comparison. If and only if the imperfect monitor of the expanded system conveys information about the agent's activity, not conveyed by the sales output number (in the sense of statistical sufficiency), can a strict Pareto improvement be achieved by expanding to the second system, independent of the beliefs and preferences of the principal and the agent [Holmstrom, 1979]. This result represents a significant step toward understanding the role and value of information within a multiperson firm and provides the managerial accountant with a theoretically correct method of comparing monitoring systems in multiperson firms. However, the comparisons discussed in this section were between a finer information system (reporting $y' = (x,z)$) and a coarser system (reporting $y = x$). What can be said if neither of the systems to be compared is finer than the other?

Comparing a Public Post-Decision Information System Producing Signal y With One Producing Signal y^T

The three types of public post-decision information system comparisons discussed so far have had one feature in common. In all cases, the comparisons were between two systems, one of which was finer than the other. That is, in all three cases, one information system reported all the data reported by the other *plus* an additional piece of data. Can agency theory provide a utility-free and belief-free way of ordering two public post-decision information systems where one is not finer than the other? The limited success that agency research has had in this endeavor is discussed now.

Gjesdal [1981] and Holmstrom [1981a] generalized their earlier analyses to make such comparisons. Let public post-decision information system η produce signal y, which need not include x as an element. Let the public post-decision information system η^T produce signal $y^T = T(y)$: where $T(\cdot)$ is any function whose sole argument is the output of system η. Again, both systems are costless. Holmstrom [1981a] then showed that a necessary and sufficient condition for any payment schedule based on signal $y^T = T(y)$ to be strictly Pareto dominated by one based on signal y, independent of the preferences and beliefs of the principal and agent, is that $y^T = T(y)$ is not sufficient for y with respect to e in the sense of statistical sufficiency. I shall refer to this as Holmstrom's second informativeness condition. Holmstrom's earlier informativeness result [1979] is a special case of this more recent one, since he uses the same condition of statistical sufficiency in both but in Holmstrom [1981a] he applies it to a more inclusive set of information system comparisons. However, Holmstrom [1981a] assumed a risk-neutral principal while Holmstrom [1979] allowed for a risk-averse principal. Gjesdal [1981] proved only the sufficient part of this result for noisy (necessity for noiseless) signals but for a risk-averse principal. Finally, the sufficient part of Holmstrom's [1981a] informativeness result dealt only with production function-information system pairs that were either sufficient or insufficient at all levels of maintenance activity (the same caveat must be made for Holmstrom [1981a] as for Holmstrom [1979]), while Gjesdal's [1981] informativeness condition was required to hold only at the preventive maintenance level which was optimal for the payment schedule based on y^T.

All of the results surveyed so far have maintained the one principal — one agent assumption of the basic agency model and maintenance example. Baiman and Demski [1980b] and more generally Holmstrom [1981a] expanded the analysis to include multiple agents. Holmstrom [1981a] showed that his second informativeness condition was necessary and sufficient for one information system to be strictly Pareto superior to another in a multiagent setting as well.[27] However, the generality of this result is limited since Holmstrom's [1981a] analysis was based on the assumption that each agent's action choice was pure rather than randomized (see the previous discussion in the third section).

In summary, agency theory research has made significant progress in analyzing the value and role of public post-decision information systems and in providing normative rules for correctly choosing between costless public post-decision information systems in multiperson firms. Holmstrom [1981a] provides the most general conditions available for the belief-free and utility-free comparison of such systems. However this result is restricted to a comparison between two public post-decision information systems such that the signal of the second system is a deterministic transformation, independent of the state realization and the agents' action choices, of the signal produced by the first system. The first system strictly Pareto dominates the second system if and only if the signal produced by the second system is not sufficient relative to the signal produced by the first, with respect to the agents' action choices. This informativeness condition provides the managerial accountant with a theoretically correct and intuitive way of structuring the choices among a class of public *post-decision* information systems.

However, much more work remains to be done in this area of agency research. First, and foremost, while Holmstrom's [1981a] result is intuitive and easy to use, it does not apply to a large set of information system comparisons. It is necessary to determine whether we can enlarge the class of public post-decision information systems for which we can make theoretically correct utility-free and belief-free comparisons. Second, can Holmstrom's [1981a] results be generalized to multiperiod settings? Finally, one significant limitation of Holmstrom's [1981a] result is that it applies to public *post-decision* information systems; that is, to information systems whose only role is to supply information for performance evaluation purposes. However, as stressed earlier, information also has a belief revision role. Gjesdal [1981] showed that the preference ordering over information systems that are used strictly for performance evaluation purposes need not be the same as the preference ordering over the *same* information systems when they are used strictly for belief revision purposes. Managerial accounting information systems are used for *both purposes simultaneously* especially in a multiperiod setting. This dual use of the output of most managerial accounting information systems further limits the applicability of Holmstrom's [1981a] result to managerial accounting choice problems.

At this point the reader should be reminded that all of the results surveyed in this section were derived in the context of the basic agency problem. The assumptions of this problem included: no pre-contract information asymmetry, no pre-decision information asymmetry, and costless information. All of the results in this section dealt with comparisons between costless unconditional post-decision information systems. The costly post-decision information systems literature is surveyed as part of the discussion of the conditional variance investigation literature. The literature in which the other information symmetry assumptions are relaxed is discussed next.

The Value of Information in the Presence of a Pre-Contract Information System

The problem of interest here is the same as the basic agency problem except that the agent or principal receives private state information (for example, about the machine's breakdown parameter θ) — not received by the other party — prior to contract negotiations. It is assumed that the uninformed individual knows the characteristics of the private pre-contract information system but not the specific signal generated.

Several interesting issues regarding the use of information arise when one allows for private pre-contract information. When the individuals *agree* on an employment contract they do so based on their utility functions and on their information. Therefore, the uninformed individual may be able to infer something about the informed individual's information from the latter's bargaining behavior. How can the uninformed extract this information in the way most useful to him? How should the informed individual bargain over the employment contract considering that his bargaining behavior may reveal some of his private information? The pre-contract information asymmetry creates problems of adverse selection that are dealt with by the design of the employment contract. (See the signaling and screening literature such as [Riley, 1979] and [Spence, 1973], where the issue of adverse selection is of central importance).

The managerial accountant's role is to design the firm's pre-decision and post-decision information systems. Thus, issues related to the value of being "better" or "worse" informed prior to the formation of the firm are outside the purview of managerial accounting. (A more fundamental issue is whether such a partial ordering over pre-contract information systems can even be established). Of considerable interest, however, is the role of pre-decision and post-decision information systems in overcoming

When a private pre-decision information system is introduced, problems of adverse selection arise, as they did in the case of asymmetric pre-contract information. In the basic agency problem, the principal knows what the cooperative preventive maintenance level is. With a private pre-decision infor- the efficiency losses due to adverse selection problems caused by the presence of pre-contract infor- mation asymmetry. For example, does Holmstrom's [1981a] ordering rule for post-decision informa- tion systems hold even in the presence of pre-contract information asymmetry? Unfortunately, such issues that do have managerial accounting implications have not yet been addressed in the agency literature.

> However, methodological results that make it easier to address these managerial accounting issues have been derived. Harris and Townsend [1981] and Myerson [1980; 1981] have established variants of the Revelation Principle for the situation in which the pre-contract information asymmetry exists. This principle states that any vector of expected utility points (one component for each individual) which can be achieved by a contract that induces the informed individuals to lie about their private information can also be achieved by a contract that induces them to tell the truth. Thus, in searching for a Pareto optimal contract for a situa- tion in which there is pre-contract information asymmetry, one need only search over the set of contracts that induce the informed individuals to reveal their private information truthfully. This principle also holds for pre-decision information asymmetry. The Revelation Principle is a significant finding since it greatly simplifies the formulation of problems with informa- tion asymmetry. It will be discussed in more detail later.

The Value of Information in the Presence of a Pre-Decision Information System

Can all the members of the firm be made better off *ex ante* if the managerial accountant improves the pre-decision information which is made publicly available? Can all members of the firm be made better off *ex ante* if the managerial accountant improves the *private* pre-decision information of one or more division managers? How should headquarters structure the capital budgeting and operations budgeting processes to reduce the budgetary slack (inefficiency) that arises when the managers of divisions have private pre-decision information? All of these issues confront the managerial account- ant of a decentralized firm, because in decentralized firms information as well as decisions are decen- tralized. Answers to questions such as those raised above are crucial for the design of a decentralized firm, including its information system.

In this section the agency literature that addresses many of these issues is surveyed. In the literature to be surveyed, the problem of interest is the same as the basic agency problem except that now in addition to the public post-decision information system, there exists a pre-decision information system. This system produces a signal with information about the machine's realized breakdown parameter. It disseminates this signal prior to the agent's preventive maintenance decision but subsequent to the employment contract agreement. This additional information system may be: public, in which case both principal and agent directly observe its signal; or it may be private, in which case *only the agent* directly observes the signal. The latter case may arise as a result of the agent testing the machine before servicing it, but not telling the principal the results of the test. In the latter case, the principal knows the characteristics of the agent's private pre-decision information system (i.e. the characteristics of the test procedure) but not the signal that it produced.

The role and value of a pre-decision information system is more complex than that of a post-decision information system. Expanding a post-decision information system to report an additional piece of information will always result in at least a weak Pareto improvement,[28] since the principal and agent can always agree to a payment schedule that ignores the additional information. However, expanding a pre-decision information system to report an additional piece of information may not result in even a weak Pareto improvement.[29] The agent generally cannot commit himself to ignore the additional information, and therefore the optimal employment contract without the additional pre-decision infor- mation is no longer necessarily self-enforcing given the additional information. This is true whether the additional pre-decision information is privately reported or publicly reported.

mation system,[30] the principal no longer even knows which level of preventive maintenance is best, since he does not have all of the information possessed by the agent. In this case, the agent's role is not only to supply preventive maintenance but also to supply expert information. Thus, the private pre-decision information system has a belief revision role. The principal's problem is to *induce* the agent to use that private information to the principal's advantage.

With a private pre-decision information system, the principal and agent can always agree that the agent will communicate his private information to the principal and that this message will affect the agent's reward. Of course, the agent will choose his message strategy to maximize his expected utility. In this case, not only does the private pre-decision information system have a belief revision role, it also has a performance evaluation role.

In the expanded agency problem that includes a pre-decision information system, three questions arise concerning the value of information: (1) do the preference-ordering rules for post-decision information systems previously discussed still hold; (2) do comparable preference ordering rules over pre-decision information systems exist; (3) given a private pre-decision information system, when will communication between agent and principal result in a strict Pareto improvement? This section reviews results with repect to the first two issues. The last question concerning the value of communication is considered later within the discussion of the value of participative budgeting.

The results of the agency literature concerning the issues related to pre-decision information are not as well developed as those discussed in regard to post-decision information. This should not be surprising since research in this area is more recent and, as discussed, the role of information is more subtle. The literature surveyed in this section finds that, in the presence of a private pre-decision information system, Holmstrom's (1979) informativeness ordering over public post-decision information systems holds as a necessary condition but no longer as a sufficient condition. In addition, expanding the basic agency problem to include either a public or a private pre-decision information system does not *necessarily* result in a Pareto improvement. However, conditions under which a Pareto improvement would result have been derived.

The Value of a Public Post-Decision Information System in the Presence of a Private Pre-Decision Information System

What results are available on the value of a public post-decision information system when the agent has access to a private pre-decision information system?

First, assume that there is no communication between agent and principal about the agent's private pre-decision information. Harris and Raviv [1979] addressed the situation in which the agent's utility function was additively separable in wealth and effort and his private pre-decision information system noiselessly reported the state (the realized machine breakdown parameter). They found that the necessary and sufficient conditions for the post-decision information system whose signal is $y' = (x,e)$ to be strictly Pareto superior to the one whose signal is $y = x$ were the same as their conditions in the case in which there was no private pre-decision information system. Holmstrom [1979] also extended his imperfect monitoring model to the private pre-decision information asymmetry context. His informativeness conditon (Holmstrom [1979]) is still necessary for the post-decision information system whose signal is $y' = (x,z)$ to be strictly Pareto superior to the one whose signal is $y = x$ when there is private pre-decision information. However, because of technical issues the informativeness conditon is no longer sufficient.

Christensen [1979] extended Holmstrom's [1979] model to allow for communication between the agent and the principal about the agent's private pre-decision signal, ξ. Of course the message, m, chosen by the agent is his utility maximizing message which is not necessarily truthful. Again, the question is when is any payment schedule based on (x,m) strictly Pareto dominated by a payment schedule based on (x,z,m) where z is an imperfect monitor of e and ξ? Christensen [1979] showed that a generalization of Holmstrom's [1979] informativeness condition is still a necessary condition. In particular, a necessary condition for a contract based on (x,m) to be strictly Pareto dominated by one based on (x,z,m) is that (x,ξ) is not sufficient relative to (x,z,ξ) with respect to $e(\xi)$. Now the agent's preventive-maintenance decision is a function of his private signal ξ. Again this generalized informativeness condition is not sufficient because of technical reasons. Further, it would seem relatively straightforward to extend the necessity part of Holmstrom's [1981a] second informativeness condition to the situation in which the agent has private pre-decision information regardless of whether communication is allowed.

As noted earlier, if communication is allowed in an agency context, the agent will choose his message strategy so as to maximize his expected utility. In choosing the employment contract the principal would have to consider its effect on the agent's message strategy. However, as previously discussed, the Revelation Principle considerably simplifies the problem formulation. The Revelation Principle states that any outcome (in terms of the expected utilities of the individuals) which can be achieved by an employment contract that does not induce the agent to reveal his private information truthfully can also be achieved by an employment contract that does. It does not say that only truth-inducing employment contracts are optimal, but that without loss of generality the researcher can restrict his search to the class of truth-inducing employment contracts. The reasoning is fairly straightforward. Assume that the optimal employment contract is nontruth inducing so that the agent's optimal message mapping is $m(\xi)$. The principal can always commit himself, under the assumed legal structure, to garble the agent's message the same way that the agent did and then use the same employment contract as before. If $m(.)$ were the agent's optimal message strategy before, his optimal strategy now must be truth-telling. Further, the agent and principal receive the same expected utility under the new system as the old. The Revelation Principle was derived in its many forms by Harris and Townsend [1981], Myerson [1979; 1980; 1981] and Christensen [1979]. Harris and Townsend [1980] derived their result based on a multiperiod, multiagent formulation in which the agents were restricted to pure strategies. Myerson's [1979; 1980; 1981] analysis was based on a single-period, multiagent analysis in which the agents were allowed to use mixed strategies. Christensen's [1979] analysis was based on a single-agent, single-period analysis.

In summary, our ability to order public post-decision information systems, independent of the preferences and beliefs of the individuals involved, is considerably reduced in situations in which the agent has private pre-decision information. Holmstrom's [1979] informativeness condition is still a necessary condition for a strict Pareto improvement to result from expanding the public post-decision information system to report an additional piece of data. However, that condition is no longer sufficient when the agent has private pre-decision information. A more subtle question however, is under what conditions can a strict Pareto improvement be achieved by allowing the agent to acquire his superior *private* pre-decision state information? This issue is addressed in the next section.

The Value of Pre-Decision Information Systems

While a better private pre-decision information system may allow the agent to be better informed and capable of making better preventive maintenance decisions, it may also reduce his motivation by reducing the risk with respect to the uncertainty of the breakdown parameter that he must face. That is, improving the agent's private pre-decision information system may exacerbate the moral hazard problem. The net effect of the counteracting forces is not obvious. In fact, as long as the agent's information about the breakdown parameter is not effectively perfect, it is not even clear that installing a *public* pre-decision information system will result in a strict Pareto improvement. The agent may still be able to use the additional pre-decision information to shirk, possibly making the principal worse off. What agency results are there concerning the value of pre-decision information systems?

When the basic agency model is expanded to include a private pre-decision information system for the agent, the analysis and results depend upon whether communication between agent and principal is allowed. For the case in which communication is not allowed, Christensen [1979] constructed an example in which making the agent better informed results in the principal being made worse off. Atkinson [1978; 1979] and Baron and Holmstrom [1980] also addressed this issue. They each found that for the case in which the firm's output is jointly observed ex post ($y = x$), if only linear payment schedules are considered, then a Pareto improvement can be achieved by allowing the agent private access to a pre-decision information system. However, for the situations investigated by Atkinson [1978; 1979] and Baron and Holmstrom [1980], linear payment schedules are not optimal. Therefore, their results need not hold when optimal contracts are considered. Further, Atkinson's [1978; 1979] unambiguous results were based on a work-neutral agent and therefore the problem of the agent using the additional information to shirk was not considered.

If communication between agent and principal with respect to the agent's private pre-decision information is allowed, more definitive results are available. Christensen [1979] again provided an example in which the principal is made worse off by allowing the agent to receive private pre-decision information even when communication is allowed. However, Baiman and Evans [1981] found sufficient conditions under which expanding the basic agency problem to include a private pre-decision information system results in at least a weak Pareto improvement. Further, they offer an example satisfying their sufficiency condition in which a strict Pareto improvement is achieved. Unfortunately, the Baiman and Evans [1981] sufficiency condition is technical and without a satisfactory intuitive interpretation. Thus the extent to which this sufficiency condition is widely applicable has not yet been established.

Thus agency research has only limited help to offer to the owner of the machine in our simple example who is trying to decide whether to provide the agent with a private pre-decision information which will improve his information about the machine's breakdown parameter. Christensen's [1979] examples point out that the principal will not necessarily benefit, and may even suffer as a result of providing the information system to the agent. Baiman and Evans [1981] established sufficient conditions under which a weak Pareto improvement can be attained by providing the agent with the private pre-decision information system, but the generality of the condition is difficult to establish. Thus the available results in this area are at best suggestive. General guidelines for when a strict Pareto improvement can be achieved by acquiring a private pre-decision information system to whose signals only the agent will have access have yet to be established. Further, what results we do have with respect to private pre-decision systems deal only with comparisons between null and nonnull information systems. The question of the value of improving an already existing private pre-decision information system is more often at issue but has not been addressed at all in the agency literature. Thus a great deal more work is necessary before we can start to understand the effect of private pre-decision information systems on the efficiency of the firm.

Summary of the Value of Information Literature

As an overall summary, the extant agency theory literature has, with varying degrees of success, analyzed parts of the managerial accountant's choice problem rather than his problem in its entirety. For example, results have been obtained with respect to the ordering of information systems whose signals are used solely for performance evaluation purposes. More limited results have been obtained with respect to the ordering of information systems whose signals are used solely for belief revision purposes. But the signals produced by managerial accounting systems are often used for both purposes. Agency research has essentially no general results on how to order such dual-purpose information systems. However, given the short period of time that the agency method of analysis has been applied to the problem, this last remark should not give agency theorists or managerial accountants cause to despair. The results of agency research have clarified our thinking about the managerial accountant's choice problem and have given us additional insight into the implications of his choices. Each new result afforded by use of the agency model has allowed us to address more subtle issues or to generalize earlier results. Thus, the results of agency research to date seem to provide a convincing argument that the agency model has the potential to serve as the basis for a useful normative theory of managerial accounting.

Evaluation of Specific Managerial Accounting Procedures from an Agency Perspective

This survey of agency research has so far focused on those results that prescribed how to rank alternative information systems; the emphasis was on the normative contribution of agency theory to managerial accounting. The objective was to see what guidelines and insight the agency model could offer to the managerial accountant with respect to *how he should* choose among alternative accounting systems.

In general the extent to which we can have confidence that our normative prescriptions for managerial accounting will result in the desired outcomes depends upon how much confidence we have that the accounting systems will be used in the way hypothesized. What is important here is not whether people think and make choices in the way hypothesized but whether their actions are consistent with those implied by the hypothesized model of choice behavior. Thus any normative theory of managerial accounting must be based on some predictive or positive model. Can the agency model, which includes a model of individual behavior within the firm, serve in both these roles and thus be a self-contained and complete model of managerial accounting? This section focuses on the agency model as a positive model of managerial accounting. In order to do so, the major question addressed is the extent to which the results of agency research with respect to the use of information are consistent with currently observed uses.

Responsibility Accounting

When information is to be used for performance evaluation the concept of responsibility accounting has traditionally been relied upon to indicate how the information should be used or organized. Responsibility accounting states that a person should be evaluated only on the basis of those factors that he controls. This is *usually interpreted* to mean that a person should be evaluated only on the basis of those *outcomes* that he affects. This implies that the firm's public post-decision information should be organized in such a way that all costs, revenues, assets, and liabilities are traced to the individual who is primarily responsible for them.

For a world of complete certainty, agency research agrees with the above interpretation of responsibility accounting. The agent is assigned a task, the principal can costlessly verify whether the agent has performed the task and pays the agent the agreed upon fee for doing so. However, if we admit *ex ante* state uncertainty while still allowing for perfect costless post-decision information ($y = (x,e)$), the results of agency research no longer agree with the implications of responsibility accounting. In this case, with a risk-averse principal, the Pareto optimal contract would call for risk sharing. Therefore, the agent's payment would be a function not only of his task performance (level of preventive maintenance supplied), for which he is totally responsible, but also of the state realization for which he has no responsibility (see, [Demski, 1976]). However, if the principal holds a diversified portfolio of investments or represents the interests of a large group of diversified shareholders, he should be effectively risk neutral and would not use the agent to share risk for other than motivational purposes. If this were the case, then agency theory and reponsibility accounting would both reward the agent strictly on the observed preventive maintenance level (e).

When imperfect post-decision information is also allowed, the results of agency research and the implications of responsibility accounting differ further. From an agency perspective, an agent should *not* be evaluated only on those costs for which he is "primarily" responsible. Rather, all available information shoud be used to learn about the agent's action choice. For example, assume that in the preventive maintenance example the principal owns two machines and that he hires two agents. Each agent supplies preventive maintenance to a different machine. The only common factor between machines is the state occurrence. Therefore $x = x_1(e_1,\theta) + x_2(e_2,\theta)$. Agent 1(2) is responsible only for $x_1(x_2)$, and therefore responsibility accounting would be interpreted to mean that his payment should be a function only of $x_1(x_2)$. However, observing x_1 and x_2 may tell the principal more about the state outcome than observing each separately. This may allow the principal to infer each agent's choice more accurately than he could by observing each machine's output separately. Thus, for motivational purposes alone it may be Pareto optimal to base agent 1's (2's) payment on x_1 *and* x_2 even though he is responsible only for $x_1(x_2)$. Baiman and Demski [1980b] and Holmstrom [1981a] demonstrate this more generally.

This two-machine example and the results of Baiman and Demski [1980b] and Holmstrom [1981a] are not inconsistent with the objective of responsibility accounting, but rather with the way that it is usually interpreted. Agency theory and responsibility accounting differ when the goal of evaluating an individual only on the basis of those factors that he controls is interpreted by managerial accounting to mean evaluate the individual only on the basis of those *outcomes* over which he exercises control. Agency research concludes that this is too narrow an interpretation of responsibility accounting. In evaluating and rewarding an agent who controls only part of the firm's output, it may be optimal to evaluate the agent on the basis of the firm's entire output. The key is that even outputs over which the subordinate exercises no influence may contain information that can be used by the supervisor to improve his assessment of the subordinate's action choice.

Budgets

Budgeting is a frequently used managerial accounting tool. Does the current agency literature find the use of managerial accounting data in budget-based schedules to be Pareto optimal? Demski and Feltham [1977, p. 337] defined a budget-based payment schedule as one which satisfies three criteria:

> 1. the worker's compensation is, in part, a function of some observable attribute(s) of the outcome resulting from his actions;
> 2. the contract specifies a budgeted (standard) outcome (attribute) level that partitions the set of possible outcomes into favorable and unfavorable subsets; and
> 3. the worker's compensation function consists of two or more functions, one defined over the favorable subset and the other defined over the unfavorable subset.

The third point implies that a budget-based contract cannot be everywhere differentiable in the observable attribute.

Demski [1976] and Wilson [1968] did not find budget-based contracts to be Pareto optimal in the situations they addressed. The use of budgets is usually associated with motivational problems, and the Demski [1976] and Wilson [1968] analyses were concerned solely with optimal risk sharing and side betting.

Demski and Feltham [1978] addressed the issue of the optimality of budget-based payment schedules but were not able to demonstrate sufficiency conditions. They did present numerical examples demonstrating the Pareto superiority of budget-based contracts over optimal linear contracts. Lewis [1980] generalized Demski and Feltham's [1978] numerical examples. Mirrlees [1974], Gjesdal [1976], Feltham [1977] and Harris and Raviv [1979] all found conditions under which budget-based contracts are not only optimal but also either induce the cooperative solution or come arbitrarily close to the cooperative solution.[31] While it is heartening to find results that do support the use of managerial accounting data in budget-based payment schedules, these latter results are limited in their positive implications since some rely on unbound penalties and all produce the cooperative solution, neither of which is usually observed in practice. Thus, the question remains: are budget-based contracts ever Pareto optimal in second-best situations? Holmstrom [1979] provides an affirmative answer.

Holmstrom [1979] characterized the optimal payment schedule for a class of problems for which the cooperative solution was not achievable. In this class of problems, which is restricted to those problems in which the payment schedule is bounded, the optimal payment schedule will be budget-based for at least two situations:

> (i) The optimal incentive function is not everywhere interior (i.e., for some monitoring signals either the maximum or minimum allowable payment to the agent will be made.).
> (ii) The agent's action affects what "state" a machine is in, but not the output given that it is in that "state."

The second condition can be illustrated in terms of the preventive maintenance example. If the agent's preventive maintenance activity affects the probability of whether the machine breaks down, but not when it will break down (after how much output has been produced), then the second condition will be satisfied. In particular if the principal is risk neutral, then the optimal payment schedule will be one constant if the machine breaks down *at any time* and a different constant if it does not break down. This payment schedule clearly satisfies the definition of a budget-based contract.

Thus Holmstrom's [1979] result is consistent with the use of managerial accounting data in budget-based contracts. But how general are the sufficiency conditions? Does the agency model predict the use of budget-based contracts for those situations in which they are actually observed and not in other situations? Research at this level of detail has not yet been attempted. The problem is that the second condition is not very general while the first is difficult to apply. In particular the first condition is with respect to the optimal contract itself rather than an exogenous variable. Therefore it is difficult to know, *a priori*, when the first condition will be satisfied. Thus, the agency model is consistent with the use of budget-based contracts. But a finer test of the agency model based on comparing the predicted and actual use of budgets awaits the development of easier-to-apply sufficient conditions.

Conditional Variance Investigation Policies[32]

The research surveyed on the value of post-decision information dealt with the value of *costless unconditional* monitoring of the agent's maintenance activity. However, by ignoring the cost of monitoring one can never explain management's use of exception reporting, sequential (multistage) audits, and conditional variance investigation, all of which are commonly used control techniques in managerial accounting. By ignoring the cost of monitoring, the question of when to investigate is reduced to a choice between always and never.

Most of the conditional-variance investigation policies observed in practice are one- or two-tail policies: Investigate if $x \leq x_L$ and/or $x \geq x_U$. The rationale for such policies is based on the statistical quality control literature. The question of interest here is whether their use is optimal in a multiperson agency setting.

Dyckman [1969] and Kaplan [1969] among others (See Kaplan's [1975] survey article) have studied the issue of when to undertake a costly investigation. All of these studies base their analyses on nonagency models in which the possibility of investigation has no motivational effects. That is, they assume that the transition probabilities between exogenously defined in-control and out-of-control states for the object of investigation are invariant to the choice of the investigation policy. While this assumption may be reasonable when the object is an automated machine, it is not when the object is a person. The value of a variance-investigation policy is based not only on the undesirable behavior that is attempted and detected, but also on the undesirable behavior that is *not* attempted because of the chosen investigation policy.

Demski and Feltham [1978] studied conditional variance investigation by starting with the basic agency model in which the monitoring system reported $y = x$. However, in their model, after the principal observes x, he has the option of gathering additional (costly and imperfect) information about the agent's preventive maintenance activity. Any additional information gathered would be public and hence would be a potential argument in the payment schedule. Using examples, they compared the effect on the expected utilities of the principal and agent of using lower-tail investigation policies with an exogenously specified payment schedule, to allowing no variance investigation at all. They left unresolved the interesting questions of when such costly lower-tail conditional variance investigation policies are Pareto optimal and what the associated Pareto optimal payment schedule would be.

Baiman and Demski [1980a] used a model similar to that used by Demski and Feltham [1978] and demonstrated that the optimal variance investigation policy was pure rather than mixed. That is, for each possible sales output (x), the principal would either order an investigation or not, but he would not use a randomized decision rule. Further, Baiman and Demski [1980a] showed that the optimal conditional variance investigation policy was not, in general, lower-tail. Because the conditional variance investigation policy has both motivational and risk-sharing implications, the optimal policy tends to be quite complex. In fact, the set of sales outputs which trigger an investigation is not, in general, a convex set.

In a subsequent paper, Baiman and Demski [1980b] identified relatively mild conditions that were sufficient for the Pareto optimality of the one-tail conditional variance investigation policy studied by Demski and Feltham [1978]. However, Baiman and Demski [1980b] showed that the payment schedule assumed by Demski and Feltham [1978] was not optimal. The Baiman and Demski [1980a, 1980b] results thus show that the use and form of a much observed managerial accounting tool is optimal within an agency context.

To put the Baiman and Demski [1980a, 1980b] results in perspective, it is important to understand how sensitive they are to the particular assumptions made. While randomized investigation policies are never optimal for the problem analyzed by Baiman and Demski [1980a, 1980b], they can be optimal for the problem analyzed by Kanodia [1980]. The major reason for the difference in results seems to be two different assumptions. Kanodia [1980] assumed that the agent observed the state realization before choosing his action and that the investigation system was perfect. Baiman and Demski [1980a, 1980b] assumed that when the agent chose his action he was no better informed than the principal and that the investigation system was imperfect.

One further point should be mentioned about both the Baiman and Demski [1980a, 1980b] and Kanodia [1980] formulations. For the solution to work, the principal must irrevocably commit himself to carry out the chosen investigation policy. Within the basic agency model formulation, the principal *knows with certainty* what action the agent actually took. Therefore, the principal does not need to consume resources for a conditional variance investigation in order to learn the agent's action choice. In fact, it is totally irrational to investigate the action choice *after the fact* in these models. However, if the principal does not irrevocably commit himself to adhere to the *ex ante* optimal investigation policy, the agent will change his action choice accordingly, making *both* worse off. Thus, we should be careful in condemning certain policies that appear *ex post* irrational, as they may be unavoidable ways of achieving *ex ante* efficiency. This point will be discussed later in the context of cost allocations.

The Baiman and Demski [1980a; 1980b] and Kanodia [1980] papers open up a new way of looking at the familiar tool of conditional-variance investigation. It still remains to be seen whether the use of the two-tail investigation policies, also observed in practice, is optimal within an agency context. Further, while these studies have rationalized different structures for conditional-variance investigation policies that are observed in practice, they certainly have not rationalized the particular parameter settings used in these policies. That is, why, if the optimal policies are a function of the production process and risk characteristics of the principal and agent, do we typically see investigation being triggered based upon simple 1σ, 2σ, or 3σ rules? An interesting study here would be to see how robust such heuristic decision rules are within a simulation study. This simulation study would allow the agent to be a rational utility-maximizing individual, while previous simulation and numerical analysis studies, such as [Magee, 1976] and [Dittman and Prakash, 1979], assumed the agent to be a machine.

One final point concerning cost variance investigation is that while there is value to *gathering the information* on which variances are computed within the agency model, there is no value to the *computation* of variances (see [Baiman and Demski, 1981b]). Any variance policy or payment schedule that is stated in terms of some deviation from a standard can be stated equally well in terms of only the observation. Thus, within the agency model there is no value to computing variances. The rationale for calculating variances must lie elsewhere, perhaps in the notion that variances serve as a convenient, easily understood means of communicating.

Cost Allocation

Probably the most often used and least understood managerial accounting procedure is joint and overhead cost allocation. Textbooks teach cost allocation procedures but then provide examples of the problems that arise when performance evaluations or operating decisions are based on allocated costs. Despite the textbook examples, evaluation and decisionmaking based on allocated costs continue to be common practice.

Zimmerman [1979] and Demski [1981] have attempted to explain the use of cost allocation within an agency context. Zimmerman [1979] shows that varying the fixed component of an individual's payment schedule may affect his incentives. One can vary this fixed component through the cost that is allocated to the individual. However, Zimmerman, [1979] does not show whether such a payment schedule form is optimal, nor does he connect this fixed part of the payment schedule to cost allocation. One does not need the existence of overhead or joint costs in order to use his analysis. Therefore, it does not provide a convincing rationale for cost allocations.

Demski's [1981] analysis is similar to Zimmerman's [1979] in that his general discussion of the optimal performance evaluation system is never related to what one would call a cost allocation procedure, i.e., a fixed cost that gets split among a group of individuals. However, Demski [1981] does emphasize that whatever value comes from overhead allocation comes solely from measuring the variables of activity on which the allocations will be made. No value arises from the allocation itself.

I would like to suggest one *very* tentative agency scenario that might lead to the allocation of costs. Recall that conditional-variance investigation was shown to be an *ex post* irrational act that was required in order to maintain the *ex ante* optimal solution. It may be possible that cost allocation is a similar phenomenon in a multiperiod setting. For example, assume that a firm wants to buy a central computer. To decide on the appropriate size, it is necessary to know the true demands of each division manager, which is privately held information. Headquarters can guess at the total demand or it can try to induce the division managers to reveal their private information. Headquarters can influence these divisional demand messages and subsequent divisional computer use through its choice of an employment contract for the division managers and by the choice of the actual decision rule that it promises to use in going from divisional demand message to computer size purchase. One type of employment contract might include a payment schedule based on an allocation of the computer's fixed cost. It may turn out that such a contract is part of the *ex ante* optimal solution. If it were, it would be necessary for headquarters to commit itself to such *ex post* ''irrational behavior'' and its undesirable effects in order to achieve the *ex ante* optimal solution. This is only a conjecture but perhaps one worth pursuing since it may produce results within a rational multiperson context that are consistent with the observed use of a *seemingly* inefficient managerial accounting procedure.

Participative Budgeting

The conjectured rationale for cost allocation was based on the desire of the principal to extract private information from the agent. This communication process is often observed as part of the capital budgeting process of the firm and results from the headquarters and divisions bargaining over the latter's capital budget. This bargaining or communication procedure is often observed in the operational budgeting processes of firms as well. The latter is often referred to as participative budgeting since the agent is allowed to participate in the setting of the standards (budgets) against which his performance will be evaluated. A particular form of this participative budgeting is Management by Objectives in which discussions between principal and agent are used to set goals for the agent for several different activities rather than for just the agent's operating cost or profit.

The behavioural literature dealing with participation has emphasized the benefits derived from the mere act of participation. (For an excellent survey of the participation literature, see Locke and Schweiger [1979]). It has stressed that those involved in a participative arrangement derive utility from the act of participating independent of how participation influences the productivity of the firm. Agency theory research has emphasized that the value of participative budgeting arises from the information transmission that takes place. This information focus in agency theory is achieved by expanding the basic agency problem to incorporate a pre-decision information system with signals available only to the agent. *Given* that the agent has private pre-decision information about the machine's realized breakdown parameter, when can a strict Pareto improvement be achieved by allowing for communication between the agent and principal subsequent to the agent receiving his private signal but prior to the firm's output being revealed? With communication, the payment schedule can be a function of the agent's message as well as the signal produced by the monitoring system. Of course, depending on the employment contract, the agent's optimal message strategy may *not* be to tell the truth. However, it can never be Pareto inferior to allow for communication since the agent and principal can agree on a payment schedule that ignores the agent's message.

Christensen [1979; 1980a; 1980b] first formulated this expanded basic agency model to allow for both the agent's private pre-decision information system and communication. However, he did not address the value of communication. Magee [1980] studied the value of participation (communication) but only in the context of an example. Ramakrishnan [1980] further analyzed Magee's example.[33]

Baiman and Evans [1981] used Christensen's [1979] formulation and found necessary and sufficient conditions for communication (participation) to be strictly valuable in the Pareto sense. If the agent's private pre-decision information is perfect, then communication has no value. Observing the firm's output in that case allows the principal to infer all he needs to know about the agent's private pre-decision information. However, if the agent's private pre-decision information is imperfect, a necessary and sufficient condition for communication to be strictly valuable is for the honest revelation of the agent's private pre-decision information to be strictly valuable. That is, if any value can be achieved with the information being honestly revealed *to all*, then a strictly positive part of that value can be achieved by giving the agent sole direct access to the information and letting him communicate in a manner that maximizes *his* expected utility. The Baiman and Evans [1981] results thus provide a rationale for participative budgeting that is an alternative to (but not inconsistent with) the rationale offered by the behavioral literature.

> While the results in this section are interesting, as with all analytical results, it is necessary to understand how sensitive they are to the assumptions made. The models employed by both Christensen [1979; 1980a; 1980b] and Baiman and Evans [1981] represent the agency labor market constraint in the same way. In order for the agent to work for the firm, his employment contract must offer him expected utility at least as great as he could get in the labor market. Since he won't receive any private pre-decision information unless and until he joins the firm, his expected utility is based on his beliefs prior to receiving his private pre-decision information. Therefore, the models assume that the labor market is such that the agent cannot quit the firm after he has received his private pre-decision information but before he takes his action (provides preventive maintenance services). Once he joins the firm it is assumed that he can be legally forced to stay and work. In actual fact, labor contracts are not enforceable to that extent. It would therefore be interesting to see whether the Baiman and Evans [1981] results still hold if the firm had to offer a contract that not only induced the agent to join the firm, but also induced him to stay even after he received his private pre-decision information. This criticism is equally valid for the research dealing with the value of information in the presence of pre-decision information.

This entire area of decentralized private information giving rise to budget slack (inefficiency resulting from asymmetric pre-decision information), budget manipulation, and participative budgeting is central to our understanding of managerial accounting and management control, but one for which we have only the most rudimentary results. A great deal of future research is possible in this area alone. In this regard, I must agree with Horngren [1977] who states that:

> The personal goals of managers (personal income, size of staff, esteem, power) will often lead to the "bargained" budget, whereby managers intentionally create slack as a protective device. . . . This seeking of slack permeates all budgeting in every conceivable sort of organization. Little has been done to counteract it. . . . Despite these attempts at counteraction, slack remains one of the major unsolved problems in budgetary control.

Standards

An important concept in managerial accounting, central to both variance investigation and budget-based contracts, is that of a standard. Standards are output or cost levels that signal whether investigation should take place; they indicate points at which the nondifferentiability of the budget-based payment schedule occur. The traditional managerial accounting literature talks about descriptions of standards such as: perfection, tight but attainable, and historical average, among others. What does the agency literature suggest concerning the correct choice of standards?

Demski and Feltham [1978] use examples to indicate that the optimal performance standards, given some nonoptimal employment contracts, could be less than or greater than expected performance. Unfortunately work in this area has not progressed much beyond Demski and Feltham's [1978] examples, except for those cases such as Mirrlees [1974], Gjesdal [1976], Feltham [1977] and Harris and Raviv [1979] in which the cooperative solution is achievable. Using Holmstrom's [1979] formulation (for which only a second-best solution is achievable) to characterize the optimal standards and their sensitivity to the particular parameters of the problem, even if only by stimulation, remains an unexplored area that could provide some valuable insights into the budgeting process and the choice of standards used in that process.

Summary of Literature with Implications for Managerial Accounting Procedures

The purpose of this section was to survey and develop the insights that agency research can offer with respect to some commonly used managerial accounting procedures and their underlying frameworks. In particular the objective was to assess the extent to which the implications of agency research are consistent with managerial accounting practice. The framework of responsibility accounting was found to be consistent with the results of agency research. However, from an agency perspective, responsibility accounting was found to be interpreted too narrowly by managerial accounting texts.

The use and form of conditional-variance investigation, budgets, and participative budgeting were all found to be consistent with the agency model of the firm. In addition, agency analysis suggested a possible rationale for the observed use of cost allocations.

Thus the agency model has been quite successful so far as a positive model of managerial accounting. Its results have been found to be consistent with a number of commonly used procedures, and it has provided much insight into the managerial accounting process. Most of the results discussed in this section were based on the basic agency problem with its single-period and single-agent assumptions. The question remains whether expanding the agency problem to incorporate multiple periods and multiple agents will increase or decrease the extent to which the results of agency research are consistent with observed practice.

SUMMARY AND CONCLUSION

The purpose of this essay was fourfold: (1) to survey and synthesize the agency literature; (2) to provide a basis for evaluating the agency model as the foundation for a normative theory of managerial accounting; (3) to develop some of the implications of agency research for commonly used managerial accounting procedures; and (4) to identify some unanswered managerial accounting questions which may be amenable to an agency-type analysis. This was accomplished by analyzing the agency model, its assumptions and limitations, and by surveying its results.

While a number of criticisms of the mathematical formulation of the agency model were made, they do not appear to cause major difficulties. It is premature to translate the results of agency research into normative guidelines for the choice and design of information systems within decentralized firms. However, agency research concerning the value of information can provide the managerial accountant with useful insights into the implications of his choice and design of these information systems. Agency results pertaining to budgets, variance investigation, and participative budgeting were found to support observed practice. Of course, these latter results were based on single-period, single-agent models that assumed an exogenous labor market. Whether similar results can be obtained when these and other assumptions are relaxed awaits further research. However, it does not appear that relaxing these assumptions will change the qualitative nature of the results and hence their positive implications. In summary, the initial results of agency research do support the assertion that the agency model will be a fruitful tool for future research in managerial accounting and may, indeed, provide a framework from which a useful theory of managerial accounting can be derived.

FOOTNOTES

[1] This is especially true of the Williamson, et. al. [1975] research. However, it is also true of the Jensen and Meckling [1976] research, since much of their analysis was based on graphs that they failed to justify. Further, while much of their analysis was in the form of comparative statistics, they restricted the entrepreneur to a fixed nonoptimal employment contract.

[2] As will be discussed later in the paper, the ordering of information systems for belief revision purposes and for performance evaluation purposes are, in general, not the same.

[3] As Demski and Feltham [1977, p. 30] note: "With the evaluator's outcome generally dependent upon his as well as the decision maker's choice, we have a game situation. Although we do not explore determination of η^* (the optimal information system) and $\chi(\eta)$ (the decision maker's decision rule) in a game setting system (but, for simplicity treat $\chi(\eta)$ as exogenously given), it should be clear that such an approach would provide a more thorough analysis of the class of problems we are addressing."

[4] For example in the Dantzig and Wolfe [1960] decomposition model each agent is *assumed* to reveal truthfully his demand for each resource given the prices announced by the owner. Jennergren [1971] shows that each agent may be acting against his own best interests by responding honestly.

[5] The Prisoner's Dilemma (Luce and Raiffa [1957]) is the classic example in which self-interest precludes cooperative behavior even though each prisoner would be strictly better off by cooperating.

[6] The problem in the Prisoner's Dilemma presents a moral hazard: Both individuals would be better off if neither confessed. But such behavior is not enforceable because the two prisoners cannot write an enforceable contract between themselves based on their confessing behavior. That is, each individual's action choice is whether to confess or not. But in the Prisoner's Dilemma, the individuals cannot write a contract between themselves which punishes or rewards each based on their respective action choices.

[7] The arguments in the agent's schedule $(I(\bullet))$ are left unspecified until later.

[8] If the principal's and agent's assessed probability distributions over some uncertain event differ strictly because of different information, they are said to have different beliefs. If they differ for reasons other than different information, they are said to have different opinions. The distinction is important in that the existence of different opinions raises possibilities of side betting on the state realization between principal and agent. Most of the agency literature assumes identical opinions and therefore suppresses the use of information for side-betting purposes. Homogeneous opinions will be assumed throughout this paper. For analyses that do assume heterogeneous opinions, see [Wilson, 1968] and [Amershi, 1979].

[9] Contracts, or more generally behavior, may also be enforced by social pressure and reputational effects. See [Schelling, 1978] for discussion of these.

[10] This is an example of "first-mover's" advantage or the advantage one can gain in negotiation situations by reducing one's own options. See [Schelling, 1960] for additional discussion of these and other game-theoretic issues.

[11] The agent's *promised* as well as actual behavior is part of the agency solution.

[12] With a pure payment schedule, for any given observed signal y, the agent would receive a specified amount I(y). With a randomized payment schedule, for any given observed signal y, the agent would receive a specified *lottery* or gamble.

[13] It is irrelevant whose utility is being maximized. By adjusting the minimum utility constraint for the other person, any Pareto optimal solution can be attained.

[14] This assumption merely restricts our attention to examining one particular Pareto optimal contract. Since K is exogenously given, there is no loss of generality in posing the problem this way.

[15] It is assumed that the preventive maintenance problem has a feasible solution. Therefore, since the principal's expected utility is being maximized, it is assumed that his maximal expected utility from devoting his capital to the firm is at least as great as what he would receive by selling it to the market, C. Therefore the constraint that the principal's maximal expected utility be at least C is dropped.

There are two formulations of the agency problem: the approach used by Mirrlees [1974] and Holmstrom [1979] (which is used here) and the Ross state-space approach [1973]. See [Amershi, 1980a] and [Ramakrishanan and Thakor, 1979] for syntheses of these two approaches and a demonstration of their equivalence.

[16] The principal is assumed to observe the firm's sales output, x, while the agent observes y which may be an imperfect monitor of x. Thus the basic agency model, as formulated here is an inappropriate model if one is interested in addressing the auditing problem in which the agent observes x but the principal does not. This survey does not discuss the auditing literature. For those interested in that literature, see [Evans, 1980] and [Ng and Stoekenius, 1979].

[17] This would occur if the monitoring system reported e and the principal could severely penalize the agent for not choosing the preventive maintenance level specified by the principal.

[18] Myerson's [1979; 1980; 1981] formulation does allow for randomized action rules by the agents. More often, the multiagent models assume away randomized action choice rules for the agents (see [Harris and Townsend, 1981], [Baiman and Demski, 1980b], and [Holmstrom, 1981a] for examples where this is done).

[19] All comparisons in this part are between costless information systems. Costs are ignored because any information system can be made to be preferred to any other merely by changing the costs of each. While the cost of an information system is important, the relative benefits of different information systems can be addressed without referring to the cost to implement and operate each.

[20] The only possible nonrandomized payment schedule based on the null information system is a constant payment schedule.

[21] If every feasible payment schedule based on the signals of public post-decision information system η can be strictly Pareto dominated by at least one feasible payment schedule based on the signals of public post-decision information system η', then the Pareto frontier associated with η' is everywhere to the right (northeast) of the Pareto frontier associated with η, which implies that η' is strictly Pareto superior to η.

[22] More precisely, the principal's marginal utility for the machine's sales output and y must be correlated.

[23] For example, assume the following problem: The firm's profit is characterized as $x = e + \delta$ where δ is uniformly distributed between 0 and 1. The principal is risk neutral. The agent is risk and work averse with a utility function represented by $\sqrt{I(\bullet)} - e^2/100$. The agent's minimum expected utility from other employment is 5. The first-best solution results in: $I(\bullet) \simeq 27.35$ and $e^* \simeq 4.78$. The following contract, based solely on x can achieve the cooperative solution:

$$I(x) = \begin{cases} 5.23^2 & \text{if} \quad x \geq 4.78 \\ 0 & \text{if} \quad x < 4.78 \end{cases}$$

[24] This condition is violated in the example in footnote 23. Since δ is uniformly distributed between [0,1], changing e changes the set of x's which have a positive probability of occurring.

[25] The cooperative solution can be achieved with the following payment schedule based on $y' = (x,e)$:
    if $e = e^*$ let $I(y')$ be the cooperative payment schedule.
    if $e \neq e^*$ let $I(y')$ be the smallest feasible payment.

[26] Even if z is independent of e but is an imperfect monitor of θ, observing both z and x may improve the principal's assessment of the agent's preventive maintenance activity. Therefore the distinction between whether z is an imperfect monitor of e or of θ is unimportant.

[27] Baiman and Demski's [1980] result was similar to the sufficiency part of Holmstrom's [1981a] result but required an additional assumption that Holmstrom showed to be superfluous.

[28] *Ex ante* no one is made worse off and one or more individuals may be made strictly better off.

[29] *Ex ante* one or more individuals may be made worse off, as a result of expanding the pre-decision information system.

[30] Again the signals of a private pre-decision information system are directly received only by the agent.

[31] Harris and Raviv's [1978] result states that any continuously differentiable contract based on x and z can be dominated by what they call a dichotomous contract based on x and z. However, they restrict themselves to a class of post-decision information systems that have a movable support. Mirrlees [1974], Gjesdal [1976], and Feltham [1977] showed this type of system can be used to either attain a cooperative solution or get arbitrarily close to one.

[32] This topic deals with the value of gathering *costly* post-decision public information and therefore would also fit in with the discussion of the value of post-decision information. However, because variance analysis is a well-known managerial accounting procedure which is both based on managerial accounting information and produces managerial accounting information, it is included here.

[33] Ramakrishnan's [1980] more general analysis is based on a model which implicitly assumes away normal hazard problems associated with the agent's action choice.

REFERENCES

Alchian, A. A. and H. Demsetz (1972), "Production, Information Costs, and Economic Organization," *American Economic Review* (December 1972), pp.777-795.

Amershi, A. (1979), "A Theory of Firms under Uncertainty and Differential Information with Accounting Implications," Unpublished Working Paper, Stanford University (1979).

Amershi, A. (1980a), "Agency Theory: Clarifications, Consolidation and Extensions," Unpublished Working Paper, Stanford University (1980).

Amershi, A. (1980b), "Strategy-Information Core Contracts and the Social Value of Information in Security Markets," Unpublished Working Paper, Stanford University (1980).

Amershi, A. and J. E. Butterworth (1979), "The Theory of Agency—A Core Analysis," Unpublished Working Paper, SFU and Ceremade (1979).

Anthony, R. N. and J. Dearden (1976), *Management Control Systems: Text and Cases,* (R. D. Irwin, Inc., 1976).

Arrow, K. J. (1973), "Optimal Insurance and Generalized Deductibles," R-1108-OEO, The Rand Corporation (February 1973).

Atkinson, A. A. (1978), "Standard Setting in An Agency," *Management Science* (September 1978), pp.1331-1361.

Atkinson, A. A. (1979), "Information Incentives in a Standard-Setting Model of Control," *Journal of Accounting Research* (Spring, 1979), pp. 1-22.

Atkinson, A. A. and G. A. Feltham (1981), "Information in Capital Markets: An Agency Theory Perspective," Unpublished Working Paper, University of British Columbia (January 1981).

Baiman, S. (1975), "The Evaluation and Choice of Internal Information Systems Within a Multiperson World," *Journal of Accounting Research* (Supplement 1975), pp.1-15.

Baiman, S. (1981), "Comments on the Concept of Fairness in the Choice of Joint Cost Allocation Methods," in Moriarity, S. (ed.), *Proceedings of the University of Oklahoma Conference on Cost Allocation* (1981).

Baiman, S. and J. S. Demski (1980a), "Variance Analysis Procedures as Motivation Devices," *Management Science* (August 1980), pp.840-848.

Baiman, S. and J. S. Demski (1980b), "Economically Optimal Performance Evaluation and Control Systems," *Journal of Accounting Research* (Supplement 1980b), pp.184-220.

Baiman, S. and J. H. Evans III (1981), "Decentralization and Pre-Decision Information," Unpublished Working Paper, University of Pittsburgh (August 1981).

Baron, D. P. and B. Holmstrom (1980), "The Investment Banking Contract for New Issues Under Asymmetric Information: Delegation and the Incentives Problem" *Journal of Finance* (December 1980), pp. 1115-1138.

Boland, L. A. (1979), "A Critique of Friedman's Critics," *Journal of Economic Literature* (June 1979), pp. 503-522.

Christensen, J. (1979), "Communication and Coordination in Agencies: An Approach to Participative Budgeting," Unpublished Ph.D. Thesis, Stanford University (August 1979).

Christensen, J. (1980a), "Communication in Agencies," Unpublished Working Paper, Odense University (1980).

Christensen, J. (1979), "Participative Budgeting: An Agency Approach," Odense University (1980b).

Demski, J. S. (1967), "An Accounting System Structured on a Linear Program," *Accounting Review* (October 1967), pp.701-712.

Demski, J. (1976), "Uncertainty and Evaluation Based on Controllable Performance," *Journal of Accounting Research* (Autumn 1976), pp.230-245.

Demski, J. S. (1981), "Cost Allocation Games" in Moriarity, S. (ed.), *Proceedings of the University of Oklahoma Conference on Cost Allocation* (1981).

Demski, J. S. and G. Feltham (1977), *Cost Determination: A Conceptual Approach* (Iowa State University Press, (1977).

Demski, J. S. and G. Feltham (1978), "Economic Incentives and Budgetary Control Systems," *Accounting Review* (April 1978), pp. 336-359.

Demski, J. S. and R. J. Swieringa (1974), "A Cooperative Formulation of the Audit Choice Problem" *Accounting Review* (July 1974), pp. 506-513.

Dittman, D. and P. Prakash (1979), "Cost Variance Investigation: Markovian Control Versus Optimal Control," *Accounting Review* (April 1979), pp. 358-373.

Dopuch, J., J. G. Birnberg and J. S. Demski (1967), "An Extension of a Standard Cost Variance Analysis," *Accounting Review* (July 1967), pp. 526-536.

Dyckman, T. R. (1969), "The Investigation of Cost Variances," *Journal of Accounting Research* (Autumn 1969), pp. 215-244.

Dye, R. A. (1980), "Optimal Contract Length," Unpublished Working Paper, Carnegie-Mellon University (April 1980).

Evans, J. H. III (1980), "Optimal Contracts with Costly Conditional Auditing," *Journal of Accounting Research* (Supplement 1980), pp. 108-128.

Fama, E. F. (1980), "Agency Problems and the Theory of the Firm," *Journal of Political Economy* (April 1980), pp. 288-307.

Feltham, G. (1968), "The Value of Information," *The Accounting Review* (October 1968), pp. 684-696.

Feltham, G. (1977), "Optimal Incentive Contracts: Penalties, Costly Information and Multiple Workers," Unpublished Working Paper Number 588, University of British Columbia (October 1977).

Friedman, M. (1953), "The Methodology of Positive Economics," in Friedman, S. (ed.), *Essays in Postive Economics* (University of Chicago Press, 1953).

Gjesdal, F. (1976), "Accounting in Agencies," Unpublished Working Paper, Stanford University (1976).

Gjesdal, F. (1981), "Accounting for Stewardship," *Journal of Accounting Research* (Spring 1981), pp. 208-231.

Gonedes, N. J. and N. Dopuch (1974), "Capital Market Equilibrium, Information Production, and Selecting Accounting Techniques: Thoeretical Framework and Review of Empirical Work," *Journal of Accounting Research* (Supplement 1974), pp.48-129.

Grossman, S. J. and O. D. Hart (1980), "An Analysis of the Principal-Agent Problem" Unpublished Working Paper, CARESS (July 1980).

Grossman, S. J. and J. Stiglitz (1976), "Information and Competitive Price Systems," *American Economic Review* (May 1976), pp. 246-253.

Groves, T. (1975), "Information, Incentives, and the Internalization of Production Externalities," in Lin, S. (ed.), *Theory and Measurement of Economic Externalities* (Academic Press, 1975).

Groves, T. and J. O. Ledyard (1976), "Some Limitations of Demand Revealing Processes," Unpublished Working Paper, Northwestern University (May 1976).

Groves, T. and J. O. Ledyard (1977), "Optimal Allocation of Public Goods: A Solution to the 'Free Rider' Problem," *Econometrica* (May 1977), pp. 373-809.

Groves, T. and M. Loeb (1975), "Incentives and Public Inputs," *Journal of Public Economics* (1975), pp. 211-226.

Groves, T. and M. Loeb (1979), "Incentives in Divisionalized Firms," *Management Science* (March 1979), pp. 221-230.

Hakansson, N. (1977), "Interim Disclosure and Public Forecasts: An Economic Analysis and a Framework for Choice," *Accounting Review* (April 1977), pp. 396-416.

Hamlen, S. S. (1980), "A Chance-Constrained Mixed Integer Programming Model for Internal Control Design," *Accounting Review* (October 1980), pp. 578-593.

Hamlen, S. S., Hamlen, W. A. and J. T. Tschirhart (1977), "The Use of Core Theory in Evaluating Joint Cost Allocation Schemes," *Accounting Review* (July 1977), pp. 616-627.

Harnett, D. and W. Hamner (1973), "The Value of Information in Bargaining," *Western Economic Journal* (March 1973), pp. 81-88.

Harris, M. and A. Raviv (1979), "Optimal Incentive Contracts with Imperfect Information," *Journal of Economic Theory* (Vol. 20, 1979), pp. 231-259.

Harris, M. and R. M. Townsend (1981), "Resource Allocation Under Asymmetric Information," *Econometrica* (January 1981), pp. 33-64.

Hayes, D. C. (1977), "The Contingency Theory of Managerial Accounting," *Accounting Review* (January 1977), pp. 22-39.

Hirshleifer, J. (1971), "The Private and Social Value of Information and the Reward to Inventive Activity," *American Economic Review* (September 1971), pp. 561-574.

Holmstrom, B. R. (1979), "Moral Hazard and Observability," *The Bell Journal of Economics* (Spring 1979), pp. 74-91.

Holmstrom, B. R. (1981a), "Moral Hazard in Teams," Unpublished Working Paper, Northwestern University (February 1981).

Holmstrom, B. R. (1981b), "Equilibrium Long-Term Labor Contracts," Unpublished Working Paper, Northwestern University (January 1981b).

Horngren, C. T. (1977), *Cost Accounting: A Managerial Emphasis,* 4th ed. (Prentice-Hall, Inc. 1977).

Jennergren, L. P. (1971), *Studies in the Mathematical Theory of Decentralized Resource-Allocation,* Unpublished Ph.D. Thesis, Graduate School of Business, Stanford University (1971).

Jensen, M. C. and W. H. Meckling (1976), "Theory of the Firm: Managerial Behavior, Agency Costs and Ownership Structure," *Journal of Financial Economics* (3, 1976), pp. 305-360.

Kanodia, C. (1980), "Optimal Monitoring and Moral Hazard," Unpublished Working Paper, U.B.C. and University of Chicago (November 1980).

Kaplan, R. S. (1969), "Optimal Investigation Strategies with Imperfect Information," *Journal of Accounting Research* (Spring 1969), pp. 32-43.

Kaplan, R. S. (1975), "The Significance and Investigation of Cost Variables: Survey and Extensions," *Journal of Accounting Research* (Autumn 1975), pp. 311-337.

Kreps, D. M. and R. B. Wilson (1981), "Sequential Equilibria," Unpublished Working Paper, Stanford University (May 1981).

Lambert, R. A. (1981), "Managerial Incentives and Short-Run vs Long-Run Optimization," Unpublished Working Paper, Stanford University (January 1981).

Lewis, T. R. (1980), "Bonuses and Penalties in Incentive Contracting." *Bell Journal of Economics* (Spring 1980), pp. 292-301.

Locke, E. A. and D. M. Schweiger (1979), "Participation in Decision-Making: One More Look," *Research in Organizational Behavior* (1979), pp. 265-339.

Loeb, M. (1975), "Coordination and Informational Incentive Problems in the Multidivisional Firm," Unpublished Ph.D. dissertation, Graduate School of Management, Northwestern University (May 1975).

Luce, R. D. and H. Raiffa (1957), *Games and Decisions* (John Wiley & Sons, Inc., 1957).

Magee, R. P. (1976), "Simulation Analysis of Alternative Cost Variance Models," *Accounting Review* (July 1976), pp. 529-544.

Magee, R. P. (1980), "Equilibria in Budget Participation," *Journal of Accounting Research* (Autumn 1980), pp. 551-573.

Marschak, J. and R. Radner (1972), *Economic Theory of Games,* Cowles Foundation Monograph 22 (Yale University Press, 1972).

Milgrom, P. and J. Roberts (1980), "Predation, Reputation and Entry Deterrence," Unpublished Working Paper, Northwestern University (June 1980).

Mirrlees, J. A. (1974), "Notes on Welfare Economics, Information, and Uncertainty," in Balch, M., McFadden, F. and S. Wau (eds.) *Essays in Economic Behavior Under Uncertainty* (North-Holland 1974).

Mirrlees, J. A. (1975), "The Theory of Moral Hazard and Unobservable Behavior-Part 1," CARESS Working Paper #80-17, Nuffield College, Oxford, 1975).

Mirrlees, J. A. (1979), "The Implications of Moral Hazard for Optimal Insurance," Unpublished Working Paper, Nuffield College, Oxford University (April 1979).

Myerson, R. B. (1979), "Incentive Compatibility and the Bargaining Problem," *Econometrica,* Vol. 47 (January 1979), pp. 61-74.

Myerson, R. B. (1980), "Optimal Coordination Mechanisms in Principal-Agent Problems." Unpublished Working Paper, Northwestern University (June 1980).

Myerson, R. B. (1981), "Mechanisms Designed by an Informed Principal," Unpublished Working Paper, Northwestern University (June 1981).

Ng, D. S. (1975), "Information Accuracy and Social Welfare under Homogenous Beliefs," *Journal of Financial Economics* (March 1975), pp. 53-70.

Ng, D. S. and J. Stoekenius (1979), "Auditing, Incentives and Truthful Reporting," *Journal of Accounting Research* (Supplement 1979), pp. 1-34.

Papoulis, A. (1965), *Probability, Random Variables and Stochastic Processes* (McGraw-Hill Book Company, 1965).

Ponssard, J. P. and S. Zamir (1973), "Zero Sum Sequential Games With Incomplete Information," *International Journal of Game Theory* (Vol. II, Issue 2, 1973), pp. 98-107.

Radner, R. (1980), "Does Decentralization Promote Wasteful Conflict?" Unpublished Working Paper, Bell Laboratories (June 1980).

Raiffa, H. (1968), *Decision Analysis* (Addison-Wesley Publishing Company, 1968).

Ramakrishnan, R. T. (1980), "Performance Evaluation and Budgeting with Asymmetric Information," Unpublished Working Paper, M.I.T. (April 1980).

Ramakrishnan, R. and A. Thakor (1979), "The Economic Theory of Agency: Synthesis and Clarification," Unpublished Working Paper, Northwestern University (August 1979).

Raviv, A. (1979), "The Design of an Optimal Insurance Policy," *The American Economic Review* (March 1979), pp. 84-96.

Riley, J. (1979), "Noncooperative Equilibrium and Market Signalling," *American Economic Review* (May 1979), pp. 84-96.

Ronen, J. and J. L. Livingstone (1975), "An Expectancy Theory Approach to the Motivational Impacts of Budgets," *Accounting Review* (October 1975), pp. 671-705.

Ross, S. A. (1973), "The Economic Theory of Agency: The Principal's Problem," *American Economic Review* (May 1973), pp.134-139.

Sappington, D. (1979), "The Non-Optimality of the First-Best Contract in the Principal-Agent Model with Asymmetric Information," Unpublished Workng Paper, Princeton University (November 1979).

Schelling, T. C. (1960), *The Strategy of Conflict* (Harvard University Press, 1960).

Schelling, T. C. (1978), *Micromotives and Macrobehavior* (W. W. Norton & Co., 1978).

Shavell, S. (1979), "Risk-Sharing and Incentives in the Principal-Agent Relationship," *The Bell Journal of Economics* (Spring 1979), pp. 55-73.

Simon, H. A., H. Guetzkow, G. Kozmetzky and G. Tyndall (1954), *Centralization vs. Decentralization in Organizing the Controller's Department* (Controllership Foundation, 1954).

Solomons, D. (1965), *Divisional Performance: Measurement and Control,* (R. D. Irwin & Co., 1965).

Spence, M. (1973), "Job Market Signalling," *Quarterly Journal of Economics* (August 1973), pp. 355-374.

Townsend, R. M. (1979), "Optimal Contracts and Competitive Markets with Costly State Verification," *Journal of Economic Theory* (October 1979), pp. 265-293.

Townsend, R. M. (1980), "Contract Length and the Gain from Enduring Relationships," Unpublished Working Paper, Carnegie-Mellon University (May 1980).

Williamson, D. E., Wachter, M. L. and J. E. Harris (1975), "Understanding the Employment Relation: the Analysis of Idiosyncratic Exchange," *The Bell Journal of Economics* (Spring 1975), pp. 250-278.

Wilson, R. B. (1968), "The Theory of Syndicates," *Econometrica* (January 1968), pp. 119-132.

Zimmerman, J. L. (1979), "The Costs and Benefits of Cost Allocation," *Accounting Review* (July 1979), pp. 504-521.

SELECTED ANNOTATED BIBLIOGRAPHY

1. Baiman, S. and J. S. Demski "Economically Optimal Performance Evaluation and Control Systems," *Journal of Accounting Research* (Supplement 1980), pp. 184-220

   Baiman and Demski analyze, within the context of the agency model, some of the uses of information in the firm's performance evaluation and control system. They first derive sufficient conditions for the optimality of the familiar one-tail variance-investigation strategy. They also show that some of the implications of responsibility accounting are nonoptimal within a multiagent firm context. Finally, they point out that the value of variance investigation and cost allocation comes from the underlying disaggregation of data and not from the computation of variances and allocations.

2. Baiman, S. and J. H. Evans III, "Decentralization and Pre-Decision Information," Unpublished Working Paper, University of Pittsburgh (August 1981).

   Baiman and Evans focus on two issues in this paper: (1) conditions under which participative budgeting between a principal and a better informed agent leads to a strict Pareto improvement and (2) conditions under which a Pareto improvement is achieved by the agent acquiring additional private pre-decision information given a participative budgeting system is already in place. They use the participative budgeting formulation introduced by Christensen [1979] to address these issues. The authors find that participative budgeting will result in a strict Pareto improvement if and only if the agent's private information is such that costless public revelation of it would lead to a strict Pareto improvement. The authors also find a sufficient condition for both individuals to be made at least weakly better off by improving the agent's private pre-decision information. This sufficiency condition is of a technical nature and has no simple interpretation.

3. Christensen, J. "Communication and Coordination in Agencies: An Approach to Participative Budgeting," Unpublished Ph.D. Thesis, Stanford University, (August 1979).

   Christensen generalizes and expands the agency model to include communication and participation. He derives necessary and sufficient conditions for a public post-decision information system to have value in his expanded model. His conditions are analogous to Holmstrom's [1979] informativeness condition. The author also demonstrates that improving the agent's private pre-decision information can leave the agent better off but the principal worse off.

4. Demski, J. S., "Cost Allocation Games," in S. Moriarity (ed.) *Proceedings of the University of Oklahoma Conference on Cost Allocation* (1981).

   Demski criticizes the recent game-theoretic cost allocation literature for first assuming the use of cost allocations and only then offering properties that the required allocation should possess. Demski suggests that a more fundamental question is why we allocate costs at all. Demski posits three possible reasons for allocating costs and derives economically valuable allocation mechanisms that are consistent with these reasons.

5. Gjesdal, F., "Accounting for Stewardship," *Journal of Accounting Research* (Spring 1981), pp. 208-231.

   Gjesdal discusses the traditional stewardship literature in accounting and demonstrates the relevance of the agency model for clarifying and advancing that literature. The author generalizes earlier work of Shavell [1979] and Holmstrom [1979] on sufficient conditions for the strict positive value of public post-decision information. The author further divides the value of this information into its incentive value and insurance value. The author also demonstrates that the ordering of information systems for decision-making and for incentives purposes are, in general, not the same. Thus when evaluating an information system that will have both decision-making (belief-revision) and incentive effects a trade-off between these two purposes will have to be made. Finally, the author finds that a sufficient condition for the agent in a two-person agency model to choose only pure strategies is that he have an additively separable utility function in wealth and effort.

6. Grossman, S. J. and O. D. Hart, "An Analysis of the Principal-Agent Problem," Unpublished Working Paper, CARESS (July 1980).

   Grossman and Hart introduce a new formulation of the two-person symmetric information agency problem. They show that this new formulation avoids many of the mathematical (existence) problems inherent in previous formulations. In addition, using their problem formulation, the authors are able to rederive and refine previous agency results as well as derive new results.

7. Holmstrom, B. "Moral Hazard in Teams," Unpublished Working Paper, Northwestern University (February 1981).

   Holmstrom examines remedies to the moral hazard problem under both certainty and uncertainty. The author shows that, under certainty, moral hazard becomes a problem for a team only when one restricts one's choice of sharing rules to the set that always allocates the team payoff in its entirety to the team members. If one retains this "budget balancing" constraint, then monitors are required to mitigate the moral hazard problem under certainty. For the uncertainty case, Holmstrom generalizes his earlier informativeness result [Holmstrom, 1979] to multiple agents and to a wider class of information system comparisons. His result is that one can partially order public postdecision information systems in terms of their Pareto effects essentially using the notion of statistical sufficiency.

8. Myerson, R. B., ''Optimal Coordination Mechanisms in Principal-Agent Problems,'' Unpublished Working Paper, Northwestern University, (June 1980).

Myerson formulates the principal-agent problem allowing for multiple agents, each with private pre-decision information, as well as allowing for randomized strategies. The author shows that, without loss of generality, the principal can restrict himself to employment contracts whereby: (1) the agents are induced to honestly report their private information, and, (2) the agents are induced to follow the decisions made by the principal based on the centralized information. This ''Revelation Principle'' greatly simplifies the analysis of agency problems with asymmetric information.

Part V

EMPIRICAL ACCOUNTING RESEARCH

EMPIRICAL accounting research employing rigorous survey methods, questionnaires, behavioural experiments with hypothesis testing, etc., is of relatively recent vintage. It began in the fifties in the area of budgeting with the behavioural surveys of Chris Argyris,[1] continued with the award winning experimental research of Andrew Stedry,[2] and has since found widespread acceptance, even more so in financial accounting and related areas. Indeed, since the late sixties, especially during the seventies and early eighties, a large number of empirical accounting studies have emerged. It is not an easy task for the uninitiated to find his way through this maze of different but often interrelated topics and broader subject areas. Even experts occasionally require some guidance, and the survey article becomes an indispensable beacon for general orientation.

In the first article, Dyckman, Gibbins, and Swieringa begin with an overview of research in Financial Statement Disclosure and Use. They conclude that "there does not appear to be a burning desire for drastic revisions or changes . . . most of the criticism . . . is not that there is necessarily something wrong with what is presently reported, but that relevant data are left out. However, there is relatively little agreement about what these relevant data are." Meanwhile, of course, inflation became more rampant and legislations on current value disclosures, filling a particularly urgent need, have been issued in the United States (*FAS No. 33*) and Canada (Section 4510 of the CICA *Handbook*). The authors also confirm the limited usefulness of financial statements for making investment decisions. They then examine research on Accounting Principles and Models, including proposals on price-level and current-value accounting. The latter was only slightly favoured over the former -- a result that may have influenced the Financial Accounting Standards Board (FASB) and perhaps even the Canadian Institute of Chartered Accountants (CICA) to ultimately opt for a combination of both.[3]

Furthermore, the following special topic areas are examined: Segment and Subsidiary Reporting (where extensive practical problems impede progress); Interperiod Reporting (where a consensus favours more frequent reporting of income data before taxes and extraordinary items, as well as product-line breakdowns); Forecast Reporting (generally favoured by stockholders who assume that the major forecast assumptions are reviewed by the auditors); and Alternative Accounting Procedures and Changes in Reporting Practice (which indicates that alternative reporting procedures may influence individual evaluations and hints at the importance of FASB and CICA exposure drafts in developing attitudes toward changes).

This first article closes with two sections on the evaluation of Research Methods and of Research Impact. The authors, as empiricists, are in a way self-critical and expose a healthy scepticism when pointing out that the large increase in empirical accounting research (especially in the form of Ph.D. dissertations) has not resulted in a dramatic increase in our knowledge, something that is partly due to the lack of rigor and of sound theoretical background and partly due to a weak interrelation with the work of others. As to the impact of behavioural accounting research upon practice, the authors could not find any confirming evidence and point at the low credibility which this research carries with practitioners (this situation may have improved somewhat in the meantime). Particular worries are the failure of researchers to consistently follow through well-conceived research plans, the often haphazard selection of topics, the neglect of cost-benefit trade-offs, and an insufficient attention to basic research.

The second paper, by Kaplan, is predominantly concerned with the relevance of accounting data for investors.[4] It begins with the relation between empirical accounting research and the market model (a topic which the first part of our last paper recapitulates and tries to bring up-to-date). The author gives free rein to his astonishment over the fact that the securities market seems to be fairly efficient in spite of the widespread ignorance among "financially knowledgeable" people. His further discussions concern the information content of both Annual Accounting Numbers (providing strong evidence that income figures do have information content -- something which gives rise to unexpected security returns and also affects security riskiness) and Interim Earning Reports and Forecasts (the meaningfulness and relevance of which is evidenced by various studies; but it is pointed out that "it is most difficult to forecast earnings for those firms whose operations are most strongly correlated with economy-wide forces, i.e., high beta firms"). Further topics discussed in the second paper are: Time Series Behaviour of Earnings (indicating the inconclusiveness between the two extremes of either regarding the earnings series as following the rhythmic trend of a "moving-average mean reverting process" or regarding them as a "martingale process" in which successive earnings are conceived as being *independent* of each other; also pointing at the paucity of evidence for justifying both the extrapolation of growth trends and the smoothing of annual earnings); Evaluations of Accounting Alternatives (discussing conflicting evidence as to whether changes in accounting procedures were or were not associated with fluctuations in pertinent stock prices); and Accounting Ratios as Predictors of Business Failures (emphasizing the relevance and importance of related profile analyses, dichotomous classification tests, multiple discrimination analysis, split sampling techniques, etc.). Kaplan, although being enthusiastic about the early phase of empirical accounting research, wonders whether the past momentum can be maintained (so far, we would worry less about the momentum than about the direction of this research). He infers that many debates about alternative accounting procedures are not worth the costs, and he doubts whether empirical research can shed light on disclosure and reporting issues. In general, he closes this article on a somewhat pessimistic note.

The third article, by Gibbins and Brennan (now Hughes), is of most recent date and fulfills a dual function in our anthology. It not only brings up-to-date some of the material discussed in the first two articles of Part V, but concentrates more on behavioural accounting research in the *judgemental and decision-making literature*.[5] The emphasis here is not only on the evaluation of financial information by investors and creditors, but also on issues relevant for the FASB and its constituency. The major conclusions of this paper are:

(i) Behavioural studies had little success in confirming the predictions of normative models of judgement and decisions, but were somewhat more successful in confirming results of simple statistical models. Nevertheless, normative as well as statistical models seem to be useful first approximations of purposeful decision making and prediction.

(ii)   Although there was little support for alternatives to historical cost-accounting models, current-cost data are viewed more positively now than in the past among persons of influence.

(iii) Users' needs are specific, and no general summary of information priorities has or will emerge. Research interest is thus shifting towards the study of thought processes involved in investment decisions.[6]

(iv)   Accounting is *not* neutral, and more attention should be paid to its role as a behavioural control process (a statement which is not only in line with our plea for a *normative* approach, but also with managerial accounting and the more recent trend towards agency theory).

(v)   Behavioural accounting has no integrated theory, and progress might have to wait for a "hybrid approach" that provides more solid theoretical foundations.

The functions of the last paper, by Clarkson and myself, are: first, to emphasize empirical accounting research based on security markets; and second, to bring the reader up-to-date in this literature as well as in the area of experimental and survey research in financial accounting.[7]

The application of various versions of the efficient market notion and of the capital asset pricing model (developed in finance theory) to accounting raised the hope that, in this way, the content of public accounting information could be properly quantified.[8] But there is hardly any *theoretical* explanation about the extent and means by which accounting information is reflected in security prices. In consequence, the expectations put on this kind of research have been greatly moderated.[9]

It is regrettable that, so far, relatively little empirical research is concerned with objectives, information goals, and, above all, the means-end relations connecting specific accounting hypotheses to different information needs. The various issues of the FASB on objectives[10] might be regarded as a first step in this direction, but they hardly turned out to be satisfactory from an academic point of view and were criticized from several quarters.[11] A recent study dealing, to some extent, with objectives and preparing the ground for the appropriate empirical research is that by Paul A. Griffin.[12] *To Explain why specific accounting hypotheses* (as regards valuation, realization, classification, aggregation, etc.) *are preferred in certain situations, and why certain conceptual accounting tools are optimal in serving particular purposes* -- this, in our mind, ought to be a major task of empirical accounting research. Had empiricists paid more attention to this task, we might today be much closer to an analytically and empirically well-balanced, general theory of accounting.

Finally, I should like to draw attention to two recent historical surveys of empirical accounting and auditing research, edited by Robert H. Ashton: (1) *The Evolution of Behavioral Accounting Research: An Overview,* and (2) *Some Early Contributions to the Study of Auditing Judgment* (both New York: Garland Publishing, 1984), as well as to his recent CGA-Research Foundation Monograph No. 6 on *Research in Auditing Decision Making: Rationale, Evidenz, and Implications* (Vancouver: 1983).

To avoid duplication, we have provided a *commom bibliography* for all four papers *at the end* of this Part V.

R.M.

FOOTNOTES

[1] *The Impact of Budgets on People* (Ithaca, N.Y.: The Controllership Foundation, 1952).

[2] *Budget Control and Cost Behavior* (Englewood Cliffs, N.J.: Prentice-Hall, Inc., 1959/1960).

[3] This is to be most welcome, because only through such a combination is it possible to separate *fictitious* from *real* holding gains.

[4] One of the first modern books paying attention to this problem was George J. Staubus' *A Theory of Accounting to Investors* (Berkeley: University of California Press, 1961).

[5] Other excellent and more comprehensive surveys in this area are offered by Robert Libby, *Accounting and Human Information Processing: Theory and Applications* (Englewood Cliffs, N.J.: Prentice-Hall, Inc., 1981); and Robert Libby and B.L. Lewis, "Human Information Processing in Accounting: The State of the Art," *Accounting, Organizations and Society* 2 (1977), pp. 245-268; and *idem*, "Human Information Processing

in Accounting 1982,'' *Accounting, Organizations and Society* (1983).

[6] We, of course, would ask: "Why is there hardly any attempt to relate those specific needs to specific accounting models?''

[7] See also the paper by B. Lev and J.A. Ohlson, ''Market-Based Empirical Research in Accounting: Review, Interpretation and Extension,'' and other papers, all presented at the 1982 Annual Accounting Research Conference (Chicago: University of Chicago, Graduate School of Business, April 1982).

[8] ''By (1) isolating the release of accounting information as much as possible from other factors which might impact on security prices, (2) separating the security price change at that point of time into a part explained by the market model as well as an unexplained part, and finally (3) hypothesizing that the unexplained part was due to the accounting information release, these researchers were able to place a number on the information content of the release, an achievement which had seemed impossible until then.'' Hein Schreuder, ''Accounting Research and Practice,'' pp. 10-11, a paper presented at the Conference on ''New Challenges to Management Research'' of the European Institute for Advanced Studies in Management, Brussels, 23-24 May 1984.

[9] Cf. William H. Beaver, *Financial Reporting: An Accounting Revolution* (Englewood Cliffs, N.J.: Prentice-Hall, Inc., 1981).

[10] Financial Accounting Standards Board, *Objectives of Financial Reporting by Business Enterprises,* Statement of Financial Accounting Concepts No. 1 (Stamford, Conn.: FASB, 1978), and its preceding ''tentative conclusions (1976)'' and ''exposure draft (1977)''.

[11] Nicholas Dopuch and Shyam Sunder, ''FASB's Statements on Objectives and Elements of Financial Accounting: A Review,'' *The Accounting Review* 55 (January 1980), pp. 1-21; David Solomons, ''Judging Accounting Policies,'' in *1978 Accounting Research Convocation,* ed. by J.J. Davies (Tuscaloosa: University of Alabama, 1978), pp. 11-26.

[12] *Usefulness to Investors and Creditors of Information Provided by Financial Reporting: A Review of Empirical Accounting Research* (Stamford, Conn.: Research Report -- FASB, 1982), especially pp. 1-3 and 17-30.

EXPERIMENTAL AND SURVEY RESEARCH IN FINANCIAL ACCOUNTING: A REVIEW AND EVALUATION*

by Thomas R. Dyckman, Michael Gibbins and Robert J. Swieringa

Reprinted from The Impact of Accounting Research on Practice and Disclosure, ed. A. Rashad Abdel-khalik and Thomas F. Keller (Durham, N.C.: Duke University Press, © 1978), pp. 48-105.

THERE is a passage in Somerset Maugham's *A Writer's Notebook* that unfortunately may apply to many researchers. It reads: "She plunged into a sea of platitudes, and with the powerful breast stroke of a channel swimmer, made her confident way towards the white cliffs of the obvious" (Maugham, 1967: p. 174).[1] The intent of this paper is to review and evaluate the recently published experimental and survey research literature in financial accounting with a view to trying, in part, to determine whether we too have been paddling powerfully towards the white clifs of the obvious.

We will review a substantial amount of literature to see what the recent experimental and survey research has to tell us about present reporting problems and about the alleged impact of financial data on individual decision-making. We will examine alternative reporting models and disclosure practice to see what choices are indicated and what improvements are suggested. We will attempt to identify important issues addressed by this research and to note any advances in our understanding of these issues.

The next three sections of the paper will review the experimental and survey research that has been done. First, we will look at the research that has focused on financial statement disclosure and use. We will then turn our attention to research that has focused on accounting principles and alternative accounting models. The final portion of our state-of-the-art review will examine research that has focused on several specific topic areas that are not easily subsumed in the previous sections.

Following this review, we will examine briefly certain aspects of the research methods used because they are important factors in explaining why we have not progressed further, what must be done in the future, and why progress will not be easy. Finally, we will evaluate the relevance and impact of this line of research on financial accounting practice. Frankly, we believe that the data support the contention that experimental and survey research has made only a modest contribution to the resolution of reporting and disclosure issues. Moreover, the results may even have been counterproductive in several instances. Our evaluation will focus on the nature of the research task, on the characteristics of the reseachers themselves, and on the nature of the environment in which the reseach task and the researchers interact.

Both our charge and our choices have constrained the scope of this review. We were asked to limit our review to developments over the past decade. Fortunately, this period includes almost all of the research activity in the area. We admit to cheating only in rare instances where we believe additional studies must be included to understand the historical perspective of more recent efforts. A review of the three bibliographies at the end of this paper will indicate the literature covered in this review. The studies which serve as the basis for our review are listed in the first bibliography. The reader will note that we have not included all the research that has been done. We have, for example, elected to omit unpublished doctoral dissertations from our review. In part, we have done this because of the unavailability of much of this research. Selective inclusion would inevitably have produced an unknown bias in our review. In addition, we have decided to restrict our review to papers that have passed the normal review process so that we would not place ourselves in the role of referees. A list of the doctoral dissertations in the area for which we have references is contained in the second bibliography.[2]

The approach we have taken generally is to evaluate the state of our knowledge and the overall contribution of the research to date. This same overview approach has been followed in the brief methods section. It could be argued that each study included should be evaluated in terms of its explicit and implicit assumptions, its research methods, its statistical tests, and so on.[3] But we believe that this would have been an inappropriate, if not impossible, approach given the time, the space, and the task allotted us. Our charge was to "examine the benefits of recent accounting research . . . and to provide guidelines for future research." It is only as the conclusions of several studies begin to suggest directions and patterns that they assist us in this task. Indeed, the same comment also applies to review papers such as ours. This paper is only a recent attempt to review and evaluate the growing literature in the area. Review papers by Birnberg and Nath (1967), Hofstedt (1972a, 1975), Rhode (1972), Green (1973) and by Gonedes and Dopuch (1974) provide further insights into the contributions and the limitations of experimental and survey research in financial accounting.

FINANCIAL STATEMENT DISCLOSURE AND USE

We begin by examining research that has focused primarily on financial statement disclosure and use. Included in this research are studies that have dealt with four overall issues: (1) the adequacy of financial statement disclosure, (2) the usefulness of financial statement data, (3) attitudes about corporate reporting practices, and (4) materiality judgements. In focusing on these issues, several different conceptual and methodological approaches have been used. Of particular relevance to this paper is the usefulness of these approaches in improving the quality of information provided to users of financial statements.

2.1. Adequacy of Disclosure.

There is almost unanimous agreement that there is more financial disclosure in corporate annual reports today than in the past. A recent survey by Opinion Research Corporation for Arthur Andersen & Company reveals that 96% of the "key publics" and 98% of the corporate executives interviewed stated that their overall impression is that there is more disclosure today than there was five to ten years ago (Opinion Research Corporation, 1974). Yet, during the last decade, there has been considerable controversy about the extent to which financial data available to investors and the public have been adequate to meet their requirements.

Studies that have focused on the adequacy of disclosure include Horngren (1955, 1956, 1957), Cerf (1961), Bradish (1965), Ecton (1969), Singhvi and Desai (1971), Buzby (1974), and Opinion Research Corporation (1974). Three overall approaches have been used in these studies. One approach has been to develop a description of how users analyze financial statements to evaluate the assumptions underlying their analysis, and to assess the implications of their analysis for various disclosure issues. This approach was used by Horngren (1955, 1956, 1957) who surveyed written reports of financial analysts and who interviewed analysts to obtain information about their use of financial statement data. He then developed a description of their use of these data, evaluated the underlying reasoning, and assessed its implications for the inclusion of funds-flow statements, price-level accounting, and disclosure of capital expenditures, depreciation, and so forth.

Another approach has been to focus on certain interest groups and to survey their perceptions and attitudes about disclosure. Studies by Bradish (1965), Ecton (1969), and Opinion Research Corporation (1974) provide examples of the use of this approach. Both Bradish and Ecton conducted open-ended interviews with limited numbers of expert users of financial statement data. Bradish interviewed several financial analysts to determine what types of information they cnsidered inadequately disclosed. Ecton interviewed the chief lending officers of seven commercial banks to determine their views of the adequacy of disclosure in financial statements submitted to them. Both Bradish and Ecton discuss specific areas of criticism and solutions proposed by the analysts and lending officers.

The survey by Opinion Research Corporation was more general in nature and broader in scope. Telephone interviews were conducted with individual shareholders and personal interviews were conducted with "key public" individuals, including corporate executives, professors, institutional investors and portfolio managers, stockbrokers and investment analysts, securities lawyers, CPAs, government officials, editors and writers, and social activists. The survey focused on overall opinions which individuals held on the adequacy of disclosure as well as on specific changes in disclosure, such as the inclusion of SEC Form 10-K, information in annual reports and forecasts of future earnings.

A third approach has been to determine the extent to which specific items of important information are disclosed in corporate annual reports. An index of disclosure is developed and then used to measure the extent of disclosure in the annual reports of a sample of companies. This approach was initially used by Cerf (1961), who developed a 31-item index of disclosure on the basis of interviews with financial analysts, an examination of analysts' reports, and a survey of a random sample of analysts. Cerf then rated the disclosures of 527 individual companies in terms of a percentage score based on the number of items in the index that were included in their annual reports. Those scores were used to calculate differences in disclosure among companies and to analyze the relationships among these differences and several other variables.

More recently, this approach has been used by Singhvi and Desai (1971) and Buzby (1974). Relying heavily on the index developed by Cerf and on interviews with four expert analysts, Singhvi and Desai developed a 34-item index which they used as a composite measure of the extent of disclosure in the annual reports of 100 listed and 55 unlisted corporations. Singhvi and Desai analyzed the relationships between disclosure and several other variables, including fluctuations in security prices.

Buzby asked a sample of financial analysts to indicate (on a five-point scale) the relative importance of 39 selected items of information in evaluating an investment in a company's common stock. He then used the responses of 131 analysts to develop a set of weighted disclosure criteria and applied these criteria to a sample of annual reports of 88 small and medium-sized companies. Buzby analyzed the extent to which each item was disclosed, the average disclosure for the items taken as a whole, and the relationship between the relative importance of an item and the extent to which it was disclosed.

Research on the adequacy of disclosure has produced at least three overall conclusions. The first is that there does not appear to be a burning desire for drastic revisions or changes in the form and content of financial statements.[4] Most users of financial statements believe that adequate financial data are available today. In addition, it appears that most of the criticism about financial disclosure is not that there is necessarily something wrong with what is presently reported, but that relevant data are left out. However, there is relatively little agreement about what these relevant data are. Where some users would like to have more detail about what is presently reported (e.g. more statistical breakdowns), others would like to have data that are presently unreported (e.g., replacement cost data) because they think these data would better help them evaluate a company's future prospects.

A second conclusion is that the trend toward increased financial disclosure apparently has not resulted in overcomplicated financial statements. Many observers have expressed concern about financial statements becoming too complex and too difficult to understand because of increased financial disclosure. Yet, responses to substantive questions on content suggested to some researchers that readers of financial statements may have little difficulty understanding these statements, although we ourselves do not entirely agree with this finding. Further, research indicates that the investing public generally is not very critical of the complexity of these statements.

A third conclusion is that there appear to be significant differences in financial disclosure between companies and that many of these differences tend to be a function of such variables as company size (as measured by total assets or number of shareholders), profitability (as measured by rate of return or earnings margin), size of the CPA firm auditing the company, and the listing status of the company. In general, companies that are larger, more profitable, audited by large CPA firms, and whose shares are traded on the New York Stock Exchange tend to be significantly better disclosers than companies that are smaller, less profitable, audited by small CPA firms, and whose shares are traded either over the counter or closely held. However, it is important to realize that these variables are probably highly intercorrelated. For example, companies traded on the New York Stock Exchange are generally those that have the largest asset size and the widest ownership distribution, and tend to be audited by large CPA firms. Thus, observed differences in disclosure between companies may merely reflect differences in listing status and the involuntary disclosure requirements associated with that status.

2.2 Usefulness of Financial Statement Data.

During the last decade, there has been considerable controversy about the extent to which financial data available to investors and the public are useful in decison-making. Studies that have focused on the usefulness of financial statement data include Soper and Dolphin (1964), Pankoff and Virgil (1970), Smith and Smith (1971), Falk (1972), Haried (1972, 1973), Falk and Ophir (1973a, 1973b), Baker and Haslem (1973), Abdel-khalik (1973, 1974a,1974b), Ronen and Falk (1973), Chandra (1974), Oliver (1974), and Libby (1975a, 1975b). Several approaches have been used in these studies.

One approach has been to ask users of financial statements to indicate the relative importance of various factors or information items in investment analysis. A list of information items or factors is developed and a sample of users of financial statements is asked to indicate (usually on a five-point scale) the relative importance of these items in making investment decisions. The mean responses for each item are used to determine the degree of importance attributed to it. In some cases, the mean responses of different samples of users or preparers of financial statements are compared. This approach, which is similar to that used by Cerf (1961) and Buzby (1974) in developing their indices of disclosure, has been used by Baker and Haslem to determine the relative importance of 33 factors to a sample of common stock investors and by Chandra to determine the relative importance of 58 information items to a sample of CPAs and to a sample of Chartered Financial Analysts (CFAs).

A second approach in the attempt to determine whether financial statement data are used in decision-making and whether their use is affected by other variables is to create a representation of a "decision" under quasi-laboratory conditions and then to study the bahaviour of the subjects who make the "decisions." Pankoff and Virgil (1970), to investigate the demand for information and the effects of information on expectations and on the quality of forecasts and decisions, constructed a laboratory stock market in which subjects purchased information, predicted closing market prices, and chose portfolios. Falk and Ophir (1973a, 1973b) used a representative investment setting to investigate the relationship between the degree of risk involved in an investment and the demands of the investor for information and the frequency of his requests for this information. Libby (1975a, 1975b) used a field experiment to investigate the use of five accounting ratios by 43 professional lending officers in evaluating the likelihood of failure of 60 firms (and ten repeat firms). Abdel-khalik (1973, 1974a, 1974b) and Ronen and Falk (1973) have used the concept of entropy as a basis for experiments on aggregation in accounting. Abdel-khalik asked respondents to estimate the probability of loan default by a hypothetical firm and to estimate the subjective probabilty of its being a good credit risk within the next three years. Ronen and Falk report the results of three laboratory experiments designed to probe the relationship between entropy and the expected value of information.

A third approach that has been used to study the usefulness of financial statement data has been to try to measure the effectiveness of the communication of these data. One way of measuring effectiveness has been to apply readability formulas to disclosures in samples of financial statements. Soper and Dolphin (1964) and Smith and Smith (1971) used this approach to measure objectively the comprehension ease level of financial statement disclosure. Another way of measuring communication effectiveness is to measure the meaning assigned to accounting terms by various interest groups. Haried (1972, 1973) and Oliver (1974) each developed semantic differentials for selected accounting concepts and terms and then sampled groups with different backgrounds and professional affiliations to measure and compare the meanings these groups assigned to those concepts and terms.

The overall conclusion that emerges from this research is that financial statements appear to be, at best, of limited value in making investment decisions. First, investors and analysts tend to consider nonfinancial statement factors to be relatively more important in making investment decisions. Investors consider factors concerned primarily with expectations to be relatively more important than financial statement data in making these decisions. Moreover, they tend to rely on stockbrokers and advisory services for their investment information and to attach only minor importance to financial statements as a source of information. Similarly, analysts tend to consider data about the general economy and the industry within which a company operates to be relatively more important than the reported financial statement data.[5] However, it appears that the perceived value of financial statement data may be affected by the perceived riskiness of an investment. Falk and Ophir (1973a, 1973b) found that use of financial statement data was highest for securities not guaranteed by the government and not traded on the stock exchange and lowest for securites traded on the stock exchange with government guarantee. In addition, it appears that income statement items are considered to be relatively more important than balance sheet items in making investment decisions.

Second, it is not clear that the use of financial statements leads to either better forecasts or better decisions. It appears that analysts want some kinds of financial statement data to the extent that they are willing to pay for them, and that their use of these data can in some instances result in slightly better forecasts of stock prices on average than if these data had not been used. However, it is not clear that these better forecasts necessarily resulted in better decisions—e.g., choosing portfolios.

There are several reasons why financial statement data might not be useful to investors and analysts. One reason may be that generally accepted accounting principles and generally accepted auditing standards reduce the usefulness of financial statement data by reducing the extent to which subjective, not easily auditable judgments are reflected in those data.[6] Another reason may be that the information content of financial statement data is known by the time the statements are available to the public. Yet, financial statement data might by useful to investors and analysts by providing them with a reasonably good (or at least better than random) history of the economic status and progress of the company. If it were not for published financial statements, some financial data might not be available during the year or at year-end. In addition, some financial data may be communicated more efficiently (in a cost-benefit sense) by using financial statements than by using other sources. Year-end financial statements also may merely confirm information otherwise obtained during the year. Investors receive information from analysts, brokers, or company officials and may tend to rely on this information because at year-end an accounting will be available in the form of audited financial statements. In this way, financial statement data may provide a useful check on the accuracy of data received from nonfinancial statement sources. However, within this context, investors' expectations about financial statement data must be specified in some way, otherwise one cannot interpret the extent to which these data tend to confirm or disconfirm their expectations.

2.3 Attitudes about Corporate Reporting Practices.

Even though the development and reformulation of accounting principles has been a slow and often controversial process, the last decade has brought about many significant changes in corporate accounting and disclosure policies. Studies that have focused on the attitudes of various interest groups about current and proposed corporate reporting practices include Nelson and Strawser (1970), Brenner and Shuey (1972), Carpenter and Strawser (1972), Copeland, Francia and Strawser (1973), and Godwin (1975).

Some of these studies have focused on preferences for alternative methods of accounting for specific transactions or events. The approach used in these studies has been to develop a questionnaire describing a transaction or event and alternative methods of accounting for it. Respondents are then asked to indicate their preferences for one of the alternative methods described. Often one of the alternative methods described has been one suggested by an accounting policy-making group (e.g., APB) in an exposure draft. Nelson and Strawser (1970) surveyed members of the Institute of Chartered Financial Analysts, the AICPA, and the American Accounting Association (AAA) to determine which of three methods of accounting for business combinations they preferred. In a follow-up study, Brenner and Shuey (1972) surveyed controllers, CFAs, and the CPAs about the use of the purchase and pooling-of-interest methods of accounting for business combinations. Similarly, Carpenter and Strawser (1972) surveyed controllers, CFAs, AAA members, and CPAs about methods of reporting accounting changes.

Other studies have focused on more general reporting issues. The approach used in these studies has been to develop a questionnaire consisting of several items and to ask respondents to indicate (usually on a five-or-seven-point scale) how much information they feel is available now to users of financial statements, how much information they feel should be available to these users, and how important the item is, in their opinion. Mean responses to the question of how much information is available now are used as measures of the respondent's perceptions of the present state of the art and mean responses to the question of how much infomation should be available are used as measures of the respondent's attitudes about what the state of the art should be. The difference between what "should be" and what "is" provides a measure of perceived information deficiency (if positive) or fulfillment (if negative). Mean responses to the question of how important the item is provide indications of relative importance. Copeland, Francia and Strawser (1973) used a questionnaire consisting of 27 items to survey the attitudes of accounting students, controllers, CPAs, CFAs, and AAA members about financial reporting practices. Mean responses for each item were analyzed by group and compared across groups. Using a slightly different approach, Godwin (1975) surveyed CPAs about the feasibility of auditing certain items and their willingness to audit 25 proposed SEC disclosures, and surveyed financial analysts and stockholders about the usefulness of these disclosures and their current accessibility to these disclosures.

The studies focusing on preferences for alternative methods of accounting for specific transactions or events have provided useful data about several controversial accounting issues. In particular, these studies have provided data about the extent to which these preferences have been consistent with those of the APB, at least for specific (though often limited) samples of CPAs and others. Yet, it appears that in evaluating these studies, it is important to consider carefully the exact wording used to obtain attitudinal data. Nelson and Strawser (1970) asked respondents to indicate which of three methods of accounting for business combinations they preferred and found that the majority of the respondents favored alternatives other than the one selected by the APB. Brenner and Shuey (1972) asked respondents about the extent to which they believed the purchase method and pooing-of-interest method were alternatives for a single business combination and the extent to which the choice of a specific method depended on the circumstances surrounding the combination. They concluded that respondents were in general agreement with the conditions set forth by the APB.

The studies focusing on more general reporting issues suggest that there are apparent intergroup attitudinal differences between students, controllers, CPAs, CFAs, and AAA members. However, it is impossible to assess the importance of these apparent attitudinal differences without some insight into how these attitudes were formed, how strongly they are held, or how they are related to behavior.

2.4. Materiality Judgments.

Research on financial statement disclosure and use has also focused on materiality judgments that affect financial reporting. These judgments concern either the collection, classification, and summarization of data about the results of a company's economic activities or the presentation of these data and related disclosure in financial statements. Research on materiality judgments has generally focused on what factors influence these judgments and on what people consider material. Studies that have focused on these topics include Woolsey (1954a, 1954b, 1973), Dyer (1973), Boatsman and Robertson (1974), Pattillo (1975), Pattilo and Siebel (1973, 1974), Rose et al. (1970), and Dickhaut and Eggleton (1975).

Research on what factors influence materiality judgments has typically involved the development of a questionnaire that consists of hypothetical cases containing a common set of situational variables and asks respondents to make materiality judgments for each case. This approach was first used by Woolsey (1954), who developed a set of ten questionnaire cases, each of which set forth specific circumstances using six different sets of figures. He then asked samples of preparers, auditors, and users of financial statements to make materiality judgments for each of the six sets of figures for each case. In a more recent study, Woolsey (1973), used a single questionnaire case involving an error found in the examination of the cost of goods sold account of a hypothetical manufacturing company to obtain materiality judgments from various groups. Similarly, Pattillo (1975) used six sets of questionnaire cases that focused on a variety of items, including extraordinary items, contingencies, accounting changes, segment reporting, interim reports, and groups of these items, to obtain materiality judgments from preparers and users of financial statements, CPAs, and educators. Both Woolsey and Pattillo focused on the amounts or range of amounts at which items were considered to be material and on the factors respondents indicated as influencing their judgments.

Boatsman and Robertson (1974) presented a sample of CPAs and a sample of security analysts with 30 hypothetical cases containing a common set of eight variables. Subjects were asked to sort the 30 cases into one of three categories according to how they believed the cases *should* be disclosed, without regard for how the cases *might* be disclosed under current practice. Boatsman and Robertson used multiple discrminant analysis to model the composite judgments of the subjects, stepwise discriminant analysis to develop separate models for the CPAs and the security analysts, and evaluated the use of a simple percent of net income rule to distinguish material from immaterial judgments.

Research on what people consider material has sought to determine how much of a difference in an accounting datum is required for a judgment of a difference and whether that difference is a constant function of the amount of the item presented. Rose et al. (1970) conducted a laboratory experiment to determine the magnitude of the percentage change in earnings per share (EPS) required before a subject would perceive a difference. On two occasions subjects were presented with pairs of EPS figures in the format of an abbreviated financial statement for a single company and asked to provide judgments about whether a share of the company's stock should be selling for essentially more, essentially the same, or essentially less from one year to another. The hypothesis was that the change in magnitude required before it could be detected was a constant function of the amount presented (Weber's Law). In a more recent study, Dickhaut and Eggleton (1975) sought to test the strength of Weber's Law over manipulations of the setting in which judgments were made, the sequence of data presentation, and the format in which standards and comparison stimuli were presented.

The overall conclusion that emerges from research on materiality judgments is that several factors, either individually or in combination, appear to influence these judgments. The relationship of an item to current year's income appears to be an important factor influencing these judgments. However, this factor also appears to combine with other factors, such as the nature of the item and characteristics of the company and its management, in influencing these judgments. Because of the simultaneous influences of these and other factors, people tend to differ somewhat in their materiality judgments, even though many of the observed differences do not appear to be statistically significant. In addition, people appear to be indifferent between footnote and line item disclosure, indicating that the decision of where to disclose may not be as difficult or as important as the decision of whether to disclose.

Finally, it appears that the use of a quantitative criterion such as a simple percent of net income may err on the side of underdisclosure.

Even though both Rose et al. and Dickhaut and Eggleton found that their results were generally consistent with the predictions of Weber's Law, the implicit psychological process that underlies this law may not be useful in determining what is material for numerical data. The fundamental proposition underlying Weber's law is that some distortion of a physical continuum occurs on a subject's psychological continuum such that the subject is an imperfect measurement device. Because there is greater measurement error at higher levels of the physical continuum, the stimuli become more indistiguishable and the just noticeable differences surrounding a particular standard increase. Weber's Law suggests a specific form the distortion will take and suggests that the relationship between a just noticeable difference and a standard will be a constant one. Yet, it is not clear that people assimilate numerical stimuli in the same manner they assimilate physical stimuli or that a similar distortion of an individual's psychological continuum is likely to result.

ACCOUNTING PRINCIPLES AND MODELS

This section reviews experimental and survey research into the general principles of financial accounting and into various alternative financial accounting models. The number of studies included in this section is not large, for two reasons. First, much of the research done has been oriented to particular financial disclosure or use issues and therefore is covered in sections 2 and 4. Second, there has been a paucity of empirical research into the fundamental nature of financial accounting information. Such research has not begun to keep up with nor to deal adequately with the large volume of theoretical writing on financial accounting models and measurement.

The discussion below will consider four not entirely unrelated areas of research: (1) general views about accounting principles; (2) "de facto" application of accounting principles; (3) price-level adjusted and current-value accounting proposals; and (4) probabilistic financial statements and allied proposals.

3.1. General Views of Accounting Principles.

This has been a popular area for researchers, especially in recent years. Research reviewed here includes Carsberg, Hope and Scapens (1974), Copeland, Francia and Stawser (1973), Fisher (1974), Flynn (1965), Francia and Strawser (1972, 1971a and 1971b), Hay (1955), Mautz (1972), Morton (1974), and Piaker and Dalberth (1973). In addition to these studies, professional journals and business publications have frequently carried reports of similar questionnaire or interview-based solicitations of views.

Letters, questionnaires, or interviews provide useful devices for "taking the pulse" of various constituencies about accounting matters. Such solicitations can be used to demonstrate readily enough both that someone "out there" cares about the various issues the researcher chooses to ask about, and that a diversity of opinion exists on the issue. Yet, such conclusions often are obvious in advance. In addition, these conclusions can be challenged on the basis of nonresponse rate, potential response bias due to the questions' context, difficulty of wording questions unambiguously, lack of connection of answers to respondents' actual behaviour, and possible arbitrariness in selecting questions to ask. Nonetheless, a carefully designed questionnaire (e.g., Hay, 1955) can provide useful data on people's thoughts about the objectives and the content of accounting reports.

Several approaches have been used to try to get beyond the compilation of views and to provide a systematic structure to the research. One approach, used by Carsberg, Hope, and Scapens (1974), has been to send identical questionnaires to members of different groups and to compare the groups' positions on each question. The research method itself cannot illuminate the reasons for any reported differences, but such findings provide possible hypotheses for more intensive follow-up research. Unfortunately, since no such follow-up research seems to have been done, any statements which go beyond the listing of differences remain speculative. A refinement of this approach has been used by Copeland, et al. (1973), and Francia and Strawser (1972, 1971a and 1971b). As we noted in Section 2.3, these studies, by using a questionnaire technique that, it was hoped, would reduce response biases, attempted to detect differences not only in direction but also in the importance of views held. This method expanded the dimensions on which differences were displayed but still provided no explanations for observed differences. However, some of the differences were intriguing. For example, Copeland, et al. (1973) asked students and accounting educators eight identical questions about proposals for improving financial reporting. The two groups differed significantly on all eight questions about deficiencies in information now available, but on only one concerning the importance of the deficiencies. Students' attitudes differed from those of analysts on all of the seven questions about information available on certain financial reporting objectives, but on only one of the seven about the importance of the information. Such tidbits are tantalizing; it is unfortunate that we are given no further insights.

Another approach, used by Mautz (1972), has been to send letters soliciting illustrative examples of circumstances that would lead to departures from usual accounting treatments to provide a focus for later seminars on the issues and for the development of a survey questionnaire. The eventual survey questions as well as the answers were empirically derived and the conclusions rooted in a context that had some applied meaning. In addition, the letters, seminars, and questionnaire responses provide varying vantage points for triangulating on the issues. For example, the importance of the context in which accounting choices are made, and their impact on the uniformity versus flexibility issue, were illuminated in useful and different ways by the various data sources.

Another approach has been to turn to the theoretical issues behind an accounting principle in designing the questionnaire and to relate the results to the theoretical questions. Morton (1974) tested specific hypotheses concerning the survey respondents' perceived relationships among relevance, understandability and bearing (direction of effect on investment decisions) of footnote disclosure and found a significant positive correlation between each pair of the three concepts. However, his study did not explore the reasons for, or causal structure underlying, the observed correlations.

3.2. "De facto" Accounting Principles.

Research in this area has consisted of mailing brief situational descriptions to CPAs and asking respondents to report how they would account for the item described. McDonald (1968) provides an early example, followed by Sterling and Radosevich (1969), Sterling (1969) and Sterling, Tollefson and Flaherty (1972).

Large variations in reported outcomes were observed, resulting apparently from differences in choice of accounting method and calculation parameters (e.g., asset life) and from incomplete accounting rules (such as for barters). The findings suggest that financial accounting measurement may not be objective; however, we have two serious reservations. First, because the situational descriptions provided were terse, practising accountants may have had to make assumptions to fit these descriptions into their useful decision rules, and such assumptions could easily have produced large variations in reported outcomes. Second, the questionnaire approach allowed no consultation with others, nor other actions that might be useful in reaching actual accounting decisions. Hence, the results may not reflect "de facto" accounting in any real sense. However, such difficulties with validity are not unique to this kind of research.

3.3. Price-Level and Current-value Accounting Proposals.

Survey and interview-based studies in this area include American Institute of CPAs' Technical Services Division (1958), Backer (1973, 1970), Brenner (1970), Estes (1968), Garner (1972), Hanna (1974 and 1972), Horngren (1955), and Rosen (1972). Experimental studies include Dyckman (1969), Heintz (1973), and McIntyre (1973).

The survey and interview-based studies were intended to examine the ultimate usefulness of price-level adjusted cost or current-value financial information. Opinions were sought primarily from presumed users of financial statements, especially analysts and bankers who were interviewed to explore their perceptions of the usefulness of various alternatives to the historical cost model. In general, three conclusions seem to emerge. First, no interest was found in replacing historical cost statements with current-value statements or with price-level adjusted historical cost statements. These alternatives have been perceived as being useful but only as supplements to the historical cost statements. Second, there was stronger interest in current-value information than in price-level adjusted historical cost information. This result apparently was due more to a lack of interest in the latter, even as supplementary information, rather than to any very great interest in the former. Third, there appears to be some confusion in the minds of survey respondents about the difference between the current-value and price-level proposals, suggesting that much of the scattered support for the latter may have been due to respondents' thinking the former was meant. Rosen (1972, p. 10) observed, ''A very small number in the Canadian business community seem to understand well the difference in effect between a price-level restatement of historical cost and replacement cost or reproduction cost. The belief that a price-level restatement equals current value must be overcome if any progress is to be made on the subject of this study.'' This point also applies to the interpretation of research results, because it is not always evident that the research questionnaire made clear the distinction between price-level adjustments and replacement cost or explained how such information would have impact on the financial statements. Copeland, et al. (1973, p. 368) asked respondents to rate ''the effects of price-level changes'' in terms of how much information ''is now available to the users of financial statements'' and ''should be available to the users of financial statements.'' The respondent might well be uncertain as to whether general or specific price-level changes were meant and whether provision of such information in the body of the statements was implied. Such uncertainty might increase with the sophistication of the respondent.

These uncertainties and ambiguities are a major barrier to interpreting the results of the nonexperimental studies in this group. The studies varied widely in the wording of questions and the conduct of the interviews. The results from four studies illustrate these variations. AICPA (1958) asked respondents, by mail, whether they were in favor of ''disclosing current dollar cost of depreciation''; 74% were in favor. Estes (1968) asked respondents, by mail, whether they considered various kinds of information ''useful''; 81% thought current-value information was useful, 70% thought price-level adjusted cost information was useful. Garner's (1972) respondents, also obtained by mail, were asked about ''need'' for current-value or price-level adjusted information; only 28% of the respondents saw a need for current-value information, and only 26% for price-level adjusted information. Hanna (1974, 1972) asked 30 analysts, in an interview setting, to ''rank alternative sets of statements (prepared by him) in terms of usefulness.'' There were four choices: historical cost only; current-value only; price-level adjusted only; and a combination of current-value and price-level adjusted. Twenty-eight analysts ranked historical cost first, all 30 ranked current value second or third, and 28 ranked price-level adjusted cost last. How much impact on the results the nature of the illustrative statements may have had was not measured, though it may have been a crucial factor. In general, these studies suggest that price-level adjusted information is not highly valued by those queried. Definite conclusions, however, remain elusive because of the ambiguities and variations referred to above.

Differences in results and methodology were just as prominent in the experimental studies as they were in the nonexperimental studies. Dyckman (1969) mailed questionnaires to analysts, while Heintz (1973) and McIntyre (1973) conducted their studies at universities, using students as subjects. Heintz's subjects made a sequence of decisons over several simulated time periods; Dyckman's and McIntyre's made decisions or evaluations once, without replication. Even though both Heintz and Dyckman used price-level adjusted statements, Heintz relied on interviews and visits with companies having experience in such adjustments to help him develop such statements, while Dyckman relied on ''reasonable assumptions'' to make his adjustments. McIntyre made both current-cost and price-level adjustments in developing his statements. In all cases, subjects were asked to make simulated investment decisions using controlled information (traditional historical cost information or proposed revised information or both) and the apparent impact of the various kinds of information on their decisions and judgments was observed. Dyckman's analysts, however, were asked to select the better investment for a described client, while Heintz's and McIntyre's students were asked to make specific forecasts. In addition to expertise differences, the analysts and students differed on task familiarity, task performance, prior expectations and viewpoints.

Suppose for a moment that the results of the three studies had shown a statistically strong preference for one of the proposed alternative accounting methods. Generalizing from such experiments nevertheless to actual decision-making contexts would still be risky. In particular, it is not clear that the information used in the manipulation contained all that is used by "real" decision-makers, nor that the contextual simulation was sufficient, nor that the subjects brought an appropriate degree of motivation to the task, nor that subjects (especially, but not exclusively, the students) knew how to make investment decisions.

Subject to such external validity caveats, however, the results of the three published experiments are not encouraging with respect to the alternative accounting methods. McIntyre found no statistically significant effects of using his price-level and current-value adjusted statements. Heintz found few effects, generally nonsignificant, of using price-level adjusted information. Dyckman found some significant effects of using price-level adjusted information, but the relationships found were not strong (statistical significance is partly a function of sample size, and Dyckman's sample was quite large). And in a critical behavioral measure of information impact, the per-share evaluation assigned by the analyst subject to the hypothetical company, no significant differences were found.

From an overall market point of view, the efficient market literature would suggest that general as well as specific price-index measures of inflation are already common knowledge. Hence, it is only to the extent that certain financial information (e.g., the age of an organization's assets) is not generally known that such information, if reported, could influence the relative structure of security prices. Thus, the conclusion would appear to be that simple disclosure of such data would be sufficient for decision-making. Moreover, for our purposes, the results suggest the difficulty of attempting to establish conclusions in behavioral studies of inflation adjustments when subjects are prevented access to other sources of information normally available (or which could be made available). This issue restricts the scope of conclusions which can be drawn from studies dealing with the impact on decison-making of inflation-adjusted data, and hence on an evaluation of the information content of inflation-adjusted data.

3.4. Probabilistic Financial Statements and Allied Proposals.

Oliver (1972) is the only published study included in this section, although there have been a number of recent dissertations in this area.[7] Oliver used an experiment to investigate the effect of "confidence interval" financial statements that put specific confidence bands around the reported numbers on the hypothetical lending decisions of bankers. No judgment was made about the quality of any decisions; rather, the study tried to detect any perturbations from the use of such altered statements. Further analysis in this area awaits a critical mass of published research efforts.

The research reviewed in this section has been successful in displaying wide ranges of opinions on issues of financial accounting principles. For example, the issue perhaps of most interest to practitioners now—the use of price-level adjusted historical cost information—has found, at most, lukewarm support. Few of the research efforts reviewed in this section have been methodologically or theoretically rigorous. The most popular kind of research has been the exploratory survey or interview but without more rigorous or more specific follow-up investigation. There has been no research to speak of on the fundamental purposes of financial accounting, and much more investigation of proposed alternative bases of financial accounting is needed before it could be said that such bases have received serious empirical investigation. More consideration is needed of the place of financial accounting information in users' decision models, and of the assumptions made by researchers about what that place is. People may not use the information in the way the experimenter thinks they do, they may not even use it in the way *they* think they do. For example, individuals may not use it if other sources are available or cheaper. They may not use it at all.

SPECIAL TOPICS

Several studies have focused on issues of what and when to report and the effects of alternate reporting methods on individual decisions within the context of special topic areas. In this section, we focus on the following five special topic areas: (1) segment and subsidiary reporting; (2) interperiod reporting; (3) forecast reporting; (4) decision effects of alternate reporting methods; and (5) effecting changes in reporting practice.

One interesting observation can be made before we begin. The behavioral research methods used by the respective researchers can be classified by the type of question addressed. The questions of what and when to report have been investigated almost exclusively by using survey research methods, interviews and questionnaires, and these methods have provided considerable data. Respondents often have been asked to identify the critical reporting issues relevant to the topic under investigation. Users of financial reports have provided information about their desires for specific information and the uses to which such information might be put. Although sometimes respondents have been asked what they would do with a specific bit of information, the responses have represented at most the stated opinions, beliefs and attitudes of those answering the question. Respondents have never been asked, however, to make either a real decision using the data involved, or to pay for the data requested.

Two other types of data occasionally have been obtained by using survey research methods. First, problems likely to be encountered in the implementation of new reporting requirements have been suggested by those who were either to provide or certify the new requirements. In rare cases information has been solicited from those who have already inplemented or tried to implement a new reporting technique. Once again the data have expressed only the attitudes, opinions, and, occasionally, the recollections of the respondents.

Issues involving the effects of alternative reporting methods on user decisions have generally been studied by designing experiments. Researchers have attempted to control the setting in which subjects respond to the data presented, hoping in this way to minimize the effects of extraneous variables which tend to confound the decision results and make interpretation difficult, if not impossible. The objective was to make inferential statements concerning cause and effect or, alternatively, associations among the variables studied.

Because many of these studies have used student subjects, extrapolation of the results to the target populations is tenuous at best. Moreover, in most of these studies it is not clear that the researcher has been able to reproduce the decision environment, and this raises questions about the validity of the responses obtained. For these and other reasons to be discussed briefly in the subsequent methods section, there typically remain at the conclusion of each separate study several contending explanatory hypotheses. The emergence of a dominant hypothesis will require a substantial number of studies designed to eliminate competing explanations. The recent work of Dopuch and Ronen (1973) provides a good example.

4.1. Segment and Subsidiary Reporting.

In one respect, research on segment and subsidiary reporting extends analysis of disclosure issues to further breakdowns of the activities of an organization. The area is a timely one, given the recent (September 30, 1975) issuance of the FASB's Exposure Draft on *Financial Reporting for Segments of a Business Enterprise*. If the draft is adopted in its present form, business enterprises would be required to report their activites in different industries and their major customers, as well as other activites. Of particular importance to us is the required disclosure of segment revenues, profitability and identifiable assets.

The research summarized in this section includes the following studies: Backer and McFarland (1968); Cramer (1968); Mautz (1968); Martin, Laiken and Haslam (1969); Stallman (1969); Backer (1970); Dascher and Copeland (1971); Crumbley and Strawser (1974); and Ortman (1975).

Supporters of segment reporting have argued for some time that the separate segments of a business are usually subject to different economic conditions, degrees of risk, and exhibit different rates of growth. A single all-inclusive report tends to average and thereby obscure these factors. The research on user attitudes suggests that the primary value of segment reporting would be to display the effects of growth, risk and economic conditions on the activites of the enterprise. With this information, analysts believe they could make better investment analyses and improve investment decisions and recommendations to individual investors. Those involved in merger and acquisition activites suggest that they could do a better job of identifying merger candidates and of appraising an acquisition decision. Bankers point out that their loan decisions would be facilitated; a bank typically has no recourse to a subsidiary's assets if it forecloses on a loan, netted payables and receivables cloud the financial position of the potential loanee, and the earnings strength of a company is more clearly suggested by separate reporting of both subsidiary and segment earnings and sales data.

Research on segment reporting suggests that extensive practical problems are likely to impede implementation. These problems, and the uses described in the previous paragraph could be deduced by logical analysis, but it is useful to discover central issues which the "experts" agree must be addressed when solutions are offered.

An initial issue requiring resolution is the definition of product lines and segments. The research indicates that this definition may be company specific, and that a more general (perhaps industry) approach may be necessary if comparability among companies is to be maintained.

A second issue is that of just when an event occurs which affects segment reporting. These events could well differ from those affecting the overall company's report. Certain cost allocations have been mentioned as particularly difficult examples. Since there is no one correct way to allocate common and joint costs, problems which influenced the firm's reported profits over time would now affect the reported segment's profits within that time period.

Even if the technical issues could be resolved, the research suggests that management may be reluctant to disclose segment earnings for competitive reasons. Even though financial executives tend to recognize that segment data may be useful to investors, they have expressed concern that investors might be confused by such data. Analysts, as might be expected, strongly favor such reporting.

The problems and attitudes discussed above, when taken together, explain why the reporting of sales by segments is common practice while separate segment income statements are rare among surveyed firms.

Segment-reporting problems are in part a result of business combinations involving diverse activities. In a study by Martin, Laiken and Haslam (1969), the authors examined reporting practices in Canada for business combinations. This extensive survey describes the accounting approach used and the reporting problems encountered by a substantial set of firms traded on the Toronto Stock Exchange. The authors conclude that in Canada there has been a rather liberal interpretation of the standards used for deciding whether a combination qualified as a pooling of interests, despite the fact that only about 5% of all combinations were accounted for as poolings. The study reveals that two of the three allowed methods of accounting for purchases resulted in roughly the same balance sheet presentation for the purchase transaction as if it had been treated as a pooling. This fact could account for the relatively infrequent use of the pooling technique in Canada. In over 50% of the cases treated as puchases, no portion of the excess over book value paid was charged against income. As the authors conclude, "The implication is clear that comparability of earnings data among these conmpanies was difficult, if not impossible, to determine since in most cases the information concerning disposition of (the) excess was not clearly spelled out (disclosed) in published annual reports."[8]

All but three of the studies in this area were based on data obtained from interviews and questionnaires. The response rates ranged from 22% to 50% with little, if any, attempt to examine possible nonresponse biases. In evaluating these studies, particular attention must also be paid to the populations sampled. In general, many of those surveyed (including businessmen) could be expected to be opposed to segment reporting. On the other hand, analysts will nearly always prefer more data, especially if the data are offered for free. High quality experimental work in this topic area would be welcome.

One experimental study on the disclosure of divisional data on investment evaluations has been attempted (Stallman, 1969). The reactions of sophisticated investors to additional disclosure were examined by focusing on their judgments of a stock's "intrinsic" or long-run value in the presence of manipulated price data together with the disclosure differences. The statistical finding that the analyst adjustments were less affected by the manipulation of price data when in the presence of the additional disclosure is cited as evidence of the value (but not the net value considering disclosure cost) of segment reporting for multi-industry companies.[9]

A related study requiring operating decisions was conducted by Dascher using less sophisticated students as subjects. The results are reported in Dascher and Copeland (1971). No statistically significant decision effects were found; yet it should be emphasized that this study differed in both the sophistication of the subjects (analysts versus students) and task (investment valuations versus operations decisions). Hence, the results should not be taken as *necessarily* conflicting.[10] Moreover, we observe that many of the difficult issues involved in segment reporting (e.g., the allocation of joint costs) are substantially reduced for consolidated firms. This was the type of disclosure involved in both of these experiments.

In a recent study by Ortman (1975), a field experiment using financial analysts was "conducted to determine the effects on investment analysis of the presence of segment data in financial statements of diversified firms." Subjects were divided into two groups, with one group receiving the additional segment data. Ortman found that "the introduction of segmented data significantly reversed the analysts' evaluations of the diversified firms presented," in the direction of what was expected, given the situation. As in similar studies, the response rate was quite low (about 25%) and there is no way of knowing if subjects acted toward the experimental situation as they would have acted toward a real one.

4.2 Interperiod Reporting.

The question of what to report has been expanded recently to deal with when to report. Specifically, should firms report on an interim basis, normally within the year, on their operations? Several studies have addressed this issue, including Bird (1969), Edwards, Dominiak and Hedges (1972), Lipay (1972), Bollom (1973) and Nickerson, Pointer and Strawser (1975). The recently adopted amendments to SEC Regulations S-X and to Form 10-Q, which significantly increase quarterly reporting requirements and expand the auditor's involvement therin, highlight the importance of this area.

The importance of interim reports is related to the intensity of analysis on the part of the user. The kaleidoscope of analysis intensity varies from the mere tracking of investments to intensive evaluation. For those in this latter category, interim reports are seen as providing the basis of short- and long-run growth predictions, estimations of sales and earnings variability, and the revision or modification of estimates, predictions and trends.

One of the major results of the attitude studies in this area is the apparent consensus about the type of data users want. As is usual with this type of research, the opinions have been expressed without concern for cost of the data and nearly always without any indication of the specific use to which the information would be put. Moreover, no attempt has been made to monitor requests coincident with decisions.

Users and potential users both appear to want more freqent reporting of two particular types of data: income data, particularly before taxes and extraordinary items; and product-line breakdowns. The tie-in with segment reporting is clear. Simultaneously and perhaps surprisingly, given the importance attached to audited yearly statements, there appears to be little enthusiasm either for seasonal adjustments to reports covering less than one year or for attestation of interim reports by independent auditors. The most general summary of what the unspecified user apparently desires is simply unaudited company reports concerning the status of those items reported annually. This is precisely what many companies are presently reporting.

Preparers have expressed little opposition to providing such interim reports, since many, if not most, of the publicly held companies are already providing much of what users appear to want reported on an interim basis. However, preparers have expressed a preference for allocations while analysts and others desire actual figures (e.g., costs). Preparers stress the revelance of allocations to long-term investors, but it is likely that a more parochial interest supports their position on this issue.

The studies reviewed indicate that, even several years ago, over 80% of the publicly held firms were reporting sales, net income before extraordinary items, and earnings per share on an interim basis. However, less than 10% were reporting even major items from the balance sheet. Quarterly reporting appears to have been the dominant form of interim-report accounting for over 90% of company-reporting practice in this area.

Only one study, Bollom (1973), was of an experimental nature. Students in a business-game setting made investment-type valuations of a seasonal business using interim vs. yearly reports under several alternative reporting techniques. The research did not find any statistically significant decision-related differences, although results cannot be generalized because of the nature of the sample involved, the experimental environment simulated and the content of the reports presented.

We have made the point here and elsewhere that obtaining the views of preparers and users is a valuable input to the policy-decision process. Yet, two warnings should be made. First, we need to be concerned with consequences. Research on what may and, where possible, what does happen when a particular proposed policy is implemented is essential to the policy decision-maker. Too little attention has been given to date by policy-makers (and researchers) to consequences, and too much to prior attitudes. Second, the information which, in users' opinions, will optimize performance may not actually do so when supplied. This substantial leap of faith is much too tenuous to support the present reliance of policy-makers on opinion research. Empirical behavioral research is needed on this point.

4.3 Forecast Reporting.

One of the more recent and more hotly contested reporting questions has been whether forecasts should become an integral element of the financial statements or of the annual report. Several recent behavioral studies have looked at this issue, including Daily (1971), Asebrook and Carmichael (1973), Carmichael (1973), Financial Executives Research Foundation (1973), Benjamin and Strawser (1974), Corless and Norgaard (1974), and Nickerson, Pointer and Strawser (1974).

Studies of the impact of reporting forecasts again have been primarily of the attitude variety. The users studied, namely investors and analysts, appeared to favor the reporting of forecasts, as would be expected given a cost-free choice. The user groups surveyed did not indicate that such forecasts should be mandated, but indicated that any forecast made should be attested to by the CPA and some estimate of the error associated with a given forecast should be provided.

Initial and fragmentary evidence has failed to show any increase in the confidence users place in a forecast when attested to by the auditor. On the other hand, more accurate forecasts, indicated by a lower error measure, did influence earnings-per-share predictions in one study (Benjamin and Strawser, 1974), and greater accuracy was associated with greater reliance on the forecast.

Stockholders surveyed indicated they considered forecasting to be part of management's job and believed it appropriate for them to be provided with management's forecasts. They assumed that the auditors would at least review the essential assumptions and verify the underlying computations, even though they were less certain about whether the historical data and the statistical methods used would be covered as part of the attest function.

Providers of forecast data—financial executives and certified public accountants—are generally against providing audited forecast data to the public. The Financial Executives Research Foundation (1973) found that 65% of the financial managers it surveyed stated they believed the financial community was doing a good job projecting the earnings of their companies. Auditors argue that they are not trained to evaluate forecast techniques and they cite a lack of the knowledge prerequisite to evaluating management's projections. Providers appear to be very concerned about the loss of independence that they believe could follow attestation as auditors become concerned with, and perhaps even responsible for, attaining the forecasted results. The specter of the auditor's legal liability for attaining the forecast is cited as a potentially reinforcing argument for their concern about the possible loss of independence.

Finally, providers appear to be uneasy about the ability of investors and potential investors intelligently to digest forecast data. One study (Nickerson, Pointer and Strawser, 1974) found that investors expected forecast errors of 10% to be maximum for any company, which suggests that the difficulty of forecasting is not affected by type of industry, product line, or other salient business characteristics. It was also noted that this particular set of users expected sales and income forecasts to be done with equivalent preciseness. Using actual company data, the Financial Executives Research Foundation (1973) found substantive differences in the accuracy of sales, expense and corporate earnings forecasts.[11]

One of the more valuable contributions to research on forecasts has been the interview study by Carmichael (1973) of the English experience. This study points to the need to educate potential consumers to the meaning of, and particularly the uncertainty inherent in, forecasts. This will not be an easy task. For example, the possible range of a forecast was not found to be, at least in England, and adequate measure of uncertainty.

This study also points to the need to clarify the paramount issue of legal responsibility associated with the attest function. Questions such as the allowable variability, and the permissibility of ex post facto explanations, and the importance of fraud and intent in determining legal liability must be resolved prior to the reporting of forecasts. This research suggests that we may be able to avoid unfortunate consequences and perhaps make more effective and efficient decisions by careful analysis of the experience of other countries.

In terms of present practice, only 3% of companies now indicate that they are providing forecasts to the public although 95% of the firms in the Financial Executives Research Foundation study (1973) prepare such forecasts for internal use. These forecasts are not audited. Criteria for judging forecast accuracy have not been established nor have the factors affecting forecast accuracy been researched.[12]

4.4 Decision Effects from Using Alternate Accounting Procedures.

Some of the more interesting behavioral research has been done in the area of reporting effects on individual decision-making. This was one of the earlier subject areas to be investigated using experimental methods. The studies influencing our review include Horngren (1959), Dyckman (1964), Dyckman (1966), Jensen (1966), Livingstone (1967), Khemakhem (1968), Barrett (1971), Elias (1972), Hofstedt (1972a), Hofstedt (1972b), Dopuch and Ronen (1973), Hawkins and Wehle (1973), Libby (1975), and Ortman (1975). These studies do not neatly fit into the previous subject areas examined. Many of them were of an experimental nature and nonstudent subjects were commonly employed.

These studies support the contention that alternative reporting procedures can influence individual evaluations. This phenomenon has been observed among students, stockholders, potential individual investors, analysts, bank loan officers, certified public accountants and financial executives as subjects. However, the extent or importance of the influence has often been less than expected.

The extent of the influence appears to depend, in part, on the nature of the particular decision and decision-maker as well as the alternate reporting techniques investigated. The different effects of alternate reporting can be mitigated by the inclusion of supplementary information in the form of schedules, footnotes or narrative form which facilitate comparability, unless the added data, whether in numerical or narrative form, conflicts with that originally supplied. Cost-benefit tradeoffs, as they relate to disclosure, have not been investigated by these studies.

The impact of alternate reporting methods also appears to be related to the characteristics of the users. More sophiciated users, in terms of their understanding and appreciation of accounting data, tend to rely more heavily on the accounting data supplied to them in financial reports, rather than on the nonaccounting portions of such reports. Unsophisticated users, on the other hand, rely more on the nonaccounting data in the financial reports. Sophisticated users are more likely to be able to perceive economic realities underlying alternative reporting methods. These user characteristics are job-related and are probably related to the user's experience as well. Therefore, the effect of alternative reporting practices is likely to be influenced by the same factors.

The nature of the experimental environment (as well as the experimental parameters) appears to influence decisions. Hence, the access to expert technical assistance will likely influence the experimental results obtained. This possibility is typically ignored in most experimental situations. The experimental environment, and hence the validity of extrapolating the results obtained, is also affected by motivation, a realistic time-decision framework, and task-familiarity. The results of the experiment (or interviews) will depend on just how these factors are controlled; whether valid generalizations can be drawn will depend on the effectiveness of the experimental environment in inducing behavior reflective of what would have been done in actual decision situations. For example, one of these studies involved (either directly or indirectly) the allocation of the subject's capital with real rewards and penalties.[13]

It should be emphasized that although the use of alternative reporting methods may result in individuals' making different investment decision, these differences do not necessarily imply inefficiencies in the market. The presence of sufficient arbitrage activity will dampen and can even remove these effects from the market.[14]

A study by Libby (1975) extended the predictability work on firm failure begun by Beaver (1966), by trying to determine whether bank loan officers could distinguish between failed and nonfailed firms in a reporting population in which 50% of the firms failed within a short period. The research indicated that "a small empirically derived set of accounting ratios allowed bankers ranging widely in backgrounds to make highly accurate and reliable predictions of business failure." Limitations of subjects (and the reality of the task) caused Libby to raise the usual cautions about generalization.

Although the research examined in this review is, by nature of this conference, restricted to financial accounting and disclosure, we cannot totally overlook the somewhat overlapping boundaries of financial reporting and managerial decisions. Khemakhem (1968)offers the observation based on his research that managerial decisions may be influenced by goals different from maximizing reported income. These could include the concern for competitive position (including survival and market share), funds (or cash) flow, and others. There can exist in some firms an interdependence among certain managerial decisions and a concern for what will be reported in the company's financial reports, known to the operation-research analyst as constrained optimization and to the behavioral scientist as "satisficing" behavior. We also note that the flow of informatio reaching the manager and the investor (beyond that contained in financial statements) is extensive and often heavily relied on in the making of decisions, including investment evaluations.

4.5 Effecting Changes in Reporting Practice

Our knowledge of what may affect the decision-making process, together with what we know about efficient capital markets, is a necessary input to accounting policy. Yet, it is not sufficient to indicate which accounting policies should be adopted. The research problems in this area have been immense, and little substantive progress has been made on them to date. Behavioral studies have, however, leap-frogged this issue and have begun to examine how changes in accounting practice can be achieved. Studies addressing this issue include Sorter and Becker (1964), Sorter, Becker, Archibald and Beaver (1966), Comiskey and Groves (1971), Copeland and Shank (1971), Rakes and Shenkir (1972), Piaker and Dalberth (1973), and Ritts (1974)

Research to date suggests that the learning-set corporate-personality characterization of companies appears to be superior to diffusion theory in explaining innovation. The characteristics of the innovation appear to be less important than the behavior set of the firm affected by it. (See also Shank and Copeland [1973].) Acceptance of this viewpoint implies that a learning set can be created by starting with easily implementable and noncontroversial reporting changes. As experience with the new reporting techniques is obtained, the approach (if not the solution) becomes transferable. The theory may suggest likely industries or companies where specific reporting changes might be implemented.

Some research also has focused on just when attitude changes related to accounting policy-board pronouncements actually take place. Psychological studies suggest that behavioral changes may precede attitude changes. Certified public accountants, for example, appear to believe that APB opinions lead ultimately to forced compliance. It may well be that the forced compliance results in the eventual acceptance of the accounting procedure as the appropriate one. The method advocated by the opinion, then, becomes the accepted norm to be defended.

The policy of the FASB is issuing exposure drafts may be a critical step in the development of attitudes supportive to the change.[15] Research suggests that major attitude changes can occur when an exposure draft is released as well as when the final opinion or standard is issued. This appears to reflect the belief that the final opinion will mirror the exposure draft. If so, then it is important that any substantive research be accomplished prior to the issuing of such drafts.

The research just reviewed points to a noticeable gap in our knowledge. To date there has been almost no research done on how companies make accounting choices. The studies of corporate personality, Sorter et al. (1964 and 1966), provide the best attempts of which we are aware, but they do not deal with the essence of the issues involved.

EVALUATION OF RESEARCH METHODS

The previous sections of this paper have provided considerable evidence of the empirical vigor of experimental and survey research in financial accounting. In the last decade, over 100 experimental and survey studies have been conducted and published, and the rate of production has increased dramatically in recent years. But the increasing volume of research activity has not resulted in a dramatic increase in our body of knowledge, partly because the empirical evidence has not been obtained in a form that allows it to be integrated with prior evidence. The accumulation of knowledge requires more than an increasing literature.

Our review of experimental and survey research in financial accounting has provided us with a relatively broad perspective. Several features of this research are evident from this perspective and we will now attempt to describe these features and some of their consequences for the accumulation of knowledge.

Based on general impressions gained from our review, the "typical" study in this area was done by an academic, often as part of a Ph.D. dissertation, with little, if any, nonuniversity financial support. The study was done in isolation from others, at a relatively rapid pace, and often published in one or more condensed versions. It made only passing reference to the work of others and provided little, if any, theoretical formulation of the problem or of the hypotheses to be tested. It usually described data-collection and data-analysis procedures in somewhat more detail; there has been, nevertheless, considerable variation in both the sophistication and rigor employed by these researchers. In presenting results, conclusions usually have been limited to those justified by statistical inference, although the discussion of these results often has gone beyond the data, implying both stronger and less equivocal results than can be justified by the research. Finally, the need for research that replicates the findings and explores the variables further has been strongly urged.

This characterization is, of course, an oversimplification and an overgeneralization. It is a composite of a number of features, each of which occurs frequently although not necessarily together in any one study. The point of the characterization is not that all of the studies reviewed have all of these features; rather, the point is that lack of theoretical emphasis, lack of ties to the work of others, and lack of rigor all are very general problems in the research reviewed and that these problems have implications for the accumulation of knowledge.

5.1 Lack of a Theoretical Emphasis.

A theory provides a guide that tells a researcher where to look for what is to be observed. Ideally, a theory hypothesizes specific outcomes under specified conditions in terms that both make it possible to test the prediction and anchor the hypotheses into a broader context of assumptions. Most of the research reviewed here has been done (or at least reported) without explicit formulation of theory. Surveys of attitudes of preparers, auditors, and users of financial statements have been done without benefit of a theory of attitude formation, of attitude change, or of the relationship between attitudes and behavior.[16] In addition, most experiments on the usefulness of financial statement data or on the effects of alternative accounting methods on decision behavior have been done without benefit of a theory of information processing or of decision-making. This lack of emphasis on theory effectively has limited data analyses in these studies to tests for differences (and occasionally to measures of the strength of realtionships), even though it has been difficult, if not impossible, to interpret meaningfully the differences observed without a theory of why they might exist or what their direction might be.

As reflected in our review, experimental and survey research has been conducted in a large number of areas and has focused on a wide variety of topics and issues. But there have been relatively few areas in which a critical mass of studies has emerged. Consequently, many studies have been in areas so little studied that researchers have had to choose between the alternatives of collecting data with little theory to guide them in its interpretation or of pausing to build the requisite theory while having little evidence to give them confidence that they were building something useful. Given such a choice, many researchers have chosen the first alternative, perhaps because it may have been the less frustrating one, or maybe the only practical one.

An alternative to building theory is to use theory previously developed in other fields and desciplines Recent experimental research in financial accounting has reflected an increased use of this alternative. For example, Abdel-khalik (1973, 1974) and Ronen and Falk (1973) have used entropy concepts to study aggregation in accounting; Rose et al. (1970) and Dickhaut and Eggleton (1975) have used Weber's Law from psychophysics to study judgments of numerical data; Boatsman and Robertson (1974) and Libby (1975a, 1975b) have used the Brunswik Lens model (Brunswik, 1952, 1956) to study judgment formation, and Ritts (1974) has used dissonance theory to explain compliance with APB Opinions. The use of theories developed elsewhere is a convenient way to formulate testable hypotheses in a financial accounting context. Whether these theories are likely to contribute to our body of knowledge will depend in part on how well they are (or can be) integrated into accounting contexts. Often the process of integrating theories developed elsewhere is as difficult and frustrating as the process of building theories. Theories which are adapted from one field to another often carry with them a type of thinking and some of the concepts of their area of origin which are not always appropriate to their application in an accounting context.

We believe that knowledge will accumulate more rapidly if researchers conducting experiments and surveys in financial accounting use theory to guide their choices of where to look for what they want to observe. We are more concerned about the use of more and better theories than we are about whether these theories are developed within an accounting context.

5.2 Lack of Ties to the Work of Others.

Independent researchers conducting studies unknown to each other usually do not design their studies to facilitate later comparisons. Researchers sometimes claim a theoretical connection to earlier studies through one or more variables common to their studies and earlier studies. Yet, they rarely detail differences in their measures of those variables and the measures used in earlier studies. For example, even though several studies used indices of disclosure to measure the extent to which companies differed in disclosure, these studies differed dramatically in the specific items included in these indices. Similarly, survey of attitudes of various individuals about corporate reporting practices used different questionnaire items to obtain measures of these attitudes.

Studies differ dramatically in the specific actors, behaviors, objects, and context of focus. Despite these differences however, researchers seldom specify how the various aspects in their studies compare with those in earlier studies. Indices of disclosure have been applied to very different samples of corporate annual reports; attitude surveys have obtained data from very different samples of users, preparers, auditors, students and academics; and experiments on the usefulness of financial statement data and on the effects of alternative accounting methods have been conducted in very different decision-making contexts and have used very different subjects. Few of these studies have attempted to compare precisely these differences and to assess their implications.

We believe that knowledge will accumulate more rapidly if researchers do not leave the task of comparing and integrating their studies with past efforts entirely to future researchers. Researchers should deliberately design their studies to dovetail in useful ways with other studies and should attempt to specify the limits and aspects of their studies with precision. In addition, future research should deliberately undertake the task of comparing two or more studies to the end of drawing new conclusions.

5.3 Lack of Rigor.

Over 75% of the studies reviewed were done in natural rather than contrived settings. Of these studies, about 60% were based on mail surveys and another 18% were experiments based on mail questionnaires. This preponderance of studies done in natural settings and relying on survey research methods is somewhat surprising in view of the academic affiliations of most of the researchers. The preference for these settings and methods probably stems from many sources, including the fact that mail survey studies can be done rapidly, at relatively low cost, can be easily adapted to current issues or topics, and so forth. However, a major consequence of the extensive use of natural settings and survey methods is the general lack of rigor. Studies conducted in natural settings and based on survey methods tend to maximize opportunities for realism and external validity or generalizability, but they run the risk of less precision and control and thereby typically exhibit low internal validity.

A natural inclination is to call for more extensive use of the laboratory method. After all, the laboratory method represents the quintessence of science, regardless of the substantive problem involved. The use of this method can imporve control and precision relative to that possible in natural settings. Yet, there is no reason to expect that the heavy reliance on natural settings and survey research methods will diminish. Therefore, it may be more useful to note some ways in which researchers can increase precision and control in conducting survey studies or survey-based experiments.

The research strategy used in surveys or survey-based experiments is the "sample survey" (Runkel and McGrath, 1972). The key attributes of this strategy are that the behaviors of interest are elicited (1) in response to predetermined stimulus inputs such as questions, presentations and instructions controlled by the researcher, and (2) in settings to which the respondents are indigenous. The typical survey is generally concerned with generalizability over respondents and therefore samples respondents from the populations to which the results are intended to be generalized. In surveys used as a basis for experiments, the concern is not only with generalizability over respondents, but also with generalizability over stimuli, and these studies usually focus as well on sampling stimulus properties that are of interest.

The sample survey provides for control by the researcher over stimulus *inputs*. However, it does not provide for control by the researcher over stimulus *conditions*. Researchers ususally assume that the effects of the behavioral setting either are muted or neutralized by its being a natural one, or that these effects are extraneous to the behavior being studied rather than being important determinants of that behavior. For example, one's preference for one method of accounting over another or one's evaluation of a hypothetical company's prospects presumably may be unaffected by when and where one answers the question. However, some features of the behavioral setting may distract or distort a subject's responses. For example, responses may be deliberately or unwittingly distorted by social pressures, or judgment errors may occur due to physical distractions peculiar to the setting.

In using the sample-survey research strategy, a researcher should take advantage of the opportunities that exist to control stimulus inputs and sample selection. The researcher should specify the populations to be sampled, should randomly draw respondents to be included, and should standardize the instructions, presentations and the phrasing of questions. The broadest sampling base possible should be used. The initial set-up cost for a sample survey is relatively high, but the cost of additional observations is relatively low. A researcher should be constantly aware of his inability to control the setting and should attempt to obtain information about it if there is reason to believe that responses may be influenced or biased by the setting and are therefore not generalizable over a wide range of settings. In this regard, and for purposes of checking responses, a post-experiment questionnaire is useful. Few studies employed such a device.

Most of the surveys and all of the survey-based experiments used a "static group comparison" research design (Campbell and Stanley, 1963). In pure form, this research design includes one group which is measured after exposure to an experimental treatment and a different group which is measured without exposure to the experimental treatment. Most of the studies reviewed were similar to this design only in that group comparisons were based on postexposure tests only. Rather than use a control group that received no experimental manipulation, most studies used several experimental groups.

The group comparison research design is vulnerable to two confounding factors. The first factor is selection. There is no assurance that the groups being compared started from equivalent levels, especially if entry into either group was voluntary or was affected by administrative or logistic convenience. Any observed differences between the groups could have come about through differential recruitment. The second factor is sampling mortality. Observed differences between groups could have come about through differential drop-out from the groups. For example, mortality may result from feelings about the experimental treatments: subjects who do not like the treatments may be more likely to drop out than subjects who like the treatments. Such differential mortality, interacting with experimental treatments, can account for differences observed between comparison groups.

True experimental designs usually control for selection biases by providing for the random assignment of subjects to experimental and control groups from a common pool of subjects. Random assignment will not always insure subgroup equivalence, but it is more likely to result in the averaging out of individual biases. However, it is difficult to use randomization when groups are not being selected from a common pool of subjects. Here, sampling procedures have to be relied upon to generate equivalent subgroups. Sampling procedures, however, cannot be relied upon to generate subgroup equivalence when response rates are low, and low response rates have been reported in almost all of the surveys and survey-based experiments reviewed. Too many studies have had more nonrespondents than respondents, and this raises questions about external validity—whether respondents are representative of the populations from which they were drawn. In addition, too many studies have reported differential response rates for comparison groups, and this raises questions about internal validity— whether experimental treatments or differential mortality rates explain observed differences between groups.

Researchers using survey research methods simply must deal with the nonresponse problem. Several practical approaches exist. First, the researcher should try to compare the characteristics and backgrounds of respondents with those of the population from which the respondents were drawn. In addition, the researcher should attempt to compare the responses of early respondents with those of late respondents as another means of testing for a response bias. A trend suggests nonrespondents might have attitudes similar to late respondents and, hence, not like the average reply. Finally, in situations where a researcher is sampling subgroups from different populations, these comparisons should be made within as well as between subgoups.

Two other technical problems pervade the analysis of differences between groups. The first is the use of multiple variables in making group comparisons. Most survey studies have dealt with a relatively large number of dependent variables. For example, some of the survey questionnaires used in these studies have included up to 50 items. Analyses of questionnaire items typically have focused on mean differences between groups on each item. Yet researchers using questionnaires with multiple items should worry about possible intercorrelations and patterns of intercorrelations betweeen responses on these items. Our supspicion is that many of these items are intercorrelated and that researchers should try to reduce the number of dependent variables through factor analysis (or some other multivariate technique) to a smaller set of orthogonal dimensions. Comparisons between groups could then be made on the basis of mean factor scores on these dimensions. The second problem is the use of multiple t tests to make pairwise comparisons between groups. Performing multiple t tests to make these comparisons overstates the probability of finding significant differences and overutilizes the sample data. Researchers interested in making multiple comparisons should consider the alternative of using a one-way analysis of variance (F test) followed by one of several procedures for examining pairwise differences between groups.[17]

Often it is more useful to measure the strength and hence the importance of the relationship rather than simply to test for significance. Significance does not necessarily imply an important relationship. The hypothesis-testing (significance-testing) procedure used by most authors is essentially a question of whether the sample size is sufficiently large to show the differences that must inevitably exist between different groups. The fact that the groups differ is trivial. This is why some indication of the strength of the relationship found is of more interest.[18]

An additional set of problems concerns surrogation of task and subject. Most, if not all, of the experiments reviewed in this paper are open to the criticism that we cannot be certain of adequate task surrogation. Does the subject treat the experimental task in a way that mirrors actual decision-making behavior? Among other problems here are the effects of alternate information sources normally available but excluded from the experiment of similar task interest, of task familiarity, of the effect of learning and of a representative reward system. The problems suggest the value of a laboratory study using the appropriate subjects. The goal is not to obtain realism per se, but rather to induce the relevant behavioral set and task characteristics. If this can be done in a simple and controlled setting, so much the better.

Finally, we observe that about 14% of the studies reviewed were experiments in which students were used as subjects, and for those that were purely experimental, students were used in more than 50%. Several critics have either raised or discussed the question of using students as subjects in experiments.[19] We do not intend to repeat that discussion here. Simply put, the issue typically raised in these discussions is whether student subjects are "good" surrogates for "real" decision-makers. In addition, we believe that the issue of rigor in laboratory methods should be raised.

In a laboratory experiment, a researcher not only manipulates variables of interest; he also creates a behavioral setting within which observations are to be made. The purpose of this behavioral setting should not be simply to mirror some naturally occurring behavioral system, but rather to highlight selected behavioral processes and certain conditions related to those processes. The laboratory experiment is not concerned only with generalizing over subjects but also over settings. Ideally speaking, if a laboratory experiment is well-conceived and well-designed to capture the intended behavioral processes, one subject should be interchangeable with another, and different subjects would be used only in the interest of replication and reliability. This, in contrast with our earlier discussion of sample surveys, leaves the generalizability over subjects as a separable issue. Surveys deal with behavior elicited in response to stimuli in settings to which the subjects are indigenous but the stimuli are not. Laboratory experiments, on the other hand, deal with behavior emitted in response to a setting to which the stimuli are indigenous but the subjects are not. Differences observed between students and other groups in surveys should, then, raise questions about generalizability over respondents. Differences observed between students and others in laboratory experiments should raise qustions about the reliability and replicability of responses to stimuli in the setting created.

AN EVALUATION OF RESEARCH IMPACT

The impact of behavioral research on accounting practice has been almost nonexistent. While the pronouncements of the APB and now the FASB may have reflected behavioral considerations, there is no clear tie-in to the behavioral research we have examined. The changes we have seen in recent years and those being considered by policy makers at this time do not reflect the findings of behavioral research nor do the official pronouncements indicate any reliance on the existing behavioral literature. The thinking of senior and influential practitioners as expressed in their writings and speeches gives little evidence of a behavioral research impact. Operating rules and requirements of major government bureaus and organizations involved with accounting reports also do not appear to reflect any behavioral research findings. We believe there are several reasons why this is the case.

First, most professionals and those in policy-making positions are not trained in behavioral science and the research they rely on is often of an interview or questionnaire variety rather than experimental.[20] Hence, they are not ideally trained by education or experience to evaluate the existing behavioral research. Yet this is critical in determining and evaluating what has been achieved, to integrate one study with others, and relate it to policy issues.

Secondly, behavioral reseach is of relatively recent vintage and has had little time to have an impact on policy-makers. The communication of research results from academic researcher to practicing accountants has not been adequate. The academic typically writes for other academics. The better experimental studies in accounting tend to be published in the *Journal of Accounting Research* and *The Accounting Review*. These journals are not the prime reading material of the practicing accountant or the policy maker. Perhaps through review and summary papers, such as those presented at this symposium, research results can be communicated to practitioners.

In addition, behavioral research is costly both in terms of time and out-of-pocket costs. Much of the research we have reviewed is the outgrowth of doctoral dissertations. While doctoral students typically spend a year or so on this requirement for their degree, such research studies, particularly if they are of the experimental variety and done in the field, may need a longer time to do them justice. Limited funds often limit samples to students or artificial groupings of practitioners (e.g., executive development programs). Doctoral students are novices at doing research and are perhaps the least competent to draw policy conclusions from their work, although they are typically asked to do so, often with unfortunate results.

Junior faculty also can neither afford the time nor command the resources for such studies. The requisites for promotion and tenure promote an interest in short-term, low-risk research endeavors. By the time a track record has been established, such that resources can be commanded and tenure attained, and longer-run research becomes appealing, the competent researcher is often entangled in the administrative jungle. Sometimes those academics in the best position to understand practice and adopt the proper research perspective are either not able to conduct the appropriate research or lack the time or inclination to do the research. On the other hand, practitioners either do not have the training, the time, or the inclination to engage in other than opinion research. Some reasons for this situation are supplied in the paragraphs that follow. Perhaps it would be useful to encourage junior faculty with research expertise to work more closely with practitioners who possess the resources, including data access, to secure potentially useful research. We note, however, that such apparent opportunities have remained unexploited for some time.

Third, those doing research must remember that formulating accounting policy is essentially a political process. The "art of the possible" plays a paramount role in the determination of what gets adopted. It may be partly for this reason that policy bodies including the FASB place so much weight on opinion research. But, as we noted earlier, this focus misses several potential benefits of research and ignores the consequences of policy decisions.[21] Research about these consequences prior to major policy decisions would make it possible to improve our knowledge of the cost-benefit tradeoffs of a proposed course of action. There is also a tendency for policy-makers to accept users' opinions concerning the optimal information set despite the shortcomings of this research approach. The question should be addressed empirically. Hawkins and Wehle (1973) note, for example, that "empirical (opinion) data alone does not lead to a resolution of the lease accounting controversy." We know of no empirical research in accounting supportive of this behavior on the part of policy-makers, and at least one study which questions it (Libby, 1975).

322

But the above represents only the top of the iceberg. Of more importance in our minds is the failure of researchers to define and follow through on a logical, well-conceived plan of research. Until they do, they should not expect practitioners and policy-makers to pay much attention to them. Let us be more specific on this point.

The selection of research topics by academic researchers has been haphazard at best. In part, this reflects the failure to tie in our resarch with the questions of professional concern. Often research is undertaken after a position has been adopted rather than when the results could be of assistance to policy formulation. The issue here is one of timing. And, given the extensive time required for certain types of behavioral studies, adequate communication at an early stage of problem analysis is critical. If the key issue is to affect policy, then more attention must be given to the policy issues of concern and less to the investigation of intellectually satisfying issues. Further, the early identification of policy issues becomes paramount.[22]

Basic research also needs more attention. First and foremost, some theory, some model of the decision process is needed to support the empirical results found and to suggest reasonable and useful research projects. Without theory, the research becomes like the nautical derelict, merely an aimless wandering. Whether such a theory is developed from psychology (information-processing models, conflict and dissonance theory, attitude formation and change models) or from economics (information economics, market choice and marginal analysis, capital asset pricing) is not the critical issue. Indeed, separate theories may all prove productive.

Yet, even with (or without) an adequate theory, proper attention must be given to the experimental design. Studies to date have not always (or even usually) done a satisfactory job of assuring internal validity. Researchers need better training in the techniques of behavioral experimentation. The fact that most of the studies suffer from important omissions in this area makes the sum total of the research on any given issue tenuous at best. The concern is one of critical mass; in most areas, we simply have not accumulated sufficient data. Failure to achieve internal validity makes it hard to evaluate the confidence a reader should place in a study and also helps explain the minimal impact achieved by behavioral research to date. Indeed, the difficulty of evaluating a given study and the knowledge that shortcomings are almost sure to exist may cause the reader to totally reject this type of research. The very integrity of the researcher may have contributed to the lack of impact. Some researchers carefully document the limitations of their studies, but if they overlook even a minor limitation found or expected by a reader, the reader may reject the study.

Behavioral research and research in general appears to suffer from a lack of credibility with the profession, a feeling that may have been partly reinforced by what the profession viewed as unsatisfactory experiences with professionally oriented research commissioned by the AICPA and by the perceived lack of interest of academicians in researching real problems and communicating the results.

A final reason for the lack of impact of behavioral research appears to be the failure of nearly every study to consider explicitly the cost-benefit tradeoffs. Investors and analysts, when asked whether additional disclosure is useful, will almost always answer in the affirmative if the information is free. While it may not be easy to quantify these aspects, it is critical that their order of magnitude be estimated before effective policy decisions can be made, keeping in mind that the learning phenomenon may drastically alter any initial relationships. Researchers have been remiss in not explicitly recognizing cost-benefit tradeoffs in their research and recommendations.

FOOTNOTES

[1] We are indebted to Karl Weick for bringing this description and its chilling implications to our attention.
[2] The third bibliography contains those papers to which we refer but which do not represent experimental or survey research. We have also included here a few papers that are relevant to our review but which were not yet available to us. Our review has not been extended to the sizable number of survey articles published

by regional or special interest journals.

[3] To our knowledge such reviews have been successful only when restricted to a very few studies. Reviews of numerous studies often fail to capture adequately what specific studies have found, let alone adequately evaluate their research methods. A substantive review of one or two research papers is itself a substantial task, as a brief examination of any issue of the *Empirical Supplement to the Journal of Accounting Research* will show.

[4] It is interesting to note that even though there have been many improvements and increases in disclosure in recent years, this conclusion is essentially the same as that offered by Roper (1948) and Sanders (1948) almost three decades ago. Perhaps, this indicates the difficulties people have in forecasting the future "state of the art."

[5] Horngren (1957) found that there was widespread agreement among security analysts that the company annual report served as the springboard for their review. He concluded that, although the annual report was not always the most important source of information, in terms of universal usage it belonged in first place among the sources.

[6] Schneider (1972), for example, wants the SEC to remove its prohibition against issuers' including "soft" information, such as sales and earnings forecasts and appraisals, in prospectuses. As he puts it, "SEC filings generally have an artificial or unreal quality. They purport to be full disclosure documents but, as a matter of convention, they exclude important types of information investors consider relevant, and stress much information investors consider irrelevant or relatively unimportant."

[7] See, for example, K.K. Chen (1974), Danos (1974), Hawkins (1974) and King (1973) in the dissertation bibliography.

[8] In this regard, it is interesting to note that the FASB is presently gathering data on the problems experienced by U.S. firms in accounting for business combinations under the relevant APB opinions.

[9] For detailed critiques of the study see the comments of McDonald and Kleinman which immediately follow Stallman's paper, and Dascher and Copeland (1971).

[10] We note that precisely this error is often made by competent researchers. As an example, Dopuch and Ronen (1973) fall into this error in evaluating the conclusions of several behavioral studies involving investment versus managerial operating decisions. See in particular their claim of "inconsistent results" on page 192.

[11] The concern here is with information processing at the individual level and hence cannot be directly extrapolated to support a position of inefficiency in the market for securities.

[12] A study by Daily (1971) suggests that firm size may not be an important factor. The Financial Executives study (1973), on the other hand, finds larger variances for smaller companies. This study found no significant effects due to type of industry, the existence of written instructions, or the use of a range presentation format.

[13] In some cases, payoffs to the subjects are included, but they are not the rewards earned from operating in the market.

[14] See Dyckman (1964), p. 286, footnote 5, for an early recognition of this fact.

[15] The point also applies to SEC releases.

[16] The conduct of many studies in this area has left the typical respondents (e.g., financial analysts) less than enthusiastic about further participation. We, like the economy, may well have used up a substantial portion of a scarce resource with relatively poorly-structured research instruments.

[17] See Winer (1971) or Morrison (1967) for a discussion of methods developed by Scheffé, Tukey, or by Newman and Keuls for examining pairwise differences between groups.

[18] A lack of significance is a good indication of an unimportant relationship. Unfortunately, the converse does not follow.

[19] See Birnberg and Nath (1967), Hofstedt (1972a), Copeland, Francia and Strawser (1973), Watson (1974), Copeland, Francia and Strawser (1974), and Abdel-khalik (1974b).

[20] We note some changes here as the FASB has done a semi-behavioral study in conjunction with its study of business combinations.

[21] The investment credit issue provides an excellent example of what happens when consequences are not given sufficient attention.

[22] Since some research will require longer lead time than we can expect, research of a basic nature unrelated to current policy issues must continue. In this way, a fund of relevant data may already exist when a policy issue arises. (We speak only of a reordering of priorities and do not wish to imply that basic research should cease.)

For bibliographic references see Common Bibliography for Part V.

THE INFORMATION CONTENT OF FINANCIAL ACCOUNTING NUMBERS: A SURVEY OF EMPIRICAL EVIDENCE*

by Robert S. Kaplan

*Reprinted from *The Impact of Accounting Research on Practice and Disclosure*, ed. A. Rashad Abdel-Khalik and Thomas F. Keller (Durham, N.C.: Duke University Press, © 1978), pp. 134-173

W HEN I was first asked to do a paper surveying empircal research in accounting, I found it difficult to believe that the world needed yet another survey on this topic. I sometimes think that there are more surveys on empirical research than there are papers to be surveyed. Nevertheless, the theme of this conference is the relevance of recent research to practice (some cynics may argue that this should guarantee both short papers and a brief conference) and most previous surveys of empirical research have been addressed more to academicians than to practitioners (see Beaver [1973] for an exception). I could thus see at least a tiny niche in which this paper might fit without flagrantly duplicating previous efforts.

It seems only prudent for me to acknowledge other survey papers and admit that I have both read and been influenced by the views in these sources. Therefore, any similarity betwen the views expressed here and the evaluations in these other papers could hardly be considered accidental. Among these other sources of surveys are Beaver (1972), (1973), (1974b), (1975), Gonedes and Dopuch (1974; Section 8), Hakansson (1971), and Lev (1974). Of these, Lev (1974) is a particularly comprehensive treatment which should be readable by many practitioners.

I have decided to classify the empirical papers into five principal subject areas: (1) information content of annual accounting numbers; (2) information content of interim earnngs reports and corporate forecasts; (3) time-series properties of accounting income numbers; (4) effect of accounting alternatives on common stock prices; and (5) predicting bankruptcy with accounting data. A separate section will be devoted to each of these subject area.

Much of the literature on the above topics builds upon extensive developments in the finance literature studying and documenting the efficiency of capital markets. We have obtained significant insights into the speed and effectiveness of capital markets in responding to information, into appropriate definitions of risk, and into methodology for testing hypotheses about various aspects of information processing and risk-and-return relationships in capital markets. Before moving to a survey of the accounting literature, I must initially summarize some important concepts in this efficient markets literature which form the basis of many of the accounting studies.

Even before that, however, I must issue a disclaimer as to what I will *not* be doing in this survey. As previously mentioned, I *am* attempting to relate the significance of recent academic research to practitioners. Consequently, I will *not* be discussing methodological details or criticizing the methodology used in the various studies. This should not be construed as tacit approval of the methodology used in each case. In fact, I have yet to read an empirical study whose methodology was beyond criticism. It does, however, represent my judgment that the surveyed papers were done in a reasonable fashion and that there is a distinct possibility that the authors' conclusions would still follow even had somewhat different procedures been used in the papers.

With this background, we are ready to start.

EFFICIENT CAPITAL MARKETS AND THE MARKET MODEL

Over the last fifteen years, a considerable amount of theoretical and empirical analysis has pointed to the conclusion that, as a good working approximation, the securities markets in which common stocks of U.S. corporations are traded are efficient with respect to publicly available information (a feature sometimes called semi-strong efficiency). We mean by this that the current price incorporates all publicly available information including the entire sequence of past prices, annual reports, accounting income numbers and ratios, macroeconomic variables such as monetary and fiscal policies, and a variety of other industry-specific and firm-specific information. The fact that this information is "included" in the current price implies that trading strategies based on such information will not yield a profit, on average, after paying transactions costs and controlling for the risk of the trading strategy. In particular, technical analysis, which is the arcane study (not unlike astrology) of past sequences of stock prices in order to predict future prices will not, on average, be a profitable way of spending one's time, unless one prefers such graphical activities for recreational or psychological reasons. Also, it is suggested that detailed perusals of annual reports, SEC filings, Alan Abelson's weekly Barron's column, or any of Professor Abraham Briloff's critical "exposés" of the frailties of the accounting profession will not yield special returns to the informed reader.

These ideas were in conflict with much prevailing Wall Street wisdom and naturally have not been widely accepted by financial analysts and many other practitioner groups, including public accountants and SEC regulators. For example, the public-accounting profession is constantly in contact with presumably financially knowledgeable individuals who show a disconcerting amount of ignorance about the assumptions under which financial reports are prepared. It is therefore hard to believe that any degree of market efficiency and rationality can exist in such a sea of ignorance and chaos. Nevertheless, the literature on this question is both lengthy and basically supportive of market efficiency. The technically inclined reader is referred to Fama (1970) and Jensen (1972) for extensive surveys of this literature, but these papers do assume a fair amount of mathematical and economic sophistication on the part of the reader. Lorie and Hamilton (1973) provide, perhaps, the most accessible discussion of the theory and evidence of efficient capital markets (see especially Chapters 4, 5, 10, 11, 12).

Some evidence in conflict with the efficiency of markets has been reported by Black (1973), Jaffe (1974), and Downes and Dyckman (1973). Despite these latter sources, most academics who have studied the evidence now accept as a highly reasonable first approximation that the market is efficient with respect to publicly available information; i.e., new information is processed rapidly and unbiasedly into security prices and no important dependencies exist which allow one to make superior predictions about future stock prices on the basis of past prices or previously available information.

The other important result that we will need from the finance literature is a concept of risk in securities markets. It is reasonable to assume that risk has something to do with possible variation of the actual return of a security or portfolio from its expected return; e.g., a 30-day government note (the U.S. government, not New York City) is considered as close as one can get to a risk-free security (it would be even better if the return were adjusted for increases in the price level over the 30-day period). Again, as a first and reasonable approximation, researchers have found that stock-price returns are normally distributed, so that the statistical variance of the actual return distribution is a reasonable measure of variation about the expected return.

Modern finance theory, however, indicates that it is incorrect to estimate the risk of individual stocks considered in isolation. Sensible risk-averse investors hold diversified portfolios of securities. Therefore, the riskiness of an individual security is judged by its effect on the riskiness of a well-diversified portfolio, how much the stock contributes to the variance of a diversified portfolio. This effect is measured by a quantity known as a stock's beta (β) which is a measure of the sensitivity of the stock's (or other asset's) return to general movements in the market.

The market, as a whole, has a β equal to 1. High-risk stocks ($\beta = 1.5$ or above) tend to increase in price faster than the market when the market is rising and to go down in price faster than the market when the market is falling (the so called go-go funds which came into prominence during the later 1960s, and some of which are still around, provide excellent illustrations of high-risk portfolios). Conversely, low-risk securities tend to increase in value slower than the market during rising markets but tend to fall less in value when the market is declining. Gold stocks and utilities are usually considered low beta securities. This relationship is summarized by the following "market model":

$$R_{it} = a_t + \beta_i R_{Mt} + \epsilon_{it} \tag{1}$$

where R_{it} is the rate of return of security i in period t, the rate by definition being equal to $(P_{it} + D_{it})/(P_{it-1})$,

with P_{it} = price of security i at the end of period t

P_{it-1} = price of security i at the end of period t-1 (or the beginning of period t)

D_{it} = dividend paid by security i during period t.

The length of the period can be a week, a month, three months, etc.

R_{Mt} is the rate of return on the market portfolio sometimes measured by Standard and Poor's Composite Index of 500 Stocks or the New York Stock Exchange Index (some other indices have also been developed for empirical studies).

Equation (1) implies that there is a linear relationship between the return on a security and the return on the market. The coefficient β_i indicates how strong the relationship is, as mentioned before. A security with β_i equal to one rises or falls, by definition, on average, about as fast as the market as a whole. The error term, ϵ_{it}, indicates that many factors affect the return on a particular security other than overall market movements. With weekly data, the linear dependence on the market explains about 15% of the return of an average security. With monthly data, the linear dependence can explain 30-40% of a security's return. While these are not impressive statistics, when one forms portfolios of say 20-25 securities, the unsystematic portion of a security's return (as represented by ϵ_{it}) averages out and only the systematic part, caused by each security's linear dependence with the market, remains. Thus, at the portfolio level, it is not surprising to find that more than 90% of a portfolio's return can be explained by its linear dependence on the market.

The β of a portfolio is a linear combination of the β_i's of the individual securities in the portfolio and is considered an excellent measure of the risk of the porfolio. The β_i's of individual stocks are to a first approximation stationary over time but, recently, the tendency for the β_i's of individual stocks to be mildly nonstationary has been documented. Portfolio β's however, tend to be much more stable over time because much of the movement in the individual β_i's in the portfolio tends to average out.

In conclusion, we obtain the important relationship that the rate of return of a security is linearly related to its risk where risk is measured by the correlation between the security's rate of return and the market's rate of return. Thus higher-risk stocks tend to have higher rates of return and vice versa. As we shall now see, accounting information may be useful in explaining either unusual returns associated with firm-specific events as measured by the residual term, ϵ_{it}, in equation (1), or the risk of a security, as measured by a security's β_i. Both roles of accounting information are important in attempting to explain or predict the price movement of a security or group of securities.

INFORMATION CONTENT OF ANNUAL ACCOUNTING NUMBERS

In this section I will survey the evidence on the relationship between accounting information derived from annual accounting numbers (those which eventually appear in annual reports) and stock-price movements. At first glance, this may look like another instance of academics attempting to prove the obvious. Any person familiar with the "real world" knows that the market reacts strongly (and perhaps overreacts) to earnings-per-share data. Almost daily, there is a column on the next to the last page of the *Wall Street Journal* analyzing the current year's earnings prospects for one or more companies. Why then is there any interest in confirming the obvious importance of earnings?

First of all, as scientists, we are still interested in seeing whether our methodologies are able to detect this relationship (between earnings and stock prices) and are able to estimate the strength of the relationship. More important, we academic accountants exist in a skeptical world in which we have to prove such relationships to our colleagues, particularly when we attempt to assert the importance of accounting information. Many of our coworkers, especially those in finance and economics, view the accounting process as a tribal rite that must be tolerated for vague institutional reasons not fully understood (except perhaps to create a demand for accountants). A common reaction is to tell us not to bother about aggregating or summarizing all the information on the firm; just to give out the basic data (i.e., cash flows) and leave the evaluation to the informed users of financial information. A prominent economist, attempting to keep accountants in their proper place, once wrote:

> A known untruth is much better than a lie, and provided that the accounting rituals are well known and understood, accounting may be untrue but it is not lies; it does not deceive because we know that it does not tell the truth, and we are able to make our own adjustment in each individual case, using the results of the accountant as evidence rather than as definitive information. (Boulding [1962; p. 55])

Further skepticism with respect to the usefulness of accounting income numbers has been provided by a prominent financial analyst:

> The accountant defines it [earnings] as what he gets when he matches costs against revenues, making any necessary allocation of costs to prior periods; or as the change in the equity account over the period. These are not economic definitions of earnings but merely descriptions of the motions the accountant goes through to arrive at the earnings number. (Treynor [1972; p. 41])

In one of the earliest empirical studies relating accounting numbers to stock prices, even one of our own found it difficult to find much association between published financial reports and stock prices:

> One factor is striking. Only a relatively small, though significant relationship was found between the rates of change of data found in corporate published reports and rates of change of stock prices.... Thus, as measured in this study, the information contained in published accounting reports is a relatively small portion of the information used by investors. (Benston [1967; p. 27-28])

It is in light of such skepticism and criticism that academic accountants have attempted to verify the importance of the numbers produced by accountants.

The earliest and most widely quoted study on this issue was performed by Ball and Brown (1968). Basically they were attempting to test the null hypothesis that the annual earnings numbers have no information content because of (1) measurement and aggregation errors of the type suggested by Boulding and Treynor, and (2) alternative and more timely sources of information about firms. The methodology they and others followed depended on an assumption of market efficiency, as described in the preceding section, that security prices incorporate all available information. To detect whether annual earnings numbers are in this set of relevant information, the researchers attempted to determine whether variation in stock prices was associated with the variability of earnings or with the act of issuing such numbers.

Ball and Brown tested whether foreknowledge of the annual earnings number was sufficient to allow an investor to earn superior returns. Certainly, we cannot attach much importance to the earnings number as a factor in determining security prices if knowledge of that number a year in advance of other investors would not allow us to outperform the market. One problem that researchers face when investigating this question is, however, evaluating a given earnings number. When I am told that company ABC's earnings-per-share (EPS) will be $3.00 next year, I don't know whether that is good news, so that I should buy the stock, or bad news. A given realization of actual earnings can only be considered favorable or unfavorable when it is compared with the market's expectation of ABC's EPS. We are all familiar with instances in which a company announced a decline in earnings but the stock rose, or announced an increase in earnings and the stock declined. Rather than view this as yet another example of market perversity, such behavior can be rational if the market, in the first case, expected a sharper decline than actually occurred or, in the second case, a higher increase.

Thus, in order to evaluate whether a given earnings number will be considered favorable or not, we need to have some measure of what the market, in aggregate, expects that number to be. Unfortunately, Ball and Brown did not have access to such expectations data, and consequently, developed some naive models of the expectations process. They used a simple time-series model of earnings expectations (i.e., next year's earnings will equal this year's earnings) as one surrogate for a firm's expected earnings. They also used a cross-sectional regression model in which the change in a firm's earnings was assumed to be consistent with its historical association with an aggregate market index of earnings. Both models produced an estimate of expected earnings. Actual earnings were then compared with these estimates and two portfolios were formed. Firms whose actual earnings exceeded "expected" earnings (called a positive forecast error) were in one portfolio and firms whose actual earnings numbers were less than expected (a negative forecast error) were in another portfolio. These portfolios were formed twelve months prior to the actual release of the earnings number to test whether foreknowledge of actual earnings would enable an investor to earn superior returns. Note that a failure to earn superior returns could be explained by two factors: either earnings are irrelevant to investors, or else earnings do matter but Ball and Brown's simple models for generating market expectation of earnings are woefully inadequate.

Fortunately, the results were positive. Stocks with positive forecast errors tended to outperform the market and stocks with negative forecast errors tended to do worse than the market. (Notice that only the sign and not the magnitude of the forecast error was used to form the two portforlios; an additional factor which would tend to mitigate against strong positive findings.) Thus, when actual income differs in whatever direction from expected income, the price of the associated security tends to move in the same direction. Of even more interest, Ball and Brown found that much of this movement occurs early in the year, well in advance of the actual release of the year's income. This is consistent with an efficient market, in which information is gathered in anticipation of the actual announcement, and stock prices are adjusted accordingly. In fact, Ball and Brown could find little price reaction by the time the actual earnings numbers were released, implying that delays in issuing these numbers cause them to be almost entirely discounted by the time they were issued. More recent evidence provides an alternative explanation: the low reaction may be caused by the increasing unrealism of the mechanical models of earnings forecasts vis-à-vis market expectations as the end of the year approaches.

It is also interesting to note that abnormal returns[1] were not realized once the annual earnings report was issued, implying that once the information is released publicly there is no opportunity for earning superior returns by careful analysis of the earnings numbers. Ball and Brown reported using a cashflow figure (they actually used operating income, which still includes noncash income items) which was not as successful in predicting the signs of abnormal returns as the net income or EPS figures.

Gonedes (1974) replicated the Ball and Brown study with a more sophisticated methodology. He used a variety of financial ratios as well as.the EPS number to generate surrogates for market expectations of firm performance. (Gonedes, however, did not use a pure cash-flow variable.) He found that the EPS variable captured most of the information content of all that was available from the accounting numbers that he tested. Both Ball and Brown, and Gonedes, point out that their tests do not describe the unique contribution of the net income or EPS figure. These income figures are correlated with many other variables (e.g., sales) and economic events relative to the firm so that even if these figures were not provided, much of the information contained in them might be generated from other sources.

Patell (1976) replicated the Ball and Brown procedure on a sample of firms for which he had management's estimate of earnings for the coming year. Thus he could test whether the procedures are sensitive to the mechanical model used by Ball and Brown to generate the market expectations of earnings. While he found that the management forecast was more accurate, ex post facto, in predicting actual earnings for the year, the margin of superiority was not great. Further, the trading strategy based on management's forecast and assumed prior knowledge of the actual earnings was only slightly better than the strategy based on the mechanical models used by Ball and Brown. Therefore, it would appear that the procedure they used to generate a surrogate for market earnings expectations is a reasonable one.

Recall that Ball and Brown only used the sign and not the magnitude of the forecast error to classify firms. Beaver (1974a) has recently investigated a strategy in which the magnitude as well as the sign of the forecast error is used to form portfolios. Presumably, firms with high positive forecast errors (large amounts of unexpected earnings) will outperform firms with lower positive forecast errors. Beaver found that the most extreme portfolios, the ones containing firms with the largest positive and negative forecast errors, had much larger abnormal returns than portfolios formed from firms whose forecast errors were moderate in magnitude. Patell (1976) formed portfolios where stocks were weighted in proportion to the *magnitude* of unexpected earnings (stocks with negative unexpected earnings [forecast errors] were sold short) and found that the weighted portfolios "outperformed" the unweighted portfolios. Thus the magnitude of unexpected earnings has information content as well as the sign.

Additional evidence on the importance of the magnitude of unexpected earnings was provided by Niederhofer and Regan (1972). They identified the 50 best and 50 worst performers on the New York Stock Exchange in 1970. Where possible, they obtained earnings predictions for these firms from the March 1970 Standard and Poors Earnings Forecaster and compared the actual 1970 earnings to these forecasts. They found that the analysts had consistently underestimated the earnings gains of the top 50 firms and overestimated the earnings for the bottom 50 firms. They concluded that "stock prices are strongly dependent on earnings changes, both absolute and relative to analysts' estimates" and that "the most important factor separating the best from the worst performing stocks was profitability."

Collins (1975) performed a particularly interesting study on the value of disclosing sales and earnings data by segments. In 1970 companies were required by the SEC to start reporting sales and profits before taxes and extraordinary items by product line. In addition, firms had to disclose line-of-business sales and earnings for the previous five years. Collins tested whether a trading strategy developed from segment-based earnings, which were not publicly available prior to 1970, would be profitable. Forecasts from segment-based earnings were compared to forecasts prepared from consolidated statements as a measure of unexpected earnings changes. During 1968 and 1969 such a trading strategy was profitable for firms which had not publicly reported either segment revenue or profit figures, but there was no significant profit from this trading strategy for firms which had voluntarily disclosed this information. This finding could not be replicated in 1970. Nevertheless, the study suggests that segment disclosure is desirable in enabling investors to anticipate changes in earnings which otherwise would be unexpected if only consolidated data were disclosed. In this case, the study is supportive of the SEC disclosure requirement and is similarly revelant to the current FASB discussion on disclosure of operating data by segments.

The above studies provide fairly convincing evidence that the procedures accountants use to arrive at a net income or EPS number do not destroy the information content of these numbers. Investors with advance knowledge of a firm's income number should be able to earn superior returns, and no other financial number has yet been found that one would rather have a year in advance than the net income number.

There is still the question of the timeliness of the annual accounting number by the time it is released; has the information content of this number already been incorporated in market expectations so that the actual announcement has little effect? Beaver (1968) investigated the magnitude of both price changes and volume of trading in the week of the earnings announcement as compared with other weeks in the year. He found that the variance of price changes (which combines the effect of both positive and negative price changes) was 70% higher in the report week than at other times of the year, implying that the announcements led to significant changes in the equilibrium prices of securities. The volume was 30% higher in the week of the announcement, which Beaver interpreted as the extent to which investors are willing to incur the transactions costs of altering their portfolios to reflect the new information contained in the earnings announcement. Both pieces of evidence tend to support the significance of new information in the annual earnings announcement.

These studies should put to rest the idea that accounting earnings are irrelevant. They have information content in that prior knowledge should enable an investor to earn superior returns, and they are timely since significant price and volume reactions do occur at the time they are released. While we are unable to measure the unique contribution of the annual earnings number relative to all other forms of available information, accounting income has been shown to play an important role in investor expectations about the future performance of the firm.

In addition to the role that accounting income numbers play in revising investor expectations about future returns, there is also the question as to whether accounting data could be used to form expectations about the systematic market risk of a security, i.e., the β_i of a stock. Typically, the β_i's of securities are estimated from a historical regression of a security's return with the market return according to equation (1). For predictions in the future it is usually assumed that the historical relation will persist and that the stock will continue to have about the same correlation with the rest of the market as it did in the past. The queston that arises is whether accounting information is used by the market in estimating the systematic risk of a firm. Also, can accounting variables be used to predict future levels of systematic risk better than simple extrapolations of past trends? This latter question is important if the firm changes its capital structure or the industries in which it operates so that historical relationships may no longer be indicative of future risk levels.

Beaver, Kettler, and Scholes (BKS) (1970) investigated the association between accounting-determined risk measures and the market risk measure. An accounting beta was defined, analogously to the market-determined beta, as the correlation of the firm's net income with a market index of earnings. A variety of other financial risk measures were also tested (for example, earnings variability, liquidity, leverage and payout). BKS found significant correlations between the accounting risk measures and the market risk measures. Thus accounting risk measures are consistent with the underlying information set used by the market in assessing the riskiness of firms. BKS even found that the accounting risk measures could be used to develop forecasts of future market-determined risk measures superior to the procedure of simply assuming that the future β_i will be the same as the present β_i. More recent evidence on the nonstationarity of β, however, enables us to make better forecasts of future β than the simple extrapolation technique employed by BKS so that the indicated superiority of the accounting-based forecasts may not now exist.

Gonedes (1973) used a slightly different methodology to test the association between accounting-based and market-based risk measures and was unable to detect a strong association between the accounting beta and the market beta as reported by BKS. He attributed the difference in findings to the use by BKS of a market price to scale the accounting numbers which may have introduced a spurious correlation with the market measure of risk.

Beaver and Manegold (1975) attempted to resolve this issue by investigating a variety of specifications to test the association between accounting- and market-based betas. They again found that "across a variety of specifications for accounting and market betas, there is a statistically significant correlation between the two." Especially at the portfolio level, where measurement errors in estimating the accounting beta for individual firms will average out, there is a strong correlation between the two risk measures. Further, this correlation is not caused by scaling the accounting measure by the market price since the effect persists when nonmarket measures are used to scale income numbers. Nevertheless, Beaver and Manegold conclude that the accounting beta appears to be only one of the explanatory factors in determining the market beta.

Gonedes (1975) reran his initial study with a different index of market earnings, and he, too, now found a statistically significant though small association between accounting and market estimates of systematic risk. While Beaver and Gonedes still disagree on some details of the appropriate methodology to use to settle this issue, it seems that both have agreed that accounting-based measures of systematic risk play a significant role (of unknown magnitude) in the market's assessments of the systematic risk of securities. Thus we now have evidence that not only are unexpected changes in earnings associated with unexpected changes in a security's market value, but also that information from the accounting numbers can be used to form expectations about the systematic risk of a security which affects the expected rate of return from holding that security. Accounting data plays a dual role—in giving rise to unexpected security returns as well as affecting the riskiness of a security. This latter effect is especially interesting since it suggests the use of a new aggregation of accounting data not previously used in traditional financial analysis (i.e., the accounting beta).

These results can give us some comfort. It would have been hard to justify our existence if we could not find any evidence of the relation of accounting data to market-based phenomena. Nevertheless, apart from this comfort, we do not have much guidance or insight for the profession. For the auditor who has to decide whether or not to disclose an item as material, or to classify an event as extraordinary, there is little in this research to offer much help. While the studies have demonstrated the importance of an accounting income number, we would not know how to choose a single accounting income number to best summarize the operations of a firm. We really have no idea how the market reacts differentially to extraordinary items, income before or after taxes, primary or fully diluted earnings, operating income or net income available for common shareholders. At this stage, we must fall back on our feelings about efficient market processing of available information to suggest more disclosure rather than less and to recommend against a heavy expenditure of resources in argument about the form of presentation or the production of a single "best" number.

INFORMATION CONTENT OF INTERIM EARNINGS REPORTS AND CORPORATE FORECASTS

The previous section documented the importance of the annual-earnings number in the process of setting equilibrium prices by investors. As pointed out in the Ball and Brown study, investors do not wait until the annual-earnings number is released to revise their expectations about the magnitude of this number. A continuing series of adjustments are made throughout the year as investors receive new information about the firm's prospects. Among the potential sources of new information for revising expectations are interim reports issued by management and the announcement, by management, of forecasts of annual earnings. At present, auditors are not responsible for either of these informational items, but there are rumblings that auditors should bear some responsibility for the process that generates the figures in these announcements.

In this section I will review the evidence on the information content of these interim reports to see whether the reports do contain information relevant to investors. A failure to find information content in such reports could be due either to the fact that they are irrelevant or that they are potentially relevant but are not taken seriously by investors because of the lack of an auditor's opinion associated with their release. Alternatively, if the reports are found to have information content, then we may conclude that it is reasonable to have companies continue to issue them, and the case for additional and costly intervention by outside auditors is made more difficult.

One of the earliest empirical studies on the value of quarterly reports was performed by Green and Segall (1967). Their objective was to make an accurate prediction of annual EPS. They wanted to see whether having the actual first quarter EPS figure for a year would enable them to make a better prediction of annual EPS than if they did not have this figure. Presumably, if the first quarter actual EPS could not be used to make a better prediction of annual EPS, it was not a worthwhile piece of information to have.

Green and Segall developed three forecasting models using annual data alone and three models which incorporated quarterly data for forecasting annual EPS. Overall they could not distinguish between the accuracy of the annual models and the quarterly models, which led them to conclude that "first quarter reports are of little help in forecasting annual EPS." This is a surprising result since, on average, knowing one fourth of a figure should enable one to make a better prediction of that figure. Green and Segall suggest that this negative finding may be caused by the arbitrary allocations of annual expenses to four quarters of operations which give an unrealistic picture of operations in any given quarter.

Green and Segall (1966) replicated their study using a large set of firms, one more quarterly model, and a different year for estimating the annual EPS. (Just how a replication of a 1967 study could appear in 1966 is one of the more intriguing aspects of publishing in academic journals.) They obtained the same general conclusions as in their first study about the difficulty of using the first quarter of actual earnings to make a better prediction of annual earnings.

Brown and Niederhoffer (1968) performed an extended replication of the Green and Segall study with a large number (519) of firms, four annual models, and eight quarterly models. They concluded that the predictors using interim information, as a group, did better than the annual predictors and that the best interim model predicted better than the best annual model. Moreover, as each additional quarterly report is received, the interim predictors' margin of superiority increased.

Green and Segall (1968) disputed the Brown and Niederhoffer conclusions, pointing out, among other things, that the worst interim predictor did more poorly than the worst annual predictor. The dialogue continued for another round (see Niederhoffer [1970] and Green and Segall [1970]) without agreement between the two groups. A dispassionate observation (I hope) on the evidence is that it has proved surprisingly difficult to develop simple forecasting rules, using quarterly data, which can be applied uniformly to all firms to make annual predictions of annual EPS which are markedly better than the predictions made solely on the basis of previous annual data. This is not to say that quarterly numbers are not without information content; just that we have been unable to devise mechanical rules that estimate annual income reasonably well.

Another approach to this problem, using the ideas of market efficiency, was taken by Brown and Kennelly (1972). Rather than take as the ultimate objective of interim reports the prediction of annual EPS, they applied the market test to see whether quarterly earnings were in the information set used by investors. Basically they used the Ball and Brown methodology, which was based on annual data, to see if advance knowledge of quarterly earnings would enable investors to earn higher profits (i.e., than from just knowing the annual EPS in advance). They claimed that "if the disaggregation of annual EPS into quarterly EPS adds information, it should reduce errors in classification for shorter periods."

They found that trading models based on advance knowledge of quarterly earnings outperformed models which used advance knowledge of annual earnings only (transactions costs being ignored). Also, the response of the market to the audited annual earnings reports was lower than the response to the unaudited interim reports. While there may be a variety of explanations for this phenomenon, it is at least consistent with investors responding strongly to interim reports even without the auditors' seal of approval. Brown and Kennelly concluded: (1) the information contained in quarterly EPS reports is useful for predicting aggregate abnormal rates of return of associated securities, and (2) disaggregating the annual EPS into its quarterly components improves the predictive ability (in terms of stock prices) by 30-40%.

Beaver (1974a) replicated the Brown and Kennelly study but formed portfolios on the basis of the magnitude of the quarterly forecast errors as well as just the sign. He too found that using quarterly data, in the weighted portfolios, produced abnormal returns superior to those obtained when annual data alone were used.

Just as Brown and Kennelly (1972) can be viewed as an extension of the Ball and Brown (1968) analysis to quarterly data, May (1971) extended Beaver's (1968) methodology for assessing the information content of the annual earnings report to quarterly reports. May found that the magnitude of price-change responses in weeks of interim and annual earnings announcements was greater than the average price change for non-announcement weeks. Also, the relative price-change response to quarterly earnings, while generally less than the response to annual earnings, was not significantly less. This was consistent with the Brown and Kennelly finding of the relevance of quarterly earnings to investor decisions. May was concerned that the comparable responses to unaudited quarterly earnings announcements and to audited annual reports suggest that "investors may be unaware of or unable to take account of the difference in quality (reliability) of quarterly and annual accounting data." An alternative explanation, which assumes the market is fully aware of the unaudited nature of interim reports, raises the question of the value of auditing annual data, at least as measured by the ability to change investor expectations.

Kiger (1972) also observed generally significant price changes as well as volume changes when interim reports are released. His methodology was somewhat different from that used in the other studies, and he investigated New York Stock Exchange firms, whereas May looked only at firms listed on the American Stock Exchange. Nevertheless his findings were consistent with the previously cited studies.

Additional evidence on the reliability of interim reports was provided by Stickney (1975). He investigated firms which were making their initial public offering more than two or three months past the close of the fiscal year and hence had to present interim data. Clearly, if there is an opportunity to inflate an interim earnings report, such companies would have the motivation to do so to improve the terms of the stock issue. Nevertheless, he found that forecasting models using these interim earnings report outperformed predictors based solely on annual data, and he could find no evidence of manipulation of these interim reports.

Patell (1976) has provided evidence for the information content of forecasts voluntarily made by company officials of annual EPS. He found a statistically significant upward price change during the week of forecast disclosure. This occurred, on average, even for firms for which the forecast was below what would have been expected based on the past earnings history of the firm. This suggests that there is some self-selection among the set of firms that voluntarily issue forecasts; even firms disclosing bad news may be trying to preclude more drastic downward revisions which the market might be making about their prospects. In general, however, forecasts which exceeded estimates of market expectations were preceded by positive price adjustments. Patell also found that the voluntarily issued forecasts were better predictors of year-end earnings than the mechanical rules on annual data used by Ball-Brown and Brown-Kennelly even though the differences were surprisingly small, especially since the forecasts were issued after part of the year had already passed. The fact that these rules performed almost as well as management's own estimates provides additional support for the value of these models in developing surrogates for market expectations of earnings.

Interestingly, the largest errors in management forecasts were associated with firms with the highest risks, as measured by β. This suggests that a significant amount of uncertainty in the accuracy of forecasts is caused by the inability of management to forecast general economic conditions for the coming year. It is therefore most difficult to forecast earnings for those firms whose operations are most strongly correlated with economy wide forces (i.e., high beta firms).

To summarize the results in this section, interim earnings reports and company forecasts provide useful information to investors. Significant price reactions are associated with the release of these reports and advance knowledge of the information contained in these reports provides the basis of profitable trading strategies for investors. While the prediction of the next annual EPS may not be the most important objective of quarterly reports, it is interesting that it has been difficult to develop models using quarterly data which are substantially more accurate than models based on annual data alone. There is no evidence, on the other hand, that investors respond less strongly to quarterly reports than to annual reports, even though quarterly reports are unaudited. The conclusions one draws from this finding differ depending upon the strength of one's prior belief there should or should not be a differential reaction to an unaudited report.

TIME SERIES BEHAVIOR OF EARNINGS

Studies described in the previous sections have indicated that changes in earnings are associated with changes in stock prices. A variety of theoretical models exist in which the value of the firm is a function of future earnings of the firm. One question that arises, then, is how can the past earnings history be used to make a prediction about future earnings and hence explain or predict stock price reactions to unexpected earnings changes. We are all familiar with, and presumably chastised by, the growth-stock cult in which a subset of firms was identified which were supposed to be able to maintain a superior rate of earnngs growth over long periods of time. Many simple valuation models also use past earnings growth as an important variable for explaining price-earning ratios.

To illustrate the issues here let us consider three hypothetical firms. Firm A's EPS for the past four years has been $1, $2, $3, and $4 respectively. Firm B's EPS has been $4, $4, $4, and $4, while firm C's EPS has been $7, $6, $5, and $4. Suppose now we are asked to predict next year's earnings for these three firms using, as evidence, only these past four years of earnings history. In order to make this prediction, it would be useful to know something about the process which generates successive earnings changes. Two extreme cases have been considered. One is the stationary process, which implies that earnings are a random variable whose expectation is either constant over time or a deterministic function of time. With a stationary process, unusually favorable earnings in a year will tend to be followed by unfavorable earnings as the earnings "revert" to their historic level (or trend line). With a stationary process, successive earnings changes are *negatively* correlated, and the most recent earnings level is not helpful in explaining the future level of earnings. If one believed that earnings followed a stationary process with no trend, one would estimate that, for next year, firm C would have higher earnings than firm B which, in turn, would have higher earnings than firm A.

An alternative process to describe the time-series properties of earnings is the martingale process. A martingale is a generalization of the now famous random walk process in which past earnings and trends are not important in predicting future earnings. With a martingale, successive earnings changes are independent over time (zero correlation instead of negative correlation as with a mean-reverting process) so that the expected value of next period's earnings would be no different from the realized value of last period's earnings. With a pure martingale process generating earnings, one would predict that next year's earnings would be $4 for firm A, B, and C; i.e., only the most recent earnings are relevant, not how the firms happened to reach that level.

If earnings are expected to follow a drift (usually positive) over time, we could be dealing with a submartingale process in which earnings other than the most recent are still irrelevant but the expected value of next year's earnings is now allowed to be greater than the most recent year's (rather than precisely equal to it).

There are a variety of other reasons for attempting to understand the time-series properties of earnings. In the previous two sections a number of researchers needed to construct a surrogate for market expectations of earnings so that realized earnings could be evaluated as being favorable or unfavorable in comparison with those expectations. The particular time-series models one will use to generate market expectations will be strongly influenced by the evidence on the distribution of successive earnings changes as described above. Also, I have described the difficulties that past researchers have had in developing predictors, using interim data, which could substantially improve upon forecasting models using annual data alone. The models that were being tested by these researchers were generated on an ad hoc basis and may be improved as we learn more about the underlying structure of the earnings process.

The evidence will also be useful in understanding the value of smoothing accounting income figures. The accounting literature is filled with articles documenting the attempts of company officials to smooth their income series. The value of trying to smooth this series depends upon the process generating earnings. Smoothing has its basis in the idea that increases and decreases in income are temporary fluctuations about a long-term trend line. Rather than allow these fluctuations to occur, companies would prefer to show a smoother rate of growth, and hence, attempt to lower income in good periods and pick up income (where possible according to GAAP of course) in bad periods. Such behavior is consistent with a feeling that earnings do follow a mean-reverting process. For if one believes that earnings follow a martingale process, one would expect an unusually good earnings report to be followed by earnings distributed randomly about this most recent level and to be unrelated to previous earnings levels. In such a situation, it makes little sense for company management to attempt to smooth their earnings. In fact, Ball and Watts (1972) claim that attempting to smooth a random walk or martingale process could lead to more variability in the earnings series rather than less.

Finally, the underlying process is important for valuing the firm when a new earnings number becomes public. With a martingale process, unexpected increases or decreases in earnings will likely be followed by subsequent earnings about this new level. Consequently, the expectation of all future incomes is changed by each earnings realization and there should be a significant price adjustment to unexpected changes. With a mean-reverting process, however, unexpected changes will likely be followed by changes in the opposite direction in future years so that the effect of one year of unexpected good or bad earnings is much smaller.

Lintner and Glauber (1967) examined whether growth rates in a variety of income measures and in sales persisted over time. They divided the post-war period into four five-year periods and computed the correlation of growth rates for a large number of U.S. companies over these four time periods. They found that the degree of dependence between successive growth rates in the income and sales numbers was extremely small. The evidence suggested, though Lintner and Glauber were reluctant to conclude, that growth rates could almost be assumed to be independent in successive time periods.

Brealey (1969) correlated the change in earnings in successive years for 700 companies over a fourteen-year period. If earnings changes were expected to persist (positive changes followed by more positive changes; e.g., we've found a "growth" stock), then there should be positive correlation between successive changes. If earnings followed a mean-reverting process (which might lead company accountants to smooth out fluctuations), then there should be negative correlations in successive changes. In fact, Brealey found that the correlations were extremely small, suggesting a martingale process in which successive earnings charges are statistically independent. Brealey concluded that simple extrapolation of earnings changes (such as assuming next year's earnings to be $5 for firm A, $4 for firm B, and $3 for firm C) is "likely to prove valueless or almost so...and may distract attention from relevant information."

Ball and Watts(1972) performed extensive statistical analysis on 451 firms using four definitions of income (net income after taxes excluding extraordinary items, adjusted EPS, net income/total assets, and net sales) during the 1947-66 time period. They found that changes in both net income and EPS are independently distributed, suggesting a martingale process. Since earnings, on average, increased over this 20-year period, they concluded that the earnings process was best described by a submartingale. Ball and Watts emphasize that their results are based on averages (means and medians), which still allows some specific firms to be outliers.

Beaver (1970) also examined the time-series properties of earnings but concentrated more on the accounting rate-of-return series than the undeflated earnings series. He found that the accounting rate of return is a mean-reverting process but the reversion (from unexpected increases or decreases) occurs over some period of time in excess of a year. He attributes this to the smoothing process induced by accounting conventions such as historical cost depreciation. Beaver describes the rate of return through the years as a moving-average mean-reverting (MAMR) process. The undeflated net income series was consistent with a martingale process.

In a subsequent paper, Beaver (1974) argues that the mean-reverting process for accounting earnings is a "straw man" that no one really takes seriously. He maintains that a moving-average mean-reverting process is also consistent with good predictors that place a large weight on the most recent observation. He also claims it is important to distinguish between earnings changes due to profitability (i.e., an increase in the rate of return earned on one's assets) and earnings changes caused by an expansion of the investment base but with underlying profitability remaining the same. For example, it would be reasonable to assume that a firm's investment base follows a martingale process which may induce a martingale process on the income earned from this base. I might add that it would be useful to deduct that component of earnings changes which is due to price-level effects and which exerts an upward bias on any earnings series examined in the post World War II period. The MAMR process proposed by Beaver assumes that each year's unexpected earnings consists of a transitory factor (as in the pure mean-reversion process) and a nontransitory factor (as in a martingale) whose effects will persist for a finite number of periods into the future.

Recent evidence by Griffin (1977) and Watts (1975) suggests that quarterly earnings may be characterized as a moving-average process in first differences. Such a process could be manipulated in a quarterly basis by management's smoothing operations.

While the evidence is still inconclusive between a martingale process and a moving-average mean-reverting one, some tentative conclusions can be drawn. Little evidence can be found to support the practice of extrapolating past growth rates of earnings into the future. It has also been difficult to find evidence of an annual-earnings process which would be amenable to smoothing by management. One possibility, which does not seem to be widely advocated in traditional financial analysis, is to use esitmates of the accounting beta for a firm (the correlation of a firm's earnings changes with economy-wide earnings changes) to estimate the change in income for a firm in the current year. In addition to the Ball and Brown (1968) and Brown and Kennelly (1972) papers, which used this as one of the models to generate an estimate of the market's expectation of earnings, Brown and Ball (1967) have documented the strong cross-sectional dependence of a firm's earnings on a market-wide-earnings index and an industry-earnings index. Thus if analysts could generate reasonable estimates of these economy and industry-wide earnings levels, they might be able to get a better prediction of a firm's change in earnings than would be possible by simply attempting to exploit the time-series properties of past earnings numbers for the firm. For the auditor, such a model would be easy to implement at the time of an audit since there should be reasonable estimates of these earnings levels by the end of a year. Such an estimate may prove useful as part of the analytic review to see whether management's presentation of income is consistent with the historical relationship.

Another study of the time-series properties of earnings was performed by Dopuch and Watts (1972). Rather than restricting the earnings process to, say, one of two arbitrary processes (martingale or mean-reverting), they allowed the data to pick out a process from a very large class of linear-autoregressive-integrated-moving-average processes, sometimes known as Box-Jenkins analysis after the principal proponents of this collection of models. Having selected the particular process which seems to best fit the historical time-series data for each firm, Dopuch and Watts attempted to see whether a switch in accounting policy would cause the time-series earnings process to change. If it did, this was construed as a material or significant change in the firm's earnings process. If an accounting change did not change the time-series process, the change could be viewed as immaterial. Testing this methodology on the net income series of eleven steel firms which switched from accelerated to straight-line depreciation, they found a significant difference in eight of these firms (only one, though, had a significant change in the series describing accounting rates of return). Two problems arise with this technique. First, Box-Jenkins analysis requires an enormous amount of time-series data to select the underlying process which presumably is remaining stationary during this time. Second, at the time an accounting change is made there is no evidence of what the future series which could enable one to determine if a different time-series model is operating will look like. It does not seem helpful to recommend that auditors should wait fifteen years to gather enough data to decide whether a change made fifteen years earlier was, in fact, material.

EMPIRICAL EVALUATIONS OF ACCOUNTING ALTERNATIVES

The existence of alternative accounting methods for reporting the same set of underlying economic effects has occupied the attention of many academic accountants, practitioners, and occasionally even the U.S. Congress. Academic accountants have written an almost uncountable number of papers on the merits and demerits of proposals accounting for cost of goods sold, depreciation, the investment credit, mergers, interperiod tax allocation, intangible drilling expenses, and leases, among others.

Practitioners have not only been involved in the above debates in the journals and in policy groups, but also have had to deal with clients who, having found it difficult to generate profits in the factory, have tried to produce profits in the controller's office. Many firms have refused to adopt LIFO because of fears of what impact the drop in reported earnings would have on their stock-price performance. (One of the few good outcomes of the recent U.S. inflation has been a considerable decrease in the number of firms willing to pay heavy indemnities to the government because of such vague and, in my opinion, misguided fears.)

If one believes in an efficient market that correctly processes all available information about a firm, then one is not likely to believe that a fully disclosed change in accounting policy, which does not affect any cash flows, is likely to have much of an impact on a firm's stock price. Even further, if a firm's market price is found to be affected by earnings changes caused by accounting method changes, we might have serious evidence in conflict with the efficiency of the market. A number of studies have investigated whether a change in a firm's accounting policy which tends to increase reported earnings can be associated with abnormal increases in the stock price of the firm.

At a very simple level, tests have been made as to whether the price-earnings ratios of conservatively reporting firms (e.g., using tax allocation before APB 11, or accelerated depreciation) differed from comparable firms that used liberal reporting policies (e.g., flow-through, and straight-line depreciation). If the market is clever about detecting such reporting differences, the P/E ratio of conservative firms should exceed that of liberal firms since the former are using procedures which will, on the same set of economic events, report lower earnings than will the latter group. Since the prices of the two groups of companies should be unaffected by differences in reporting policies, the P/E ratios of the two groups would have to differ. Unfortunately, there are a number of problems associated with building defensible models of P/E ratios (see Gonedes-Dopuch [1974], Section 8) so that one is reluctant to draw definitive conclusions from such studies. Nevertheless, the studies generally found that there were differences in the P/E ratios, of the expected sign, between liberal and conservative firms.

A number of studies have now been performed which examine the stock-price reaction around the announcement of annual earnings for the year in which a company switched a particular accounting policy. The period immediately after date of announcement was selected because the difference in annual earnings from one year to the next would seem to be largest for the first year in which the new accounting policy was in effect. Thus, if the market was to be fooled by a reported earnings increase caused by an accounting change, the maximum impact would likely occur for the first year of the change when the earnings comparison with the prior year would be most dramatic.

Kaplan and Roll (1972) examined two sets of companies; one set switched to the flow-through method (from deferral) for the investment credit, the other set switched from accelerated depreciation to straight line. While a small (and still unexplained) positive effect was noticed around the time of the earnings announcement, this effect was temporary and there were no permanent increases in price caused by adopting either of these more liberal accounting policies. In fact, firms which switched depreciation methods seemed to do worse than the market, implying that such changes were undertaken when the firm was anticipating hard times.

Ball (1972) examined a large number of accounting changes of many different types. He found that shareholders of firms which tend to make such changes have generally received lower than normal returns prior to the year in which the switch was made. The year of the accounting change itself did not exhibit any unusual stock price behavior. He concluded that changes in accounting tehnique were not associated with market-price adjustments.

Sunder (1973) examined the stock price performance of firms that switched from FIFO to LIFO and from LIFO to FIFO. This is an interesting test since firms switching from FIFO to LIFO will report lower earnings at the same time that their economic earnings have improved because of a lower tax bill. Conversely, firms switching from LIFO to FIFO will report higher earnings, which they hope the market will respond to and thereby overcome the negative impact of their much higher tax bill (e.g., more than $50 million for Chrysler in 1970). The evidence indicated that firms switching to LIFO did not encounter any negative price reactions in the stock market. In fact, the average price of these stocks rose 5% more than would be expected, given general market movements, during the year in which the accounting change was made. The sample of firms that switched from LIFO to FIFO was too small to yield definitive conclusions, but there was a tendency for the stock prices of these companies to decline after this accounting change, which increased nominal earnings. A subsequent paper, which controlled for changes in the riskiness of these firms (Sunder [1975]), indicated no effect for the LIFO to FIFO switchers but the positive effect for the FIFO to LIFO firms persisted. Thus switching from LIFO to FIFO seems a particularly expensive and fruitless way to improve one's stock price, and we now have evidence that the market will not penalize and may even reward the share prices of firms that voluntarily report lower earnings and pay lower taxes.

Patz and Boatsman (1972) investigated the price performance of oil exploration companies around the time that the Accounting Principles Board issued a draft statement requiring companies which previously used full-cost accounting to switch to the successful-efforts method. If adopted, the earnings of such companies would be sharply lowered. If the market could not perceive that such an earnings decrease was merely due to an accounting convention and not to any fundamental economic forces, one might expect the share prices of full-cost companies to be adversely affected. Patz and Boatsman found that there was no adverse effect on the share prices of such companies, which is again consistent with predictions made from a premise of market efficiency.

Merger accounting has been a particularly inflammatory topic in accounting and financial circles. Many observers felt that the growth of conglomerates in the 1960s was attributable to their ability to avoid accounting for the excess of costs over book value of acquired companies through use of the pooling-of-interests method. The more stringent conditions imposed by APB 16 and 17 for merger accounting may even have been considered by some to have led to the decline in merger activity since their promulgation. Most of the controversy centers on the amortization of goodwill associated with a purchase price in excess of book value, an expense which has no effect on the cash flows of the firm. It should not be difficult for an intelligent analyst or investor, familiar with the terms of a merger, to compute such an amortization charge himself if he thought that that was the appropriate adjustment to make. Therefore, the pooling vs. purchase controversy is another instance of an argument over an alternative form of presentation which should not matter in an efficient market. Hong, Mandelker, and Kaplan (1978) investigated 159 mergers during the 1954-64 time period; 122 of these used pooling of interests and had positive goodwill associated with the merger, 37 used purchase accounting to amortize positive goodwill. Despite the use of pooling of interests, which some observers feel leads to inflated earnings, there was no tendency for the 122 pooling firms to earn abnormal returns around the merger date. On the contrary, there was a tendency for firms using purchase accounting to have positive excess returns around the time of the merger. This effect is probably not due to the use of purchase accounting, per se, but could be due to a selection mechanism whereby firms which choose purchase accounting may have been doing well and could therefore "afford" the decrease in reported earnings caused by amortizing goodwill. In any case, we have additional evidence that earnings increases caused solely by accounting conventions do not translate into higher stock prices.

The above studies concentrated on stock-price reactions at the time immediately following an earnings change or important event (APB announcement, a merger) took place. The studies found, in general, that no abnormal price movements were caused by an accounting change at that time. Once a company has switched to a more liberal accounting policy though, it will typically report higher earnings year after year than if it had continued to use the more conservative method. If the market somehow lost track of what set of accounting policies a firm was using, a possibility much more likely before the extensive disclosure rules in recent years, it might not realize that differences in earnings between two companies could be due to their using different accounting policies. Jacobs and Kaplan (1975) compared the stock-price rates of return between two sets of companies from 1962 to 1968; one set used straight-line depreciation and the other used accelerated depreciation for financial reporting. Both sets used accelerated depreciation for tax purposes. They found that there were no significant differences in the rates of return between the two sets of firms even though the accelerated firms, as a group, were reporting lower earnings than they could while still following generally accepted accounting principles.

The evidence is consistent that the market does not respond to earnings increases which are caused by cosmetic changes in accounting policy. There is even evidence which suggests that companies which change accounting policies in an attempt to increase earnings (or reduce losses) are in the midst of, or anticipating, poor operating results. As a consequence, investors may perceive such manipulations as a negative signal by management about the current and future profitability of the firm. Additional anecdotal evidence on this point occurred earlier this year when both Ford and Chrysler suddenly decided that the flow-through method was more appropriate to account for the investment credit. Coincidentally and within one day of each other, the two auto companies switched accounting methods; this changed a $97.9 million loss in the first quarter for Ford into a $10.6 million loss.

Similar beliefs about the incredible naïveté of the market were expressed in a recent *Business Week* (July 28, 1975) article about establishing deferred tax accounts for oil companies now that the depletion allowance has been repealed. Whatever the merits of deferred tax accounting, one should hardly conclude that this type of earnings restatement should have much effect on the market. Yet two top oil company executives were quoted as saying: "This is going to make oil stocks look a lot less attractive because many investors do not look beyond the net income figure." And "It's going to make equity financing almost impossible at the worst possible time." The writer of the article concluded that reducing the retained-earnings figures of these companies (through a retroactive charge) will cause a major increase in debt-equity ratios which would make borrowing more difficult and affect the financial decisions of the firms. Surely, it doesn't take very much "efficiency" in the market to make such statements appear ludicrous. Only if the market and commercial lenders were wildly inefficient could such statements ever begin to attain plausibility. Enough said!

A different approach has been taken by some to evaluate the impact of accounting alternatives on the market. Recall that in the Ball and Brown (1968) and Brown and Kennelly (1972) studies (among others), mechanical models were used to generate surrogates for market expectations of earnings. These surrogates were then compared to actual earnings to form portfolios and assess the profitability of knowing the earnings numbers one year in advance. Beaver and Dukes (1972) investigated whether the profitability of such a strategy could be affected by changing the accounting method used to measure earnings. In particular, they wished to determine whether earnings prepared under the deferral method for tax allocation would yield lower abnormal returns (because the method involved more allocations and was further from actual cash flows) than earnings generated under the flow-through method. It turned out that the deferral earnings seemed to be most consistent with the information in security prices, with flow-through (or nondeferral) and cash flow less consistent, respectively. In a subsequent paper, Beaver and Dukes (1973) viewed tax allocation as an issue of accelerated depreciation rather than of determining a deferred tax-liability account. They found that an earnings measure based on a depreciation charge somewhat greater than straight line was most highly associated with stock-price changes.

In a similar study, Dukes (1976) found that capitalizing R & D expenditures is more consistent with security prices than the actual expensing procedures that were used in his sample of companies. Foster (1975) also found that the earnings numbers of insurance companies had a higher association with security prices when unrealized capital gains and other adjustments were included in income than when these items were excluded, as they are in reporting normal or statutory income.

One implication of these latter studies is that the information that the market uses to assess performance of companies is broader than just reported earnings. Items in footnote disclosure such as R & D expenditures or market value of securities appear to be used by investors even though these items may not have been flowed through the income statement. As such, these findings are consistent with the studies reported earlier in this section which found that the market could properly evaluate the effects of alternative accounting techniques and respond to footnote disclosure.

It is not true, however, that these studies can be used to determine the most preferred accounting alternative, i.e., the one whose use leads to the highest association with stock-price changes. Theoretical reasons why stock-price reactions cannot be used to infer the market preferences for an accounting alternative are developed in Gonedes-Dopuch (1974). Preferences for alternative information systems ultimately require an analysis of social-welfare considerations which cannot be decided merely by stock-price associations. On a practical basis, accountants attempting to generate measures that have maximum association with market prices would eventually be driven to define accounting income as the change in market value over the period.

ACCOUNTING RATIOS AS PREDICTORS OF BUSINESS FAILURE

Of all the material surveyed in this paper, I believe that the research done in predicting bankruptcies has the most immediate relevance to practicing auditors. While it is important that net income not be in error by more than a material amount and that inventories not be valued at above cost or market, auditors get into much of their troubles when they give an unqualified opinion to a firm which shortly thereafter goes bankrupt. Analytic techniques which help an auditor decide when a firm is approaching default or insolvency would seem to offer significant benefits in reducing legal and insurance expenses. A fair number of studies have been performed which indicate that such techniques exist.

Beaver (1966) examined 30 financial ratios of a paired sample of 79 failed and 79 nonfailed firms from 1954—64. The ratios were in six broad categories: cash flow, net income, debt to total asset, liquid asset to total asset, liquid asset to current debt, and turnover. In his first analysis, he compared the mean values of each of the ratios between the failed and nonfailed firms. This profile analysis revealed substantial differences in the mean ratios between the two sets of firms and the mean difference increased as the year of failure approached (financial statements for up to five years before the actual failure event having been examined).

A second analysis was a dichotomous classification test in which each of the ratios was used to see how well it could discriminate between failed and nonfailed firms. The cash flow to total debt ratio had the strongest ability to predict failure, followed closely by net income to total assets. Each of these two ratios correctly classified 87% of the firms based on the last financial statements issued before failure (of the firms that actually failed, of course). The cash-flow to total-debt ratio correctly classified 78% of firms based on financial statements issued five years before failure. These flow ratios were substantially better in predicting bankruptcies than the liquid-asset ratios advocated in much traditional financial analysis.

Altman (1968) extended Beaver's univariate analysis to allow for multiple predictors of failure (Beaver considered the effects of using only one ratio at a time). Altman used multiple discriminant analysis (MDA), which attempts to develop a linear function of a number of explanatory variables to assign a value to a qualitative dependent variable, e.g., bankrupt or nonbankrupt. Since financial ratios are highly intercorrelated, it is difficult to predict which variables work well together in predicting bankruptcy from examining the effects of variables taken one at a time. Altman had a matched sample of 33 bankrupt and 33 nonbankrupt manufacturing corporations (1946—65) with assets between $1—$25 million. Twenty-two financial ratios, based on data one period before bankruptcy, were examined and Altman eventually selected five of these to be included in his final discriminant function:

1. Working capital/Total assets (liquidity),
2. Retained earnings/Total assets (age of firm and cumulative profitability),
3. Earnings before interest and taxes/Total assets (profitability),
4. Market value of equity/Book value of debt (financial structure),
5. Sales/Total assets (capital turnover rate).

Unfortunately, Altman was not able to use a cash-flow variable, which Beaver found to be the most discriminating in his study; apart from other accruals, Altman did not have depreciation figures.

Running split sample techniques, Altman was able to classify correctly more than 90% of the firms. With a new sample of 25 bankrupt firms, Altman's discriminant function correctly predicted 24 of them would go into bankruptcy. With a sample of firms that had negative earnings but which did not go bankrupt, only 14 of 66 were predicted to go into bankruptcy. One additional company which was classified as bankrupt did subsequently go into bankruptcy. For the original sample, but going back three years before bankruptcy, 48% of the firms were correctly predicted—note, however, that this is below the naïve, ex post facto, sample selection prediction that one half of the firms would go bankrupt.

A number of subsequent studies also confirmed the value of the multiple discriminant technique. Blum (1969) examined 115 failed companies (1954—68) with a paired sample of another 115 nonfailed firms and was able to classify correctly more than 90% of these firms based on financial ratios computed within a year of bankruptcy. Edmister (1972) was able to discriminate correctly 39 out of 42 cases of small business failures using multiple discriminate analysis. Edmister found that dividing company ratios by the average ratio for companies in the same industry improved the classificational ability of the test. Deakin (1972) examined 13 ratios for 32 failed and 32 nonfailed firms (1964—70). He replicated Beaver's methodology and again found that the cash-flow to total-debt ratio had the best discriminating ability of any single ratio though his classification results were not as good as Beaver's. He then constructed a discriminant function using all 14 variables with disappointing results—the function was highly nonstationary in each of five years prior to failure and on a new sample of 11 failed and 23 nonfailed firms, eight of these were incorrectly predicted on the basis of financial ratios computed in the year prior to failure. These results were likely caused by Deakin's inclusion of too many highly intercorrelated variables in the discriminant function. Wilcox (1973) tested a bankruptcy model he developed from an underlying probabilistic model (called the gambler's ruin problem). While this simple model at least has some theoretical underpinning, the statistical analysis is too informal to allow us to draw definitive conclusions as to its value.

Altman (1973) developed a discriminant function to predict railroad bankruptcies. In companies selected from many industries, normal variation in financial ratios across industries weaken the discriminating ability of these ratios. The railroad industry is unique in having had enough bankruptcies in recent history to enable a statistical analysis of factors that could predict bankruptcy for this industry by itself. From an initial list of 14 ratios, Altman developed a discriminant function based on 7 ratios. The model was derived from 21 bankruptcies in the 1939—70 period by comparing the ratios for each of the bankrupt railroads with the industry average for the year of bankruptcy. (There are some problems with this methodology which are not worth getting into here.) When the model was applied to the estimating sample, only one bankrupt firm was misclassified as healthy while every industry observation was correctly classified, not an unsurprising result given the large number of independent variables used and the strong serial correlation of industry averages from year to year.

The model was applied to a randomly selected group of 50 railroads between 1946 and 1969. Six railroads were classified as bankrupt prone, two did go bankrupt, one discontinued all railroad operations, two were merged into larger systems, and one was operated by the Canadian government. None of those classified as nonbankrupt had gone bankrupt by 1970. The model was also tested on 55 large railroads in 1970. Of these, 14 were classified as bankruptcy candidates. Of the 14, six were already in bankruptcy, five had been classified by railroad analysts as being on the brink of failure, and the other three were controlled by larger, more solvent railroads (with a deep pocket, presumably).

In a good summary article for this section, Altman and McGough (1974) describe the relation between the multiple-discriminant analysis prediction of failure and an auditor's qualification or disclaimer as to the going-concern nature of the firm. They used the five-variable discriminant function developed in Altman's 1968 paper. Of 34 companies entering bankruptcy since 1970, 28 of them would have been predicted to be bankruptcy candidates based on multiple-discriminant analysis of their last financial statement. In only 16 of these 34 companies did the auditors indicate going-concern problems in their opinion.

Of a sample of 21 companies which had a going-concern problem expressed in the auditor's opinion, six did subsequently go bankrupt and all six would have been predicted by the MDA model. Seven of these firms have recovered and are no longer receiving a qualified opinion; of these seven, five had MDA scores which would not have predicted bankruptcy. Thus, this study certainly suggests that a multivariate model could be of significant help for auditors attempting to assess the going-concern probability of a firm.

Despite the reasonable success of multiple-discriminant analysis for predicting bankruptcy, I think that much better and more powerful statistical techniques can be used to work on this important problem. MDA is a rather heuristic technique with only limited tests of significance and internal checks on its validity available. Samples have been mostly drawn on a matched-pair basis when there is no logical reason why there have to be as many failed as nonfailed firms in a sample. As a consequence, most tests are made on samples of failed firms. The auditor's task, however, is to assess the validity of the methodology on *all* firms and then see which get misclassified. If only a .5% of all firms fail each year, but the model predicts that each year 10% are bankruptcy candidates, we cannot expect auditors to qualify their opinion on 10% of their clients. More work has to be done to relate levels of ratios to the norms for an industry, as Edmister did. Also the impact of inflation on net income figures and on the desirability of including more debt in the capital structure needs to be included.

As I said in the introduction to this section, I believe this area offers the most potential for research impact on practice. It is therefore disappointing that statistical analyses done to date have been so cursory. Even granting the limitations of MDA, it might still be interesting for auditors to apply Altman's discriminant function to their clients' numbers this year to see how many of their clients they should start to worry about. At the very least, such a test could be the first step in an analytic review. Failure to pass this test might lead to more stringent testing of the marketability of inventory and the collectibility of receivables.

SUMMARY

How do we evaluate the impressive number of empirical studies of the information content of accounting messages? I am very positive and enthusiastic about the contribution of empirical research over the last ten years. Nevertheless, I view the future possibilities for empirical accounting research with much less optimism. While I reserve the right to change my mind in the light of new research, I now think that we are unlikely to maintain the momentum of empirical research into the next ten years. But first, let us start with the good news.

The studies in Section 3 demonstrate that accounting numbers do have information content. The stock market responds to the release of these numbers and stock-price revisions are associated with unexpected changes in earnings. Moreover, the income number produced by accounting procedures appears to be more closely associated with the underlying economic operations of the firm than are cash-flow variables. Interim reports including quarterly announcements and corporate forecasts of earnings are also viewed as timely information sources and are used by the market in forming expectations about the future prospects of the firm. This occurs despite the unaudited nature of these reports.

We have gained much knowledge about the time-series behavior of earnings. In particular, the idea of growth stocks which can maintain a steady percentage growth of earnings, over a period of several years, has been shown to be the exception rather than the rule. Simple models in which next year's earnings equal this year's appear to forecast better than extrapolation of past growth trends into the future.

A number of studies have shown that the market is able to evaluate properly the increase in earnings caused by fully disclosed changes in accounting policy. Such changes and accompanying earnings increases are fully discounted by the market so that there is no apparent benefit from this earnings manipulation. If anything, earnings increases manufactured in the controller's office may be viewed by the market as a negative signal about the firm's future prospects for sustaining earnings from continuing operations.

The concept of an efficient market which processes all available information in an unbiased and timely manner has important implications for accounting policy-makers. For one thing, it implies that many debates about selection among various forms of accounting procedure may not be worth the resources currently devoted to them. Typically, disclosure of the particular procedure used by the firm, along with enough supplementary data to enable the computation of income and balance sheet effects under alternative procedures, is a relatively costless course of action. In many cases, enough information already exists in footnote disclosure to permit alternative income and valuation computations.

An efficient market also implies that we should not be greatly concerned about whether readers can understand more complex and complete disclosure. Worries about the naïve investor seem misplaced since, to an excellent approximation, such investors face a fair game in which stocks are correctly priced according to risk-return relationships. As long as such investors hold diversified protfolios and avoid incurring heavy transactions costs by excessive trading, they can expect about the same return, for their level of risk, as more sophisticated investors. Accountants need not feel either paternalistic or responsible for investors who hold improperly diversified portfolios or who trade constantly on every piece of information that emerges in the marketplace.

An efficient market also gives some guidance on a limited set of accounting policies such as marketable securities. Once one accepts the idea that the market is rational and that prices respond to all available information, then there can be little justification for valuing securities at other than market value. Current policy, in which securities are written down to market value (below cost) only when the decline is expected to be permanent, implies that the accountant has greater knowledge and insight than all the participants in the market. If the accountant could know which price declines were only temporary, he would be silly to be spending his time verifying receivables and signing opinions. Much more profitable opportunities would await him. Again, as long as the market value of securities is disclosed somewhere in the financial statements this is not a crucial issue, but it provides an example of how research can occasionally give a clear preference for an accounting procedure. More extensive policy implications that follow from the idea of market efficiency, and the empirical evidence in support of this idea, are presented in Beaver (1973), and the reader is referred to this highly readable source.

What then are my reservations about the future value of empirical research in accounting? I think that we have now gotten all the easy results and that major new findings are going to be much harder to obtain. In effect, we have taken an extremely important advance in finance, tested it successfully on a variety of accounting data, and drawn some straight-forward conclusions from this research. Current research is involved with cleaning up some of the past studies by controlling for or testing a number of factors that were not included in the original research. Future work may extend our testing procedures from NYSE firms to OTC firms which may be more representative of most of the clients of CPA firms. At best, though, these studies will confirm the findings of the earlier studies by showing that the results follow even under more careful testing or using a more sophisticated methodology, and the conclusions from such studies will therefore be consistent with our current beliefs.

I am more pessimistic about the ability of empirical research to give us many insights into many varied and important questions now confronting the accounting profession. While it is typical, when confronted with a difficult policy issue, to call for more research on the question, it is not clear to me how empirical research in particular can provide much guidance in current debates over issues which involve costly disclosure. An example of such an issue is how or whether to adjust financial statements for the effects of inflation or changes in the price level of specific assets. As another example, should quarterly statements or earnings forecasts be audited? Both issues potentially involve having more information disclosed but with some cost associated with such disclosure. (While general price level accounting may be the least costly of the above possibilities, many critics, myself excluded, argue that the benefits are commensurate with or even below these low costs.) At present, empirical research cannot offer much help for policy-makers trying to decide whether to implement any of the above proposals. The situation is even worse than this, though. Let us assume that a new form of costly disclosure is selected. Present methodology does not allow us to look at the subsequent price and return series to make a judgment as to whether there has been an improvement in resource allocation or any form of social welfare to warrant the costs of increased disclosure. I find this a particularly frustrating state of affairs.

I should mention one particularly ambitious and clever attempt at such a policy evaluation. Benston (1973) tried to determine whether there were any measurable benefits from the Securities Exchange Act of 1934 which established more costly disclosure requirements. Benston could not find any empirical measure of market performance that improved in the post-SEC area. Unfortunately, many other factors could have led to this finding besides the ineffectiveness of the SEC (see Gonedes-Dopuch [1974], Section 8), so that we are unable to conclude from this study alone that the SEC has had no positive impact on the functioning of securities markets.

Therefore, I am unable to conclude this survey of ten years of empirical research in accounting with an optimistic forecast of what the next ten years of such research will yield. On particular issues, the evidence from empirical research may be used to provide support for a particular alternative. I have already mentioned the marketable securities question. Another possibility for future research is to incorporate the recent advances in the pricing of options and convertible securities so as to improve drastically the current arbitrary and irrational features of computing earnings-per-share in APB 15. The research cannot be used to justify the computation and disclosure of a figure such as fully diluted earnings per share, but since policy-makers have decided that such a figure should be computed, research can be used to derive a figure that has some basis in economic theory and evidence. A third area where empirical research may prove useful is on materiality in financial reports. By observing market responses to unexpected changes in financial statements, we might be able to determine the sensitivity of the market to small differences in reported income. Thus, on particular issues, empirical research may provide a significant amount of guidance. We should not expect, however, that such research will resolve many of the fundamental disclosure and reporting issues addressed by the FASB and the SEC.

For bibliographic references see Common Bibliography for Part V.

FOOTNOTES

[1] An abnormal return is the return in excess of what would be expected given the stock's systematic risk, β, and the market return, i.e., for a period, t, in which the market return was R_{Mt}, a stock with risk β and return R_{jt} would have an abnormal return equal to $R_{jt} - \beta R_{Mt}$.

BEHAVIORAL RESEARCH AND FINANCIAL ACCOUNTING STANDARDS*

by Michael Gibbins and Patricia Hughes

The authors thank participants in research workshops at the University of Alberta, the University of British Columbia, and the University of Washington for their very helpful comments on earlier drafts of this chapter.

*Reprinted from *Usefulness to Investors and Creditors of Information Provided by Financial Reporting: A Review of Empirical Accounting Research,* ed. Paul A. Griffin (Stamford, Connecticut: Financial Accounting Standards Board, © 1982), Chapter 6, pp. 99-134.

Vast amounts of research effort are being given to the study of the ways in which people use information and make decisions. Behavioral research, as it applies to financial accounting, uses empirical methods (such as field studies, protocol analyses, interviews, and questionnaires) arising from psychology and similar disciplines to seek general explanations of how accounting information is used. This area of research is at present young, unfocused, and conceptually underdeveloped. However, a review of the research to date uncovers interesting possibilities for future study as well as potential shortcomings of such study in general.

Because conceptions of behavioral research and the Financial Accounting Standards Board's interest in it vary, it is best to begin by clarifying the scope of our review. The analysis concentrates on the issues of efficiency and effectiveness of standard setting in accounting rather than on normative (and political) questions about the existence of the FASB or its own preferences for outcomes. We focus on the behavior of investors, creditors, and similar decision makers—the principal users of general purpose financial reports (see Concepts Statement 2, paragraphs 22-26). The behavior of managers, auditors, and others will be referred to where relevant, but we make no systematic review of the extensive behavioral literature in areas such as management accounting, auditing, and personnel management (in public accounting). Moreover, the bulk of the work reviewed deals with the behavior of *individuals* rather than organizations or markets, which are dealt with in other chapters [of the book edited by Griffin].

This chapter has two major parts. The first reviews the behavioral research relevant to the evaluation of financial information by investors and creditors. The second attempts to draw conclusions that we hope are of interest to the FASB and its constituency. These conclusions are based on the research itself, and on certain characteristics of the research that should be considered when evaluating the contribution it makes to a discussion of issues raised in this and other chapters.

Before we go further, we must emphasize that, so far, strong conclusions of direct applicability to standard setters have eluded us.

Behavioral research in financial accounting emphasizes descriptive explanations of the world as it is and, as such, is not particularly well suited to examining the *desirability* of alternative accounting standards. In our review and conclusions, therefore, we try to clarify not only what is known but also the limits of that knowledge. We wish to inform the reader about the kinds of topics studied in behavioral accounting and allied research and to explain how the orientation of that research tempers the conclusions that can be drawn.

REVIEW OF BEHAVIORAL RESEARCH IN FINANCIAL ACCOUNTING

Large amounts of behavioral research could be considered relevant to this review, so we have tried to avoid sins of omission by taking a broad view in this section. One difficulty with this approach is that no conceptual framework for relating behavioral research to investment and lending decisions and standard setting exists. Notwithstanding periodic commentary about this situation (e.g., Gonedes and Dopuch [1974]; American Accounting Association [1977a]; Dyckman, Gibbins, and Swieringa [1978, pages 79-81]), researchers have failed to rally to any generally agreed solution. As a result, we have adopted a simple and somewhat arbitrary scheme for classifying the behavioral research we review:[1]

1. People's response to information in general
2. Additional issues related to financial accounting
3. Specific users of accounting information
4. Influences of the accounting environment on action

Most of the research cited or reviewed deals with the behavior of *individuals* rather than that of groups, markets, or other aggregates. We believe that the aggregate effects of individual behavior are important in evaluating the contribution of behavioral financial accounting research. Unfortunately, there is a paucity of behavioral research on either aggregate behavior or the link between the individual and the aggregate. Questions of aggregation are discussed in the second part of this chapter.

PEOPLE'S RESPONSE TO INFORMATION IN GENERAL

As stated earlier, a great amount of research attention is being given to the ways in which people use information and make decisions. A recent bibliography of empirical research, for example, includes more than 850 articles and books on the subject (Naylor [1979]). Relevant to this study are four interrelated results drawn from the literature reviewed:

1. In studying how people make choices, empirical results do not compare well with results predicted by models of how one ought to behave in a given situation (normative models).
2. People are not really conscious of their own decision-making styles or, in most cases, what information is important to their decisions.
3. Some statistical models are fairly robust approximations of the way judgments are made. Such models often outperform the decisions or judgments made by people.
4. People's responses in making decisions reflect a variety of simplifications, fixations, and perceptual distortions of their environment.

We examine each of these results below, citing key studies where appropriate.

Predictions from Decision Models

Many attempts have been made to test empirically the predictive ability of normative (rational) models of judgment and decision making. Overall, the findings indicate little predictive success for such models, suggesting that they are poor representations of actual behavior. The normative theory of decision making based on "subjective expected utilities" has been extensively studied in this regard (e.g., Slovic, Fischoff, and Lichtenstein [1977]). The evidence is reasonably clear: People make choices that are inconsistent, contaminated by supposedly irrelevant considerations, or otherwise improper in terms of the prescriptions of the theory. Nobel laureate Herbert Simon (1979) summarized the state of affairs:

> . . . The refutation of the theory has to do with the *substance* of the decisions, and not just the process by which they are reached. It is not that people do not go through the calculations that would be required to reach the [subjective expected utility] decision—neoclassical thought has never claimed that they did. What has been shown is that they do not even behave as if they had carried out those calculations, and that result is a direct refutation of the neoclassical assumptions. [page 507]

Other decision-making models have encountered similar difficulties. An example is the well-known "Bayesian probability revision model" that considers the activity of revising an event's estimated probability on the basis of new information. People's revisions of probability assessments do not follow the Bayes model well in that they are often "conservative," that is, they give less weight to arriving information than the model prescribes. An example of conservative behavior would be changing one's estimate of the probability of loan default from one percent to two percent upon the arrival of new information, whereas the Bayes formula would revise the probability to greater than two percent. There is much debate about the phenomenon of "conservatism," but the principal findings have led many researchers to claim that the Bayesian model is fundamentally invalid as an explanation of the way people evaluate probabilities (Kahneman and Tversky [1972, page 450]; Hogarth [1975, page 273]; Shafer [1978]).

These theories of decision making, of course, involve only one image of humans as processors of information (Libby [1976]; Watts and Zimmerman [1979]). Among the more empirically oriented alternative models of choice behavior are some that are rational in spirit yet adjusted to meet empirical realities. Simon (1979) has argued that rationality is bounded by several human limitations in processing information. Such limitations include failure to adequately consider new evidence (anchoring), inability to make proper probability judgments, and preoccupation with personal experience. Additionally, Kahneman and Tversky (1979) suggest that people edit information and hence change its meaning before using it in decision making (Newman [1980]). Some of the newer approaches reflect entirely different conceptions of the choice process. March (1978), for example, suggests that people may reasonably prefer ambiguity and lack of coherence concerning their tastes, preferences, and inclinations to act. Finally, Nisbett and Wilson (1977) and Weick (1979) have questioned the conventional interpretation of rational behavior (i.e., consistent with prescribed "rational" axioms), suggesting that rationality might be viewed as rationalization—as an attempt to explain behavior to ourselves after the fact, rather than as a determinant of behavior.

An important assumption in the normative theory of investment choice, referred to in other chapters, is that investors use information (e.g., financial statements) to assess the probabilities of future returns to various investment alternatives. In such a context, information is useful only if it allows an "improved" assessment of uncertain returns. Unfortunately, this concept of information, and the kinds of probability assessments it implies, have received little behavioral investigation in accounting as yet, though some work on developing ways of getting managers to verbalize the probability of occurrence of events has begun (Chesley [1978]). Recent findings pertaining to judgment processes (see reviews by Hammond, McClelland, and Mumpower [1980]; Hogarth [1980]; Einhorn and Hogarth [1981]) are undoubtedly consistent with the concept of information in terms of its role to change or confirm beliefs, but direct connections between the concept and the evidence are still only speculative.

As explained elsewhere in this chapter, behavioral research is still struggling with the identification of major components of people's decision making, both in accounting and in general.

The relationship between normative decision models and behavioral research findings has been a matter of much debate (Mock and Vasarhelyi [1978]; Hilton [1980]; Butterworth, Gibbins, and King [1981]; Einhorn and Hogarth [1981]). Once considered divergent schools of thought, the normative and behavioral frameworks now appear to have a lot in common—mostly as a result of more precise analytical expressions of the observed behavior. The debate has doubtless had positive effects. For example, taking normative models as first approximations of purposeful decision making has drawn attention to decision aids and other methods of improving decisions (Slovic et al. [1977, pages 17-28]). Accountants have long recognized the value of such aids. Much of standard presentation in financial statements, such as the notes, calculations of earnings per share, and so on, are directed at helping people use the information more effectively. Behavioral evaluation of the design of decision aids in financial accounting has not yet begun, though there is some progress in the auditing area (e.g., Chesley [1978]) and in research on computer aids (e.g., Benbasat and Dexter [1979]).

Lack of Self-Knowledge about Decision Making

People, including those with apparent expertise in the decision or judgment to be made, are not consciously aware of their own decision-making thought processes. For example, Gray (1979) claims that people's ability to *make* judgments exceeds their ability to understand how they *reached* those judgments. The evidence is mixed, however. Some studies have found that auditors exhibit substantial understanding of the factors that affect their judgments (Ashton [1974]; Schultz and Gustavson [1978]). Savich (1977) and Wright (1977a and 1979) also found good understanding among business students. However, all but Savich's study used a statistical research technique known as the "Brunswik lens model," a technique that requires a large number of repetitive decisions in a tightly controlled setting. This may encourage the research participant to develop a simple decision strategy just to cope with the repetition (Ashton [1974]). Similarly, Nisbett and Wilson (1977) suggest that people's reports on their own thought processes are based on their own theories about what seems plausible in the situation, rather than on any true introspection. Consequently, what appears to be "self-knowledge" may be a function more of the situation than of the person.

People also tend to be overconfident in their judgments, compared with the confidence implied by reasonable statistical models (e.g., Slovic et al. [1977]). This is a fairly persistent phenomenon and seems to involve a failure to understand the limitations of the information being used in the judgment, though Gibbins (1982) demonstrates that statistical models may support higher confidence than had been thought.

The Robustness of Simple Statistical Models of Judgment

For years psychologists have recognized that simple statistical models tend to perform well in representing decision makers, or in competing with them (Meehl [1954]). One class of models, called *linear models*, assumes that the various pieces of information "add together" in terms of their combined effect on the decision or judgment.[2] Certain simple models may even predict a person's own judgments better than that person could predict alone. For example, if error in the information leads to noise or uncertainty, the simple statistical model, which ignores the noise, may cope better than an ostensibly sophisticated human who might be confused or sidetracked by it (Slovic et al. [1977, page 12]; Ogilvie and Schmitt [1979]). Moreover, composites of people's judgments often outperform all but the most successful individuals (Libby [1975a]; Wright [1979]). Such findings are frequent (Libby [1975b]; Wright [1977b]; Abdel-khalik and El-Sheshai [1980]) though not universal (Libby [1976]; Libby and Lewis [1977]; Libby and Blashfield [1978]) and may be a function partly of the research instruments.

Yet little is really known about how people actually combine information in reaching a decision. While the above simple models appear to be approximating *some* fundamental underlying processes, it is not obvious what those are. However, researchers such as Eggleton (1976) and Biggs (1979) are attempting to generate deeper understanding by developing ways of "tracing" people's use of information through a decision, and by trying to model the brain's storage and retrieval processes.

In sum, the conclusions drawn in most of the literature suggest that while the simple statistical models are not necessarily valid representations of a decision maker's actual thought processes, they can be useful aids in predicting or replacing the human's decision tasks (Dawes [1979]).

Simplifications, Distortions, and Fixations

A tendency observed in many studies is that people seem to simplify the situation when making decisions, particularly if the task is complex or repetitive. These simplifications take many forms, including a disregard for information and a failure to recognize changes in the situation since the previous decision.

One class of simplifications, dubbed heuristics, applies rules of thumb to the information used. Heuristics, for example, may give too much importance to immediately available information or to the imagined results of an alternative action. A previous result may be given too much importance as well or be remembered as having been better than it actually was. The concept of "materiality" in accounting and auditing is a generally accepted heuristic based on the size of the discrepancy relative to expectations. (For studies of materiality and other simplifying techniques, see Patillo [1976], Hofstedt and Hughes [1977], Dyckman et al. [1978], Firth [1979], and Moriarity and Barron [1979].)

Another simplification that has received considerable attention from accounting researchers is the so-called functional-fixation hypothesis: People stick doggedly to previously used ways of evaluating information because they fail to recognize the changing aspects of the situation. The hypothesis has been supported in experimental settings and as such appears to be valid (Ashton [1976]; Chang and Birnberg [1977]; Abdel-khalik and Keller [1979]; Swieringa, Dyckman, and Hoskin [1979]). For example, Abdel-khalik and Keller reported that the investment officers and securites analysts who participated in their study . . .

> . . . indicated an understanding of the impact of switching to LIFO on reported earnings and on cash flows. In spite of this apparent understanding, respondents generally preferred a firm using FIFO over an identical firm that had decided to switch to LIFO in an inflationary economy. . . .Our explanation is consistent with the posited hypothesis of functional fixation— subjects do not readily change the weights assigned to reported earnings in forming expectations about the prospects of the firm. [page 50]

It is not yet known how people choose heuristics (or similar decision rules) or to what range of phenomena they might apply. In a recent experiment, Abdel-khalik and El-Sheshai (1980) found that default predictions by lending officers were more affected by the officers' choice of information than by the officers' use of the chosen information. In other words, it is what a person selects as information and not how that is combined with other data that is important. Neither is it known whether biases in individuals' decisions affect stock market or other aggregate behavior; they may "cancel out" or otherwise be mitigated in the aggregation process.

To summarize, behavioral research on the whole has shown generally inconclusive results about people's decision making. There are, however, a few valuable results. Normative decision models, despite their broad conceptual appeal, appear to be poor representations of what people actually do. People's judgments can be represented better by simple statistical models based on empirical analysis. Also, people are not very aware of their own thought processes, which seem subject to a variety of biases and distortions.

ADDITIONAL ISSUES RELATED TO FINANCIAL ACCOUNTING

Though there has been much nonbehavioral research and other writing on accounting measurement (including the FASB's Statements of Financial Accounting Concepts), behavioral investigation of accounting measurement concepts has been sparse. Dyckman et al. (1978, pages 53-55) reported several studies in the early 1970s on aggregation and entropy (i.e., loss of information through aggregation), communication effectiveness, reliability, and semantic meaning, but there have been few recent studies. Adelberg (1979) and Moriarity (1979) demonstrated intriguing techniques for assessing communication effectiveness. Adelberg asked respondents to try to fill in randomly deleted words from financial statement narratives. Moriarity translated financial reports into schematic human faces and asked respondents to use them in bankruptcy predictions. Ashton (1977) proposed a consensus approach to the evaluation of objectivity, and Belkaoui (1978) suggested that the accounting "language" be examined using linguistic techniques. Interest continues in how (as distinct from what) accounting information is communicated, but no general conclusions have yet emerged.

There has been some research on financial statements containing numbers expressed as confidence intervals or ranges (Birnberg and Slevin [1976]; Keys [1978]; Collins and Yeakel [1979], but the evidence is that such statements are not helpful to users. Keys, for example, found that bank officers' decisions on loans were not affected by the presence of confidence interval information. Apparently users feel comfortable with single-figure estimates, and some believe that the presence of ranges implies inaccuracy in the accounting information.

There is a large amount of literature questioning the adequacy of historical cost financial statements in the present inflationary environment and suggesting alternative ways of producing inflation-adjusted reports. In spite of this, Dyckman et al. (1978, pages 63-66) reported that behavioral studies had generally discovered that decision makers had little interest in inflation-adjusted numbers or in other alternatives to the traditional historical cost model. Benston and Krasney (1978) also found little enthusiasm for alternatives to historical cost among investment officers in life insurance companies, particularly among the more experienced officers. Additionally, Eyes and Tabb (1978) found that bank managers did not strongly desire inflation-adjusted statements. More recently, a study conducted by Louis Harris and Associates (1980) for the Financial Accounting Foundation indicates that the current cost data is viewed more positively now than in the past by a variety of influential persons. A survey by Arthur Young & Company (1981) shows that preparers favor current cost over constant dollar information, although many respondents oppose both. And two additional surveys (Casey and Sandretto [1981]; Schwarzbach and Swanson [1981]) indicate that managers are beginning to use the changing prices data for decision making. A FASB Research Report by Frishkoff (1982) reviews those and other studies in more detail.

The results of a business game task (Benbasat and Dexter [1979]) support the contention that users prefer to draw their own conclusions from information about economic events, rather than being given summarized information that might obscure the events and doubtless contains assumptions about users' particular needs. However, not all of the users studied by Benbasat and Dexter preferred the nonaggregated information; those who did prefer it did not perform any better in the task.

Proposals to supplement financial statements with information on a firm's management of human resources and attention to various "social responsibilities" have received reasonable research effort, some of it behavioral. Most behavioral research, though, has found little enthusiasm for information regarding the use of social or human resources (Hendricks [1976]; Flamholtz and Cook [1978]; Buzby and Falk [1979]; Snowball [1979]). However, Williams (1980) reports some evidence of interest in such data by managers for their own performance evaluations, and Schwan (1976) observed some effects on decisions of bankers, as did Acland (1976), who studied analysts.

To conclude, behavioral research has uncovered little support for alternatives to the historical cost financial accounting model and has as yet given only scattered attention to the underlying measurement characteristics of that model. Behavioral financial accounting research has produced rather less conclusive results than has the more general decision-making research reviewed in the previous section.

SPECIFIC USERS OF ACCOUNTING INFORMATION

We now turn to the large amount of behavioral research concerned with the needs of particular users of financial statements. Dyckman et al. (1978) commented:

> ... More sophisticated users, in terms of their understanding and appreciation of accounting data, tend to rely more heavily on the accounting data supplied to them in financial reports, rather than on the nonaccounting portions of such reports. Unsophisticated users, on the other hand, rely more on the nonaccounting data....Sophisticated users are more likely to be able to perceive economic realities underlying alternative reporting methods. These user characteristics are job-related and are probably related to the user's experience as well. Therefore, the effect of alternative reporting practices is likely to be influenced by the same factors. [page 76]

These conclusions were based largely on survey research published in the late 1960s and early 1970s.

Since then, additional experimental research (conducted in laboratories and other controlled settings) has examined individual differences among information users (Driver and Mock [1975]; Savich [1977]; McGhee, Shields, and Birnberg[1978]; Benbasat and Dexter [1979]; Lusk [1979]; Pratt [1980]). These recent studies normally have used student subjects and have focused principally on differences in personality and "style" of information use (e.g., preference for complex versus simplified information). Such studies involve sorting student users into groups and examining differences among groups, and so do not provide much detail about the use of accounting information by individuals.

Surveys of preferences for information by various user groups, which were plentiful in the early 1970s, have almost disappeared from the academic accounting literature. They are also rare in professional accounting journals. Recent studies include only a sprinkling of user groups: Epstein (1975), Lewellen, Lease, and Schlarbaum (1977), and Reckers and Stagliano (1980) studied individual investors; Ferris (1976) and Chandra and Greenball (1977) studied managers; Fuller and Metcalf (1978) and Carper, Barton, and Wunder (1979) studied financial analysts; and Benjamin and Stanga (1977) and Most and Chang (1979) studied a variety of users.

The findings from these studies and the earlier ones examined by Dyckman et al. (1978) are often contradictory. For example, Epstein (1975) reported that financial statements are of little value (or at least are little used) in making investment decisions, whereas Most and Chang (1979) reported the opposite, that is, repondents felt financial statements were very useful in such decisions. Such contradictory findings may be a function of differences in the questions asked (most are surveys), response rates, alternatives provided, and other differences in research approach. The methodological difficulties and contradictory results of surveys, together with people's earlier-noted lack of conscious awareness of their own use of information, make survey results hard to interpret, although some conclusions may tentatively be drawn.

Investors have difficulty understanding financial statements and show little interest in using them. Financial analysts are more able and inclined to use financial statements but do not appear to depend very much on them and do not see much value in the inclusion of information (e.g., forecasts) that they already develop for themselves. As remarked in Chapter 4,[of the book edited by Griffin] the SEC's Advisory Committee on Corporate Disclosure (1977) found that analysts relied on more informal sources of information. Nevertheless, Patton (1976) surveyed users of municipal financial statements and found some interest in improving the statements' format. In a subsequent study, however, Patton (1978) did not succeed in establishing experimentally that varying the degree of funds consolidation in such statements made a difference to municipal officers' estimates of interest rates for the debt of other municipalities.

A large subset of behavioral research in this area has focused on bankers and loan officers (Kennedy [1975]; Libby [1975a, 1975b, 1979a, and 1979b]; Estes and Reimer [1977]; Eyes and Tabb [1978]; Stanga and Benjamin [1978]; Abdel-khalik and El-Sheshai [1980]; Casey [1980b]; Zimmer [1980]). Much of this has involved carefully controlled experimental settings, with considerable emphasis on providing the bankers and loan officers with realistic tasks. Because the phenomena of interest vary from study to study, the specific tasks and surrounding information vary also. For example, in one study, Libby (1979a) used only audit reports, with no accompanying financial statements; in a second study, Libby (1979b) used full financial statements, including an audit report and a "management evaluation" and an "uncertainty" report; Casey (1980b) used ratios only; and Abdel-khalik and El-Sheshai (1980) used a set of 18 ratio and trend numbers computed from the statements. No particular picture of bankers' and loan officers' decision processes has therefore emerged, but it is clear that these people do use financial statements in their credit decisions, that they are sensitive to information related to credit risk, and that they seem to pay attention to only a few dimensions of each set of information (as we might expect from the earlier discussion on decision makers' simplifications of their environment).

The conclusion drawn from behavioral research on particular users of financial statements is that users' needs are specific and relate to each job, decision-making task, or environment. No general summary of needs or informational priorities has emerged; indeed, the research suggests that none will emerge. Researcher interest is thus shifting away from the earlier (optimistic) attempts to summarize users' general-purpose needs or preferences and toward the study of the actual thought processes inherent in making investment decisions. Several of the above-noted studies of bankers and loan officers are typical of this newer, "human information processing" approach. There is also increased interest in the environmental factors affecting users' decisions, to which we turn next.

INFLUENCES OF THE ACCOUNTING ENVIRONMENT ON ACTION

This section considers the reponse of individuals to financial information in relation to the informational, organizational, and economic *environment* of accounting and reporting. We hope that by examining some behavioral concepts relevant to that environment, a richer understanding of individual response and action may develop. This section presents some environmental influences offered by behavioral research as relevant to understanding a person's response to accounting information. Some of the points made are tentative, for much of the research is recent and little has been conducted yet in the financial accounting area. However, the discussion provides necessary background to the conclusions we draw later. The environmental picture we outline is a highly interactive one; the points discussed, therefore, are highly interrelated.

(1) Most people who come in contact with accounting information do not act in isolation but, instead, interact as members of organizations, professions, or other groups. (See Hayes [1977] for a demonstration of this in a management accounting setting.) In so interacting, people respond and contribute to an array of processes that cause organizations to act and, hence, change. Those processes can be subtle, are often political, and are frequently not explicitly directed to the organization's goals (Cohen and March [1974]; March [1978]; Weick [1979]).

The conception of an organization's actions as not necessarily deliberate, even though individuals within the organization may act deliberately, is causing many researchers on organizational behavior to rethink their discipline. This is contributing to an increased interest in studying the ways organizations actually decide things (similar to the earlier-noted increased interest in "human information processing" at the individual level). Interest in this conception also reflects the increasing awareness that study of individual behavior does not necessarily provide insights about the aggregate behavior of organizations or markets. We touch on the issue of organizational choice later in this section.

(2) People, to a degree, cause or create their own environment. Their actions, a part of the ongoing events, in effect physically shape or determine their world. Under this view, prophecies can indeed be self-fulfilling. Further, because the effects of their own (and others') acts are often not easily observable, people construct explanations based on what they perceive to be happening, which may not always coincide with what actually is happening (Nisbett and Wilson [1977]). Their learning is in relation to an environment that may at first be hypothetical but that through their actions may gain some physical reality. For example, if an investor has some belief about the market's behavior (e.g., prospects will improve) and acts accordingly, that investor's acts will contribute, even if in only a small way, to the events that determine whether or not the belief is founded.

(3) It has been theorized (e.g., Weick [1979]) that organizational behavior is a product of dual tendencies to stability and change. Such tendencies are generally thought to operate in a kind of balance. Information, for example, is needed both about ongoing environmental change and about the organization's accumulated experience and wisdom. An imbalance toward the former would tend to produce erratic or stop-and-go policies through attempts to respond to every change, while an imbalance in the other direction would produce a tendency to stagnation through lack of response to change. Information such as financial statement data no doubt contributes both to the assessment of future returns to the investor and to the assessment of past behavior by the investor's agents (management). How such dual roles work, which role is predominant in a particular setting, and how they affect each other is largely unknown (Butterworth et al. [1981]). But, as noted in Chapter 4, [of the book edited by Griffin] research effort (none of it as yet behavioral) is now being directed to the role that (accounting) information plays in organizations' contractual arrangements and other mechanisms.

(4) Organizations' reward and management systems constitute massive constraints on a person's response to accounting information. An analyst who fails to respond to an accounting change may recognize the information but respond instead to the firm's guidelines concerning investment in particular industries. This response may be similarly influenced if there is to be an evaluation by a method believed to be insensitive to the accounting change. Similarly, an auditor facing a conflict with a client about an accounting policy will consider the business risk involved, the probability of losing the client, and so on. Behavioral research has not yet contributed to a substantial understanding of the organizational settings within which people respond to financial accounting information, though recent "human information processing" research offers promise in this regard.

(5) The role of financial accounting information as a control system on individual behavior is important, perhaps more important than its role as a basis for predictions (Butterworth et al. [1981]). Recent work on the economic theory of principal and agent relationships and its implications for financial accounting (Watts and Zimmerman [1978 and 1981]; Atkinson and Feltham [1981]), information evaluation (Uecker [1978 and 1980]), and behavior that anticipates information (Prakash and Rappaport [1977]) is giving new attention to the traditional but heretofore neglected concepts of stewardship and control. Accounting information *influences* behavior. It not only provides neutral information for decision making, but it also motivates, influences, and otherwise induces behavior by way of feeding back the results of decisions in a variety of ways and by acting as a "scoring system" for measuring results. For example, if a bond indenture imposes restrictions on management's actions on the basis of particular accounting results, there must be a way of calculating those results. Future behavioral accounting research is likely to give more emphasis to control and feedback effects and less to a decision maker's ability to make predictions using accounting numbers.

(6) Even if the individual decision maker is responding entirely without the assistance of others and is using accounting information to decide on how to respond, the role of that information can be understood only if it is related to the individual's available information sources. If shareholders do not use financial statements in making decisions, then what do they use? Epstein (1975, page 71) conjectures that they ask their stockbroker for advice. But how does the broker formulate this advice? We have noted that analysts, for example, rely extensively on information from informal sources. What informal information systems are used?

The existence of other information sources means that financial accounting information must be evaluated on the basis of marginal benefits and costs. Regarding marginal benefits, an investor who believes profits are a function of uncontrollable market effects would have little incentive to seek better information for investment decisions. As Watts (1977) commented with respect to individuals' willingness to vote in elections, the incremental benefits are negligible. Even if there were a perceived marginal benefit, it may not outweigh the marginal costs. Lack of interest in changing the content of financial reports, therefore, does not necessarily imply no desire for information; it may simply indicate a perceived excess of marginal costs over marginal benefits. Marginal analysis, moreover, must take into account any other existing sources of similar information. Lev (1976) observes that financial statements do not and should not monopolize the provision of information to the capital markets. In the inflation-accounting area, for example, if a decision maker requires information on the effects of inflation but can and does estimate most of the effects from other sources, an improved financial accounting standard, even if perfect, can provide only a limited benefit. That benefit might not be worth the incremental cost to implement the new standard. Evaluations of this sort may well influence potential respondents to the FASB, who are aware of their information alternatives, to express little enthusiasm for accounting changes.

(7) The set of individuals whose actions are relevant to standard setting is very broad: included are analysts, auditors, creditors, managers, regulators, shareholders, union members, and so on (Watts and Zimmerman [1978 and 1979]; Dopuch and Sunder [1980]). This breadth, combined with our earlier remarks about the role of financial accounting as a behavioral control system, suggests that major effects of financial accounting information will be observed not only in stock prices after the new information is released, but also in altered behavior of managers, auditors, and others during the periods before and after first public disclosure. If an accounting standard is changed to assist investors in adapting to changing external circumstances, its result may be to alter managerial behavior or investor expectations so as to head off stock price fluctuations that would otherwise have occurred. In other words, lack of effect on stock prices can be evidence that the accounting change is working, not that it is ineffective.

(8) External forces such as increased regulation, endemic inflation, and increasing business internationalization (Brennan [1979]; Gray [1980]; Scott and Troberg [1980]) are likely to affect various user groups differently and to affect the role financial accounting plays in influencing each group's behavior. The role of financial accounting information may be quite subtle. Stock market behavior, for example, will not necessarily reflect that role if external events affect the market differently than they do other components of the economy. Shank, Dillard, and Murdock (1980) interviewed financial managers about their responses to the FASB's Statement 8 on foreign currency translation and found that, in spite of an apparent lack of reaction by stock markets to the standard, the managers undertook action in the foreign currency area that would increase expected costs and risk levels, in order to preserve "desired" relationships in accounting numbers.

In summary, a consideration of the statement user's decision environment and the factors that influence it as studied by other researchers provides behavioral financial accounting researchers with examples of potential contributions. Yet to be explored are accounting's role as a behavioral control system and its role in organizational decision making. The environmental review also raises issues that may help to explain the earlier-noted lack of conclusiveness of behavioral financial accounting research, for example, the problems of making deductions about market behavior and the need for marginal cost and benefit alternatives as part of the research in the use of accounting information.

CONCLUSIONS AND IMPLICATIONS FOR STANDARD SETTING

This section draws conclusions of interest to the FASB and its constituency from the preceding review and makes connections to points raised in other chapters[of the book edited by Griffin]. Because behavioral financial accounting research has not been particularly oriented to standard-setting issues, because individual research results have seldom been conclusive, and because we wish to avoid potentially misleading speculation, our conclusions must be general ones.

Financial accounting is a difficult subject to study using behavioral methods, because such methods emphasize empirical fact finding and do not deal well with questions of desirability (of alternative standards, of the FASB's political effects, etc.) Setting financial accounting standards involves not only an assessment of what likely effects will occur, but also an evaluation of whether those effects are desirable for all affected parties. Empirical research's focus on assessing the effects therefore produces results that, from a standard setter's viewpoint, are incomplete. While research on questions of social desirability may be conducted by appealing to integrated theories in economics, decision theory, and statistics, empirical behavioral accounting research has no integrated theory. It is not in the nature of the underlying behavioral disciplines to provide such theory. Real progress in behavioral research on financial accounting issues may therefore have to await the development of a hybrid approach, such as the empirical study of people's responses to information prepared in accordance with rules deemed desirable by others.

BEHAVIORAL ACCOUNTING RESEARCH RELATES TO INDIVIDUALS, NOT AGGREGATES

Virtually all the research reviewed has been directed at the behaviors and perceptions of individual decision makers who use accounting information. Of course, the information is usually aggregated to develop descriptions of average perceptions, to distinguish the responses of different types of decision makers, and so on, but the behavior of such aggregates as firms, markets, or professions has seldom been studied. As has been noted already, aggregate behavior is likely to have properties not deducible from separately observed individual actions (Milgram and Toch [1968]; Beaver [1972]; Schelling [1978]). Further, the processes by which individual actions or values are aggregated into market or social behavior have been subjected to only rudimentary analytical or behavioral analysis as yet (e.g., Schelling [1978]; Demski [1980]; Plott and Sunder [1981]). Schelling, for example, developed simple models to explain what happens when the collective good of the aggregate (such as a nation wanting reduced energy consumption) is not matched by the wishes of each individual (a person who will suffer if heat is absent and who knows that the use of fuel makes no real difference to total consumption). Plott and Sunder studied the formation of "security markets" in a controlled laboratory setting.

The FASB appears to have an interest in both aggregate and individual behavior. On the one hand, the Board's mandate—to set generally accepted accounting standards—implies an interest in general effects that might be observed in such aggregates as stock markets, professions, organizations, or governments. The FASB's publications (e.g., Concepts Statements 1 and 2) make references to efficient resource allocation—an aggregate concept. On the other hand, those same FASB publications refer to individual investors, creditors, and people without access to sophisticated analysis. Regardless of how aggregation works, it is composed somehow of individual actions—and certain ones may significantly impact the whole (e.g., powerful individuals or those involved in precedent-setting court cases). Our discussions with academic researchers indicate agreement that the FASB should be concerned with aggregate behavior but no agreement that the Board should be concerned with individual behavior.

If the factors explaining individual behavior cannot be assumed to translate readily into aggregate behavior, specific conclusions about market or organizational effects from behavioral research at the individual level cannot be drawn without conjecture. If the FASB is concerned with both levels of behavior, it should encourage research that would build connections between the two. For instance, a useful connection would relate the limitations of individuals' decision making (e.g., heuristics, biases, functional fixation, conservatism) to market behavior. Are such limitations also evident in market behavior? And if not, why not? Attempts to improve financial accounting will be frustrated if they are ignored or distorted by the presumed beneficiaries.

On the other hand, research reviewed in other chapters [of the book edited by Griffin] indicates that the market is neither unresponsive nor naive with respect to understanding the impacts of changes in accounting methods. This suggests, from an aggregate perspective, that the expenditure of resources by a body such as the FASB to alter financial reporting so as to, for example, reduce functional fixation, make probability revisions less conservative, or otherwise "improve" individuals' decision making may not be needed.

If our economic and societal institutions have some sophistication with respect to the problems of relating financial accounting information to individual behavior, these institutions are likely to bring about changes to mitigate such problems. For example, if people have difficulty with complex accounting information, a profession (e.g., analysts) arises to cope with the problem and, in the process, becomes part of the mechanism of informational use itself. If an efficient and effective method of adjustment exists for a given difficulty, changing financial accounting to deal with that difficulty may be not only unnecessary but inefficient. The relative efficiencies of the present methods of adjustment and the proposed financial accounting change must be known in order to evaluate whether the change is worthwhile.

SETTINGS IN WHICH ACCOUNTING IS USED ARE NOT WELL SPECIFIED

The uses of financial accounting information are varied and complex. Certainly, uses extend beyond making investment decisions. Moreover, the role that such information plays, even in investment settings, is unclear. Accounting information is used together with other information, so that the contribution of such information (or of accounting standards) must be argued on marginal grounds. Behavioral research can assist in untangling settings in which information is used and possibly can permit such marginal analysis. However, it has not yet done so except in one or two isolated cases, such as in experimental studies of bankers and financial analysts.

DECISION MAKING IS NOT WELL UNDERSTOOD

Behavioral research on the use of financial accounting information has produced generally inconclusive findings. The processes of people's decision making, revision of probabilities, and formation of perceptions are not well known. Moreover, there has been little success in applying such concepts as rationality or consistency to empirical research on information use. In short, it has been difficult to demonstrate clearly that accounting information matters to individual investors, creditors, analysts, etc., notwithstanding the studies reviewed in other chapters [of the book edited by Griffin] that find evidence of market effects—produced unquestionably by many individuals acting in response to information.

To be sure, the behavioral findings suggest caution when making assumptions about how people use accounting information, in particular about assuming that the user carefully weighs all the facts before making a decision. An interesting corollary to this discussion concerns the concept of rationality (e.g., paragraph 34 of Concepts Statement 1). We believe that concept is empirically elusive. Reference to it in accounting standards would not seem to help in predicting the effects of such standards, especially since, given the behavioral findings, the concept implies inappropriate expectations about users' decision-making behavior.

If the FASB is interested in the behavior of individuals, it should encourage research into decision makers' actual thought processes. Assumptions in economics and decision theory appear to be descriptively invalid and, since alternative theories of decision making are not well developed, there is somewhat of a vacuum in this important area of research.

ACCOUNTING INFORMATION IS NOT NEUTRAL

Because accounting information has many uses and seems to have behavioral effects, it gains characteristics of a control system in addition to its role as a "dispassionate" information system. At least three such aspects appear relevant to financial accounting. First, people are influenced to act in accordance with the way their actions are reported. There are, therefore, issues regarding education and persuasion to consider in the development of financial accounting standards. If the FASB's directives contain declarations about cause and effect that users can be persuaded to believe (e.g., current cost information improves forecasts of enterprise cash flows), those users' actions, by reflecting (for better or worse) such declarations, can partly determine whether the declarations are true (for example, that current cost data do indeed predict cash flows better). Second, the FASB, by designing features of the accounting information structure, prescribes or promotes certain decision-making approaches or biases, or triggers decision makers' "heuristics" or other rules of thumb. Third, if an accounting standard does have effects on individual behavior, those effects are unlikely to be the same from person to person or from group to group. In the research reviewed, little support for widespread change in financial accounting has been detected. Rather, the research suggests that various personal, institutional, and informational variables interact so substantially that one would not predict similar evaluations of a standard's effects or neutrality by different individuals or groups. The behavioral research here is consistent with arguments advanced elsewhere against the general desirability of particular standards (Demski [1973]; American Accounting Association [1977a]; Dopuch and Sunder [1980]).

SURVEYS SHOULD BE USED WITH CARE

One means of obtaining broadly based opinions about accounting alternatives is to conduct questionnaire surveys of various groups of presumed users. Lack of consistency in survey results and people's lack of awareness of their own thought patterns imply, however, that surveys of users' preferences for or confidence in accounting alternatives are unlikely to be reliable indicators of the real impact of accounting alternatives.

Surveys have a variety of uses, nonetheless, including adding credibility to the Board's conclusions (as part of the FASB's due process system) and developing political commitment or consensus. Hence, we are not advocating discontinuance of surveys as part of the FASB's research function. However, we caution that surveys should be supplemented with detailed empirical analyses, such as in-depth case studies, experimental investigations, and other procedures, to verify the survey findings. Also, we suggest that the use of survey results to rank accounting alternatives should not be encouraged. Direct evidence of decision behavior should be sought in preference to self-reports on informational preferences.

A FINAL COMMENT

In this chapter, we have considered behavioral research published primarily within the accounting literature. Conclusions about the implications of that research for standard setting have been drawn. Several of those conclusions, however, point to a lack of reliable findings, due in part to the fact that behavioral research in accounting is a young and relatively unfocused discipline. We hope that this chapter has informed the reader about the present state of the research and has made a good case for additional research to improve our understanding of the complex relationships between financial accounting information and individual behavior. However, we have not been able to identify key implications of *immediate* relevance to accounting policymakers. The body of "solid" research findings as yet is small, especially compared with the number of unresolved questions and unexplored issues. Only as our knowledge expands will more direct implications be evident.

For bibliographic references see Common Bibliography for Part V.

FOOTNOTES

[1] For behavioral accounting research earlier than 1975, the reader is referred to Dyckman et al. (1978) for financial accounting studies; American Accounting Association (1976) for managerial accounting studies; and Gibbins (1977) for auditing studies. In addition, reviews specifically related to ''human information processing'' research, which emphasizes individuals' thought processes rather than their behavior, are available. (See, for example, American Accounting Association [1977b] and Libby and Lewis [1977].)

[2] A simple linear model could appear as follows: $Y = aX_1 + bX_2 + cX_3$. Each variable is measured numerically. Y represents the decision or judgment that is explained by pieces of information X_1, X_2, and X_3. Since each piece of information is of differing importance, they are each weighted differently (by a, b, and c, respectively). Y is referred to as the dependent variable, the Xs are independent variables, and a, b, and c are coefficients.

A REVIEW OF MARKET RESEARCH IN FINANCIAL ACCOUNTING

by Peter Clarkson and Richard Mattessich

FINANCIAL ACCOUNTING RESEARCH BASED ON SECURITY MARKETS

Market based research is designed to examine the use of financial accounting information as reflected in the capital markets. Much of this literature builds on developments in finance dealing with the portfolio selection problem and the related capital asset pricing model (CAPM),[1] as well as the concept of informationally efficient capital markets (the efficient market hypothesis, EMH).[2] The intent of this section is to provide a review of empirical research (market based research) in financial accounting. Previous surveys in this area include the papers by Beaver [1972, 1973], Gonedes and Dopuch [1974], Lev [1974], Kaplan [1975], Lev and Ohlson [1982], and the book by Dyckman, Downes, and Magee [1975].

EFFICIENT CAPITAL MARKETS AND THE MARKET MODEL

Most empirical studies in market based accounting research rest on either or both of the following assumptions: (1) capital markets are efficient; and (2) the CAPM offers an acceptable description of economic reality. To begin with, an assumption of efficiency justifies the use of capital markets for testing the relevance of accounting information. Under the EMH, it is assumed that the current price of a security reflects all publicly available information (past price, annual reports, economic data, etc.) as soon as it becomes available; i.e., securities markets are efficient with respect to publicly available information (semi-strong efficiency). The implication is that, on average, such information will not yield any net benefit after controlling for the risk of the trading strategy. In general, the literature promotes the belief in market efficiency as a reasonable first approximation to the real world, but some evidence against the efficient market hypothesis has been reported [Ball 1978, Black 1973, Brown 1978, Joy and Jones 1979, Latane and Jones 1977, and others]. Thus it is *assumed* that new information is processed rapidly and without bias during the formation of security prices.

The assumed validity of the CAPM often underlies the use of a return risk adjustment and abnormal rates of return as an appropriate vehicle for recognizing this information content. Risk is usually interpreted as the possible variation of the actual return of a security (or portfolio) from its expected return. Since pertinent research regards such returns as normally distributed, statistical variance is held as the measure of this variation.

Given that the risk-averse investor[3] will hold a well-diversified portfolio, the riskiness of an individual security should be judged by its effect on the riskiness of the portfolio (i.e., how much the stock contributes to the variance of a well-diversified portfolio). Consequently, only risk that cannot be avoided through diversification (systematic risk) should be of concern. This risk is associated with changes in rates of return on the market as a whole and is described by a parameter known as a *stock's beta*, β. The market (or the average of all securities) has a beta of 1 by construction. High beta securities ($\beta > 1$) tend to change in price faster than the market, while low beta securities ($\beta < 1$) tend to change slower than the market.

This relationship between security returns and the market can be characterized by the following "market model":

$$R_{it} = a_i + \beta_i \cdot R_{mt} + \mu_{it}$$

where R_{it} = rate of return for security i in period t

R_{mt} = rate of return on the market portfolio in period t

μ_{it} = residual term for security i in period t

The coefficient β indicates *the strength of the assumed linear relationship between the return of a security and the return on the market*. The error term, μ, allows for the presence of factors other than the market which can affect the return on a particular security. It is this residual portion of a security's return that one hopes to explain through a consideration of accounting data. In a portfolio situation, this residual should net to zero, leaving only the security's dependence on the market. Accounting information may be useful in explaining abnormal returns associated with firm specific events as measured by the residual term, μ, or the risk of a security as measured by the security's β.

INFORMATION CONTENT STUDIES

A growing literature concerns itself with information content studies, which have the task of analyzing the marginal information contribution of specific accounting data. Most such studies are of the "announcement type," examining whether parameters (mean or variance) of the stock return distribution have changed, given the pertinent information announced. Research in this area distinguishes between studies that deal with the announcement of earnings and those that deal with other accounting data (e.g., declared dividends).

(a) Earnings Announcements

The earliest and most widely quoted study, by Ball and Brown [1968], was an attempt to determine whether variations in stock prices are associated with the variability of earnings or with the publication of these earnings. Their study assumed market efficiency and *examined the correlation between unexpected annual earnings changes and residual stock returns*. They found that, whenever there was a discrepancy between actual income and expected income, the price of the associated security tended to move in the same direction as the unexpected earnings change. In addition, it was determined that much of this movement occurs early in the year, well in advance of the actual earnings announcement, a result consistent with the EMH. These findings were based on a naive earnings expectation model, which assumes that expected future earnings are determined by and are equal to current earnings; hence the unexpected earnings for any period becomes the difference between the current period's earnings and that of the previous period. Ball and Brown relied only on the sign of the unexpected earnings to classify firms.

Gonedes [1974] replicated the Ball and Brown study using a more sophisticated approach to generate investor earnings expectations and again found that the *income announcement captured most of the information content* that was available. It was also suggested that the income figures are correlated with many other variables, so the information could be generated through other sources. In an effort to improve on the measurement of the unexpected element of earnings, Patell [1976] substituted management's earning forecasts in lieu of Ball and Brown's naive model and found that *a trading strategy based on these forecasts was only slightly better.* Beaver [1974] also extended the Ball and Brown methodology *to incorporate the size rather than just the sign of unexpected earnings,* and found that *the most extreme portfolios,* those containing stocks of firms with the largest unexpected earnings, *had the highest residual returns. In a similar vein, Beaver, Clark, and Wright [1979], and Niederhoffer and Regan [1972] also found the magnitude of unexpected earnings to be highly correlated with the magnitude of residual returns.*

The Ball and Brown approach has been applied in numerous related contexts. Within the earnings context, it has been used to examine the information content of the quarterly earnings reports. Brown [1970], Brown and Kennelly [1972], Deakin, Norwood, and Smith [1974], Firth [1976], and Foster [1975, 1977] all report confirmation of the existence of a statistical association between (unexpected) earnings and (residual) returns using quarterly data.

Alternative approaches for examining the information content of earning announcements have focused on the variance of the residual returns and/or the volume of trading. Beaver [1968] examined annual earnings announcements by investigating both the residual variance and the trading volume in the week of the earnings announcement as compared to the non-report period and found both pieces of evidence supportive of the conjecture that annual earnings announcements have information content. Hagerman [1973], Kiger [1972], May [1971], and McNichols and Manegold [1982] employed similar approaches and enjoyed similar findings with respect to interim reports. In addition, Morse [1981], and Patell and Wolfson [1981] used the Beaver variance tests, but applied to more finely partitioned return data (e.g., daily data), yet with no significantly different results. Patell and Wolfson [1979, 1981] have also examined the anticipated information content of earnings and detected a fairly accurate anticipation of quarterly earnings announcements.

In summary, it appears that earnings announcements (both quarterly and annual) do provide the securities market with useful information. Moreover, these results do not seem to be influenced by the specific methodology employed or by the choice of time periods or the specific exchange in which the securities are traded. Recently, Holthausen and Verrechia [1981] hypothesized that earnings information content is determined by four factors: (1) the number of common signals received before the annual earnings announcement; (2) the precision of these signals; (3) the precision of the annual announcement; and (4) the covariance between prior signals and the annual announcements. Richardson [1982] developed a similar model and has tested it empirically.

(b) Other (Non-Earnings) Financial Data

Somewhat less emphasis has been placed on studies of information content regarding financial data other than earnings and security prices. However, there are some areas which cannot be ignored. To begin with, examination of the information content of dividend announcements has generally led to the conclusion that unexpected earnings and unexpected dividends do not convey identical information (see Aharony and Swary [1980], Ashley [1962], Griffen [1976], Laub [1976], Penman [1980], and Pettit [1972, 1976]). That is to say, dividend data appear to be informative after consideration of earnings information, and vice versa. In addition, management earnings forecasts (Foster [1973], Gonedes, Dopuch, and Penman [1976], Patell [1976], and Penman [1978]) appear to contain significant supplementary information content.

Collins [1975] examined the value of disclosing sales and earnings data by segment, and found such disclosure desirable and beneficial for anticipating earnings changes. Foster and Vickrey [1978] provided some statistically weak evidence that information is disclosed in 10-K reports.[4] Foster [1981] examined the interesting question of interdependencies in accounting information.

In addition to the role that accounting data play in revising investor expectations about future returns, there arises the question of whether accounting data can be used to form expectations about the systematic market risk of a security, i.e., β. Beaver, Kettler, and Scholes [1970], Beaver and Manegold [1975], and Gonedes [1973, 1975] have examined this issue; while there were some conflicting results, some connection between accounting based and market based risks,[5] especially at the portfolio level, was disclosed. This suggests that information from accounting numbers can be used to form expectations about the systematic risk of a security.

The question of using quarterly reports to predict annual earnings figures was explored by Brown and Kennelly [1972], Brown and Niederhoffer [1968], and Green and Segall [1966, 1967, 1968]. In general, the findings suggest that predictors using interim information perform marginally better than annual data.

In summary, these results seem to contradict the argument that accounting information in general, and earnings announcements in particular, are irrelevant. In this way, evidence has been provided that financial statements play an important role in investor expectations about the future performance of the firm.

ACCOUNTING ALTERNATIVES

The existence of alternative accounting methods has been an open area for academics for some time. Until recently, research in this area was strictly concerned with investors' reaction. The idea is straightforward: rational investors are not concerned with the packaging of the information. In a sense, the EMH demands this behaviour. Recent research has extended the subject to examine managerial motives for selecting accounting techniques and the effects of such selections on the value of firms.

While some changes in accounting methods may merely serve cosmetic purposes, others will have cash-flow consequences; thus a distinction between the two types of changes should be made. With respect to the case of no direct cash-flow effects, Beaver and Dukes [1972], and Kaplan and Roll [1972] examined the association between stock returns and earnings based on deferral versus the flow through method of accounting for the investment tax credit; they found no permanent effects on price. Archibald [1967, 1972], Beaver and Dukes [1973], and Kaplan and Roll [1972] looked at firms switching from accelerated to straight line depreciation (showing a positive effect) or employing the former for reporting purposes and the latter for tax purposes (showing no effect). Ball [1972] studied four hundred thirty cases of various accounting changes and concluded that investors were able to distinguish between the real and the "cosmetic" effects on earnings. Eskew [1975], and Patz and Boatsman [1972] report that investors in oil and gas stocks are able to adjust for differences between the "full cost" and "successful efforts" methods of accounting for explorations. Hong, Kaplan, and Mandelker [1978] found no statistically significant price reaction at the merger date to firms which used the pooling method to record mergers as opposed to the purchase method.

For accounting changes which have substantive direct cash-flow effects, these effects are generally due to tax implications of the accounting changes. Papers dealing with switches from LIFO to FIFO and from FIFO to LIFO include those by Abdel-khalik and McKeown [1978], Brown [1980], Ricks [1982a], and Sunder [1973, 1975], and provide somewhat conflicting results. The most recent studies suggest an adverse market reaction for the firms switching to LIFO. This result must for obvious reasons be treated as somewhat discomforting.[6]

Although an accounting change, such as from accelerated to straight line depreciation, might have no immediate or direct effect on cash flows, other determinants of stock and bond values could still be affected. For example, management compensation is generally a function of reported earnings.

Thus one must also address the fundamental question of what managers' motives may be for selecting among alternative accounting techniques. Collins, Rozeff, and Dhaliwal [1981], Holthausen [1981], Gonedes [1976], Leftwich [1981], Watts [1974, 1977], and Watts and Zimmerman [1978] have turned their attention to this matter, though not in a completely satisfactory manner.

IMPACT OF ACCOUNTING REGULATIONS

Evaluation of consequences is, or at least should be, an integral and ongoing part of any regulatory process. Presumably, financial market consequences are of particular relevance to accounting regulators. This subsection will consider some of the studies dealing with various kinds of regulation and with the information disclosure based on such regulation.

Eskew and Wright [1976], Foster [1975], Gonedes [1975, 1978], and Manegold [1981] considered APB Opinion No. 9 — Extra-ordinary and Special Items — concluding that the classification of special items provides investors with relevant information. Abdel-khalik, Thompson, and Taylor [1978], Bowman [1980], Finnerty, Fitzsimmons, and Oliver [1980], and Ro [1978] examined FASB No. 13 — Lease Capitalization — and concluded that there was a slight market reaction to its release. Dukes [1976] and Vigeland [1981] implied that security prices were not affected by FASB No. 2, which requires firms to expense R and D outlays. Dukes [1978] and Shank, Dillard, and Murdock [1980] failed to observe a security price response to the implementation of FASB No. 8 — Foreign Currency Translation. Abdel-khalik and McKeown [1978], Arbel and Jaggi [1978], Beaver, Christie, and Griffen [1980], Freeman [1982], Gheyara and Boatsman [1980], and Ro [1980, 1981] all failed to detect a price or volume reaction to the SEC regulation concerning the disclosure of replacement cost data — FASB No. 33.

TIME-SERIES BEHAVIOUR OF EARNINGS

Time-series studies are closely related to forecasting issues because their results are supposed to indicate to what extent past earning records can be employed to explain and, above all, predict the market price of company shares under the impact of surprise changes in earnings. The studies of Albrecht, Lookabill, and McKeown [1977], Ball and Watts [1972], Beaver [1970], Brealy [1969], Brooks and Buckmaster [1980], Dopuch and Watts [1972], Foster [1977], Griffin [1977] Hopwood and McKeown [1981], Lev [1976], Lookabill [1976], Lintner and Glauber [1967], Watts [1975], and Watts and Leftwich [1977] are concerned with this issue. One may conclude from them that quarterly earnings follow a moving-average process in first differences; such earnings might be amenable to manipulative smoothing by management, but evidence as regards the smoothing of annual earnings processes is difficult to find.

FINANCIAL FAILURE STUDIES

Studies focusing on the prediction of business failure include those by Altman [1968, 1973], Altman, Avery, Eisenbeis, and Sinkey [1981], Altman, Haldeman, and Narayanan [1977], Altman and McGough [1974], Beaver [1966], Blum [1969], Deakin [1972a], Edmister [1971], Eisenbeis [1977], Joy and Tollefson [1975], Ohlson [1980], Pinches [1980], Scott [1981], Vinso [1979], and Wilcox [1973]. The major research thrust in this area has been to seek empirically validated characteristics that distinguish distressed from non-distressed firms (e.g., Beaver [1966], Altman [1968], and Ohlson [1980], the latter two of which used multivariate techniques). The success rate in classifying firms based primarily on financial ratios typically exceeds 90 per cent. The common statistical tool employed is multi-discriminate analysis (MDA).

SUMMARY

The research considered in this section has dealt primarily with the relationship between financial accounting information and the reaction of users to its release as reflected through capital market activity. The basic conclusions resulting are as follows:

(1) Accounting data convey useful and timely information to users (this conclusion primarily pertains to the announcements of earnings, while the impact of other data is somewhat less definitive).

(2) Market effects of changes in accounting techniques appear to indicate that investors behave rationally, especially when the broader picture, including management motivation for selecting accounting alternatives, is examined.

(3) Regarding the impact of accounting regulation on the security market, it is satisfying to observe that, in the few cases which have attracted considerable research attention, results appear to be consistent and even conclusive.

The ultimate test of accounting, however, lies in its usefulness and, as yet, the precise meaning of usefulness (and therefore the role of accounting data and their benefit to society) has not been addressed directly in the context of market based research.

EXPERIMENTAL AND SURVEY RESEARCH IN FINANCIAL ACCOUNTING

Behavioural research, as it applies to financial accounting, uses empirical methods (such as field studies, protocol analysis, interviews and questionnaires) arising from psychology and similar disciplines to seek general explanations of how accounting information is used. This section examines a substantial amount of literature on recent experimental and survey research and its conclusions about present reporting problems as well as the alleged impact of financial data on individual decision making. Previous review papers supplying insights into the contributions and limitations of behavioural research in financial accounting are, among others, Birnberg and Nath [1967], Hofstedt [1972b, 1975], Rhode [1972], Green [1973], Gonedes and Dopuch [1974], and Dyckman, Gibbins and Swieringa [1978].

THE USE OF FINANCIAL STATEMENTS

Here, the focus is on research examining the needs of various users of financial statements and, in particular, on the extent to which financial data available to investors and the general public meet the needs of various decision making processes. The issues under consideration include: usefulness of financial statement data; adequacy of disclosure; materiality judgements that affect financial reporting; and reporting effects on individual decision making.

The major studies that have concentrated on various aspects of the contemplated usefulness of financial statements and their data are by Abdel-khalik [1973, 1974a, b], Abdel-khalik and El-Sheshai [1980], Baker and Haslem [1973], Benjamin and Stanga [1977], Carper, Barton, and Wunder [1979], Casey [1980], Chandra [1974], Chandra and Greenball [1977], Epstein [1975], Estes and Reimer [1977], Eyes and Tabb [1978], Falk [1972], Falk and Ophir [1973a, b], Ferris [1976], Fuller and Metcalf [1978], Haried [1972, 1973], Kennedy [1975], Lev [1976], Lewellen, Lease, and Schlarbaum [1977], Libby [1975a, b, 1979a, b], Most and Chang [1979], Oliver [1974], Pankoff and Virgil [1970], Patton [1976, 1978], Reckers and Stagliano [1980], Ronen and Falk [1973], Smith and Smith [1971], Soper and Dolphin [1964], Stanga and Benjamin [1978], and Zimmer [1980].

These studies employed different approaches, and derived, at times, contradictory results. One of the approaches commonly employed involved asking the users of financial statements to indicate the relative importance of information items in investment analysis; another attempted the representation of decisions under quasi-laboratory conditions, examining to what extent financial statement data are used in decision making; finally, some tried to evaluate the effectiveness of the communication of these data by measuring the "comprehension ease level" of financial statement disclosure. The overall conclusion which follows from these studies is that *investors and analysts tend to consider nonfinancial statement factors to be relatively more important than financial statement data in making investment decisions* (although they do seem to pay attention to some dimensions of the financial data). In addition, it is not clear whether the use of financial statements is of greater importance to the forecasting area or to the decision making area.

Studies to determine the adequacy of financial data available to investors and the public were authored by Horngren [1955, 1956, 1957] who examined interviews and written reports of financial analysts, Cerf [1961] who designed an index of disclosure for specific items, likewise based on interviews with analysts, and whose work stimulated similar studies by Singhvi and Desai [1971] and Buzby [1974], and finally Bradish [1965], Ecton [1969], and Opinion Research Corporation [1974] who surveyed various groups as to their perceptions and attitudes toward disclosure. The three basic approaches used in this research were: (1) to develop a description of how users analyze financial statements to evaluate the assumptions underlying their analysis; (2) to focus on certain interest groups, and to survey their perceptions and attitudes about disclosure; and (3) to determine the extent to which important information is disclosed in annual reports. The conclusions of these studies confirm a general reluctance toward revision or drastic change of the traditional financial statement presentation. Furthermore, it seems that from the perspective of the users, the trend toward increased disclosure has not as yet over-complicated the statements; also, there appear to be significant differences in disclosure among firms, conditional on such variables as firm size, profitability, size of auditing firm, and the listing status of the firm.

Analysis of factors influencing *judgements of materiality* are found in Boatsman and Robertson [1974], Dickhaut and Eggleton [1975], Firth [1979], Hofstedt and Hughes [1977], Moriarity and Barron [1979], Pattillo [1975, 1976], Pattillo and Siebel [1973, 1974], Rose, Beaver, Becker, and Sorter [1970], and Woolsey [1954a, b, 1973]. The methods span the spectrum from questionnaires to experiments, typically using hypothetical cases and requiring respondents to make materiality judgements for each case. The conclusions drawn from these studies suggest that *several individual or combined factors appear to influence materiality decisions.* The predominant factor is the *size of the pertinent item in relation to the size of the firm's profit,* but interdependence of this factor with others (characteristics of a specific item, of management, of type of firm, etc.) complicates the situation. A secondary conclusion shows the apparent indifference of statement users toward line disclosure versus footnote disclosure.

The effects of reporting on individual decision making are revealed in a less well defined collection of research. The latter ranges from the examination of users' preferences for alternative reporting practices and the influence of alternative reporting procedures on individual evaluations, to the influence of environmental factors on users' decisions. Studies directed toward the question of user preferences include Benbasat and Dexter [1979], Brenner and Shuey [1972], Carpenter and Strawser [1972], Copeland, Francia, and Strawser [1973], Driver and Mock [1975], Godwin [1975], Lusk [1979], McGhee, Shields, and Birnberg [1978], Nelson and Strawser [1970], Pratt [1980], and Savich [1977]. These studies for the most part employed questionnaires with two distinct focal points. The first focal point was the preference for alternative methods of accounting for specific transactions, while the second was a measure of perceived information deficiency through a consideration of the difference between what "ought to be" and what "is". The studies focusing on preferences in special issues have provided useful data about several controversial accounting issues, while research concentrating on more general reporting issues suggests that there are apparent attitudinal differences between groups of users.

Studies which consider the influence of alternative reporting procedures were conducted by Barrett [1971], Dopuch and Ronen [1973], Dyckman [1964, 1966], Elias [1972], Hawkins and Wehle [1973], Hofstedt [1972a, b], Horngren [1959], Jensen [1966], Khemakhem [1968], Libby [1975a], Livingstone [1967], and Ortman [1974]. The conclusion reached by these investigations seems almost trivial: alternative reporting procedures can influence individual evaluations; however, the extent of the influence is often less than expected. In addition, the impact of a specific reporting method appears to be related to the characteristics of the pertinent user and the type of his decision. The nature of the experimental environment also appears to influence user decisions.

Studies on the influence of environmental factors are summarized by Gibbins and Brennan [1982] who point to papers by Atkinson and Feltham [1981], Brennan [1979], Butterworth, Gibbins, and King [1981], Cohen and March [1974], Dopuch and Sunder [1980], Epstein [1975], Gray [1980], Hayes [1977], Lev [1976], March [1978], Nisbett and Wilson [1977], Prakash and Rappaport [1977], Scott and Troberg [1980], Shank, Dillard, and Murdock [1980], Uecker [1978, 1980], Watts [1977], Watts and Zimmerman [1978, 1979], and Weick [1979]. The conclusions are that *environmental factors are highly interactive and have a considerable influence on users' decisions,* and that users' needs are specific and relate to each job, decision making task, or environment. No general summary of needs or informational priorities has emerged or seems likely to emerge in the near future.

ACCOUNTING PRINCIPLES AND RELATED MATTERS

Research considered in this subsection deals with the general issue of users' views regarding current accounting principles. Specific attention is directed at the subissues of modified financial statements (price-level and/or current-value adjusted statements and probabilistic statements) and of effecting change in reporting practice. The following studies have been concerned with probing the attitude of the public, financial analysts, or other users of accounting data toward present accounting principles and their eventual alternatives. McDonald [1968], Sterling [1969], and Sterling, Tollefson, and Flaherty [1972] asked respondents how to report certain items presented to them. Carsberg, Hope, and Scapens [1974], Copeland, Francia, and Strawser [1973], and Francia and Strawser [1971a, b, 1972] sent identical questionnaires to members of different groups and received significantly different answers from those groups. Further research in this area was done by Mautz [1972] and Morton [1974] who tested specific hypotheses as to the respondents' understanding of financial statements. Ball [1972], Kaplan and Roll [1972], and Sunder [1973, 1975] examined firms switching certain accounting methods (e.g., depreciation, FIFO versus LIFO), while Patz and Boatsman [1972] examined the share-price performance of oil exploration firms under the impact of switching from "full-cost accounting" to "the successful-efforts method." Hong, Mandelker, and Kaplan [1978] investigated a large number of mergers using "pooling of interests" and other methods. Jacobs and Kaplan [1975] compared stock-price rates of return among companies using different depreciation methods. Further studies on related topics are Abdel-khalik and Keller [1979], Ashton [1976], Beaver and Dukes [1972], Chang and Birnberg [1977], Dukes [1976], Gonedes and Dopuch [1974], and Swieringa, Dyckman, and Hoskin [1979].

This area of accounting principles still remains a most important overall topic for research, and a carefully designed questionnaire can provide useful data on people's thoughts about the objectives and the content of accounting reports — even in the face of critical challenges such as potential biases and the nonresponse rate. The major studies intended to examine the ultimate usefulness of price-level adjusted and/or current-value information include AICPA Technical Service Division [1958], Arthur Young Company Survey [1981], Backer [1970, 1973], Benston and Krasney [1978], Brenner [1970], Casey and Sandretto [1981], Dyckman [1969], Estes [1968], Garner [1972], Hanna [1972, 1974], Heintz [1973], Horngren [1955], McIntyre [1973], Rosen [1972], and Schwarzbach and Swanson [1981]. The results of these studies indicate that *there is no particular desire among financial state-*

ment users to abandon the traditional approach, but merely to supplement it. The preference for such a supplement favours the current-value information as opposed to the price-level adjusted historical cost information. It should be noted, however, that some confusion was found in the minds of the respondents about the difference between the two supplemental disclosures. There are recent indications that *managers are beginning to use the changing price data for decision making.* A FASB Research Report by Frishkoff [1982] should be referred to for a more detailed review of these and other studies in this area.

There have been several investigations into the impact of "confidence" interval financial statements (i.e., financial statements containing numbers expressed as confidence intervals or ranges), such as those by Birnberg and Slevin [1976], Collins and Yeakel [1979], Keys [1978], and Oliver [1972]. The evidence is that users feel comfortable with single-figure estimates and do not find probabilistic statements helpful.

Particularly difficult problems are associated with research directed toward the expression of preferences for specific accounting policies (e.g., Watts and Zimmerman [1978]), and little progress has been made in this area. As a result, research studies have turned to examine how changes in accounting practice can be achieved, i.e., effecting changes in reporting practice. Studies addressing this issue include those by Brennan [1979], Comiskey and Groves [1971], Copeland and Shank [1971], Dopuch and Sunder [1980], Gray [1980], Piaker and Dalberth [1973], Rakes and Shenkir [1972], Ritts [1974], Scott and Troberg [1980], Shank, Dillard, and Murdock [1980], Sorter and Becker [1964], and Sorter, Becker, Archibald, and Beaver [1966]. This research suggests that *major attitude changes can occur when an exposure draft is released or when the final opinion or a standard is issued;* thus the policy of issuing exposure drafts may be a critical step in the development of attitudes supportive to the change. In other words, the general view expressed in these studies is that a learning process can be initiated by starting with easily implementable and noncontroversial reporting changes.

In summary, the studies considered in this subsection have displayed a wide range of opinions on issues of financial accounting principles. However, there has been no substantial research addressed to the fundamental purposes of financial accounting, i.e., to a consideration of the place financial accounting fills in the users' decision model.

ADDITIONAL REPORTING ISSUES

This section has been designed to deal with the following three, somewhat distinct, reporting issues which, for the purpose of completeness, should not be overlooked: (1) the need to report on separate segments of a business (segment and subsidiary reporting); (2) the question of when and how to report (interperiod reporting); and (3) the question of whether forecasts should become a part of the financial statements.

It has been argued that, since *different segments of a company often develop at drastically different rates and in different directions,* a single all-inclusive report tends to average and thereby to obscure the true position. The research considered includes Acland [1976], Backer [1970], Backer and McFarland [1968], Benbasat and Dexter [1979], Buzby and Falk [1979], Cramer [1968], Crumbley and Strawser [1974], Dascher and Copeland [1971], Flamholtz and Cook [1978], Hendricks [1976], Martin, Laiken, and Haslam [1969], Mautz [1968], Ortman [1974], Schwan [1976], Snowball [1979], Stallman [1969], and Williams [1980]. This research suggests that *extensive practical problems are likely to impede implementation,* including definition of product lines and segments, the question of timing of events, and allocation of costs. In addition, it is suggested that, even if the technical issues are resolved, *management is reluctant to make such reports.* On the other hand, *users in general appear to be in favour of segmented reporting.* They prefer to draw their own conclusions rather than being given summarized information that might obscure the events and that contains assumptions about users' particular needs.

The question of *when to report and how frequently* (on an interim basis) has been dealt with in such studies as those by Ball and Brown [1968], Beaver [1968, 1974a], Bird [1969], Bollom [1973], Brown and Kennelly [1972], Brown and Niederhoffer [1968], Edwards, Dominiak, and Hedges [1972], Green and Segall [1966, 1967, 1970], Kiger [1972], Lipay [1972], May [1971], Nickerson, Pointer, and Strawser [1975], and Stickney [1975]. The conclusions indicate a general agreement among financial statement users that *more frequent reporting (at least quarterly) of income data before taxes, extraordinary items, and a product-line breakdown is highly desirable*. However, these opinions are necessarily given without overt consideration of the additional costs which interim reporting would cause. Preparers have expressed little opposition to providing such interim reports.

Studies dealing with the question of *whether forecasts should become an integral element of the financial statements* include Asebrook and Carmichael [1973], Benjamin and Strawser [1974], Carmichael [1973], Corless and Norgaard [1974], Daily [1971], Financial Executives Research Foundation [1973], Nickerson, Pointer, and Strawser [1974], and Patell [1976]. Stockholders indicated that they considered forecasting to be part of management's job and appeared to favour the reporting of forecasts. However, there was *no evidence that users were interested in having forecasts attested by the auditor*. Providers of forecast data are generally opposed to providing audited data (as are auditors).

SUMMARY

This paper has provided a review and updating of experimental and survey research in financial accounting. Its relatively broad perspective reveals several features of interest and concern. Some anxiety must be expressed as to the lack of behavioural considerations given by pronouncements. Several key factors seem to contribute to this situation, including the fact that behavioural research is of relatively recent vintage, and is costly in terms of time and out-of-pocket expenses; furthermore, formulating accounting policy is essentially a political process. Thus it can be argued that more attention must be given to policy issues and to the development of some form of theory which ties the empirical results to a coherent whole; additional consideration must also be given to the problem of experimental design. In summary, behavioural research still seems to suffer from a lack of credibility.

Another feature of concern to be noted is that aggregate behaviour has at least some properties that cannot be inferred by deduction from separately observed individual actions. Above all, the process of decision making, the revision of probabilities, and the formation of perceptions are not well known. Moreover, there has been little success in applying such concepts as rationality or consistency to empirical research on information use. In short, it has been difficult to demonstrate clearly how or if accounting information matters to individual statement users. Furthermore, the processes by which individual actions and preferences are aggregated into market or social behaviour have been subjected to only rudimentary analytical or behavioural analysis.

For bibliographic references see Common Bibliography to Part V.

FOOTNOTES

[1] Fama [1976, pp. 383-417].

[2] Sharpe [1964, pp. 425-452].

[3] The assumption of risk aversion means that an investor will reject a fair gamble, because the disutility of the loss is greater than the utility of an equivalent gain.

[4] The 10-K report is an annual report required by the SEC within ninety days after the end of each fiscal year. Financial Statements and notes to the statements required in the 10-K report give substantially more information than other financial statements distributed by companies.

[5] The accounting risk can be given as the covariability of a firm's earnings with the earnings of all other firms (accounting beta).

[6] One would expect the switch from FIFO to LIFO to have a positive tax effect on the firm.

COMMON BIBLIOGRAPHY TO PART V

Abdel-khalik, A. Rashad. "The Effect of Aggregating Accounting Reports on the Lending Decision: An Empirical Investigation." *Journal of Accounting Research Supplement* to Vol 11 (1973). (2.2; experiment by mail; bank loan officers.)

Abdel-khalik, A. Rashad. "The Entropy Law, Accounting Data and Relevance to Decision-Making." *The Accounting Review* (April 1974a): 271-83. (2.2; experiment by mail; bank loan officers.)

Abdel-khalik, A. Rashad. "On the Efficiency of Subject Surrogation in Accounting Research." *The Accounting Review* (October 1974b): 743-50. (2.2; experiment by mail using bank loan officers and "take home" experiment using MBA students.)

Abdel-khalik, A. R.; Thompson, R.B.; and Taylor, R.E. "The Effect of Reporting Leases off the Balance Sheet on Bond Risk Premiums: Two Exploratory Studies." In *Economic Consequences of Financial Accounting Standards: Selected Papers*, pp. 101-58. Financial Accounting Standards Board, Research Reports, July 1978.

Abdel-khalik, A. Rashad, and El-Shesai, Kamal M. "Information Choice and Utilization in an Experiment on Default Prediction." *Journal of Accounting Research* (Autumn 1980): 325-42.

Abdel-khalik, A. Rashad, and Keller, Thomas F. *Earnings or Cash Flows: An Experiment on Functional Fixation and the Valuation of the Firm.* Studies in Accounting Research, no. 16. Sarasota, Fla.: American Accounting Association, 1979.

Abdel-khalik, A. R., and McKeown, J.C. "Understanding Accounting Changes in an Efficient Market: Evidence of Differential Reaction." *The Accounting Review* (October 1978): 851-868.

Acland, C. Derek. "The Effects of Behavioural Indicators on Investor Decisions: An Exploratory Study." *Accounting, Organizations and Society* nos. 2/3 (1976): 133-42.

Acland, C. Derek. "The Effect of Human Resource Information on Investment Decision Making: An Accounting Experimental Study." University of North Carolina at Chapel Hill, 1973. (Experiment by mail; Canadian analysts.)

Adelberg, Arthur Harris. "A Methodology for Measuring the Understandability of Financial Report Messages." *Journal of Accounting Research* (Autumn 1979): 565-92.

Advisory Committee on Corporate Disclosure. *Report of the Advisory Committee on Corporate Disclosure to the Securities and Exchange Commission.* Washington, D.C.: U.S. Government Printing Office, Nov. 3, 1977.

Aharony, J., and Swary, I. "Quarterly Dividend and Earnings Announcements and Stockholders' Returns: An Empirical Analysis." *Journal of Finance* (March 1980): 1-12.

Ajinkya, B.B. "An Empirical Evaluation of Line of Business Reporting." *Journal of Accounting Research* (Autumn 1980): 343-61.

Albrecht, William Steve; Lookabill, Larry L.; and McKeown, James C. "Time-Series Properties of Annual Earnings." *Journal of Accounting Research* 15 (Autumn 1977): 226-44.

Altman, Edward. "Financial Ratios, Discriminant Analysis, and the Prediction of Corporate Bankruptcy." *Journal of Finance* (September 1968): 589-609.

Altman, Edward. "Predicting Railroad Bankruptcies in America." *Bell Journal of Economics and Management Science* (Spring 1973): 184-211.

Altman, E.I.; Avery, R.B.; Eisenbeis, R.A.; and Sinkey, J.F. *Application of Classification Techniques in Business, Banking and Finance.* Greenwich, Conn.: JAI Press, 1981.

Altman, E.I.; Haldeman, R.G.; and Narayanan, P. "Zeta(TM) Analysis: A New Model to Identify Bankruptcy Risk of Corporations." *Journal of Banking and Finance* (June 1977): 29-54.

Altman, Edward, and McGough, Thomas. "Evaluation of a Company as a Going Concern." *Journal of Accountancy* (December 1974): 50-57.

American Accounting Association, Committee on Concepts and Standards — Management Planning and Control. "Managerial Accounting Literature Abstracts." (Mimeographed.) Sarasota, Fla.: American Accounting Association, October 1976.

American Accounting Association, Committee on Concepts and Standards for External Financial Reports. *Statement on Accounting Theory and Theory Acceptance.* Sarasota, Fla.: American Accounting Association, 1977a.

American Accounting Association, Committee on Human Information Processing. "Report of the Committee on Human Information Processing." (Mimeographed.) Sarasota, Fla.: American Accounting Association, 1977b.

American Institute of C.P.A.'s Technical Services Division. "Opinion Survey on Price-Level Adjustment of Depreciation." *Journal of Accountancy* (April 1958): 36-42. (3.3; mail survey; businessmen, analysts and educators.)

Arbel, A., and Jaggi, B. "Impact of Replacement Cost Disclosures on Investors' Decisions in the United States." *International Journal of Accounting* (Fall 1978): 71-82.

Archibald, T.R. "The Return to Straight-Line Depreciation: An Analysis of a Change in Accounting Methods." *Journal of Accounting Research Supplement* to Vol. 5 (1967), *Empirical Research in Accounting: Selected Studies, 1967,* pp. 164-180.

Arnold, Donald F., Sr. "The Feasibility of Measuring Income Concepts Defined by 'Alternative' Accounting Principles." SUNY Buffalo, 1972. (Test application of revised accounting reports following alternative principles; practicing accountants.)

Arthur Young & Company. *Financial Reporting and Changing Prices: A Survey of Preparer's Views and Practices.* New York: Arthur Young & Company, 1981.

Asebrook, R.J., and Carmichael, D.R. "Reporting on Forecasts: A Survey of Attitudes." *Journal of Accountancy* (August 1973): 38-48. (4.3; mail survey; CPAs, financial executives, analysts.)

Ashley, J.W. "Stock Prices and Changes in Earnings and Dividends: Some Empirical Results." *Journal of Political Economy* (February 1962): 82-85.

Ashton, Robert H. "The Predictive-Ability Criterion and User Prediction Models." *The Accounting Review* (October 1974): 719-32.

Ashton, Robert H. "Cognitive Changes Induced by Accounting Changes: Experimental Evidence on the Functional Fixation Hypothesis." *Journal of Accounting Research Supplement* to Vol. 14 (1976), *Studies on Human Information Processing in Accounting,* pp. 1-17.

Ashton, Robert H. "Objectivity of Accounting Measures: A Multivariant-Multidimensional Approach." *The Accounting Review* (July 1977): 567-75.

Ashton, Robert H. *The Evolution of Behavioral Accounting Research: An Overview.* New York: Garland Publishing, 1984.

Ashton, Robert H. *Some Early Contributions to the Study of Auditing Judgment.* New York: Garland Publishing, 1984.

Atkinson, A.A., and Feltham, G.A. "Information in Capital Markets: An Agency Theory Perspective." Working Paper. Vancouver: Faculty of Commerce, University of British Columbia, January 1981.

Backer, Morton. *Financial Reporting for Security Investment and Credit Decisions.* New York: National Association of Accountants, 1970. (3.3, 4.1; interviews; analysts, bankers, executives.)

Backer, Morton. *Current Value Accounting.* New York: Financial Executives Research Foundation, November 1973. See also report on this research in Morton Backer, "A Model for Current Value Reporting." *The CPA Journal* (February 1974): 27-33. (3.3; interviews; analysts, bankers, CPAs.)

Backer, Morton, and McFarland, Walter B. *External Reporting for Segments of a Business.* New York: National Association of Accountants, 1968. (4.1; interviews; analysts, commercial bankers, and executives.)

Bacon, Leonard A. "An Exploratory Study of the Role of Financial Disclosure of Accounting Data in the Development of the Stock Exchange and Capital Growth in Mexico City." University of Mississippi, 1973. (Interviews; various Mexican officials.)

Baker, M. Kent, and Haslem, John A. "Information Needs of Individual Investors." *Journal of Accountancy* (November 1973): 64-69. (2.2; mail questionnaire; investors in the Washington, D.C. area.)

Ball, Ray J. "Anomalies in Relationships Between Securities' Yields and Yield Surrogates." *Journal of Financial Economics* (June-September 1978): 103-126.

Ball, Ray J. "Changes in Accounting Techniques and Stock Prices." *Journal of Accounting Research Supplement* to Vol. 10 (1972), *Empirical Research in Accounting: 1972*, pp. 1-38.

Ball, Ray J., and Brown, Philip. "An Empirical Evaluation of Accounting Income Numbers." *Journal of Accounting Research* (Autumn 1968): 159-78.

Ball, Ray J., and Watts, Ross. "Some Time Series Properties of Accounting Income." *Journal of Finance* (June 1972): 663-81.

Banz, R.W. "The Relationship Between Return and Market Value of Common Stocks." *Journal of Financial Economics* (March 1981): 3-18.

Bariff, Martin L. "A Study of the Impact of Replacement Cost Data on Individual Investment Behavior." University of Illinois, 1973. (Laboratory and mail experiment; businessmen and analysts.)

Barrett, M. Edgar. "Accounting for Intercorporate Investments: A Behavioral Field Experiment." *Journal of Accounting Research Supplement* to Vol. 9 (1971): 50-92. (Pages include discussion comments.) (4.4; experiment by mail; analysts.)

Beard, Larry Holden. "The Effect on Projections of Alternative Disclosures of an Accounting Change: A Behavioral Investigation." University of Georgia, 1974. (Experiment; accountants, financial executives, analysts.)

Beaver, William. "Financial Ratios as Predictors of Failure." *Journal of Accounting Research Supplement* to Vol. 4 (1966): 71-127. (Pages include discussion comments).

Beaver, William. "The Information Content of Annual Earnings Announcements." *Journal of Accounting Research Supplement* to Vol. 6 (1968), *Empirical Research in Accounting: 1968*, pp. 87-92.

Beaver, William. "The Time Series Behavior of Earnings." *Journal of Accounting Research Supplement* to Vol. 8 (1970), *Empirical Research in Accounting: 1970*, pp. 62-99.

Beaver, William. "The Behavior of Security Prices and Its Implications for Accounting Research (Methods)." *The Accounting Review Supplement* to Vol. 47 (1972), *Committee Reports*, pp. 407-37.

Beaver, William. "What Should Be the FASB's Objectives?" *Journal of Accountancy* (August 1973): 49-56.

Beaver, William. "The Information Content of the Magnitude of Unexpected Earnings." Stanford University Working Paper, presented to the 1974 Stanford Research Seminar (1974a).

Beaver, William. "The Evolution of Security Price Research in Accounting." Stanford University Working Paper, presented to the 1974 American Accounting Association Doctoral Consortium (1974b).

Beaver, William. "Financial Statements: Issues of Preparation and Interpretation." Stanford University Working Paper, presented to the 1975 Stanford Research Seminar (1975).

Beaver, William; Christie, A.A.; and Griffin, P.A. "The Information Content of SEC Accounting Series Release No. 190." *Journal of Accounting and Economics* (August 1980): 127-57.

Beaver, William; Clarke, R.; and Wright, W. "The Association Between Unsystematic Security Returns and the Magnitude of the Earnings Forecast Error." *Journal of Accounting Research* (Autumn 1979): 316-40.

Beaver, William, and Dukes, R.E. "Interperiod Tax Allocation, Earnings Expectations, and the Behavior of Security Prices." *The Accounting Review* (April 1972): 320-32.

Beaver, William, and Dukes, R.E. "Delta-Depreciation Methods: Some Empirical Results." *The Accounting Review* (July 1973): 549-59.

Beaver, William; Kettler, Paul; and Scholes, Myron. "The Association Between Market Determined and Accounting Determined Risk Measures." *The Accounting Review* (October 1970): 654-82.

Beaver, William, and Manegold, James. "The Association Between Market-Determined and Accounting-Determined Measures of Systematic Risk." *Journal of Financial and Quantitative Analysis* (June 1975): 231-84.

Belkaoui, Ahmed. "The Impact of the Disclosure of 'Pollution Control' Information on the Investors: A Behavioral Field Experiment and a Market Reaction Investigation." Syracuse University 1972. (Experiment; subjects unknown.)

Belkaoui, Ahmed. "Linguistic Relativity in Accounting" *Accounting, Organizations and Society*, no. 2 (1978): 97-104.

Benbasat, Izak, and Dexter, Albert S. "Value and Events Approaches to Accounting: An Experimental Evaluation." *The Accounting Review* (October 1979): 735-49.

Benjamin, James J., and Stanga, Keith G. "Differences in Disclosure Needs of Major Users of Financial Statements." *Accounting and Business Research* (Summer 1977): 187-92.

Benjamin, James J., and Strawser, Robert H. "The Publication of Forecasts: An Experiment." *Abacus* (December 1974): 138-46. (4.3; experimental simulation; students.)

Benston, George J. "Published Corporate Accounting Data and Stock Prices." *Journal of Accounting Research Supplement* to Vol. 5 (1967), *Empirical Research in Accounting: 1967*, pp. 1-14, 22-54.

Benston, George J. "Required Disclosure and the Stock Market: An Evaluation of the Securities Exchange Act of 1934." *American Economic Review* (March 1973): 132-55.

Benston, George J., and Krasney, Melvin A. "DAAM: The Demand for Alternative Accounting Measurements." *Journal of Accounting Research Supplement* to Vol. 16 (1978), *Studies on Accounting for Changes in General and Specific Prices: Empirical Research and Public Policy Issues*, pp. 1-30.

Biggs, Stanley F. "An Empirical Investigation of the Information Processes Underlying Four Models of Choice Behavior." In *Behavioral Experiments in Accounting II*, pp. 35-81. Edited by Thomas J. Burns. Columbus: The Ohio State University, 1979.

Bird, Francis A. "Interperiod Comparability in Financial Reporting." *Journal of Accountancy* (June 1969): 51-56. (4.2; mail survey, analysts.)

Birnberg, Jacob G., and Nath, Raghu. "Implications of Behavioral Science for Managerial Accounting." *The Accounting Review* (July 1967): 468-79.

Birnberg, Jacob G., and Slevin, Dennis P. "A Note on the Use of Confidence Interval Statements in Financial Reporting." *Journal of Accounting Research* (Spring 1976): 153-57.

Black, Fischer. "Yes, Virginia, There is Hope: Tests of the Value Line Ranking System." *Financial Analysts' Journal* (September-October 1973): 10-14.

Blum, Mark P. "The Failing Company Doctrine." Ph.D. dissertation, Columbia University, 1969.

Blume, Marshall. "Betas and Their Regression Tendencies." *Journal of Finance* (June 1975): 785-95.

Boatsman, James R., and Robertson, Jack C. "Policy-capturing on Selected Materiality Judgments." *The Accounting Review* (April 1974): 342-52. (2.4; on-site experiment; analysts and CPAs.)

Bollom, William J. "Toward a Theory of Interim Reporting for a Seasonal Business: A Behavioral Approach." *The Accounting Review* (January 1973): 12-22. (4.2; business game experiment; students.)

Boulding, Kenneth. "Economics and Accounting: The Uncongenial Twins." In *Studies in Modern Accounting Theory*, p. 44-55. Edited by W. Baxter and S. Davidson. Homewood, Illinois: Irwin, 1962.

Bowman, R.G. "The Debt Equivalence of Leases: An Empirical Investigation." *The Accounting Review* (April 1980): 237-53.

Bradish, Richard D. "Corporate Reporting and the Financial Analyst." *The Accounting Review* (October 1965): 757-66. (2.1; interviews; analysts.)

Brandon, C.H. "The Disclosure of Forecasts in Annual Reports." University of Georgia, 1972. (Experiment; students.)

Brealey, Richard A. *An Introduction to Risk and Return from Common Stocks.* Cambridge: M.I.T. Press, 1969.

Brealey, Richard A. *Security Prices in a Competitive Market.* Cambridge: M.I.T. Press, 1971.

Brennan, W. John, ed. *The Internationalization of the Accounting Profession.* Toronto: The Canadian Institute of Chartered Accountants, 1979.

Brennan, W. John. "Investment Analysis and Generally Accepted Accounting Principles." University of Michigan, 1972. (Experiment; apparently analysts.)

Brenner, Vincent C. "Financial Statement Users' Views of the Desirability of Reporting Current Cost Information." *Journal of Accounting Research* (Autumn 1970): 159-66. (3.3; mail survey; stockholders, bankers, analysts.)

Brenner, Vincent C., and Shuey, Ronald E. "An Empirical Study of Support for APB Opinion No. 16." *Journal of Accounting Research* (Spring 1972): 200-208. (2.3; mail survey; analysts, CPAs, controllers.)

Brooks, L.D., and Buckmaster, D.A. "First Difference Signals and Accounting Income Time Series Properties." *The Journal of Business Finance and Accounting* (Autumn 1980): 437-54.

Brown, Philip. "The Impact of the Annual Net Profit on the Stock Market." *The Australian Accountant* (July 1970): 277-282.

Brown, Philip, and Ball, Ray. "Some Preliminary Findings on the Association between the Earnings of a Firm, Its Industry, and the Economy." *Journal of Accounting Research Supplement* to Vol. 5 (1967), *Empirical Research in Accounting: 1967*, pp. 55-77.

Brown, Philip, and Kennelly, John. "The Information Content of Quarterly Earnings: An Extension and Some Further Evidence." *Journal of Business* (July 1972): 403-15.

Brown, Philip, and Niederhoffer, Victor. "The Predictive Content of Quarterly Earnings." *The Journal of Business* (October 1968): 488-97.

Brown, R.M. "Short-Range Market Reaction to Changes in LIFO Accounting Using Preliminary Earnings Announcement Dates." *Journal of Accounting Research* (Spring 1980): 38-63.

Brown, S.L. "Earnings Changes, Stock Prices and Market Efficiency." *The Journal of Finance* (March 1978): 17-28.

Brunswik, E. *The Conceptual Framework of Psychology.* Chicago: The University of Chicago Press, 1952.

Brunswik, E. *Perception and the Representative Design of Experiments.* Berkeley, Calif.: University of California Press, 1956.

Bullara, Ruth M. "The Effect of Accounting for Combinations on Investor Decisions." University of Texas at Austin, 1973. (Mail survey; analysts.)

Butterworth, John E.; Gibbins, Michael; and King, Raymond. "The Structure of Accounting Theory: Some Basic Conceptual and Methodological Issues." Prepared for the Clarkson, Gordon Foundation Research Symposium, "The Nature and Role of Research to Support Standard-Setting in Financial Accounting in Canada."

(Mimeographed.) Toronto: Clarkson, Gordon Foundation, May 1981. [Now published as: *Research to Support Standard Setting in Financial Accounting: A Canadian Perspective, Proceedings of the 1981 Research Symposium*. Edited by Sanjoy Basu and J. Alex Milburn. Toronto: Clarkson, Gordon Foundation, 1982.]

Buzby, Stephen L. "Selected Items for Information and Their Disclosure in Annual Reports." *The Accounting Review* (July 1974): 423-35. (2.1; mail survey; analysts.)

Buzby, Stephen L., and Falk, Haim. "Demand for Social Responsibility Information by University Investors." *The Accounting Review* (January 1979): 23-37.

Cadenhead, Gary M. "Circumstantial Variables in Accounting for Inventories." Stanford University, 1969. (Questionnaires and interviews; company officers, etc.)

Campbell, Donald T., and Stanley, Julian C. *Experimental and Quasi-Experimental Designs for Research*. Chicago: Rand McNally & Co., 1963.

Carmichael, D.R. "Reporting on Forecasts: A U.K. Perspective." *Journal of Accountancy* (January 1973): 36-47. (4.3; interviews; United Kingdom accountants.)

Carpenter, Charles G., and Strawser, Robert H. "Disclosure of Changes in Accounting Methods." *Journal of Accounting Research* (Spring 1972): 209-16. (2.3; mail survey; controllers, accounting educators, analysts, CPA's.)

Carper, William Brent; Barton, M. Frank, Jr.; and Wunder, Haroldene F. "The Future of Forecasting." *Management Accounting* (August 1979): 27-31.

Carsberg, Bryon; Hope, Anthony A.; and Scapens, R.W. "The Objectives of Published Accounting Reports." *Accounting and Business Research* (Summer 1974): 162-73. See also K.V. Peasnell, "The Objectives of Published Accounting Reports: A Comment," *Accounting and Business Research* (Winter 1974): 71-76; and Carsberg, et al. "The Objectives of Published Accounting Reports: Reply to a Comment," *Accounting and Business Research* (Spring 1975): 152-56. (3.1; interviews and mail questionnaires; United Kingdom accountants.)

Carter, Clairmont P., Jr. "Sources of Substantial Authoritative Support for Accounting Principles: A Theoretical and Empirical Investigation." Kent State University, 1971. (Mail questionnaire; analysts, financial executives, CPA's, accounting educators.)

Casey, Cornelius J., Jr. "The Usefulness of Accounting Ratios for Subjects' Predictions of Corporate Failure: Replication and Extensions." *Journal of Accounting Research* (Autumn 1980): 603-13.

Casey, Cornelius J., Jr., and Sandretto, Michael J. "Internal Uses of Accounting for Inflation." *Harvard Business Review* (November/December 1981): 149-56.

Cassidy, D.B. "Investor Evaluation of Accounting Information: Some Additional Empirical Evidence." *Journal of Accounting Research* (Autumn 1976): 212-229.

Cattanach, Richard L. "An Inquiry into the Informational Needs of Stockholders and Potential Investors." Arizona State University, 1972. (Mail survey; analysts.)

Cerf, Alan R. *Corporate Reporting and Investment Decisions*. Berkeley, Calif.: Institute of Business and Economic Research, 1961. (2.1; interviews, mail survey; analysts.)

Chandra, Gyan. "A Study of the Consensus on Disclosure among Public Accountants and Security Analysts." *The Accounting Review* (October 1974): 733-42. (2.2; mail survey; CPAs and analysts.)

Chandra, Gyan, and Greenball, Melvin N. "Management Reluctance to Disclose: An Empirical Study." *Abacus* (December 1977): 141-54.

Chang, Davis L., and Birnberg, Jacob G. "Functional Fixity in Accounting Research: Perspective and New Data." *Journal of Accounting Research* (Autumn 1977): 300-12.

Chen, Kung-Kong. "Removing the Appearance of Certainty from Accounting Information: A Behavioral Experiment." University of Texas at Austin, 1974. (Classroom experiment; MBA students.)

Chen, Rosita S.C. "The Behavioral Implications of the Stewardship Concept and Its Effects on Financial Reporting." University of Illinois, 1973. A portion of the dissertation, without the empirical results, appears in Rosita S.C. Chen, "Social and Financial Stewardship," *The Accounting Review* (July 1974): 533-43. (Mail survey; apparently accountants.)

Chesley, G.R. "Subjective Probability Elicitation Techniques: A Performance Comparison." *Journal of Accounting Research* (Autumn 1978): 225-41.

Clay, Raymond J., Jr. "An Analysis of Selected Annual Reports as an Input into the Investment Decision Process of Bank Trust Investment Officers." University of Kentucky, 1974. (Questionnaires and interviews; bankers.)

Cohen, Michael D., and March, James G. *Leadership and Ambiguity: The American College President*. Report prepared for the Carnegie Commission on Higher Education. New York: McGraw-Hill, Inc., 1974.

Collins, Daniel W. "SEC Product-Line Reporting and Market Efficiency." *Journal of Financial Economics* (June 1975): 125-64.

Collins, D.W.; Rozeff, M.S.; and Dhaliwal, D.S. "The Economic Determinants of Market Reaction to Proposed Mandatory Accounting Changes in the Oil and Gas Industry: A Cross-Sectional Analysis." *Journal of Accounting and Economics* (May 1981): 37-72.

Collins, D.W.; Rozeff, M.S.; and Salatka, W.K. "The SEC Rejection of SFAS No. 19: Tests of Market Price Reversal." *The Accounting Review* (January 1982): 1-17.

Collins, Frank, and Yeakel, John A. "Range Estimates in Financial Statements: Help or Hindrance?" *Journal of Accountancy* (July 1979): 73-78.

Comiskey, E.E., and Groves, R.E.V. "The Adoption and Diffusion of an Accounting Innovation." *Accounting and Business Research* (Winter 1971): 67-75. (4.5; mail survey; company officers.)

Committee on Behavioral Science Content of the Accounting Curriculum. "Report of the Committee." *The Accounting Review Supplement* to Vol. 46 (1972): 247-85.

Copeland, Ronald M.; Francia, Arthur J.; and Strawser, Robert H. "Students as Subjects in Behavioral Business Research." *The Accounting Review* (April 1973): 365-72. See also David J.H. Watson, "Students as Surrogates in Behavioral Business Research: Some Comments;" and Copeland, et al., "Further Comments on Students as Subjects in Behavioral Business Research," both in *The Accounting Review* (July 1974): 530-33 and 534-37, respectively. (2.3, 3.1; mail survey; controllers, CPAs, analysts, accounting educators.)

Copeland, Ronald M., and Shank, John K. "LIFO and the Diffusion of Innovation." *Journal of Accounting Research Supplement* to Vol. 9 (1971): 196-230. (Pages include discussion comments.) (4.5; mail survey; company officers.)

Corless, John C., and Norgaard, Corine T. "User Reactions to CPA Reports on Forecasts." *Journal of Accountancy* (August 1974): 46-54. (4.3; mail survey of analysts and classroom questionnaire of MBA students).

Cramer, Joe J., Jr. "Income Reporting by Conglomerates — Views of American Businessmen." *Abacus* (August 1968): 17-26. (4.1; mail survey; business executives.)

Crooch, Gary M. "An Investigation of Investors' Financial Statement Knowledge." Michigan State University, 1970. (Mail survey; stockholders.)

Crumbley D. Larry, and Strawser, Robert H. "Allocation of Income Taxes in Segmented Financial Statements." *The CPA Journal* (July 1974): 35-38. (4.1; mail survey; management accountants.)

Cumming, John, Jr. "An Empirical Evaluation of Possible Explanations for the Differing Treatment of Apparently Similar Unusual Events." University of Illinois, 1972. (Mail questionnaire; company officers.)

Custer, Henry L., Jr. "The Courts' Concepts of Accounting Principles as Revealed by Court Decisions." University of Alabama, 1970. (Search of court records for accounting interpretations.)

Daily, R. Austin. "The Feasibility of Reporting Forecasted Information." *The Accounting Review* (October 1971): 686-92. (4.3; interviews; company executives.)

Danos, Paul Peter. "Confirmability Level Financial Statements: A Theoretical and Empirical Assessment." University of Texas at Austin, 1974. (Mail survey; CPA firm partners, analysts.)

Dascher, Paul E. "The Behavioral Impact and Implications of Varying Approaches to Market Segment Reporting: An Empirical Study." Pennsylvania State University, 1969. (Experiment; students.)

Dascher, Paul E., and Copeland, Ronald M. "Some Further Evidence on 'Criteria for Judging Disclosure Improvement.'" *Journal of Accounting Research* (Spring 1971): 32-39. (4.1; experiment; students.)

Davidson, Lewis F. "Impact of Various Forms of Accounting Statement Presentation and Disclosure on Decision Making Behavior: An Empirical Study in Communication and Information Theory." Pennsylvania State University, 1968.

Dawes, Robyn M. "The Robust Beauty of Improper Linear Models in Decision Making." *American Psychologist* (July 1979): 571-82.

Deakin, Edward B. III. "A Discriminant Analysis of Business Failure." *Journal of Accounting Research* (Spring 1972a): 167-79.

Deakin, Edward B. III. "On the Usefulness of Annual Report Information for Common Stock Investment Decisions." University of Illinois, 1972b. (Experiment and interviews; bankers.)

Deakin, E.B.; Norwood, G.R.; and Smith, C.H. "The Effect of Published Earnings Information on Tokyo Stock Exchange Trading." *International Journal of Accounting* (Fall 1974): 124-36.

Demski, Joel S. "The General Impossibility of Normative Accounting Standards." *The Accounting Review* (October 1973): 718-23.

Demski, Joel S. "The Value of Financial Accounting." Research Paper, Graduate School of Business, Stanford University, January 1980.

Denham, Ross A. "A Theoretical and Empirical Study of Net Income Normalized As Earnings Per Share Data." University of Minnesota, 1972. (Apparently mail survey; CPAs, analysts.)

Dickhaut, John W., and Eggleton, Ian R.C. "An Examination of the Processes Underlying Comparative Judgments of Numerical Stimuli." *Journal of Accounting Research* (Spring 1975): 38-72. (2.4; classroom experiment; MBA students.)

Dopuch, Nicholas, and Ronen, Joshua. "The Effects of Alternative Inventory Valuation Methods — An Experimental Study." *Journal of Accounting Research* (Autumn 1973): 191-211. (4.4; classroom experiment; MBA students.)

Dopuch, Nicholas, and Sunder, Shyam. "FASB's Statements on Objectives and Elements of Financial Accounting: A Review." *The Accounting Review* (January 1980): 1-21.

Dopuch, Nicholas, and Watts, Ross. "Using Time-Series Models to Assess the Significance of Accounting Changes." *Journal of Accounting Research* (Spring 1972): 180-94.

Downes, David, and Dyckman, Thomas. "A Critical Look at the Efficient Market Empirical Research Literature as It Relates to Accounting Information." *The Accounting Review* (April 1973): 300-17.

Driver, Michael J., and Mock, Theodore J. "Human Information Processing, Decision Style Theory, and Accounting Information Systems." *The Accounting Review* (July 1975): 490-508.

Dukes, R.E. *An Empirical Investigation of the Effects of Statement of Financial Accounting Standards No. 8 on Security Return Behavior.* Financial Accounting Standards Board, 1978.

Dukes, R.E. "An Investigation of the Effects of Expensing Research and Development Costs on Security Prices." In *Proceedings of the Conference on Topical Research in Accounting, 1975*, pp. 147-93. New York University, 1976.

Durham, Winferd. "Ratings of Accounting Concepts by Businessmen." University of Northern Colorado, 1973. (Survey; businessmen.)

Dyckman, Thomas R. "On the Investment Decision." *The Accounting Review* (April 1964): 285-95. (4.4; classroom experiment; students.)

Dyckman, Thomas R. "On the Effects of Earnings — Trend, Size and Inventory Valuation Procedures in Evaluating a Business Firm." In *Research in Accounting Measurement*, pp. 175-85. Edited by Jaedicke et al. American Accounting Association, 1966. (4.4; classroom experiment; students and business executives.)

Dyckman, Thomas R. *Investment Analysis and General Price-Level Adjustments: A Behavioral Study.* AAA Accounting Research Study #1. American Accounting Association, 1969. (3.3; experiment by mail; analysts.)

Dyckman, Thomas R.; Downes, David; and Magee, Robert. *Efficient Capital Markets and Accounting: A Critical Analysis.* Englewood Cliffs, N.J.: Prentice-Hall, 1975.

Dyckman, Thomas R.; Gibbins, Michael; and Swieringa, Robert J. "Experimental and Survey Research in Financial Accounting: A Review and Evaluation." In *The Impact of Accounting Research on Practice and Disclosure*, pp. 48-105. Edited by A. Rashad Abdel-khalik and Thomas F. Keller. Durham, N.C.: Duke University Press, 1978.

Dyer, Jack Lawson. "Search for Objective Materiality Norms in Accounting and Auditing." University of Kentucky at Lexington, 1973. (Questionnaire; auditors.)

Ecton, William W. "Communication through Accounting — Bankers' Views." *Journal of Accountancy* (August 1969): 79-81. (2.1; mail survey; bankers.)

Edmister, R.O. "An Empirical Test of Financial Ratio Analysis for Small Business Failure Prediction." *Journal of Financial and Quantitative Analysis* (March 1972): 1477-93.

Edwards, James W.; Dominiak, Geraldine F.; and Hedges, Thomas V. *Interim Financial Reporting.* New York: National Association of Accountants, 1972. (4.2; interviews; analysts, bankers, executives.)

Eggleton, Ian R.C. "Patterns, Prototypes, and Predictions: An Exploratory Study." *Journal of Accounting Research Supplement* to Vol. 14 (1976), *Studies on Human Information Processing in Accounting*, pp. 68-131.

Einhorn, Hillel J., and Hogarth, Robin M. "Behavioral Decision Theory: Processes of Judgment and Choice." *Journal of Accounting Research* (Spring 1981): 1-41.

Eisenbeis, R.A. "Pitfalls in the Application of Discriminant Analysis in Business, Finance, and Economics." *The Journal of Finance* (June 1977): 875-900.

Elias, Nabil. "The Effects of Human Asset Statements on the Investment Decision: An Experiment." *Journal of Accounting Research Supplement* to Vol. 10 (1972): 215-40. (Pages include discussion comments.) (4.4; mail experiment using analysts and classroom experiment using students.)

Epstein, M.J. *The Usefulness of Annual Reports to Corporate Shareholders.* Los Angeles: Bureau of Business and Economic Research, California State University, 1975.

Eskew, R.K. "An Examination of the Association Between Accounting and Share Price Data in the Extractive Petroleum Industry." *The Accounting Review* (April 1975): 316-24.

Eskew, R.K., and Wright, W.F. "An Empirical Analysis of Differential Capital Market Reaction to Extraordinary Items." *Journal of Finance* (May 1976): 611-28.

Estes, Ralph W. "An Assessment of the Usefulness of Current Cost and Price-Level Information by Financial Statement Users." *Journal of Accounting Research* (Autumn 1968): 200-07. (3.3; mail survey; analysts, bank loan officers and credit men, financial executives.)

Estes, Ralph W., and Reimer, Marvin. "A Study of the Effect of Qualified Auditors' Opinions on Bankers' Lending Decisions." *Accounting and Business Research* (Autumn 1977): 250-59.

Estes, Thomas G., Jr. "An Investigation of Compliance with Desirability of Depreciation Disclosure Requirements in Accounting Principles Board Opinion Number 12." University of Arkansas, 1971. (Mail survey; analysts.)

Etnier, Donald E. "The Switch from LIFO: Disclosure Methods and Their Effect upon Investors' Decisions." University of Minnesota, 1973. (mail experiment; analysts.)

Eyes, Alan D., and Tabb, J. Bruce. "Bank Managers' Use of Financial Statements." *The Accountants' Journal* (April 1978): 81-85.

Falk, Haim. "Financial Statements and Personal Characteristics in Investment Decision Making." *Accounting and Business Research* (Summer 1972): 209-22. (2.2; field investigation; bankers.)

Falk, Haim, and Ophir, Tsvi. "The Influence of Differences in Accounting Policies on Investment Decisions." *Journal of Accounting Research* (Spring 1973a): 108-16. (2.2; interview-based simulation; bankers.)

Falk, Haim, and Ophir, Tsvi. "The Effect of Risk on the Use of Financial Statements by Investment Decision-Makers: A Case Study." *The Accounting Review* (April 1973b): 323-38. (2.2; interview-based simulation; bankers.)

Fama, Eugene F. "Efficient Capital Markets: A Review of Theory and Empirical Work." *Journal of Finance* (May 1970): 383-417.

Ferris, Kenneth R. "The Apparent Effects of Profit Forecast Disclosure on Managerial Behaviour: An Empirical Examination." *Journal of Business Finance & Accounting* (Autumn 1976): 53-66.

Fetters, Michael L. "Accounting for Extraordinary Gains and Losses: An Empirical Analysis of the Behavioral Consequences." University of Wisconsin, 1973. (Mail experiment; analysts.)

Financial Accounting Standards Board. Exposure draft of proposed statement of financial accounting standards: *Financial Reporting for Segments of a Business Enterprise*. Stamford, Conn.: Financial Accounting Standards Board, September 30, 1975.

Financial Executives Research Foundation. "How Accurate are Forecasts?" *Financial Executive* (March 1973): 26-32. (4.3; mail survey; financial managers.)

Finnerty, J.M.; Fitzsimmons, R.N.; and Oliver, T.W. "Lease Capitalization and Systematic Risk." *The Accounting Review* (October 1980): 631-39.

Firth, Michael. "The Impact of Earnings Announcements on the Share Price Behavior of Similar Type Firms." *Economic Journal* (June 1976): 296-306.

Firth, Michael. "Consensus Views and Judgment Models in Materiality Decisions." *Accounting, Organizations and Society*, no. 4 (1979): 283-95.

Fisher, J. "Financial Information and the Accounting Standards Steering Committee." *Accounting and Business Research* (Autumn 1974): 275-85. See also critical comments on this research: T.A. Lee, "Empirical Research into Information Utility and Acceptability," *Accounting and Business Research* (Spring 1975): 140-44. (3.1; interviews and mail survey; wide variety of United Kingdom, North American and European bankers, practicing accountants and others.)

Flamholtz, Eric, and Cook, Ellen. "Connotative Meaning and Its Role in Accounting Change: A Field Study." *Accounting, Organizations and Society*, no. 2 (1978): 115-39.

Flynn, Thomas D. "Corporate Executives View Accounting Principles." *Journal of Accountancy* (June 1965): 31-36. (3.1; letter to heads of business firms.)

Foster, George. *Financial Statement Analysis*. Englewood Cliffs, N.J.: Prentice-Hall, 1978.

Foster, George. "Intra-Industry Information Transfers Associated with Earnings Releases." *Journal of Accounting and Economics* (December 1981): 201-32.

Foster, George. "Stock Market Reaction to Estimates of Earnings Per Share by Company Officials." *Journal of Accounting Research* (Spring 1973): 25-37.

Foster, George. "Accounting Earnings and Stock Prices of Insurance Companies." *The Accounting Review* (October 1975): 686-89.

Foster, George. "Quarterly Accounting Data: Time-Series Properties and Predictive-Ability Results." *The Accounting Review* (January 1977): 1-21.

Foster, T.W. III, and Vickrey, D. "The Information Content of Stock Dividend Announcements." *The Accounting Review* (April 1978): 360-70.

Francia, Arthur J., and Strawser, Robert H. "Perceptions of Financial Reporting Practices by Accounting Educators: An Empirical Study." *The Accounting Review* (April 1971a): 380-84. (2.3, 3.1; mail survey; accounting educators.)

Francia, Arthur J., and Strawser, Robert H. "Perceptions of Financial Reporting Practices by CPAs." *Journal of Accountancy* (December 1971b): 84-86. (2.3, 3.1; mail survey; CPAs.)

Francia, Arthur J., and Strawser, Robert H. "Attitudes of Management Accountants on the State of the Art." *Management Accounting* (May 1972): 21-24. (2.3, 3.1; mail survey; controllers.)

Freeman, R.N. "The Disclosure of Replacement Cost Accounting Data and Its Effect on Transaction Volumes: A Comment." *The Accounting Review* (January 1981): 177-80.

Freeman, R.N. "Alternative Measures of Profit Margin: An Empirical Study of the Potential Information Content of Current Cost Accounting." Working Paper, University of California at Berkeley, 1982.

Frishkoff, Paul. FASB Research Report. *Financial Reporting and Changing Prices: A Review of Empirical Research*. Stamford, Conn.: FASB, 1982.

Fuller, Russell J., and Metcalf, Richard W. "Management Disclosures: Analysts Prefer Facts to Management's Predictions." *Financial Analysts' Journal* (March/April 1978): 55-57.

Garner, Don E. "The Need for Price-Level and Replacement Value Data." *Journal of Accountancy* (September 1972): 94-98. (3.3; mail survey; analysts, bankers, accountants, businessmen.)

Gheyara, K., and Boatsman, J. "Market Reaction to the 1976 Replacement Cost Disclosures." *Journal of Accounting and Economics* (August 1980): 107-25.

Gibbins, Michael. "A Behavioral Approach to Auditing Research." In *Symposium on Auditing Research II*, pp. 141-86. Audit Group at the University of Illinois at Urbana-Champaign: The Board of Trustees of the University of Illinois, 1977.

Gibbins, Michael. "Regression and Other Statistical Implications for Research on Judgment Using Intercorrelated Data Sources." *Journal of Accounting Research* (Spring 1982): 121-38.

Gibbins, Michael, and Brennan, Patricia. "Behavioral Research and Financial Accounting Standards." In *Usefulness To Investors and Creditors of Information Provided by Financial Reporting: A Review of Empirical Accounting Research*, pp. 99-134. Edited by Paul A. Griffin. Stamford, Conn.: Financial Accounting Standards Board, 1982.

Gleim, Irvin N. "The Content of Broker-Dealer Research Reports Prepared for Institutional Investors and Their Implications for Corporate Financial Reporting." University of Illinois, 1971. (Analysis of brokers' actual research reports.)

Godwin, Larry B. "CPA and User Opinions on Increased Corporate Disclosure." *The CPA* (July 1975): 31-35. (2.3; mail survey; CPAs, analysts, investors.)

Gonedes, Nicholas J. "Evidence on the Information Content of Accounting Messages: Accounting-Based and Market-Based Estimates of Systematic Risk." *Journal of Financial and Quantitative Analysis* (July 1973): 407-44.

Gonedes, Nicholas J. "Capital Market Equilibrium and Annual Accounting Numbers: Empirical Evidence." *Journal of Accounting Research* (Spring 1974): 26-62.

Gonedes, Nicholas J. "A Note on Accounting-Based and Market-Based Estimates of Systematic Risk." *Journal of Financial and Quantitative Analysis* (June 1975): 355-65.

Gonedes, Nicholas J. "Class Discussion Notes, Section 8." University of Chicago, 1976.

Gonedes, Nicholas J., and Dopuch, Nicholas. "Capital Market Equilibrium, Information Production, and Selecting Accounting Techniques: Theoretical Framework and Review of Empirical Work." *Journal of Accounting Research Supplement* to Vol. 12 (1974): 48-169. (Pages include discussion comments.)

Gonedes, Nicholas J.; Dopuch, Nicholas; and Penman, S.H. "Disclosure Rules, Information-Production, and Capital Market Equilibrium: The Case of Forecast Disclosure Rules." *Journal of Accounting Research* (Spring 1976): 89-137.

Gray, Clifton W. "Ingredients of Intuitive Regression." *Organizational Behavior and Human Performance* (February 1979): 30-48.

Gray, S.J. "The Impact of International Accounting Differences from a Security-Analysis Perspective: Some European Evidence." *Journal of Accounting Research* (Spring 1980): 64-76.

Green, David O. "Behavioral Science and Accounting Research." In *Accounting Research, 1960-1970: A Critical Evaluation*, pp. 93-134. Edited by Nicholas Dopuch and Lawrence Revsine. Urbana, Ill.: Center for International Education and Research in Accounting, University of Illinois, 1973. (Pages include discussion comments.)

Green, David O., and Segall, Joel. "The Predictive Content of Quarterly Earnings: A Replication." *Journal of Accounting Research Supplement* to Vol. 4 (1966). *Empirical Research in Accounting: 1966*, pp. 21-36.

Green, David O., and Segall, Joel. "The Predictive Content of Quarterly Earnings." *The Journal of Business* (January 1967): 44-55.

Green, David O., and Segall, Joel. "Brickbats and Straw Men: A Reply to Brown and Niederhoffer." *The Journal of Business* (October 1968): 498-502; "Return of Strawman." *The Journal of Business* (January 1970): 63-65.

Griffin, Paul A. "The Time Series Behavior of Quarterly Earnings: Preliminary Evidence." *Journal of Accounting Research* (Spring 1977): 71-83.

Griffin, Paul A. "Competitive Information in the Stock Market: An Empirical Study of Earnings, Dividends and Analysts' Forecasts." *Journal of Finance* (May 1976): 631-50.

Hagerman, R.L. "The Efficiency of the Market for Bank Stocks: An Empirical Test." *Journal of Money, Credit and Banking* (August 1973): 846-55.

Hakansson, Nils. "Empirical Research in Accounting, 1960-1970: An Appraisal." In *Accounting Research, 1960-70: A Critical Evaluation*, pp. 137-73. Edited by Nicholas Dopuch and Lawrence Revsine. Urbana, Ill.: Center for International Education and Research in Accounting, University of Illinois, 1973.

Hammond, Kenneth; McClelland, Gary H.; and Mumpower, Jeryl. *Human Judgment and Decision Making: Theories, Methods, and Procedures*. New York: Praeger Publishers, 1980.

Hanna, John R. "An Application and Evaluation of Selected Alternative Accounting Income Models." *The International Journal of Accounting Education and Research* (Fall 1972): 135-67. (3.3; interviews; Canadian analysts.)

Hanna, John R. *Accounting Income Models: An Application and Evaluation*. Special Study No. 8. Hamilton, Ontario: The Society of Industrial Accountants, 1974. (3.3; interviews; Canadian analysts.)

Haried, Andrew A. "The Semantic Dimensions of Financial Statements." *Journal of Accounting Research* (Autumn 1972): 376-91. (2.2; factor analysis of semantic differential scales; students, some CPAs.)

Haried, Andrew A. "Measurement of Meaning in Financial Reports." *Journal of Accounting Research* (Spring 1973): 117-45. (2.2; mail and group administered questionnaire; CPAs, analysts, attorneys, investment club members, students.)

Harvey, David W. "A Test of the Usefulness of Financial Statements Prepared with a Communication-Theory-Derived Aggregation Criterion." University of Minnesota, 1972. (Mail experiment; analysts.)

Hawkins, David F., and Wehle, Mary M. *Accounting for Leases.* New York: Financial Executives Research Foundation, 1973. (4.4; interviews and mail survey; financial executives.)

Hawkins, Ennis M. "A Study of the Probabilistic Nature of Financial Statements." Texas Technological University, 1972. (Mail experiment; analysts.)

Hay, Robert D. "Management Thinking Concerning Corporate Annual Reports." *The Accounting Review* (July 1955): 444-50. (3.1; mail survey; company officers.)

Hayes, David C. "The Contingency Theory of Managerial Accounting." *The Accounting Review* (January 1977): 22-39.

Heintz, James A. "Price-Level Restated Financial Statements and Investment Decision Making." *The Accounting Review* (October 1973): 679-89. (3.3; laboratory experiment; students.)

Henderson, Murray Scott. "Some Factors Influencing the Annual Reports of North American Corporations." University of California at Los Angeles, 1969. (Questionnaires and interviews; apparently company officers.)

Hendricks, James A. "Human Asset Accounting and Its Relation to Stock Investment Decisions: An Empirical Study." University of Illinois, 1974. (Experiment; subjects unknown.)

Hendricks, James A. "The Impact of Human Resource Accounting Information on Stock Investment Decisions: An Empirical Study." *The Accounting Review* (April 1976): 292-305.

Hilton, Ronald W. "Integrating Normative and Descriptive Theories of Information Processing." *Journal of Accounting Research* (Autumn 1980): 477-505.

Hofstedt, Thomas R. "Some Behavioral Implications of Aggregation in Accounting Reports." Stanford University, 1970. (Experiment; students.)

Hofstedt, Thomas R. "Some Behavioral Parameters of Financial Analysis." *The Accounting Review* (October 1972a): 679-92. (4.4; classroom experiment; MBA students and business executives.)

Hofstedt, Thomas R. "The Processing of Accounting Information: Perceptual Biases." In *Behavioral Experiments in Accounting*, pp. 285-315. Edited by Thomas J. Burns. Ohio State University, 1972b. (Pages include discussion comments.) (4.4; classroom experiment; MBA students.)

Hofstedt, Thomas R. "A State of the Art Analysis of Behavioral Accounting Research." Working Paper, Stanford University, October 1975.

Hofstedt, Thomas R., and Hughes, G. David. "An Experimental Study of the Judgment Element in Disclosure Decisions." *The Accounting Review* (April 1977): 379-95.

Hofstedt, Thomas R., and Kinard, James C. "A Strategy for Behavioral Accounting Research." *The Accounting Review* (January 1970): 38-54.

Hogarth, Robin M. "Cognitive Processes and the Assessment of Subjective Probability Distributions." *Journal of the American Statistical Association* (June 1975): 271-91.

Hogarth, Robin M. *Judgement and Choice: The Psychology of Decision.* Chichester, England: John Wiley, 1980.

Holthausen, R.W. "Evidence on the Effect of Bond Covenants and Management Compensation Contracts on the Choice of Accounting Techniques." *Journal of Accounting and Economics* (March 1981): 73-109.

Holthausen, R.W., and Verrecchia, R. "The Change in Price Resulting from a Sequence of Information Releases." Working Paper, University of Chicago, July 1981.

Hong, Hai; Mandelker, Gershon; and Kaplan, Robert. "Pooling vs. Purchase: The Effects of Accounting for Mergers on Stock Prices." *The Accounting Review* (January 1978): 31-47.

Hopwood, W.S., and McKeown, J.C. "An Evaluation of Univariate Time-Series Earnings Models and Their Generalization to a Single Input Transfer Function." *Journal of Accounting Research* (Autumn 1981): 313-22.

Horngren, Charles T. "Security Analysts and the Price Level." *The Accounting Review* (October 1955): 575-81. (2,1; 3.3; interviews; analysts.)

Horngren, Charles T. "The Funds Statement and Its Use by Analysts." *Journal of Accountancy* (January 1956): 55-59. (2.1; interviews and examination of reports; analysts.)

Horngren, Charles T. "Disclosure: 1957." *The Accounting Review* (October 1957): 598-604. (2.1; interviews; analysts.)

Horngren, Charles T. "Increasing the Utility of Financial Statements." *Journal of Accountancy* (July 1959): 39-46. (4.4; mail survey; analysts.)

Jacobs, Bruce, and Kaplan, Robert. "Accounting Alternatives and the Steady State Rates of Return of Stock Prices." GSIA Working Paper #54-74-75, Carnegie-Mellon University. Presented to the 1975 Stanford Research Seminar (1975).

Jaffe, Jeffrey F. "Special Information and Insider Trading." *The Journal of Business* (July 1974): 410-28.

Jain, Tribhowan N. "A Study of the Effects of Alternative Methods of Accounting for Income Taxes on Term Loan Decisions." Michigan State University, 1970. (On-site experiment; bankers.)

Jensen, Michael. "Capital Markets: Theory and Evidence." *Bell Journal of Economics and Management Science* (Autumn 1972): 357-98.

Jensen, Robert E. "An Experimental Design for Study of Effects of Accounting Variation in Decision Making." *Journal of Accounting Research* (Autumn 1966): 224-38. See also Thomas R. Dyckman, "Observations on Jensen's Experimental Design for Study of Effects of Accounting Variations in Decision Making;" and Robert

E. Jensen, "A Rejoinder;" both in *Journal of Accounting Research* (Autumn 1967): 221-29 and 230-61, respectively. (4.4; experiment by mail; analysts.)

Joy, O.M., and Jones, C.P. "Earnings Reports and Market Efficiencies: An Analysis of the Contrary Evidence." *The Journal of Financial Research* (Spring 1979): 51-63.

Joy, O.M., and Tollefson, J.O. "On the Financial Applications of Discriminant Analysis." *Journal of Financial and Quantitative Analysis* (December 1975): 723-39.

Kahneman, Daniel, and Tversky, Amos. "Subjective Probability: A Judgment of Representativeness." *Cognitive Psychology* (July 1972): 430-54.

Kahneman, Daniel, and Tversky, Amos. "Prospect Theory: An Analysis of Decision under Risk." *Econometrica* (March 1979): 263-91.

Kaplan, Robert S. "The Information Content of Financial Accounting Numbers: A Survey of Empirical Evidence." Presented at a Symposium on the Impact of Research in Financial Accounting and Disclosure on Accounting Practice, Duke University, December 1975. [Now published in *The Impact of Accounting Research on Practice and Disclosure*, pp. 134-73. Edited by A. Rashad Abdel-khalik and Thomas F. Keller. Durham, N.C.: Duke University Press, 1978] (1975)

Kaplan, Robert S., and Roll, Richard. "Investor Evaluation of Accounting Information: Some Empirical Evidence." *The Journal of Business* (April 1972): 225-57.

Karadbil, Laura L. "On the Disclosure Function of Financial Reporting for Intercorporate Investments in Controlled Corporations." The American University, 1971. (Mail survey; company officers.)

Keller, Robert J. "Disclosure of Projected Financial Information in Corporate Annual Reports." Louisiana State University, 1973. (Mail survey; analysts, CPAs, English chartered accountants.)

Kennedy, Henry A. "A Behavioral Study of the Usefulness of Financial Ratios." University of Washington, 1971. (Simulation study; bank loan officers, analysts.)

Kennedy, Henry A. "A Behavioral Study of the Usefulness of Four Financial Ratios." *Journal of Accounting Research* (Spring 1975): 97-116.

Keys, David E. "Confidence Interval Financial Statements: An Empirical Investigation." *Journal of Accounting Research* (Autumn 1978): 389-99.

Khemakhem, Abdellatif. "A Simulation of Management-Decision Behavior: 'Funds' and Income." *The Accounting Review* (July 1968): 522-34. (4.4; business game experiment; analysts and students.)

Kiger, Jack E. "An Empirical Investigation of NYSE Volume and Price Reactions to the Announcement of Quarterly Earnings." *Journal of Accounting Research* (Spring 1972): 113-28.

Kinard, James C. "The Effect of Variations in the Timing and Ordering of Presentation of Otherwise Identical Information on Expectations." Stanford University, 1969. (Laboratory experiment; students.)

King, Thomas E. "The Information Content of Accounting Reports as a Criterion for Selecting from among Alternative Accounting Methods." University of California at Los Angeles, 1973. (Laboratory experiment; apparently students.)

Kretschmar, Carl G. "Annual Financial Reporting Requirements: A Critical Analysis of Sensitivity to Investor Desires." Indiana University, 1969. (Interviews, analysts, CPAs.)

Kroener, Peter M. "The Effects of the Unattested Part of the Annual Report on the Evaluation of the Company — an Empirical Study." Indiana University, 1973. (Classroom experiment; apparently students.)

Ladley, Herbert Vern. "A Business Simulation Study of the Behavioral Implications of Price Level Adjustments to Financial Statements." George Washington University, 1970. (Simulation experiment; students.)

Landry, Maurice. "Circumstantial Variables in Accounting for the Precomputed Income of Finance Companies." University of California at Los Angeles, 1970. (Questionnaires and interviews; company officers.)

Latane, H.A., and Jones, C.P. "Standardized Unexpected Earnings -- A Progress Report." *Journal of Finance* (December 1977): 1457-66.

Laub, P.M. "On the Information Content of Dividends." *Journal of Business* (January 1976): 73-80.

Leftwich, R. "Evidence on the Impact of Mandatory Changes in Accounting Principles on Corporate Loan Agreements." *Journal of Accounting and Economics* (March 1981): 3-36.

Lev, Baruch. *Financial Statement Analysis: A New Approach*. Englewood Cliffs, N.J.: Prentice-Hall, 1974.

Lev, Baruch. "On the Adequacy of Publicly Available Financial Information for Security Analysis." In *Financial Information Requirements for Security Analysis*, pp. 123-43. Edited by A. Rashad Abdel-khalik and Thomas F. Keller. Durham, N.C.: Graduate School of Business Administration, Duke University, December 1976.

Lev, Baruch, and Ohlson, J.A. "Market Based Empirical Research in Accounting: Review, Interpretation and Extension." *Journal of Accounting Research Supplement* to Vol. 20 (1982). *Current Research Methodologies in Accounting: A Critical Evaluation.*

Lewellen, Wilbur G.; Lease, Ronald C.; and Schlarbaum, Gary G. "Patterns of Investment Strategy and Behavior among Individual Investors." *The Journal of Business* (July 1977): 296-333.

Liao, Shu Sheng. "An Empirical Investigation of the Behavioral Assumptions of the Entity Concept: A Study of Management's Perceptions of the Business Firm." University of Illinois, 1971. (Questionnaires; business managers.)

Libby, Robert. "Accounting Ratios and the Prediction of Failure: Some Behavioral Evidence." *Journal of Accounting Research* (Spring 1975a): 150-61. (4.4; information processing analysis; bankers.)

Libby, Robert. "The Use of Simulated Decision Makers in Information Evaluation." *The Accounting Review* (July 1975b): 475-89. (4.4; information processing analysis; bankers.)

Libby, Robert. "Man versus Model of Man: Some Conflicting Evidence." *Organizational Behavior and Human Performance* (June 1976): 1-12.

Libby, Robert. "Bankers' and Auditors' Perceptions of the Message Communicated by the Audit Report." *Journal of Accounting Research* (Spring 1979a): 99-122.

Libby, Robert. "The Impact of Uncertainty Reporting on the Loan Decision." *Journal of Accounting Research Supplement* to Vol. 17 (1979). *Studies on Auditing -- Selections from the "Research Opportunities in Auditing" Program,* pp. 35-57. (1979b)

Libby, Robert, and Blashfield, Roger K. "Performance of a Composite as a Function of the Number of Judges." *Organizational Behavior and Human Performance* (April 1978): 121-29.

Libby, Robert, and Lewis, Barry L. "Human Information Processing Research in Accounting: The State of the Art." *Accounting, Organizations and Society,* No. 3 (1977); 245-68.

Lintner, John, and Glauber, Robert. "Higgledy Piggledy Growth in America." Presented to the Seminar for the Analysis of Security Prices, University of Chicago, May 1967. Printed in *Modern Developments in Investment Management.* Edited by James Lorie and Richard Brealey. New York: Praeger, 1972.

Lipay, Raymond J. "What's Happening with Interim Financial Reporting?" *Financial Executive* (October 1972): 28-34. (4.2; mail survey; company executives.)

Livingstone, John L. "A Behavioral Study of Tax Allocation in Electric Utility Regulations." *The Accounting Review* (July 1967): 544-52. (4.4; published data used to make behavioral inferences.)

Lookabill, L.L. "Some Additional Evidence on the Time Series Properties of Accounting Earnings." *The Accounting Review* (October 1976): 724-38.

Lorie, James, and Hamilton, Mary. *The Stock Market: Theories and Evidence.* Homewood, Ill.: Irwin, 1973.

Louis Harris and Associates, Inc. *A Study of the Attitudes toward and an Assessment of the Financial Accounting Standards Board.* Stamford, Conn.: Financial Accounting Foundation, 1980.

Lusk, Edward J. "A Test of Differential Performance Peaking for a Disembedding Task." *Journal of Accounting Research* (Spring 1979): 286-94.

Manegold, J.G. "Time-Series Properties of Earnings: A Comparison of Extrapolative and Component Models." *Journal of Accounting Research* (Autumn 1981): 360-73.

March, James G. "Bounded Rationality, Ambiguity, and the Engineering of Choice." *The Bell Journal of Economics* (Autumn 1978): 587-608.

Martin, Samuel A.; Laiken, Stanley N.; and Haslam, Douglas F. *Business Combinations in the '60s: A Canadian Profile.* Toronto and London, Ont.: Canadian Institute of Chartered Accountants and The School of Business Administration, University of Western Ontario, 1969. (4.1; questionnaires and interviews; executives.)

Mautz, Robert K. *Financial Reporting by Diversified Companies.* Financial Executives Institute, 1968. (4.1; mail survey; business executives, investors.)

Mautz, Robert K. *Effect of Circumstances on the Application of Accounting Principles.* New York: Financial Executives Research Foundation, 1972. See also report on this research, Robert K. Mautz, "Uniformity or Flexibility in Accounting," *Financial Executive* (August 1973): 26-30. (3.1; letters, seminars, questionnaires; executives, financial executives, analysts, CPAs.)

May, Robert. "The Influence of Quarterly Earnings Announcements on Investor Decisions as Reflected in Common Stock Price Changes." *Journal of Accounting Research Supplement* to Vol. 9 (1971). *Empirical Research in Accounting: 1971,* pp. 119-63.

McCabe, Robert K. "Communication and Accounting: An Empirical Investigation into the Level of Language Complexity, Meaning Compatibility and the Attitudes of Analysts Toward the Usefulness of External Financial Reports, Management Credibility and Auditor Credibility." University of Colorado, 1973. (Mail questionnaire; analysts.)

McDonald, Daniel L. "A Test Application of the Feasibility of Market Based Measures in Accounting." *Journal of Accounting Research* (Spring 1968): 38-49. (3.2; experiment by mail; CPAs.)

McGhee, Walter; Shields, Michael D.; and Birnberg, Jacob G. "The Effects of Personality on a Subject's Information Processing." *The Accounting Review* (July 1978): 681-97.

McGillivray, Robert E. "Income Concepts Used by Bank Loan Officers in a Metropolitan Environment." North Texas State University, 1974. (Simulation; bankers.)

McIntyre, Edward V. "Current-Cost Financial Statements and Common-Stock Investments Decisions." *The Accounting Review* (July 1973): 575-85. (3.3; laboratory experiment; students and some business executives.)

McNichols, M., and Manegold, J. "Financial Disclosure and the Behavior of Security Prices: An Empirical Investigation." Working Paper, University of California at Los Angeles, February 1982.

Meehl, Paul E. *Clinical versus Statistical Prediction: A Theoretical Analysis and a Review of the Evidence.* Minneapolis: University of Minnesota Press, 1954.

Milgram, S., and Toch, H. "Collective Behavior: Crowds and Social Movements." In *Handbook of Social Psychology*. Edited by Gardner Lindzey and E. Aronson. 2nd ed. Reading, Mass.: Addison-Wesley Publishing Company, Inc., 1968. Vol. 4: *Group Psychology and Phenomena of Interaction,* pp. 507-10.

Miller, Thomas I. "An Inquiry into the Feasibility of External Reporting of Forecasted Financial Information." University of Arkansas, 1973. (Mail survey; analysts, CPAs, controllers.)

Min, Han Ki. "A theoretical and Empirical Investigation into Publication of Forecasts." University of Oklahoma, 1974. (Mail survey; analysts, CPAs, managers.)

Mock, Theodore J., and Vasarhelyi, Miklos Antal. "A Synthesis of the Information Economics and Lens Models." *Journal of Accounting Research* (Autumn 1978): 414-23.

Moore, Charles K. "The Impact of Alternative Presentations of Income Tax Expense on Selected Decision Behavior -- An Empirical Study." Texas Technological University, 1973. (Mail experiment; business executives, bankers, analysts.)

Moriarity, Shane. "Communicating Financial Information through Multidimensional Graphics." *Journal of Accounting Research* (Spring 1979): 205-24.

Moriarity, Shane, and Barron, F. Hutton. "A Judgment-Based Definition of Materiality." *Journal of Accounting Research Supplement* to vol. 17 (1979). *Studies on Auditing -- Selections from the "Research Opportunities in Auditing" Program,* pp. 114-35.

Morrison, D.F. *Multivariate Statistical Methods.* New York: McGraw-Hill, 1967.

Morse, D. "Price and Trading Volume Reaction Surrounding Earnings Announcements: A Closer Examination." *Journal of Accounting Research* (Autumn 1981): 374-83.

Morton, James R. "Qualitative objectives of Financial Accounting: A Comment on Relevance and Understandability." *Journal of Accounting Research* (Autumn 1974): 288-98. (3.1; mail survey; auditors, financial executives, security and credit analysts.)

Most, Kenneth S., and Chang, Lucia S. "How Useful Are Annual Reports to Investors?" *Journal of Accountancy* (September 1979): 111-13.

Naylor, J.C. "A Bibliography of Research Related to Human Judgment and Choice Behavior." Research Paper, Purdue University, August 1979.

Nelson, Kenneth, and Strawser, Robert H. "A Note on APB Opinion No. 16." *Journal of Accounting Research* (Autumn 1970): 284-89. (2.3; mail survey; analysts, CPAs, accounting educators.)

Newman, D. Paul. "Prospect Theory: Implications for Information Evaluation." *Accounting, Organizations and Society,* no. 2 (1980): 217-30.

Neyhart, Charles A., Jr. "Treatment of Accounting Changes: An Attitudinal Investigation." Pennsylvania State University, 1973. (Mail questionnaires; bank loan officers, analysts, financial executives.)

Nickerson, Charles A.; Pointer, Larry B.; and Strawser, Robert H. "Attitudes of Financial Executives toward Interim Financial Statements." *The CPA Journal* (March 1975): 21-24. (4.2; mail survey; financial executives.)

Nickerson, Charles A.; Pointer, Larry B.; and Strawser, Robert H. "Published Forecasts -- Choice or Obligation?" *Financial Executive* (February 1974): 70-73. (4.3; mail survey; stockholders of a single company.)

Niederhoffer, Victor. "The Predictive Content of First-Quarter Earnings Reports." *The Journal of Business* (January 1970): 60-62.

Niederhoffer, Victor, and Regan, Patrick, "Earnings Changes, Analysts' Forecasts, and Stock Prices." *Financial Analysts' Journal* (May-June 1972): 65-71.

Nisbett, Richard E., and Wilson, Timothy DeCamp. "Telling More Than We Can Know: Verbal Reports on Mental Processes." *Psychological Review* (May 1977): 231-59.

Ogilvie, John R., and Schmitt, Neal. "Situational Influences on Linear and Nonlinear Use of Information." *Organizational Behavior and Human Performance* (April 1979): 292-306.

Ohlson, J.A. "Probabilistic Prediction of Bankruptcy: Some Recent Evidence." *Journal of Accounting Research* (Spring 1980): 107-31.

Oliver, Bruce L. "A Study of Confidence Interval Financial Statements." *Journal of Accounting Research* (Spring 1972): 154-66. (3.4; classroom experiment; bankers.)

Oliver, Bruce L. "The Semantic Differential: A Device for Measuring the Interprofessional Communication of Selected Accounting Concepts." *Journal of Accounting Research* (Autumn 1974): 299-316. (2.2; factor analysis of semantic differential scores obtained by mail; CPAs, accounting educators, analysts, security dealers, financial executives, bankers, investment bankers.)

Opinion Research Corporation. *Public Accounting in Transition.* Arthur Andersen and Company, 1974. (2.1; telephone survey of shareowners, interviews of chief exectuvie and chief financial officers, interviews of "key public" including professors, portfolio managers, analysts, brokers, lawyers, accountants, government officials, business press and corporate social activists.)

Ortman, Richard F. "The Effects on Investment Analysis of Alternative Reporting Procedure for Diversified Firms." *The Accounting Review* (April 1974): 298-304. (4.1 and 4.4; experiment by mail; Canadian analysts.)

Pankoff, Lyn D., and Virgil, Robert L. "Some Preliminary Findings from a Laboratory Experiment on the Usefulness of Financial Accounting Information to Security Analysts." *Journal of Accounting Research supplement* to vol. 8 (1970): 1-61. (Pages include discussion comments.) See also Lyn D. Pankoff and Robert

L. Virgil, "On the Usefulness of Financial Statement Information: A Suggested Research Approach," *The Accounting Review* (April 1970): 269-79. (2.2; laboratory experiment; analysts.)

Patell, James. "Corporate Earnings Forecasts: Empirical Tests and Consumption-Investment Model." Ph. D. dissertation, Carnegie-Mellon University, 1976.

Patell, J.M., and Wolfson, M.A. "Anticipated Information Releases Reflected in Call Option Prices." *Journal of Accounting and Economics* (August 1979): 117-40.

Patell, J.M., and Wolfson, M.A. "The Ex Ante and Ex Post Price Effects of Quarterly Earnings Announcements Reflected in Option and Stock Prices." *Journal of Accounting Research* (Autumn 1981): 434-58.

Pattillo, James W. "Materiality: The (Formerly) Elusive Standard." *Financial Executive* (August 1975): 20-27. (2.4; mail questionnaire; preparers, users and auditors of financial statements.)

Pattillo, James W. *The Concept of Materiality in Financial Reporting,* vol. 1. Research study. New York: Financial Executives Research Foundation, 1976.

Pattillo, James W., and Siebel, Jerry D. "Materiality in Financial Reporting." *Financial Executive* (October 1973): 27-38. (2.4; mail survey; preparers, users and auditors of financial statements.)

Pattillo, James W., and Siebel, Jerry D. "Factors Affecting the Materiality Judgment." *The CPA Journal* (July 1974): 39-44. (2.4; mail questionnaire; business executives, CPAs.)

Patton, James M. "Standardization and Utility of Municipal Accounting and Financial Reporting Practices: A Survey." *Governmental Finance* (May 1976): 15-20.

Patton, James M. "An Experimental Investigation of Some Effects of Consolidating Municipal Financial Reports." *The Accounting Review* (April 1978): 402-14.

Patz, Dennis, and Boatsman, James. "Accounting Principle Formulation in an Efficient Markets Environment." *Journal of Accounting Research* (Autumn 1972): 392-403.

Pearl, Daniel. "User Information in Corporate Reports: An Examination of the Availability of User Information in Corporate Reports Prepared for the Primary and Secondary Markets." University of Minnesota, 1969. (Mail survey; analysts.)

Penman, S.H. "Voluntary Disclosure of Earnings Forecasts." Working Paper, University of California at Berkeley, 1978.

Penman, S.H. "Tests of Dividend-Signalling: A Comparative Analysis." Working Paper, University of California at Berkeley, 1980.

Petro, Freddie A. "A Study of Accounting for Long Term Leases in the Financial Statements of the Lessee and the Lessor." University of Arkansas, 1973. (Mail survey; CPAs, analysts, accounting educators.)

Pettit, R.R. "Dividend Announcements, Security Performance, and Capital Market Efficiency." *Journal of Finance* (December 1972): 993-1007.

Pettit, R.R. "The Impact of Dividend and Earnings Announcements: A Reconciliation." *The Journal of Business* (January 1976): 86-96.

Piaker, Philip M., and Dalberth, James. "Acceptance of Changes Among Accountants: An Examination of Attitudes Toward Current Controversies." *The CPA Journal* (February 1973): 132-38. (3.1, 4.5; mail survey; CPA practitioners, accounting educators.)

Pinches, G.E. "Factors Influencing Classification Results From Multiple Discriminant Analysis." *Journal of Business Research* (December 1980): 429-56.

Plott, Charles R., and Sunder, Shyam. "Efficiency of Experimental Security Markets with Insider Information: An Application of Rational Expectations Models." Social Science Working Paper 331, revised. Pasadena: Division of the Humanities and Social Sciences, California Institute of Technology, January 1981.

Prakash, Prem, and Rappaport, Alfred. "Information Inductance and Its Significance for Accounting." *Accounting, Organizations and Society,* no. 1 (1977): 29-38.

Pratt, James W. "Extending the Certified Public Accountants' Attest Function to Quarterly Financial Reports of Publicly Owned Companies." University of Southern California, 1972. (Mail survey; analysts, CPAs.)

Pratt, Jamie. "The Effects of Personality on a Subject's Information Processing: A Comment." *The Accounting Review* (July 1980): 501-06.

Radebaugh, Lee H. "Accounting for Price Level and Exchange Rate Changes of U.S. Firms with Manufacturing Subsidiaries in Brazil." Indiana University, 1972. (Interviews and questionnaires; company officers.)

Rakes, Ganas K., and Shenkir, William B. "User Responses to APB Opinion No. 19." *Journal of Accountancy* (September 1972): 91-94. (4.5; Mail survey; analysts.)

Rao, Kailas J. "An Evaluation and Empirical Study of the Disclosure of Accounting Policies in Published Financial Statements." University of Oklahoma, 1974. (Mail survey; analysts.)

Reckers, Phillip M.R., and Stagliano, A.J. "How Good Are Investor's Data Sources?" *Financial Executive* (April 1980): 26.

Reinoso, Ricardo C. "The User Assumptions Underlying Generally Accepted Accounting Principles: An Empirical Study of a Credit Grantor as a User of Financial Statements." University of North Carolina at Chapel Hill, 1971. (Observational study of the use of financial statements by the commercial lending operation of one large bank.)

Rhode, John Grant. "Behavioral Science Methodologies with Applications for Accounting Research: References and Source Materials." *The Accounting Review Supplement* to vol 47 (1972). *Report of the Committee on Research Methodology in Accounting,* pp. 494-504.

Richardson, Gordon D. "Determinants of the Information Content of Annual Earnings Announcements and the Association Between Information Content and Insider Trading Activity." A Research Proposal, Cornell University, January 1982.

Ricks, William E. "The Market's Response to the 1974 LIFO Adoptions." *Journal of Accounting Research* (Autumn 1982a): 367-87.

Ricks, William E. "Market Assessment of Alternative Accounting Methods: A Review of the Empirical Evidence." *Journal of Accounting Literature* (Spring 1982b): 59-102.

Ritts, Blaine A. "A Study of the Impact of APB Opinions on Practicing CPAs." *Journal of Accounting Research* (Spring 1974): 93-111. (4.5; experiment by mail; CPAs.)

Ro, B.T. "The Disclosure of Capitalized Lease Information and Stock Prices." *Journal of Accounting Research* (Autumn 1978): 315-40.

Ro, B.T. "The Adjustment of Security Returns to the Disclosure of Replacement Cost Accounting Information." *Journal of Accounting and Economics* (August 1980): 159-89.

Ro, B.T. "The Disclosure of Replacement Cost Accounting and its Effect on Transaction Volumes." *The Accounting Review* (January 1981): 70-84.

Ronen, Joshua. "Some Effects of Sequential Aggregation in Accounting on Decision-Making Behavior." Stanford University, 1970. (Experiment; students, business executives.)

Ronen, Joshua, and Falk, Gideon. "Accounting Data and the Entropy Measure: An Experimental Approach." *The Accounting Review* (October 1973): 696-717. (2.2; classroom experiments; MBA students.)

Roper, Elmo. *A Report on What Information People Want About Policies and Financial Conditions of Corporations.* Vols. 1 and 2. New York: Controllers' Institute Foundation, 1948. (2.1; mail survey; investors.)

Rose, Jerry; Beaver, William; Becker, Selwyn; and Sorter, George. "Toward an Empirical Measure of Materiality." *Journal of Accounting Research Supplement* to Vol. 8 (1970): 138-56. (Pages include discussion comments.) (2.4; classroom experiments; students.)

Rosen, Lawrence S. *Current Value Accounting and Price-Level Restatements.* Toronto: Canadian Institute of Chartered Accountants, 1972. (3.3; interviews; variety of Canadian accountants, executives, analysts.)

Runkel, Philip J., and McGrath, Joseph E. *Research on Human Behavior: A Systematic Guide to Method.* New York: Holt, Rinehart and Winston, Inc., 1972.

Sadhwani, Arjan. "Accounting for Land Development." Michigan State University, 1972. (Questionnaires, interviews; apparently company officers.)

Salzarulo, William P. "The Use of a Policy Capturing Approach to Assess the Relevance of Non-Financial Statement Information in Investment Decisions." University of Colorado, 1973. (Information processing analysis; analysts.)

Sanders, Thomas H. *Company Annual Reports to Stockholders, Employees and the Public.* Andover, Mass.: Andover Press, 1948. (2.1; interviews, questionnaires; financial executives, analysts and stockholders.)

Savich, Richard S. "The Use of Accounting Information in Decision Making." *The Accounting Review* (July 1977): 642-52.

Schelling, Thomas C. *Micromotives and Macrobehavior.* New York: Norton & Company, Inc., 1978.

Schmidt, Lester L., Jr. "An Evaluation of the Entity Theory as a Partial Solution to the Non-Comparability Enigma of Inter-Firm Income Statement Analysis." University of Arkansas, 1971. (Questionnaires; analysts, CPAs.)

Schneider, Carl W. "Nits, Grits, and Soft Information in SEC Filings." *University of Pennsylvania Law Review* 121 (1972): 254-305.

Schultz, Joseph J., Jr., and Gustavson, Sandra G. "Actuaries' Perceptions of Variables Affecting the Independent Auditor's Legal Liability." *The Accounting Review* (July 1978): 626-41.

Schwan, Edward S. "A Study of the Effects of Human Resource Data on Bankers' Decisions about a Firm." University of Colorado, 1973. (Experiment by questionnaire; bankers.)

Schwan, Edward S. "The Effects of Human Resource Accounting Data on Financial Decisions: An Empirical Test." *Accounting, Organizations and Society* nos. 2/3 (1976): 219-37.

Schwarzbach, Henry R., and Swanson, Edward P. "The Use of Replacement Cost Accounting Information for Decision Making during Inflationary Times." *Journal of Contemporary Business* (August 1981): 65-76.

Scott, George M., and Troberg, Pontus. *Eighty-eight International Accounting Problems in Rank Order of Importance: A DELPHI Evaluation.* Sarasota, Fla.: American Accounting Association, 1980.

Scott, J. "The Probability of Bankruptcy: A Comparison of Empirical Predictions and Theoretical Models." *Journal of Banking and Finance* (September 1981): 317-44.

Shafer, Glenn. "Two Theories of Probability." Technical Report no. 1. National Science Foundation Grant MCS78-01887. Department of Mathematics, The University of Kansas, October 1978.

Shank, John K., and Copeland, Ronald M. "Corporate Personality Theory and Changes in Accounting Methods -- An Empirical Test." *The Accounting Review* (July 1973): 494-501. (4.5; published data used to infer corporate personality.)

Shank, John K.; Dillard, Jesse F.; and Murdock, Richard J. "FASB No. 8 and the Decision-Makers." *Financial Executive* (February 1980): 18-23.

Sharpe, W.F. "Capital Asset Prices: A Theory of Market Equilibrium Under Conditions of Risk." *Journal of Finance* (September 1964): 425-42.

Simon, Herbert A. "Rational Decision Making in Business Organizations." *The American Economic Review* (September 1979): 493-513.

Singhvi, Surendra S., and Desai, Harsha B. "An Empirical Analysis of the Quality of Corporate Financial Disclosure." *The Accounting Review* (January 1971): 129-38. (2.1; interviews; analysts.)

Slovic, Paul; Fischoff, Baruch; and Lichtenstein, Sarah. "Behavioral Decision Theory." *Annual Review of Psychology* (1977): 1-39.

Smith, James E. "A Critical Analysis of the Application of Communication Theory to Accounting Communications with Published Financial Statements." University of Arizona, 1972. (Interviews, questionnaires; CPAs, analysts.)

Smith, James E., and Smith, Nora P. "Readability: A Measure of the Performance of the Communication Function of Financial Reporting." *The Accounting Review* (July 1971): 552-61. (2.2; readability analysis.)

Snowball, Doug. "Human Resource Accounting Information: A Comment concerning Demand Characteristics." *The Accounting Review* (January 1979): 199-204.

Soper, Fred J., and Dolphin, Robert, Jr. "Readability and Corporate Annual Reports." *The Accounting Review* (April 1964): 358-62. (2.2; readability analysis plus judges of readability.)

Sorter, George H. "An 'Events' Approach to Basic Accounting Theory." *The Accounting Review* (January 1969): 12-19.

Sorter, George H.; Becker, Selwyn W.; with the assistance of T.R. Archibald and W. Beaver. "Corporate Personality as Reflected in Accounting Decisions: Some Preliminary Findings." *Journal of Accounting Research* (Autumn 1964): 183-96. (4.5; field study; business managers plus behavioral inferences from published data.)

Sorter, George H.; Becker, Selwyn W.; Archibald, Ross; and Beaver, William H. "Accounting and Financial Measures as Indicators of Corporate Personality -- Some Empirical Findings." In *Research in Accounting Measurement*, pp. 200-10. Edited by Jaedicke et al. American Accounting Association, 1966. (4.5; field study; business managers plus behavioral inferences from published data.)

Stallman, James C. "Toward Experimental Criteria for Judging Disclosure Improvement." *Journal of Accounting Research Supplement* to Vol. 7 (1969): 29-54. (Pages include discussion comments.) (4.1; experiment; analysts.)

Stanga, Keith G., and Benjamin, James J. "Information Needs of Bankers." *Management Accounting* (June 1978): 17-21.

Stark, Maurice E. "Accounting for Initial Franchise Fees." University of Missouri, 1972. (Mail experiment; analysts, CPAs, accounting educators.)

Sterling, Robert R. "A Test of the Uniformity Hypothesis." *Abacus* (September 1969): 37-47. (3.2; mail questionnaire; CPAs.)

Sterling, Robert R., and Radosevich, Raymond. "A Valuation Experiment." *Journal of Accounting Research* (Spring 1969): 90-95. (3.2; mail questionnaire, CPAs.)

Sterling, Robert R.; Tollefson, John O.; and Flaherty, Richard E. "Exchange Valuation: An Empirical Test." *The Accounting Review* (October 1972): 709-821. (3.2; experiment by mail; CPAs.)

Stickney, Clyde. "Window Dressing the Interim-Earnings Report: An Empirical Assessment for Firms Initially Going Public." *The Journal of Business* (January 1975): 87-97.

Strawser, Robert H. "An Inquiry into the Financial Reporting Practices of Commercial Banks." University of Maryland, 1969. (Mail survey; bankers, CPAs, analysts.)

Sunder, Shyam. "Relationships Between Accounting Changes and Stock Prices: Problems of Measurement and Some Empirical Evidence." *Journal of Accounting Research Supplement* to Vol. 11 (1973). *Empirical Research in Accounting: 1973,* pp. 1-45.

Sunder, Shyam. "Stock Price and Risk Related to Accounting Changes in Inventory Valuation." *The Accounting Review* (April 1975): 305-15.

Swieringa, Robert; Dyckman, Thomas R.; and Hoskin, Robert E. "Empirical Evidence about the Effects of an Accounting Change on Information Processing." In *Behavioral Experiments in Accounting II,* pp. 225-59. Edited by Thomas Burns. Columbus: The Ohio State University, 1979.

Thompson, John Allen. "An Inquiry into the Nature of Earnings Per Share with Emphasis on the Usefulness and Predictive Ability of Primary and Fully Diluted Earnings Per Share Concepts." University of Arkansas, 1974. (Mail survey; CPAs, analysts.)

Treynor, Jack. "The Trouble with Earnings." *Financial Analysts' Journal* (September-October 1972): 41-46.

Uecker, Wilfred C. "Unattested Management Representations in the Annual Report: A Potential Source of Bias in the Evaluation of the Firm?" University of Texas at Austin, 1973. (Classroom experiments; students.)

Uecker, Wilfred C. "A Behavioral Study of Information System Choice." *Journal of Accounting Research* (Spring 1978): 169-89.

Uecker, Wilfred C. "The Effects of Knowledge of the User's Decision Model in Simplified Information Evaluation." *Journal of Accounting Research* (Spring 1980): 191-213.

Vigeland, R.L. "The Market Reaction to Statement of Financial Accounting Standards No. 2." *The Accounting Review* (April 1981): 309-25.

Vinso, J.D. "A Determination of the Risk of Ruin." *Journal of Financial and Quantitative Analysis* (March 1979): 77-100.

Warren, Robert L. "A Critical Examination of External Reporting of Changes in Financial Position with Emphasis on the Impact of Accounting Principles Board Opinion No. 19 and on the Usefulness of 'Fund Flow' Information." University of Arkansas, 1973. (Mail survey; controllers, analysts, bankers.)

Waters, Edwin D. "Some Criteria for Materiality Decisions in Financial Reporting for Small Businesses." University of Alabama, 1971. (Interviews; CPAs.)

Watson, David J.H. "Students as Surrogates in Behavioral Business Research: Some Comments." *The Accounting Review* (July 1974): 530-33. (See also the Copeland, Francia and Strawser listing).

Watts, Ross L. "The Information Content of Dividends." *The Journal of Business* (April 1973): 191-211.

Watts, Ross L. "Accounting Objectives." Working Paper No. 7408, University of Rochester, 1974.

Watts, Ross L. "The Time Series Behavior of Quarterly Earnings." Working Paper, University of Rochester, presented to the 1975 Stanford Research Seminar (1975).

Watts, Ross L. "Corporate Financial Statements: A Product of the Market and Political Processes." *Australian Journal of Management* (April 1977): 53-75.

Watts, Ross L., and Leftwich, R.W. "The Time Series of Annual Accounting Earnings." *Journal of Accounting Research* (Autumn 1977): 253-71.

Watts, Ross L., and Zimmerman, Jerold L. "Towards a Positive Theory of the Determination of Accounting Standards." *The Accounting Review* (January 1978): 112-34.

Watts, Ross L., and Zimmerman, Jerold L. "The Demand for and Supply of Accounting Theories: The Market for Excuses." *The Accounting Review* (April 1979): 273-305.

Watts, Ross L., and Zimmerman, Jerold L. "Auditors and the Determination of Accounting Standards." Working Paper No. GPB 78-06, revised. Graduate School of Management, The University of Rochester, November 1981.

Weick, Karl E. *The Social Psychology of Organizing*. Reading, Mass.: Addison-Wesley Publishing Company, Inc., 1979.

Wilcox, Jarrod. "A Prediction of Business Failure Using Accounting Data." *Journal of Accounting Research Supplement* to Vol 11 (1973) *Empirical Research in Accounting: 1973*, pp. 163-79.

Williams, Paul F. "The Evaluative Relevance of Social Data." *The Accounting Review* (January 1980): 62-77.

Winer, B.J. *Statistical Principles in Experimental Design*. 2nd ed. New York: McGraw-Hill, 1971.

Woolsey, Samuel M. "Development of Criteria to Guide the Accountant in Judging Materiality." *Journal of Accountancy* (February 1954a): 167-73. (2.4; mail survey; preparers, auditors and users of financial statements.)

Woolsey, Samuel M. "Judging Materiality in Determining Requirements for Full Disclosure." *Journal of Accountancy* (December 1954b): 745-50. (2.4; mail survey; preparers, auditors and users of financial statements.)

Woolsey, Samuel M. "Materiality Survey." *Journal of Accountancy* (September 1973): 91-92. (2.4; mail survey; preparers, auditors and users of financial statements.)

Wright, William F. "Self-Insight into the Cognitive Processing of Financial Information." *Accounting, Organizations and Society*, no. 4 (1977a): 323-31.

Wright, William F. "Financial Information Processing Models: An Empirical Study." *The Accounting Review* (July 1977b): 676-89.

Wright, William F. "Properties of Judgment Models in a Financial Setting." *Organizational Behavior and Human Performance* (February 1979): 73-85.

Zehms, Karl M. "Municipal Finance Reporting." University of Wisconsin, 1970. (Interviews, mail questionnaires; municipal financial officers.)

Zimmer, Ian. "A Lens Study of the Prediction of Corporate Failure by Bank Loan Officers." *Journal of Accounting Research* (Autumn 1980): 629-36.

Part VI

MANAGERIAL AND INSTITUTIONAL ACCOUNTING, AND AUDITING

Our own first article begins with a concise historical synopsis and then offers a survey of present-day management accounting, its problems and future prospects. Attention is paid to the following topics:

Systems Philosophy as the Most Basic Influence (indicating the impact of such philosophically and systems oriented management scientists as Churchman and Ackoff[1] upon management accounting).

Electronic Data Processing and Management Information Systems as the Strongest Influence (pointing at the technical as well as human-behavioural aspects of this, from a practical point of view, all-important area).

The Shifting Influence of Operations Research (an area that may not have quite fulfilled the expectations many of us harboured two decades ago but which, nevertheless, had notable impact upon management accounting by introducing it to quantitative methods — for details of the latter, see the second article of the current Part, by Kaplan).

The Significance of Information Economics (including Agency Theory) for Management Accounting (recapitulating, from a somewhat different angle, a topic discussed in considerable detail by Baiman in Part IV).

Speculations about the Future (pivoting on management accounting's trend towards specialization and fragmentation). This section distinguishes between *the object-area* (efficiency control, performance evaluation, optimizing and satisfying goals) and *the meta-area* of management accounting (dealing with the environmental and behavioural interrelations) and argues against a substitution of the former by the latter, but for both complementing each other. Furthermore, emphasizing the object-area means that a unifying, organizing framework must grow out of the very core of accounting and cannot be grafted on at the periphery. This section also examines the possibility of *counterbalancing* the ongoing fragmentation of management accounting; the remedy might be a truly integrated and general, but flexible, accounting theory. Unfortunately, the new generation of accounting researchers seems to be overwhelmed by the same onesidedness so characteristic of positivists and some other epistemologists. As Rescher points out:

> Contemporary philosophers of science have been so concerned with issues of ontogenesis that they have abandoned the issue of phylogenesis. . . . It is understandable why this subject of the disciplinary taxonomy and morphology of science should have fallen into neglect. To some extent, the nominalistic tendencies of recent philosophy have militated against devising synoptic schemes. The growing stress in philosophy on matters of microscopic detail and the aversion to large-scale synthesis are also a hindrance.[2]

Our article concludes with some insights derived from physics (the entropy law), information theory[3] (negentropy), biology (the "value function" of mutations) and from the environmental stress caused by modern technology, relating these insights to management accounting.

The second article, by Kaplan, surveys the "Application of Quantitative Models in Managerial Accounting." This author does not deny that the early hopes in quantitative methods were fulfilled; although he points out that those methods are still not sufficiently integrated in most cost accounting texts, he predicts a change in attitude.[4] The following topics are here discussed:

Cost-Volume-Profit Analysis (in this area, important developments are attributed to the explicit and formal recognition of production limitations, to the recognition of uncertainties, together with the debate over the probabilistic-distributional properties of sales and profits, and to the application of linear and nonlinear programming).

Performance Evaluation and Variance Analysis (referring to algebraic and matrix representations of standard costing; variances based on opportunity losses; the introduction of an *ex post* variance and its analysis — indicating the loss caused by management's failure to adapt to changing conditions; the application of linear programming to mix- and yield-variances; trade-offs between timeliness and accuracy of information and related aspects; as well as some reference to simulation studies). Regrettably, the area of budget simulation — pioneered by ourselves[5] and important enough to penetrate even the mainframe as well as microcomputer software market (see *FALCON/FORECAST* time-sharing system and *PLUSPLAN* by Deloitte, Haskins & Sells, as well as the spread-sheet computer programmes *VISICALC, SUPERCALC,* and the *1-2-3* program by Lotus Development Corp.) — has been ignored in this article.

Variance Investigations (referring to the extension of industrial quality control to the analysis of cost variances, incorporating cost-benefit considerations into those models, and hinting at the fact that model-building in this area seems to be far ahead of practical application).

Cost Behaviour (pointing out that the author has "been unable to find any statistical study explicitly devoted to estimating variable costs for a C-V-P analysis,"[6] which leads him, rightly, to deplore the gap between constructing more and more elaborate management accounting models, on one side, and the scarcity of statistical estimations of cost parameters, on the other).

A considerable part of the paper is devoted to the problem of Cost Allocations. Kaplan regards "the biggest triumph" in this area to be the matrix approach to allocating costs from service to producing departments. He discusses the evolution of this approach as well as the mathematical programming models devoted to the allocation of joint and by-product costs, to depreciation-allocation, to the planning of capital investments, and, finally, to the allocation of overheads to products.

The last section deals briefly with the important topic of Transfer Pricing. It too has been explored as a possible area for applying mathematical programming models, but with less success in practical applications. Kaplan concludes the paper by considering two possible future directions: first, information economics and incentive contracting (i.e., agency theory), which are presently pursued intensively by accounting researchers, as previously emphasized; and second, more widespread application and testing of existing models in actual practice, together with subsequent improvements. To keep the historical records straight, it should be added that the first major book applying analytical methods (axiomatics, set theory, matrix algebra, linear programming, and models in FORTRAN symbolism) systematically to accounting, *in general,* did not fail to apply quantitative models also to the subarea of management accounting.[7]

The third article, by Vatter, refers to institutional or nonbusiness accounting (for governmental agencies, hospitals, religious organizations, universitites, foundations, etc.). For lack of much research in this area, this "State of the Art" report concentrates mainly on reviewing Robert Anthony's Research

Report, *Financial Accounting in Nonbusiness Organizations — An Exploratory Study of Conceptual Issues* (Stamford, Conn.: Financial Accounting Standards Board, 1978). This report searches for principles underlying institutional accounting (e.g., to distinguish operating from capital flows, to establish "recognition" instead of *realization* criteria, to find substitutes for, or modifications to, depreciation, and to deal with other ideosyncrasies) and for alternative models, i.e., *Operating Statements* and *Financial Flow Statements*. Since institutional accounting covers many subareas, alternative statement forms are proposed, based on and ranging from pure cash-flow models to quasi-business accounting models. Vatter examines these models and subjects them to occasional criticism.

Meanwhile, publications in this area have also appeared in Canada: for example, Arthur Beedle's *Accounting for Local Government in Canada: The State of the Art*[8] and two exposure drafts of the CICA's Public Sector Accounting and Auditing Committee.[9] But, considering the immense amount of funds that local as well as federal governments and other nonprofit institutions spend on behalf of the public (and often in most questionable ways), the research in this area is pitifully small. This fact alone justifies the inclusion of institutional accounting in our anthology.

The last article, by Joyce and Libby, deals with the young and fast-growing area of behavioural research in auditing. This excellent and lucidly written paper begins with an outline of three major paradigms and methodologies employed in this area, which are discussed in greater detail in the last part of the paper: 1. The Policy-Capturing Paradigm employs either of two techniques, the analysis of variance (ANOVA), or a multi-dimensional scaling (MDS). The ANOVA technique enables the researcher to observe the *cues* (and their weights) that an auditor uses in attaining his judgements and shows how his judgement varies from case to case, while the MDS technique identifies the cues on which the judgements of auditors differ and indicates the weight each auditor attributes to each cue; 2. The Probabilistic Judgement Paradigm is based on normative decision theory and requires the researcher's elicitation of subjective probabilities, which the auditor attributes to the occurrence of future events; it also requires the eventual revision of such probabilities in the light of new data (Bayes' Theorem); 3. The Predecisional Behaviour paradigm is appropriately applied to contexts vaguely structured and with ill-defined tasks; auditors are required to think aloud while performing their tasks; the resulting protocol-tapes are subsequently analyzed by the researcher.

The major part of this paper deals with a survey of the various areas of behavioural audit research: Internal Control Evaluation (most extensively applied, resulting in a relatively good consensus on auditors' evaluations of internal control but a low consensus on the planning of tests); Internal Auditing (less frequently studied but bringing forth a valuable set of quality criteria); Materiality (finding little agreement among auditors on this issue, except in the case of the item of net income); Analytical Review (asking auditors to provide ranges of sales and other values beyond which they would investigate changes in gross profit percentages); Probability Elicitation (examining alternative elicitation techniques and revealing that different techniques lead to different probability assessments); Source Credibility (examining auditors' sensitivity to the reliability of information sources and suggesting that auditors possess sufficient sensitivity to adjust their judgements to pertinent changes); Disclosure Decisions (limited to a case of contingent liability); and other issues, such as Actuarial Judgements, The Effect of Uncertainty Disclosure on Lending Decisions by bankers, and Audit Reports.

From a practical point of view, behavioural research in auditing seems to be one of the most successful applications of empirical accounting research. The reasons for the favourable response on the part of public accountants lie in the increasing competition among auditing firms, in a growing number of litigations against them, and in the fact that minor and inexpensive procedural modification in auditing can lead to considerable cost reduction and an improvement in general effectiveness.

In closing the commentary to Part VI we should like to draw attention to R.S. Kaplan's paper "The Evolution of Management Accounting" which would have been included in this anthology, were it not for the late date of its publication (in *The Accounting Review,* July 1984, pp. 390-418). It not only offers an excellent survey of the history of cost and management accounting in America since 1850, but also deals with current problems such as: (1) the thorny and, in a way, still unresolved issue of transfer pricing; (2) the limitations of agency theory, and the need for an extension into the areas of production, managerial innovation, knowledge and creativity, as well as transaction costs;

(3) the need for studying what actual managers do rather than what they ought to do according to microeconomic theory; (4) the urgent attention to novel manufacturing processes (Flexible Manufacturing Systems, CAD/CAM computer-integrated manufacturing, and robotics); (5) the dangers of the domination of financial accounting regulations over managerial accounting; (6) the short-run opportunistic behavior of many managers; (7) the significance of nonfinancial goals and measures in addition to profits over the long-run; (8) the need for integration of management accounting with organization theory and other management areas.

R.M.

FOOTNOTES

[1] For further details on the contributions of Ackoff, Churchman, and Simon to systems theory, see R. Mattessich, "The Systems Approach: Its Variety of Aspects," *Journal of the American Society for Information Science* 33 (November 1982), pp. 385-394, especially 387-393.

[2] Nicholas Rescher, *Cognitive Systematization — A Systems-Theoretic Approach to a Coherentist Theory of Knowledge* (Oxford: Basil Blackwell, 1979), pp. 198-199.

[3] For an excellent survey of the interdisciplinary significance of information, See Fritz Machlup and Una Mansfield, eds., *The Study of Information: Interdisciplinary Messages* (New York: John Wiley & Sons, Inc., 1983).

[4] Meanwhile, several text books have appeared which confirm Kaplan's prediction: e.g., A. Belkaoui, *Cost Accounting* (Chicago: Dryden Press, 1983); A.W. Corcoran, *Costs: Accounting, Analysis and Control* (New York: J. Wiley & Sons, Inc., 1978); M.J. Mepham, *Accounting Models* (Afferton-Stockton: Polytech Publishers Ltd., 1980), the only one that takes budget simulation into consideration; and one by R. S. Kaplan himself, *Advanced Management Accounting* (Englewood Cliffs, N.J.: Prentice-Hall, Inc., 1982).

[5] See Richard Mattessich "Budget Models and System Simulation," *Accounting Review* 36 (July 1961), pp. 384-397; and, above all, *idem, Simulation of the Firm through a Budget Computer Program* (Homewood, Ill.: R.D. Irwin, Inc., 1964; facsimile reprinted in Ann Arbor: University Microfilms International, 1979).

[6] This statement is somewhat perplexing in the face of Kaplan's own work in this area, and of a series of important pioneering studies in the statistical estimation of cost curves by economists such as Joel Dean (beginning almost half a century ago with his "Statistical Determination of Costs with Special Reference to Marginal Costs," *Studies in Business Administration* 7, 1936), and, above all, of the book by J. Johnston, *Statistical Cost Analysis* (New York: McGraw-Hill, Inc., 1960). That such studies were designed for cost-volume-profit analyses is indicated by J. Dean, *Managerial Economics* (New York: Prentice-Hall, Inc., 1951), pp. 247-346.

[7] See R. Mattessich, *Accounting and Analytical Methods* (Homewood, Ill.: R.D. Irwin, Inc., 1964); reprinted in the "Accounting Classics Series" (Houston, Texas: Scholars Book Co., 1977), especially pp. 193-205, 333-408, and 466-495.

[8] Vancouver, B.C.: The Canadian Certified General Accountants' Research Foundation, 1981. This 272-page study also offers a bibliography of over one hundred entries referring to Canada and the U.S.A.

[9] *Exposure Draft — Introduction to the Public Sector Accounting and Auditing Recommendations* (Toronto: Canadian Institute of Chartered Accountants, 1982); and *Exposure Draft — Disclosure of Accounting Policies* (Toronto: CICA, 1982).

THIS symposium reflects the diversity of present-day management accounting, and the trend toward diversification can be understood best from an evolutionary point of view. Among the many implications of this trend, the most important one seems to be the fragmentation and eventual disintegration of management accounting. The latter might happen unless some counteracting forces can be mustered which infuse greater coherence into this discipline.

MANAGEMENT ACCOUNTING: PAST, PRESENT, AND FUTURE*

by Richard Mattessich

HISTORICAL SYNOPSIS

Thus, we should begin with a glance into the past. However, this is not a paper on accounting history, and I shall restrict myself to a concise overview of the evolution of management accounting, the roots of which are to be found in the scientific management movement, in microeconomics, and, above all, in cost accounting. Indeed, there are experts who regard management accounting as cost accounting with a dash of orientation towards the decision-making processes of managers. And cost accounting, although having made its appearance almost as early as the double-entry technique, in its modern version is a typical child of the first industrial evolution, coming of age only in our century.

Up to the middle of the twentieth century, the major concerns of cost accounting were the following:

1. Measurement and analysis of manufacturing costs, of goods produced, sold, in stock, and so on, *independent* of any physical inventory taking.
2. Measurement of and improved control over product costs, departmental costs, administrative and marketing costs, by dogmatic costing procedures.
3. Implementation of highly developed cost systems evolving out of "factory cost control."[1]
4. Budgeting of costs and revenues of certain segments of the enterprise, occasionally even of the entire firm.

The fifties brought forth the advent of *Management Accounting* (W. F. Vatter's

*Reprinted from *Management Accounting 1980; Proceedings of the University of Illinois Management Accounting Symposium*, ed. H. Peter Holzer (Urbana-Champaign: University of Illinois, © 1980), pp. 209-240.

textbook of 1950 already bears the title *Management Accounting*), and with it came the harvest of seeds sown in earlier decades:

1. The broad application of cost-volume studies, break-even charts, standard costing and variance analysis for the purpose of "managerial control."
2. The flowering of direct or marginal costing.
3. The borrowing from and occasional competition with operations research,[2] as well as the introduction of mathematical, satistical, and econometric techniques.

The sixties articulated the trend begun in the preceding decade:

1. It showed a decline in the development of formal cost accounting systems.[3]
2. A shifting towards a broader application of O.R.-techniques and microeconomics, as well as the recognition of different costing procedures for different purposes.[4]
3. Paying more heed to new insights in the area of investment theory and capital budgeting.
4. Introducing electronic data processing and simulation methods to budgeting[5] and cost analysis.
5. Beginnings of "exposure control" arising from the growing external intervention in internal managerial processes.[6]

It was in the seventies that the trend of diversification accelerated under the impact of a combination of circumstances:

1. The influence of the *systems approach and cybernetics* made a more holistic view palatable, and induced management accountants to look beyond the confines of the traditional cost accounting framework. Books like Churchman's *Prediction and Optimal Decision*, *Challenge to Reason*, and *Systems Approach*,[7] may have had, in this regard, a much stronger long-term influence than many management accountants might be aware of. Management accountants began to realize that such notions as cost, efficiency, improvement, and so forth, can be defined and measured correctly only when comprehending the norms and goals of the larger social system in which management and its accounting frame is embedded. In addition to such holistic considerations, the theoretical and practical insights of cybernetics, as the theory of control and control information, may have had an indirect or informal impact on management accounting.
2. The influence of *behavioral research* upon academic accounting came about through the training of young accounting scholars in behavioral subjects and organization theory which incited them to apply the newly acquired empirical tools and methods to financial as well as to management accounting. This too forced the latter to go far beyond the boundaries of the traditional framework. The pioneering works of Argyris[8] and of Stedry[9] in the fifties undoubtedly gave the initial impetus to this behavioral-empirical movement.
3. *Electronic data processing* enabled an extension of the traditional management analaysis to new aspects of the firm, thus furthering the developement of more integrated *management information systems*. The novel models were much more complex than the old ones and, above all, were often no longer limited to the input-output aspects and the financial flows so well reflected in the traditional double classificational system. This development also led to a broadening of the technical training of future management accountants. Indeed, the new technical details to be mastered in this area are so comprehensive that they might easily jeopardize the fundamental scientific education of future management accountants.
4. The influence of microeconomics and statistical decision theory upon management accounting reinforced itself through the application of *information economics* (including "agency theory") to our discipline. This I consider one of the most significant theoretical aspects of modern management accounting, and I regret that, so far, it has not sufficiently been taken into consideration at this symposium. For this reason, I have reserved the third section of my synthesis to a discussion of the essence and objectives of this relatively new but important sub-area of our discipline.

PRESENT TRENDS OF MANAGEMENT ACCOUNTING

Systems Philosophy as the Most Basic Influence

Management accounting is an applied and purpose-oriented discipline; as such, the most appropriate frame of analysis seems to be that of systems theory and its underlying instrumental methodology and philosophy. As I have previously hinted at, it was the impact of the systems theoretic literature of Churchman, Ackoff and others which helped to liberate management accounting from its narrow traditional confines. It is no coincidence that Churchman in a primarily philosophic work *Prediction and Optimal Decision*, confesses that

> In a very general sense we are talking about managerial accounting in this book, if I understand the true intent of this term. The "profit maker" doesn't have to be the manager of a business organization. Business organizations were discussed because one can talk about them more concretely than other organizations. But the moral is general. What are the United Auto Workers trying to accomplish? Increased takehome pay, fringe benefits, old-age security, guaranteed wage, and so on, for their members. Did they make a profit last year? The question is legitimate because profit is not a word reserved only for the activities of the entrepreneur. The UAW certainly had costs. Count in its outlays for staff, and buildings, among others, as well as the time spent by its members at meetings. Count in lost work opportunity of its members. Count in, too, its "opportunity costs"—the failures to act when it could have, the delays in processing grievances. The UAW had a "return" in terms of the objectives outlined above. Is it sensible to ask for a managerial accounting system for labour organizations?[10]

But the impact of systems philosophy was by no means limited to the extension of management accounting techniques to nonprofit, government, and other nonbusiness institutions. The critical attitude of this philosophic approach led, at least in some quarters of management accounting, to a process of soul searching. Although the results of this process did not burst forth spectacularly, they emerged slowly during the ensuing decade. Apart from the broadening of its boundaries, management accounting became deeper in the sense of exploring the layers of the hierarchy of systems in which it found itself embedded. The realization that many norms and values ought to be derived from those deeper layers, though not yet universally acknowledged, has influenced scientific research, government and business practices as well as popular movements and protests (for example, against nuclear power plants and other environmental hazards). This philosophy also convinced some of us that management accounting and other applied sciences need a great deal more methodological exploration before we can expect to explain scientifically why we do what we do in such areas as technology, business, and politics.[11] All of this, I hope, has made many of us more openminded towards such issues as the discussion of "Intuition" in this symposium.[12] Today we realize that "intuition" is not necessarily the opposite of "reason" but an important ancestor and occasional rival of reason, certainly one which still plays an eminent role in business, politics, and art.

Electronic Data Processing (EDP) and MIS as the Strongest Practical Influence

EDP and MIS are not only closely related to each other but are also tied to the systems approach which embraces them like a mother her children. Nevertheless, the subject of this section is diametrically opposed to that of the preceding one. While the latter encompasses a fundamental, fairly general, and abstract philosophic area whose influence was creeping, the former is highly practice oriented, and its spectacular influence on management accounting cannot be missed by anyone. In two decades the electronic computer has pervaded all practical aspects of management accounting, those of the small business no less than those of the gigantic multinational corporation. And this influence may well continue at an accelerated pace. In the focus of every applied science are the practical instruments to be designed for relatively specific purposes. And no applied science can afford to neglect its technical aspects; thus due recognition was given in two papers included in this symposium by G. B. Davis and by J. W. Buckley and P. O'Sullivan. The paper by Davis reveals the somewhat vague and precarious relationship between management accounting and MIS, as well as the diverse views about this relationship. Davis acknowledges the strong technological bias, but also stresses the trend toward more "behavioral" and "human" aspects encountered in MIS. The paper by Buckley and O'Sullivan dealing with the relationshop between "Control Theory and Accounting" is more programmatic in nature. Apart from some historical and fundamental conceptual aspects, it pleads for the acceptance of *formal* control theory within management accounting, and thus was bound to arouse some reaction at the symposium. I have little to add to this presentation except to mention the fact that to my knowledge it was Herbert Simon who in a classic paper "On the Application of Servomechanism Theory in the Study of Production Control"[13] first introduced control theory to our discipline. I also might refer to Baetge's comprehensive effort to apply control theory to accounting and business administration.[14]

Behavioral Research as a Growing Influence

There is little doubt that the seventies brought forth the first major boom of behavioral research in accounting. And it is a special pleasure to have in our midst Professor Argyris, the scholar who started this significant trend in the early fifties. Behavioral research was crucial for the empirical-experimental development of our discipline. Previously, accounting was descriptive and analytical, at best, but with the advent of behavioral research, it has become a truly empirical science, occasionally even an experimental one. Of course, it will take some time to consolidate this kind of management accounting research, and to extract from it academically as well as practically fruitful theories; but the launching pad is now available and the first batteries of missiles have successfully been catapulted.

Whether managerial accounting will benefit more from this behavioral trend than financial accounting is difficult to assess at this stage. The first contributions—of Argyris[15] and Stedry[16]—certainly grew out of management accounting, and the impression of many of us during the sixties was that behavioral accounting research would belong predominantly to this area. This did not prove to be the case; on the contrary, behavioral research in financial accounting has become more abundant than in managerial accounting. But this might be a passing shift, and there seems to be little doubt that behavioral research in management accounting has a good potential to further grow in depth and breadth. That it fits well into the holistic, systems theoretic trend of our discipline is illustrated by Professor Argyris' present paper.

The Shifting Influence of Operations Research (OR)

During the fifties and early sixties, various subareas of OR exercised a strong influence upon management accounting. Many of us took it for granted that this would be a continuing influence. However, there seems to be sufficient evidence that this expectation did not materialize. Perhaps the reason lies in the general reaction which OR experienced during the seventies. Even operations researchers or former OR-experts admit this reaction openly. Let me quote Ackoff who together with Churchman and Arnoff[17] wrote the first best selling textbook of OR:

> In my opinion, American Operations Research is dead even though it has yet to be buried. I also think there is little chance for its resurrection because there is so little understanding of the reasons for its demise. (p. 1)
> . . . By the mid 60s it had gained widespread acceptance in academic circles. In my opinion this gain was accompanied by a loss of its pioneering spirit, its sense of mission, and its innovativeness. Survival, stability, and respectability took precedence over development, and its decline began. . . (p. 2)
> . . . As a result OR came to be identified with the use of mathematical models and algorithms rather than the ability to formulate management problems, solve them, and implement and maintain their solutions in turbulent environments. . . (p. 3)
> . . . I submit that OR was once a corporate staff function because corporate executives believed it could be useful to them. It was pushed down because they no longer believed this to be the case, and they correctly perceived that if it had any use it was in the bowels of the organization, not the head. My observation of a large number of American corporations reveals that when it could no longer be pushed down, it was pushed out. . . (p. 4)

. . . Systems are wholes which lose their essential properties when taken apart. Therefore, they are wholes which cannot be understood by analysis. This realization, in turn, gave rise to synthetic or systems thinking. Three steps are involved in this process. First, a thing to be understood is conceptualized as a part of one or more larger wholes, not as a whole to be taken apart. Then understanding of the larger containing system is sought. Finally, the system to be understood is explained in terms of its role or function in the containing system. Analysis of a system reveals its structure and how it works; it yields know-how, not understanding. It does not explain *why* a system works the way it does. Systems thinking is required for this. . . (p. 8)

. . . The universe that appears to be mechanistic when sliced by cause-and-effect, appears to be *teleological* when sliced by producer-product. Moreover, the teleology revealed is *objective*; it makes it possible to operationally define, observe, and measure such phenomena as free-will, choice, function, role, and purpose. Systems thinking, expansionism, and objective teleology provide the intellectual foundation for what I believe can justifiably be called the *Systems Age*. The world-view they yield does not discard that of the Machine Age but incorporates it as a special case. Machines are understood as purposeful systems and purposeful systems are no longer conceptualized as machines. The Post Industrial Revolution is as logical a consequence of systems thinking as the Industrial Revolution was of mechanistic thinking.[18]

I fully subscribe to Ackoff's assertion which strongly supports my own remark that "the recent infatuation of many administrative scientists with mathematics might give way to a greater concern with philosophic issues. . ." "*Systems analysis is about to play the same stimulating role for the philosophy of the second half of the twentieth century as evolution theory did for the second half of the nineteenth century.*"[19] In the light of Ackoff's remarks, it may not be surprising that also at this symposium, the pertinent OR contribution by Professor Cooper does not refer to a business application but to one concerning government agencies and a "national goals accounting system;" it does, furthermore, not concern a narrow technique but one with broad application to "accountability, audit and evaluation," opening new ways to "efficiency measurement." Thus, this paper too might fall in line with the more holistic systems outlook than with the atomistic viewpoint of typical operations research.

As to the specific OR-applications to management accounting, R. S. Kaplan has provided an excellent and comprehensive survey referring to more than eighty publications.[20] In this survey, he discusses the most important quantitative models and studies belonging to the following six major areas: (1) Cost-Volume-Profit Analysis, (2) Performance Evaluation and Variance Analysis, (3) Variance Investigations, (4) Cost Behavior (fixed and variable), (5) Cost Allocations (reciprocal service department costs, depreciation and capital investment and overhead costs), and (6) Transfer Pricing. In the concluding remarks, Kaplan notes the usefulness of quantitative models to management accounting due to the fact that these models "greatly aided our ability to think about these issues correctly."[21] Indeed, so far the benefit of OR-application in our discipline lies predominantly in the area of conceptual clarification. And it is mainly for this reason that we agree with Kaplan's expressive regret that current textbooks (with the exception of the one by Dopuch, Birnberg, and Demski[22]) have not attempted to integrate quantitative methods with cost and managerial accounting. Kaplan's prediction that "managerial or cost accounting textbooks will begin to adopt the integrated approach taken by Dopuch, Birnberg, and Demski (1974) and start to discard the piecemeal ostrich-like approach," may well come true during the eighties. But Kaplan too is not overly optimistic as regards future prospects to match past achievements in this area. He hopes or at least desires that the next decade will produce applied research, demonstrating that the OR-models or management accounting do have practical usefulness, and revealing further areas still to be explored.

THE SIGNIFICANCE OF INFORMATION ECONOMICS FOR MANAGEMENT ACCOUNTING

General Background

During the sixties and seventies, the notion of ''information'' moved into the foreground; it permeated all areas of business administration and particularly academic accounting. the major task of management accounting is now conceived as the designing of efficient information systems serving certain managerial needs among which *performance control* and *simulation* of alternative scenarios predominate. The growing eminence of ''information'' was due to the impact of EDP and the MIS-approach rather than due to any theoretical development in economics. But in the sixties, information economics[23] was just ready to put rigorous tools at the disposal of young management accounting researchers to tackle the task of evaluating alternative information systems by analytical means. Thus for the first time, it became possible to formulate scientific criteria for determining the value of a specific information as well as the value of an entire information system. Such a criterion obviously is a prerequisite for comparing the efficiency of various management information systems and for selecting the most satisfactory one among them. Furthermore, this approach enables us to analyze many fascinating aspects of management information systems by means of greatly enriched decision-theoretical models.

I have the impression that this important subarea of accounting is still insufficiently appreciated by many management accountants, in spite of the fact that it might be of greater relevance to managerial than to financial accounting. Indeed, the fact that it has only been mentioned fleetingly in one or the other of the papers at this symposium proves my suspicion and furthermore compels me to outline, at this late stage, the relation between information economics and management accounting, and to sketch the development of recent research in this border area. But before doing so, let me add that the blame for this relative neglect lies partly with the information economists themselves. They seem to be among the best mathematicians in the accounting profession, and as such are prone to be somewhat aloof; thus, they may not have taken enough time, trouble, and care to translate their objectives and research results into a language understandable to most academic accountants. But there is hope that this deficiency will be remedied in the not too distant future. Feltham and Demski, the two leading pioneers in this area, are presently preparing a new issue in the Accounting Research Series of the AAA designed to review recent research in information economics and its implication for accounting. Futhermore, a textbook on *The Analysis of Management Accounting Information* is presently being written by Butterworth and Amershi. Furthermore, it must be admitted that the results of this research area have hardly attained practical applicability. Nevertheless, management accounting cannot afford to ignore this important theoretical development.

Distinction and Cooperation between Analytical and Behavioral Research

Academic accounting, including of course, management accounting, has reached a stage in which the specialization between the empiricist and the analytical accountant has become better discernible than it was several decades ago. During the sixties, *analytical or a priori* accounting tried to establish itself as a legitimate area of specialization. It is today distinct from empirical or behavioral accounting, in a similar way as theoretical physics is distinct from experimental physics, or as basic medical research is distinct from clinical research. This emancipation of analytical accounting was facilitated by two events, first by what Carl Nelson called the ''golden age of a *priori* research in accounting'' during the sixties (for more details see Mattessich[24]), and second by the somewhat later advent of genuine behavioral research in accounting. Without the latter, this process of mutual emancipation and polarization of those two areas of specialization would hardly have been possible. Although specialization harbors many dangers, it might be of great benefit to accounting. The three prerequisites are the following:

1. Analytical and empirical accountants would have to model their collaboration on the cooperative and fruitful teamwork encountered between theoretical and experimental physicists, astronomers, and other natural scientists;
2. For economic, methodological, and pedagogical reasons, analytical and behavioral accounting research will have to be integrated into a coherent overall framework of accounting theory;
3. The theoretical achievements must be practice oriented and must find ultimate application.

This will not merely require a more realistic and *instrumental* attitude on the part of the theoreticians,[25] but also a great deal of theoretical insight and goodwill on the part of practitioners.

There can be no doubt that "information economics accounting" is the direct descendent of the *a priori* research which pioneered rigorous analytical thinking in accounting during the late fifties and the sixties. But as the former has been advanced by a new generation of accountants, one thoroughly trained in mathematical economics, econometrics, statistics and decision theory, and other quantitative techniques, the approach is somewhat different from that of the sixties, and a father-and-son dichotomy is clearly discernible. While our generation (the older one) was concerned with a search for the basic assumptions and consequences underlying the typical accounting framework, the younger generation of analytical accountants is prone to disregard the double-classificational aspects and thus the traditional and peculiar features of the accounting framework. Their search is for details and specific consequences of the information economic model and its practical application to those tasks which, so far, the typical accounting model has fulfilled. Most of these researchers seem to distrust the double classificational input-output model and aim less towards fundamental improvement of the traditional deterministic accounting measures than towards establishing new concepts requiring many stochastic measures.[26] From an economics point of view, their activity belongs to "normal science" in the sense of Thomas Kuhn[27] because it is a puzzle-solving activity that fills many gaps and enriches the deductive framework of economic-statistical decision theory which dominates modern economics. But from the accounting viewpoint, it might have to be considered as "revolutionary scientific" activity in the Kuhnian sense because it introduces a paradigm into our discipline which, at least for accounting, must be regarded as quite novel. This paradigm, in my view, is to be found in the search for *analytical, probabilistic procedures* capable of determining the optimal or satisfactory *accounting-information structure required for a specific task*. Although the desirability of such a goal is hardly new, until recently no theory has been available that could accomplish such a task in any analytical and rigorous fashion. Since Jacob Marschak and others created the foundation of such a theory for economics, the legitimate and urgent question has arisen whether, and if so, to what extent this theory is applicable to accounting, and which further enrichments are required to adapt it to the many detailed problems and questions posed by a relatively practical discipline such as ours. This challenge has been taken up by a group of young accountants during the second half of the sixties and has been brought to some preliminary fruition, harboring further promises for the future. And one should assume that such an achievement is a matter of joy and pride to every scientifically oriented accountant.

Cost Determination from a Novel Point of View

But why is this trend of particular relevance to management accounting? To explain this, I should like to put special emphasis on Demski and Feltham's book on *Cost Determination: A Conceptual Approach*.[28] This work, so far, is the most comprehensive statement of "information economics accounting" and its foundations; its title reveals the relevance to cost and managerial accounting but not its information economics ancestry. Demski and Feltham aim at the development of a conceptual scheme for the evaluation of information and measurement alternatives. Thus, these authors are concerned with the optimal or, at least, satisfactory choice of the right information and information source under various personal and impersonal constraints and dependencies. Thereby special attention is paid to the distinction between the choices to be made by the accountant and those to be made by the entrepreneur (in contrast to previous publications by Feltham[29] and Demski and Feltham[30] where only the accountant, as a decision-maker, is explicitly recognized). Now the accountant must make information decisions, such as the choice of the pertinent accounting system, which not only concern his own actions, but also those of the entrepreneur. However, the reaction of the latter are exogenously specified and are here not yet taken into consideration within the model itself. Some preliminary insight into this kind of analysis may be gained by comparing three *major phases in the evolution of management accounting*.

1. *The historical communication approach* which, according to Demski and Feltham, dominated the accounting literature until the early sixties and still is encountered in theory and practice. Its hallmark lies in the attempt *to announce dogmatically a unique set of rules for measuring costs* whereby the most frequently used basis is that of historical or acquisition cost. Hence, the matching principle (of financial accounting) and the predominance of allocation over valuation, as well as the belief into *absolute* and global cost measures, are the major characteristics of this approach.

2. *The user decision-model approach* which came into bloom with the advent of Management Accounting, although its origin can be traced to the twenties. It is a more specific and purpose-oriented method which constructs different cost and decision models for diverse decision categories, such as investment, or pricing, or production decisions. Since those models are frequently based on microeconomic theory and operations research, the principles of *opportunity costs* and of *marginal costing* often play a dominant role. Thus the notion of absolute truth of the preceding approach is abandoned, and a *relative* truth notion is promulgated under Clark's slogan of "different costs for different purposes."[31] In spite of this more enlightened view and several related improvements, this approach is no less rejected by Demski and Feltham, for in their view both approaches suffer from the following three basic defects:

> First, truth—even if desirable— cannot be obtained without incurring a cost. Measurement consumes resources. Hence, consideration of measurement cost must be an integral component of any theory of cost measurement. Of course, the two approaches do imply cost-benefit tests. The historical communications approach is based on the belief that differentiating among users is not worthwhile, whereas the user decision model approach is based on the belief that such differentiation is worthwhile. The difficulty, however, is that cost-benefit analysis is not an integral, explicit part of either approach.
>
> Second, users operate in an uncertain world and explicit recognition of uncertainty casts doubt on the concept of a true cost, which implicitly presumes a certain world. As developed in Chapter 2, under uncertainty, a cost measure's value does not derive from how closely it represents an abstract concept but rather the state partition it induces. Hence, whether one measure or another is closer to, say, marginal cost is largely immaterial; the relevant question is what each reveals about an uncertain future.
>
> Third, the concept of a true cost (whether conditional or absolute) is likely to be both illusory and irrelevant in a multiperson world. Two people in an organization are likely to possess different beliefs and tastes and therefore may react differently to particular measurements. Furthermore, communication between them may involve distortion or bluffing, such as when a manager communicates "tight" cost standards to a subordinate.[32]

Thus the new "information evaluation approach" is claimed to be superior because (1) it incorporates *a systematic cost benefit analysis* of managerial accounting itself; (2) it takes into consideration *uncertainty* by operating with stochastic models; and (3) it introduces two *subjective functions, that is, the preference function as well as the belief function,* and carries the realization of the cost concept that began in management accounting to its logical conclusion, abandoning even the conditional notion of a "true cost."

The Analysis of Simplifications and Further Aspects

From the point of view of theoretical analysis, it will be difficult to disagree with this claim of superiority, but from a practical point of view, the critical question concerns the extent to which stochastic models, systematic cost benefit analysis, subjective preference, and belief functions can be employed in field work. However, the theoretical insights of this new, analytical approach are promising enough to promote it, even without any great chance of immediate application in actual practice. The first benefit accrues in form of an original analysis that not only introduces the distinction between the *modification* and the *simplification* of an information evaluation model but, above all, tries to investigate to what extent such modifications and simplifications of the pure or ideal model are meaningful.

Modifications (which lead to the same optimal actions as the ideal model) are encountered in cases of aggregation and multi-period problems, while typical *simplifications* of cost determination (which lead to less than optimal actions, hence deviations from the results of the ideal model) consist of various substitutions: for example, substituting linear for nonlinear cost functions, deterministic for stochastic parameters, standardized distribution functions for nonstandardized ones, as well as neglecting risk attitudes, and so on. To my mind, however, the most frequently encountered simplifications are substitutions of historic costs for market values, or for present values. As imaginative as this analysis and its mathematical presentation is, it suffers from a major weakness. As the modified and simplified models are the decision maker's result of substituting the detailed action variables or state variables through surrogate variables and parameters, one would expect from such an analysis some insight into the formal and material relations between ideal model and simplified model. In other words, the ultimate goal of such an analysis should be the *deductive* inference of the simplified system from the ideal system on the basis of the major constraints encountered in a specific situation. The revelation of such inferences *per se* would be a formidable task, even if one would know what the ideal model looks like, but in most cases that knowledge too is elusive. A further criticism refers to the previously mentioned self-imposed restriction of the Demski and Feltham[33] approach, as pointed out by Baiman:

> However, unless one allows the user's decisions to be optimal responses to the chosen managerial accounting and control system one can gain little insight into the behavioral implications of the accounting system. A more complete analysis would allow all individuals affected by the choice of the accounting system to react to it rationally. In particular, what each person takes as given in making his own decision should be consistent with optimizing behavior on the part of all persons.[34]

According to Baiman, even a team-theoretic approach *à la* Marschak and Radner which starts from a single objective, would not reveal the *motivational* role of managerial accounting and control systems. Thus, there exist several basic gaps in this kind of analysis. And if we are grateful to our information economics accountants for having shown us the first steps in the right direction, we should not close our eyes to the fact that the major task, of matching *analytically* a given information purpose to its proper system structure, is still an unsolved issue.

A great merit of the Demski and Feltham analysis lies in stressing that costs and values are the result of actions and preferences, and that the determination of these costs in turn facilitates and influences the choice of actions.[35] Accordingly, they distinguish between three types of cost determination: (1) specification of the cost components of the objective function; (2) communication of cost information from the accountant to the entrepreneur; and (3) processing of cost information. Further contributions are the following: (a) analysis of production functions as basis for cost functions, thus revealing the many necessary conditions rarely given in actual practice. This shows how complex the situation becomes when one attempts to apply such cost determination to the construction of conventional cost functions. (b) Presenting alternatives of (simplified) cost determination in short-term cost analyses through specific examples (aggregation problems, linear approximation, approximation to step-functions, decision decomposition, cost allocation, long-term average cost functions, problems of machine replacement and amortization, suppression of uncertainty, and such). All this enhances one's awareness that neither costs nor methods of cost determination can be labeled as true or false, since both are context dependent—what is correct or acceptable in one situation may be incorrect or unacceptable in another. (c) An attempt to extend this two-person analysis to a truly multiperson analysis involving persons external to the firm: the difficulties hereby encountered (for example, due to the interpersonal aggregation of preference functions as expressed in Arrow's incompleteness theorem[36]) offers *a strong hint that information economics may, indeed, be more beneficial to managerial* than to financial accounting, at least as long as the multiperson analysis cannot overcome those basic obstacles.

Of course, "information economics accounting" is neither a two-man show nor a one-book affair, and due recognition must also be given to other authors and publications of which those in the bibliography are merely a representative sample. The major topics falling under the heading of the information evaluation may now be summarized as follows:

1. The evaluation of specific information as well as of entire information systems, and the choice of satisfactory or optimal management accounting systems by enriched models of statistical decision theory.
2. An analysis of diverse factors influencing the value of information, such as accuracy (see, for example, Hilton, Swieringa and Hoskin[37]), degree of aggregation, relevance, and timeliness.
3. An examination of evaluation techniques and application of sensitivity analysis, bounds on information values, decision analysis, user questionnaires, and potentiality of prediction.
4. Information and performance evaluation in a *multiperson and multiperiod context under competitive and cooperative conditions*. Recent works by Itami,[38] Demski and Feltham,[39] and Feltham and Matsumura[40] are pointing in this direction. While Itami, as well as Demski and Feltham, examine budgeting situations in which the focus is on the control relation between foreman or department head, on one side, and top budgeting director or management, on the other, Feltham and Matsumura refer to the agency theory of Jensen and Meckling [41] which focuses on the control relationship between management as an agent and the shareholders as the principal.
5. Various subproblems and refinements of the preceding items, such as the problem of private versus public information in capital markets and similar situations, evaluation of optimal strategies of investigating various performance measures, auditing such measures under various circumstances (where management has direct influence upon the choice of auditors or on audit performance, for example), lack of superior information affecting shareholders as well as management, situations where management has access to additional information between the time of management contract and choice of managerial action, or where management's actions affect effort and risk characteristics of outcome, and so on.

Of course, the application of information economics to management accounting is not the only area somewhat neglected at this symposium. A series of topics which in recent years has found attention in the pertinent literature ought to be mentioned in this connection: cost allocation problems, human resource accounting, the agency theory, the contingency theory (of organizational behavior as applied to accounting—see Hayes,[42] and Tiessen and Waterhouse[43]) and even "zero-based budgeting." It is true that some of these areas are either more of practical than theoretical interest (zero-based budgeting), and others have been subsumed under the general topic of behavioral research (contingency theory), but some areas (human resource accounting) might have deserved separate treatment. Among these, the agency theory of Jensen and Meckling[44] and its elaboration and adaptation to management accounting seems to be especially noteworthy.

The Agency Theory as a Potential Basis for an Analytical Theory of Management Accounting

The basic ideas of what is nowadays called the "agency theory" are found in Jensen and Meckling's renowned article.[45] These ideas constitute *a theory of the firm* capable of taking into account the motivational behavior of managers, the management costs and, under certain circumstances, the ownership structure of the capital employed in the firm. This theory is an attempt not only to overcome the bloodless "market theory of the firm" of traditional economics, but also to successfully compete with alternative attempts of conceiving a meaningful behavioral theory of the firm, as advanced by O. E. Williamson, Baumol, Cyert and March, and others. The Jensen and Meckling theory has had an astonishing impact upon business economists, and especially upon young analytical accounting researchers, but many of the pertinent papers are, at this time, still unpublished working papers or dissertations. A comprehensive survey of those unpublished as well as published contributions[46] is offered by Baiman.[47]

The main concern of the agency theory is with "control and information relations" manifested in the search for the most preferred feasible contract[48] between *principal* (owner, shareholder, superior, or even insurer) and his *agent* (management, department head, subordinate, or the insured) who may enter with each other into one among alternative contracts. The agency contract delegates to the agent the responsibility to manage an entity (firm, department, workplace, or other risk situation expected to yield a return or *outcome*) in compensation for a share in the outcome. Depending on the contract or *sharing rule*, the agent's share may range from a fixed remuneration to a percentage of the total outcome and eventual penalties for imperfect fulfillment of the contract, thus transferring more or less of the enterprise risk to the agent. Although both principal and agent are assumed to be profit and/or utility maximizers aiming toward a common goal, their particular interests are likely to conflict since the agent may tend to maximize his own utility at the cost of the principal's profit (by not being efficient, active, or honest enough). Thus, an information or management accounting system is required (1) to inform principal and agent about the total outcome, and (2) eventually to supply further information signals to principal and/or agent at various stages to facilitate the agent's task as well as of monitoring the agent's activity by the principal. In cases where the principal can observe the agent's activity, there is *no moral hazard involved* ("first best solutions"), and the optimal sharing rule lies in a fixed remuneration of the agent with penalties on the agent whenever the principal's information reveals the agent's imperfect conformance to the contract (cost and frequency of monitoring can be reduced, up to a point, by increasing the agent's penalty provided the information is perfect enough to avoid unjustified penalties). But usually the monitoring activity is too costly, and thus the agent is left to act in his own interest ("second best solutions"). Thus the ultimate share going to principal, on one side, and to the agent, on the other, might not only depend on the total outcome but also on the particular information available to principal and agent respectively.

The agency theory is many things to many people, but as hinted at above, it may be regarded as the natural extension and continuation of the application of information economics to management accounting. At least, this theory fits nicely into the general program of information economics, since the valuation of information systems plays a decisive role in agency theory. Indeed, it is within this framework that finally a differentiation between the objectives of the principal (for instance, the shareholders) and the agent (management) is incorporated as an integral part of the theory. In this way, information economics accountants are able to analyze important *motivational aspects* (such as manifested in the different preferences for different accounting systems among managers versus owners) and also to test the "multiperson rationality" of the agency theory on traditional accounting practice or, perhaps, *vice versa* to criticize practice in the light of this new theory.

Of course, the agency theory offers primarily an *analytical* framework that roots in utility or profit maximization as well as in the remaining paraphernalia of neoclassical economics, together with statistical decision and game theory and the related rationality assumptions. Therefore this theory is unlikely to reconcile the dichotomy between what Alfred Whitehead so aptly called the "simple-minded scholar" and the "muddle headed scholar." *The gulf between the analytical, economics-oriented accountant, on one side, and the more pragmatic academic accountant, on the other, might thus rather be widened in future.* Yet this theory may strengthen another no less important bond, that between the *analytical* and the *behavioral* accounting scholar. The need for such a theory is genuine because of the theory's considerable potential for putting management accounting into a broader and, above all, more coherent context, for offering a more rigorous presentation, and for clarifying important analytical as well as behavioral aspects. In question is only the impact of the accruing ultimate results. In other words, will those results be truly revolutionary, or will they be fairly self-evident and thus merely enable better confirmation of what we have known all along. Even the latter is a worthwhile task, but it is the hope for the former that makes our hearts beat faster. Finally, one should also face the most pessimistic alternative according to which those results would turn out to be merely the residual of an increasingly sophisticated analysis which has long passed its point of diminishing marginal return—though in science that "marginal return" can often be evaluated correctly only decades or centuries later. Since the ever increasing complexity of economic models is sooner or later bound to lead into the realm of decreasing incremental benefit, all those competing possibilities seem to us, at present, of fairly equal likelihood, perhaps somewhat biased in favor of the second alternative of better confirming previously gained insights. Apart from two things, the impressive ingenuity of building intricate models and the scholarly rigor of argumentation, so far, the major achievement of the agency theory lies indeed in demonstrating that ''the procedures advocated in the managerial accounting literature and the philosophy which generates them are consistent with the results of agency theory.''[49] This means that aside from some adjustment (such as for taking into consideration optimal risk sharing between principal and agent), the *principles of traditional responsibility accounting* (according to which ''a manager's performance should be judged on the basis of only those items subject to his control,''[50]) are confirmed by the agency theory as useful guidelines for designing accounting systems. It also means that the major instruments of management accounting, such as periodic budgeting, standard costing with variance analysis, and so on, can be regarded as constituting a ''Pareto-efficient contract.'' One of the most crucial tasks, however, has hardly begun, that of relating this impressive ''economic theory'' for management accountants to the daily purpose-oriented details of academic management accounting theory proper (which consists in the formation and testing of specific purpose-oriented hypotheses about realization, valuation, allocation, classification, and so forth). To our mind, a prerequisite for the emergence of an instrumentally useful management accounting theory is the connecting of the latter object-area to the meta-area of the agency theory.

SPECULATIONS ABOUT THE FUTURE

Fragmentation or Unification?

Since Adam Smith's famous book,[51] economists and laymen have greatly increased their awareness of the advantages of specialization and the division of labor. And practitioners as well as scientists have applied specialization with great benefit; indeed, there is little indication that this trend has come to a halt. The progressive accumulation of knowledge makes further diversification inevitable, and in spite of its inherent dangers, it would be in vain to plead against it. Thus the accompanying danger of fragmentation has to be counteracted in a different fashion. The ideal solution would be to link the individual fragments or topics of management accounting to each other in a way similar to the impressive integration of the many diverse areas of physics and chemistry. But I harbor little hope that our discipline is ready for such a feat. For this reason I should like to present to you a more realistic solution for overcoming the dangers of fragmentation.

First of all, we should recognize that present-day management accounting consists of two major areas which I should like to distinguish by labeling the first *the object area*, and the second, the *meta-area* of management accounting (this distinction should not be confused with the more frequently encountered distinction between object language and meta-language). The object area comprises relatively well-defined objectives such as efficiency control, performance evaluation, optimizing and satisficing of goals and subgoals, budgeting and budget simulation, and so forth *under a given set of goals and environmental constraints*. All these objectives pivot on the *input-output relations* of the entity to be managed; and it is for this reason that the *double classification model* forms the core of these basically atomistic object models. Thus this area is also concerned with the general and specific assumptions about the aggregation, classification, realization, valuation, and similar aspects.

The meta-area, in contrast, deals with the normative as well as positive aspects of the environment in which those object models are embedded. *It neither regards the goals nor all constraints as endogenous variables*, but examines interrelations of environmental and thus behavioral influences upon changing goals and constraints.[52] Here one aims toward the construction of more holistic models and thus has to observe the multidimensionality of a truly comprehensive outlook. For this reason not only the physical but also the conceptual environment plays a decisive role. *Sooner or later accountants will be compelled to observe a more precise semantics*, one that recognizes, for example, a hierarchical order in which *accounting systems* merely constitute a subset of *accountability systems* (for example, a military commander is accountable for the reckless exposure of his troops, and a murderer is accountable for his criminal deed; but in all these cases, the accountability exists outside of any accounting system). Similarly, accounting systems may be regarded as subsets of control systems, the latter as subsets of information systems, and so on. Therefore a *general* concern with control systems or information systems lies outside accounting proper. The attempt to substitute meta-models for object models, although occasionally encountered among the young turks of accounting research, seems to us doomed to failure in managerial accounting; what we need is not substitution but complementation of the latter by the former. This insight alone could go far in keeping a tight check on the centrifugal forces within our discipline. Because, on one side, it would enable us to derive the input-output models of management accounting from the basic assumptions of the general accounting framework through specific interpretations; and on the other side, it would offer a picture of behavioral and social influences acting upon management accounting and determining those specific interpretations. For decades I have been pleading for a systematic separation of *uninterpreted (or semi-interpreted) calculus of accounting* (as presented by Mattessich[53]) and *specific purpose-oriented interpretations*. Although I am no longer alone in regarding this as the only realistic solution towards a general theory of accounting (combining a firm basis with great flexibility as to a variety of information purposes), and in spite of the fact that a pertinent article[54] received wide recognition through the AICPA literature award, my plea has fallen on deaf ears as far as the most important relevant publication is concerned: the reader of the AAA-Report on *Statement on Accounting Theory and Theory Acceptance* == is left with the impression that its authors were not even aware that many academic disciplines (from physics to probability theory) had solved the thorny problem of constructing a general theory by clearly distinguishing between a common basis or uninterpreted calculus, on one side, and further interpretations on the other. Had SATTA paid more attention to this crucial issue, it might well have assumed a less pessimistic and more constructive attitude; then it would also have admitted that a general theory need not comprise all possible interpretations, but merely the features common to *all* accounting systems together with "place-holders" for interpretations.

What are the Conditions of a General Theory?

First of all, a general theory of management accounting would itself constitute a fragment of a more comprehensive theory. To benefit from the economic advantages of the scientific approach and to avoid unnecessary fragmentation, we should attempt to derive our theory of management accounting by means of interpretations of a truly general theory of accounting comprising all micro- and macro-areas of our discipline. The individual object models would then be attained by further and more specific interpretations. But in order to choose the correct interpretations, we are in need of the previously mentioned meta-models of our discipline. I thus envisage this subdiscipline of management accounting as an intersection and interaction of two comprehensive frameworks, one that provides the basic assumptions and theorems of the input-output model characteristic for *all* accounting systems, and the other supplying the more or less *specific interpretations* to those basic assumptions on the basis of shifting social norms and other environmental constraints. This kind of integration seems to me the first precondition for preventing further fragmentation.

A second condition lies in the awareness of the advantages of a more unified system of management accounting. I have previously hinted at the economic advantages which follow from *preventing* costly and unnecessary repetitions in all these subareas through the creation of a common uninterpreted or semi-interpreted calculus. But this economic advantage may, in our discipline at least, not be as decisive as the pedagogical and methodological benefits inherent in such a common basis. Without such a common basis, accounting as an independent discipline may no longer have a *raison d'être*. A dissolution not only of the superdiscipline of accounting, but also of such subdisciplines as management accounting, might be the natural consequence. Whether the regrouping of these areas into a classificational scheme with novel academic disciplines is desirable or not, is difficult to judge at this stage. But as an accountant who prefers an evolutionary to a cataclysmic development of his discipline, I may be permitted to defend my own value judgements.

A third condition lies in the general awareness of the nature of the double-classification model. The neglect which this model has suffered in the hands of the younger generation of academic accountants may be explained by two factors. The first is a natural reaction to what they regard as a symbol of the past, representing mere description without any analytical challenge. The second, not unrelated to the first, lies in a misunderstanding of the nature of the double-classificational model. They regard it as an occasionally convenient but purely coincidental classification device, thereby overlooking the empirical and general "physical" foundation underlying this conception.

In my view, the double classification principle has its ultimate root (though not its historical justification) in the *law of conservation* (of matter and energy), the *first* law of thermodynamics. And it is much more than a coincidence that *Heisenberg's S-Matrix Theory* and the various *gauge theories of particle physics* are nowadays recognized as "accounting systems of nature." Thereby many interactions between nuclear and subnuclear particles are precisely accounted for, such that in terms of energy equivalents (including such properties as electrical charge, spin, and so on), the total output equals its total input. It may sound farfetched to bring consideration of physics into management accounting, but it seems much less so if the *second* law of thermodynamics, the *Law of Entropy*, is also taken into consideration. Georgescu-Roegen reminds us that the law of entropy is an *economic* and not a mechanistic law of nature, that "our whole economic life feeds on low entropy,"[56] that "the basic nature of the economic process is entropic and that the Entropy Law rules supreme over this process and over its evolution."[57] Through this law the total (thermal) energy of the universe is separated into two disinct categories: (i) the *free* or *available* energy for activating change and (ii) the *bounded* or *"wasted" energy* which no longer is available to instigate any kind of change or transformation.

CONCLUSION

All this leads to a series of insights which in the long run cannot be ignored by management accountants.

1. In a closed system the free energy is becoming scarcer with the passage of time while the wasted energy and thus the entropy are constantly increasing.
2. Our production and service activities are all transformation processes in which some free energy is converted into some bounded energy at an *accelerated* rate. In other words, all of man's economic activity speeds up nature's conversion of free into bounded energy.
3. In the face of such insights, man can no longer be regarded as a producer of goods and services; he is merely a converter of energy from one form into another through "wasteful" processes.[58]
4. Market prices can no longer be regarded as a rational basis for valuation, at least not insofar as nonrenewable resources are concerned because such market prices are based on demand and short-term supply which neglects long-range scarcities.
5. What management accountants regard as "profit" in the extraction of nonrenewable resources, constitutes, to a considerable extent, *not income but capital consumption* when looked at from a long-term macro point of view.
6. Thus the accountant's notions of equilibrium between total inputs and outputs, his distinction between flows and stocks, cost and capital, income and expenses, and so on, have their ultimate roots in the first two laws of thermodynamics.

A further link between physics and management accounting is found in *the information notion.* Since entropy can be interpreted as a measure of disorganization (the greater the proportion of bounded to free energy within a system, the greater its entropy or degree of disorganization) the inverse notion of *negentropy* can be interpreted as a measure of the *degree of organization* as well as of the *degree of information.*[59] This provides a link to biology which exploits the information notion of communication theory for illuminating the processes of cell division and the production of enzymes and other proteins. To regard the sequence of the purines and pyrimidines of a specific DNA-structure as a sequence of signals conveying "meaningful" information, is much more than a mere analogy to human information transmission. Nevertheless, questions arise: (1) To what extent does the information notion used in management accounting (such as in information economics accounting) deviate from the information notion of biology? (2) Is it possible to reconcile these two information concepts for the purpose of a systems theory satisfying the needs of both disciplines?

As far as I can see, the fundamental difference between these two information notions lies in the information economists' assertion that only those data constitute information that are capable of changing the belief (that is, the probability distribution) of the information recipient. But how could the DNA-molecule of a chromosome change the belief in the information recipient which might be some RNA-molecules, the task of which is to initiate the production of some enzymes or other proteins? How can we explain this dischotomy? Is it a mere breakdown of analogy? Or should information economists change their conception of information? Or are we using one and the same term for two entirely different phenomena? Yet these two information notions can easily be reconciled as soon as information economists admit that a change in belief does not constitute the ultimate criterion of information but merely an intermediate one. Belief is a special kind of disposition that sooner or later results in an *action* which therefore must be regarded as the ultimate criterion. And this information-induced action is encountered in economics and management accounting no less than in biochemistry. To the surprise and possible shock of some accountants, one could mention many more basic connections between the natural sciences and management accounting. For example, there is the fascinating, and for economists and management accountants highly relevant, disclosure of the Nobel laureat Manfred Eigen (1971) that the most primitive life processes already possess a *division of labor in which the tasks of information and legislation are exercised by the DNA-structures while the evaluative-executive tasks are fulfilled by the protein structures in such a way that* (depending on the survival and propagation potential of the organism) a *"value function" can be attributed to new information*[60] (for example, caused by a mutation). If I mention such instances, it is merely to indicate that management accountants might do well in future *not* to restrict their vision to the social environment in which their discipline is embedded, but also to study its interrelations with the more basic sciences. I firmly believe that out of this much enlightenment would accrue, and I sincerely hope that such broader perspective and a more holistic outlook will become a major trait of our discipline in the remaining two decades of this waning century.

This, however, does not mean that we should abandon the practice orientation of our discipline. Indeed, this orientation is presently not at all what it ought to be; it calls for much improvement. At the end of my synthesis I cannot be silent about a glaring contradiction staring into our faces. On the one side, we on this continent have developed the most sophisticated management accounting and control theories that mankind has ever possessed; on the other side, we daily witness a lack of adequate control that pervades the entire fabric of our society. From the failure of top management to control the work attitude of employees, to frustrated shareholders who are powerless to control a management that no longer regards shareholders as *de facto* owners of the company but merely as a necessary evil for procuring cheap capital, and finally to governments who squander the wealth of their constituents by the most wasteful spending practices and inflationary policies, almost everywhere some breakdown of control systems is evident. What has happened to management accounting and social controls in actual practice? Have they become mere instruments of pretense? Have these controls been wrested out of the hands of those for whose benefit they were designed? Or have the controls themselves become cancerous and gone out of control because of too much bureaucracy and information overload? The fact that on other continents different and often simpler management accounting practices and control measures have led to much higher efficiency, should make us pause and contemplate some serious questions. What has gone wrong? And why are we toiling to improve management accounting? Is *complexity* the crux of our dilemma? Or do we have to conclude that without ethical restraints and a sufficiently strong moral basis, a social control mechanism can operate, in the longrun, neither properly nor to the satisfaction of all parties concerned?

FOOTNOTES

1. See Gordon Shillinglaw, "Old Horizons and New Frontiers: The Future of Managerial Accounting" (1980).
2. R. Mattessich, "Operations Research and Accounting: Competitors or Partners?" *Review of Economics and Business* (August 1961): 7-14.
3. L. J. Benninger, "Cost Accounting" in *Handbook of Business Administration,* ed. H. B. Maynard (New York: McGraw-Hill, 1967), p. 10.21.
4. Compare with the development of cost accounting in Central Europe. See Hanns-Martin W. Schoenfeld, *Cost Terminology and Cost Theory: A Study of Its Development and Present State in Central Europe* (Urbana, Ill.: Center for International Education and Research in Accounting, 1974).
5. R. Mattessich, *Accounting and Analytical Methods* (R. Irwin, 1964; reprint ed., Houston, Texas: Scholars Book, 1977), Chapt. 9; and idem., *Simulation of the Firm through a Budget Computer System* (R. Irwin, 1964; reprint ed., Ann Arbor: Microfilm International, 1979).
6. Cf Shillinglaw, "Old Horizons."
7. C. W. Churchman, *Prediction and Optimal Decision: Philosophical Issues of a Science of Values* (Englewood Cliffs, N.J.: Prentice-Hall, 1961); idem., *Challenge to Reason* (New York: McGraw-Hill, 1968); and idem., *The Systems Approach* (New York: Dell Publications, 1968).
8. C. Argyris, *The Impacts of Budgets on People* (Ithaca, N.Y.: The Controllership Foundation, 1952).
9. A. C. Stedry, *Budget Control and Cost Behavior* (Englewood Cliffs, N.J.: Prentice-Hall, 1959-60).
10. Churchman, *Prediction,* pp. 67-68.
11. Compare with R. Mattessich, *Instrumental Reasoning and Systems Methodology* (Dordrecht/Boston: D. Reidel, 1978).
12. C. W. Churchman, "Intuition and Information" (1980).
13. Herbert A. Simon, "On the Application of Servomechanism Theory in the Study of Production Control," *Econometrics,* vol. 20 (1952):247-68.
14. J. Baetge, ed., *Betriebswirtschaftliche Systemtheorie,* 2nd ed. (Opladen: West deutscher Verlag, 1974); and idem., *Betriebswirtschaftliche Kontrolltheorie* (Opladen: West deutscher Verlag, 1975).
15. Argyris, *Impact of Budgets.*
16. Stedry, *Budget Control.*
17. C. W. Churchman, R. L. Ackoff, and E. L. Arnoff, *Introduction to Operations Research* (New York: John Wiley and Sons, 1957).
18. R. L. Ackoff, "The Future of Operational Research Is Past and Resurrecting the Future of Operational Research" (Paper presented at the national meeting of the Operational Research Society [U.K.], Philadelphia. The Wharton School, 1978), pp. 1-9.
19. Mattessich, *Instrumental Reasoning,* pp. 11 and 3.
20. R. S. Kaplan, "Application of Quantitative Models in Managerial Accounting: A State of the Art Survey," *Robert Beyer Lecture Series 1977* (Madison: Graduate School of Business, University of Wisconsin, 1977), pp. 30-71.
21. Ibid., p. 60.
22. N. Dopuch, J. G. Birnberg, and J. Demski, *Cost Accounting,* 2nd ed. (New York: Harcourt, Brace, Jovanovich, 1974).
23. As developed by Jacob Marschak; for a collection of his pertinent articles see, J. Marschak, *Economic Information, Decision and Prediction,* Vol. I (Dordrecht/Boston: D. Reidel, 1974). See also J. Marschak and R. Radner, *Economic Theory of Teams* (New Haven: Yale University Press, 1972), and others.
24. R. Mattessich, "On the Evolution of Theory Construction in Accounting: A Personal Account," *Accounting and Business Research* (U.K.) (Spring 1980).
25. R. Mattessich, "Instrumental Aspects of Accounting" in *Accounting for a Simplified Firm: Seventeen Essays Based on a Common Example,* ed. R. R. Sterling and A. L. Thomas (Houston, Texas: Scholars Book, 1979), pp. 335-51.
26. For a discussion of the connection between statistical decision models and the information economic model, see Mattessich, *Instrumental Reasoning,* pp. 219-24.
27. T. S. Kuhn, *The Structure of Scientific Revolutions* (Chicago: University of Chicago Press, 1962).
28. J. S. Demski and G. A. Feltham, *Cost Determination: A Conceptual Approach* (Ames, Iowa: Iowa State University Press, 1976).
29. G. A. Feltham, "The Value of Information," *Accounting Review* (October 1968): 684-96.
30. J. S. Demski and G. A. Feltham, "Forecast Evaluation," *Accounting Review* (April 1972).
31. J. M. Clark, *Studies in the Economics of Overhead Costs* (Chicago: University of Chicago Press, 1923).
32. Demski and Feltham, *Cost Determination,* pp. 7-8.
33. Ibid.

[34] S. Baiman, "Multiperson Analysis in Managerial Accounting: A Survey" (Working Paper, Graduate School of Industrial Administration, Carnegie-Mellon University, 1979), pp. 1-2.

[35] Demski and Feltham, *Cost Determination*.

[36] K. J. Arrow, *Social Choice and Individual Values*, 2nd ed. (New York: J. Wiley & Sons, 1951).

[37] R. W. Hilton, R. J. Swieringa, and R. E. Hoskin, "Perception of Accuracy as a Determinant of Information Value" (Working paper, Graduate School of Business and Public Administration, Cornell University, 1979).

[38] H. Itami, *Adaptive Behavior: Management Control and Information Analysis*, Studies in Accounting Research No. 15 (American Accounting Association, 1977).

[39] J. S. Demski and G. A. Feltham, "Economic Incentives in Budgetary Control Systems," *Accounting Review* (April 1978): 336-59.

[40] G.A. Feltham and E. M. Matsumura, "Cost Variance Investigation: An Agency Theory Perspective" (Working paper of the Faculty of Commerce and Business Administration, University of British Columbia, 1979).

[41] M. C. Jensen and W. H. Meckling, "Theory of the Firm: Managerial Behavior, Agency Cost and Ownership Structure." *Journal of Financial Economics*, no. 3 (1976): 305-60.

[42] D. C. Hayes, "The Contingency Theory of Managerial Accounting," *Accounting Review* (January 1977):22-39; idem., "The Contingency Theory of Managerial Accounting: A Reply," *Accounting Review* (April 1978): 530-33.

[43] P. Tiessen and J. H. Waterhouse, "The Contingency Theory of Managerial Accounting: A Comment," *Accounting Review* (April 1978): 523-29.

[44] Jensen and Meckling, "Theory of the Firm."

[45] Ibid.

[46] For example, S. Baiman, "The Evaluation of Choice of Internal Information Systems within a Multiperson World," *Journal of Accounting Research* (Spring 1975): 1-15; J. Demski, "Uncertainty and Evaluation Based on Controllable Performance," *Journal of Accounting Research* (Autumn 1976): 230-45; and Demski and Feltham, "Economic Incentives," pp. 336-59.

[47] Baiman, "Multiperson Analysis."

[48] In many cases, this would be an *"ex ante* Pareto efficient contract." Such a contract would maximize the principal's expected utility of his share as a function of various information signals, given some information about the agent prior to the contractual agreement; it would also enable the agent to maximize his own expected utility with the guarantee of a minimal expected utility. But Amershi and Butterworth have shown that under certain circumstances other than Pareto-efficient solutions (for example, "Nash solutions") may be superior. See A. M. Amershi and J. E. Butterworth, "The Theory of Agency with Diverse Beliefs" (Working paper, Faculty of Commerce and Business Administration, University of British Columbia, 1979).

[49] Baiman, "Multiperson Analysis," p. 35.

[50] C. T. Horngren, *Cost Accounting—A Managerial Emphasis*, 3rd ed. (Englewood Cliffs, N. J.: Prentice-Hall, 1972), p. 163.

[51] Adam Smith, *An Inquiry into the Nature and Causes of the Wealth of Nations* (1776).

[52] Compare with Mattessich, *Instrumental Reasoning*, pp. 37-52.

[53] Mattessich, "Towards a General and Axiomatic Foundation"; idem., *Analytical Methods;* idem., *Die wissenschaftlichen Grundlagen des Rechnungswesens* (Düsseldorf: Bertelsmann, 1970); and idem., "Aspects of Accounting."

[54] R. Mattessich, "Methodological Preconditions and Problems of a General Theory of Accounting," *Accounting Review* (July 1972): 469-87.

[55] American Accounting Association, *Statement on Accounting Theory and Theory Acceptance* (Sarasota, Fla.: AAA, 1977).

[56] N. Georgescu-Roegen, *Energy and Economic Myths* (New York: Pergammon Press, 1976), p. 277.

[57] Ibid., p. 283.

[58] Ibid., and idem., *The Entropy Law and the Economic Process* (Cambridge, Mass.: Harvard University Press, 1971); and E. F. Schumacher, *Small Is Beautiful, A Study of Economics As If People Mattered* (London: Sphere Books, 1974).

[59] L. Szilard, "Über die Entropieverminderung in sinem therms dynamischen System bei Eingriffen intelligenter Wesen," *Zeitschrift fürPhysik*, vol. 53 (1929): 840-56; C. E. Shannon, *The Mathematical Theory of Communication* (Urbana: University of Illinois Press, 1949); and L. Brillouin, *Science and Information Theory*, 2nd ed. (New York: Academic Press, 1962).

[60] Manfred Eigen, "Selforganization of Matter and the Evolution of Biological Macromolecules," *Die Naturwissenschaften*, Vol. 58: 465-528.

BIBLIOGRAPHY

Ackoff, R. L. "The Future of Operational Research Is Past and Resurrecting the Future of Operational Research." Manuscript for the presentation at the national meeting of the Operational Research Society (U.K.), Wharton School, 1978

American Accounting Association, *Statement on Accounting Theory and Theory Acceptance* (SATTA). Sarasota, Fla,: 1977

Amershi, A. M., and Butterworth, J. E. "The Theory of Agency with Diverse Beliefs." Working Paper, Faculty of Commerce and Business Administration, University of British Columbia, Vancouver, 1979.

Argyris, C. *The Impact of Budgets on People*. Ithaca, New York: The Controllership Foundation, 1952.

_____. "Some Inner Contradictions in Management Information Systems." *Management Accounting Symposium 1979*. Edited by H. Peter Holzer. Urbana-Champaign: University of Illinois, 1980.

Arrow, K. J. *Social Choice and Individual Values*. 2nd ed. New York: J. Wiley and Sons, Inc., 1951

Baetge, J. *Betriebswirtschaftliche Systemtheorie*. Opladen: Westdeutscher Verlag, 1974.

_____, ed. *Betriebswirtschaftliche Kontrolltheorie*. Opladen: Westdeutscher Verlag, 1975.

Baiman, S. "The Evaluation of Choice of Internal Information Systems within a Multiperson World." *Journal of Accounting Research* 13 (Spring 1975): 1-15.

_____. "Multiperson Analysis in Managerial Accounting: A Survey." Working Paper, Graduate School of Industrial Admininstration, Carnegie-Mellon University, 1979.

*Beaver, W. H., Kennelly, J. W., and Voss, W. M. "Predictive Ability as a Criterion for the Evaluation of Accounting Data." *Accounting Review* (October 1968): 675-83.

Benninger, L. J. "Cost Accounting." in *Handbook of Business Administration*. Edited by H. B. Maynard. New York: McGraw-Hill, Inc., 1967, pp. 10.11 to 10.22.

*Boyd, D. F. and Krasnow, H. S. "Economic Evaluation of Management Information Systems." *IBM Systems Journal* (March 1963): 2-23.

Brillouin, L. *Science and Information Theory*. 2nd ed. New York: Academic Press, 1962.

Buckley, J. W. and O'Sullivan, P., "Control Theory and Management Accounting," *Management Accounting Symposium 1980*. Edited by H. Peter Holzer. Urbana-Champaign: University of Illinois, 1980.

*Butterworth, J. E. *Accounting Systems and Management Decision: An Analysis of the Role of Information in the Managerial Decision Process*. Ph.D. dissertation, University of California at Berkeley, 1967.

*_____. "The Accounting System as an Information Function." *Journal of Accounting Research* (Spring 1972): 1-27.

*_____, and Amershi, A. M. "The Analysis of Management Accounting Information." University of British Columbia, 1980.

*_____, and Feltham, G. A. "Mathematical Decision Models in Management Accounting." Working Paper No. 204, Faculty of Commerce and Business Administration, University of British Columbia, 1972.

Churchman, C. W. *Prediction and Optimal Decision: Philosophical Issues of a Science of Values*. Englewood Cliffs, N.J.: Prentice-Hall, Inc., 1961.

_____. *Challenge to Reason*. New York: McGraw-Hill Book Co., 1968.

_____. *The Systems Approach*. New York: Dell Publications, 1968.

_____. "Intuition and Information," *Management Accounting Symposium 1980*. Edited by H. Peter Holzer. Urbana-Champaign: University of Illinois, 1980.

_____, Ackoff, R. L., and Arnoff, E. L. *Introduction to Operations Research*. New York: John Wiley and Sons, 1957.

Clark, J. M. *Studies in the Economics of Overhead Costs*. Chicago: University of Chicago Press, 1923.

Cooper, W. W. "The Impact of Quantitative Methods," *Management Accounting Symposium 1980*. Edited by H. Peter Holzer. Urbana-Champaign: University of Illinois, 1980.

Davis, G. B., "Management Information Systems and Management Accounting," *Management Accounting Symposium 1980*. Edited by H. Peter Holzer. Urbana-Champaign: University of Illinois, 1980.

*Demski, J. S. *Information Analysis*. Reading, Mass.: Addison-Wesley Publishing Co., 1972.

*_____. "Information Improvement Bounds." *Journal of Accounting Research* (Spring 1972): 58-76.

*_____. "Choice among Financial Reporting Alternatives." *Accounting Review* (April 1974): 221-32.

_____. "Uncertainty and Evaluation Based on Controllable Performance." *Journal of Accounting Research* (Autumn 1976): 230-45.

*_____ and Feltham, G. A. "Forecast Evaluation." *Accounting Review* (April 1972).

_____and_____. *Cost Determination: A Conceptual Approach* (Ames: The Iowa State University Press, 1976).

*_____and_____. "Economic Incentives in Budgetary Control Systems." *Accounting Review* (April 1978): 336-59.

*Dickson, G. R., Senn, J. A., and Chervany, N. L. "Research in Management Information Systems: The Minnesota Experiments." *Management Science* (May 1977): 913-22.

Dopuch, N., Birnberg, J. G., and Demski, J. *Cost Accounting*. 2nd ed. New York: Harcourt, Brace, Jovanovich, 1974.

*Driver, M. J. and Mock, T. J. "Human Information Processing, Decision Style Theory, and Accounting Information Systems." *Accounting Review* (July 1975): 490-508.

*Feltham, G. A. *A Theoretical Framework for Evaluating Changes in Accounting Information for Managerial Decisions*. Ph.D. dissertation, University of California at Berkeley, 1967.

*_____. "The Value of Information." *Accounting Review* (October 1968): 684-96.

*_____. *Information Evaluation*. Sarasota, Florida: American Accounting Association, 1972.

*_____ and Demski, J. S. "The Use of Models in Information Evaluation." *Accounting Review* (October 1970): 623-40.

*_____ and Matsumura, E. M. "Cost Variance Investigation: An Agency Theory Perspective." Working Paper of the Faculty of Commerce and Business Administration, University of British Columbia, 1979.

Georgescu-Roegen, N. *Energy and Economic Myths*. New York: Pergammon Press, 1976.

_____, *The Entropy Law and the Economic Process*. Cambridge, Mass.: Harvard University Press, 1971.

Hayes, D. C. "The Contingency Theory of Managerial Accounting." *Accounting Review* (January 1977): 22-39.

_____. "The Contingency Theory of Managerial Accounting: A Reply." *Accounting Review* (April 1978): 530-33.

Hilton, R. W., Swieringa, R. J., and Hoskin, R. E. "Perception of Accuracy as a Determinant of Information Value." Working Paper, Graduate School of Business and Public Administration, Cornell University, 1979.

Horngren, C. T. *Cost Accounting—A Managerial Emphasis*. 3rd ed. Englewood Cliffs, N.J.: Prentice-Hall, Inc., 1972.

*Itami, H. *Adaptive Behavior: Management Control and Information Analysis*. American Accounting Association, 1977.

Jensen, M. C., and Meckling, W. H. "Theory of the Firm: Managerial Behavior, Agency Cost and Ownership Structure." *Journal of Financial Economics* (1976): 305-60.

Kaplan, R. S. "Application of Quantitative Models in Managerial Accounting: A State of the Art Survey." In *Robert Beyer Lecture Series 1977*. Madison: Graduate School of Business, University of Wisconsin, 1977, pp. 30-71.

Kuhn, T. S. *The Structure of Scientific Revolutions*. Chicago: University of Chicago Press, 1962.

*MacCrimmon, K. R. "Descriptive and Normative Implication of the Decision Theory Postulates." In *Risk and Uncertainty*, edited by K. Borch and J. Mossin, 1974.

Marchak, J. *Economic Information, Decision and Prediction*. 3 vols. Dordrecht/Boston: D. Reidel Publishing Co., 1974.

_____ and Radner, R. *Economic Theory of Teams*. New Haven: Yale University Press, 1972.

Mattessich, R. "Operations Research and Accounting: Competitors or Partners?" *Review of Economics and Business* (August 1962): 7-14.

_____. *Die wissenschaftlichen Grundlagen des Rechnungswesens*. Düsseldorf: Bertelsmann, 1970.

_____. "Methodological Preconditions and Problems of a General Theory of Accounting." *Accounting Review* (July 1972): 469-87.

_____. *Accounting and Analytical Methods*. Homewood, Ill.: R. Irwin, Inc., 1964. Reprint. Houston, Tex.: Scholars Book Co., 1977.

_____. *Simulation of the Firm through a Budget Computer System*. Homewood, Ill.: R. Irwin, Inc., 1964. Reprint. Ann Arbor/London: Microfilm International, 1979.

*_____. "Information Economics and the Notion of Management Information Systems." *Information Systems and Organizational Structures*. Edited by E. Grochla and N. Szyperski. Berlin/New York: Walter De Gruyter, 1975, pp. 342-62.

_____. *Instrumental Reasoning and Systems Methodology*. Dordrecht/Boston: D. Reidel Publishing Co., 1978. Paperback edition, 1980.

_____. "Instrumental Aspects of Accounting." In *Accounting for a Simplified Firm: Seventeen Essays Based on a Common Example*. Edited by R. R. Sterling and A. L. Thomas. Houston, Tex.: Scholars Book Co., 1979, pp. 335-51.

_____. "On the Evolution of Theory Construction in Accounting: A Personal Account," in the special issue on Accounting History of *Accounting and Business Research* (U.K.) Spring 1980.

Mock, T. J. "Comparative Values of Information Structures." *Journal of Accounting Research* (1969 Supplement): 124-59.

_____. "Concepts of Information Value and Accounting." *Accounting Review* (October 1971): 765-78.

_____. *Measurement and Accounting Information Criteria*, Accounting Research Study No. 13 (Sarasota, Fla.: American Accounting Association, 1976).

Nolan, R. L. and Seward, H. H. "Measuring User Satisfaction to Evaluate Information Systems" in *Managing the Data Resource Function*, edited by R. L. Nolan. St. Paul: West Publishing, 1974, pp. 253-75.

414

Schoenfeld, H. M. W. *Cost Terminology and Cost Theory: A Study of its Development and Present State in Central Europe.* Urbana-Champaign: Center for International Education and Research in Accounting, 1974.

Shillinglaw, G. "Old Horizons and New Frontiers: The Future of Managerial Accounting," *Management Accounting Symposium 1980.* Edited by H. Peter Holzer. Urbana-Champaign: University of Illinois, 1980.

Simon, H. A. "On the Application of Servomechanism Theory in the Study of Production Control." In *Economica.* vol. 20, 1952, pp. 247-68.

*Slovic, P. and Lichtenstein, S. "Comparison of Bayesian and Regression Approaches to the Study of Information Processing in Judgement." *Human Judgement and Social Interactions.* Edited by L. Rappoport and D. A. Summers. 1973.

Smith, A. *An Inquiry into the Nature and Causes of the Wealth of Nations.* 1776.

Stedry, A. C. *Budget Control and Cost Behavior.* Englewood Cliffs, N.J.: Prentice-Hall, Inc., 1959/60.

Swieringa, R. J. "Behavioral Implications of Planning and Control Systems," *Management Accounting Symposium 1980.* Edited by H. Peter Holzer. Urbana-Champaign: University of Illinois, 1980.

Szilard, L. "Uber die Entropieverminderung in einem thermodynamischen System bei Eingriffen intelligenter Wesen." *Zeitschrift für Physik* (1929): 840-56.

Thomas, A. L. *The Allocation Problems in Financial Accounting.* Sarasota, Fla.: AAA, 1969.

————. *The Allocation Problem: Part Two.* Sarasota, Fla.: American Accounting Association, 1974.

Tiessen, P. and Waterhouse, J. H. "The Contingency Theory of Managerial Accounting: A Comment." *Accounting Review* (April 1978): 523-29.

*Uecker, W. C. "A Behavioral Study of Information System Choice." *Journal of Accounting Research* (Spring 1978): 169-89.

Vatter, W. J. *Managerial Accounting.* Englewood Cliffs, N.J.: Prentice-Hall, Inc., 1950.

————

*Indicates that the work is representative of "information economics accounting."

APPLICATION OF QUANTITATIVE MODELS IN MANAGERIAL ACCOUNTING: A STATE OF THE ART SURVEY[1]*

by Robert S. Kaplan

Reprinted from Management Accounting — State of the Art, Beyer Lecture Series 1976-77 (Madison, Wisconsin: Dept. of Accounting and Information Systems, University of Wisconsin, © 1977), pp. 29-71.

IN reviewing articles written 10 to 15 years ago which introduced quantitative analysis to management accounting, one is struck by the optimism of the authors who predicted a substantial impact of these models on the field. Unlike most such predictions, I believe that the hope of these early writers was fulfilled. A large literature has emerged over the past 15 years which demonstrates the usefulness of quantitative models in a wide variety of managerial accounting problems. As in most fields, there is a lag in conveying these advances to students. A key indicator of what is being taught to students is the content of textbooks in an area. That quantitative methods are not yet well integrated into cost accounting texts is indicated by the appearance of a separate chapter, usually the last one in the book, entitled, "Quantitative Decision Techniques," "Cost Accounting and Mathematics," or "Short-Run Optimization Models" (actual titles from a random selection of books in my office). Many other texts do not even take this radical a step and choose to ignore altogether the existence of quantitative models as an aid to good cost accounting, and hence, are virtually indistinguishable from texts written 15 years ago.

One text that successfully integrates quantitative material with cost accounting is Dopuch, Birnberg and Demski [1974].[2] Even with this unique niche in the market, I understand that sales of this text are not ruining the competition. This could be explained by at least three reasons.[3] Reason one suggests that there is little contribution from the inclusion of quantitative material so that little is lost by ignoring it in cost accounting texts. Reason two is that even though the material is useful, most students entering a cost accounting course are not prepared for linear programming, decision theory, and regression analysis. The third reason is similar to the second except that it is the faculty teaching such a course who are ill-prepared to handle technical material.

I will try to show in this survey that the quantitative material is relevant and actually essential to properly understand cost accounting issues. Therefore, I discard reason one and must attribute the relatively slow introduction of quantitative techniques into the cost accounting course by a combination of reasons two and three.[4] Unfortunately, one of these is easier to remedy in the short run than the other. Nevertheless, I predict that managerial or cost accounting textbooks will begin to adopt the integrated approach taken by Dopuch, Birnberg and Demski [1974] and start to discard the piecemeal ostrich-like approach (if I don't talk about it in my book, maybe it will go away) of most other cost accounting texts. When this happens, we may expect to see a much greater impact on practice of the advances of the past 15 years than is now apparent.

Before embarking on this survey of quantitative models and managerial accounting, I must indicate the scope of the effort. I have decided not to include articles whose quantitative approach involved nothing more analytic than high school algebra. This is not a criticism of these articles since for many applications advanced mathematical techniques are unnecessary. I just don't consider these articles as demonstrating the advantages of sophisticated quantitative models. My definition of a quantitative technique for purposes of this survey includes linear algebra, probability and decision theory, statistical analysis and mathematical programming. I am excluding the burgeoning literature on information economics and incentive systems since this area now requires a survey paper by itself. The paper will be organized by subject matter in managerial accounting rather than by type of technique used. Thus, the reader can see that I am focusing on the User Decision Model or Conditional Truth Approach which falls chronologically and methodologically between the True Cost Approach of traditional cost accounting and the Costly Truth Approach of the pure decision theorists (see Horngren [1975] for description of these approaches). Thus when discussing the value of a particular model for a given decision, I will not be concerned with the costs of formulating, estimating, implementing or using the model. Since these costs are actually quite significant in practice, one can view the subsequent discussion as describing an upper bound on the potential value of incorporating formal decision models into an internal planning and control system.

The subjects to be covered in this survey include: C-V-P Analysis, Performance and Variance Analysis, Variance Investigations, Cost Allocations — Reciprocal and Joint, Cost Behavior — Fixed and Variable, and Transfer Pricing. I will not cover the subjects of capital budgeting and production planning. Even though these areas depend on relevant accounting data and much has been written on these subjects in the accounting literature, they are not the prime responsibility of cost accountants.

As a final note, I cannot perform such a survey without editorializing about some of the papers along the way. Such editorializing represents my attempt to organize the literature and distinguish between innovative and pedestrian papers. It is a signal to students reading this survey that even in the leading academic accounting journals, there is considerable variation in the quality and contribution of published papers.

COST-VOLUME-PROFIT ANALYSIS

Cost-Volume-Profit (C-V-P) analysis identifies short-run fixed and variable costs for products, assumes a constant selling price for each product (with no cross-elasticities of demand), and computes breakeven sales figures and overall profitablity as a function of sales volume. The basic equation of C-V-P analysis is: Profits = Sales Quantity * (Selling Price - Variable Costs) - Fixed Costs. C-V-P analysis highlights the variable contribution margin of each product, implying that the high contribution margin products are more profitable than the low contribution margin products. It is a useful exercise especially for companies who previously only looked at products on an absorption or full-cost basis. Management science models have contributed two significant extensions to this traditional C-V-P analysis. First, the production limitations introduced by scarce resources have been recognized through mathematical programming models. Second, uncertainty has been introduced by allowing sales and subsequently prices and costs also to be random variables. In both cases we must give credit to Bob Jaedicke for having written the first article describing the application of these methods.

Jaedicke [1961] addressed C-V-P analysis for a multiproduct firm with numerous production constraints. He pointed out the limitations of breakeven analysis in such an environment and correctly recognized that in a constrained production environment, high contribution margin products are not necessarily the most profitable. One wants to maximize production and sales of those products that have maximum contribution margin per unit of scarce resource consumed. If production is constrained by only a single resource, it is a simple exercise to rank products by their contribution margin per unit of scarce resource consumed. But in the more typical multiple constraint environment, the ranking is not so obvious or even possible. In this case, linear programming provides an optimal product mix, balancing contribution margin of individual products with the resources available for production. Dopuch [1963] also pointed out that linear programming is the logical extension of breakeven and C-V-P analysis in a multiproduct multiconstrained production environment.

Charnes, Cooper and Ijiri [1963] showed how linear programming could be used to identify all the feasible product mix combinations which yield breakeven products. In addition the model could be used to identify product mixes that maximize profits or, if profitable operation is impossible to achieve, come closest to having the firm break even. This paper also introduced the relationship between the spread sheet of double entry bookkeeping and a matrix system of linear constraints. This system leads to a network representation of the accounting process. Ijiri, Levy and Lyon [1963] elaborated on the relationship between the spread sheet representation and a linear programming model, and integrated the optimizing tool into a financial planning model.

A significant generalization of these models was achieved in Ijiri [1965, Chapter 2] who demonstrated how a nonlinear revenue function (i.e., when selling price is a function of quantity sold) and a nonlinear cost function including semifixed and semivariable costs could be incorporated into the mathematical programming analysis. By using piece-wise linear representations (or approximations) of these nonlinear functions, Ijiri showed how this more complex environment could still be modeled in the linear programming framework, a significant advantage given the ready availability and efficiency of LP codes as contrasted with nonlinear programming algorithms.

Finally, while the above papers focus on price, variable costs and sales quantities, Groves, Manes and Sorenson [1970] consider the fixed cost component in C-V-P or breakeven analysis. If a product is not produced at all during a period, perhaps a substantial amount of fixed costs normally associated with that product could be escapable. Such a situation requires 0-1 integer variables to subtract the fixed costs from overall profits if any positive amount of the product is produced but ignore the fixed costs if zero amount is selected in the optimal product mix. This is a standard type of integer programming model called the fixed charge problem and, among the class of integer programming problems, is a relatively easy one to solve.

This we can see how the traditional linear contribution margin, breakeven analysis model has been expanded to include multiple products, multiple constraints on production (and sales), nonlinear revenue and cost functions, and escapable fixed costs. This progression has highlighted the key feature of the product mix decision maximizing contribution margin per unit of scarce resource consumed — and demonstrated that departures from the simple linear assumptions can be handled relatively easily within the mathematical programming framework.

The second principal extension of C-V-P analysis has been to allow uncertainty in the various parameters of the model. Jaedicke and Robichek [1963] assumed that the sales quantity was normally distributed with known mean and standard deviation. (Apparently Bierman [1963] independently modeled this situation too.) Since linear combinations of normally distributed random variables are also normally distributed, profit in this model was distributed normally and one could now compute, in addition to expected profits, the probability of breaking even, or in general the probability of achieving any particular profit level. Having the entire probability distribution of profits was felt to be more useful than just knowing the sales level for breakeven or the sales required to achieve a given level of profitability.[5]

Johnson and Simik [1971] made the straightforward extension to the multiple product situation. With multiple products one needs to know the vector of means and the covariance matrix among products to obtain the parameters of the normal distribution for profits. As we know from portfolio theory, the variance of profits is reduced when the products are negatively correlated or independent. As the intercorrelations of sales for the multiple product increases, the variance of profits increases.

In a subsequent paper, Johnson and Simik [1974] derive bounds for the variance of profits when one assumes a general rather than normal, distribution for sales. One can note in the managerial accounting literature that anytime someone presents a model assuming a normal distribution for a random variable, a paper will shortly follow showing how the analysis can be "significantly generalized" by not making such a parametric assumption. The paper then goes on to show how, given a variance, Chebyschev's inequality or some variant thereof can get an upper bound on a confidence interval without making any assumption on the distributional form of the random variable. Johnson and Simik [1974] take this process one step further by assuming that the manager does not even know the variance of sales, just the maximum possible range. (Just why a manager has no idea about the variance of a random variable but has an excellent estimate of the minimum and maximum values of the variable is never explained.) Confidence intervals based on the most dispersed probability distribution consistent with these range estimates are then computed. As is typical in these nonparametric papers, the embarrassing comparison between the widths of confidence intervals produced by using a Chebyschev inequality and those produced assuming a normal distribution is not made. Buzby [1974] also generated a Chebyschev inequality paper for C-V-P analysis.

Dickinson [1974] pointed out that if the mean and variance of the sales distribution are estimated from past data, then the profit random variable is distributed according to a t-distribution (rather than normal) and that the variance of profit follows a chi-squared distribution.

In addition to quibbling about the form of the distribution for sales quantities, another stream of research has investigated the implications of having selling price and variable cost be random variables too. Jaedicke and Robichek [1963] implicitly assumed that multiplying a normally distributed sales quantity with a normally distributed price minus variable cost random variable would yield a normally distributed gross profit random variable. That this is not true was pointed out by Ferrara, Hayya and Nachman [1972]. Assuming the two normal random variables being multiplied together are independent, the product will tend to normality as the coefficient of variation (σ/μ) of each random variable goes to zero. Without being greatly concerned about the market conditions that would imply that selling price and amount sold are statistically independent quantities, Ferrara et al. used simulation studies and X^2 tests for normality to conclude that one could assume the product is normally distributed if the coefficient of variation of the two independent variables is less than 12 percent.

Hilliard and Leitch [1975] pointed out the problems of assuming price and quantity to be independent. Also, that assuming sales was normally distributed implied a positive probability for negative sales. They assumed that sales quantity and contributed margin (price less variable cost) are bivariate lognormally distributed. This assumption eliminates the possibility of negative sales and of selling prices below variable costs, and has the nice additional property that the product of two bivariate lognormal random variables is also lognormally distributed. Thus, we can allow for uncertainty in price and quantity and statistical dependence between price and quantity and still have a closed form expression for the probability distribution of gross profit. Lau and Lau [1976], however, pointed out that sums and differences of lognormally distributed random variables are not lognormally distributed, so that Hilliard and Leitch cannot assume that price and variable cost are marginally lognormally distributed and have contribution margin also be lognormally distributed. Similarly, if fixed costs are assumed to be lognormally distributed too, net profits will not be lognormally distributed. Also, assuming a lognormal distribution with given mean and variance automatically implies a skewness value for the population.

Given this debate over the distributional properties of sales and profits, one can adopt the old management science rule: When all else fails, simulate! Liao [1975] describes such a procedure including a curve fitting algorithm to obtain a closed form distribution for the profit random variable. This procedure enables one to assume any distribution whatsoever for the various random variables and still obtain an approximation to the distribution of profits.

One final distributional extension remained. Armed with our knowlege from portfolio theory in finance, we now know that it is not variance or total risk that is the best summary of uncertainty, even for normally distributed random variables. Since the firm consists of a portfolio of projects, and since stockholders hold a portfolio of firms, we should be concerned with the covariation or systematic risk of an uncertain project. Therefore we can trace the articles in the managerial accounting literature that point this out to each area dealing with uncertainty. Ozan and Dyckman [1971] made this point for the cost variance investigation decision. For the C-V-P analysis under uncertainty case, Magee [1975] provided this service.

Morrison and Kaezka [1969] went back to the deterministic C-V-P model and attempted to characterize the effect on profits if sales quantities and selling prices are related in some manner. The analysis, which makes some use of calculus, is remarkable mainly by addressing this topic and performing all the analysis without ever mentioning the concepts of demand curves and elasticities.

In all this discussion and debate over distributional assumptions, we apparently have lost track as to why we are attempting to get a probability distribution for sales and profits. Presumably, it is because it will aid us in decision making but the decision making aspects of the problem have been suppressed or ignored as we forge ahead with bivariate distributions and Chebyschev's inequality. Bierman and Dyckman [1971] do provide a decision theory approach to breakeven analysis and uncertainty by computing quantities such as the expected loss given that a loss occurs (an expected partial loss) and the ratio of expected partial loss to expected partial gain. An advantage of assuming a normal distribution of profits is that we can easily compute quantities such as the expected value of perfect information (called the expected partial loss by Bierman-Dyckman) and the expected value of sample information to obtain bounds on the gain associated with reducing the uncertainty in profits. To date, this approach has not been advocated in the managerial accounting literature.

To summarize this section, it is conceptually easy to allow for uncertainty in C-V-P analysis though certain distributional problems arise when multiplying random variables of price and quantity together. It's doubtful whether this technical issue causes this extension not to be used in practice. I am unaware of any reference indicating that C-V-P analysis under uncertainty has had much impact on the world. Rather than continue to explore technical details associated with the distributional assumptions, it may seem wise at this point to find out why this material is apparently not being used in practice. Maybe it's because even though the original article appeared 14 years ago, it has yet to be discussed in most of the principal cost accounting textbooks, a point I made previously in the introduction.

Another explanation for the lack of acceptance is the absence of any empirical or case studies in this area illustrating actual successes associated with using this technique. I have undertaken to perform the first empirical study of "C-V-P analysis under uncertainty." In reviewing the papers for this section, I found seven papers or comments which used the words in quotes in the preceding sentence. Four of them capitalized the "u" in under while three of them used a small "u." This phenomenon was not explained either by journals or authors since successive articles by the same authors in the same journals (e.g., Johnson and Simik [1971] and [1974], and Hilliard and Leitch [1975] and [1976]) switched conventions from one paper to the next. Admittedly this is not a major empirical contribution, but I hope it at least points the way to further empirical rather than normative work in this area.

PERFORMANCE EVALUATION AND VARIANCE ANALYSIS

Standard cost systems are a traditional method for measuring and controlling cost deviations. In teaching standard cost analysis it is easy to overwhelm students with a mass of seemingly arbitrary definitions and instructions for computing variances from standard cost. A series of articles in the 1960's (Kwang and Slavin [1962], Zannetos [1963], and Hasseldine [1967], among others) developed algebraic representations of standard cost systems to facilitate understanding of variance analysis among the mathematically literate. Frank and Manes [1967] went one step further by providing a linear algebraic formulation of standard cost systems which enabled them to use matrix operations in computing variances. Corcoran [1966] developed a linear algebraic approach to process costing to demystify the units lost units cost computation. These studies, while clarifying some of the computations in a variance analysis, did not introduce new ways of analyzing performance.

Samuels [1965] was perhaps the first to exploit a linear programming formulation of the firm's production opportunities to compute a variance based on opportunity losses. He suggested that the dual prices on the scarce resources be used to charge departments which overuse the scarce resources of the firm and thereby deprive the firm of more profitable production opportunities. He also suggested that dual prices be used to ration the scarce resources but failed to realize that this would cause managers to be indifferent between producing the optimal product mix and not producing at all (since the best they can do is break even on a marginal cost basis). Nevertheless, this paper was the first to recognize the possibility of integrating the control system with the formal decision models used by the firm.

The seminal article (in my opinion) in this area is Dopuch, Birnberg and Demski [1967]. The authors identify three types of variances, only two of which had been previously analyzed. A Type 1 variance is due to normal random variation when the process is in statistical control (see Deming [1975] for an excellent and simple discussion of "statistical control"). A type 2 variance is caused when the process has changed and is no longer in a state of statistical control. The contribution of the paper is to identify that there are two causes of a Type 2 variance. The first type, labeled Type 2a, is controllable if detected and the process can be reset back to its previous level of performance. This is the traditional type of variance and is the subject of an entire literature on cost variance investigations to be discussed in a subsequent section.

The second type of variance, a 2b, is caused by a permanent change in process. It cannot be corrected even if detected. In this situation, an investigation would usually be thought to be wasted because no useful action by management could be taken. The paper, however, points out that knowing of a change in the parameters of the process could be beneficial if it enabled managers to change the decisions they would make. In order to model the benefits associated from learning of a permanent change in the cost levels of a process, one needs to know the formal decision model being used by managers so that we can compare the benefits from new optimal decisions with those obtained using the decisions based on the old cost data. This computation of an opportunity loss variance, associated with not knowing of the change in the parameters of the process, is illustrated with an economic order quantity model from inventory theory and a linear programming model for optimal product mix decisions.

Demski [1967a] and [1967b] provides extended examples of this opportunity loss or ex post variance. The first paper uses the traditional price-output model of economists, equating marginal cost and marginal revenue at the optimal scale of output, as the example of the formal decision model. Demski [1967b] provides the most comprehensive discussion of the ex post analysis. He shows how this analysis provides a new benchmark, the ex post optimum conditional on the actual changes in the environment, in addition to the traditional comparison of planned versus actual results. This enables him to decompose the total variance of actual minus planned results into a forecasting variance, equal to the planned outcome minus the ex post optimum, and an opportunity loss variance, equal to the ex post optimum minus the actual outcome. The opportunity loss variance is a measure of how much was lost by not adapting decisions to the permanent changes that occurred during the period. The analysis is executed in the context of a linear programming model of the firm's product mix decision. Ronen [1970] develops an ex post analysis of the firm's capacity and output decisions in the context of the economic model of long and short-run cost curves. In a subsequent section, I will describe a mathematical programming approach to this joint capacity and output decision. Wolk and Hillman [1972] give an example of how a linear programming model can be used to properly evaluate mix and yield variances. The analysis would have been more complete had they analyzed the variances in the context of the ex ante and ex post optimums developed by Demski.

Cushing [1968], in commenting on Demski's ex post linear programming model, takes particular note of the assumption that all deviations from planned or standard parameters occur at the beginning of the period and that the manager could have implemented a change in action (to achieve the ex post optimum) at that time. Itami [1972] extends Demski's LP model to allow for all changes in the environment to become known at some intermediate point in the period. Itami shows that in this case, the manager should take an initial decision conditional on knowing of the arrival of new information at this intermediate point and his beliefs about the possible realizations of this new information. When this new information arrives, the manager should then adapt his plan to the ex post optimum. The driving assumption behind this model is the existence of finite capacity so that the manager cannot simply wait until he receives information on all the relevant parameters and then produce according to the optimum plan in the time remaining to the end of the period. Itami provides extensive analysis of this model including a variance analysis to describe the "adaptability" of the manager to the receipt of the new information. One particularly important characterization is that there is increasing marginal cost associated with delay in receipt of the new information.

Ijiri and Itami [1973] provide an additional illustration of the information timing approach to ex post analysis and adaptive behavior. They consider a production smoothing problem with a quadratic cost structure, i.e., produce for total demand in a period by attempting to equalize production on a daily basis. The results from Itami's linear programming under uncertainty model readily extend to this environment. A generalization is also achieved by allowing for the receipt of intermediate but imperfect information during the period. Thus we can begin to model the more realistic situation where there is a trade-off between the timeliness and the accuracy of information. This generalizes Itami's assumption for the LP model, that perfect information arrives at a single intermediate point during the period.

Demski, in a series of three papers, attempted to evaluate the usefulness of the ex post analysis approach by comparing performance with this scheme with performance generated using more traditional direct and full absorption costing systems. In what comes as close to empirical research as any in the managerial accounting literature, Demski explored the consequences of the three costing systems using multiperiod production scheduling simulation models. Demski [1969] evaluated the three costing systems by comparing the ability of each system to predict the opportunity loss incurred by the firm each period. The results were somewhat inconclusive because of limitations in the nature of adaptive behavior permitted in the model and also because of the tenuous nature of the predictive ability evaluation criterion in this context.

Demski [1970] and [1971] provides a more interesting setting for comparing the three cost systems by allowing the variances produced from each cost system to influence the future performance of the manager. In effect, Demski has postulated a behavioral model of how managers react to their evaluations, based on past performance, to achieve future cost levels. In addition, managers determine actual production to maximize their performance measurement under direct, fully absorbed, or ex post costing systems. Results varied as a function of the experimental situation but the ex post metric tended to yield significantly higher profits than the other two schemes when demand was most variable and when there were significant opportunities for changing decisions as the environment changed. A problem with all simulation studies is the difficulty of generalizing from the specific situation that was modeled. But these studies did point out an interesting gap in our knowlege which, if corrected, would make such experiments highly important and useful. The models are quite complex but we really have little trouble accepting the optimizing models used by managers to maximize profits.

Nor do we have trouble in constructing a cost accounting and control system based on direct, full or ex post costing. The weak link in the simulation model is in what Demski calls the "implementation interface," that is, how do signals from the control system affect the behavior and performance of the individuals being monitored. At this stage, we must look to the models being developed by behavioral accountants who frequently chide their more mathematically inclined colleagues for not paying adequate attention to behavioral consequences of cost accounting systems. Yet when we wish to incorporate such consequences in our models, we find the models available from the behavioral accounting literature woefully inadequate. This was the situation seven or eight years ago when Demski was conducting his simulation experiments and it is not obvious to me that we have received any further insights in the "implementation interface" since then.

To summarize this section, the existence of formal planning models in a firm provides new opportunities for the accountant to determine the value of more accurate information by assessing the consequences of changes in decisions made with finer information. The formal models also provide a context in which deviations from planned results can be evaluated in terms of an opportunity loss suffered by not revising decisions given changes in the environment. The concept of timeliness of information in enabling managers to adapt to new estimates has also been introduced in the context of formal decision models.

VARIANCE INVESTIGATIONS

Any standard cost system will generate a myriad of (accounting) variances each period. If the standard cost system is to act as a control mechanism, those variances or deviations which appear to be the most significant should be investigated to determine their source and to correct the process if possible. Using the nomenclature introduced in the preceding section, the problem is to determine when a variance is of Type 1, due to normal statistical variation, and when it is of Type 2, caused by a change in the parameters of the process being controlled. We do not wish to investigate Type 1 variances, but do wish to investigate Type 2a variances caused by a controllable shift in the process. If we do investigate and discover a Type 2b variance so that we cannot return to the previous standard, the principal benefit of such an investigation is to alert us to possible changes in our decision model as discussed in the preceding section.

An extensive literature has developed relating ideas in industrial quality control to the variance investigation decision. This literature attempts to aid accountants in distinguishing between Type 1 and Type 2a variances. I have recently performed an extensive review and synthesis of this literature (see Kaplan [1975a]) and hence will not cover this area here in much depth at all. In the survey, I identified two dimensions along which previous studies could be classified. The first dimension is whether the investigation decision is made on the basis of a single observation (the most recent) or a past sequence of observations. The second dimension is whether the costs and benefits associated with the investigation decision are explicitly included in the model or whether the decision is based on arbitrary statistical confidence limits. A control chart approach in which an investigation is signaled if the most recent cost report is more than two standard deviations from the expected value is an example of a model based on a single observation with costs and benefits from the investigation decision not considered. A model in which the probability of the process being out of control is revised each period as a new cost report is received and an investigation signaled when the discounted future expected benefits from an investigation exceed the costs (as determined by optimizing a multi-period dynamic programming model) is an example of a model which uses a past history of observations and explicitly incorporates a benefit/cost analysis of the investigation decision.

While the latter approach seems intuitively appealing (ignoring estimation and implementation costs, see Magee [1976]), some difficult problems still remain. It seems particularly difficult to capture the effects of Type 2b variances, when an investigation is undertaken in anticipation of resetting the process back to its standard cost level but such resetting proves impossible. Similarly, the problem of investigating low cost (favorable variance) reports is difficult to model. Should we undertake such an investigation in anticipation of resetting the standard to a more stringent level, or are we conducting an investigation to determine whether quality or other longer term objective is being compromised in order to achieve short-run low costs? A number of cited studies also had difficulties by assuming that the benefits from an investigation are exogenous rather than endogenously determined by future cost savings when operating in control. These issues and a variety of other technical points are discussed in considerable detail in Kaplan [1975a] to which the interested reader is referred. Also, no model has suggested that, unlike the industrial quality control setting, the threat of investigation of an unfavorable variance may affect the probability of going out-of-control.

A conclusion from this survey of cost variance models was that the ratio of papers advocating the use of statistical models for signaling the existence of a Type 2a variance to the number of successful applications of even simple versions of these models is uncomfortably high (perhaps even infinite). At this point the models appear to be far ahead of practice and so far ahead that we have little guidance in knowing what the crucial remaining issues are, if any. We have no evidence on the stochastic process which tends to shift the mean of generated cost data away from standard cost levels and no studies on the magnitude of costs associated with wasted investigations or opportunity losses incurred for not investigating variances soon enough. It is not clear that there is much fertile ground left for developing more elaborate models in this area without a data base on the type and magnitude of problem we are dealing with here.

COST BEHAVIOR — FIXED AND VARIABLE

Normally in a cost accounting text, a section on cost behavior is adjacent to or contained in the chapter on Cost-Volume-Profit analysis. Why then have I deferred discussing this topic until after sections on performance measurement and investigation? The simple answer is that I have been unable to find any statistical study explicitly devoted to estimating variable costs for a C-V-P analysis. One could presume from this lack of attention that the problem is trivial and not worthy of consideration. But this is clearly not the case. In order to estimate short-run variable costs, one needs to worry about the appropriate time period for estimation, whether the relevant cost data are collected over this time period, the impact of changing price levels and how to adjust prior years' data to make them consistent with current year's data, the impact of technological change, problems in aggregating product lines together into a homogeneous product class, and the impact of varying product mixes. If we are adopting the linear programming approach to C-V-P analysis, there are problems associated with estimating the technological coefficients and the capacities of each scarce resource. Even in what should be a straightforward variable cost account such as direct labor, there are problems if vacation and sick pay are expensed as used or if payroll taxes, such as unemployment and social security which are eliminated once earnings exceed a certain level, are expensed as incurred.

While account analysis may apparently avoid some of these problems (e.g., this account is fixed, this one is variable, this one is 60 percent fixed and 40 percent variable), this approach is going to be misleading when applied to overhead accounts and may even be fooled with prime cost accounts. Therefore, I find it surprising and disturbing that no statistical research has been devoted to problems associated with estimating fixed and variable costs for product mix and output decisions. What statistical research has been done to estimate fixed and variable costs has been in the context of developing a flexible budget so that variations in actual cost from standard can be adjusted for changes in activity level. It is for this reason that this discussion appears after the performance measurement and investigation sections.

My informal search turned up Comiskey [1966] as the first U.S. study to estimate costs as a function of activity levels.[6] Comiskey performs a cross-sectional study of the determinants of cost for 83 branches of a consumer loan company. While the model appeared to have explanatory power, as determined by a statistically significant R^2 value, no t-tests on the significance of individual coefficients were offered. Moreover, when the model was used to predict the costs of a set of five branches, only a point estimate was provided and not a statistical probability interval which could have been computed if a distributional assumption on the error term was made. Thus the model was unable to signal when a deviation from the model's prediction was statistically significant.

The lack of statistical inference in Comiskey's model was pointed out by Jensen [1967], who also discussed a variety of pitfalls that await the researcher who attempts to use regression analysis to explain or predict short-run cost behavior. Among these problems are heteroscedasticity,[7] multicollinearity of independent variables, error term correlated with levels of the independent variables, and autocorrelation of the error term. Benston [1966] also provided an extensive discussion of the opportunities and pitfalls for accountants using regression analysis. Perhaps the admonitions of Benston and Jensen were too discouraging because I was unable to find another study which described the actual use of regression analysis to explain or predict cost behavior. This lack is even more anomalous when compared to the extensive and sophisticated use of econometric techniques by empirical researchers investigating financial accounting issues, particularly in a capital market context. There appears to be a conflict between managerial accountants and data. This aversion leads to management accountants developing more and more elaborate models, thereby imposing heavier demands on statistical procedures which must eventually be used to estimate parameters of these models. But we really have very little knowledge of our ability to estimate the parameters of even the simplest models we talk about in class and describe in our cost accounting textbooks.

Because of an out-of-print collection of papers edited by David Solomons, I am aware of two British studies on estimating short-run marginal cost. Oliver [1962] performed a cross-sectional study of the costs of issuing motor vehicle licenses in England and Wales. The study was reasonably sophisticated (it even worried about and detected heteroscedasticity) and illustrated the types of statistical procedures one can perform in such studies. Perhaps more germane for accountants, Mansfield and Wein [1958] performed a multiple regression study of the costs of a railroad freight yard as an input to a control chart for costs. There likely are other examples of short-run cost studies in the journal Applied Statistics, but I have not undertaken a literature review of this source.

My own work in developing improved planning and control systems for hospitals led me into statistical studies of the determinants of marginal costs in a variety of hospital departments and patient units. My early trials and tribulations (including discovering the value of an accrual rather than cash system for estimating these costs) are described in Kaplan [1974b] where I attempted to indicate the types of problems one encounters when estimating variable costs as well as the insights one might get from carefully analyzing the statistical output.

Follow-up work for estimating how nursing hours vary with patient days is described in Kaplan [1975b]. This paper shows how the statistical probability intervals one obtains from the regression equation can be used as an input to a control chart approach to the cost variance investigation decision. It raises some statistical issues as to how non-stationarities in cost behavior should be modeled, e.g., should one assume that the fixed cost coefficient or the variable cost coefficient has changed? Questions of aggregation across similar departments and seasonalities are also discussed. The main message from these two papers, however, is that statistical analysis can give one a quick handle on estimating the fixed and variable costs needed for a flexible budgeting approach. The statistical approach also provides a natural link into the cost variance investigation decision by providing standard errors of estimates, a feature not available when judgment or account classification is used to determine flexible budgets. In addition, a careful look at the data will suggest certain features about the process or organization being modeled that may not be apparent when one first confronts the investigation.

In order to have credibility for our models, we need additional studies of estimation and implementation problems. The normative models described in this survey place demands on the accuracy and reliability of parameter estimates. These estimates are not trivial to obtain and in some cases may require more thought and effort than the models themselves. If one is looking for new research opportunities in management accounting, the estimation and implementation issues would appear to offer more promise than additional extensions to theoretical and unused models.

COST ALLOCATIONS

Since accountants devote a great deal of attention to allocating costs among periods, departments, and products, it is fitting that an extensive literature has developed on the use of quantitative models to achieve reasonable and occasionally even rational cost allocations. The topics to be covered in this section are the allocation of interacting service department costs, joint and by-product costs, depreciation, and overhead costs. The latter two categories are actually special cases of joint costs but are usually treated separately from the traditional joint product cost problem.

Reciprocal Service Department Costs

Perhaps the biggest triumph of mathematical modeling to cost accounting has been the matrix approach to allocating costs from interacting service departments to revenue producing departments. Previously when allocating costs of service departments that provided services to each other (e.g., a power department providing heat and light to administrative offices which, reciprocally, provide personnel and payroll services to employees in the power department), a somewhat arbitrary step down or sequential procedure was advocated. A sequential procedure was thought to be necessary because of the apparent circularity in the relationship among interacting service departments. This circularity was more apparent than real, however, since the relationships could be modeled easily by a system of simultaneous linear equations. Williams and Griffin [1964] were the first to point out this application of linear algebra and to show how the allocations could be accomplished via matrix inversion and multiplication. Churchill [1964], virtually simultaneously and coincidentally, also pointed out the role of matrix algebra for this problem. Livingstone [1969] placed the problem in a more general setting by showing that it was a special case of input-output analysis.

Manes [1965] questioned the particular system of equations used by Williams and Griffin and the other authors. These equations charged a service department for the services it used from other service departments. Manes pointed out that one could also give a service department credit for services that it provided to other service departments. With this motivation, he developed a different system of linear equations to allocate costs and arrived at a different set of cost allocations. Building upon Manes' questioning of the original system of equations, Minch and Petri [1972] developed a third set of equations to reallocate service department costs. A principal advantage of the Minch-Petri method was that only diagonal matrices needed to be inverted so that the computations could be done without a digital computer.

Kaplan [1973] worked from a model which assumed that all the service department costs were variable. Using this model, only the original set of equations (proposed by Williams et al.) were shown to be consistent with the costs of providing service to revenue and other service departments in the firm. This paper provided an economic interpretation for some of the intermediate cost allocations that are produced by the matrix method and identified the opportunity cost or transfer price for use of a service department's output. In addition, the paper showed that the correct matrix method was indifferent between treating self-service costs explicitly (e.g., a power department must provide heat and light to itself) or just allocating on the basis of external service provided.

Thus, despite some initial uncertainty as to the properties of various methods for reallocating reciprocal costs, the use of matrix methods for computing a reallocated set of service department costs is now established and unambiguous. The value of using these methods versus the traditional step down procedure depends on the structure of inter-relationships among service departments. If the departments can be ordered so that in a matrix of allocations all the positive entries appear on or below the main diagonal, the step down and matrix methods will yield identical answers. The allocations from the two methods will differ most markedly when it is impossible to order departments so that no significant coefficients appear above the main diagonal of an allocation matrix.

Joint and By-Product Costs

The use of formal decision models, especially mathematical programming models to allocate joint costs, is one of the more intriguing yet controversial applications of quantitative models to managerial accounting. Many accountants and almost all economists argue that any allocation of joint costs (including overhead and depreciation over time) is arbitrary and serves no useful purpose. Yet, over the last 15 years, mathematical programming models of a firm's decision problem have yielded, in addition to the optimal decision rule, allocations based on the dual variables from the programming model. These allocations permit an overall or global decision problem to be decomposed into a system of much smaller problems. By using the allocations derived from the global model, managers solving their local or suboptimal problem will be motivated to achieve the solution that is globally optimum for the firm.

This is not an uninteresting property and would seem to be a necessary condition for any cost allocation scheme, i.e., that local decision making is not distorted by the allocation. Thus we can achieve a cost allocation that is rational, being based on a decision model of the firm, and is not capricious or arbitrary. But a fundamental problem still remains. The "correct" allocation is derived from a global model of the firm which also generates the set of optimal local decisions. Since the firm must know the optimal local decisions in order to derive the shadow prices that allocate the joint costs, why should we be concerned with the property that local decision makers will also accept these decisions as locally optimal after the cost allocation process? I don't have a very good or even a not-so-good response to this objection. About the best I can do is indicate in what direction future research may eventually provide a justification for this practice.

A desire for cost allocations (apart from external reporting or regulatory requirements) must arise because of decentralization. Therefore a justification for cost allocations will likely require an explicit treatment of uncertainty and information specialization which are among the principal motivations for decentralization. One approach that might prove interesting is to assume that central management has a simple, but not complete, representation of the production and sales opportunities available for each of its divisions or product lines. This simple model is solved and the dual variables used to allocate joint common costs to local managers. Local managers with a more complete representation of their actual production and sales opportunities will solve their local maximization problem incorporating the costs imputed by the central management. One would hope to be able to show that the solution arrived at by the local managers incorporating the allocated costs is superior to the solution which they would have obtained in the absence of any cost allocations. In spirit, this approach is similar to the simulations of the implementation interface performed by Demski to evaluate the ex post performance model, but in practice the methodology described above could be quite different. With this background and explicit reservation about the uses of the produced cost allocations, let us now survey the results we do have.

Manes and Smith [1965] were the first in the accounting literature to point out the use of a mathematical programming model in a joint cost setting. Using a simple two-product example with separable nonlinear revenue functions (i.e., each product has a downward sloping demand curve), Manes and Smith showed that if free disposal is permitted, it may not be optimal to always produce and sell the maximum available of each product. In the situation where the optimal solution is to not sell all of one of the products, all of the joint costs should be allocated to the other products. The product not sold to capacity can then be considered a by-product. Manes and Smith did not see all of the structure that was available from the nonlinear programming problem and the Kuhn-Tucker conditions as evidenced by their remark "when all of each of the outputs is sold . . . then the accountant must fall back on one of the traditional joint cost allocating methods . . . ." Bierman [1967] provided a more detailed example of the joint cost problem introduced by Manes and Smith. He showed how the first order (necessary) conditions for a maximum did not always lead to the globally optimum solution, again because of the failure to model the free disposal assumption. Bierman introduced the concept of allocating joint costs proportional to the marginal revenues obtained from the optimal product mix.

Weil [1968] provided the correct conceptual framework for this joint cost problem by showing that in general the joint costs can be obtained from the Lagrange multipliers of the nonlinear maximization problem. With a linear joint cost function, the dual variables (or Lagrange multipliers) on the individual product output constraints will sum to the per unit joint cost and hence provide a basis for allocating the joint cost. If a product is not sold or processed to the maximum available, its dual variable will be zero and it will not receive any allocation of joint costs. In the more general situation where all joint products are produced and sold to capacity, the allocation will be proportional to the marginal revenues of the products. The joint costs produced by this allocation represent opportunity costs for each product; they represent the maximum the firm should pay for an additional unit of the product by itself. Also, if each product is assigned to a different product manager who is told to maximize profits and all products are charged to the managers at the allocated joint cost, the amount demanded by each manager will exactly equal the global solution.

The solution produced by this Lagrange multiplier allocation procedure is very different from those produced by any of the traditionally recommended joint cost allocation schemes. Because the allocation is proportional to the net revenue produced by the last unit sold, the profitability across product lines is influenced substantially by the profitability of this marginal unit and the allocation can be strongly affected by relatively small shifts in the demand curves. Nevertheless, it is the only joint cost allocation that represents the opportunity cost of each product and that can serve as a basis for decentralized decision making.

Hartley [1971] formulates a linear programming model to obtain the optimal decisions in a joint cost setting with processing costs after split-off, constant prices, and production and sales constraints. He also notes the importance of the free disposal asssumption. The objective of Hartley's paper is to provide a framework for optimal decisions in a joint cost setting, not to allocate joint costs to the intermediate and final products. Jensen [1973] suggests that Hartley's linear model is inadequate to properly handle sales constraints and the sensitivity of sales to price. He proposes that these features be modeled directly by a quadratic programming formulation which assumes a linearly declining demand curve for each product. The value of a nonlinear representation had previously been recognized, of course, by Manes, Smith, Bierman and Weil. Jensen [1974] provides an extended example of the allocations produced by a nonlinear programming formulation of the joint cost problem with units either sold immediately after the split-off point or after further processing. While having an extended discussion of this approach in the accounting literature is desirable, I could find little in this paper that was not directly implied by Weil's formulation.

Depreciation and Capital Investment

It may seem unusual to include a discussion of depreciation, which is basically a financial accounting topic, in a paper on managerial accounting models. But the acquisition of fixed plant and equipment and its use over time is analogous to the acquisition of a common input material to be processed into separate products. Depreciation is an allocation of a joint cost over time rather than over products. Despite this similarity, there has been little attempt until recently to develop a unified framework for discussing the two related issues.[8] The mathematical programming framework presented in the previous section apparently provides this framework, and in the process, gives us a much more satisfying model for capital budgeting decisions.

The use of mathematical programming models for planning capital investments is a relatively recent phenomenon even in the economics literature.[9] Turvey [1969] and Littlechild [1970] are the important papers in this area and Baumol [1971] embellished the model somewhat. Previously, it was common for economists to talk about capital expansion as part of a long-run marginal cost curve. This approach assumes that capital assets can be continuously bought and sold to adjust capacity. In fact, it is probably more realistic to assume that for most firms capital assets, once acquired, will be used within the firm for their remaining economic lives. In this case, each capital acquisition is associated with an increase in the capacity of the firm for a number of periods into the future. In a multiperiod setting, one can assume a demand curve for the firm's outputs for the present and future periods, a cost function for acquiring capacity in each period, and a set of constraints limiting output in each period to available capacity. Thus the firm can jointly determine price, output, and new investment in a mathematical programming model which maximizes discounted gross revenues less variable operating costs and costs of acquiring capacity, subject to capacity constraints on output. Note that capacity becomes a continuous decision variable within this model rather than the accept/reject variable for lumpy projects used in traditional capital budgeting.

Just as in the joint cost model, the dual variables or Lagrange multipliers from the nonlinear programming model may be interpreted as the opportunity cost of the capacity resources. If the acquisition cost of new capacity is linear, the dual variables in all future periods will sum to the acquisition cost and, hence, can be used to rationally allocate the acquisition cost to all future periods, that is, the dual variables serve as depreciation charges. Further, price in each period is set equal to the variable operating cost plus the dual variable for capacity (the opportunity cost of capacity) for that period. If there is excess capacity in a period, then price is simply short-run variable cost. Finally, the decentralization property also holds. If a manager is charged for capacity at a rate given by the depreciation charge for a period (i.e., the dual variable), but is left free to choose price and output, the manager will select the price and output given in the global plan and will demand just the amount of capacity that is being supplied by the global model. I find these to be interesting possibilities to pursue, since the model allows price, output and investment to be jointly determined, simultaneously. Most current capital budgeting models assume a given output and price and then determine whether a particular investment is worthwhile.

It is interesting that the derived depreciation schedule assuming stationary demand is quite different from the "theoretically correct" annuity depreciation method advocated by many accountants to equalize rates of return in all periods. To date, there has been little exploitation or investigation in the accounting literature of the properties and implications of the derived depreciation schedule from the mathematical programming formulation. Relating this development to ROI and residual income measurements would seem to be an interesting exercise.

Overhead

Last and perhaps least of our trilogy of joint costing problems is the allocation of overhead to products. I hesitate to even raise the subject since the debate between direct costers and full costers has rarely sought the dignified ground of formal mathematical models and models of maximizing behavior. This is surprising from at least one point of view since one of the best criticisms that full costers fling at direct costers is that with limited production capacity, direct costs considerably underestimate the opportunity costs of producing a given product mix. Yet full costers, relevant costers and even cost obviators have not formulated the model from which the opportunity costs could be generated. Note that the nonlinear programming model for capacity expansion and depreciation described in the previous section does generate an opportunity cost for capacity in each period which can easily be interpreted as a depreciation or overhead charge for providing capacity in that period.

In Kaplan and Thompson [1971], we present a model which enables overhead to be allocated to products proportional to their use of scarce resources. Two types of overhead charges are identified. One is associated with charges that could be directly traced to each capacity resource. These costs are allocated to products proportionately to their use of each capacity resource. Costs of resources which are not used to capacity cannot be allocated to products directly; i.e., there are no charges associated with the use of surplus resources. Costs not traceable to scarce capacity resources are lumped into a common overhead pool and allocated to products proportionately to their profitability.[10] The interesting feature of this allocation is that the identical product mix would be chosen both before and after the overhead allocation so that the process at least yields an allocation procedure that does not distort optimal decisions, a feature not common to most overhead allocation schemes.

One reason given by many managers for a fully allocated cost scheme is for guidance on pricing decisions. In a subsequent paper, Kaplan and Welam [1973] extend the constant price linear programming model to a nonlinear programming model, allowing price and costs to be a function of output. Again it is possible to fully allocate overhead costs using the dual variables from the programming model in such a way that the optimal solution after the allocation is identical to the preallocation optimal solution. Thus, the message of first choosing price and output and then to allocate overhead, not the reverse, is again justified.

Colantoni, Manes and Whinston [1969] develop a mathematical programming model for a firm which wishes to maximize profits when prices are proportional to fully allocated costs. This is a reasonable representation for firms bidding on cost-plus contracts from a government agency or for firms satisficing by achieving a given markup over "costs." It turns out that if the markup percentage is the same for all jobs, and fixed costs are always allocated to activities, then the problem reduces to ordinary profit maximization. More complicated situations are also analyzed in this paper.

Itami and Kaplan [1976] compute average unit costs for multiple products which can be produced in a variety of ways on differing production processes so that there is no unique variable cost for any product. Using an activity analysis framework, a special type of linear programming problem, average unit costs are computed which in some sense summarize the alternative production processes used to produce each good, the use of joint products, and some activities such as overtime, power, and supervision which are normally treated separately as overhead costs.

Thus, mathematical programming models of a variety of managerial decisions can be used to derive costs that impute the opportunity costs associated with producing the optimal level and mix of output. These allocations are more defensible than those traditionally advocated in the cost accounting literature since they are derived from a rational model of maximizing behavior for the firm. The allocations are still not completely defensible since, given that we have the model of maximizing behavior for the firm, it is not clear what is added by allocating joint costs, acquisition costs, or overhead costs to products or time periods. The allocations can motivate optimal decisions at a decentralized level but these decisions had already been determined from the centralized model. A succinct and not completely frivolous conclusion from these sections is: We're not telling you to allocate, but if you must, use one of the models described here.

TRANSFER PRICING

Transfer pricing has received extensive attention not only in the accounting literature but also in the economics and management science journals. It is a complex and controversial subject which I will barely touch on in this survey. The principal reason for discussing it at all is that mathematical programming models have been widely discussed as an approach to computing transfer prices. Dopuch and Drake [1964] provide the first general discussion for accountants of the use of programming techniques for transfer pricing. Manes [1970] provides an excellent illustration of the use and limitations of transfer prices derived from a linear programming model of the firm by working through a numerical example based on the Birch Paper transfer pricing case. Manes shows that the programming approach allocates profits to those divisions that are most tightly constrained, thereby providing incentives for division managers to underestimate their capacity or to be sure never to have excess capacity.

Large changes in transfer prices occur as divisions reach or recede from capacity. Also, small changes in the firm's opportunity set lead to dramatic reallocations of intrafirm profitability. Further, it is not clear who should get credit for the imputed profits (dual variables) associated with constraints other than production or capacity constraints. In short, the linear programming approach appears promising for this problem but has substantial and perhaps insurmountable problems associated with its use. Even more than in the joint cost cases, one must admit that if central management has a good representation of the opportunity set and production technology of the firm, then attempts to use this information to assign profits to divisions may lead to more difficulties than benefits. As an additional problem, when the dual prices from a linear program are used as transfer prices, some of the linear programs representing the divisional models are degenerate and the global optimum may not be achieved at the local level. Kydland [1975] provides a form of hierarchical decomposition which can avoid this problem in certain cases.

Onsi [1970] discusses a mathematical programming approach to the transfer price problem but one must be less than confident about his recommendations since they are based on the dual variables from two constraints, one of which is simply 1.5 times the other. Just how one can get two useful dual variables from essentially one constraint is an unsolved problem at this time. For additional discussion of quantitative approaches to transfer pricing, one can start with the survey by Abdel-khalik and Lusk [1974] and the references cited in this paper. My personal evaluation is that the ideas have been around for many years, and I doubt whether programming approaches are going to have much influence on the transfer pricing issue. The problem of getting reliable information from subordinates as an input to the model while knowing that this information will then be used as a basis to evaluate their performance seems very difficult to deal with at this time, especially since the transfer prices are very sensitive to the locally produced information on production and sales opportunities.

CONCLUSIONS AND RECOMMENDATIONS

I hope that the reader who has survived this far into the paper will agree that I have demonstrated the basis for a statement made in the opening paragraph of the paper on the usefulness of quantitative models for a variety of topics in managerial accounting. The models have formalized the way we talk about various issues and in many cases greatly aided our ability to think about these issues correctly, e.g., consider the improvement in discussion of joint costs that results from understanding the interaction between demand and output through the Kuhn-Tucker conditions. What are the prospects for similar advances over the next 10 years? I would not look for a continuation of the type of models described in this paper. Given the topics commonly taught in a managerial accounting course, it's hard to identify areas where new management science models are going to have a substantial impact on the way we think about these problems. There are still some issues on the margin which are worth exploring but not enough to support a major stream of research.

I can see two major directions for research in managerial accounting, only one of which is actively being pursued now; the other, unfortunately, is not quite as glamorous and is closer to being development work rather than research. The direction being actively pursued, of course, is the research on information economics and incentive contracting (see Demski et al. [1976] and Demski and Feltham [1976] for examples of this genre). This research models information as a commodity to be bought and sold just like wheat and widgets. The research to date indicates that despite the apparent similarity of information to other economic commodities, there are unique and difficult problems associated with acquiring and selling information. The research has involved very simple models and many simplifying assumptions but its data requirements are even more severe than most of the quantitative models surveyed in this paper. In addition to estimates of model parameters, one needs to know the cost of supplying various types and aggregations of information and the preferences and beliefs of the diverse participants affected by the choice of information system and incentive contract.

It is my impression that useful, implementable results from this research should not be expected over the next decade. (Recall that my operational definition of a useful, implementable result is one that gets incorporated into a standard cost accounting text in something other than an introductory or throw away final chapter, well separated from the principal messages of the book.) Nevertheless, this research represents the fundamental basis for managerial accounting concepts and should be explored to see where it leads us. The research certainly makes us more humble and less confident about advocating to our students certain popular procedures which ignore incentive effects of measurement systems or the diverse beliefs and preferences that may exist within an organization. It motivates us to introduce information cost and incentive issues in at least a qualitative way when discussing planning and control systems.

The other direction in which managerial accounting research might go relates to points I have made throughout the paper. In answer to the question I posed at the beginning of the paper as to why the quantitative models have had so little apparent impact on practice, I placed the blame on the failure of popular textbooks to incorporate new material. Perhaps this criticism was too harsh. What is apparently needed is some evidence that these quantitative models do have a favorable benefit-cost ratio in practice. Rather than extensions of existing models, it would be helpful to have confidence that already existing models have some utility. I would like to see some studies on the problems of estimating and implementing these models in actual situations with some estimate of the perceived benefits and acceptance of these models. Without such evidence, it is difficult to know where models need further extensions, e.g., is it really important to be concerned about the precise distribution of profits in a C-V-P analysis under uncertainty?

The activity of worrying about estimation and implementation problems of models is different from the basic research many academics cherish and are rewarded for. Yet at some stage, if we wish to maintain our ties to an actual profession, we should be concerned with the interaction between the two groups and not let our research and teaching activities be isolated from each other. I believe that if we had some good papers describing estimation and implementation experiences and some detailed cases written which captured these experiences, the introduction of the quantitative models into both teaching and practice would be hastened. Moreover, these experiences should set the stage for additional research on problems identified during the application of the quantitative techniques. At this time, the models have gotten ahead of the problems and we could use a consolidation phase to evaluate the practicality and payoff of what has already occurred and to learn what important remaining problems have not been addressed to date.

FOOTNOTES

[1] Helpful comments on an earlier draft were supplied by Stan Baiman.

[2] Bierman and Dyckman [1971] also incorporate extensive analytic models.

[3] In fact, other factors could be working. For example, Birnberg claims that the book would sell better if it had more than one chapter devoted to behavioral effects, while Dopuch and Demski claim that the book has a limited audience because it has too many chapters on behavioral science models.

[4] A fourth explanation will be discussed throughout the survey and summarized in the conclusion.

[5] An unfortunate characteristic of authors writing on this subject is to start with the claim that not controlling for risk and uncertainty may severely limit the usefulness of C-V-P analysis. This claim continues to be made despite a complete lack of evidence of financial executives stating that they would use C-V-P analysis much more if only it could handle risk and uncertainty. Moreover, there is no evidence that once the articles have appeared, C-V-P analysis has been embraced by managers because the distribution of profits can now be computed. It behooves researchers to be a little more modest about how breathlessly the world is waiting for their new model, and perhaps they should only suggest that their paper describes an incremental improvement to current practice and may prove useful in certain circumstances (and that it is unlikely to be hazardous to a company's wealth).

[6] I am excluding the numerous econometric studies on the long-run cost and production functions of firms.

[7] Accusing a study of having problems with heteroscedasticity is almost a knee-jerk reponse for critics of empirical studies. I recommend that in the future, anyone wishing to make this accusation be forced to obtain the data set and perform the necessary adjustments to eliminate this 18-letter condition. My experience has been that heteroscedasticity effects usually show up in the third significant digit of estimated coefficients.

[8] A preliminary version appears in Atkinson [1975].

[9] I am not counting the integer programming models of how to optimally select discrete investment opportunities under capital rationing.

[10] This second allocation rule which allocates overhead proportional to relative contribution margin, can be done on an a priori basis. Thus, unlike the other joint cost allocation schemes described in this section, it can be implemented without solving the global model first to obtain the dual variables.

REFERENCES

Abdel-khalik, A. Rashad and Edward J. Lusk, "Transfer Pricing Synthesis." *The Accounting Review,* Vol. 49 (January 1974). S-23.

Atkinson, Anthony A., "Cost Allocation and Valuation: A Programming Perspective," Carnegie-Mellon U. Working Paper, 1975.

Baumol, William J., "Optimal Depreciation Policy: Pricing the Products of Durable Assets," *Bell Journal of Economics and Management Science,* Vol. 2 (Autumn 1971), 638-56.

Benston, George J., "Multiple Regression Analysis of Cost Behavior," *The Accounting Review,* Vol. 41 (October 1966), 657-72.

432

Bierman, Harold, *Topics in Cost Accounting and Decision* (New York: McGraw-Hill, 1963), 36-40, 44-46.

Bierman, Harold, "Inventory Valuation: The Use of Market Prices." *The Accounting Review,* Vol. 42 (October 1967), 731-7.

Bierman, Harold, and Thomas R. Dyckman, *Managerial Cost Accounting* (New York, Macmillan, 1971).

Bradley, Hugh E., "Setting and Controlling Budgets with Regression Analysis." *Management Accounting* (November 1969), 31-34, 40.

Buzby, Stephen, "Extending the Applicability of Probabilistic Management Planning and Control Models." *The Accounting Review,* Vol. 49 (January 1974), 42-49.

Charnes, A., W. W. Cooper, and Y. Ijiri. "Breakeven Budgeting and Programming to Goals." *Journal of Accounting Research,* Vol. 1 (Spring 1963), 16-41.

Churchill, Neil, "Linear Algebra and Cost Allocations: Some Examples." *The Accounting Review,* Vol. 39 (October 1964), 894-904.

Colantoni, Claude S., Rene P. Manes, and Andrew Whinston, "Programming Profit Rates and Pricing Decisions." *The Accounting Review,* Vol. 44 (July 1969), 467-81

Comiskey, Eugene E., "Cost Control by Regression Analysis." *The Accounting Review,* Vol. 41 (April 1966), 235-38.

Corcoran, A. Wayne. "A Matrix Approach to Process Cost Reporting." *Management Accounting,* Vol. 48 (November 1966), 48-54.

Cushing, Barry E., "Some Observations on Demski's Ex Post Accounting System." *The Accounting Review,* Vol. 43 (October 1968), 668-71.

Deming, W. Edwards, "On Some Statistical Aids Toward Economic Production." *Interfaces,* Vol. 5 (August 1975), 1-15.

Demski, Joel, "Analyzing the Effectiveness of the Traditional Standard Cost Variance Model." *Management Accounting,* Vol. 48 (October 1967a), 9-19.

Demski, Joel S., "An Accounting System Structured on a Linear Programming Model." *The Accounting Review,* Vol. 42 (October 1967b), 701-12.

Demski, Joel S., "Predictive Ability of Alternative Performance Measurement Models." *Journal of Accounting Research,* Vol. 7 (Spring 1969), 96-115.

Demski, Joel, "The Decision Implementation Interface: Effects of Alternative Performance Measurement Models." *The Accounting Review,* Vol. 45 (January 1970), 76-87.

Demski, Joel, "Implementation Effects of Alternative Performance Measurement Models in a Multivariate Context." *The Accounting Review,* Vol. 46 (April 1971), 768-78.

Demski, Joel, and Gerald Feltham, "Economic Incentives in Budgetary Control Systems." Stanford Working Paper, presented to Accounting Research Seminar, Stanford University, August 1976.

Demski, Joel, Gerald Feltham, Charles Horngren, and Robert Jaedicke, "A Conceptual Approach to Cost Determination" (Ames: Iowa State University Press, 1976).

Dickinson, J. R., "Cost-Volume-Profit Analysis Under Uncertainty." *Journal of Accounting Research,* Vol. 12 (Spring 1974), 182-87.

Dopuch, Nicholas. "Mathematical Programming and Accounting Approaches to Incremental Cost Analysis." *The Accounting Review,* Vol. 38 (October 1963), 745-53.

Dopuch, Nicholas, Jacob G. Birnberg, and Joel Demski, "An Extension of Standard Cost Variance Analysis." *The Accounting Review,* Vol. 42 (July 1967), 526-36.

Dopuch, Nicholas, Jacob Birnberg, and Joel Demski, *Cost Accounting.* Second Edition (New York: Harcourt Brace Jovanovich, 1974).

Dopuch, Nicholas, and David F. Drake, "Accounting Implications of a Mathematical Programming Approach to the Transfer Price Problem." *Journal of Accounting Research,* Vol. 2 (Spring 1964), 10-24.

Ferrara, William L., and Jack C. Hayya, "Toward Probabilistic Profit Budgets." *Management Accounting* (October 1970).

Ferrara, William L., Jack C. Hayya, and David A. Nachman, "Normalcy of Profit in the Jaedicke-Robichek Model." *The Accounting Review,* Vol. 47 (April 1972), 299-307.

Frank, Werner and Rene Manes, "A Standard Cost Application of Matrix Algebra." *The Accounting Review,* Vol. 42 (July 1967), 516-25.

Groves, Roger, Rene Manes, and Robert Sorensen, "The Application of the Hirsch-Dantzig 'Fixed Charge' Algorithm to Profit Planning: A Formal Statement of Product Profitability Analysis." *The Accounting Review,* Vol. 45 (July 1970), 481-89.

Hartley, Ronald V., "Decision Making When Joint Products are Involved." *The Accounting Review,* Vol. 46 (October 1971), 746-55.

Hasseldine, C. R., "Mix and Yield Variances." *The Accounting Review,* Vol. 42 (July 1967), 497-515.

Hilliard, Jimmy E., and Robert A. Leitch, "Cost-Volume-Profit Analysis Under Uncertainty: A Log Normal Approach." *The Accounting Review,* Vol. 50 (January 1975), 69-80; also, "A Reply," *The Accounting Review,* Vol. 51 (January 1976), 168-71.

Horngren, Charles T., "Management Accounting: Where Are We?" in *Management Accounting and Control* (Madison: University of Wisconsin-Madison, 1975).

Ijiri, Yuji, *Management Goals and Accounting for Control* (Chicago: Rand McNally, 1965).

Ijiri, Yuji, and Hiroyuki Itami, "Quadratic Cost-Volume Relationship and Timing of Demand Information." *The Accounting Review*, Vol. 48 (October 1973), 724-37.

Ijiri, Y., F. K. Levy, and R. C. Lyon, "A Linear Programming Model for Budgeting and Financial Planning." *Journal of Accounting Research*, Vol. 1 (Autumn 1963), 198-212.

Itami, Hiroyuki, "Evaluation of Adaptive Behavior and Information Timing in Management and Control," unpublished Ph.D. dissertation, GSIA, Carnegie-Mellon University (August 1972).

Itami, Hiroyuki, and Roberts S. Kaplan, "An Activity Analysis Approach to Unit Costing with Multiple Interactive Products." Carnegie-Mellon Working Paper 72: 75-76 (May 1976).

Jaedicke, Robert K., "Improving Break-Even Analysis by Linear Programming Techniques." NAA Bulletin, Vol. 42 (March 1961), 5-12.

Jaedicke, Robert K., and Alexander A. Robichek, "Cost-Volume-Profit Analysis Under Conditions of Uncertainty." *The Accounting Review*, Vol. 39 (October 1964), 917-26.

Jensen, Daniel L., "Hartley's Demand-Price Analysis in a Case of Joint Production: A Comment." *The Accounting Review*, Vol. 48 (October 1973), 768-70.

Jensen, Daniel L., "The Role of Cost in Pricing Joint Products: A Case of Production in Fixed Proportions." *The Accounting Review*, Vol. 49 (July 1974), 465-76.

Jensen, Robert E., "A Multiple Regression Model for Cost Control Assumptions and Limitations." *The Accounting Review*, Vol. 42 (April 1967), 265-73.

Johnson, Glenn L., and S. Stephen Simik, "Multiproduct C-V-P Analysis under Uncertainty." *Journal of Accounting Research*, Vol. 9 (Autumn 1971), 278-86.

Johnson, Glenn L., and S. Stephen Simik, "The Use of Probability Inequalities in Multiproduct C-V-P Analysis Under Uncertainty." *Journal of Accounting Research*, Vol. 12 (Spring 1974), 67-79.

Kaplan, Robert S., "Variable and Self-Service Costs in Reciprocal Allocation Models." *The Accounting Review*, Vol. 48 (October 1973), 738-48.

Kaplan, Robert S., "Management Accounting in Hospitals: A Case Study." in J. L. Livingstone and S. Gunn, *Accounting for Social Goals: Budgeting and Analysis of Non-Market Projects* (New York: Harper and Row, 1974), 131-48.

Kaplan, Robert S., "The Significance and Investigation of Cost Variances: Survey and Extensions." *Journal of Accounting Research*, Vol. 13 (Fall 1975a), 278-96.

Kaplan, Roberts S., "Analysis and Control of Nurse Staffing." *Health Services Research*, Vol. 10 (Fall 1975b), 278-96.

Kaplan, Robert S., and Gerald Thompson, "Overhead Allocation via Mathematical Programming Models." *The Accounting Review*, Vol. 46 (April 1971), 352-64.

Kaplan, Robert S., and Ulf Peter Welam, "Overhead Allocation with Imperfect Markets and Nonlinear Technology." *The Accounting Review*, Vol. 49 (July 1974), 477-84.

Kwang, Ching-wen, and Albert Slavin, "The Simple Mathematics of Variance Analysis." *The Accounting Review*, Vol. 37 (July 1962), 415-33.

Kydland, Finn, "Hierarchical Decomposition in Linear Economic Models." *Management Science*, Vol. 21 (May 1975), 1029-39.

Lau, Amy Hing-Ling and Hon-Shiang Lau, "CVP Analysis under Uncertainty — A Log Normal Approach: A Comment." *The Accounting Review*, Vol. 51 (January 1976), 163-67.

Liao, Mawsen, "Model Sampling: A Stochastic Cost-Volume-Profit Analysis." *The Accounting Review*, Vol. 50 (October 1975), 780-90.

Littlechild, S. C., "Marginal Cost Pricing with Joint Costs." *Economic Journal*, Vol. 80 (June 1970), 323-34.

Livingstone, J. Leslie, "Input-Output Analysis for Cost Accounting, Planning and Control." *The Accounting Review*, Vol. 44 (January 1969), 48-64.

Magee, Robert P., "Cost-Volume-Profit Analysis, Uncertainty and Capital Market Equilibrium." *Journal of Accounting Research*, Vol. 13 (Autumn 1975), 257-66.

Magee, Robert P., "A Simulation Analysis of Alternative Cost Variance Investigation Models." *The Accounting Review*, Vol. 51 (July 1976), 529-44.

Manes, Rene, "A New Dimension to Breakeven Analysis." *Journal of Accounting Research*, Vol. 4 (Spring 1966), 87-100.

Manes, Rene, "Birch Paper Company Revisited: An Exercise in Transfer Pricing." *The Accounting Review*, Vol. 45 (July 1970), 565-72.

Manes, Rene P., "Comment on Matrix Theory and Cost Allocation." *The Accounting Review*, Vol. 40 (July 1976), 640-43.

Manes, Rene, and Vernon L. Smith, "Economic Joint Cost Theory and Accounting Practice." *The Accounting Review*, Vol. 40 (January 1965), 31-35.

Mansfield, Edwin, and Harold H. Wein, "A Regresson Control Chart of Costs." *Applied Statistics,* Vol. 7 (March 1958), 48-57.

Minch, Roland, and Enrico Petri, "Matric Models of Reciprocal Service Cost Allocation." *The Accounting Review,* Vol. 47 (July 1972), 576-80.

Morrison, Thomas A., and Eugene Kaczka, "A New Application of Calculus and Risk Analysis to Cost-Volume-Profit Changes." *The Accounting Review,* Vol. 44 (April 1969), 330-43.

Oliver, F. R., "A Cross-section Study of Marginal Cost." *Applied Statistics,* Vol. 11 (June 1962), 69-78.

Onsi, Mohamed, "A Transfer Pricing System Based on Opportunity Cost." *The Accounting Review,* Vol. 45 (July 1970), 535-43.

Ozan T., and T. Dyckman, "A Normative Model for Investigation Decisions Involving Multi-Origin Cost Variances." *Journal of Accounting Research,* Vol. 9 (Spring 1971), 88-115.

Ronen, Joshua, "Capacity and Operating Variances: An Ex Post Approach." *Journal of Accounting Research,* Vol. 8 (Autumn 1970), 232-52.

Samuels, J. M., "Opportunity Costing: An Application of Mathematical Programming." *Journal of Accounting Research,* Vol. 3 (Autumn 1965), 182-91.

Solomons, David, *Studies in Cost Analysis.* Second Edition (Homewood, Ill: Irwin, 1968).

Turvey, Ralph, "Marginal Cost." *Economic Journal,* Vol. 79 (June 1969), 282-99.

Weil, Roman L., "Allocating Joint Costs." *American Economic Review,* Vol. 58 (December 1968), 1342-5.

Williams, T. H., and C. H. Griffin, "Matrix Theory and Cost Allocation." *The Accounting Review,* Vol. 39 (July 1964), 671-78.

Wolk, Harry I., and Douglas Hillman, "Materials Mix and Yield Variances: A Suggested Improvement." *The Accounting Review,* Vol. 47 (July 1972) 549-55.

Zannetos, Zenon S., "On the Mathematics of Variance Analysis." *The Accounting Review,* Vol. 38 (July 1963), 528-33.

STATE OF THE ART — NON-BUSINESS ACCOUNTING*

by William J. Vatter

*Reprinted from *The Accounting Review* 54 (July 1979): 574-584.

SINCE the beginning of 1978, several publications have evidenced a renewed interest in those areas of accounting which are somewhat outside the purview of business-oriented thought — governments, quasi-public institutions (such as hospitals, societies, and clubs), religious organizations, universities and colleges, foundations and the like. The first to appear was a proposed revision of a chapter from *Governmental Accounting, Auditing and Financial Reporting*, published in 1968 by the Municipal Finance Officers Association. This chapter on Principles was circulated by the National Council on Governmental Accounting for comments to be returned by June 15. This is an improvement on the pattern of principles that has been developing since 1934, but no drastic changes in the well-established pattern are observable.

Some time before this, the Financial Accounting Standards Board (FASB) had commissioned a research study by Robert N. Anthony, entitled *Financial Accounting in Nonbusiness Organizations: An Exploratory Study of Conceptual Issues*. This was completed and published by the FASB in May, 1978, as a Research Report, in continuation of the Board's interest in conceptual developments in accounting. Following its usual practice, the Board arranged hearings to discuss written comments on the report on October 12 and 19, and a last one on November 3. The written comments were to be submitted by September 11. To facilitate this, a ten-page "Discussion Memorandum" was circulated on June 15: this was a statement of the issues raised in the Report with additional questions added.

At this writing (December, 1978) nothing further has been released by FASB except an 11-page "Overview" written by Anthony, entitled "Financial Accounting Concepts in Non-business Organizations." This paper calls attention to the need for a unifying theme from which concepts related to *both* business and non-business accounting might be developed. The author suggests that "capital maintenance" could serve as a starting point to build the conceptual framework. The argument for this is that both groups must balance inflows and outflows so as to avoid the erosion of capital if they are to survive. In the business firm, this produces an emphasis on earnings to cover costs, including the cost of capital. Capital maintenance concerns the non-business organization in the pattern of operating "within the budget" — a "break-even" case of capital maintenance. On the assumption that this unifying idea could be accepted, Anthony proceeds to show that only a few major questions would need to be resolved:

(1) A principle must be developed that will distinguish operating inflows from capital inflows.
(2) Principles are needed to establish when the non-business inflows are to be recognized; realization from sales of goods or services may not be adaptable to non-business inflows.
(3) While a business charges depreciation to match expirations of capital costs with revenue, non-business organizations acquire capital assets by grants or legislation, and principles must span this gap.
(4) There are other problems, such as volunteer services, gains and losses, and the measurement of income from endowments, but these are not difficult.

This result would be desirable, but the major difficulty lies in motivation; the business firm is motivated by the hope of augmenting its capital to produce growth from profits; the typical non-business organization has no such motivation, because its capital (indeed, practically all of its inflows except service charges) is supplied by asking for it, or having a legislature appropriate it. The basic point of California's Proposition 13 is that there is no way to provide motivation for governmental cost reduction and efficiency except to limit the supply of resources. Perhaps there is a way to control motivations in non-business organizations.

The only other item which this reviewer has found in current publications is a six-page condensed (typographically as well as rhetorically) "Analysis of the FASB Anthony Report," published by the Municipal Finance Officers Association. It is a digest of the report with an appendix that adds the questions posed in the discussion memorandum to a repetition of Anthony's 16 issues, but it offers no evaluation or comment.

Thus, the developments of the year with respect to non-business accounting are limited to the content of the Research Report, which is reviewed at length in the following pages.

THE ANTHONY REPORT

The report opens with a brief review of the current situation regarding the field of "non-business" accounting. There are a number of statements of accounting procedures applicable to such organizations as general or municipal governments, colleges and universities, independent schools, hospitals and other health and welfare agencies, churches, clubs, and museums. In addition, there are five AICPA Audit Guides, as well as a pending "Statement of Position," which when approved will apply to most non-profit institutions not now covered. Several states have laws which spell out the principles to be followed by their governmental units, but these are not consistent with publications of the National Council on Governmental Accounting, nor with the AICPA Audit Guides. In about half of the 50 states, the state accounting systems are on a cash basis, or some other basis not consistent with NCGA positions. A research study covering the reports of 46 cities indicated that more than half of them did not comply with NCGA principles. Some reports in the municipal area are seriously deficient. Jan Lodal is cited (p. 4):

> New York is perhaps the outstanding example of such a situation, having "balanced" its books according to its own self-imposed financial policies and system while accumulating a true deficit of $4 billion.

Anthony adds, "some users find existing financial reports deficient in that they provide fragmented information, are unnecessarily inconsistent in format and terminology with financial reports of business enterprises, and therefore are difficult to understand"(p. 4).

These and other considerations are seen as pointing to a need for action of the sort which has been the work of the FASB, and especially the need for a conceptual framework — "a set of broad, internally consistent fundamentals, and definitions of key terms." The purpose of the Anthony report is "to identify the problems that would be involved in arriving at one or more statements of objectives and basic concepts of financial reporting of non-business organizations."

The report does not attempt to define a "non-business organization," but the term "should be understood to include, roughly, governmental and other non-profit organizations" (p. 7). A more precise definition is deferred to Chapter 5.

The definition does not really emerge there, either, being lost in a complex of arguments concerning the criteria to be applied in establishing distinctions between business and non-business organizations.

There is, however (p. 8), a list of 25 non-profit organizations from an exposure draft dated April 1, 1978 of the AICPA Accounting Standards Subcommittee on Nonprofit Organizations. This list is fairly exhaustive, and it is "useful background for thinking about the problem." Anthony sets up two categories of non-profit organizations: Type A which includes "non-profit organizations [which] obtain their financial resources entirely, or almost entirely, from revenues realized from selling goods or rendering services" (p. 9), and Type B which obtain "a significant amount of financial resources from sources other than the sale of goods and services"(p. 10).

By way of further clarification of the scope of the study, the author gives his reasons for excluding the subjects of internal accounting, budgetary information, special purpose reports, and standards, as such. Human resource and social accounting as well as the measurement concept (departures from historical cost) are excluded, except that "depreciation on replacement cost, and the computation of endowment earnings in periods of changing price levels are exceptions to the basic approach." Issues having to do with multi-level and consolidated reports, affiliated and ancillary organizations, or overlapping of interests are excluded as matters of standards rather than concepts. There are six pages of premises of the study, mostly concerned with the accounting model, references to earlier studies, and assumptions about users of financial information.

The plan of the report is given:

Chapter 2.   Problems of identifying users and their information needs.
Chapter 3.   Alternative concepts of reporting; Operating versus Financial Flow Statements.
Chapter 4.   Alternative concepts regarding certain items reported in Financial Statements.
Chapter 5.   Three basic issues regarding the appropriate boundaries for a set of accounting concepts for non-business organizations.

A section is devoted to special terminology, but since these definitions are restated more concisely (in a longer list which does not include "spending"), we defer discussion of them here. However, we note that

> *Spending* has to do with the resources used in an accounting period. It is an intentionally vague term, broad enough to encompass the alternative specific concepts of encumbrance, expense, expenditure, or cash disbursement. Its only purpose is to permit statements to be made that do not imply a preference for one of these specific concepts. It is *not* recommended for use in a concepts statement; a concepts statement should use one or more of the specific terms, depending on the approach that is finally decided upon (p. 30).

Chapter 2 is concerned with two of the 16 basic issues. One is identifying the principal classes of users of non-business reports; the other is identifying the information needs of these users that can be met by general purpose financial reports.

The list of users includes: (1) Governing Bodies, (2) Investors and creditors, (3) Resource-providers, (4) Oversight Bodies (i.e., regulatory agencies or committees of legislatures), and (5) Constituents (taxpayers, the general public, participants in a health maintenance organization, or members of a club or fraternal organization). The author recognizes the lack of sharp distinctions among these groups. They overlap; they are not exhaustive; not all of them are found in every organization; their importance varies as between different entities and at different times; they are not equally competent; nor do they all have sufficient time to form positive judgments from the review of financial reports. There are other groups who use financial information that are not included, because their needs are highly individual or special, and cannot be considered in formulating a conceptual framework.

Based upon this configuration of users, the general nature of user needs for information is set up in four categories: (1) Financial Viability, (2) Fiscal Compliance, (3) Management Performance, and (4) Cost of Services Provided. *Financial Viability* comprises more than the usual tests of solvency and liquidity; also involved are (a) the nature of resource inflows (the degree of confidence that the resource-flows from given sources may be depended upon to continue at given levels) and (b) resource transferability (whether resources can be transferred to achieve various purposes, or whether they are restricted to specified activities). In part, viability. . .

> is indicated by the relationship between resource inflows and resource outflows during a period. This is analogous to the concept of "earnings" in a business enterprise, which also shows the difference between resource inflows (i.e., revenues and gains) and resource outflows (i.e., expenses and losses) (p. 49).

But on the immediately preceding page, the "earnings" concept was rejected:

> In analyzing the type of information needed by those interested in nonbusiness organizations, this approach [earnings] seems inadequate for two reasons. First, earnings, or profitability, as such is not an appropriate concept in a nonbusiness organization, almost by definition. Second, the groups of users identified in the preceding section have needs that cannot be satisfied by an "earnings" amount, or by a number that is analogous to it (p. 48).

Fiscal compliance refers to the spending mandates legally prescribed, (appropriations, or conditions with respect to grants) or by expressed intentions of the governing body. Users seek assurance that these mandates have been complied with, and that resources have been used for the intended purposes. *Management performance* is a matter of. . .

> how well the money was spent, to the extent that accounting can shed light on this. (The terms "stewardship" and "accountability" are often used for this idea, but these terms are used by some people to refer to compliance only.) (p. 50).

Thus, user needs for information about management performance are merely mentioned; since budgetary information has been excluded from consideration, it is difficult to see how users could appraise performance except by using cost of services performed, which is discussed as follows:

> Citizens are interested in how much their government spends for recreational facilities as compared with roads. Prospective donors may be interested in the amount a college spends for its library compared with its athletic program. . . . Creditors, for example, may have doubts as to the long run viability of an organization that spends what is believed to be an inordinate amount for administration. . . . [U]sers also need program spending information that has a time dimension. They need to know whether current constituents receive an equitable amount of services as contrasted with that which is to be provided to future constituents (pp. 50-52).

To the writer, it seems obvious that this emphasis on comparison really suggests the clear superiority of *expense* (rather than expenditure) as a measure of current period costs. The report, however, passes over this point in the attempt to remain "neutral."

The chapter closes with some observations on the difficulty of measuring goal attainment as expressed in money; the lack of unanimity as to the items included in user needs and their relative importance; and the limitations of financial reports in the attempt to report such things as the reputation of the organization, the ability of its personnel, and the quality of the services provided.

Chapter 3 is concerned with how financial reports can best meet the needs of users. First, there is a summary of the general contents of the three basic financial reports used in the business area — the Income Statement, the Statement of Changes in Financial Position, and the Balance Sheet. The Balance Sheet is here viewed as of minor importance; when that issue is raised (No. 14, discussed at p. 114f.), Anthony concludes:

> In short, no conceptual issue that is peculiar to the balance sheet has been identified. This may, however, be an oversight. In order to provide an opportunity to raise and discuss issues

that may exist, the following is included in the list of issues: . . . Are there conceptual issues related to the balance sheet? (p. 115).

The author's position is that a thorough consideration of the various flow statements would answer the question of how things might appear (and what should appear) on a Balance Sheet.

Ten definitions are presented as special terminology (four of which were discussed at length in Chapter 1) (pp. 30-31). These are condensed here. *Financial Resource Inflows* are all financial resources made *available*, [reviewer's italics] during an accounting period that increase an organization's equity. They consist of *Operating Inflows* and *Capital Inflows*. Operating Inflows are related to operations of the current period and include (1) *Revenues* and (2) *Other Operating Inflows*. (Gains and losses are excluded for simplicity.) Revenues are amounts realized in exchange for goods and services during the current period. Other operating inflows (Non-revenue inflows) include "all operating inflows other than revenues." (After giving examples, the author adds, "to the extent that these inflows are related to the operating activities of the current period") (p. 61). *Capital Inflows* include "all financial inflows other than operating inflows" but again, after giving examples, a phrase is added: "to the extent that these [capital] inflows are intended for the benefit of activities of future periods" (p. 61). *Asset Conversions* are transactions that "convert an asset or liability into another asset or liability but that do not result in a change in the organization's equity" (p. 61). *Expenses* are the "monetary measure of the amounts of goods and services used for operating activities of the current period" (p. 61). *Expenditures* are the "monetary measure of the [total] amounts of goods and services acquired during the current period, whether or not used in operating activities of that period" (p. 61). *Operating Statement*—A report showing "operating inflows, expenses, and the difference between them during the current period" (p.61). A *Financial Flow Statement* reports "*some or all* [reviewer's italics] of the financial resource inflows, expenditures, and/or asset conversions during the current period" (p. 61). (The italics added by the reviewer cover the case illustrated as Statement F (p. 65) and further discussed herein, below, p. 441 of this paper.) The definitions of expense and expenditure are worth a comment. The cost of goods and services used during a period would include depreciation as a cost of using an asset during the period, as well as the cost of future payments which will be required to compensate employees for vacations, leave pay, or pensions *earned* during the period even though they may be payable in the future, one or many periods hence. Expenditure would not include these items, but would include purchased goods in inventory at the end of the current period.

This terminology is applied to a number of illustrative reports, the first of which is an Operating Statement which is *not* a "financial flow statement," i.e., one which recognizes current period costs measured as *expenses*. To distinguish this from the other (financial flow) reports, the operating statement has no identifying symbol other than its title, while the financial flow statements are lettered A, B, C . . . F.

The Operating Report shows Revenues (400), Endowment Earnings (80), Grants for Operations (60), and Total Operating Inflows (540). This amount is reduced by Expenses (510) to arrive at "Operating Excess" (30). "Operating Excess" unfortunately suggests redundance, indulgence, or superfluity. It might have been replaced by "increase in Current Equity from Operations," or, more simply, "Operating Margin."

Financial Flow Statement A begins with the "Operating Excess" from the operating statement and adds "Noncash Expenses" (20) to obtain 50 as Total from Operations. To this are added Increase in Borrowing (38) to show Total Sources (88). Additions to Inventory (55) and Transfers to Plant (40) — a total of 95 — are subtracted from the Total Sources (88) to arrive at a Decrease in Cash (7). The "Transfer to Plant" suggests that there may be a plant "group of accounts," but there is no other mention of that possibility.

Financial Flow Statement B is one that could be used to replace the operating statement by integrating its content within it. But the expense data in the first operating statement are replaced by expenditure data. Thus, while the Operating Inflows remain at 540, total Expenditures are 545, and the Inflow from Operations becomes an *Out*flow of 5. This outflow is covered by the Increase in Borrowing (38), making the net Total Sources (33). Deducting the Transfers to Plant (40) (but *not* the Addition to Inventory (55), which was included in operating expenditures), the Decrease in Cash is again 7.

Financial Flow Statement C is in another form, showing three funds. The Operating Fund is represented only by the label, "Same as A or B." But Statement A showed Inflow from Operations (50) — adding Depreciation (20) to Operating Excess (30), while Statement B showed Operating *Outflows* of 5. Statement B omits Additions to Inventory (55) since it is included in Operating Expenditures. These items offset each other, but it is confusing to treat them this way, having the remainders taken care of in a separate report.

Statement C is different from the earlier ones, as transactions are added to the discussion. There are now Endowment Gifts (140) added to the Monetary Capital Flows Fund, together with Endowment Income (70), and Endowment Gains (20), which total to 230 of Inflows to the Fund. The outflow consists of only the 80 previously included as Endowment Earnings in the Operating Inflows. The Plant Fund also has two additional transactions, Additional Borrowing (25) and Grants for Plant (70). Thus, the "Plant Fund" part of Statement C combines the Additional Borrowing (25) and Grants for Plant (70) with the Transfers of 40 shown in earlier reports to get Total Sources of 135. A deduction for Depreciation of (20) reduces the Plant Increase to 115. Note that the 20 of depreciation is an *expense* in the plant group of accounts, but does not affect operations in any way. Operating expenditures in Statement B were 545, which is expense of 510 plus inventory additions of 55 *minus* depreciation of 20. This is the correct *expenditure* figure, but it does *not* include depreciation.

There is still another difficulty here. The reader may have noticed that Endowment Earnings (80) (in the *operating* statement) has become Endowment Income (70) in the Monetary Capital Flows. Evidently some of the 70 income plus 20 gains was retained in the Monetary Capital Flows Fund, in the form of cash.

Financial flow Statement D arranges Revenues (400), Endowment Income and Gains (90), Endowment Gifts (140), both Operating and Plant Borrowing (63), and both Current and Plant Fund Gifts (130) to produce Total Sources (823), less the sum of Operating Expenditures (545), Endowment Fund Investments (of Gifts) (135), and Plant Additions (126), or 806 for Total Uses, to yield a Cash Increase of 17. The Investment of Endowment Gifts (135) and the Plant Additions of (126) are new items; they were not in Statement C. The Cash Increase (17) is explained as the sum of Endowment Cash Increase (15) and Plant Cash (9), less the Decrease in Operating Cash (7).

Financial Flow Statement E is an aggregated statement (which shows the consolidation of all funds; it is set up to be accompanied by an Operating Statement). Because of this, it begins by adding "Operating Excess" (30), and Depreciation (20) to show the Total from Operations (50). The other inflows are Endowment Income (10) — the net after eliminating the Transfer to Operations (80) — Endowment Gifts (140), Additional Borrowing (63) and Grants for Plant (70), to show Total Sources (333). The uses are: Additions to Inventory (55), Additional Investments (135), and Additional Plant (126), a total of 316, which leaves the Net Increase in Cash (17). These totals, 333 (Sources) and 316 (Uses), are considerably smaller than those shown in Statement D, because the Sources in the Operating Statement were left out by showing only the Net Operating Excess added to depreciation, as in Statement A, to show 50 of Sources from Operations. Allowing for this, the difference in Total Sources is explained — 823 less 333 is 490, the amount of Total Inflows in the Operating Statement; but although the Endowment Earnings (80) was eliminated in the aggregation, the Grants for Operations (60) should not have been eliminated, for it was not an interfund transfer. The Total Sources must be 393, not 333.

Applying the same approach to the Total Uses, reducing it by 430 to correct for the 60 error in excluding grants, we get 806 − 430 = 376, the indicated amount of Uses as corrected. This result would show the Increase in Cash as 393− 316 or 77, not 17, as stated; something else is amiss. The answer is that Statement E started with the Total from Operations as 50, taken from Statement A (based on the original Operating Statement), when it should have used the expenditure-based figures from Statement B, which shows the difference between Operating Inflows (540) and Expenditures (545) as an outflow of 5, instead of the inflow of 50 in Statement E. This difference would bring the Cash Increase to 17, the correct amount, but the 55 of Additions to Inventory (shown *explicitly* in Statement E) would then not have been shown there; in an expenditure-based report, that item is included in Operating Expenditures as in Statement D, not as a separate "Use" as in Statement E.

While all this may seem trivial, this reviewer sees it as a reasonable argument against the use of different concepts and financial reports (especially the latter) for non-business and business organizations.

Finanial Flow Statement F. This method of presenting the result of activities for a period in a non-business organization reflects a basic difference from any of the preceding examples. It starts by adding Revenues (400) and Endowment Income and Gains (90) — leaving out the transfer this time — to get a "subtotal" (490). Expenses (510) are subtracted from this amount to leave an unlabeled deficit of 20. This, in turn, is covered by adding Gifts of Operations (60) to produce "Operating Excess" of 40. Capital Gifts — for Endowment (140) and for Plant (70) — total 210, are added to produce Increase in Capital (250). Borrowings of both kinds (63), the Additional Endowments (135), and the New Plant (126) do not appear. An explanation of the "Increase in Capital" (250) — not furnished in the text — is:

"Operating Excess" per expense-based computation,		$ 50
Less Cash Income retained in Endowment Fund		10
Operating Excess per Statement E		$ 40
Add: Gift to Increase Endowment	$140	
Gift to Finance part of New Plant	70	210
"Increase in Capital"		$250

The Total Increase in Capital (even by the definition implied) is 260, not 250. The 10 Cash left in the Endowment Fund is Income, and it is as much an Increase in Capital as Revenue less Expense. Whether Borrowings of 63, Plant Additions of 126 and Cash Income of 10 ought to be ignored in a Financial Flow Statement is not, in this reviewer's opinion, a moot question!

The remainder of the report is devoted to the dicussion of 14 remaining issues, which are listed here as they appear in the report:

Issue Three	Do users need a report of operating flows that is separate from a report of capital flows?
Issue Four	Do users need an operating statement?
Issue Five	Do users need a report of cost of services performed?
Issue Six	Should financial flow statements report encumbrances as well as, or instead of, expenditures?
Issue Seven	Do users need a single, aggregated set of financial statements for the organization rather than separate financial statements for each fund group? If the latter, what criteria should determine the composition of fund groups?
Issue Eight	Are there conceptual issues related to the balance sheet?
Issue Nine	How should the nonrevenue operating inflows of an accounting period be measured?
Issue Ten	How should endowment earnings be measured?
Issue Eleven	Under what circumstances, if any, should a charge for the use of capital assets be recorded as an item of spending?
Issue Twelve	Should pension costs be accounted for as spending in the period in which the related services were rendered?
Issue Thirteen	Under what circumstances, if any, should donated or contributed services be reported as an item of expense at their fair value?
Issue Fourteen	How, if at all, should business organizations be distinguished from other organizations for the purpose of developing accounting concepts?
Issue Fifteen	Should the federal government and/or state governments be excluded from the applicability of financial accounting concepts for non-business organizations?
Issue Sixteen	Should a single set of concepts apply to all types of non-business organizations, or should there be one set for governmental organizations and one or more additional sets for non-governmental, non-business organizations?

Issues Three through Eight are discussed in the remainder of Chapter 3, Issues Nine through Thirteen are dealt with in Chapter 4, and the last three are the focus of attention in Chapter 5. In the

125 pages or so used for these expositions, each of these 14 issues is thoroughly discussed in a general pattern, as follows: (a) introductory background, (b) statement of the issue, (c) arguments for each approach to that issue, (d) arguments against, and (e) comments of various kinds. This mode is in keeping with the intention expressed on page 29, where the author wrote the following about these issues:

> Background material. . . is intended to be entirely descriptive; if any value judgments are inferred, their inclusion is unintentional. . . Relevant considerations relating to the issue are listed. Essentially, these are pros and cons for each of the alternative ways of resolving the issue.
>
> It should be emphasized again that the study stops at this point. There is no attempt to weigh the relative merits to the various pros and cons, and hence to arrive at a conclusion or recommendation on the issue. This is the task for the next stage, if and when the FASB decides to develop objectives and basic concepts. . . .

This approach has the result of bringing to the fore (so far as can be seen) every position that *could* be taken by anyone connected with the study. The fact that the 53 advisors listed immediately after the preface were drawn from various organizations would tend to sharpen the issues and bring up whatever pros and cons appeared to be relevant. The group contained eight CPA firm partners, five accounting educators, 12 from various governmental organizations, six from hospitals and other health and welfare institutions, four from investment firms, three finance officers of universities, three from foundations, two from church organizations, and each from ten other kinds of organizations, such as the Community Fund, a professional society, a pension fund, a museum, and a bank. With such a group of participants, one would expect that no large stone or even a small pebble would remain unturned. Some examples are given below, to elucidate:

> [T]hose who favor the "expenditure" approach may refer to either of two expenditure definitions. One group favors the bugetary expenditure approach in which expenditures are recorded only for those items for which appropriations or similar resources have been provided in the current period; they would omit, for example, pensions and other liabilities that do not come due until the future and that will be discharged by appropriations or other resources expected to be provided at that time. Those who favor this definition maintain that there is no reason to record a liability if no provision is made in a current appropriation for discharging this liability. . . .
>
> Those who favor the conventional definition of expenditures, in which all liabilities are recorded as soon as they exist, maintain that to do otherwise is to present misleading financial information (p. 84).

In discussing the problem of timing (largely solved in business accounting by the concept of realization), the report takes the position that (pp. 123 ff):

> In general, an asset is recorded when the organization receives either cash or the unconditional right to cash or to equivalent resources. . . . [that have a] high probability of being received. . . .
>
> The revenue recognition concept stated above is a generalization that is amplified, applied to specific situations, and even changed on an exception basis by accounting standards. For example, the recognition of revenue on certain types of long-term construction contracts, and for certain precious metals are exceptions to the basic concept. . . .
>
> Although there are differences of opinion on the treatment of specific types of operating inflows. . . ., it is roughly accurate to say that there are two general approaches to the measurement of such [non-business] inflows in an accounting period. These are here labeled the "matching" alternative and the "availability" alternative. . . .
>
> A useful way of sharpening the distinction between these two alternative approaches. . . is to examine the differences that would result in the recording of certain types of transactions.
>
> Assume that property taxes are levied in November 1977, are payable in 1978, and are to finance municipal services in 1978. In the matching alternative, these property taxes would be operating inflows in 1978. In the availability alternative, there is some doubt as to whether the property taxes should be counted as operating inflows in 1977 (on the grounds that the tax levy can be used as the basis of tax anticipation notes in 1977) or whether they should be counted as operating inflows in 1978 when they are actually payable. (This doubt would be resolved in an accounting standard.)
>
> . . . if dues intended to finance 1978 services were received in 1977, they would be operating inflows in 1978 under the matching alternative, but they would be operating inflows in 1977

under the availability alternative. Dues intended for 1978 activities not paid by the end of 1978, but for which payment is expected, would be operating inflows for 1978 under either alternative.

The subject of depreciation of capital assets occupies 13 pages in which the methodology related to computations is not an issue (in keeping with earlier exclusions). The following alternatives are proposed as background for dicussion (pp. 137-38):

1. Do not depreciate assets. Omit depreciation expense from the operating statement.
2. Record depreciation expense when the corresponding grant, contract, or user charge of a service or program includes depreciation as one of the applicable elements of cost.
3. Record depreciation expense when the governing body intends to use the funds derived from operating activities to replace the assets being depreciated.
4. Record depreciation expense when the governing body intends to use funds derived from operating activities to replace the assets being depreciated *if* it sets aside in a special fund an amount equal to the depreciation expense.
5. Record debt service payments as an expense, in lieu of depreciation, for assets whose acquisition is financed by bond issues with a maturity substantially equivalent to the useful life of the asset.
6. Record depreciation expense for assets whose acquisition was financed by endowment funds when the depreciation amount is returned to the endowment fund.
7. Record depreciation on fixed assets to be acquired in the future, but do not depreciate fixed assets currently on hand.
8. Do not record depreciation for assets that constitute the organization's "infrastructure" (e.g., roads, dams, bridges, sewer and water distribution systems, educational buildings). Record depreciation for other depreciable assets.
9. Depreciate all depreciable assets, as in business organizations.

. . . In discussing the above alternatives, some people make a distinction between real property and personal property. They tend to favor a depreciation mechanism for furniture, equipment, automobiles, and other personal property on the grounds that these items have a relatively short life and there is a relatively steady need to provide for their replacement. . . (pp. 138-39).

Opponents of depreciation accounting recognize that under some circumstances the costs that are reimbursed through fees, grants, or contracts specifically include an allowance for depreciation or a charge for the use of facilities that amounts to the same thing. They deny, however, that this practice is a valid reason for reporting depreciation expense on the financial statements; the calculation of the reimbursement should be separate from financial reporting. They maintain that if the fixed assets were donated or appropriated in a capital budget, the effect of such a practice would be to collect double payment for them, once at the time of donation or appropriation for the asset acquisition, and the second time via user charges paid by current clients (p. 142).

With regard to Issue Fifteen, whether federal and/or state governments should be "excluded from the applicability of financial accounting concepts for non-business organizations," some of the arguments are:

Creditors. . . know that the unique power of the federal government to create money provides better assurance of repayment than can be inferred from any financial statement analysis. . . .

. . . The national debt differs in its essential nature from the liabilities of other organizations; in particular, there is no expectation that the national debt is a meaningful claim on assets listed on an accounting balance sheet.

The federal government is sovereign. The Comptroller General has statutory authority to set accounting standards for federal agencies. . . . It is therefore questionable whether any useful purpose is served by suggesting that concepts developed by another organization, such as the FASB, should be applicable to the federal government (p. 176).

CONCLUSION

This long and tedious discourse has taken liberties in correcting a few mistakes, offering some critical comments, and quoting extensively to present a sample — certainly not conclusive, perhaps inadequate, and possibly colored by the reviewer's own predilections, but nevertheless a sample — of what the report presents. The report is the culmination of much time and effort in producing it, and the problems dealt with are complex and difficult to evaluate. The author and those who helped him are to be commended for attempting to uncover the gaps that seem to exist between business-oriented accounting, and applications of it that are made to fit "non-business" situations. Those who will work through the report as the reviewer has done will gain at least a partial appreciation of what those gaps are, even if no ways can be found to bridge them.

Financial support for this paper was provided by Peat, Marwick, Mitchell & Co. Many parts of this paper rely heavily on Biddle and Joyce [1979], Joyce and Biddle [1981a, 1981b], Libby [1981] and especially Libby and Lewis [1981]. We wish to thank our coauthors Garry Biddle and Barry Lewis for their gracious consent to our use of many of their ideas in this paper.

BEHAVIORAL STUDIES OF AUDIT DECISION MAKING*

*by Edward J. Joyce
and Robert Libby*

PRIOR to the early 1970's, the auditor's professional judgment had not been the subject of systematic study. Today, less than ten years later, a sizeable literature on this topic exists. We attribute this development to three primary factors. First, the dramatic increase in litigation against auditors in the early 1970's accentuated the importance of improving the *effectiveness* of audits. Second, as the pressures of litigation began to subside somewhat in the late 1970's, competition among auditors for clients increased. This has led to an increased emphasis on improving the *efficiency* of audits. Finally, a conceptual framework for studying and evaluating auditor judgment under uncertainty—Brunswik's Lens Model[1]—became known to audit researchers. The increased concern about the quality of audit decision making and the existence of a mature, experimentally-based paradigm well suited to its study has been responsible for the rapid growth of the audit judgment literature.

The purpose of this paper is to review and assess the implications of this literature. The reader will note that we have defined the relevant literature as what is popularly known as human information processing (HIP) research in auditing. We feel that this category comprises the most influential of the behavioral studies in auditing.

HIP RESEARCH IN AUDITING

The great majority of HIP research in auditing has been conducted within three paradigms: (1) the policy-capturing paradigm, (2) the probabilistic judgment paradigm, and (3) the predecisional behavior paradigm. This section of the paper briefly introduces each paradigm.

*Reprinted from *Journal of Accounting Literature* 1 (Spring 1982): 103-123.

In the following section, we discuss the applications of these paradigms to particular audit judgment topics. The research methodologies employed within each paradigm are then evaluated. The last two sections of the paper deal with implications of the research for audit practice and suggestions for future research.

Policy-Capturing Paradigm

The objective of policy-capturing research is to build mathematical representations of auditors' judgment policies. Audit researchers have employed both analysis of variance (ANOVA) and multidimensional scaling (MDS) as modeling techniques.

ANOVA has been the single most popular policy-capturing technique used by audit researches. It has been used to model (1) internal control judgments [Ashton, 1974; Joyce, 1976; Mock and Turner, 1979; Ashton and Kramer, 1980; Ashton and Brown, 1980; Hamilton and Wright, 1981], (2) internal audit evaluations [Gibbs and Schroeder, 1979], (3) materiality judgments [Moriarity and Barron, 1976, 1979; Hofsted and Hughes, 1977], (4) actuarial judgments [Schultz and Gustavson, 1978], and (5) uncertainty disclosure decisions [Libby, 1979b].

In ANOVA studies, the researcher constructs a set of audit cases that are systematically different from one another. By observing how an individual auditor's judgments change from case to case, the researcher is able to estimate (via inferential statistics) how important certain factors (cues) in the audit cases are to that auditor. (The important factors are those that account for the most variance in the ANOVA of auditor judgments). The researcher also assesses the extent of consensus *among* auditors by correlating their judgments over the same set of cases.

Unlike ANOVA, MDS permits judgments to be modeled without a prespecification and manipulation of cues. This is advantageous in situations where judgments are made on the basis of cues that are ill-defined and not easily quantifiable. (Both ANOVA and MDS are described in more detail later in the paper).

Probabilistic Judgment Paradigm

Audits are conducted in an uncertain world. As the process of auditing has become more formalized, the role of the auditor in the audit process has changed. Increasingly, auditors are asked to make *explicit* estimates of the probabilities of uncertain events (e.g., the probability that an internal control system will fail to detect a material error). Probability elicitation research is concerned with developing techniques that provide good measures of auditors' subjective beliefs [Felix, 1976; Crosby, 1980, 1981; Solomon and Wilson, 1980; Kinney and Uecker, 1981].

As evidence is collected and evaluated in the course of an engagement, the auditor must revise his subjective beliefs. The audit research on heuristics and biases attempts to assess the quality of these revisions [Gibbins, 1977; Uecker and Kinney, 1977; Biddle and Joyce, 1979; Bamber, 1980; Joyce and Biddle, 1981a, 1981b; Kinney and Uecker, 1982]. Heuristics are informal judgment procedures that are intuitively appealing but lead to judgments that are sometimes inconsistent with normative principles of decision making. Research in this area is concerned with the identification of audit situations where such non-normative behavior will occur.

Predecisional Behavior Paradigm

Research conducted within the policy-capturing paradigm employs a ''black box'' design—that is, the judgment process of the auditor is inferred entirely from the relationship between the factors supplied by the researcher (input) and the final judgments made by the auditor (output). No attempt is made to look inside the black box. In contrast, research in the predecisional behavior paradigm attempts to obtain some data on how the black box works (that is, on the *process* of making judgments). Data are obtained from the auditor *prior* to the final judgment.

Two auditing studies have been conducted within this paradigm. Weber [1980] compared the memory structures of EDP audit experts and students in recalling EDP control features. Biggs and Mock [1980] had auditors think aloud while performing an internal control task.

In the next section, we review the applications of the above research paradigms to particular audit issues.

AUDIT ISSUES STUDIED

Internal Control Evaluation

The most studied aspect of auditor judgment has been auditor evaluations of an internal control quality and the audit program planning implications thereof. Because objective criteria for determining the true quality of an internal control system or the appropriate amount of audit work to perform in a subsystem do not exist, judgmental *consensus* or agreement among auditors has been the focal point of this research.

Judgmental consensus has long been a matter of concern for the profession. A major objective of professional training in degree programs and continuing professional education is to promote consensus in professional judgment. Within public accounting firms, detailed procedure manuals and review processes serve the same purpose. Finally, when auditor judgments are questioned in litigation or regulatory proceedings, successful defense often entails establishing a professional consensus (via expert witnesses) that the defendant acted in a prudent manner.

Most of the internal control studies replicated and/or extended the work of Ashton [1974] on internal control evaluation and Joyce [1976] on audit program planning. Ashton and Kramer [1980], Ashton and Brown [1980], and Hamilton and Wright [1981] substantially replicated Ashton [1974].

In Ashton [1974], each of 63 auditors from four different firms evaluated the quality of the internal control systems for payroll for 32 hypothetical systems. The 32 systems were generated from a fractional ANOVA design with six dichotomously scaled (yes-no) internal control factors (cues). The consensus among the evaluations of the different auditors was rather high. The average correlation among their judgments was .70. On average, the two separation of duties factors accounted for most of the variation in the auditors' judgments.

Joyce [1976] studied the consensus among auditors in audit program planning. Thirty-five auditors evaluated either 20 or 36 cases where five cues related to the accounts receivable subsystem were manipulated in ANOVA designs. For each case, the auditors indicated the number of man-hours they would plan for five categories of audit work. The consensus among the auditors on the audit program planning task was low. The average correlation among the auditors was .37. On average, the single separation of duties factor accounted for the most variance in the auditors' judgments.

Ashton and Kramer [1980] compared the internal control evaluations of students and auditors in identical tasks. Thirty undergraduate students completed Ashton's [1974] payroll internal control instrument. They found that the students were less predictable than the auditors (74 percent versus 86.6 percent) and placed less emphasis on separation of duties (36.9 percent versus 51.4 percent). Consensus among the students (.66) was slightly lower than that found by Ashton [1974] but still moderately high.

Ashton and Brown [1980] added two cues to the Ashton [1974] instrument to produce a more complex task. Thirty-one auditors (most with one to three years of experience) evaluated the internal control systems for 128 cases from a fractional factorial design plus 32 repeat cases. The two additional cues related to rotation of duties and the use of background inquiries for new employees. The results were virtually identical to Ashton [1974]. Separation of duties was the most important aspect of the auditors' judgments of internal control. Consensus was moderately high. The average correlation was .67. The rotation of duties cue had little effect on the auditors' judgments.

Hamilton and Wright [1981] investigated the effect of experience on internal control judgments. The subjects were 17 practicing auditors from a single office of a national public accounting firm. Five dichotomously scaled internal control factors were manipulated in a completely crossed factorial design. Each subject made evaluations of internal control quality for the 32 different internal control cases for payroll generated by the ANOVA design. A moderately high level of consensus was found between the internal control evaluations of the subjects. The average correlation was .66. In addition, separation of duties factors accounted for most of the explained variance in the subjects' responses. These findings are consistent with Ashton [1974]. Hamilton and Wright [1981] also reported that subjects with greater than three years of experience exhibited greater consensus than the less experienced subjects.

In a substantial departure from the Ashton paradigm, Mock and Turner [1979] sacrificed some internal validity for the sake of a much richer and representative set of experimental materials. The variables manipulated within an extremely detailed set of background data were internal control changes (fair to weak or weak to strong) and the level of detail in the instructions related to internal control. Each of the subjects (71 seniors and two supervisors from Big Eight firms) evaluated only one case, a departure from the within-subjects designs employed in the studies disussed above. The experimental task was to make sample-size judgments for four audit tests. Consistent with Joyce's [1976] findings, considerable differences in the sample-size judgments among the subjects (within experimental conditions) were observed.

In a study employing verbal protocols, Biggs and Mock [1980] extended the audit sample-size selection research of Mock and Turner [1979] discussed above. Two experienced and two inexperienced audit seniors thought aloud while making sample-size selections for the detailed case developed by Mock and Turner [1979]. While the small number of subjects studied makes generalization difficult, the more experienced auditors employed decision strategies that seemed to be markedly different from the inexperienced auditors. The authors also reported that all of the auditors attended to a much greater proportion of the available information than was indicated in the rationale memos produced by the subjects in the Mock and Turner study [1979]. Consistent with Joyce [1976] and Mock and Turner [1979], major between-subject differences in sample-size decisions were observed.

In one of a series of experiments designed to test for the existence and prevalence of use of the anchoring and adjustment heuristic in auditor judgments, Joyce and Biddle [1981a] examined the effect of changes in internal control systems on the extensiveness of substantive tests. The subjects were 132 practicing auditors from a Big Eight firm. Each subject made recommendations on the extent of substantive tests for two internal control systems. One system had strong internal control and the other had weaker internal control. The order in which the extensiveness recommendations were made was manipulated between subjects. Anchoring could not account for the results. Instead, the subjects apparently employed a contingent adjustment strategy where they made large adjustments when internal controls became weak and small adjustments when internal controls became stronger. The extensiveness of the substantive tests recommended by the subjects was not just a function of the quality of internal control of the system at hand, but of the quality of the internal control system evaluated immediately before. Large individual differences in the work-extensiveness judgments of the subjects were also observed.

Weber [1980] administered a free recall experiment to experienced EDP auditors and accounting students. A list of fifty computer controls from five categories was read in a random order and the subjects were instructed to write down as many of these controls as they could remember. In general, the experts remembered more of the controls than did the students. In addition, the experts tended to remember the controls in clusters conforming to the five categories of controls; no such clustering was observed among the students. These results suggest that expertise is related to the organization of memory.

The main findings of the above studies are consistent: (1) a fairly high degree of consensus among auditors on evaluation of internal control, and (2) little consensus on the planning of substantive tests. The latter finding is disturbing in that while consensus does not ensure accuracy, its absence may be considered *prima facie* evidence of inaccuracy.

Internal Auditing

Gibbs and Schroeder [1979] studied auditors' evaluations of the competence of internal audit staffs using a completely crossed factorial design. Each of the 146 managers and partners who participated in the experiment evaluated 32 cases. Five cues were dichotomously scaled and manipulated in the design: continuing education, educational background, knowledge of auditing trends and techniques, knowledge of company operations, and the amount of supervision. The latter two cues were most important in the group ANOVA model that was estimated. Substantial consensus among the auditors on this task was indicated by the high proportion of variance (68.5 percent) explained by the ANOVA. A major contribution of the study is a list of 54 internal audit department quality criteria obtained from a survey of 143 managers and partners from Big Eight firms and 111 internal auditors.

Materiality

Boatsman and Robertson [1974] modeled the materiality judgments of 18 CPAs and 15 security analysts. Thirty different cases were constructed from eight factors in a representative design. The subjects each classified the cases into one of three disclosure categories: no disclosure, footnote disclosure, and line item dislosure. Percentage of net income was the most important factor. No difference between the materiality judgments of the CPAs and analysts was found.

Moriarity and Barron [1976, 1979] employed conjoint measurement techniques in the study of auditors' materiality judgments. In Moriarity and Barron [1976], 15 partners from eight large public accounting firms ranked 18 cases by the materiality of an error in the estimate of depreciable life causing a decrease in earnings of $.5 million. Three variables were manipulated in a full factorial design: net income, earnings trend, and firm size. The net income effect was easily the most important. The authors report differences in the functional forms of the design models estimated for the auditors as well as differences in their implicit scaling and weighting of the cues.

In their second [1979] study, Moriarity and Barron examined the "overall preaudit materiality" judgments of auditors. The subjects were eight audit partners from four offices of a major public accounting firm. Each subject responded to 30 cases generated from the manipulation of five variables. Once again the income effect was strongest. The authors also report little agreement among the judgments of the auditors.

Ward [1976] assessed consensus among the factors employed by auditors in materiality decisions. Included were legal, technical, professional, personal, and environmental factors. Ward had the subjects order the importance of the factors using a sort technique. A statistically significant but unimpressive amount of agreement was observed between the subjects on this task. Thus this study provides further evidence of individual differences in the audit materiality judgments of auditors.

Hofstedt and Hughes [1977] manipulated three materiality factors in an ANOVA design. Nineteen MBA students assumed the role of auditors and estimated the probability that they would recommend disclosure of losses from the write-off of an unconsolidated subsidiary. Significant individual differences were observed among the subjects. On average, the magnitude of the loss relative to operating income was the most important factor.

The literature on materiality judgments is too small to make sweeping generalizations. Apart from the importance of net income, there appears to be little agreement among auditors on how to make materiality judgments. This is not surprising given the lack of formal guidelines for its assessment. Each auditor is left to develop his (her) own. This would appear to be an area where firms, in the absence of specific authoritative guidelines, might explore the development of formal models. One way in which firms might proceed is discussed in the section on suggestions for future research.

Analytical Review

In one of the two experiments on anchoring, Kinney and Uecker [1982] tested for the effect of unaudited book values on the intuitive analytical review judgments of practicing auditors. The authors hypothesized that the auditors' assessments of the reasonableness of unaudited book values would be anchored on those values in spite of their irrelevance in a classical statistics sense.

Subjects were given audited sales, cost of sales, gross profit, and gross profit percentage data for the two preceeding years and unaudited book values for the current year. The experimental task was to provide a range of values beyond which they would investigate a change in the gross profit percentage. A total of 154 auditors provided usable responses. Mean upper and lower control limits were, on average, a direct function of book value. While more research is needed, the results here suggest that less informal analytical review techniques may be advantageous.

Probability Elicitation

Four studies in this area [Felix, 1976; Crosby, 1980, 1981; Kinney and Uecker, 1982] have examined the convergence of alternative elicitation techniques. Felix [1976] assessed the prior probability distribution of ten practicing auditors using an equivalent prior sample (EPS) method and a bisecting method. The subjects first received brief training on probability and then were instructed to specify their prior probabilities for error rates for two attributes of an order-receiving, shipping, and billing system. The bisecting method was employed to permit a comparison with an earlier study by Corless [1972], which had reported large within-subject and between-subject differences in the probability distributions elicited from a bisecting method and a fixed-interval method. Like Corless, Felix compared the distributions from the two methods on the basis of quartile values. Somewhat smaller differences than those reported by Corless were observed.

Instead of comparing the distributions elicited via different techniques on the basis of the ratio of mean difference in quartile values to the average quartile value, Crosby [1981] employed a statistical significance test. Auditors assessed their prior probability distributions for the error rate for one attribute of a system using both an EPS model and a direct estimation of fractiles. The subjects received written explanations of the methods, but, unlike the Felix study [1976], they received no training. The distributions from each method were tested for significant differences in central tendency and dispersion. The null hypotheses of no differences in means, medians, variance, and 90 percent credible intervals were not rejected. (Note, however, that failure to reject the null hypothesis at conventional p-values is an extremely weak test for identifying differences.) The hypothesis of no difference in the 50 percent credible interval was rejected.

Crosby [1980] then computed the Bayesian sample sizes that would result from the probability distributions assessed by the subjects under the two elicitation techniques. The Bayesian sample sizes computed from the EPS input were smaller than those computed from the fractile method input. The Bayesian sample sizes from *both* methods, however, were smaller than those from judgmental and classical sampling methods. Since no "correct" sample size is known, we cannot conlcude which method is best.

The second of the two experiments in Kinney and Uecker [1982] investigated the difference in auditors' evaluations of compliance sampling results between use of a fractile assessment method and a risk assessment method. A total of 169 auditors evaluated one of four sample results and assessed the 95th percentile population error rate (fractile assessment method) or the probability that the population error rate exceeded eight percent (risk assessment method). The two methods employed were suggested in the proposed *Statement of Auditing Standards* on audit sampling [AICPA, 1979] as means for judgmentally controlling beta risk in the evaluation of compliance sample results.

The authors hypothesized that, due to anchoring, use of the fractile assessment method would understate the achieved upper precision limit for the population error rate, and use of the risk assessment method would overstate it. Using classical evaluations of the sample results as criteria, their hypotheses were confirmed: the fractile assessment method was more likely to lead to excessive Type II errors (too frequently concluding that a population error rate is acceptably low) and the risk assessment method more likely to lead to excessive Type I errors (too frequently concluding that a population error rate is unacceptably high). Kinney and Uecker [1982] argue that since Type II errors are more costly than Type I errors, the risk assessment method is preferable.

The only study in this section that did not address the issue of convergence among elicitation techniques was Solomon and Wilson [1980]. Instead they examined the relative consensus in probability estimates made by interactive audit teams, individual staticized audit teams, and individual auditors. The authors report increased consensus in an interactive or staticized team format over individual auditor judgments.

The research reviewed above generally indicates that different elicitation methods lead to different probability assessments, which can lead to different audit decisions. The choice of elicitation method does indeed make a difference. The choice of a ''best'' method from a cost-benefit standpoint is not clear from the research. A good deal of intuition must be combined with the present research results for a choice to be made. This research has had an impact, however. The Sampling Standards Task Force, for example, has revised the proposed *Statement of Auditing Standards* [1979] to exclude the fractile assessment method on the basis of the results of Kinney and Uecker [1982].

Source Credibility

Joyce and Biddle [1981b] and Bamber [1980] have examined auditor sensitivity to the reliability of information sources in different contexts. In two experiments, Joyce and Biddle had a total of 182 practicing auditors etimate the probability of collection of a large past-due accounts receivable. The subjects were provided with both (1) base rate data concerning the unconditional probability of collection and (2) data specific to the account in question. The reliability of the source of the latter was manipulated. The first experiment employed a between-subjects design and the second a within-subjects design. In the between-subjects design where the subjects were unaware of the reliability manipulation, the auditors did not differentially weight the data by source. In the within-subjects design where the subjects were aware of the reliability manipulation, they weighted the more reliable source more heavily. The findings suggest that auditors may not attend to important factors such as source reliability unless those factors are made salient.

In a within-subjects design, Bamber [1980] manipulated the technical ability (70 percent, 80 percent, or 90 percent reliable) of hypothetical senior accountants and tested whether audit managers differentially weighted their work. The subjects assessed the reliability of the control system for sales and receivables based on compliance tests conducted by a senior accountant and his recommendation. Bamber found that the managers' reliability judgments were significantly affected by the reliability of the hypothetical seniors. No between-subjects tests were conducted.

The research on this topic is too limited to have produced any definitive conclusions. Thus far it appears that auditors adjust their judgments in the appropriate direction to reliability changes if they are aware of the changes (as they are in a within-subjects design). Whether they do so when reliability is not such a salient factor, as in the real world, is another matter.

Judgmental Evaluation of Sample Results

While formal statistical procedures are often employed to determine appropriate sample sizes and to interpret sample results, there exist many audit situations where such procedures are not cost-effective. In these situations the unaided intuitive judgment of the auditor must be employed. A fundamental principle of statistics is the inverse relationship between sample size and sampling error. Gibbins [1977], Uecker and Kinney [1977], and Biddle and Joyce [1979] explored auditors' understanding of this elementary relationship. In spite of the statistical sophistication of most of the subjects, a substantial minority in all three studies made judgmental errors. While the auditors performed better than most subjects tested by psychologists (including university researchers), the limited research suggests that the relationship between sample size and sampling error be given increased emphasis in university auditing courses and in firms' continuing-education courses.

Disclosure Decisions

Lewis [1980] explored the consensus among auditors' decisions within a case involving dislosure of a contingent liability. Unlike prior consensus studies, Lewis operationalized the experiment within an expected utility framework. Materiality was manipulated in a between-subjects design. The author found a greater degree of homogeneity among the auditors in the high-materiality condition than among those in the low-materiality condition.

Other Issues Studied

The studies reported above had one factor in common: they studied the professional judgments of *auditors*. Several other studies have been conducted where the judgments studied were not those of auditors, but of professionals whose judgments are of interest to auditors.

Actuarial Judgments. Schultz and Gustavson [1978] used ANOVA to model the judgments of five actuaries, one each from five of the six United States insurers of accounting firms. Each actuary judged the probability of a valid claim in 32 different cases (and four repeat cases) produced from the five dichotomously scaled cues: (1) number of accountants in the firm, (2) percentage of write-up work performed, (3) rotation of accountants among clients, (4) size of clients, and (5) financial condition of clients. Consensus among the actuaries was very low. The average correlation among the actuaries' judgments was .12.

The Effect of Uncertainty Disclosures on Lending Decisions. In Libby [1979b], 34 commercial loan officers from four large commercial banks made loan recommendations and interest premium decisions for twelve cases. Factors manipulated in the ANOVA design included a verbal evaluation of management (positive versus negative), level of financial statements (75th versus 25th percentile statistics from *RMA Annual Statement Studies*), the disclosure of a litigation uncertainty, the issuance of a "subject to" qualification, and a supplemental expert report predicting the outcome of the litigation. In addition to the financial statements and management evaluations, the disclosure of the litigation and the supplemental report had large effects on the bankers' risk assessments. However, addition of the auditor's "subject to" qualification had no effect.

Audit Reports. Libby [1979a] employed MDS to test the similarity of auditors' and bankers' perceptions of the meanings of alternative audit reports. Thirty Big Eight audit partners and 28 "money center" commercial lenders evaluated the similarity of the messages intended by ten different audit reports (unqualified, different types of uncertainty and scope qualifications and disclaimers). A two-dimensional (cue) model was constructed. The auditors' and bankers' perceptions were compared using three methods. All methods indicated highly similar perceptions of the reports' intended messages.

EVALUATION OF THE HIP RESEARCH METHODOLOGIES

There are no free lunches in research. No matter how brilliantly executed a study may be, its contribution to knowledge is constrained by the limitations of its research strategy. Different strategies possess different strengths and weakness. In this section, we briefly discuss the strengths and weaknesses of the research methods commonly employed within the three experimental paradigms introduced previously.

Policy Capturing Paradigm

ANOVA. ANOVA studies are most useful where the objective is to assess an auditor's cue weighting policy while eliminating the effect of confounding variables. The experimental cases are constructed such that the intercue correlations are zero. Each cue is first partitioned into two or several discrete levels (e.g., high-low, yes-no, increasing-decreasing), and hypothetical cases are formed by taking *all* unique combinations of cue values (a completely crossed design) or a systematically determined subset of these combinations (a fractional design).

Fractional designs are commonly employed because they can model a subject's utilization of a given number of cues with considerably fewer hypothetical cases than would be required with a completely crossed design. The price of this advantage is the inability to assess certain interactions and the possible confounding of main effects with higher order interactions. Since few studies of human judgment have discovered interactive cue utilization, fractional designs appear to be the cost-effective alternative.

While ANOVA designs permit unambiguous estimates of cue importance in individual auditor judgments by avoiding the problem of multicollinearity among the cues, they do so at some cost. The hypothetical cases constructed from ANOVA designs are almost certainly unrealistic. They are unrealistic because cues in the real world are correlated with one another, and frequently these correlations are quite high. The subject is thus responding to cases which are, in part, unrepresentative of the situation to which we would like to generalize (some aspect of the real world). When the basic structure of the task is changed so that it is no longer representative of the real world task faced by the subject, the behavior of the subject may also change, and thus the experimental results may not be generalizable.

MDS. As mentioned above, ANOVA requires the explicit selection and partitioning of the important cues by the experimenter. Many judgments, however, are made based on cues which are ill-defined and not easily quantifiable ex ante. MDS techniques permit human judgments to be studied without a prespecification of cues. Subjects make judgments concerning multidimensional objects and MDS identifies the cues or dimensions on which judgments of objects differ and indicates the perceived position of each object on each cue. In addition, individual or group cue weights can be measured. A major conceptual difference between ANOVA and MDS is that in MDS "perceived" cue values replace the "objective" cue values preselected by the experimenter in ANOVA.

MDS is especially helpful in exploratory research since it places fewer constraints on the experimental design and thus permits the study of more realistic decision problems than does ANOVA. It also permits the subject to judge the objects on the basis of his own perceptual framework rather than the framework implicit in cues prespecified by the experimenter.

However, again these benefits are gained at considerable cost. For most MDS models, distribution theories upon which statistical significance can be judged are not available. Further, ex post identification of the cues relied upon by the auditor is often open to differing interpretations and the effects of intercorrelated cues cannot be disentangled. Finally, MDS builds a perceptual model whose relation to actual audit decisions may be less than obvious.

Probabilistic Judgment Paradigm

The application of normative decision theory to auditing [Kinney, 1975] provides the theoretical basis for probabilistic judgment research in auditing. Such normative models require (among other things) that the auditor (1) estimate a subjective probability distribution over possible states of nature and (2) revise his beliefs in accordance with Bayes' Theorem. The first requirement has led to research on probability elicitation while the second requirement has led to research on heuristics used in the revision of beliefs.

Probability elicitation. The primary issues in probability elicitation are (1) how well the subject can express his subjective beliefs through a particular elicitation technique and (2) the correspondence between the subject's subjective beliefs and reality. To date no study in an audit context with auditor subjects has addressed these issues. (See [Chesley, 1976, 1977, 1978] for examples in nonaudit contexts.) The primary reasons for the latter are the difficulty in obtaining a criterion for assessing how well an elicitatin technique has succeeded in capturing the unobservable subjective beliefs of a subject, and ignorance of the distribution of objects (e.g., errors) in the real world.

The probability elicitation research in auditing has instead focused on the issue of convergence between techniques (i.e., the similarity of results obtained from different elicitation methods).

Heuristics and biases. Where auditors can express their beliefs as subjective probabilities, normative principles of decision making require that these beliefs be revised (when information is received) in accordance with Bayes' Theorem. Two psychologists, Daniel Kahneman and Amos Tversky, have conducted a series of experiments which indicate that in at least some circumstances people revise their beliefs via processes fundamentally different from Bayes' Theorem. Tversky and Kahneman [1974] have identified some rules of thumb or heuristic judgment procedures to account for the observed discrepancies from Bayes' Theorem. Much of the audit research in this area has attempted to identify audit situations where heuristics are likely to be employed by auditors *and where such use would lead to costly decision errors.*

The psychology on which this auditing research is based is new and constantly evolving. (See [Einhorn and Hogarth, 1981] for a recent review.) The heuristics of Tversky and Kahneman are tentative constructs and remain to be integrated into a comprehensive theory of human judgment. Presently, little is known about how the information processing capabilities of humans interact with task structure to result in heuristic employment. Thus, it is difficult to predict the situations in which particular heuristics will be employed. To date, the research in this area has had a distinctively ad hoc flavor.

Predecisional Behavior Paradigm

Many important audit judgments involve ill-defined tasks where the auditor must search for information and generate and evaluate hypotheses. For the most part, the research conducted within the policy-capturing and probabilistic-judgment paradigms has provided the subjects with (1) well-defined tasks, (2) relevant information, and (3) prespecified possible responses. The subjects play a rather passive role in these highly structured decision situations.

Increased concern for the dynamics of problem definition, hypothesis formation, and information search in less structured contexts more representative of the real world has led to the development of research methodologies suitable for examining these aspects of predecisional behavior. The primary advantages offered by these techniques are the provision of a richer level of detail and the ability to provide sequential measures of decision behavior.

The audit research in this paradigm has analyzed verbal protocol data collected by having subjects think aloud into a tape recorder while performing the task. The tapes were transcribed and the protocols classified into predetermined categories relevant to the researchers' hypotheses.

While verbal protocols permit the development of relatively detailed time-dependent models of decision making, they do so at a price. Among the disadvantages are (1) the sheer volume of data collected in such studies which limits the number of subjects that can be studied, and (2) the lack of objective coding techniques. This makes the analysis arduous and the communication of the results quite difficult. Reports of verbal protocol studies are usually quite long and difficult to read, even when the results from just a few subjects are presented.

IMPLICATIONS FOR AUDIT PRACTICE

The consistency and consensus of audit judgments has been the focal point of much of the research we have discussed. This issue has also generated a great deal of interest among practicing accountants (see e.g. [Elliott, 1981; Holstrum, 1981]). Perhaps because of—or at least coincident with—these research findings, a number of public accounting firms have developed what is known in the judgment literature as "expert measurement and mechanical combination models." These models substitute structure for part of the audit judgment process to ensure that all important variables are evaluated and then combined into a decision in a consistent fashion. When employing these models, auditors measure parameters that are most efficiently measured subjectively by experts. Once the parameter estimates have been supplied, they are processed mechanically via the model. One example is the Peat, Marwick, Mitchell & Co. [1980] system for sample-size determination in substantive testing.

The method entails use of decision tables and equations that mechanically combine the auditor's expert judgments of the following parameters: (1) the size of aggregate errors in the account for which assurance is to be provided, (2) the results of internal control review and compliance tests, (3) the existence of overlapping substantive tests, (4) the prior probability of error, (5) level of sample stratification, and (6) characteristics of the distribution of dollar values. The output of the model is sample size.

Other firms are applying different expert measurement and mechanical combination techniques that also should achieve higher levels of consensus in audit planning. For example, Deloitte, Haskins, & Sells has developed a system which links evaluation of control components to specific substantive tests, and Touche, Ross & Co. has developed sampling reliability decision tables. At this point, no system directly considers the effect of prior periods' control evaluations, the importance of which is suggested by Joyce and Biddle [1981a]. This issue provides a useful direction for further research.

When a firm decides to restructure a portion of the audit decision process, policy-capturing techniques such as ANOVA can aid the firm in developing its new policies. Alternative rules for combining different factors can be modeled mathematically or graphically. By identifying different cue-weighting strategies implicit in the policy alternatives, differences are made *explicit* and can be discussed more directly. Libby [1981] demonstrates this approach by analyzing an experimental decision table developed by Touche, Ross & Co. to combine required overall level of assurance, internal control evaluation, and analytical review results in setting sampling reliability levels. A graphical presentation of cue weights and the implicit tradeoffs between the three factors provides a more systematic basis for evaluation than one by one consideration of each of the 18 values in the decision table. The approach may also aid in developing compromises when policy makers disagree because the models, in a sense, lay everyone's cards on the table. Research evaluating this decision aid might produce important benefits.

Other components of audit practice could benefit from similar research. For example, auditing firms spend millions of dollars each year selecting, training, and evaluating personnel. Policy-capturing research could play a major role in analyzing firms' selection and evaluation policies. In-house research usually involves tabulating success rates for employees from different schools or with different types of degrees. This research could be expanded to analyze the relative importance of various factors in hiring decisions (e.g., grade-point, appearance, etc.) and these "cue weights" could be compared with future success statistics for accepted candidates.[2] Such research might even result in the development of expert measurement and mechanical combination models where interviewers' evaluations of oral communication skills, professional demeanor, etc. could be combined with statistical information such as grade-point average.

Studies of the auditor as an intuitive statistician also appear to have affected practice by increasing the acceptance of statistical methods for sampling and analytical review. The academic research has coincided with considerable developmental work by most large CPA firms. Studies indicating a lack of understanding of elementary statistical relationships by many auditors and a lack of consensus among auditors' judgmental sample sizes have received the greatest attention. In addition to increasing the application of statistical models, at least one firm has altered its training materials to warn auditors of commonly made errors. As mentioned above, evidence suggesting that use of alternative probability elicitation methods often leads to different audit decisions has also led the Auditing Standards Board to exclude the fractile assessment method from the proposed *Statement of Auditing Standards* [AICPA, 1979]. We expect that as we develop a better understanding of the limitations of the auditors' intuitive statistical abilities, we may observe a complete elimination of judgmental procedures in this area.

Behavioral studies of the effectiveness of different audit techniques are a new and useful research area. The results to date concerning audit confirmations suggest that minor modifications in procedures can lead to improved effectiveness at little cost. In response to these studies, at least one firm has redesigned its procedures. Investigations of the effectiveness of other procedures are bound to be conducted in response to auditors' continuing efforts to increase audit efficiency and effectiveness.

In other areas of audit policy making, less progress has been made. Many of these questions, such as the need to alter the audit reporting structure, are more difficult to address directly. While we have a better understanding of the impact of uncertainty qualifications on lending decisions, even in this limited area, our knowledge is far from complete. In the materiality area, we are at a similar stage of development. Major contributions in these and other important areas must await the painstakingly slow development of a systematic body of literature. Unfortunately, this is the nature of the research process.

SUGGESTIONS FOR FUTURE RESEARCH

As the above review indicates, there is no shortage of auditor judgment problems to explore, and we believe this is largely responsible for the rather fragmented nature of the research. Much of the literature consists of single, isolated studies. The internal control area is the only one where a systematic literature of some size has developed—and this area is by no means exhausted.

The early internal control studies emphasized internal validity while the later studies emphasized realism. Neither type, *by itself*, could have produced results as impressive as those produced by the different approaches together. The generality of the findings has been greatly enhanced. We recommend a multi-method approach to other auditor judgment problems as well. No single research design, methodology, or strategy is sufficient to explore any problem. Multiple methods with offsetting strengths and weaknesses are the best way to enhance the external validity of research findings. Below we suggest some potential avenues for future research.

Almost all of the research on auditor internal control judgments has employed orthogonal designs. The lack of consensus found in audit planning may be, in part, an artifact of this design. For example, suppose that an internal control system with only two mutually exclusive control attributes existed: Control 1 and Control 2. Assume in the population of client firms that all clients had either both controls or neither. Note that an auditor judgment policy which gave 100 percent of the weight to Control 1 and none to Control 2 would produce the same judgments as an auditor judgment policy which gave 100 percent of the weight to Control 2. While an orthogonal design would indicate no consensus, the *real world* implications of such vastly different judgment policies would be zero. Orthogonal designs, by definition, yield cases where cue intercorrelations are zero. In audit populations, control features are probably highly correlated. Thus the different weighting policies found to exist among auditors in orthogonal designs may overstate the real world differences in auditor judgments. Different auditor *policies* might lead to similar auditor *judgments*.

To explore this issue, information about the empirical relationships among control systems is necessary. Firms in a particular industry might be sampled in an effort to obtain such data from several control sytems. A research design with representative intercue correlations could then be used to develop an experiment where specialists in the selected industry would serve as subjects. Consensus among the judgments of these auditors could then be assessed.

Virtually all studies of auditor decisions that have assessed consensus have reported considerable differences among the judgments of auditors. In spite of concern over lack of consensus, no study of the relationship between error magnitude, direction, and cost has been attempted. It is quite possible that a variety of combinations of audit procedures would produce the same amount of evidence at nearly the same cost. In this case, the interpretation of consensus studies becomes less obvious. This represents another possible area for future research.

Thus far, the issue of learning has not been addressed in judgmental research in auditing. Learning is important in a profession as dynamic as auditing because it requires that constant additions to the expertise of auditors be made. Psychological research in learning has shown that learning can be difficult enough in static complex environments. We would expect it to be even more so in dynamic complex environments.

Recent research into decision framing or structuring (e.g. [Tversky and Kahneman, 1981]) has interesting implications for auditing. For example, in the review of audit work, the supervisor, manager, or partner may unconsciously adopt the same perspective or decision frame as the auditor whose work is being reviewed. This might lead each reviewer to repeat the same erors. Research in this area could test for the existence of this problem and might lead to techniques that help reviewers avoid the problem.

Accounting research on heuristics and biases reflects the developing nature of the underlying psychological research. However, a variety of interesting avenues for audit research still remain open. An area with great potential is the "data salience" question. Recent research suggests that the perceived importance of data, e.g., base rates, is a function of a variety of task characteristics. This suggests the possibility that firms' policy makers could alter audit programs to direct the auditor's attention to important information (e.g., source credibility) and away from irrelevant factors. Simple pencil and paper attention directing devices may provide some of the most useful decision aids for auditors.

In the training area, further study of the differences between the cognitive processes of expert and novice auditors might lead to improved training methods where both substantive material *and* processing skills can be taught. Further, studies of the effectiveness of educational programs that sensitize auditors to their cognitive limitations are in order.

The above suggestions obviously represent only a small portion of the interesting judgment related auditing problems in need of research. In the short time period over which the research discussed in this paper was conducted, we have experienced a significant increase in research activity. Further, the research has already begun to affect auditing practice, particularly in developing consensus in audit planning decisions and in increasing the acceptance of statistical sampling techniques in place of judgmental methods. A continuation of this research will likely produce further changes which improve the effectiveness or efficiency of the auditor.

FOOTNOTES

[1] Brunswik's lens model is a general structure which highlights many important characteristics of decision making under uncertainty. It portrays the individual judging an event which cannot be directly observed (e.g., future business failure) through a "lens" of cues (e.g., accounting ratios) whose relationships to both the event and the judge are uncertain. The interaction between the individual and the environment is described by a number of relationships, including those among the cues, those between the cues and the criterion event, those between the cues and the judge's response, and those between the criterion event and the judge's response. These relationships are used to explain the accuracy of the judge's response usually in terms of the predictive ability of the information, the predictability (consistency) of the judge, and the accuracy of his (her) cue weighting. For a detailed description of the model, see [Libby, 1981].

[2] Although a thorough evaluation requires a sampling of rejected candidates, this analysis still provides useful information.

REFERENCES

American Institute of Certified Public Accountants (1979), *Statistical Sampling, Proposed Statement of Auditing Standards*.

Ashton, R. H. (1974), "An Experimental Study of Internal Control Judgments," *Journal of Accounting Research* (Spring 1974), pp.143-157.

Ashton, R. H., and Brown, P. R. (1980), "Descriptive Modeling of Auditors' Internal Control Judgments: Replication and Extension," *Journal of Accounting Research* (Spring 1980), pp.268-277.

Ashton, R. H., and Kramer, S. S. (1980), "Students as Surrogates in Behavioral Research: Some Evidence," *Journal of Accounting Research* (Spring 1980), pp.1-15.

Bamber, E. M. (1980), "Expert Judgment in the Audit Team: An Examination of Source Credibility," Unpublished Manuscript, The Ohio State University.

Biddle, G. C., and Joyce, E. J. (1979), "The Role of Sample Size in Probabilistic Inference in Auditing," Unpublished Manuscript, University of Chicago.

458

Biggs, S. F., and Mock, T. J. (1980), "Investigation of Auditor Information Search Processes in the Evaluation of Internal Controls," Working Paper 2-80-6, University of Wisconsin-Madison.

Boatsman, J., and Robertson, J. (1974), "Policy Capturing on Selected Materiality Judgments," *The Accounting Review* (April 1974), pp.342-352.

Chesley, G. R. (1976), "The Elicitation of Subjective Probabilities: A Laboratory Study in an Accounting Context," *Journal of Accounting Research* (Spring 1976), pp.27-48.

_____ (1977), "Subjective Probability Elicitation: Congruity of Datum and Response Mode," *Journal of Accounting Research* (Spring 1977), pp. 1-11.

_____ (1978), "Subjective Probability Elicitation Techniques: A Performance Comparison," *Journal of Accounting Research* (Autumn 1978), pp.225-241.

Corless, J. (1972), "Assessing Prior Distributions for Applying Bayesian Statistics in Auditing," *The Accounting Review* (July 1972), pp.556-566.

Crosby, J. (1980), "Implications of Prior Probability Elicitation on Auditor Sample Size Decisions," *Journal of Accounting Research* (Autumn 1980), pp.585-593.

_____ (1981), "Bayesian Statistics in Auditing: A Comparison of Probability Elicitation Techniques," *The Accounting Review* (April 1981), pp.355-365.

Einhorn, H., and Hogarth, R. M. (1981), "Behavioral Decision Theory: Processes of Judgment and Choice," *Annual Review of Psychology, 32,* pp.53-88.

Elliott, R. K. (1981), "The Future of Audit Research," *The Auditor's Report* (Fall, 1981), pp.3-4.

Felix, W. L. (1976), "Evidence on Alternative Means of Assessing Prior Probability Distributions for Audit Decision Making," *The Accounting Review* (October 1976), pp.800-807.

Gibbins, M. (1977), "Human Inference, Heuristics and Auditors' Judgment Processes," Presented at the Canadian Institute of Chartered Accountants Auditing Research Symposium, Laval University, November 1977.

Gibbs, T. E., and Schroeder, R. G. (1979), "Evaluating the Competence of Internal Audit Departments," in *Symposium on Auditing Research III,* Department of Accountancy, University of Illinois, Urbana.

Hamilton, R. E., and Wright, W. F. (1981), "The Evaluation of Internal Controls Over Payroll," Unpublished Manuscript, University of Minnesota.

Hofstedt, T., and Hughes, E. (1977), "An Experimental Study of the Judgment Element in Disclosure Decisions," *The Accounting Review* (April 1977), pp.379-395.

Holstrum, G. L. (1981), "Audit Judgment Research," *The Auditor's Report* (Fall, 1981), pp.3-4.

Joyce, E. J. (1976), "Expert Judgment in Audit Program Planning," *Studies in Human Information Processing in Accounting,* Supplement to the *Journal of Accounting Research.* pp.29-60.

_____, and Biddle, G. (1981a), "Anchoring and Adjustment in Probabilistic Inference in Auditing," *Journal of Accounting Research* (Spring 1981), pp.120-145.

_____, and_____ (1981b), "Are Auditor's Judgments Sufficiently Regressive?" *Journal of Accounting Research* (Autumn, 1981), pp.323-349.

Kinney, W. R. (1975), "A Decision Theory Approach to the Sampling Problem in Auditing," *Journal of Accounting Research* (Spring 1975), pp.117-132.

_____, and Uecker, W. C. (1982), "Mitigating the Consequences of Anchoring in Auditor Judgments," *The Accounting Review* (January 1982), pp.55-69.

Lewis, B. L. [1980], "Expert Judgment in Auditing: An Expected Utility Approach," *Journal of Accounting Research* (Autumn 1980) pp.594-602.

Libby, R. [1979a], "Bankers' and Auditors' Perceptions of the Message Communicated by the Audit Report," *Journal of Accounting Research* (Spring 1979), pp.99-122.

_____[1979b], "The Impact of Uncertainty Reporting on the Loan Decision," *Studies on Auditing—Selections from the Research Opportunities in Auditing Program,* supplement to *Journal of Accounting Research.* pp.35-37.

_____[1981], *Accounting and Human Information Processing: Theory and Applications.* Englewood Cliffs, NJ: Prentice Hall, Inc.

_____, and Lewis, B. L. [1981], "Human Information Processing Research in Accounting: The State of the Art in 1981," Unpublished Manuscript, University of Michigan.

Mock, T. J., and Turner, J. L. [1979], "The Effect of Changes in Internal Controls on Audit Programs," in T. J. Burns (ed.), *Behavioral Experiments in Accounting II.* Columbus, Ohio: College of Administrative Science, Ohio State University.

Moriarity, S., and Barron, F. H. [1976], "Modeling the Materiality Judgments of Audit Partners," *Journal of Accounting Research* (Autumn 1976), pp.320-341.

_____, and_____ [1979], "A Judgment-Based Definition of Materiality," *Studies on Auditing—Selections from the Research Opportunities in Auditing Program,* supplement to *Journal of Accounting Research,* pp.114-135.

Peat, Marwick, Mitchell, & Co. [1980], *Auditing Sample,* ASB 1980-6. New York: Peat, Marwick, Mitchell & Co.

Schultz, J. J., and Gustavson, S. G. [1978], "Actuaries' Perceptions of Variables Affecting the Independent Auditor's Legal Liability," *The Accounting Review* (July 1978), pp.626-641.

Solomon, I., and Wilson, B. M. [1980], "Audit Team Consensus: An Empirical Investigaton," Unpublished Manuscript, University of Arizona.

Tversky, A., and Kahneman, D. [1974], "Judgment under Uncertainty: Heuristics and Biases," *Science, 185,* pp.1124-1131.

_____, and_____ [1981], "The Framing of Decisions and the Psychology of Choice," *Science* (January 1981), *211,* pp.453-458.

Uecker, W., and Kinney, W. R. [1977], "Judgmental Evaluation of Sample Results: A Study of the Type and Severity of Errors Made by Practicing CPAs," *Accounting Organizations and Society, 2,* pp.269-275.

Ward, B. H. [1976], "An Investigation of the Materiality Construct in Auditing," *Journal of Accounting Research* (Spring 1976), pp. 138-152.

Weber, R. [1980], "Some Characteristics of the Free Recall of Computer Controls by EDP Auditors," *Journal of Accounting Research* (Spring 1980), pp.214-241.

SELECTED ANNOTATED BIBLIOGRAPHY

1. Ashton, R. H. An Experimental Study of Internal Control Judgments. *Journal of Accounting Research* (Spring 1974), pp. 143-157.

   The two principal goals of this study were to determine (1) whether auditors make the same internal control evaluations when faced with the same circumstances at different times (judgmental consistency) and (2) whether different auditors make the same internal control evaluations in the same circumstances (judgmental consensus). The relative importance of different internal control factors was also assessed. In the context of extensive background information, 63 auditors evaluated 32 cases, which varied on the values of six internal control factors. Six to thirteen weeks later, the same auditors evaluated the 32 cases a second time. The auditors' judgments were highly consistent over the two administrations of the experiment; the average correlation between the two sets of judgments was .81. Consensus among the auditors' judgments was assessed by computing the correlation between each pair of auditors' judgments. The average correlation was .70, indicating a high degree of consensus. The two most important internal control factors related to the separation of duties.

2. Boatsman, J. and Robertson, J. Policy Capturing on Selected Materiality Judgments. *Accounting Review* (April 1974), pp. 342-352.

   This study examined whether CPAs and security analysts agree on judgments of materiality. It also investigated the importance of different factors in materiality judgments and whether different rules were used for different types of disclosure items. In the experiment, 18 CPAs and 15 analysts classified 30 cases into one of three disclosure categories (none, footnote, line item). Each case was represented by eight different factors. The authors found no significant difference between the CPAs' and analysts' judgments, and the effect of an item on net income was the most important factor. Gains and losses on the disposal of fixed assets were judged differently than accounting changes or uncertainties.

3. Gibbins, M. Human Inference, Heuristics and Auditors' Judgment Processes. Presented at the C.I.C.A. Auditing Research Symposium, Laval University, Quebec, November 1977.

   Gibbins investigated whether auditors understand the relationship between sample size and sample variance in the context of auditing sales invoices of two different sized departments for proper handling of discounts. Thirty-seven experienced auditors were asked whether the smaller or larger department would have more days where sales disounts were 10% above average. Since the sample size for the smaller department is smaller, its variance will be larger, resulting in a greater percentage of outliers more than 10% above average. Only 51% of the auditors answered the question correctly. This suggests that nearly half of the practicing auditors did not understand this important relationship.

4. Joyce, E. J. Expert Judgment in Audit Program Planning. *Journal of Accounting Research* (Supplement 1976), pp. 29-60

   Joyce determined whether Ashton's findings [1974] of consistent and consensual internal control evaluations result in consistent and consensual audit planning decisions. Thirty-five auditors evaluated either 20 or 36 audit cases (including 4 cases administered twice) where five internal control factors were varied. For each case, the auditors indicated the number of man-hours they would allocate to each of five areas of audit work. The average correlation between the two administrations of the four repeated cases was .863 indicating that the auditors' decisions were highly consistent over time. However, different auditors made widely varying audit planning decisions in the same circumstances (low consensus). The average correlation between each pair of auditors' internal control judgments found by Ashton [1974] was *not* reflected in similar audit planning decisions. Again, separation of duties was the most important internal control factor.

5. Lewis, B. L. Expert Judgment in Auditing: An Expected Utility Approach. *Journal of Accounting Research* (Autumn 1980), pp. 594-602.

   Lewis measured consensus among auditors' preferences for outcomes resulting from a disclosure decision. Seventy six experienced auditors rated the desirability of six combinations of three disclosure alternatives (accrue, footnote, no disclosure) and two items relating to the client's potential liability (client liable and client not liable). In addition, the materiality of the litigation was varied. As measured by the average correlation among the auditor's judgements, average agreement was .63 and .73 for the low- and high-materiality cases, respectively. This suggests that there is a greater agreement on the consequences of a disclosure decision in more material cases. Some small, but significant, between-firm differences were also uncovered.

6. Libby, R. The Impact of Uncertainty Reporting on the Loan Decision. *Journal of Accounting Research* (Supplement 1979), pp. 35-57.

   This study assessed the impact of disclosure of litigation uncertainty on commercial lending decisions. Thirty-four commercial loan officers from major banks made loan recommendations for twelve cases where the financial statements, management evaluations, and litigation uncertainty dislosure were varied. The results suggest that the disclosure of litigation uncertainty had a large effect on the loan officers' decisions as did the financial statements and management evaluations. However, when presented with the results of an in-house evaluation of the litigation uncertainty (as was required by bank policy), the addition of the auditor's qualification had no effect on the loan officers' decisions. This suggests that at major banking institutions, where in-house evaluations of litigation are normally conducted, the auditor's decision to qualify may have liitle impact.

BIOGRAPHICAL NOTES ON CONTRIBUTORS

STANLEY BAIMAN is currently Associate Professor of Business Administration at the Graduate School of Business, University of Pittsburgh. He was formerly a member of the faculty of the Graduate School of Industrial Administration, Carnegie-Mellon University. During 1977/78, he was a visiting faculty member at Stanford University's Graduate School of Business, where he earned his Doctorate in 1974. Dr. Baiman's research interests include the application of agency theory to managerial accounting and auditing. He is currently a member of the Editorial Boards of the *Journal of Accounting and Economics,* the *Journal of Accounting Research*, and *The Accounting Review.*

JOHN E. BUTTERWORTH is Associate Professor in the Faculty of Commerce and Business Administration at the University of British Columbia and was previously with Johns Hopkins University. He served as Chairman of the Accounting and MIS Division at U.B.C. and was a visiting professor at the European Institute for Advanced Studies in Management, Brussels; at Queen's University, Kingston; and at the University of Paris; furthermore, he was a guest lecturer at many other universities.

Born in Manchester, England, he took his undergraduate studies at Cambridge University, and his graduate studies at the University of California, Berkeley, where he acquired a Ph.D. degree in 1967. Previous to this, he worked for more than a decade in actual practice as a manager and company director in Ireland. He is the recipient of the Canada Council's Leave Fellowship, the Samuel Bronfmann Foundation Faculty Award, and the McKinsey Foundation Doctoral Thesis Award, as well as several other research grants.

Dr. Butterworth has published in *The Accounting Review*, the *Journal of Accountinq Research*, *Stochastics* and other journals, and he has contributed to several books.

CHARLES CHRISTENSON is Royal Little Professor of Business Administration at Harvard University and Chairman of the Control area of the Harvard Business School faculty. He has a B.Sc. from Cornell University and M.B.A. and D.B.A. degrees from Harvard

University; he has taught at Harvard since 1959, with the exception of one year in which he was deputy for management systems to the Assistant Secretary of the Air Force. For a number of years, he has taught a doctoral seminar on systems theory and scientific method.

In his book, *Strategic Aspects of Competitive Bidding for Corporate Securities* (1965), Dr. Christenson formulated the theory of decision-making by syndicates, out of which, in its subsequent development by Robert Wilson, grew agency theory. He is also coauthor of *Managerial Economics: Text and Cases* (with Vancil and Marshall); *Public Management: Text and Cases* (with Bower); and *Management Decision Sciences: Cases and Readings* (with Berry and Hammond).

PETER CLARKSON is a Ph.D. Candidate in Accounting at the University of British Columbia. He currently holds a Deloitte, Haskins & Sells Doctoral Fellowship. Mr. Clarkson has received degrees from the University of Western Ontario and the University of Windsor, where he subsequently had an appointment as a Lecturer in the Faculty of Business Administration. His principal areas of academic interest revolve around the effects of differential information on capital market equilibrium.

MASAKO N. DARROUGH is an Assistant Professor and a Postdoctoral Fellow in Accounting at the University of British Columbia, where she is involved in research in the areas of Accounting, Economics, and Finance. After receiving a Ph.D. in Economics at U.B.C., she taught Economics at the University of Guelph and the University of Santa Clara.

She has published in a number of journals, including the *Canadian Journal of Economics*, the *International Economic Review*, *The Journal of Business*, *Economics Letters*, *Public Finance*, the *Review of Economics and Statistics*, and the *Journal of Economic Behavior and Organization*; she has contributed to *Management by Japanese Systems* (edited by Sang M. Lee) and *Economic Models of Criminal Behavior* (edited by John M. Heineke). Dr. Darrough has also edited a book entitled *Biological Differences and Social Equality* (published by Greenwood Press).

THOMAS R. DYCKMAN is presently the Ann Whitney Olin Professor of Accounting at Cornell University and previously taught at the University of California, Berkeley. He also serves as a consultant to the Financial Accounting Standards Board on research matters. He received his Ph.D. degree from the University of Michigan in 1961. In 1981-82, he served as President of the American Accounting Association, after having been Director of Research in 1977-79.

Dr. Dyckman has received the AICPA Award for Notable Contribution to the Accounting Literature (once alone and once jointly with D.H. Downes and R.P. Magee), and his publications have appeared in *The Accounting Review*, *The Journal of Accounting Research*, *The Journal of Accounting and Economics*, *The Journal of Accountancy*, *Management Science*, *The Journal of Business*, *The Financial Analyst's Journal*, *Accounting, Organizations and Society*, *Decision Sciences*, and *The Review of Economics and Statistics*, as well as other journals. In addition, he has authored and coauthored seven books in accounting, statistics, and mathematics.

GERALD A. FELTHAM has a distinguished Professorship at the University of British Columbia, endowed by the Certified General Accountants Association of B.C. He was previously an Assistant Professor at Stanford University and at the University of Alberta, and he received his Ph.D. from the University of California at Berkeley.

He grew up in Saskatchewan, where he took his undergraduate studies and acquired the designation of Chartered Accountant. Dr. Feltham is a McKinsey Foundation Post-Doctoral Fellow, a Killam Senior Fellow (U.B.C.), and held a Leave Fellowship from the Social Sciences and Humanities Research Council. He served as Chairman of the Accounting and MIS Division at U.B.C., on the Editorial Board of *The Accounting Review*, and is presently on the Editorial Boards of the *Journal of Accounting and Economics* and *Management Science*.

Dr. Feltham is the author and coauthor, respectively, of two books and has published well-known articles in *The Accounting Review* and the *Journal of Accounting Research*, as well as in other journals and books. He won the AAA Competitive Manuscript Award in 1968, and received (jointly with

J. Demski) the 1970 AICPA Award for Notable Contribution to the Accounting Literature. Dr. Feltham has served on several committees of the AAA.

MICHAEL GIBBINS is Associate Professor in the Faculty of Commerce at the University of British Columbia and has recently assumed the Chairmanship of its Accounting and MIS Division. He is a native of British Columbia and received his B.Comm. at U.B.C.; he earned an M.B.A. at York University and a Ph.D. at Cornell and held an Assistant Professorship at Queen's University (1971-73). In 1966, he qualified as a C.A. with Deloitte, Haskins & Sells and spent more than seven years in public practice in British Columbia and Toronto. From 1967 to 1971, he was Assistant Director of Education and Secretary of the National Board of Examiners of the CICA; he has served on a number of committees of professional associations since 1980 and is Vice-president of the Canadian Academic Accounting Association. He is presently a member of the Board of Governors of the School of Chartered Accountancy (ICABC). He spent his sabbatical year (1981/82) with Deloitte, Haskins & Sells in Toronto.

Dr. Gibbins is a member of the Editorial Boards of *The Accounting Review*, the *Journal of Accounting Research*, and *Auditing: A Journal of Practice and Theory*. He has presented invited research papers at about twenty universities and research symposia since 1977. He is the author and coauthor of more than twenty articles and book chapters, which have appeared in such publications as *The Accounting Review*, the Journal of Accounting Research, *CA Magazine*, and *FASB Research Reports*. His principle research interest is in behavioural aspects of information flow and use, both at the individual decision-maker level and at the organizational level.

NILS H. HAKANSSON is currently the Sylvan C. Coleman Professor of Finance and Accounting at the University of California, Berkeley. He was born in Sweden and received his Ph.D. from U.C.L.A. in 1966. He is a former member of the faculty at U.C.L.A. as well as at Yale. Dr. Hakansson is a Certified Public Accountant and spent three years with Arthur Young Company. He has twice been a Visiting Scholar at Bell Laboratories in New Jersey and was, in 1975, the Hoover Fellow at the University of New South Wales. He is also a Fellow of the Accounting Researchers International Association. He has written and lectured extensively in the areas of accounting, finance, and the economics of information.

SHAILESH HARIBHAKTI is managing partner of Haribhakti & Co., a leading firm of Chartered Accountants in India; since 1981, he has been Visiting Faculty Member at the Indian Institute of Management, Ahmedabad (1981-1983). He received his B.Comm. degree from the University of Bombay. He is a Chartered Accountant, Cost Accountant, and a Certified Internal Auditor. During 1979/80 he worked with Arthur Young & Co. in Chicago. He has written numerous articles in accounting and economic journals and is presently preparing a textbook in cost accounting. He has been an active member of the Institute of Chartered Accountants of India and was elected to their Council in 1982.

PATRICIA HUGHES is about to receive her Ph.D. in Accounting from the University of British Columbia, is currently an Assistant Professor at UCLA, and holds a Deloitte, Haskins & Sells Doctoral Fellowship. She received other degrees at Duke University and the University of Pittsburgh and is a member of Beta Gamma Sigma. Her dissertation is a theoretical and empirical study of accounting disclosure as a means of resolving the informational asymmetry between insiders in a firm and investors. Her principal area of academic interest is the empirical testing of hypotheses of information economics and of agency and signaling theories (especially the testing of hypotheses about managers' choices in connection with disclosure, bonding and monitoring activites, as well as financial decisions).

YUJI IJIRI is the Robert M. Trueblood Professor of Accounting and Economics at the Graduate School of Industrial Administration of Carnegie-Mellon University and was previously with Stanford University as well as with the Tokyo office of Price Waterhouse and Company.

He received an LL.B. degree from Ritsumeikan University and his C.P.A. designation in Japan, an M.S. degree from the University of Minnesota, and a Ph.D. from Carnegie-Mellon University (then Carnegie Institute of Technology). Dr. Ijiri has been a consultant to Gulf Oil Corporation, the Ford Foundation, the AICPA, the FASB, and the National Science Foundation.

Dr. Ijiri is the author and coauthor of many books and numerous articles[1] and has received *four* times the AICPA Award for Notable Contribution to the Accounting Literature (in 1967 jointly with R. Jaedicke, and in 1972 jointly with R. Kaplan). He has served on the Board of Nominations of the Accounting Hall of Fame and on many committees of the American Accounting Association; he was its Vice-President in 1974/75 and is currently its President. Dr. Ijiri's association with the Canadian Certified General Accountants' Research Foundation began with the first issue of the organization's Monograph Series, *Historical Cost Accounting and Its Rationality* (1981), which he authored.

EDWARD J. JOYCE is an Associate Professor of Accounting at the Graduate School of Management, University of Minnesota, a position which he has held since 1981. Prior to that, he taught at the University of Michigan and at the University of Chicago. He received his B.S.B.A. from Ohio State University and his M.A.S. and Ph.D. from the University of Illinois at Urbana.

Dr. Joyce has been on the Editorial Boards of the *Journal of Accounting Research* and *The Accounting Review*. He served on several committees of the AAA, and he was a member of the Consulting Committee for a FASB Monograph submission. He was codirector of the Big Ten Consortium and is a consultant for Sunbeam Corporation and Honeywell.

Dr. Joyce's publications include articles in the *Journal of Accounting Research*, the *Journal of Accounting Literature*, and in the *Symposium on Auditing Research III* and *IV* (Department of Accountancy, University of Illinois).

ROBERT S. KAPLAN is Dean of the Graduate School of Industrial Administration at Carnegie-Mellon University. He received a B.S. and M.S. in Electrical Engineering from M.I.T. and a Ph.D. in Operations Research from Cornell University. Dr. Kaplan was selected as the AAA Distinguished International Lecturer for 1982-83. He serves as Consulting Editor for the *Journal of Accounting and Economics*, is on the Editorial Board of the *Journal of Accounting Research*, and was a consulting editor for the *Accounting Review* from 1977 to 1982. He has also been a consultant to CPA firms and financial institutions on the application of statistical methods to auditing and financial analysis. He serves on the Board of Directors of the Pittsburgh Branch of the Federal Reserve Bank of Cleveland and on the Board of Directors of the Pittsburgh Chamber of Commerce. He was Chairman of the AACSB Task Force on the Supply of and Demand for Ph.D.'s for Business Schools that produced a highly publicized study on the shortage of Business School faculty.

In 1971, Dr. Kaplan received the AICPA Award for Notable Contribution to the Accounting Literature (jointly with Y. Ijiri). He has contributed more than forty articles to monographs and leading professional journals in accounting and management science. His textbook, *Advanced Management Accounting*, was published in March 1982 by Prentice-Hall.

RAYMOND D. KING is an Assistant Professor of Accounting at the University of Oregon. Prior to joining the University of Oregon faculty, he held a similar position at the University of British Columbia. He is a C.P.A. who received his B.S. from Montana State University, his M.B.A. from the University of Montana, and his Ph.D. from the University of Oregon. His Ph.D. Dissertation, concerning valuation of convertible bonds, received special recognition by the College.

Dr. King's recent works (apart from the article reprinted in *Part IV*) include: "Convertible Bond Valuation: An Empirical Test;" and "Convertible Bonds: Debt Equity Values."

ROBERT LIBBY is Professor of Accounting at The University of Michigan Graduate School of Business Administration. He received his B.S. from Pennsylvania State University, his M.A.S. and Ph.D. from the University of Illinois at Urbana-Champaign, and previously taught at the University of Chicago. He is a C.P.A. and has served as a member of the Editorial Board of *The Accounting Review* and of the *Journal of Accounting Research*.

Dr. Libby has authored numerous articles, including "The Impact of Uncertainty Reporting on the Loan Decision" *(Journal of Accounting Research);* "Behavioral Models of Risk Taking in Business Decisions: A Survey and Evaluation" *(Journal of Accounting Research);* "The Use of Simulated Decision Makers in Information Evaluation" *(The Accounting Review);* he has also written *Accounting and Human Information Processing: Theory and Applications* (Prentice-Hall, 1981).

RICHARD V. MATTESSICH is Arthur Andersen & Co. Alumni Professor of the University of British Columbia. He held academic Chairs at the Ruhr University Bochum (codirector of its Institute of Management and Management Science) and at the University of Technology of Vienna (where he founded and directed the Institute of Industrial Administration and Methodology); he was Professor and Department Head at Mt. Allison University and held a tenured Associate Professorship at the University of California in Berkeley (and was a founding member of its Center for Management Science). He was a Visiting Professor at the Free University of Berlin, the University of St. Gallen (Switzerland), the University of Canterbury in Christchurch (N.Z.), and the Management Academy in Graz, and has been guest lecturer at a dozen other universities.

He was born in Trieste but grew up in Vienna, where he acquired a degree in Engineering, a degree in Business Administration, and a Doctoral Degree in the Economic Sciences (1945). For ten years, he practiced as an engineer, accountant, economist (as a Research Fellow of the Austrian Institute of Economic Research), and internal auditor (Prudential Assurance Co. of England) and is a Chartered Accountant. Dr. Mattessich is a Ford Foundation Fellow (U.S.A.), a Distinguished Erskine Fellow (N.Z.), a Killam Senior Fellow (U.B.C.), and has received grants and fellowships from the Canada Council, the Social Sciences and Humanities Research Council, and other institutions; in 1980, he was elected a regular member of one of the national academies of Italy. Recently he has become a corresponding member of the Austrian Academy of Sciences. For five years, he served as an Editor of the Monograph and Reprint Series of the Faculty of Commerce and Business Administration at U.B.C. and is presently an Associate Editor of the *Journal of Business Administration;* he is also a member of the Board of Editors of *Economia Aziendale* and of the International Editorial Advisory Board of "Philosophy and Methodology of the Social Sciences" of the *Theory and Decision Library.*

As an author, editor, and coeditor, Dr. Mattessich has eleven books bearing his name and over one hundred scholarly articles (published in *The Accounting Review,* the *Journal of Accounting and Business Research* and its predecessor: *Accounting Research,* the *Journal of Accounting Research,* *Management Science,* the *Quarterly Review of Economics and Business, Zeitschrift für betriebswirtschaftliche Forschung,* as well as other journals and books).[2] In 1973, he received the AICPA Award for Notable Contribution to the Accounting Literature. Furthermore, he served on several committees of the AAA and the CICA, as Secretary-Treasurer of the International House at U.B.C., on the Council to the Executives of the Association of University Instructors of Business Administration (BRD), on the Board of Nominations of the "Accounting Hall of Fame," on the Social Sciences and Humanities Research Council of Canada's Consultative Group on Management and Administrative Studies, and on the Board of Governors of the School of Chartered Accountancy (ICABC).

SHYAM SUNDER is Professor of Accounting at the Graduate School of Management, University of Minnesota at Minneapolis. Previously, he was a faculty member at the University of Chicago and Visiting Professor at the Indian Institute of Management at Ahmedabad, the California Institute of Technology, and the University of British Columbia. He received his Master's and Doctoral degrees in Industrial Administration (1972 and 1974, respectively) from the Graduate School of Industrial Administration of Carnegie-Mellon University. After an undergraduate degree in Engineering, he worked in industry for four years.

In 1982, Dr. Sunder (jointly with N. Dopuch) received the AICPA Award for Notable Contribution to the Accounting Literature. In 1975, he was named winner of the AAA's Manuscript Award. He has been a member of the Editorial Board of the *Journal of Accounting Research* since 1979 and served as its Associate Editor during 1980/82. He has been a member of the Board of Editors of the *Journal of Accounting and Economics* since its founding in 1978 and of *The Accounting Review* during 1978-81.

Dr. Sunder's research work includes a monograph and articles in academic journals of accounting, finance, and economics, and in the financial press. His studies of the stock market reaction to the LIFO method of accounting and of the profitability of the oil and gas industry have received wide attention. His recent articles include: "Efficiency of Controlled Security Markets with Insider Information: An Application of Rational Expectation Models," *Journal of Political Economy* (August 1982), coauthored; "Simpson's Reversal Paradox and Cost Allocation," *Journal of Accounting Research* (Spring 1983); and "Stationarity of Market Risk: Random Coefficient Tests for Individual Stocks," *Journal of Finance* (September 1980).

ROBERT J. SWIERINGA is Professor of Accounting at Cornell University, having joined the faculty in 1974. He received his Ph.D. from the University of Illinois in 1969 and has taught at Stanford University. He is an Associate Editor of *The Accounting Review* and of *Management Science* and serves on the Editorial Boards of *The Journal of Accounting Research, Accounting, Organizations and Society*, and *Abacus*.

Dr. Swieringa's research interests are primarily in the area of behavioral accounting. He has published in *The Journal of Accounting Research, The Accounting Review, The Journal of Accountancy, Accounting, Organizations and Society, Decision Sciences*, and other journals and has coauthored four books. His publications have dealt with such topics as behavioral approaches to internal control evaluation, behavioral effects of participative budgeting systems, heuristics used by individuals in processing accounting information, effects of accounting changes on information processing, and perceptions of determinants of information value.

DANIEL B. THORNTON is Associate Professor of Accounting, Faculty of Management Studies, University of Toronto; he is also Visiting Associate Professor of Accounting, School of Business, Queen's University. A Chartered Accountant, he earned his Ph.D. from York University in 1978, holding a Seagram's Business Faculty Award. Dr. Thornton's primary publications and research interests are in Financial Accounting Theory and the role of generally accepted accounting principles in contracts and capital markets.

WILLIAM J. VATTER is Professor *emeritus* of the University of California at Berkeley, where he was active for fifteen years. For about twenty years, he was with the University of Chicago and previously with Miami University, Oxford, Ohio. He was also Fulbright Professor at Melbourne University, Australia, during 1955/56.

Dr. Vatter holds a B.A. degree in Business, *summa cum laude*, from Miami University (1934), an M.B.A. and Ph.D. degree from the University of Chicago (1946), and is a Certified Public Accountant. In 1962/63, he chaired the Committee on Concepts and Standards of the AAA, was its Vice-president in 1969/70, Honorary Fellow of the Australian Society of Accountants, Fulbright Research Scholar under the AAA's auspices in 1964, and was a Fellow of the ARIA in 1974.

Dr. Vatter has over seventy publications to his credit, consisting of articles, several monographs, books, and research reports covering a wide range of subjects in Financial and Managerial Accounting. Dr. Vatter is listed among the nineteen "Significant Contributors to Accounting Thought in the 20th Century," together with *four* other former members of the "Berkeley School of Accounting" (Hatfield, Moonitz, P.W. Bell, and Mattessich), as presented in the historical work: *The Development of Accounting Theory* (1982), edited by M.J. Gaffikin and M.J. Aitken.

ROSS L. WATTS is Associate Professor of Accounting and Finance at the Graduate School of Management of the University of Rochester. He joined Rochester's faculty in 1971, after earning his Ph.D. from the University of Chicago. Prior to that, he was an Instructor in Finance and Accounting at the University of Chicago during 1969/70. From 1974 to 1975, he was Professor of Commerce at the University of Newcastle (Australia) and in 1981 was Visiting Special Lecturer at Monash University in Australia. Dr. Watts has twice been a distinguished faculty member at the Doctoral Consortium of the American Accounting Association and has also been a visiting faculty member at the Consortium for Canadian Ph.D. Students in Accounting. He received the A.C.A. from the Institute of Chartered Accountants in Australia in 1964 and has six years' experience in public accounting in that country.

Dr. Watts has published widely in first-rate accounting and finance journals. In 1979 and again in 1980 (jointly with J.L. Zimmerman), he won the AICPA Award for Notable Contribution to the Accounting Literature. Founding Co-editor of the *Journal of Accounting and Economics*, Professor Watts is also an Associate Editor of the *Journal of Financial Economics* and a member of the Advisory Board of *Chase Financial Quarterly*.

MURRAY C. WELLS migrated to Australia from New Zealand in 1967 and was appointed a Professor of Accounting at the University of Sydney in 1975. In 1982-83, he was President of the New South Wales Division of the Australian Society of Accountants, and in 1983, he was Visiting Professor at the University of Glasgow.

Dr. Wells has been a Trustee of the American Academy of Accounting Historians and has served on several committees of the American Accounting Association. He is the editor of *Abacus*, was the first secretary of the Pacioli Society, and launched Sydney University's MBA programme. His interests are in the history and theory of cost and financial accounting. He is the author of two books, the editor of three others, and has published numerous articles in Australia and overseas.

JEROLD L. ZIMMERMAN is an Associate Professor of Accounting at the Graduate School of Management of the University of Rochester. He joined the University of Rochester faculty in 1974, after receiving his Ph.D. degree from the University of California, Berkeley.

Dr. Zimmerman is a founding Editor of the *Journal of Accounting and Economics*. He won the American Accounting Association Manuscript Contest in 1977. In 1978 and 1979 (jointly with R.L. Watts), he received the AICPA's Award for Notable Contribution to the Accounting Literature. He is presently collaborating with Watts on a forthcoming book — *Positive Theories of the Determination of Accounting Procedures*. Dr. Zimmerman's publications have appeared in such journals as: the *Journal of Accounting and Economics*, *The Accounting Review*, *Journal of Accounting Research*, *Journal of Business*, and *Chase Financial Quarterly*.

FOOTNOTES

[1] Further biographical and bibliographical details can be found in M.J. Gaffikin and M.J. Aitken, eds., *The Development of Accounting Theory: Significant Contributors to Accounting Thought in the 20th Century* (New York: Garland Publ. Co., 1982), pp. 206-222.

[2] Further biographical and bibliographical details can be found in *Who's Who in America* (43rd ed., 1984) and in M.J. Gaffikin and M.J. Aitken, eds., *The Development of Accounting Theory: Significant Contributors to Accounting Thought in the 20th Century* (New York: Garland Publ. Co., 1982), pp. 173-194. Unfortunately, this historical work contains several inaccuracies in Mattessich's personal data and other errors.

INDEX OF NAMES